ENTANGLED LEGALITIES BEYOND THE STATE

Law is usually understood as an orderly, coherent system, but this volume shows that it is often better understood as an entangled web. Bringing together eminent contributors from law, political science, sociology, anthropology, history and political theory, it also suggests that entanglement has been characteristic of law for much of its history. The book shifts the focus to the ways in which actors create connections and distance between different legalities in domestic, transnational and international law. It examines a wide range of issue areas, from the relationship of state and indigenous orders to the regulation of global financial markets, from corporate social responsibility to struggles over human rights. The book uses these empirical insights to inform new theoretical approaches to law, and by placing the entanglements between norms from different origins at the centre of the study of law, it opens up new avenues for future legal research. This title is also available as Open Access.

NICO KRISCH is a professor of international law at the Graduate Institute for International and Development Studies in Geneva.

GLOBAL LAW SERIES

The series provides unique perspectives on the way globalization is radically altering the study, discipline, and practice of law. Featuring innovative books in this growing field, the series explores those bodies of law which are becoming global in their application, and the newly emerging interdependency and interaction of different legal systems. It covers all major branches of the law and includes work on legal theory, history, and the methodology of legal practice and jurisprudence under conditions of globalization. Offering a major platform on global law, these books provide essential reading for students and scholars of comparative, international, and transnational law.

Series Editors

M. E. A. Goodwin
Tilburg University
Randall Lesaffer
Tilburg University
David Nelken
King's College London
Han Somsen
Tilburg University

Books in the Series

Intimations of Global Law
Neil Walker
Legalized Families in the Era of Bordered Globalization
Daphna Hacker
Transnational Sustainability Laws
Phillip Paiement
The Sociology of Law and the Global Transformation of Democracy
Chris Thornhill
Authority and the Globalisation of Inclusion and Exclusion
Hans Lindahl
Property Law in a Globalizing World
Amnon Lehavi
The Law of the List: UN Counterterrorism Sanctions and the Politics of Global Security Law
Gavin Sullivan
Democratic Crisis and Global Constitutional Law
Christopher Thornhill
The Redress of Law: Globalisation, Constitutionalism and Market Capture
Emilios Christodoulidis
9/11 and the Rise of Global Anti-Terrorism Law
Arianna Vedaschi and Kim L. Scheppele
On Tyranny and the Global Legal Order
Aoife O'Donoghue

ENTANGLED LEGALITIES BEYOND THE STATE

Edited by

NICO KRISCH

Graduate Institute of International and Development Studies, Geneva

CAMBRIDGE
UNIVERSITY PRESS

CAMBRIDGE
UNIVERSITY PRESS

University Printing House, Cambridge CB2 8BS, United Kingdom

One Liberty Plaza, 20th Floor, New York, NY 10006, USA

477 Williamstown Road, Port Melbourne, VIC 3207, Australia

314–321, 3rd Floor, Plot 3, Splendor Forum, Jasola District Centre, New Delhi – 110025, India

103 Penang Road, #05–06/07, Visioncrest Commercial, Singapore 238467

Cambridge University Press is part of the University of Cambridge.

It furthers the University's mission by disseminating knowledge in the pursuit of education, learning, and research at the highest international levels of excellence.

www.cambridge.org
Information on this title: www.cambridge.org/9781108843065
DOI: 10.1017/9781108914642

First published 2022

A catalogue record for this publication is available from the British Library.

Library of Congress Cataloging-in-Publication Data
Names: Krisch, Nico, editor.
Title: Entangled legalities beyond the state / edited by Nico Krisch, Graduate Institute of International and Development Studies, Geneva.
Description: Cambridge, United Kingdom ; New York, NY : Cambridge University Press, 2022. | Series: Global law series | Includes papers "presented . . . the Hong Kong annual conference of the International Society of Public Law, and also at a conference on 'Multiple Legalities: Conflict and Entanglement in the Global Legal Order' which I convened with Hannah Birkenkötter from Humboldt University as part of the OSAIC group"–ECIP preface. | Includes bibliographical references and index.
Identifiers: LCCN 2021019498 (print) | LCCN 2021019499 (ebook) | ISBN 9781108843065 (hardback) | ISBN 9781108823791 (paperback) | ISBN 9781108914642 (epub)
Subjects: LCSH: Legal polycentricity–Congresses. | Law and globalization–Congresses. | International and municipal law–Congresses. | Conflict of laws–Congresses.
Classification: LCC K236 .E58 2022 (print) | LCC K236 (ebook) | DDC 340.9–dc23
LC record available at https://lccn.loc.gov/2021019498
LC ebook record available at https://lccn.loc.gov/2021019499

ISBN 978-1-108-84306-5 Hardback
ISBN 978-1-108-82379-1 Paperback

CONTENTS

CONTRIBUTORS

KIRSTEN ANKER, Associate Professor at Faculty of Law, McGill University. PhD (University of Sydney), LLB (University of Sydney), BSc (physics, University of Sydney).

LARRY CATÁ BACKER, Professor of Law and International Affairs, Pennsylvania State University. BA (Brandeis University), MPP (Harvard University Kennedy School of Government), JD (Columbia University).

TOBIAS BERGER, Assistant Professor in Politics and International Relations, Free University of Berlin. PhD (Free University of Berlin), MPhil (political theory, University of Oxford), BA (politics and development studies, SOAS, University of London).

TOMER BROUDE, Professor, Bessie and Michael Greenblatt QC Chair in Public and International Law at the Hebrew University of Jerusalem Faculty of Law and Department of International Relations; Academic Director of the Minerva Center for Human Rights, Hebrew University of Jerusalem. SJD (University of Toronto), LLB (Hebrew University of Jerusalem), BA (Department of International Relations, Hebrew University of Jerusalem).

FRANCESCO CORRADINI, PhD candidate in international law at the Graduate Institute of International and Development Studies (IHEID). MA (international law, IHEID), BA (political science and international relations, University of Padua).

KEITH CULVER, Professor of Management and Associate Dean for Regional Innovation Practice, University of British Columbia.

ANTOINE DUVAL, Senior Researcher at the T.M.C. Asser Instituut. PhD (European University Institute), MA (law and political science, Paris 1 Panthéon-Sorbonne), MA (law, University of Cologne), MA (law, European University Institute).

JULIA ECKERT, Professor, Chair for Political Anthropology at the Institute of Social Anthropology at the University of Bern. PhD (sociology, Free University of Berlin).

MICHAEL GIUDICE, Associate Professor in the Department of Philosophy at York University, Toronto. PhD (philosophy, McMaster University), MA (philosophy, McMaster University), BA (philosophy and law in society, University of New Brunswick).

CAROLINE HUMFRESS, Professor in Medieval History, University of St Andrews, Director of the University of St Andrews' Institute of Legal and Constitutional Research and Postgraduate Convenor of the MLitt in Legal and Constitutional Studies. PhD (University of Cambridge), MA (University of Cambridge), BA (University of Cambridge).

MACHIKO KANETAKE, Assistant Professor of Public International Law and coordinator of the Master's Program in Public International Law, Utrecht University. PhD (Kyoto University), LLM (London School of Economics), MA (law, University of Sheffield).

NICO KRISCH, Professor of International Law at the Graduate Institute of International and Development Studies (IHEID). PhD (law, University of Heidelberg).

GRÉGOIRE MALLARD, Professor in the Department of Anthropology and Sociology and Director of Research at the Graduate Institute of International and Development Studies (IHEID). PhD (Princeton University).

RALF MICHAELS, Director at the Max Planck Institute for Comparative and International Private Law in Hamburg, Global Law Professor at Queen Mary University of London and Professor of Law at Hamburg University. LLM (University of Cambridge).

TOMÁŠ MOROCHOVIČ, PhD candidate in international law at the Graduate Institute of International and Development Studies (IHEID). LLM (University of Exeter), LLB (King's College London).

AUREL NIEDERBERGER, postdoctoral researcher at the Global Governance Center, Graduate Institute of International and Development Studies (IHEID). PhD (IHEID).

LUCY LU REIMERS, PhD candidate in international law at the Graduate Institute of International and Development Studies (IHEID). MA (international law, IHEID), BA (political science and law, Ludwig Maximilian University of Munich).

BRIAN Z. TAMANAHA, John S. Lehmann University Professor at Washington University School of Law. BSc (University of Oregon), JD (Boston University School of Law), SJD (Harvard Law School).

PREFACE

Entanglement may appear a strange term for an inquiry in law. Many will think it does not have anything to do with law at all, but rather with threads, nets or wire. Some may think it has to do with relationships – especially complicated ones – but not the kinds of relationships that help us to make sense of legal structures. Both views have a point, and paradoxically pursuing legal entanglements is attractive in part because they have a point. What we try to do with this volume is to take us away from the familiar, to break with some traditional frames, and thus to pave the way for thinking afresh about law, especially law beyond the confines of the state.

In this endeavour, 'entanglement' helps not only to unsettle but also to reconstruct. By pointing us towards relationships, it helps to shift our gaze to the ways in which legal norms and legal systems are not self-standing entities but are instead tied up in relationships with others (other norms and legal systems) that often are crucial to understanding the identity of each part as well as the character of the whole. In many contexts of legal practice, litigants draw on norms from a wide variety of origins – domestic and international, sub-state and transnational, public and private – to persuade courts of their cases. Law, whether in finance, environment, human rights, trade, sports or corporate accountability, is not one law but is pieced together out of a great many layers by skilled attorneys, civil society actors, business representatives and government lawyers. In the end, law is the product of the ways in which the relationships of its different parts are construed.

Using the notion of entanglement is a way of highlighting the interwoven character of much of law, and it urges us to understand better on which terms such an entanglement takes place. This is what the present volume hopes to achieve. Bringing together a stellar group of scholars – from law, political science, sociology, anthropology and history – it shows us how actors entangle and disentangle law in a variety of contexts, and how this forces us to change the way we should think about law and legal order more broadly. It takes into view a highly diverse set of issues – ranging from family law disputes in Bangladesh to the Chinese Belt and Road Initiative and the making of global standards by the Financial Stability Board – and it uses insights about legal practices in these contexts to advance our theorization of law. In all of this, law appears neither as one nor as many, but as somewhere in-between. Entanglement points to this in-between character and highlights the challenge we face when trying to square such practices into the frame of unitary, well-ordered legal systems we are accustomed to as a result of the legal theories of the twentieth century.

The volume has been a long time in the making. The idea of entanglements was born in the discussions Francesco Corradini, Lucy Lu Reimers and I had on our 'Interface Law' project – a project that was itself part of a broader, interdisciplinary research group in which we were trying to understand 'Overlapping Spheres of Authority and Interface Conflicts in the Global Order' (OSAIC, because everything these days needs an acronym). In our project, we were trying to reconstruct the norms actors use to structure the relations between different legal orders, but we soon realized that we could not capture much of what we were seeing with the typical vocabulary of conflict and reception norms. We thus needed to look elsewhere and began to draw more widely from legal anthropology and sociology, from historical studies and from legal theories long outside the mainstream. Students of legal pluralism, of postmodern interlegalities or of historical legal entanglements had begun to describe aspects of the phenomenon we were interested in, and we built on their findings in order to generate a broader account of how law was shaped by interactions between norms from different contexts beyond the typical frame of legal systems.

In the spring of 2018, we gathered a group of colleagues in Geneva for a workshop exploring further the entanglements we began to see. Many of these colleagues, and a few new members of the group, have taken our discussions further and contributed to this volume. We presented some of our work collectively at the Hong Kong annual conference of the International Society of Public Law, and also at a conference on 'Multiple Legalities: Conflict and Entanglement in the Global Legal Order', which I convened with Hannah Birkenkötter from Humboldt University of Berlin as part of the OSAIC group. I am grateful to the participants in these different events for their intense engagement with our ideas and papers.

Entangled Legalities is the product of many minds and hands – most obviously the minds and hands of the contributors to whom I owe much gratitude. My special thanks go to our Interface Law team – Lucy and Francesco from the beginning, and later also Tomáš Morochovič, who not only moved us forward in substance but also handled many of the practical aspects of editing the volume with great professionalism and efficiency. The Graduate Institute of International and Development Studies, and especially Camila Morais Silva, provided excellent practical and logistical support throughout. And all this was rendered possible by generous funding from the Swiss National Science Foundation through project grant 100011E-170996, as well as the Deutsche Forschungsgemeinschaft which supported the overall OSAIC research group with project grant no. 277531170.

We hope the volume will inspire many to new explorations of law – and help them to look at the law in a different way. We believe that many of our insights are true not only for today's globalized world but reflect relatively common features of law throughout history – perhaps with the (limited) exception of the twentieth-century modern state. That law is characterized by multiplicity, and by interconnections between its multiple parts, is neither good nor bad; it is just normal. Focusing on this normality, and tracing how law is created out of entanglement, should open up many fruitful avenues for future work. With this volume we have tried to make a beginning.

ABBREVIATIONS

ACHPR	African Charter on Human and People's Rights
AI	artificial intelligence
AIDCP	Agreement on the International Dolphin Conservation Program
AML	anti-money laundering
AML/CFT	anti-money laundering and countering the financing of terrorism
ANSI	American National Standards Institute
BCBS	Basel Committee on Banking Supervision
BIS	Bank for International Settlements
BITs	bilateral investment treaties
BLA	Baloch Liberation Army
BRI	Belt and Road Initiative
CAC	Codex Alimentarius Commission
CAS	Court of Arbitration for Sport
CAT	Committee against Torture
CBD	Convention on Biodiversity
CCSI	Columbia Center on Sustainable Investment
CED	Committee on Enforced Disappearances
CEDAW	Convention on the Elimination of All Forms of Discrimination against Women
CERD	Committee on the Elimination of Racial Discrimination
CESCR	Committee on Economic, Social and Cultural Rights
CETA	Comprehensive Economic and Trade Agreement
CFT	countering the financing of terrorism
CIEL	The Centre for International Environmental Law
CITES	Convention on International Trade in Endangered Species
CJEU	Court of Justice of the European Union
CMW	Committee on Migrant Workers
CPC	Communist Party of China
CPF	counter-proliferation finance
CPSS	Committee on Payment and Settlements Systems
CRC	Committee on the Rights of the Child
CRPD	Committee on the Rights of Persons with Disabilities

CSR	corporate social responsibility
DPRK	Democratic People's Republic of Korea
DSU	Dispute Settlement Understanding
EC	European Communities
ECHR	European Convention on Human Rights
ECtHR	European Court of Human Rights
EIA	Environmental Impact Assessment
EO	Executive Order
ESIA	environmental and social impact assessment
ETP	Eastern Tropical Pacific
FATF	Financial Action Task Force
FET	fair and equitable treatment
FIFA	Fédération Internationale de Football Association
FIFA RSTP	FIFA Regulations on the Status and Transfer of Players
FNLMA	First Nations Land Management Act
FPIC	free, prior and informed consent
FRF	Romanian Football Federation
FSAP	Financial Sector Assessment Program
FSB	Financial Stability Board
FSF	Financial Stability Forum
FTA	Free Trade Agreement
G7	Group of Seven
G10	Group of Ten
G20	Group of Twenty
G2G	government-to-government
GATT	General Agreement on Tariffs and Trade
GMOs	genetically modified organisms
HRC	UN Human Rights Committee
IACrtHR	Inter-American Court of Human Rights
IAEA	the International Atomic Energy Agency
IAIS	International Association of Insurance Supervisors
IASC	International Accounting Standards Committee
IBS	international banking standard
ICCPR	International Covenant on Civil and Political Rights
ICJ	International Court of Justice
ICSID	International Centre for Settlement of Investment Disputes
IFC	International Finance Corporation
IIA	international investment agreement
ILA	International Law Association
ILC	International Law Commission
ILO	International Labour Organization
IMF	International Monetary Fund

IOSCO	International Organization of Securities Commission
ISDS	investor–state dispute settlement
ISEAL	International Social and Environmental Accreditation and Labelling
ISO	International Organization for Standardization
JCPOA	the Joint Comprehensive Plan of Action
MEAs	multilateral environmental agreements
MFLO	Muslim Family Law Ordinance
MOFCOM	China's Ministry of Commerce
MOU	memorandum of understanding
NAFTA	North American Free Trade Agreement
NCPs	National Contact Points
NGO	non-governmental organization
OBOR	One Belt One Road
OECD	Organisation for Economic Co-operation and Development
OFAC	Office of Foreign Assets Control
OHCHR	Office of the United Nations High Commissioner for Human Rights
OIC Agreement	The Agreement on Promotion, Protection and Guarantee of Investments among member States of the Organization of the Islamic Conference
PCA	Permanent Court of Arbitration
PoE	panel of experts
PPMs	processing and production methods
PRC	People's Republic of China
RSPO	Roundtable for Sustainable Palm Oil
SASF	semi-autonomous social field
SFT	Swiss Federal Tribunal
SGBs	sports governing bodies
SPS Agreement	Agreement on Sanitary and Phytosanitary Measures
SR	Special Representative
SWIFT	Society for Worldwide Interbank Financial Telecommunication
TBT Agreement	Agreement on Technical Barriers to Trade
TEDs	turtle excluder devices
TPP	Trans-Pacific Partnership
TTIP	Transatlantic Trade and Investment Partnership
UDHR	Universal Declaration of Human Rights
UEFA	Union Européenne de Football Association
UEFA FFP	UEFA Club Licensing and Financial Fair Play Regulations
UN	United Nations

UNCED	United Nations Conference on Environment and Development
UNCITRAL	United Nations Commission on International Trade Law
UNCTAD	United Nations Conference on Trade and Development
UNDRIP	United Nations Declaration on the Rights of Indigenous Peoples
UNFCCC	United Nations Framework Convention on Climate Change
UNGPs	United Nations Guiding Principles on Business and Human Rights
UNSC	United Nations Security Council
UNSCR	United Nations Security Council Resolution
VCLT	Vienna Convention on the Law of Treaties
WADA	World Anti-Doping Agency
WADC	World Anti-Doping Code
WTO	World Trade Organization
WTO DSB	WTO Dispute Settlement Body

1

Framing Entangled Legalities beyond the State

NICO KRISCH

1.1 Introduction

Law tends to make its appearance in the singular. We think of a legal order as a relatively integrated whole, as a system in which the different parts play a defined role and display a certain amount of coherence, if only because there are rules that regulate what happens when different norms conflict and because there are judges to decide unclear cases. We also expect law to be coherent and orderly as a matter of normative judgement – under the rule of law, we need to be able to know what the law requires from us. The unitary legal system then appears as both an analytical frame and an evolutionary achievement.

Yet in many contexts, law does not actually appear in the singular but in the plural. Norms from different origins become relevant in the same situation, and they often come with divergent prescriptions or at least orientations. Their relations are not predefined but remain to be determined through the social interplay of actors. State law interacts with local, Indigenous and religious law; norms from international and transnational law are used alongside domestic law and national regulation. These norms are not limited to neatly separated spheres but instead often address, directly or indirectly, the same set of actors and the same kind of behaviour. Yet they do not form part of a common legal order – they are entangled rather than integrated.

Such entanglement is the focus of the present volume. We regard entanglement as a common state of affairs in law – and likely a more common one than legal 'systems' with aspirations of hierarchy, order and coherence, as depicted in the standard image of law in the context of the modern, Western nation state. Legal entanglement was typical before the modern state arose, has been present within many states throughout, and has arguably increased with the rise in importance of transnational and international rules.

In this volume, we focus primarily on contemporary forms of entanglement, with a particular eye on encounters 'beyond' the state, both in the relation of state law with non-state law (especially of an Indigenous or religious kind) as well as the relation of different legalities in the transnational sphere. We inquire into the contexts in which entanglement occurs: the different bodies of norms, institutions and actors involved, as well as the dynamics they create. We also inquire into the legal forms it generates: the ways in which actors construe the relations between different norms, which are increasingly central to defining the shape of the overall order. And we are interested in the consequences entanglement has for conceptions of legal order more broadly – how do we need to adjust our understanding of 'law' if it is entangled rather than systemic?

This framing chapter sets the scene for the volume by defining key concepts, developing the theoretical frame and setting out the questions and *problématiques* animating the volume while highlighting the contributions of the different chapters. It begins by clarifying the concept of 'entanglement' in law (Section 1.2) and then explores some historical instantiations to generate a backdrop against which to theorize its contemporary forms (Section 1.3). The chapter then develops expectations as to where we can observe entanglement and what the actors and dynamics behind it are (Section 1.4). It outlines a typology of the legal forms in which we can expect entanglement to be reflected (Section 1.5), and then lays out some implications of entangled legalities for our conceptualization of legal order (Section 1.6).

1.2 Legal Entanglement

The notion of entanglement is not typically used in the legal context. It is common in quantum physics where it denotes a phenomenon in which different particles relate to one another in such a way that the 'state of each of them cannot be described independently of the state of the other(s)'.[1] In a related vein, in the study of history the notion of 'entangled histories' has come to emphasize the importance of relations between interconnected societies. This approach was originally driven

[1] See Wikipedia entry on 'quantum entanglement', https://en.wikipedia.org/wiki/Quantum_entanglement.

by the insight that the histories of European and extra-European societies cannot be understood without taking into account the continuous connections between them.[2] Unlike comparative approaches which inquire into similarities and differences, entangled histories are interested 'in processes of mutual influencing, in reciprocal or asymmetric perceptions, in entangled processes of constituting one another',[3] and especially in 'the constitutive role which the interaction between Europe and the extra-European world has played for the specificities of modernity in the different societies'.[4]

Similarly, the idea of *histoire croisée* focuses on intercrossings between different objects of inquiry – intercrossings that potentially transform these objects themselves.[5] In cultural studies more broadly (and well beyond the particular focus on postcoloniality), the notion of cultural entanglements has been used to highlight 'the aspects of agency, processuality and the creation of something new which is more than just an addition of its origins' from different contexts, and the importance of liminal spaces in which different cultures come into particularly close encounters.[6]

In the study of law, proponents of legal pluralism have done most to trace 'entanglements' between different legal orders, even if they have not always called them thus.[7] The first phase of legal pluralism often focused on the simultaneous, parallel existence of different legal systems in the same social field, often with an eye on the relationship of formal and informal law, state law and custom, particularly in traditional societies. This gave way over time to a broader appreciation of similar phenomena in other contexts, including states in the Global North. Later pluralist scholarship also moved away from an image of separate legalities and

[2] S. Randeria, 'Geteilte Geschichte und verwobene Moderne', in N. Jegelka, H. Leitgeb, and J. Rüsen (eds), *Zukunftsentwürfe: Ideen für eine Kultur der Veränderung* (Campus Verlag, 1999), pp. 87–96.

[3] J. Kocka, 'Comparison and Beyond' (2003) 42 *History and Theory* 39–44, at 42.

[4] S. Conrad and S. Randeria, 'Einleitung: Geteilte Geschichten - Europa in einer postkolonialen Welt', in S. Conrad, S. Randeria and R. Roemhild (eds), *Jenseits des Eurozentrismus* (Campus Verlag, 2013), pp. 32–70, at p. 40.

[5] M. Werner and B. Zimmermann, 'Beyond Comparison: *Histoire Croisée* and the Challenge of Reflexivity' (2006) 45 *History and Theory* 30–50, at 38.

[6] P. W. Stockhammer, 'Conceptualizing Cultural Hybridization in Archaeology', in P. W. Stockhammer (ed.), *Conceptualizing Cultural Hybridization: A Transdisciplinary Approach* (Springer, 2011), pp. 43–58, at pp. 47–8.

[7] K. Günther and S. Randeria, *Recht, Kultur und Gesellschaft im Prozess der Globalisierung* (Programmbeirat der Werner Reimers Konferenzen, 2001), p. 85.

came to stress the 'complex and interactive relationship' between different forms of ordering and their intertwined nature.[8] Some authors have found intersecting legalities, or 'interlegality', to be the condition of postmodern law.[9]

In recent years, in a 'third phase' of legal pluralism, these approaches have found broader application to law under conditions of globalization, taking into more direct view relations between domestic, international and transnational law.[10] The connections between these three phases, or approaches, are not always clear-cut, and in Chapter 17 Brian Z. Tamanaha highlights the discontinuities as well as the problems in borrowing from the two former to inform the latter approach. Legal historians, too, have begun to inquire more closely into legal entanglements. Inspired by frames from the study of history, the emphasis of this historical work is on openness, entanglement being seen as characterized by 'complex intertwined networks, with no beginning and no end, and a difficulty to fix the own point of departure'.[11]

This passage suggests, as in much of legal pluralist writing and works on interlegality, that the entanglements that come into focus here are primarily about mutual de facto influences and the travelling content of legal norms. Legal transplants and the substantive reception of legal forms and institutions are recurring themes,[12] in a somewhat similar way to archaeologists studying the material entanglement of objects that are created in imitation of, and borrowing from, foreign examples.[13] The perspective tends to be that of an outside observer tracing such influences, even if the participants in legal discourse (or the different legal

[8] S. E. Merry, 'Legal Pluralism' (1988) 22 *Law & Society Review* 869–96, at 873; J. Griffiths, 'What Is Legal Pluralism?' (1986) 18 *The Journal of Legal Pluralism and Unofficial Law* 1–55, at 17–18.

[9] B. de Sousa Santos, 'Law: A Map of Misreading – Toward a Postmodern Conception of Law' (1987) 14 *Journal of Law and Society* 1279–302; B. de Sousa Santos, *Toward a New Legal Common Sense: Law, Globalization, and Emancipation* (Cambridge University Press, 2002).

[10] Günther and Randeria, *Recht, Kultur und Gesellschaft im Prozess der Globalisierung*; R. Michaels, 'Global Legal Pluralism' (2009) 5 *Annual Review of Law & Social Science* 1–35; P. Zumbansen, 'Transnational Legal Pluralism' (2010) 1 *Transnational Legal Theory* 141–89; P. S. Berman, *Global Legal Pluralism: A Jurisprudence of Law Beyond Borders* (Cambridge University Press, 2012).

[11] T. Duve, 'Entanglements in Legal History: Introductory Remarks', in T. Duve (ed.), *Entanglements in Legal History: Conceptual Approaches* (Max Planck Institute for European Legal History, 2014), pp. 3–25, at p. 8.

[12] Duve (ed.), *Entanglements in Legal History.*

[13] Stockhammer, 'Conceptualizing Cultural Hybridization in Archaeology', p. 50.

discourses intersecting here) continue to emphasize traditional frames.[14] Many pluralists have long lamented the fact that legal discourse ignored such growing mutual influences and remained wedded to ideas of closed, unitary legal orders.[15]

Yet also from the perspective of the actors involved in them, legal orders have always had aspects defining their relations with other bodies of norms. Conflict-of-law norms for foreign law and norms about the reception of international law in domestic legal orders are the most prominent examples.[16] If anything, globalization has enhanced the pressure on defining and developing these interface norms further – the global universe of norms is ever more populated, with overlapping norms and authority spheres in many, if not most, issue areas. Participants in legal discourses can choose to ignore this multiplicity and merely focus on their own legal order, but when other norms have strong social backing ignoring them can be costly in terms of legitimacy and often also compliance. In a context of multiplicity, defining relations becomes central for actors to stake out their positions.[17]

As a result, bodies of norms become 'entangled' not only as a matter of fact, but also in discursive construction. It is such connections which we, unlike much of the classical pluralist literature, take into focus in this volume. Actors – litigants, judges, dispute settlers, observers, addressees – make claims about the relation of norms from different backgrounds, and they thus define and redefine the relative weights and interconnection between the norms at play. They also define the extent to which norms are perceived to form part of broader assemblages – in the relatively stable and firm mode of modern state legal orders, or in more porous ways, with a more open interplay of norms and characterized more through their linkages across boundaries than any strong form of belonging to an order as such.[18] The production of tertiary

[14] Günther and Randeria, *Recht, Kultur und Gesellschaft im Prozess der Globalisierung*.

[15] See, e.g., G. Teubner, 'The King's Many Bodies: The Self-Deconstruction of Law's Hierarchy' (1997) 31 *Law & Society Review* 763–88.

[16] See Chapter 16 by Michaels.

[17] See also M. Delmas-Marty, *Ordering Pluralism: A Conceptual Framework for Understanding the Transnational Legal World* (Bloomsbury, 2009); N. Krisch, *Beyond Constitutionalism: The Pluralist Structure of Postnational Law* (Oxford University Press, 2010), chapter 8.

[18] The notion of 'bodies of norms' is meant to capture this possibility of looser assemblages, the boundaries and strength of which are themselves produced through discourses in and around law. It is also meant to capture that norms tend to come in clusters or patterns, especially when they are institutionally produced.

norms – norms about the recognition of one legal order by another, as in Ralf Michaels' chapter – is one example here. The different contributions to the volume trace the ways in which relations between norms from different origins are construed in social practice – thus taking a primarily external perspective, though interested in the forms participants in legal discourses have at their disposal.

When we focus on legal entanglement here, we mean such discursive entanglement: the universe of statements that link different bodies of norms with one another. This is similar to the 'relational' (as opposed to 'material') entanglement in cultural studies: an entanglement in which the difference in origin remains visible even if the object is embedded in a different practice.[19] In a context of growing multiplicity, this entanglement becomes stronger – where various norms are seen to apply to the same situation, actors will often be forced to clarify the relation they see between them, and we move towards a greater 'centrality of the margins'.[20] As actors engage in this practice, they also redefine the overall order as such: they construe the weight of different norms in that order, the relative strength of their claims over behaviour or institutions. And through this, they remake the law. If we understand law as ultimately socially constructed,[21] a shift in the ways in which actors relate different parts of the legal order to one another reshapes the law itself.

Where entanglement is particularly pronounced, we might even end up in a situation in which – just as in quantum physics – 'the state of each [body of norms] cannot be described independently of the state of the other(s)';[22] a situation of enmeshment, or even the creation of a new, hybrid form. But entanglement, in the way we use it here, remains distinct from full integration into a new form. Where norms are widely accepted as part of a common legal order, they are integrated rather than entangled. Likewise, when one body of norms is not linked with another by relevant actors, they remain separate. Entanglement comes in different degrees, but it sits between, and is distinct from, both separation and integration.

[19] Stockhammer, 'Conceptualizing Cultural Hybridization in Archaeology', p. 50.

[20] N. Walker, 'Beyond Boundary Disputes and Basic Grids: Mapping the Global Disorder of Normative Orders' (2008) 6 *International Journal of Constitutional Law* 373–96.

[21] See, e.g., B. Z. Tamanaha, *A General Jurisprudence of Law and Society* (Oxford University Press, 2001).

[22] See Wikipedia entry on 'quantum entanglement', https://en.wikipedia.org/wiki/Quantum_entanglement.

1.3 Entanglement before and around the State

Entanglement was, by all accounts, a defining feature of many legal orders before the emergence and consolidation of the modern state. Even Roman law, often associated with system and coherence, is an impressive example of multiple fora, rules and practices, between which litigants and dispute settlers navigated their way. In Chapter 13, Caroline Humfress gives a vivid account of this complex interplay, tracing how actors reasoned out the application of different norms and, especially at the margins of the late Roman Empire, generated connected, but not integrated, legal orderings of their own.

Yet perhaps the most prominent expression of entangled legalities is to be found in medieval Europe. From the eleventh century onwards, law became increasingly systematized through legislation and codification, but the *corpus iuris* of much secular law was still made up of rules drawn ('received') from a wide variety of sources, including Roman law and customary usages. These rules retained their character as Roman law, *ius commune*, etc., but they were transformed through the reception process in a way that made them more compatible than they might have otherwise been.[23] Codifications, reflections of the law applied on the ground, consequently contained elements from many different bodies of norms. The eleventh-century *Usatges de Barcelona* used rules of Visigoth and Roman origin just as well as secular and ecclesiastical ones; the German *Sachsenspiegel* of the early thirteenth century meshed an account of local custom with rules from imperial legislation and some from canon law. In the French law of the period, multiple local customs stood alongside royal law, with royal courts applying only those customs they deemed 'reasonable', often taking as guidance canon law or the learned Roman law taught at universities.[24]

Scholars have described the resulting structure as a 'patchwork of accommodations', in stark contrast with the idea of an integrated order or system.[25] Judges in this structure could not merely rely on one set of rules but had to navigate between norms from a wide variety of contexts,

[23] H. J. Berman, *Law and Revolution: The Formation of the Western Legal Tradition* (Harvard University Press, 1983), p. 2.

[24] Ibid., pp. 470–1, 504, 511.

[25] S. P. Donlan and D. Heirbaut, '"A Patchwork of Accommodations": Reflections on European Legal Hybridity and Jurisdictional Complexity', in S. P. Donlan and D. Heirbaut (eds), *The Laws' Many Bodies: Studies in Legal Hybridity and Jurisdictional Complexity, c1600–1900* (Duncker & Humblot, 2015), p. 9.

with greater emphasis on the substantive appropriateness of the rule finally chosen than on its pedigree.[26] In their pragmatic ways, these judges inevitably entangled the multiple bodies of norms at play. This structure slowly gave way, with the emergence and consolidation of the modern nation state, to a focus on one, national law and the attempt to shape it through binding codifications. But the transition was winding and protracted, with many pockets of entanglement persisting for a long time.[27] In Germany, for example, legal plurality continued to be prominent until the late nineteenth century. Judges based their decisions on a confluence of local laws, *ius commune* and various other sets of norms until the legislative and judicial unification of many areas of law after the creation of the German state.[28]

Entanglements remained particularly strong in borderlands in which different authorities and legal traditions intersected. French Flanders and the Roussillon, acquired by France from the Netherlands and Spain in the seventeenth century, experienced long periods of interwoven application of French laws, local customs and previously governing rules, thereby pursuing accommodation and avoiding clashes of authority.[29] Yet more pronounced was multiplicity in imperial structures, inside and outside Europe.[30] In the Holy Roman Empire, a prime example of jurisdictional complexity, the law applied was 'a mixture' of a variety of legal sources, meshing Roman and canon law with imperial prescriptions and

[26] Donlan and Heirbaut, '"A Patchwork of Accommodations"', p. 21.

[27] See the contributions in Donlan and Heirbaut (eds), *The Laws' Many Bodies*.

[28] See N. Jansen, 'Law and Political Domination: Historical Observations, Conceptual Reflections, and Some Questions for Discussion' (2018) 16 *International Journal of Constitutional Law* 1176–85; M. Löhnig, 'Killing Legal Complexity: The Jurisprudence of the German Reichsgericht in the First Years of its Existence', in S. P. Donlan and D. Heirbaut (eds), *The Laws' Many Bodies: Studies in Legal Hybridity and Jurisdictional Complexity, c1600–1900* (Duncker & Humblot, 2015), pp. 249–70.

[29] A. Wijffels, 'Ancien Régime France: Legal Particularism under the Absolute Monarchy', in S. P. Donlan and D. Heirbaut (eds), *The Laws' Many Bodies: Studies in Legal Hybridity and Jurisdictional Complexity, c1600–1900* (Duncker & Humblot, 2015), pp. 81–108; B. Durand, 'Pluralism in France in the Modern Era – Between the "Quest for Justice" and "Uniformity Through the Law": The Case of Roussillon', in S. P. Donlan and D. Heirbaut (eds), *The Laws' Many Bodies: Studies in Legal Hybridity and Jurisdictional Complexity, c1600–1900* (Duncker & Humblot, 2015), pp. 169–92.

[30] See L. Benton and R. J. Ross (eds), *Legal Pluralism and Empires, 1500–1850* (New York University Press, 2013); J. Duindam, J. D. Harries, C. Humfress and H. Nimrod (eds), *Law and Empire: Ideas, Practices, Actors* (Brill, 2013).

territorial and local rules.[31] In the British Empire, jurists in England and abroad 'liberally mixed sources of common, civil, and natural law, principles of equity, and the law of nations' when grappling with colonial situations.[32] Here and elsewhere, imperial and local legalities overlapped, and imperial subjects navigated the different bodies of norms and jurisdictions, often choosing sites and norms beneficial for them individually and creating 'relational fields' of law along the way.[33]

With the consolidation of the modern state, complexity and entanglement were reduced but not entirely suppressed. The 'cuts' between different elements of modern, liberal law, highlighted by Julia Eckert in Chapter 15, have also always been contested. 'Negotiations' between state and non-state law, traced in pluralist scholarship, persisted both in Europe and elsewhere, albeit with major variations.[34] In recent decades, increasing societal diversity has sparked renewed interest in the relation of state and religious jurisdictions, especially on issues of family law.[35] Such issues are often dealt with in a conflict-of-laws frame, with special attention to public policy exceptions, but they evoke larger issues of primacy between state law, human rights and religious precepts, as reflected in Tobias Berger's chapter on Bangladesh. The greater salience of these issues, especially in Western countries, stems in part from the rise of multicultural claims over the past decades. These claims have also directed renewed attention to the relation between state and Indigenous legal orders.[36] In this collection, the contributions by Kirsten Anker

[31] P. Oestmann, 'The Law of the Holy Roman Empire of the German Nation', in H. Pihlajamäki, M.D. Dubber, and M. Godfrey (eds), *The Oxford Handbook of European Legal History* (2018), pp. 731–59.

[32] R. J. Ross and P. J. Stern, 'Reconstructing Early Modern Notions of Legal Pluralism', in L. Benton and R. J. Ross (eds), *Legal Pluralism and Empires, 1500–1850* (New York University Press, 2013), pp. 109–42, at p. 130.

[33] K. Barkey, 'Aspects of Legal Pluralism in the Ottoman Empire', in L. Benton and R. J. Ross (eds), *Legal Pluralism and Empires, 1500–1850* (New York University Press, 2013), pp. 83–107, at pp. 94–103. See also S. E. Merry, 'Colonial Law and Its Uncertainties Forum: Maneuvering the Personal Law System in Colonial India: Comment' (2010) 28 *Law and History Review* 1067–72, at 1068.

[34] Merry, 'Legal Pluralism'; M. A. Helfand (ed.), *Negotiating State and Non-state Law: The Challenge of Global and Local Legal Pluralism* (Cambridge University Press, 2015).

[35] See, e.g., M. A. Helfand, 'Religious Arbitration and the New Multiculturalism: Negotiating Conflicting Legal Orders' (2011) 86 *NYU Law Review* 1231; M. Maclean and J. Eekelaar (eds), *Managing Family Justice in Diverse Societies* (Bloomsbury, 2013).

[36] See, e.g., J. Tully, *Strange Multiplicity: Constitutionalism in an Age of Diversity* (Cambridge University Press, 1995); K. Gover, *Tribal Constitutionalism: States, Tribes, and the Governance of Membership* (Oxford University Press, 2010).

(Chapter 3) and by Keith Culver and Michael Giudice (Chapter 14) draw on this latter debate. They use the example of relations between the Canadian state and First Nations and trace how traditional, hierarchical legal conceptualizations can be, and are being, transformed into ones of entanglement.

The rise of transnational and international legalities over the past few decades has exacerbated the perceived multiplicity of legal orders and has helped to remove legal pluralism from the obscurity it long suffered in many mainstream accounts of law.[37] One important driver for this development, especially for European scholars, has been the constitutional indeterminacy of the European Union. Protracted conflict between national constitutional courts and the European Court of Justice led many to diagnose a form of (constitutional) pluralism in Europe.[38] For international lawyers, the long debate on fragmentation within the international legal order as well as the increasingly dense relations between domestic and international layers of law generated greater interest in the construction of these relations.[39] Both as concerns the EU and international law, 'entanglement' is probably a better descriptor of complex realities than (integrated or separate) legal systems.

One important aspect of the new 'global legal pluralism' has been the broader focus on different kinds of legalities – formal and informal, public and private.[40] The concept of law used in this debate typically goes beyond a traditional, Hartian frame and borrows from understandings used by legal pluralists with more anthropological backgrounds. The boundaries of the concept remain contested, and are often blurred,[41] but they tend to include as a minimum 'institutional normative

[37] See, e.g., Berman, *Global Legal Pluralism*.

[38] N. MacCormick, *Questioning Sovereignty: Law, State, and Nation in the European Commonwealth* (Oxford University Press, 1999); N. Krisch, 'Europe's Constitutional Monstrosity' (2005) 25 *Oxford Journal of Legal Studies* 321–34; G. De Búrca and J. H. Weiler (eds), *The Worlds of European Constitutionalism* (Cambridge University Press, 2011).

[39] M. Koskenniemi, 'The Fate of Public International Law: Between Technique and Politics' (2007) 70 *The Modern Law Review* 1–30; J. E. Nijman and A. Nollkaemper (eds), *New Perspectives on the Divide between National and International Law* (Oxford University Press, 2007); Krisch, *Beyond Constitutionalism*.

[40] See, e.g., Berman, *Global Legal Pluralism*; N. Krisch, 'Pluralism in International Law and Beyond', in J. d'Aspremont and S. Singh (eds), *Concepts for International Law: Contributions to Disciplinary Thought* (Edward Elgar, 2019), pp. 691–707.

[41] See B. Z. Tamanaha, 'Understanding Legal Pluralism: Past to Present, Local to Global' (2008) 30 *Sydney Law Review* 375–411.

orders' – bodies of norms associated with certain institutions, formal or informal, for their interpretation or enforcement.[42] Customary and religious law form part of the 'law' on this account, just as many of the informal norms – soft law, standards, etc. – that are institutionally produced and monitored, accepted by actors in the respective fields as carrying significant weight, and are often more consequential than formal rules.[43] It is such a broader understanding of law that underlies the present volume. Not all chapters necessarily employ the same approach – some have a focus on more formal norms, others stretch the notion of law well into non-normative forms of governance.[44] Chapters 14 and 17 by Culver and Giudice and by Tamanaha are most explicit in theorizing the concept of law as such, and in many of the other chapters we can witness how the most consequential entanglements straddle the boundaries of formal law and create linkages with, and among, less formal legalities.

1.4 Dynamics of Entanglement

Entanglement is not the same everywhere. Some cultures have been shaped more, some less, by interactions with others, and so it is in law. Not all law is equally entangled – some legal relations are characterized by a high degree of interaction between different bodies of norms, others not. And while such interaction depends on legal multiplicity, on overlapping claims associated with norms from different origins, multiplicity is not sufficient to bring it about. Even where different, potentially competing norms are present, we may find them to be not entangled but integrated into a common whole, as in many federal states in which there is one legal order and federal law is recognized to trump legislation at the state level.

When we look beyond the state, it is not immediately clear why, in contexts of intense multiplicity, degrees of entanglement vary as much as they do. Contrast the European Union, where national and EU law have

[42] See K. Culver and M. Giudice, *Legality's Borders: An Essay in General Jurisprudence* (Oxford University Press, 2010); M. Del Mar, 'Legality as Relative Institutionalisation: MacCormick's Diffusionism and Transnational Legal Theory' (2014) 5 *Transnational Legal Theory* 177–217.

[43] N. Krisch, 'The Decay of Consent: International Law in an Age of Global Public Goods' (2014) 108 *American Journal of International Law* 1–40; J. Pauwelyn, R. Wessel and J. Wouters (eds), *Informal International Lawmaking* (Oxford University Press, 2012).

[44] Contrast, for example, Chapters 4 and 6 by Backer and Kanetake.

been deeply entangled since the 1960s, with the Andean Community where, despite a similarly strong central court and formal setup, national and community rules have remained far more distant.[45] Or compare the differences across countries in the ways global women's rights relate to national legal discourses – sometimes kept at a distance, sometimes leading to mutual influences of a transformative kind.[46] In all these cases, encounters would be possible in the liminal space of overlapping norms, but actual encounters do not always happen, and if they do they do so in widely varying forms and intensities.

Understanding such variation would require a detailed contextual analysis in each case, and it is bound to be impossible to generalize broadly across historical and institutional contexts. Tamanaha, for example, emphasizes in Chapter 17 the contrast between relations among legalities that reflect diversity in modes and visions of life – as between state law and customary law in many, especially postcolonial societies – and legal multiplicity fostered by a proliferation of regulatory or adjudicatory institutions of more or less the same kind. But based on existing studies and the analyses in this volume, we can develop some observations and conjectures about the actors, pathways and dynamics through which legal entanglement comes about and develops.

1.4.1 Actors

On which path entanglement comes about (and whether it does) will always depend on the actors present and relevant in a given context – it is through them that entanglement is 'brought to life'.[47] Relations between bodies of norms are often construed by judges and other dispute settlers, but not only or perhaps not even primarily. They are also built by lawmakers, such as governments formulating legislation and treaties defining the relation with other rules; by regulators devising common norms and drawing on them in their regulatory practice; by international organizations producing statements about the weight of one body of norms vis-à-vis another. This volume contains many

[45] See, e.g., K. J. Alter and L. R. Helfer, 'Nature or Nurture? Judicial Lawmaking in the European Court of Justice and the Andean Tribunal of Justice' (2010) 64 *International Organization* 563–92.

[46] P. Levitt and S. E. Merry, 'Vernacularization on the Ground: Local Uses of Global Women's Rights in Peru, China, India and the United States' (2009) 9 *Global Networks* 441–61.

[47] See especially Chapters 2 and 13 by Berger and Humfress.

examples of this type, such as attempts by the Chinese government to entangle different legalities, transnationally through the Belt and Road Initiative and domestically through the social credit system, explored in Chapters 4 and 5 by Larry Catá Backer and Tomer Broude. International bodies are the focus of other contributions, as in Machiko Kanetake's account of the UN Human Rights Committee's efforts to create linkages with domestic courts in Chapter 6, or Grégoire Mallard and Aurel Niederberger's inquiry in Chapter 9 into the way in which norms on counter-proliferation finance are circulating between regulators and institutions such as the UN Security Council or the Financial Action Task Force.

Yet the scope of relevant actors goes well beyond the governmental sphere. As already noted in the imperial context, individual litigants often play key roles in determining by whom legal claims are decided, and they present arguments about which norms ought to apply and how.[48] Lawyers advising clients generate understandings of how different laws relate; international law firms, in particular, are important producers of legal knowledge in this respect.[49] Civil society groups, business associations and private norm addressees are often active in fostering views on how one body of norms interacts with another – they need to navigate a pluralist order, and their statements will have a particular weight in areas where more authoritative actors are absent. For example, as emerges from Eckert's chapter on struggles over rights violations in the context of global value chains, entanglement will often be driven by a 'mobilisation of law from below'. More generally, if we think of law as a social practice, it is a broad range of societal and official actors whose practices constitute legal orders and the relations of norms among them.[50] Actors are situated, and this situation shapes their way of regarding the multiple norms at play. Where actors – for example dispute settlers – are closely tied to one body of norms, we can expect them to be more reticent bridge-builders than actors with a self-understanding that is less clearly defined. This is most obvious in the context of national courts. Where judges understand themselves as part of a state's authority structure, tasked first and foremost with applying that state's law, they are unlikely

[48] See Chapter 13 by Humfress.

[49] See also Günther and Randeria, *Recht, Kultur und Gesellschaft im Prozess der Globalisierung*, pp. 52–9.

[50] See generally Chapter 17 by Tamanaha; and the emphasis on a 'user theory of jurisdiction' in Chapter 13 by Humfress.

to draw openly on norms from other origins.[51] However, not all national judges are alike. Common law judges, for example, might be more open than their civil law colleagues to creating linkages with norms from various sources out of an understanding of law that is encompassing rather than tied to a particular political authority.[52] Which actors are tasked with resolving a particular conflict – and what background they have – will then often have strong repercussions for the kind and strength of resulting connections. Humfress' chapter, with its focus on the different engagements with Roman law by military officials, clerics and tribal leaders in the resolution of an individual dispute, brings this point out nicely.

Variations in situatedness might also help to explain, for example, the relative unwillingness of courts tasked with the interpretation of a particular instrument to consider norms from other origins, compared with the attempts of, say, the International Court of Justice to provide a (somewhat) more ecumenical reading of international law.[53] A body tasked with the interpretation of less well-defined areas of law, such as the Court of Arbitration for Sport, is likely to sense greater freedom in creating linkages with norms from different origins.[54] And dispute settlers who, like arbitrators appointed ad hoc, are not beholden to a particular political or legal order, can be expected to draw on a broader range of norms than their more directly committed counterparts.

Non-governmental actors – and especially those that are not tasked with enforcing a particular legal order – are more generally less committed in principle, and they are likely to be more flexible in using and drawing upon different legalities: they may perhaps be seen to inhabit the 'liminal spaces' in which entanglements tend to flourish.[55] This is probably also true for actors who, like regulators, understand themselves as lawmakers rather than law-appliers and therefore may feel less

[51] See J. Resnik, 'Law as Affiliation: "Foreign" Law, Democratic Federalism, and the Sovereigntism of the Nation-State' (2008) 6 *International Journal of Constitutional Law* 33–66.

[52] See Chapter 6 by Kanetake; also H. P. Glenn, 'Transnational Common Laws' (2005) 29 *Fordham International Law Journal* 457–71.

[53] Y. Shany, 'International Courts as Inter-Legality Hubs', in J. Klabbers and G. Palombella (eds), *The Challenge of Inter-Legality* (Cambridge University Press, 2019), pp. 319–38. See also Corradini, Chapter 7, on investment tribunals.

[54] See Chapter 10 by Duval.

[55] On those liminal spaces, see Stockhammer, 'Conceptualizing Cultural Hybridization in Archaeology', pp. 45–51.

constrained by considerations of what the law in force is on a given issue. Yet, as Broude highlights in Chapter 5, individual actors tend to approach the multiple legalities potentially relevant in a given situation from a particular, and highly bounded, perspective – their situatedness will often make them see, or prioritize, certain norms rather than others, and it is crucial to understand these perspectives for an account of how and why legalities become entangled (or not).

1.4.2 *Pathways*

There are many paths to entanglement, and the discussion so far has already suggested some important ones. The *ideational* context of actors – most clearly in the case of judges – is bound to condition whether they construe legal orders as one or as separate, and whether they see them as open or closed. The space for and possibilities of entanglement are likely to vary historically and geographically as a result. For a judge in seventeenth-century Germany, entangling may have been the norm, whereas his late twentieth-century counterpart will have approached the plurality of norms through a prism of clearly separated (and internally integrated) legal spheres. Likewise, actors in many developing countries may be more used to navigating different normative orders than their colleagues in the Global North, even if there remains important variation. On the other hand, actors with a firm international law background applying formal international legal rules may be less open to applying norms from other sources than those engaged in the application of informal or transnational norms. The intense practice of linking norms from different origins by bodies such as the National Contact Points under the Organisation for Economic Co-operation and Development (OECD) Guidelines for Multinational Enterprises, traced by Tomáš Morochovič and Lucy Lu Reimers in Chapter 12, reflects a very open imagination of the law to be applied. At the same time, international lawyers will tend to regard different issue-specific regimes as part of one international legal order and seek to construe harmonious relations between them.[56] That said, the communities of practice actors form part of will often shape the way they construe linkages; this comes out particularly clearly in Chapter 11 in Francesco Corradini's portrayal

[56] H. Birkenkötter, 'International Law as a Common Language across Spheres of Authority?' (2020) 9 *Global Constitutionalism* 318–42.

of how investment and human rights communities differ in their construction of the nexus between norms from these areas.[57]

A second ideational pathway works through resonance. Norms from other origins may be appealing for their substantive content but also for the aura of progress they come with, the Zeitgeist they represent or the fit they produce with existing commitments. Likewise, the actors creating such norms may appear as appealing – as embodying the right values, as culturally superior, etc., sometimes as a result of hegemonic scripts.[58] Linkage on this basis is, however, likely primarily when the norms in question resonate with norms and values in the target context.[59] Such resonance does not only have to do with the 'actual' content of the respective norms but also, and perhaps primarily, with the ways in which those norms are framed and construed in societal and political discourses. If such construction allows enhancing beliefs and values that are already widely held, linkages succeed more easily, but they may come at the cost of greater distance from the way in which those norms are understood in the contexts they originate from.

Other pathways relate more directly to *rational choices*. Relevant actors often stand to gain from linkages between different bodies of norms – litigants, for example, may see the mobilization of law from a variety of sources as beneficial to their cause, as detailed in Eckert's chapter. They may also use them to relativize or circumvent unfavourable local norms or obtain advantageous remedies.[60] Sometimes, they will be led to draw freely on relevant norms from different origins – state law, religious law, or international norms.[61] In Berger's chapter on the entanglement of state and non-state law in Bangladesh, activists make liberal use of multiple normative registers, including religious and international law, to carve out space for marginalized actors.

[57] See also S. Taekema, 'Between or beyond Legal Orders: Questioning the Concept of Legal Order in Light of Interlegality', in J. Klabbers and G. Palombella (eds), *The Challenge of Inter-Legality* (Cambridge University Press, 2019), pp. 69–88, at pp. 78, 84.

[58] See Chapter 15 by Eckert.

[59] Levitt and Merry, 'Vernacularization on the Ground'; T. Berger, *Global Norms and Local Courts: Translating the Rule of Law in Bangladesh* (Oxford University Press, 2017).

[60] L. Benton, *Law and Colonial Cultures: Legal Regimes in World History, 1400–1900* (Cambridge University Press, 2002) p. 137; Barkey, 'Aspects of Legal Pluralism in the Ottoman Empire', p. 100.

[61] See J. Eckert, 'What Is the Context in "Law in Context"?', in S. P. Donlan and L. Heckendorn Urscheler (eds), *Concepts of Law: Comparative, Jurisprudential, and Social Science Perspectives* (Routledge, 2016), pp. 225–36.

Linkages with different bodies of norms can create space, but they can also serve to strengthen authority. For example, transnational regulators may enhance their own position by linking up with bodies of norms produced by other, reputed institutions, as detailed in Corradini's chapter on global financial regulation, and in particular the efforts of the Financial Stability Board, to weave a common set of norms. Another prominent example are national courts who, by linking their domestic legal order to European Community law, created space for themselves vis-à-vis political branches and hierarchically superior courts.[62] In Antoine Duval's chapter on the making of a transnational *lex sportiva*, it is the Court of Arbitration for Sport that bolsters its authority – and wards off potential challenges by other courts – by drawing together rules and laws of very different pedigree.

In this picture, stronger, more autonomous actors would likely be more resistant to closer entanglement, while weaker, more vulnerable ones would seek it to bolster their own position and authority.[63] Corradini's chapter on investment and human rights law suggests that increasing legitimacy challenges for investment law might push actors, including arbitrators, to seek stronger entanglements, at least rhetorically. In contrast, Lucy Lu Reimers' chapter on international trade law shows how a relatively strong institution – the World Trade Organization (WTO) – has been able to use linkages strategically and selectively, while avoiding unfavourable entanglements. In Backer's chapter, algorithmic techniques of governance can subsume other legalities, but typically on their own terms and potentially dominating them as a consequence of technological change. Taking the different, competing norms into account may appear as the path of least resistance, but it may also help to create space to come to a preferred conclusion.

A further major pathway, too often neglected, is *coercion*, broadly conceived. Metropolitan law in imperial settings may have at times held some appeal or benefits, but in many cases local actors have woven it into their legal arguments because of a relation of domination – expressed, for example, through imperial judges who needed to relate 'their' law to the norms operative on the ground, or through local judges who thereby

[62] K. J. Alter, *Establishing the Supremacy of European Law: The Making of an International Rule of Law in Europe* (Oxford University Press, 2001).

[63] This may help to explain patterns in judicial borrowing by international courts; see E. Voeten, 'Borrowing and Nonborrowing among International Courts' (2010) 39 *The Journal of Legal Studies* 547–76.

reaffirmed loyalty and obedience to imperial rulers.[64] But coercion is not confined to the distant past. Today, for example, the adoption of World Bank rules on resettlement in the context of infrastructure programmes on the part of borrowing states is often a matter of conditionality and necessity rather than persuasion or attraction.[65] In Chapter 11, Corradini points to the coercive aspects of conditionality in the implementation of international financial standards by the International Monetary Fund. Backer's chapter highlights hierarchical forms of entanglement in the Chinese social credit system as well as transnational credit rating agencies. Broude's chapter traces the imperial character of entanglements brought about by the Chinese Belt and Road Initiative. Mallard and Niederberger's contribution to this volume also stresses the coercive aspect as it traces the hegemonic origins of intertextual entanglements in the new legal order of counter-proliferation finance. In their compelling reading, the circulating references between different kinds of rules – formal and informal, international and national – reinforce each other's authority but also serve to hide their origins in US policies.

1.4.3 Dynamics

Entanglements may be gradual and smooth, but often they are characterized by a dialectical dynamic – one in which actors favour proximity between different bodies of norms but they also seek a certain distance, and they thus construe the relation as neither strict separation nor full integration into one order. Just as processes of globalization are characterized by the dual tendencies of assimilation and fragmentation, entanglement is an in-between state which often oscillates between these poles.[66]

This is perhaps most obvious when entanglement comes about, at least in part, through coercion. Pressure to adopt certain norms is then likely to be countered by attempts to create distance at the same time, as in the case of local law faced with metropolitan legislation in (post)colonial

[64] See, e.g., Benton, *Law and Colonial Cultures*, chapter 4.

[65] See S. Randeria, 'The State of Globalization: Legal Plurality, Overlapping Sovereignties and Ambiguous Alliances between Civil Society and the Cunning State in India' (2007) 24 *Theory, Culture & Society* 1–33.

[66] See Z. Bauman, 'On Glocalization: Or Globalization for some, Localization for some Others' (1998) 54 *Thesis Eleven* 37–49; Conrad and Randeria, 'Einleitung: Geteilte Geschichten', pp. 41–2.

contexts.[67] This is visible today, for example, in the continuing struggle of Indigenous peoples against the supremacy claims of (settler) state law or in attempts to counter state law demands by emphasizing the autonomy of Sharia law.[68] But the tension between proximity and distance can be observed more widely. In the postnational context, it will often reflect a tension between factors militating for closer linkage – for example the harmonization of markets, or universal human rights claims – and an insistence on autonomy and the freedom to decide differently. The latter is relatively obvious in 'vertical' relations when actors insist on the autonomy of smaller units, for example national institutions vis-à-vis international rules.[69] Kanetake's chapter shows how UN human rights bodies accommodate potential resistance by leaving national actors significant flexibility when it comes to giving international decisions domestic legal weight, and how national courts use (and sometimes extend) this space in a variety of ways. Approaching the question from the local angle, Berger's chapter traces the complex interplay between proximity and distancing in the approaches of different actors to multiple available norms, from Islamic to state and international human rights law, in debates over a ban on Islamic fatwas in Bangladesh.

Yet we can also observe an insistence on autonomy in other, more 'horizontal' contexts, for example when actors seek to defend the values driving international human rights law or international economic law from being contaminated by the respective other.[70] Reimers' chapter on the interaction between international trade and environmental law provides a vivid account of this dynamic. The more particular bodies of norms are linked with distinct values, institutions and constituencies, the more linkages may create concerns about heteronomy and provoke calls for greater distance. In the end, the portrayal of certain relations as 'vertical' or 'horizontal' is also a product of how an entanglement is socially construed – as we can see, for example, in Culver and

[67] On the latter, see e.g. Barkey, 'Aspects of Legal Pluralism in the Ottoman Empire', pp. 101–3.

[68] See Chapters 3, 14 and 17 by Anker, Culver and Giudice, and Tamanaha.

[69] The 'vertical' and 'horizontal' dimensions of entanglement are helpful as heuristic tools to structure the inquiry, but it should be noted that they are themselves products of how the relation between different bodies of norms are related. Indigenous and state law, for example, can be understood as standing in either the one or the other relation; the politics of this choice are reflected in Chapter 14 by Culver and Giudice.

[70] P. Alston, 'Resisting the Merger and Acquisition of Human Rights by Trade Law: A Reply to Petersmann' (2002) 13 *European Journal of International Law* 815–44.

Giudice's discussion of the relation of Canadian state and indigenous laws in Chapter 14, the question of whether a relation should be seen as one or the other can be highly contested and consequential. Attempts at linkage can make entanglements appear as more vertical, attempts at distancing can make them more horizontal.

The need to create, or insist on, distance is likely to be, in part, a function of the character of the entangled norms. Where these are informal and soft, actors retain space and autonomy even in the face of close linkages. The examples of corporate social responsibility norms, in Morochovič and Reimers' chapter, or global financial standards, in Corradini's contribution, are cases in point here – as Corradini emphasizes, the creation of unified financial standards has long been hampered by an insistence on autonomy on the part of both national governments and various international bodies. In hard law contexts, for example in domestic courts, the stakes of entanglement will often be higher and a clear definition of relations more consequential.

The dialectic of proximity and distancing also has a temporal dimension. Linkages often have long-term effects, especially when they concern not only individual norms but whole sets of norms or legal orders. A norm defining the status of international law in the domestic legal order, for example, has relevance for an unlimited number of interactions between both legal orders in the future. The effects of such linkage, however, are often difficult to predict for the actors involved, and attention may well be drawn to them only when problems arise and a particular issue becomes politicized.[71] As tighter forms of coupling emerge and come to apply to increasingly consequential and salient issues, they can be expected to provoke political contestation and resistance which will often seek to disrupt more routinized forms of interaction and may result in mechanisms for reclaiming distance. Even if issue-specific, this politicization may lead to calls for redefining the linkage more broadly. In this vein, contestation around issues of terrorism and voting rights for prisoners has engendered a general movement in the UK for greater distance from judgements of the European Court of Human Rights.[72]

[71] M. Zürn, M. Binder and M. Ecker-Ehrhardt, 'International Authority and Its Politicization' (2012) 4 *International Theory* 69–106.

[72] See M. Madsen, 'The Challenging Authority of the European Court of Human Rights: From Cold War Legal Diplomacy to the Brighton Declaration and Backlash' (2016) 79 *Law and Contemporary Problems* 141–78, at 170–1.

1.5 A Variety of Forms

If we can indeed expect a push towards greater proximity, accompanied by certain forms of distancing that prevent full integration, the result is likely to be the emergence of new types of norms at the interfaces between different parts of the legal order – norms that, instead of governing behaviour directly, define the relation and applicability of primary norms (on behaviour) as well as secondary norms (on powers to make and interpret the law).[73] With this volume, we aim at gaining a clearer picture of the shape of these norms – 'tertiary norms', as Michaels describes them in Chapter 16.

In a context of entanglement, interface norms are likely to reflect the dialectic dynamics in Section 1.4 – strengthening ties between different bodies of norms but preserving discretion or safety valves that help to recalibrate relations in times of tension.[74] Yet how these norms are construed will often differ across actors. This is most obvious in the jurisprudence of different courts, for example in differences in interpretation of the proper relationship of human rights and international humanitarian law.[75] But it is at least equally observable outside the courtroom, for example in the conflict over the relationship of the TRIPS (Trade-Related Aspects of Intellectual Property Rights) Agreement with international human rights and world health law as regards access to essential medicines. Here, the World Health Assembly and the (then) UN Human Rights Commission urged an interpretative coupling of the different areas, while neither the WTO's eventual Doha Declaration on the TRIPS Agreement and Public Health nor the implementing decision mention other bodies of law at all – despite the fact that, as a political matter, these other bodies were obviously important for the eventual *rapprochement* of the WTO.[76] Corradini's chapter on investment and human rights, and Reimers' on trade and environment,

[73] See Krisch, *Beyond Constitutionalism*, pp. 285–96.

[74] In a similar vein, Kjaer highlights the proliferation of 'connectivity norms' in the global order; see P. F. Kjaer, 'Global Law as Inter-contextuality and as Inter-legality', in J. Klabbers and G. Palombella (eds), *The Challenge of Inter-legality* (Cambridge University Press, 2019), pp. 302–18, at p. 304.

[75] See, e.g., A. E. Cassimatis, 'International Humanitarian Law, International Human Rights Law, and Fragmentation of International Law' (2007) 56 *International & Comparative Law Quarterly* 623–39.

[76] See on the contest L. R. Helfer, 'Regime Shifting: The TRIPS Agreement and New Dynamics of International Intellectual Property Lawmaking' (2004) 29 *Yale Journal of International Law* 1, at 42–5.

trace other cases of actors' diverging views over the relationship between two bodies of norms, and they highlight especially the interactive and temporal dimension of the construction of the relationship. Interface norms themselves are contingent: claims about them vary across actors and times. Stable relations between bodies of norms may emerge from convergence among concerned actors on the substance or on the norms governing the interfaces, but such convergence may well prove elusive.

Getting closer to these interfaces means that we cannot limit ourselves to considering the formal rules that govern these relations or the occasional pronouncement of a court – too much of the postnational legal order only has loose connections with courts or other formal dispute settlers. Instead, we need to take into view the ways in which different kinds of actors – norm-makers, addressees, dispute settlers and other concerned societal actors – construe these relations and resolve (potential) conflicts between different norms. We thus need to get closer to the 'social life' of postnational law in order to understand the way it works.[77] This is brought out in this volume by, for example, Eckert's account of the construction of entanglements 'from below' which zooms in on societal actors and their struggles behind the legal façade, or in Humfress' insistence on a user theory of jurisdiction that starts from the ways in which litigants draw on particular authorities to navigate different layers of law.

The relations brought about through societal action can be a mere matter of fact and influence between different bodies of norms. But they will also often be the result of, and reflected in, discursive statements – in the overlapping bodies of norms themselves or in statements about them from relevant actors. The production of interface norms is then the result not so much of a one-off determination, but of a process of law – a process whose analysis will often benefit from sociological and anthropological methods to complement the work of lawyers, as evident from the multidisciplinary contributions to this volume.[78]

[77] See also Taekema's suggestion that a practice orientation is key to understanding interlegality in Taekema, 'Between or Beyond Legal Orders'.

[78] See generally S. F. Moore, *Law as Process: An Anthropological Approach* (Routledge & Kegan Paul, 1978).

1.5.1 Towards a Typology

What then are the norms and practices that structure the relations between different bodies of norms? Practice has generated a host of tools and approaches in this respect,[79] and we can distinguish three main types: reception norms, overarching norms and – situated between them – straddling practices. The two former form part of the common repertoire of inter- and intra-systemic norms – they reflect the dichotomy between the (external) conflict of laws and the (internal) conflict of norms[80] – while the latter blur system boundaries and suggest an alternative structure, characterized by looser couplings.

Reception norms. Reception norms are the typical form through which a legal system deals with norms from the outside; they reproduce the inside/outside distinction and define the ways in which outside norms enter a given body of norms. Michaels' tertiary norms, as developed in Chapter 16, fall into this category as they are designed to regulate the relations of one legal system with others. Reception norms include norms performing an accommodating function in the regulation of the interaction between bodies of norms.[81] They can reflect closer as well as more distanced relations, though they remain short of actual integration. They can thus range from the exclusion of outside norms to fixed references, potentially coupled with conditions of a procedural or substantive kind. Examples of the latter are conflict-of-law norms that specify in which circumstances foreign norms are applied by national courts; norms about the effect and hierarchical status of outside norms in the domestic legal order; or norms of the *Solange* kind that recognize the direct effect of (regional or international) norms if these fulfil certain – procedural or substantive – conditions, for example equivalent protection. More flexible reception norms embody greater discretion, for example in requirements of taking norms from other authority spheres 'into account', or in practices granting them 'persuasive authority', thus giving them weight

[79] See, e.g., Delmas-Marty, *Ordering Pluralism*; D. Pulkowski, *The Law and Politics of International Regime Conflict* (Oxford University Press, 2014); A. Peters, 'The Refinement of International Law: From Fragmentation to Regime Interaction and Politicization' (2017) 15 *International Journal of Constitutional Law* 671–704.

[80] R. Michaels and J. Pauwelyn, 'Conflict of Norms or Conflict of Laws? Different Techniques in the Fragmentation of Public International Law' (2012) 22 *Duke Journal of Comparative & International Law* 349–76.

[81] See R. Michaels, 'On Liberalism and Legal Pluralism', in M. Maduro, K. Tuori and S. Sankari (eds), *Transnational Law: Rethinking European Law and Legal Thinking* (Cambridge University Press, 2014).

but no conclusive effect.[82] Kanetake's chapter traces the many such forms the United Nations treaty bodies and domestic courts use to calibrate their relations, providing for both linkage and flexibility by using open criteria, such as 'due consideration'.

Overarching norms. Typical for the intra-systemic dimension, overarching norms regulate relations centrally and with binding character for the different bodies of norms involved. This can involve classical conflict norms, such as *lex specialis* or *lex posterior*. It can also involve norms about hierarchies, as between constitutions and ordinary statutes or secondary legislation, between federal and state law in federal orders, between *ius cogens* and other international rules or between obligations under the United Nations Charter and other international obligations under Article 103 of the Charter. Overarching norms can also be construed as substantive integrating rules or principles, such as human rights, sustainable development or democracy/good governance, which create normative expectations throughout the entire system – often expressed, in international law, as rules of 'customary' or 'general' international law.[83] Equally more flexible are interpretative connections that allow actors space to define relations, such as principles of harmonizing interpretation or requirements not to interpret certain rules 'in isolation' from other parts of the legal order.[84] On the other hand, overarching rules can also be seen to protect the autonomy of certain parts of the order, through constitutional limits on interference, the recognition of the self-contained character of certain suborders, *lex specialis* claims or rules which delimit regulatory spheres, as between agreements with different sets of parties.

Straddling practices. The third (and perhaps most interesting) category comprises norms and practices that straddle different bodies of norms without being seen to belong to either, thus blurring the boundaries between them. Given the prevailing systemic imagery, such practices have found less attention so far, even if – as we have seen in the brief historical survey in Section 1.3 – they seem to have formed an important part of the entangled legalities of the past. Such norms and practices will also tend to be less clearly developed and are likely to appear in more inchoate forms. We can observe them, for example, in courts weaving

[82] See also Krisch, *Beyond Constitutionalism*, pp. 286–96.
[83] See Chapters 7 and 8 by Corradini and Reimers.
[84] See, e.g., C. McLachlan, 'The Principle of Systemic Integration and Article 31(3)(C) of the Vienna Convention' (2005) 54 *International and Comparative Law Quarterly* 279–320.

together different bodies of norms in order to come to a solution in a given case. For example, the Court of Appeal of England and Wales, in a case concerning the implementation of UN sanctions, used the notion of 'conciliation' to bring together UK primary and secondary legislation, the European Convention on Human Rights as well as obligations deriving from UN Security Council resolutions in a harmonious fashion, rather than stipulating rules of hierarchy or re-enacting the boundaries between legal systems.[85] Other boundary-blurring norms may be hybrid norms, multi-sourced equivalent norms[86] or open concepts used to provide a pathway between different bodies of norms. Examples here include due diligence principles that allow for connections between the national and transnational regulation of multinational companies, or the notion of 'core labour rights' developed by the International Labour Organization and allowing for flexible references in a multitude of other codes, public and private. These forms mirror the 'intertextuality' traced by Mallard and Niederberger in counter-proliferation finance.[87] Open concepts are also visible in Berger's account of the Bangladeshi Supreme Court's navigation of the boundary between state and religious law (and international human rights).

Such straddling practices are particularly visible in contexts less structured by ideational frames of modern state law. Humfress emphasizes the importance of jurisgenerative practices of actors, rather than formalized norms and relations between them, in the making of law in Chapter 13 on the Eastern Roman Empire. Similar observations pertain to contemporary contexts with a lesser degree of formalization and weaker boundaries than typically found in the state context. Some of the National Contact Points under the OECD Guidelines for Multinational Enterprises, for example, have emerged as quasi-judicial dispute settlement bodies and have drawn on various bodies of norms to ground their findings, as Morochovič and Reimers detail in Chapter 12. Some of the norms they use – such as the requirement of 'free, prior and informed consent' – are drawn from other bodies of norms but used as if they were free-floating principles applicable throughout. Similarly, Duval traces how the Court of Arbitration for Sport uses both publicly and privately

[85] England and Wales Court of Appeal, Judgment of 30 October 2008, *A, K, M, Q & G* v. *HM Treasury* [2008] EWCA Civ 1187.

[86] T. Broude and Y. Shany (eds), *Multi-sourced Equivalent Norms in International Law* (Bloomsbury, 2011).

[87] See also Kjaer, 'Global Law as Inter-contextuality and as Inter-legality'.

produced norms in its effort at weaving together *lex sportiva*'s 'tapestry'. Such references build lasting connections between different norms, even in the absence of (systemic) reception norms. We can observe similar phenomena on the regulatory side, as Corradini shows in Chapter 7. The Financial Stability Board (FSB), for example, has sought to connect standards from various transnational and international standard-setters, public and private, formal and informal, through its *Compendium of Standards*, with fifteen 'key standards' singled out as requiring particular attention. Through the *Compendium*, the FSB seeks to build a more integrated order out of the existing multiplicity, though one that functions not in the form of a system but through a web with less stable linkages and hierarchies. Other bodies in global financial governance play their part in weaving this web. The resulting structure is not sustained through firm general rules about relations, but rather through contingent, sometimes ad hoc, acts of linking, referencing and distancing, with a potential consolidation occurring only over time.[88]

Another intriguing yet highly challenging form of entanglement is highlighted in Backer's chapter on algorithmic techniques of governance. With the rise of such forms of governance, the linkages between different bodies of norms created through algorithms and ratings become a central concern, and one so far hardly understood. This is especially so as algorithmic governance – just as the many indicators and rankings in contemporary governance in and beyond the state – operationalizes, but typically does not lay open, the normative choices and preferences that go into the weighing of different types of norms and expectations.[89]

1.6 Entangled Order

In some of its forms, entanglement can appear as the antithesis of order and system. A multitude of actors producing varying links between norms, sometimes closer, sometimes more distant, but always somehow in flux: this picture seems to be in stark contrast to the ideal of a rule of law. Yet the landscape that emerges from this volume is not as dark or drastic – in many contexts it is quite the opposite.

[88] See also N. Krisch, F. Corradini and L. L. Reimers, 'Order at the Margins: The Legal Construction of Interface Conflicts over Time' (2020) 9 *Global Constitutionalism* 343–63.

[89] See also K. E. Davis, A. Fisher, B. Kingsbury and S. E. Merry (eds), *Governance by Indicators: Global Power through Classification and Rankings* (Oxford University Press, 2012).

1.6.1 *Conflict and Consolidation*

Legal entanglement will often be seen as prone to conflict – more clearly defined relations, either the separation or the integration of different bodies of norms, seem to promise greater stability. Stanley Hoffmann's famous dictum about the European Community, which he saw as occupying an unstable middle ground between international cooperation and the creation of a new state, exemplifies this widespread view.[90] Today, similar assessments often accompany the diagnosis of regime complexity and interface conflicts between different institutions and norms in the global order.[91]

Whether this assumption of conflictivity is empirically justified is not obvious,[92] however, and how it applies to different forms and degrees of entanglement even less so. Entangled relations do not have to be unstable at all; they can display a high degree of consolidation around the norms that govern interactions. This is especially so if addressees as well as dispute settlers adopt a conciliatory rather than confrontational attitude.[93] Even if underlying tensions persist, the relative openness of such entanglements, and the frequent accommodation of both linkage and distancing just mentioned, may actually help to provide flexibility and the necessary safety valves to adjust to changing or unforeseen circumstances.[94]

In fact, in several of the chapters in this volume, closer entanglements are construed precisely to respond to, and ward off, challenges to the legitimacy of a certain body of norms. These challenges stem from, for example, human rights (as in Duval's story of the Court of Arbitration for Sport or Corradini's of international investment law) or environmental concerns (as in Reimer's chapter on trade law). On the other hand, more distant entanglement is sometimes sought to defuse conflicts that would be caused by too integrated a relation – as in the move

[90] S. Hoffmann, 'Obstinate or Obsolete? The Fate of the Nation-State and the Case of Western Europe' (1966) 95 *Daedalus* 862–915.

[91] See, e.g., D. W. Drezner, 'The Tragedy of the Global Institutional Commons', in M. Finnemore and J. Goldstein (eds), *Back to Basics: State Power in a Contemporary World* (Oxford University Press, 2013), pp. 280–310.

[92] See C. Kreuder-Sonnen and M. Zürn, 'After Fragmentation: Institutional Density, Regime Complexes and Interface Conflicts' (2020) 9 *Global Constitutionalism* 241–67.

[93] See Peters, 'The Refinement of International Law'; T. Megiddo, 'Beyond Fragmentation: On International Law's Integrationist Forces' (2019) 44 *Yale Journal of International Law* 115–48.

[94] See Krisch, *Beyond Constitutionalism*, chapter 7.

towards a more equal status for Indigenous groups (Chapters 3 and 14 by Anker and Culver and Giudice), or towards greater leeway for national courts vis-à-vis international human rights adjudication (Chapter 6 by Kanetake). Legal entanglement, on the evidence presented here, does not eliminate conflict, but it might help to reduce problems associated with stronger integration or a strict separation of norms that express different, sometimes competing values. It might also, as in Berger's chapter on the struggle over the prohibition of *fatwas* in Bangladesh, simply help to delay a more principled, clear-cut response to a societal conflict, creating time and space for other processes to do their work.

Once open and contested, interactions between different bodies of norms will also often develop into more settled relations over time. This can be observed, for example, in the evolution of human rights-based contestation in international economic law which we have traced in an earlier article. What initially appeared as destabilizing challenges – of World Bank authority, or earlier corporate social responsibility rules – led to an adjustment and transformation which, despite some continuing uncertainties, has led to new consolidation.[95]

1.6.2 Beyond Legal Systems

Entanglement also stands in some tension with the way law and legal order have been imagined throughout the past century. Much of the notion of law, inspired by the image of domestic legal systems, was linked to the idea of system – to an orderly structure held together either in form or in content, and distinguishable from its outside. It is the systemic character, brought about by the union of primary and secondary rules, that for H. L. A. Hart and many theorists after him, distinguishes modern law from less developed forms of obligation.[96] Others, including non-positivists such as Ronald Dworkin, have focused on coherence and integrity as hallmarks of law.[97]

From all these perspectives, entanglement is a challenge.[98] It is a limited challenge, at least in formal terms, when we deal with reception

[95] Krisch, Corradini and Reimers, 'Order at the Margins'.

[96] See only H. L. A. Hart, *The Concept of Law* (Clarendon Press, 1994); J. Raz, *The Concept of a Legal System: An Introduction to the Theory of Legal System* (Clarendon Press, 1980).

[97] See R. Dworkin, *Law's Empire* (Harvard University Press, 1986); S. Shapiro, *Legality* (Harvard University Press, 2011).

[98] See also Tamanaha, 'Understanding Legal Pluralism'.

norms and overarching norms – here, entanglement is integrated into the legal system through the system's own rules about identity and boundaries. Yet even here, the particular rules required to deal with the relations with others have not been overly well theorized. Reception norms, traditionally seen as relatively marginal, pose theoretical problems because, as a matter of fact, they do not operate solely within the system but depend on accommodating rules and practices in other systems. Where interactions between different bodies of norms are intense, the potential for divergences and substantial incoherence grows, posing a challenge for the rule of law aspirations often associated with law, and especially with the systemic image of law. And while a description of law that operates with closure and hierarchies may still have some formal validity (within each of the interacting systems), it captures less of the social reality of a legal order.[99] In Chapter 16, Michaels draws our attention to the challenge of plurality for a Hartian legal theory and begins to develop a response by introducing 'tertiary' norms and clarifying their scope and functioning. He highlights in particular that such tertiary norms need to reflect a recognition not just from the officials or addressees of the particular legal system concerned but also from other legal systems with which it stands in relations.

The theoretical challenge grows further when we turn to the straddling practices mentioned in Section 1.5. The more these blur the boundaries of different legal systems, the less they can be integrated into a systemic image of the law, even one relying on a multiplicity of systems. The idea of a 'web' – in which different norms, and bodies of norms, form connections with one another, with the whole only emerging from these connections – then becomes yet more attractive.[100] As Culver and Giudice demonstrate in Chapter 14, such a web may rest on a conceptualization that builds upon but modifies a Hartian approach, by emphasizing mutual references between legal institutions.[101] This might also provide a frame in which systemic and non-systemic expressions of law can coexist, distinguished primarily by the strength and stability of the connections between particular norms and bodies of norms. Culver and

[99] See also the discussion in Taekema, 'Between or Beyond Legal Orders'; G. Palombella, 'Theory, Realities, and Promises of Inter-Legality', in J. Klabbers and G. Palombella (eds), *The Challenge of Inter-Legality* (Cambridge University Press, 2019), pp. 363–90, at pp. 374–8.

[100] F. Ost and M. Van de Kerchove, *De la pyramide au réseau?: pour une théorie dialectique du droit* (Publications Fac St Louis, 2002).

[101] See also Culver and Giudice, *Legality's Borders*.

Giudice demonstrate the analytical but also the normative appeal of entanglement over more systemic, hierarchical models by using the example of state–First Nations relations in Canada.

Much theorizing about networks in law, often inspired by Niklas Luhmann's systems theory, has taken the perspective of an external observer, seeking to bring to light the real workings of a social system represented otherwise by the actors involved in it – to reveal 'the hard-core reality of a trompe d'oeil'.[102] Yet, as our volume shows, a networked reality may well be visible also in the legal discourses themselves. Linkages and entanglements are processed and produced internally to legal practice, through various kinds of norms and practices connecting and straddling different bodies of norms. Often enough, these linkages may connect individual norms, rather than 'bodies' of norms as such, thus taking us yet further away from the notion of closed systems.[103] A pluralist jurisprudence will then have to give an account of not only the inter-systemic dimension,[104] but also the trans-systemic, networked character of law, as in Boaventura de Sousa Santos' interlegality.[105]

This is bound to have repercussions on the nature of legal reasoning, well beyond the particular forms of interface norms constructed to deal with the margins. Where actors understand law as a web rather than a hierarchical system, we can expect them to turn away from the ambition of principled solutions – valid throughout the system – and shift towards forms of practical, localized and perhaps provisional accommodation. Inconsistencies within the law are then not so much elements to be eliminated, but instead normal occurrences in an order of multiplicity that need to be processed and navigated.[106] As indicated by Broude's chapter on the many attitudes of actors towards the entangled legalities they are confronted with, 'navigating' may in any event be a more accurate description of the approach to legal reasoning appropriate in this context. However, as Eckert astutely highlights in her contribution,

[102] Teubner, 'The King's Many Bodies', 765.

[103] See D. Burchardt, 'Intertwinement of Legal Spaces in the Transnational Legal Sphere' (2017) 30 *Leiden Journal of International Law* 305–26.

[104] This is the dominant perspective in, for example, N. Roughan and A. Halpin (eds), *In Pursuit of Pluralist Jurisprudence* (Cambridge University Press, 2017).

[105] See, e.g., de Sousa Santos, *Toward a New Legal Common Sense.*

[106] See, e.g., H. P. Glenn, *The Cosmopolitan State* (Oxford University Press, 2013), chapter 14; M. Del Mar, 'Legal Reasoning in Pluralist Jurisprudence', in N. Roughan and A. Halpin (eds), *In Pursuit of Pluralist Jurisprudence* (Cambridge University Press, 2017), pp. 40–63; Taekema, 'Between or beyond Legal Orders'.

such a 'navigating' stance (and the turn away from systematicity) may well undermine one of the core sources of hope associated with the law – the hope for coherence and universality.

This image suggests a deeper inquiry into the theoretical foundations underlying competing imaginations of law. The contrast between 'post-modern' (complex and multivalent) and 'modern' (orderly and systemic) approaches to law is useful here,[107] but other directions need to be equally included. Anker's chapter pursues one of these by showing how Indigenous approaches to law have a more natural affinity to entanglement, based on an ontology in which law is merely part of the relations that already exist in symbiotic ecosystems. Taking into view such conceptions of law, and more broadly those animating the historically widespread forms of legal entanglement around the world, should help to situate the image of law in the modern state that most of our jurisprudence has been built around. This image – the systemic, hierarchical and exclusive one – may well constitute the exception rather than the rule.

1.7 Conclusion

If law is typically understood in the singular, our focus on entangled legalities traces the implications of its appearance in the plural. Legal multiplicity can, of course, just mean that different legal orders exist side by side, with occasional contact, as in the traditional conflict-of-laws paradigm between national legal orders. But where interactions are more frequent and intense, the relations between different legal orders (and more broadly, different bodies of norms) move to the centre of attention. The legal order as such can then no longer be understood without an account of the ways in which its different parts are entangled.[108] In this volume, we try to understand the contours of such entanglement better. We ask what entanglement may mean in law and whether it can give a useful account of the relations between different norms, especially in the context of law beyond the state. We try to understand the forms through which actors produce entanglement and what kind of order results from their efforts at weaving norms from different origins together – or at keeping them apart. Entanglement, in our approach, does not denote

[107] See also D. Burchardt, 'The Twilight of Legal Order? On the Current Challenges Faced by the Concept of a Legal System' (2018) 9 *Transnational Legal Theory* 110–46.

[108] See also Chapters 14 and 16 by Culver and Giudice and Michaels.

merely any form of de facto interaction; it seeks to capture linkages expressed in discursive statements about the relation of multiple norms, namely legal statements about the relations of different norms and legal orders.

We conjecture that in today's globalized world, the burgeoning multiplicity of norms has engendered more entanglement than was the norm in the heyday of consolidated legal orders within nation states. In this respect it may present greater similarities with pre-national legal orders (and continuities with lesser-studied aspects of law in and around modern states) and connect with a neo-medievalist interpretation of the postnational constellation.[109] Yet this volume is not intended to present a comprehensive empirical picture of legal entanglements in the past or present. It primarily seeks to draw attention to a phenomenon that helps us to observe law differently, and to develop a better understanding of the causes, forms and consequences of this phenomenon. With this, we hope to shift the focus, to begin to see entanglement as a normal state of law, and initiate broader enquiries into entangled legal orders.

[109] See J. Friedrichs, 'The Meaning of New Medievalism' (2001) 7 *European Journal of International Relations* 475–501.

PART I

Entangling State Law

2

Denial, Deferral and Translation

Dynamics of Entangling and Disentangling State and Non-state Law in Postcolonial Spaces

TOBIAS BERGER

2.1 Introduction

Legal entanglements unfold in a curious space. They emerge in-between different sets of norms, which are neither fully integrated nor kept entirely apart.[1] This position in-between various sets of norms is inherently unstable, so that legal entanglements need ardent work of creation, maintenance and constant renewal. Entanglements thus need to be made and unmade by specific actors who are situated in historically shaped yet malleable contexts where different sets of norms overlap and coincide. This chapter focuses on the ways in which different actors entangle international, state and non-state law in postcolonial societies. While undoubtedly a very heterogeneous category that unavoidably escapes reductionist attempts at homogenization, I argue that those places where colonial powers institutionalized plural legal orders as explicit strategies for the consolidation of their rule constitute a privileged site for the investigation of entangled legalities. It is from these sites that systemic images of law, as they have been problematized in Chapter 1, have been forcefully attacked. As Renisa Mawani argues, 'Law, in all of its plurality – including Western, customary, and personal law – is conventionally viewed as geographically situated and territorially bound to national and imperial polities. What the comparative and transnational turn has revealed is that law was also itinerant, moving with imperial authorities and colonial subjects, and connecting imperial jurisdictions in the process.'[2] Itinerant laws have thus produced historically grown legal

[1] See the definitional discussion in Chapter 1.

[2] R. Mawani, 'Law and Colonialism', in A. Sarat and P. Ewick (eds), *The Handbook of Law and Society* (Wiley-Blackwell, 2015), pp. 417–32, at p. 426.

entanglements affecting socio-legal dynamics in most of the world today. Yet laws hardly ever travel by themselves.

This chapter consequently analyses (some of) the actors that make law move and the dynamics in which they seek to make and unmake certain legal connections. Focusing on judges and activists of non-governmental organizations (NGOs), it identifies three modes in which dynamics of distancing and approximation between different sets of norms can unfold: denial, deferral and translation. Whereas denial refers to a state where empirically existing entanglements are acknowledged but their legal as well as normative validity is denied, deferral denotes a situation of precarious balance in which a given relationship between interwoven sets of norms cannot be altered, as this would leave one or more of the involved parties deeply dissatisfied. Thriving on imprecision and ambiguity, the politics of deferral thus denotes a strategy of leaving the final arrangements between different bodies of norms open and unsettled. Finally, rather than aiming to unmake entanglements, as in the case of denial, or postponing conclusive settlements between competing sets of norms, as in the case of deferral, translation refers to the proactive transformation of norms that occurs as they move back and forth between different contexts. In all three modes – denial, deferral and translation – multiple normativities do not merely coexist but are brought to life and are related to each other through the ardent work of individual actors. They are the main protagonists of this chapter.

After having discussed the ways in which colonial legacies have historically shaped and continue to strongly affect entanglements between international, state and non-state law in postcolonial spaces (Section 2.2), I turn to the discussion of denial, deferral and translation as three distinct modes through which actors seek to navigate highly complex entangled legal landscapes (Section 2.3). The remainder of the chapter then turns to the analysis of the dynamics in which legalities become entangled in Bangladesh as a postcolonial space par excellence (Section 2.4). More precisely, I focus on three instances to illustrate these dynamics: first, the Supreme Court's attempt to ban Islamic fatwas in 2001 (denial); second, the violent protests this has triggered and the subsequent decision of the Appellate Division of the Supreme Court to stay the verdict for over a decade (deferral); and third, the work of local activists who, regardless of constitutional developments, seek to carve out emancipatory spaces for marginalized people by simultaneously drawing on multiple normative registers, including Islamic and international human rights norms (translation).

2.2 Colonial Entanglements

Today's legal entanglements unfold in long historical trajectories in which colonial encounters have played a decisive role.[3] On the one hand, law was a key instrument of colonial rule. It was, in the words of Martin Chanock, 'the cutting edge of colonialism, an instrument of the power of an alien state and part of the process of coercion'.[4] As an instrument of coercion, law was crucial for the facilitation of the extraction of land, labour and mineral resources from the colonized as well as for the organization of highly unequal trade networks and market exchanges.[5] Yet beyond its function as a tool for domination, Sally Engle Marry has argued that law also had constitutive effects; it not only enabled extraction but also 'transformed conceptions of time, space, property, work, marriage, and the state'.[6] Embedded in broader systems of domination, colonial laws thus significantly altered not only the material infrastructures of colonized societies but also deeply transformed diverse systems of knowledge deployed to navigate various aspects of everyday life. While colonial projects varied significantly across time and space, as well as between different colonizing empires, most, if not all, European colonial projects operated through the making and unmaking of legal entanglements whose shape and direction were frequently the subjects of intense debate in both the colonies and the metropoles. In these debates, arguments ranged from the wholesale transfer of metropolitan laws to the wide-ranging reliance on seemingly indigenous laws in systems of indirect rule. Yet even in the latter case, colonialism's legal entanglements had far-reaching effects on colonized societies. Rather than simply relying on pre-existing 'traditional' or 'customary' authority, colonial projects operating through various forms of indirect rule strongly altered Indigenous legal forums. Importantly, the kind of legal pluralism that emerged and continues to significantly shape legal dynamics in most of the world today was thus not a factual state of affairs but a project to be realized. As Lauren Benton argues, 'colonial powers sought simultaneously to

3 For an extended version of this argument, see also T. Berger, 'The "Global South" as a Relational Category: Global Hierarchies in the Production of Law and Legal Pluralism' (forthcoming) *Third World Quarterly*.

4 M. Chanock, *Law, Custom, and Social Order: The Colonial Experience in Malawi and Zambia* (Cambridge University Press, 1985), p. 4.

5 J. L. Comaroff, 'Reflections on the Colonial State, in South Africa and Elsewhere: Factions, Fragments, Facts and Fictions' (1998) 4 *Social Identities* 321–61, at 325.

6 S. E. Merry, 'Law and Colonialism' (1991) 25 *Law & Society Review* 889–922, at 890–1.

establish limited jurisdiction and to reinforce – and in some cases create – Indigenous legal forums. As with indirect rule, legal pluralism as a colonial project often required the creation of "traditional" authority and the reification of legal practices and sources of law that had existed formerly only as fluid elements of a flexible legal process.'[7]

While the constitutive effects of colonial laws on colonized societies have been carefully documented, recursive effects on the colonizing societies have received less attention. In the legal histories of Western Europe and North America, narratives of autonomous legal evolutions still predominate. Yet the constitutive effects of colonial encounters cut both ways. Although highly unequal, these encounters did not merely constitute the unilateral imposition of legal templates. Instead, recent scholarship has shown how even core aspects of European legal systems remain poorly understood if conceptualized without the transnational entanglements in which they emerged. Rather than being only peripheral to legal developments in Europe, colonies frequently had to serve as laboratories for legal innovation and new regulatory techniques. As John Comaroff has argued, 'the terrain of the colonized became a testing ground from which emanated new lawfare, new technologies of order and regulation. These sometimes confined themselves to the colonial frontier itself. But sometimes they were taken back to the metropole, there to alter its social lineaments.'[8] At times, the alterations that resulted from the retransfer of legal innovation to the metropole were far-reaching. One example is the legal institution of property as a cornerstone of liberal social and political orders developing in Western Europe. As Brenna Bhandar has shown, the emergence and current shape of modern property laws in the United Kingdom are inseparable from colonial expansions since the eighteenth century.[9] In her account, the validation of formal ownership via the registration of land titles in state-regulated regimes institutionally emerged in the colonies of South Australia and British Colombia, long before a similar regime became implemented in the United Kingdom on a national scale.[10] Perhaps

[7] L. Benton, *Law and Colonial Cultures: Legal Regimes in World History, 1400–1900* (Cambridge University Press, 2002), p. 128.

[8] J. L. Comaroff, 'Colonialism, Culture, and the Law: A Foreword' (2001) 26 *Law & Social Inquiry* 305–14, at 311.

[9] B. Bhandar, *Colonial Lives of Property: Law, Land, and Racial Regimes of Ownership* (Duke University Press, 2018).

[10] Ibid., pp. 77–114.

ironically, the subsequent prevalence of private property as a formally sanctioned, state-recognized institution became a key marker of civilizational achievements while, conversely, its absence turned into a key justificatory trope for colonial settlements.[11] The ensuing 'racial regimes of ownership', as Bhandar aptly calls them, fundamentally shaped processes of social and political transformation in both the colonies and the metropoles. At an equally fundamental level, Nasser Hussain has shown how notions of the rule of law, and exceptions to this rule of law in terms of emergency powers, were at the heart of nineteenth-century colonial governance in India and Jamaica, which, in turn, decisively 'affected the development of Western legality'.[12] These accounts of the entangled legalities in which modern notions of property as well as 'the rule of law' as cornerstones of legal systems emerged powerfully undermine inward-looking narratives of teleological (legal) development in either the Global North or the Global South.

2.3 Dynamics: Denial, Deferral and Translation

Those places where colonial powers institutionalized plural legal orders as explicit strategies for the consolidation of their rule constitute privileged sites for the investigation of entangled legalities. Here, both state and non-state law have not developed in isolation but invariably bear the traces of the transnational entanglements in which they emerged. Significantly shaping different sets of legal norms as well as the respective relationships between them, the effects of these transnational entanglements have been enduring, reaching well into the postcolonial period. In the postcolonial period, at least three different kinds of entanglements can be observed in previously colonized, plural legal orders. First, international financial institutions and multilateral donor agencies continue to entangle state legal systems transnationally. These entanglements encompass both the substantive legal provision, generally along liberal lines, and the facilitation of material legal infrastructures like courtrooms or digital devices. Contemporary transnational legal entanglements thus take myriad forms, often enumerated by international actors in terms of 'laws passed, people trained, computers

[11] C. W. Mills, *The Racial Contract* (Cornell University Press, 1997).

[12] N. Hussain, *The Jurisprudence of Emergency: Colonialism and the Rule of Law* (University of Michigan Press, 2003), p. 3.

provided, buildings erected'.[13] Second, transnational entanglements also continue shaping the operation of non-state legal systems. These entanglements stem from various sources, including (again) international donor organizations that have recently rediscovered non-state justice institutions as seemingly 'local' and 'authentic' avenues for the promotion of human rights and the rule of law.[14] Yet diaspora communities also entangle non-state justice institutions in broader webs of conflict resolution beyond the confines of the nation state, thus embedding seemingly local courts in wider networks of normative and legal reasoning.[15] Finally, state and non-state law in postcolonial contexts are not only transnationally embedded but also interact with each other. The ensuing entanglements can take various forms. They can surface as formal legal integration, for example, when non-state justice institutions are recognized by state authorities under conditions of adherence to certain substantive and/or procedural requirements. In addition, entanglements can also emerge through officials performing functions across different systems. Marlies Bouman provides a powerful example of such entanglement in her analysis of the complicity of police officers in the facilitation of non-state justice in Botswana, where 'chiefly courts are in fact tolerated, or even supported, by the official police forces, although their adjudication activities are in violation of various national laws'.[16] Beyond formal integration, state and non-state law thus also become entangled in quotidian practices of conflict resolution.

What emerges in these entanglements is a dynamic movement of approximation and distancing, as actors navigate the complex space in-between state and non-state law. As argued in Chapter 1, this space in-between emerges as entanglements '[are often] characterized by a dialectical dynamic – one in which actors favour proximity between different bodies of norms but they also seek a certain distance, and they

[13] D. Desai and M. Woolcock, 'Experimental Justice Reform: Justice for the Poor: Lessons from the World Bank and Beyond' (2015) 11 *Annual Review of Law and Social Science* 155–74, at 163.

[14] T. Berger, 'Global Village Courts: The United Nations and the Bureaucratization of Non-state Justice in the Global South', in R. Niezen and M. Sapignoli (eds), *Palaces of Hope: The Anthropology of International Organizations* (Cambridge University Press, 2017), pp. 198–219.

[15] A. Hoque, 'Land, Development and the Political Class: In a Translocal "Londoni" Village' (2020) 54 *Contributions to Indian Sociology* 215–35.

[16] M. Bouman, 'A Note on Chiefly and National Policing in Botswana' (1987) 19 *Journal of Legal Pluralism and Unofficial Law* 275–300, at 291.

thus construe the relation as neither strict separation nor full integration into one order'. In what follows, I introduce three distinct modes in which the dynamics of entangling (and disentangling) legalities can unfold: denial, deferral and translation. *Denial* constitutes a radical form of distancing. It does not concern so much the repudiation of the actual existence of the entanglements of different sets of norms as empirical phenomena but denies their legal validity as much as their normative desirability. Entangled legalities are thus portrayed as pathologies to be overcome by the actors involved. In the case of entanglements between state and non-state law, denial as a way of (almost) unmaking entanglements frequently relies on teleological narratives reproducing rather than challenging idealized notions of law as a unitary and coherent system. Interestingly, the denial of one set of entanglements might well coincide with simultaneous demands for new but different entanglements. Liberal critics of the pathologies of non-state institutions, for example, often rely on international norms concerning human rights to make their case for severing the ties between state law and its local non-state counterparts. In these cases, entangled legalities are evaluated against the backdrop of a spatial imagination in which 'the international' is seen as the reservoir of normatively desirable order, whereas 'the local' becomes the source of backwardness, poverty and strife.[17] State law is sought to be entangled with the former, also to distance it from the latter.

In contrast to the denial of legal entanglements, *deferral* aims at keeping a precarious balance between different forces in place. Often this involves undermining aspirations to unity and coherence usually associated with state law. Instead of producing certainty, the politics of deferral flourishes in the realm of the uncertain and undecided. It enables cohabitation precisely because it does not conclusively settle issues or conflicts, which cannot be settled, or cannot be settled in a way acceptable to all parties involved. Noah Salomon provides a striking example of the politics of deferral in his analysis of 'The Ruse of Law' in Sudan. Analysing the politics of religious diversity in the 1990s, he shows how, in the run-up to the 2005 Comprehensive Peace Agreement, only the suspension of the questions of applicability of Islamic religious principles to non-Muslims enabled progress in otherwise stalled negotiations between the north and the south. In Salomon's words, in the negotiations it seemed 'that the consensus was that the building of a state that respects

[17] R. Rao, *Third World Protest: Between Home and the World* (Oxford University Press, 2010), p. 45.

religious diversity was only possible *in spite of the law* – that is, when the law was unequally or inconsistently applied – and not by crafting a law that would be acceptable to all'.[18] Here, a unitary and consistent legal system is deliberately eschewed for inconsistency and a status of deferred legal certainty. Interestingly, the resulting uncertainty is often a source of stability rather than chaos. While scholars operating within the kind of unitary images of law outlined in Chapter 1 unavoidably understand uncertainty as a source of trouble and strife, the notion of legal entanglements opens the analytical space to appreciate the stabilizing function of uncertainty. Precisely because the conflictual relationship between different sets of norms is not brought into hierarchical order but is kept open and thus dynamic (or 'uncertain'), entangled legalities can have de-escalating effects in situations where seemingly irreconcilable differences coincide.

The third mode through which actors navigate entangled legalities is *translation*. Rather than aiming to unmake entanglements, as in the case of denial, or postponing specific settlements between competing sets of norms (as with deferral), translation refers to the proactive transformation of norms that occurs as they move back and forth between different contexts. Its focus is less on conceptualizing the ways in which different sets of norms are temporarily coupled or decoupled but rather on the myriad ways in which external ideas enter specific sets of norms. Translations usually involve two kinds of change that occur simultaneously.[19] On the one hand, the content of norms changes, at times quite considerably. As Walter Benjamin argued in his seminal reflection of 'The Task of the Translator', translations are inherently creative as much as productive processes. Instead of simply transferring ideas from one language (or one context) into another, translations constitute proactive innovations of new meanings. This, in turn, challenges the idea of 'the original' as an authoritative reference point to which any translation would need to seek as close a proximity as possible. Instead, proximity in meaning might well arise from a seeming distance to the original. In the beautifully poetic words of Benjamin, 'no translation would be possible if, in accord with its ultimate essence, it were to strive for

[18] N. Salomon, 'The Ruse of Law: Legal Equality and the Problem of Citizenship in a Multireligious Sudan', in W. F. Sullivan, R. A. Yelle and M. Taussig-Rubbo (eds), *After Secular Law* (Stanford University Press, 2011), pp. 200–20, at p. 203.

[19] T. Berger, *Global Norms and Local Courts: Translating the Rule of Law in Bangladesh* (Oxford University Press, 2017).

similarity to the original. For in its continuing life, which could not be so called if it were not the transformation and renewal of a living thing, the original is changed.'[20] On the other hand, as the content of norms changes, the contexts in which they are translated are also altered. In processes of translation as well as in instances of denial and deferral, the boundaries of Razian legal systems, both inwards and outwards, become rather fuzzy. To illustrate the modes of denial, deferral and translation, the remainder of this chapter turns to the analysis of entangled legalities in contemporary Bangladesh.

2.4 Entangled Legalities in Bangladesh

As a highly transnationalized socio-political space, Bangladesh exemplifies the properties of postcolonial statehood and the correlative legal entanglements so far discussed. Since its inception Bangladesh has been a highly aid-dependent country. Labelled as a 'perpetual basket case' by Henry Kissinger in the 1970s,[21] it subsequently became a testing ground for development practices and ideas as well as a focal point for developmental innovations.[22] At the same time, the country's legal landscape is characterized by historically grown and deeply anchored plurality. In Sarah White's paraphrase of Joel Migdal, Bangladesh remains 'a weak state in a strong society'.[23] The resultant legal entanglements between international, national and local sets of norms as well as between state and non-state law unfold in a long historical trajectory reaching back to the British colonial state in India. Before turning to the analysis of three instances of denial (Section 2.5), deferral (Section 2.6) and translation (Section 2.7), I first briefly sketch some pertinent aspects of this trajectory.

Having been part of the colonial state in India, Bangladesh emerged from the so-called second partition on the Indian subcontinent. The first had resulted in the separation of India and Pakistan upon the eve of independence in August 1947. Based on the 'two-nation theory' and the

[20] W. Benjamin, 'The Translator's Task' (1997) 10 *TTR: traduction, terminologie, rédaction* 151–65, at 155.

[21] C. Bell, 'Kissinger in Retrospect: The Diplomacy of Power-Concert?' (1977) 53 *International Affairs* 202–16.

[22] D. Lewis, *Bangladesh: Politics, Economics, and Civil Society* (Cambridge University Press, 2011).

[23] S. White, 'NGOs, Civil Society, and the State in Bangladesh: The Politics of Representing the Poor' (1999) 30 *Development and Change* 307–26.

assertion that Hindus and Muslims constituted two different nations and consequently ought to inhabit distinct nation states, Pakistan emerged as a bifurcated state with two geographically disconnected wings, separated by more than 1,000 kilometres of Indian territory. In many ways an unviable political project from the outset, tensions in Pakistan quickly rose, especially between the eastern and western wings. Escalating over questions of political representation, the distribution of resources and – above all – national language, these tensions resulted in a short but bloody war of independence in 1970–1, leaving between one and three million dead and more than ten million refugees in neighbouring India. Based on an ethnolinguistic nationalism built around the Bengali language as the most decisive marker of identity for the inhabitants of what was then still East Pakistan, the independence movement sought to undermine Pakistan's raison d'être as the homeland for all Muslims on the subcontinent by advocating a secular rather than religious identity for the future state-to-be. After the surrender of the Pakistani troops, following Indian aerial intervention in December 1971, Sheikh Mujibur Rahman and the Awami League as leaders of the independence movement consequently established secularism, together with socialism, nationalism and democracy, as constitutive principles of the newly born state of Bangladesh.[24]

Since its inception the state of Bangladesh has existed in a web of multiple, at times overlapping, entangled legalities. From the British colonial state in India, it inherited a bifurcation between secular Civil and Criminal Codes and a set of religious personal laws governing questions of marriage, divorce, inheritance and the custody of children. While based on religious precepts, the colonial state heavily intervened in the interpretation of religion. Relying on orientalist scholarship and excessively scripture-based understandings of religion, the colonial state codified religious laws whose content diverged significantly from the quotidian practices of (religious) legal interpretation in India. As Michael Anderson has argued, 'colonial administrators may never have changed Islamic legal arrangements quite so profoundly as when they were trying to preserve them'.[25] Departing from the colonial interpretation of religious law, the Pakistani state also engaged in substantial

[24] W. van Schendel, *A History of Bangladesh* (Cambridge University Press, 2009).

[25] M. R. Anderson, 'Islamic Law and the Colonial Encounter in British India', in D. Arnold and P. Robb (eds), *Institutions and Ideologies: A SOAS South Asia Reader* (Curzon Press, 1993), pp. 165–85, at p. 169.

religious law reform. From the Pakistani period, the postcolonial state in Bangladesh inherited the 1961 Muslim Family Laws Ordinance (MFLO). In many ways a radical piece of legislation, the MFLO altered inheritance patterns for orphaned grandchildren in ways considered by many religious authorities in direct contravention of Shar'ia law.[26] Until today, this provision of the MFLO is subject to vocal protest, most recently during large-scale rallies of the Hefazat-e-Islami movement in Dhaka in 2013, demanding (in addition to twelve further points) the 'abolishment of anti-Islamic inheritance laws'. Besides altering the law of inheritance, the MFLO also established a central role for the state in the administration of Muslim family law.

It prohibits the practice of so-called 'verbal divorce' (effected by a husband uttering the word 'talaq' three consecutive times). Under the MFLO, all Muslim marriages have to be registered with the state, and any divorce of such marriage can only take effect if submitted in writing to the chairman of the local administrative council and subject to a ninety-day mediation phase aimed at the restoration of marital life. While welcomed by women's rights organizations, the MFLO provoked severe resistance among the community of religious scholars in Pakistan who understood it to be a direct attack on their authority.[27]

From the liberation movement, the state inherited the initial emphasis on secularism as a foundation of the state. Yet this notion of secularism was always subject to interpretation and contestation. Between 1975 and 1991, Bangladesh was governed by two military dictatorships, both of which deployed religious language as a legitimating device.[28] The first dictator, General Ziaur Rahman, changed the principle of secularism to an emphasis on 'absolute trust and faith in the Almighty Allah' in the preamble as well as a new subclause (1A) of the Bangladeshi constitution. The second one, General Husain Md. Ershad, altered the constitution in 1988 by introducing the Eighth Amendment that declared Islam to be the

[26] M. J. Nelson, *In the Shadow of Shari'ah: Islam, Islamic Law, and Democracy in Pakistan* (Columbia University Press, 2011); M. J. Nelson, 'Inheritance Unbound: The Politics of Personal Law Reform in Pakistan and India', in S. Khilnani, V. Raghavan and A. K. Thiruvengadam (eds), *Comparative Constitutionalism in South Asia* (Oxford University Press, 2012), pp. 219–46.

[27] M. Ahmad, 'The MFLO of Pakistan' (1993) 10 *International Journal on World Peace* 37–46, at 42–3.

[28] A. Riaz, '"God Willing": The Politics and Ideology of Islamism in Bangladesh' (2003) 23 *Comparative Studies of South Asia, Africa and the Middle East* 301–20.

state religion.[29] Ershad's amendment encountered strong resistance from both secular and religious forces within the country, as the strongest Islamic political party, the Jamaat-e-Islami, denounced Ershad's move as 'hypocritical' and 'not genuinely Islamic'.[30] A 2010 Supreme Court verdict reinstated secularism as a cornerstone of the constitution and banned Islamic parties.[31] Through the following Fifteenth Amendment of the Constitution in 2011, Article 1A was deleted and replaced by Article 8 (1) stating that '[t]he principles of nationalism, socialism, democracy, and secularism [. . .] shall constitute the fundamental principles of state policy'. At the same time, however, Article 2A was left intact, declaring that '[t]he state religion of the Republic is Islam, but the State shall ensure equal status and equal right in the practice of the Hindu, Buddhist, Christian and other religions'.[32]

Finally, the complex constitutional history also encompasses ongoing transnational entanglements in the form of obligations under international treaties. Bangladesh has signed the Convention on the Elimination of All Forms of Discrimination Against Women (CEDAW, signed in 1984), the Convention on the Rights of the Child (signed in 1990), the International Covenant on Economic, Social, and Cultural Rights (signed in 1998) and the International Covenant on Civil and Political Rights (signed in 2000), all of which have become powerful tools in the hands of Bangladeshi human rights organizations in their struggles against myriad forms of discrimination. In these struggles, local organizations need to navigate a complex web of entangled legalities, comprising a discrete set of state laws, often still exhibiting the imprint of colonial authorship, various forms of local non-state law, including religious

[29] Ershad's amendment also further 'indigenized' national identify by changing the spelling of 'Bengali' to 'Bangla' and 'Dacca' to 'Dhaka'.

[30] Riaz, 'God Willing', 308–11.

[31] This decision currently seems highly controversial as in the run-up to the national elections in January 2014, the Election Commission has withdrawn the registration of the Jamaat-e-Islami. A High Court verdict from November 2013 confirmed the deregistration of the Jamaat-e-Islami. The judges argued that although Islam is the state religion under article (2A), 'the Jamaat had misinterpreted Islam from its inception' (quoted in *The Dhaka Tribune*, 4 November 2013).

[32] *Constitution of the People's Republic of Bangladesh*, P.O. No. 76 of 1972, 4 November 1972, website of the Bangladeshi Ministry of Law, http://bdlaws.minlaw.gov.bd/sections_detail.php?id=367&sections_id=24549, accessed 7 November 2013. This is the slightly altered version of 2011. The earlier version from 1988 read: '[t]he state religion of the Republic is Islam, but other religions may be practiced in peace and harmony in the republic'. Quote taken from www.law.emory.edu/ifl/legal/bangladesh.htm, accessed on 7 November 2013.

precepts and customary conventions, and a liberal international architecture at least partially anchored in state law.

In what follows, I analyse denial, deferral and translation as three modes in which human rights organizations seek to navigate these entanglements. To scrutinize these processes of entangling and disentangling legalities, I focus in particular on the question of the legal status of fatwa. While the precise definition of fatwa is itself subject to ongoing debates, at its most basic fatwa refers to a non-binding decision issued by a learned religious authority on a point of Islamic law or practice.[33] Yet who exactly qualifies as a learned scholar authorized to issue fatwa, the weight of fatwa in light of competing legal precepts and the precise scope of which kinds of questions are actually governed and governable under Islamic law remain subjects of contention, and not only in Bangladesh.[34] In Bangladesh, these questions gained judicial salience with a High Court judgement issued in 2001.

2.5 Denial

On 1 January 2001, a Division Bench of the High Court Division of the Supreme Court of Bangladesh delivered what many national and international observers at the time considered to be a landmark judgement. On its own initiative and without having been approached by any party, the court has issued a *suo moto* ruling in reaction to a news item reported in the Bangladeshi newspaper *Daily Bangla Bazar Patrika* on 2 December 2000. The ruling questioned local authorities of Naogaon district regarding their failure to act against an illegal fatwa. The fatwa had directed a young woman of Naogaon to undertake an intervening marriage after an alleged verbal divorce to restore marital life with her previous husband. According to the news report, Saiful Chunnu of Naogaon village had pronounced 'talaq' ('divorce') to his wife Shahid more than a year ago, yet the couple had reconciled and continued marital life. As Saiful Chunnu spent a few days away from their village on family business, a neighbour claimed to have heard the pronouncement of 'talaq' and issued a fatwa directing Shahid to undergo a so-called

[33] D. Siddiqi, 'Islam, Gender, and the Nation: The Social Life of Bangladeshi Fatwas', in D. Heath and C. Mathur (eds), *Communalism and Globalization in South Asia and Its Diaspora* (Routledge, 2011), pp. 181–203, at pp. 200–1.

[34] W. B. Hallaq, *The Impossible State: Islam, Politics, and Modernity's Moral Predicament* (Columbia University Press, 2013).

hilla (intervening) marriage with another man from the village. Upon his return and learning about the forced hilla marriage, Saiful Chunnu refused to continue their marriage and sent Shahid back to her father's house. While highlighting the persistence of patriarchal power relations, the case is rather unambiguous in the legal terms of the state. Both intervening hilla marriages and verbal divorce (whether by uttering 'talaq' once or thrice) are in violation of Section 7 of the MFLO; in addition, causing people to believe that they will become objects of Divine displeasure is punishable under Section 508 of the Penal Code.[35] The court's condemnation of the local authorities' failure to act is thus neither surprising nor controversial.

While singling out the fatwa case from Naogaon, the court's verdict unfolds against the backdrop of deeper societal controversies over fatwa practices. As Dina Siddiqui has shown, since the early 1990s approximately thirty-five to sixty fatwa cases have annually gained attention in the national press.[36] This does not mean that fatwa are a recent phenomenon; it only indicates the increased visibility of certain kinds of fatwa verdicts after the return to electoral democracy in 1990 and the correlative improvements in freedom of speech. The fatwa cases that attract the attention of a larger audience often involve extreme displays of violent enforcement, frequently targeted against women's bodies. One of the first fatwa cases discussed at the national level was the case of Nurjahan in 1993. After having obtained a divorce from her first husband, Nurjahan rejected the proposal of an influential member of the village community and decided, instead, to marry a landless youth of her choice. Enraged by the refusal, the influential village elder initiated a shalish court and prompted a local religious figure to issue a fatwa against Nurjahan and her second husband for adultery. Although the same figure had previously verified the state-sanctioned divorce of Nurjahan and her first husband, he subsequently disputed the validity of the divorce papers produced in the shalish session, in which Nurjahan, her husband and the guests attending their wedding party were condemned to acts of severe public humiliation. Based on her meticulous reconstruction of the complexity of local power structures, Dina Siddiqui has shown how

[35] F. Pereira, 'Introduction' (2002) 4 *Interventions* 212–14; S. Hossain, 'High Court Nails Fatwa' (2002) 4 *Interventions* 220–3; A.-U. Zaman, 'Fatwa and the High Court' (2002) 4 *Interventions* 233–6.

[36] D. Siddiqi, 'Crime and Punishment: Laws of Seduction, Consent, and Rape in Bangladesh' (2011) 1 *Social Difference Online* 46–54, at 47.

Nurjahan's case cannot be read exclusively through the lens of seeming adherence to religious moral precepts. Instead, she shows how the fatwa aims to reaffirm intersecting power structures, including patriarchal control and class domination.[37] Yet these complexities are frequently lost in both liberal international and secular-nationalist narratives of fatwa violence. As Siddiqui argues, in Bangladesh:

> Understandings of the 'fatwa-frenzy' were also overdetermined by the specific trajectory of secular nationalism [. . .], in which Islam had always been the Other of the nation. Within this context, fatwas came to signify the contamination of secular national space by the backwardness of religious law. Accordingly, fatwas could be read as antinational phenomena attached to Islam, rather than one located in the complex conditions of modernity.[38]

It is this broader discursive universe, in which questions of fatwa verdicts intimately link to questions of national identity and the legacies of the liberation movement that the High Court's verdict is articulated in January 2001.

As argued earlier in this section, the verdict against the specific fatwa under scrutiny seems neither surprising nor especially controversial. Much more controversial than the condemnation of the individual case, however, were the broader implications that the court sought to extrapolate from the case it had decided to pursue. First, it concluded that all fatwa are illegal. As the court argued: 'Fatwa means legal opinion which, therefore, further means legal opinion of a lawful person or authority. [The] [l]egal system of Bangladesh empowers only the Courts to decide all questions relating to legal opinion on the Muslim and other Laws as in force. We, therefore, hold that any fatwa including the instant one are all unauthorised and illegal.'[39] Furthermore, the court called upon parliament to make the issuing of fatwa a punishable offence, even if the fatwa was not executed. In addition, the court's verdict also recommended the inclusion of the (until today highly controversial) MFLO in the Friday sermons and argued for the creation of a unitary education system, including religious educational institutions:

37 Siddiqi, 'Islam, Gender, and the Nation', p. 189.

38 D. Siddiqi, 'Transnational Feminism and "Local" Realities: The Imperiled Muslim Woman and the Production of (In)Justice' (2011) 9 *Hawwa* 76–96, at 81.

39 Quoted in the *Daily Star Law Report*, 7 January 2001. Reproduced in 'The Fatwa in Question Is Wrong' (2002) 4 *Interventions* 228–32, at 231.

> Before parting with this matter, we find it necessary to answer a question as to why a particular group of men, upon either getting education from maddrasah or forming a religious group, are becoming fanatics with wrong views. There must be defect in their education and their attitude. As a short measure, we recommend that study of Muslim Family Laws Ordinance must be introduced in all schools and that the Khatibs in all the mosques must be directed to discuss the Ordinance in their Friday sermons. As a long-term measure, we recommend an unified education system and an enactment to control the freedom of religion subject to law, public order and morality within the scope of Article 4 (1) of the Constitution. The State must define and enforce public morality. It must educate society.[40]

In effect, this line of argument amounted to a hardly concealed attack on entrenched religious authorities and their standing within established local power structures. Rather than limiting itself to the already justiciable prosecution of the violence inflicted under the seeming cover of religious justification, the verdict constitutes a radical attempt at affirming the superiority of the state over societal sources of law and legal reasoning *tout court*. What is remarkable about the case decided on 1 January 2001 is thus neither the indictment of the inaction of local state authorities nor the condemnation of the individual fatwa but the vehemence with which it draws much broader conclusions about the relationship of state and non-state law, especially in its religious manifestations. By calling upon the state to enforce public morality and educate society, it seeks to disentangle the complex legal architecture of family relations, especially in rural parts of the country, from religious influences. This denial as a radical form of distancing, which aims at the creation of the greatest distance possible between entangled legalities, unsurprisingly encountered strong resistance. Demanding the subordination of state law to religious principles, several Islamic organizations, including both political parties and religious educational institutions, organized a general strike, disrupting public life and leading to violent confrontation with law enforcement agencies. Religious scholars also appealed the judgement in the Appellate Division of the Supreme Court. The Supreme Court, in turn, stayed the verdict exactly two weeks after it had been first pronounced. Attempts at denying the entanglements between the state laws and religious authorities (however defined) had come to a standstill. What emerged, instead, was a politics of deferral.

[40] Ibid.

2.6 Deferral

After the Supreme Court had stayed the verdict in January 2001, initially for a mere six weeks, it took more than a decade before the legal status of fatwa was to reappear at the court. Confronted with hardened positions between secular-nationalist and religious camps, the court decided not to pursue the case further. Instead of aiming for legal clarity, the court settled for a politics of deferral where the legal status of fatwa remained undecided. Initially, the deferral coincided with a change in political climate. While the original judgement was passed during the last days of the Awami League-led government, in October 2001 the Bangladesh Nationalist Party (BNP), in coalition with three smaller parties, including religious ones, won the elections. Although recent scholarship has shown how the ideological differences between the Awami League and the BNP seem exaggerated in both public imagination and scholarly discourse,[41] the BNP's return to power in 2001 did amplify the voice of small yet highly organized Islamic political parties. Operating in a precarious balance of different political forces, the erstwhile very vocal defendants of the so-called 'fatwa ban' settled for a strategy of deferral, especially at the constitutional level. While the case seemed to be lingering and almost forgotten, its deferral was actually not caused by inaction but hard work, requiring myriad interventions to make sure that no judgement was forthcoming. One close observer and longstanding participant in the judicial contestation over the status of fatwa summarized the politics of deferral that emerged as follows:

> And then [after the Supreme Court had stayed the verdict in 2001], we ran a ten-year job to make sure that this case did not get heard too early, because at various points there were very worrying constructions of the bench and so on – and we were worried that if the case got heard that we would end up with a Supreme Court finding [. . .] saying that there is a fundamental right to issue fatwa.[42]

The decision on the constitutional status of fatwa thus remained undecided – until 2011.

In 2011, the Appellate Division of the Supreme Court reopened the case and endorsed, at least in part, the appeal that had been filed against the initial High Court verdict on the illegality of fatwa. Contra the High

[41] M. Hassan and S. Nazneen, 'Violence and the Breakdown of the Political Settlement: An Uncertain Future for Bangladesh?' (2017) 17 *Conflict, Security & Development* 205–23.

[42] Interview by author with senior legal counsel, Dhaka, January 2012.

Court judgement, it declared fatwa legal, but only if it was (1) passed by a 'learned person', and (2) only applied to 'religious matters'. Yet on both of these important qualifications the judgement remained conspicuously vague. It neither defined the ingredients necessary to qualify as a 'learned person' nor delineated what precisely constituted a 'religious matter'. The ambiguity surrounding the judgement further increased as the Supreme Court did not publish the full judgement until 2015, forty-four months after the verdict had been actually passed and communicated as a brief statement.[43] When the full judgement was eventually published, it still refrained from these crucial specifications of what qualifies 'properly educated persons' to issue fatwa in 'religious maters', and what exactly these religious matters comprised. Even as the Supreme Court formerly settled the case, the politics of deferral thus continued, as the precise status of fatwa within the complex legal architecture of Bangladesh remained an unsettled question and open to competing interpretations.

While deferring the conclusive settlement on the constitutional status of fatwa required the continuous work by the parties involved in the case, it also allowed human right's activists to disentangle the legal condemnation of violence against women from broader questions about the status of religious law. While these broader questions remained deferred, the judgement nonetheless explicitly stated that 'no punishment including physical violence or mental torture in any form can be imposed or implicated on anybody in pursuance of [a] fatwa'.[44] The Supreme Court's judgement thus overturned the High Court's decision to ban fatwa in 2001 but upheld another High Court decision from 2010 on the illegality of extrajudicial punishment. This 2010 High Court decision, in turn, came in response to three writ petitions filed by five prominent human rights organizations in Bangladesh, the Bangladesh Legal Aid and Services Trust, Ain-o-Shalish Kendro, Bangladesh Mahila Parishad, BRAC and Nijera Kori. These organizations are exceptionally skilful socio-legal actors, and their strategic choices have paved a distinct pathway to legal entanglement. Most of the organizations had already been at the forefront of the judicial process leading to the fatwa ban in 2001. A decade later, their

[43] A. Sarkar, 'Fatwa Must Not Violate Laws, SC Says in Full Verdict', *Daily Star*, 26 January 2015, www.thedailystar.net/fatwa-must-not-violate-laws-61702.

[44] Quoted in T. Huda, 'Zero Tolerance for Fatwas that Violate Human Rights', *Daily Star*, 23 December 2017, www.thedailystar.net/opinion/human-rights/zero-tolerance-fatwas-violate-human-rights-1509055.

writ petitions constitute an attempt at disentangling the inflection of violence, often against women, from questions of Islam and Islamic law. Starting from the observation that the first judgement declaring fatwa illegal was 'very poorly reasoned', one human rights activist describes how these five organizations at the time 'thought that somehow we had to clarify this whole question: what is a fatwa, what is not a fatwa, and what is the nature of this violence? And to bring the conversation, the discussion, the judicial exercise back to a discussion about the constitution and law, rather than religion and religious rights. We had to take it out of that space.'[45] Taking the violence perpetrated against women out of the space of contestations over religious-cum-legal authority is an act of disentanglement. It aims to dissociate the pathologies of patriarchal power structures in Bangladesh from questions of religious rights within a constitutional framework. At the same time, while disentangling questions of violence and questions of fatwa, the argumentative architecture built carefully by the five human rights organizations did include new entanglements with international norms. As the activist already cited argues, in the final court hearing the organizations were very careful to advance the following argument:

> we as Bangladeshi organisations working in Bangladesh within the framework of the Bangladesh constitution, but also within the framework of International Human Rights obligation that pertain on our government, have this interpretation. Our interpretation is that we want to have a very clear condemnation of the violence perpetrated in the name of fatwa. We do not want a debate what is and is not fatwa under religious law, we are not before a religious court, but before a constitutional court, so we want a constitutional interpretation. Our constitution clearly says: all forms of cruel and degrading punishment are prohibited.[46]

This argument, in turn, was supported by frequent references to CEDAW and its strict condemnation of all kinds of cruel and degrading punishments. The making and unmaking of legal entanglements in this case illustrates the importance of strategic choices of individual actors. As outlined in Chapter 1, strategic choices constitute one of the possible pathways in which entangled legalities come about. In this case, entangling and disentangling legalities coincided as Bangladeshi human rights organizations very deliberately sought to forge certain connections while releasing others.

[45] Interview by author with senior legal counsel, Dhaka, January 2012.
[46] Ibid.

2.7 Translation

The processes of distancing and approximation analysed as 'denial' and 'deferral' in Sections 2.5 and 2.6 play out in a context of confrontation between secular-nationalist and Islamic narratives deployed by different actors to lay claims upon the state and its constitutional order. At times, these claims have been laid quite violently, for example, in the repeated physical attacks on secular women's rights NGOs by seemingly religious actors throughout the 1990s or in the equally violent crackdown on members of the Jamaat-e-Islami by the seemingly secular Awami League government in the run-up to the 2014 election. While the dividing line between the religious and the secular is frequently staged in exceedingly violent spectacles in Bangladesh, recent scholarship has cast serious doubts on the social embeddedness of this divide. Analysing the confrontation between religious actors and secular NGOs over questions of women's economic empowerment in rural areas throughout the 1990s, Sarah White has shown how 'the substance of the NGO–"Mullah" confrontation lay indeed in the symbolic, or political, capital that each side could derive from it, rather than this signifying any more structural antagonism between "Islam" and the expansion of women's economic activity'.[47] Analysing the multifaceted dynamics of entangled legalities in rural Bangladesh thus requires moving beyond the confines of both secular and religious elite discourses as they circulate in Dhaka's higher judicial institutions and national media outlets. In contrast to urban elites, the grassroots-level fieldworker and activists in rural Bangladesh often need to navigate significantly more complex legal landscapes that eschew dichotomous confrontations between Islam and secular nationalism.[48]

To carve out emancipatory spaces for poor and marginalized people, and women in particular, activists in rural Bangladesh simultaneously draw on multiple, often quite different, normative registers. While the upper echelons of Bangladesh's vibrant NGO sector frequently disregard piety and religious registers as tools for local struggles, Elora Shehabuddin has shown how grassroots-level staff of these organizations regularly draw on religious arguments in their everyday work. The

[47] S. C. White, 'Beyond the Paradox: Religion, Family and Modernity in Contemporary Bangladesh' (2012) 46 *Modern Asian Studies* 1429–58, at 1441.

[48] E. Shehabuddin, *Reshaping the Holy: Democracy, Development, and Muslim Women in Bangladesh* (Columbia University Press, 2008), p. 30.

examples she cites range from Islamic condemnations of violence against women (for example by invoking the example of the Prophet Mohammed) to religious sanctions for girls' education and the use of contraception.[49] Often materially dependent on international funding, this kind of grassroots-level activism in rural Bangladesh thus needs to straddle the normative expectations of very different audiences. Elsewhere, I have argued that the notion of translation offers a productive way to capture the work local activists do in their attempts to straddle these different normative expectations as well as the different legal systems in which these expectations are embedded.[50] Rather than distancing or approximation, the notion of translation refers to the transformation of legalities that occurs as norms move back and forth between different contexts where they become embedded in deep webs of pre-existing institutions, practices and normative aspirations. In what follows, I use this notion of translation to illustrate a third mechanism by which different legalities become entangled.

I analysed a series of such translations between 2011 and 2012 throughout my field research on the recursive interactions between transnational liberal norms and local non-state justice institutions in Bangladesh.[51] Responding to a growing fatigue with conventional rule of law reform programmes that exclusively target state institutions, mostly in the Global South, non-state justice institutions have recently reappeared on the agenda of international donor organizations as one possible avenue for the promotion of human rights and the rule of law. One of the largest projects this recent interest in non-state justice institutions has given rise to aims at 'activating' the village courts in Bangladesh. The village court is a quasi-formal institution whose setup and operational logic closely resembles the non-state institution of the shalish. Yet, in contrast to the shalish, the state does recognize the village courts as legitimate sites for the trial of minor civil and criminal cases if they adhere to certain procedural requirements laid down in the 2006 Village Court Act. This focus on civil and criminal cases renders the village courts a seemingly secular institution, as in Bangladesh (like in India and Pakistan) the respective Civil and Criminal Codes are based on secular law, whereas Family Law is based on religious sources codified by the state, for example, in the MFLO discussed in Section 2.4. As several

[49] Ibid., p. 102.
[50] Berger, *Global Norms and Local Courts.*
[51] Ibid.

representatives of international donor agencies confirmed throughout my fieldwork, one key attraction of the village courts as sites for interventions was precisely their seeming ability to bypass the entire 'fatwa *problematique*' discussed in Sections 2.5 and 2.6.[52] As they understood the village courts as quasi-formal institutions dealing with conflicts governed by secular law, they simply did not expect religious arguments or religious authorities to figure prominently in their project activities.

Contra their expectations, religion did figure prominently as the field-workers and court assistants employed by local NGOs at grassroots levels for the implementation of the project regularly engaged in vivid religious argumentations. Many of these argumentations involved women's standing in processes of conflict resolution, which – in turn – frequently escaped neat distinctions between civil, criminal and family disputes. Often, questions of physical insult or disputes over land ownership are intimately tied to family conflicts, rendering distinctions between different sets of state law difficult in practice. In reality, religious lines of argument played important roles as the resolution of conflicts falling under civil or criminal law repeatedly required the simultaneous intervention in disputes within the realm of family law. In these interventions, religious arguments were drawn upon. In the case of fatwa, for example, many fieldworkers and court assistants argued that local religious authorities lacked the training to give binding interpretations of Islamic law. Similarly, they emphasized the religious obligation of husbands to issue security payments before marrying their wives (morhana) and maintained that verbal divorces without the state-prescribed ninety-days mediation phase were, in fact, 'Un-Islamic'. Ironically, while international donor agencies sought to strengthen quasi-formal institutions for the resolution of civil and criminal conflicts, the fieldworkers and court assistants implementing the project argued, in many ways, that only the state had both the authority and the legitimacy to interpret Islamic family law. These acts of translation entangle international and local legalities in novel ways, thus allowing grassroots-level employees of Bangladeshi NGOs to carve out participatory spaces for women in a discursive environment otherwise characterized by a dichotomous confrontation between Islam and secular nationalism.

[52] Interview by author with representative of the United Nations Development Program, Dhaka, March 2012.

2.8 Conclusions

As a paradigmatic developing country, Bangladesh exemplifies the complexities of legal entanglements as they unfold in most of the world. Indeed, as argued in Chapter 1, the ideal type of closed, coherent and unitary legal systems that carefully guard their boundaries with clearly defined reception norms while ordering internal plurality hierarchically and unambiguously has been historically the exception rather than the rule. Navigating complex and contradictory legal landscapes often requires the mastery of 'straddling practices', in which the boundaries between different sets of norms loosen at the edges and become more fuzzy. As I have argued in this chapter, the conditions of postcolonial statehood are highly conducive to zooming in on these fuzzy rather than clearly demarcated boundaries between different legal systems. Theorizing legal entanglements from the postcolonial space of Bangladesh, I have identified three distinct modes in which actors seek to forge specific entanglements between different sets of norms. In the case of denial, empirically existing entanglements are acknowledged while their normative and legal validity is denied. Deferral as a mode of entanglement eschews fixity and, instead, thrives on ambiguity and imprecision. Here, the precise relationship between different sets of norms is deliberately left open by postponing a conclusive verdict on their hierarchical order. In contrast to legal theorists who equate imprecision with disorder and instability, the empirical excavation of processes of continued deferral as a mode of entanglement in Bangladesh has shown how it actually can become a source of stability in situations where a given relationship between different sets of norms should not be altered without leaving at least one party deeply dissatisfied. Yet, as I have shown, also keeping the final arrangements between competing sets of norms unsettled requires continued and ardent work; the mere fact that nothing seems to change is no indication of inaction but is instead the product of continued legal labour by multiple actors, in the case at hand primarily NGOs and representatives of religious institutions. Like denial and deferral, translation as a mode of entangling legalities also depends on the proactive work of individual actors. In translations, the content of norms is transformed as they move back and forth between different contexts. While resonating in the receiving context, translations nonetheless retain the mark of the foreign, thus constituting a particular kind of entanglement in which norms are neither fully integrated nor wholly kept apart but made recognizable across different contexts. Denial, deferral and translation constitute different pathways to legal entanglements. As I have shown in this chapter, social and legal conflicts do not, as frequently assumed in legal scholarship, unfold as disputes over the precise meaning and interpretation of individual legal norms. Instead, they also, and often even primarily, unfold as contestations over which of these pathways to take.

3

To Be Is to Be Entangled

Indigenous Treaty-Making, Relational Legalities and the Ecological Grounds of Law

KIRSTEN ANKER

3.1 Introduction

How are we entangled? I invite you to breathe in. Can you feel the air enter your nostrils and lungs, and then be expelled? Try it again. With some practice you may no longer feel 'you' and 'the air', but simply a sensation that appears in consciousness. From this and a multitude of other metabolic processes, your body is literally constructed and deconstructed daily through exchanges – the activities of breathing, eating, shedding – with your environment. At an atomic level, it is not even easy to tell where the boundary between the self and the environment lies. Between the electrons and the nucleus that make up the apparent solidity of your skin is a distance the equivalent of something like that between the Sun and Jupiter. Electrons that are 'part of' your skin can be discharged in a current, and, indeed, have no distinct location (or other definite properties) but exist as a set of probable states expressed as a wave function (indeed, as energy).[1]

The human minds that find these aspects of quantum mechanics counterintuitive have evolved, slowly and over millennia, a form of intuition matched to the mechanics of what is visible and touchable,[2] a musculoskeletal system adapted to gravity on earth, and a nervous system capable of responding to prevalent threats and resources in furtherance of survival. Generalized throughout ecosystems, this

[1] M. Humphrey, P. Pancella and N. Berrah, *Quantum Physics* (Alpha Books, 2015), chapter 9.

[2] This may correspond to Newtownian physics or even earlier theories: see B. Sherrin, 'Common Sense Clarified: The Role of Intuitive Knowledge in Physics Problem Solving' (2006) 43 *Journal of Research in Science Teaching* 535–55.

physical, chemical and biological interconnectivity entangles everything from whales to weather patterns.[3] The way things appear to us is a product of an interaction of the properties of matter and motion with our sensory-motor system (although we can play around with those perceptions, as in the breathing meditation above). This 'life of the body' then proves integral to the development of even the most abstract of conceptual schemas, whether because reasoning relies metaphorically on basic physical properties like shape, size, distance, motion, up/down, now/later, inside/outside and containment, or because, as a neuroscientist might put it, 'imagining and doing use a shared neural substrate'.[4] That is, we learn to think together with human and non-human others; through them, we humans co-constitute our 'selves'. Forms – selves, types, categories, concepts – are neither mind nor thing, say ecologists of mind, but a process of pattern production and propagation in which we participate with the rest of the world, both present and absent.[5]

Following the first order of physical interdependence, this second order of semantic emergence from the material is also related to the inseparability of observer and observed. For example, were we to measure or observe the location of those electrons above, we would find that our choice of apparatus affects the phenomenon that is observed, such as in the famous wave–particle experiment for light.[6] Interaction with laboratory equipment causes the wave function to collapse into a definite state.[7] Further, to understand what an electron is, we would first need to examine the material conditions that provide it with meaning and some definite sense of existence; doing so, we would inevitably find a network of humans and non-humans – scientists and lab technicians, microscopes and particle accelerators, but also funding agencies,

[3] K. Balaramen, 'Whales Keep Carbon Out of the Atmosphere', Scientific American, 11 April 2017, www.scientificamerican.com/article/whales-keep-carbon-out-of-the-atmosphere/.

[4] V. Gallese and G. Lakoff, 'The Brain's Concepts: The Role of the Sensory-Motor System in Conceptual Knowledge' (2005) 22 *Cognitive Neuropsychology* 455–79, at 456.

[5] E. Kohn, *How Forests Think: Towards an Anthropology beyond the Human* (University of California Press, 2013), pp. 20, 37. On constitutive absences, see T. W. Deacon, *Incomplete Nature: How Mind Emerged from Matter* (Norton, 2006), p. 3.

[6] See R. Feynman, R. Leighton and M. Sands, *The Feynman Lectures on Physics* (Addison-Wesley, 1965), Vol. 3, §1-4–§1-6, www.feynmanlectures.caltech.edu.

[7] And once one aspect of that state is measured – its location, for instance – other of its properties can no longer be determined, as per Heisenberg's uncertainty principle: see ibid., §1-8.

manufacturers and policy-makers, as well as a shared system of signs and representations.[8]

I have begun with the lessons of (to take them in rough order) mindfulness, dialectics, quantum mechanics, ecology, phenomenology, cognitive psychology, evolutionary semiotics, anthropological post-humanism and actor-network theory to make the point that you and I have multiple ways of grasping entanglement. However, my purpose in this chapter is not to then notice that law is yet another 'thing' that becomes entangled or is made by entanglement, although I hold this to be sometimes a useful way of seeing the world. Socio-legal theory, for example, has embraced the dialectic idea that 'law' and 'society' are co-constituted through processes of argumentation, proof, naming and claiming, record-keeping, monitoring and all forms of performance, discipline, enactment, representation and discourse. Intersecting legal orders may produce particular formulations of one another through processes of 'recognition', on which social actors act, so that those actors then become in some measure part of the changing reality of each of those orders.[9] Rather than entangled legalities, though, in this text I am interested in legalities of entanglement – forms of legality adapted to the ontological entanglement in which we find ourselves. It has been noted that one reason for the various ecological crises we face is that dominant forms of law have become dysfunctionally oblivious to human interdependence with the living world.[10] Seeking to understand or develop legalities of entanglement engages with the normative project of developing what has been labelled 'Earth jurisprudence' or law imagined in ecological terms.[11]

In this chapter, I would like to suggest ways in which many Indigenous legalities provide examples of law borne out of entangled ways of being. From where I am writing, in Canada, invoking Indigenous legalities also engages with the normative project of settler-colonial reconciliation and

[8] K. Barad, *Meeting the Universe Halfway: Quantum Physics and the Entanglement of Matter and Meaning* (Duke University Press, 2007), p. 22.

[9] See K. Anker, *Declarations of Interdependence: A Pluralist Approach to Indigenous Rights* (Ashgate, 2014).

[10] F. Capra and U. Mattei, *The Ecology of Law: Toward a Legal System in Tune with Nature and Community* (Berrett-Koehler Publications, 2015); K. Bosselman, *The Principle of Sustainability: Transforming Law and Governance*, 2nd ed. (Routledge, 2016); F. Ost, *La Nature Hors la Loi, l'Ecologie à l'Épreuve du Droit* (La Découverte, 1995).

[11] P. Burdon (ed.), *Exploring Wild Law: The Philosophy of Earth Jurisprudence* (Wakefield Press, 2011).

the call for the recognition of Indigenous law *as law*.[12] Indeed, political philosopher James Tully's recent work on sustainable constitutionalism would have us see that the 'ecological problem' and the 'reconciliation problem' are intricately connected.[13] The disembedding of European peoples from their environments – produced by phenomena like the enclosure of the commons and industrialization – and the colonizing dispossession of Indigenous peoples were driven by similar forces and ideologies.[14] Indeed, some would go further and describe plantation colonies as the historical engine for industrial capitalism and its ecological fallout.[15] In the present, efforts towards Indigenous reconciliation are continually thwarted by the pressures of extractive economics, as well as the assumption of state dominion over land through its monopoly over sovereignty and the rule of law.[16] So, on the one hand, reconciliation cannot occur without a reckoning with the ecological pathologies of the reigning legal, economic and political systems. On the other hand, solutions to ecological crises that do not address the colonial suppression of Indigenous law and knowledge, Tully argues, will 'fail to discern and realize a good, sustainable relationship [with the Earth] because such a relationship is discovered and learned through practice. [. . .] Indigenous peoples and their practical knowledge systems have co-evolved with the ecosystems in which they have co-inhabited, learned from, shaped and been shaped.'[17]

As state institutions and citizens grapple with the issue of how to 'make space for' and recognize Indigenous legal orders, a reverse formulation of the question of coexistence appears that is much more deeply challenging both to state sovereignty and its form of legality: how can

[12] V. Napoleon and H. Friedland, 'Gathering the Threads: Developing a Methodology for Researching and Rebuilding Indigenous Legal Traditions' (2015–16) 1 *Lakehead Law Journal* 16–44, at 20.

[13] J. Tully, 'Reconciliation Here on Earth', in J. Tully, J. Borrows and M. Asch (eds), *Resurgence and Reconciliation: Indigenous–Settler Relations and Earth Teachings* (University of Toronto Press, 2018).

[14] See K. Polanyi, *The Great Transformation: The Political and Economic Origins of Our Times* (Beacon Press, 2001) on the market society or V. Plumwood on a form of gendered rationality in *Feminism and the Mastery of Nature* (Routledge, 1993) and *Environmental Culture: The Ecological Crisis of Reason* (Routledge, 2002).

[15] D. Haraway, 'Anthropocene, Capitalocene, Plantationocene, Chthulucene: Making Kin' (2015) 6 *Environmental Humanities* 159–65.

[16] See H. King and S. Pasternak, *Canada's Emerging Indigenous Rights Framework: A Critical Analysis* (Special Report of the Yellowhead Institute, 2018), https://yellowheadinstitute.org/rightsframework/.

[17] Tully, 'Reconciliation Here on Earth', p. 84.

newcomers find a place for themselves in Indigenous legal orders?[18] It is my argument that attempting to find such a place leads us to a different take on both the reconciliation and the Earth jurisprudence project. First, tentative answers to the question of coexistence require not simply trying to understand the competitive overlap of Indigenous and non-Indigenous legal orders, for example, as they vie for jurisdiction over forestry or child protection matters, nor the mutual normative or ideological influences that may historically have created 'intersocietal law'[19] or now lead to entanglement in the nature of mutual impacts, transplants and borrowings between legal traditions.[20] Rather, these questions require looking to the way Indigenous law speaks to the deeper ontological entanglement in which all things – including Indigenous peoples, newcomers and their legal orders – are implicated in each other. For the Earth jurisprudence project, this engagement with Indigenous legalities leads us away from mere intellectual recognition of symbiosis and planetary limits and towards embodied practices of entanglement.

Beginning with a brief overview of Canadian history through the lens of pluralist legal encounters, the centrepiece of which is the conclusion of treaties between European colonial (and, post-1867, Canadian federal) authorities and Indigenous peoples, I argue, borrowing a framework developed by Anishinaabe legal scholar Aaron Mills, that such a view largely relies on a contractual, and thus liberal, understanding of legality.[21] I then shift to exploring the legalities out of which Indigenous practices of treaty-making emerged. As Robert Williams Jr. puts it, treaties are 'a way of imagining a world of human solidarity

[18] See for instance, L. S. G. Finch, 'The Duty to Learn: Taking Account of Indigenous Legal Orders in Practice', paper presented at the 'Indigenous Legal Orders and the Common Law' British Columbia Continuing Legal Education Conference (Vancouver, November 2012), www.cerp.gouv.qc.ca/fileadmin/Fichiers_clients/Documents_deposes_a_la_Commission/P-253.pdf, 20.

[19] B. Slattery, 'The Generative Structure of Aboriginal Rights' (2007) 38 *Supreme Court Law Review* 595–628; J. Webber, 'Relations of Force, Relations of Justice' (1995) 33 *Osgoode Hall Law Journal* 623–60.

[20] B. Miller, 'An Ethnographic View of Legal Entanglements on the Salish Sea Borderlands' (2014) 47 *UBC Law Review* 991–1023.

[21] A. Mills, 'What Is a Treaty? On Contract and Mutual Aid', in J. Borrows and M. Coyle (eds), *The Right Relationship: Reimagining the Implementation of Historical Treaties* (University of Toronto Press, 2017). My objective is to bring that work to bear on the theme of this volume, so that the difference between 'entangled legalities' and 'legalities of entanglement' comes more sharply into focus.

where we regard others as our relatives'.[22] Following the lead of Williams and a number of other Indigenous scholars, I understand treaty jurisprudence as growing out of a deep appreciation for entanglement as constitutive of our being. Human treaties, if you like, are the reiteration of similar patterns of interdependence beyond the human. Further, I have learned that treaties were – and are – extended as invitations to newcomers to enter into relations with the peoples of Turtle Island[23] and the broader webs of their connections with local ecologies. Responding to an invitation confounds the colonial dynamics of recognition, in which Indigenous law is rendered legible to state institutions or individuals;[24] it is also different to simply stepping back or carving out a space for Indigenous law so as to avoid appropriating what is not mine, because it is about law as the practice of relationships rather than as an object of knowledge or appropriation. Finally, the invitation to invigorate ontological interdependence also has critical consequences not just for rethinking the liberal monad of the contractual conception of treaties, but for several other separations foundational to modern legal theory, such as the division between culture and nature, mind and matter, and subject and object. It gives me a way of drawing the lessons of entanglement from above into a relational mode for law generally.

3.2 Colonial Encounters and Normative Pluralism

Colonial encounters in North America produced a range of plural legal phenomena when the 'visitors who never left' – European fishers, fur traders, religious orders, soldiers, farmers, entrepreneurs and others – were variably integrated into local kinship networks, trade alliances and treaties, and when the original peoples – Mi'kmaq, Innu, Eeyou, Anishinaabe and Haudenosaunee fishers, hunters, agriculturalists, warriors, medicine people and others – were variably integrated into imported forms of education, economics and law. Historical accounts demonstrate different degrees and kinds of entanglement. In the terminology used in Chapter 1 by Nico Krisch, one can see the adoption, from

[22] R. Williams, *Linking Arms Together: Indian Treaty Visions of Law and Peace 1600–1800* (Routledge, 1999), p. 113.

[23] A common name for North America deriving from widespread creation stories that recount the emergence of the land from the back of a turtle.

[24] See G. Coulthard, *Red Skin, White Masks: Rejecting the Colonial Politics of Recognition* (University of Minnesota Press, 2014) and A. Simpson, *Mohawk Interruptus: Political Life across the Borders of Settler States* (Duke University Press, 2014).

early times, of Indigenous protocols by colonists as a *strategic pathway to mutual benefit*. In conducting trade and diplomatic business, colonial officials would give gifts, exchange wampum belts and perform abbreviated parts of the Haudenosaunee condolence ceremony for greeting allies:[25] these norms were likely adopted to 'create space to come to a preferred conclusion'.[26] Conciliatory approaches led in some places to ad hoc forms of criminal and civil justice that represented compromises between differing conceptions of crime and punishment. For instance, in New France, the individual responsibility for French *habitants* confronted the Innu practice of compensating crimes like murder with goods or human substitution.[27] The emergent norm for intercultural murder in New France for 150 years – that Aboriginal culprits would be delivered to French authorities, who would then pardon them with the exchange of ceremonial gifts – could be a *connecting norm*, 'weaving together different bodies of norms in order to come to a solution in a given case'.[28] Again, in Krisch's terms, we can see *interface norms* providing for varying degrees of engagement. The Treaty of Albany from 1701 describes complimentary, but distinct, areas of jurisdiction in which wrongs or injuries committed by the English or Dutch against Indians would be punished by the governor at New York, and, conversely, wrongs committed by 'Indians belonging to the Sachims' against the English or Dutch would be punished by the Sachims.[29] American law similarly recognized limited tribal sovereignty and treated it as foreign law subject to private international law rules.[30] Elsewhere, the common law 'doctrine of continuity' promoted the recognition of local Indigenous 'customs' within colonial legal categories and incorporated them as

[25] M. Pomedli, 'Eighteenth-Century Treaties: Amended Iroquois Condolence Rituals' (1995) 19 *American Indian Quarterly* 319–39; A. Wallace and T. Powell, 'How to Buy a Continent: The Protocol of Indian Treaties as Developed by Benjamin Franklin and Other Members of the American Philosophical Society' (2015) 159 *Proceedings of the American Philosophical Society* 251–81; J. R. Miller, *Compact, Contract, Covenant: Aboriginal Treaty-Making in Canada* (University of Toronto Press, 2009), pp. 11–32.

[26] See Chapter 1.

[27] Webber, 'Relations of Force and Relations of Justice'; R. White, *The Middle Ground: Indians, Empires, and Republics in the Great Lakes Region, 1650–1815* (Cambridge University Press, 1991).

[28] See Chapter 1.

[29] J. Borrows and L. Rotman, *Aboriginal Legal Issues: Cases, Materials and Commentary*, 4th ed. (LexisNexis, 2012), pp. 14–16.

[30] M. Walters, 'The "Golden Thread" of Continuity: Aboriginal Customs at Common Law and Under the *Constitution Act, 1982*' (1999) 44 *McGill Law Journal* 711–52.

British law.[31] The longstanding practice of making trade and diplomatic agreements formalized into an official British treaty-making policy with the Royal Proclamation of 1763, which provided for an 'interface norm' of consent for the settlement of lands occupied by Indigenous 'nations' – such lands would only be settled if 'ceded to or purchased by' the Crown at 'some public Meeting or Assembly of the said Indians'.[32] These so-called 'cession' treaties extended from Ontario in the east to parts of British Columbia in the west from the 1780s to 1921; their written texts read as a transaction in which Indigenous parties promise to 'cede, release and surrender' their lands to the Crown in exchange for small reserves, contingent hunting and fishing rights over the remainder of their territories, payments and other promises like the provision of education or medicine. An earlier era of treaties secured 'friendship' between the British and their Indigenous allies.[33] The undertakings of the Royal Proclamation itself were the subject of the Treaty of Niagara in 1764, at which 2,000 representatives of twenty-four Indigenous Nations from the eastern regions of North America gathered to 'join hands' in the Covenant Chain of friendship and alliance, in continuity of such treaties with European colonists dating back to the 1600s.[34]

Treaty-making thus constituted the central 'interface norm' for Indigenous and colonial polities for an extended period. Later, the balance of power shifted in favour of the Europeans. Following confederation in 1867 the Canadian state assumed jurisdiction over Indigenous peoples as subjects, and instigated a policy of assimilation.[35] After a century or more of official state denial of the existence or relevance of Indigenous law, the constitutional recognition of 'Aboriginal and treaty rights' with the promulgation of s. 35 of the Canadian Constitution Act in 1982 opened the door to wider consideration of the place of Indigenous legal orders, jurisdiction and sovereignty in modern Canada. For historic treaties, constitutional recognition has meant

[31] J. Borrows, 'With or Without You: First Nations Law (in Canada)' (1996) 41 *McGill Law Journal* 629–65.

[32] King George III of England, Royal Proclamation issued 7 October 1763, https://exhibits.library.utoronto.ca/items/show/2470.

[33] Such as the 'Covenant Chain' treaties in the seventeenth century, and the 'Peace and Friendship' treaties in the eighteenth century: see Miller, *Compact, Contract, Covenant*, chapter 2.

[34] Ibid., pp. 70–3.

[35] For a comprehensive history, see J. R. Miller, *Skyscrapers Hide the Heavens: A History of Native-Newcomer Relations in Canada*, 4th ed. (University of Toronto Press, 2018).

reversing the prevailing judicial stance that they were unenforceable either because First Nations lacked the capacity of an 'independent power', or because treaties were understood simply as gestures of political good will and not as binding legal obligations.[36] Further, courts now undertake to interpret the written treaties as manifesting the parties' common intention in light of their distinct motivations and understandings, and the cultural and linguistic differences between the parties.[37] While the written text remains the core of treaty interpretation for the courts, research on the transcripts of treaty negotiations, as well as oral histories passed through generations, has led to an academic consensus that the Indigenous signatory parties to the 'cession' treaties could not have intended to surrender their land; that an understanding of their relationships to land – and of their constitutional orders more generally – supports only that the treaty parties were agreeing to share the land and enter into ongoing relationships with the newcomers.[38]

3.3 Indigenous Treaty Jurisprudence

It is my contention that to see these interpretive differences with respect to treaties in terms of different things that are consented to misses the forest for the trees. For the whole structure of a contractual-style agreement as the interface between normative orders – the means by which individual norms might become entangled – treats contract as a neutral meta-norm. However, an attentive turn to Indigenous treaty jurisprudence shows up the ways in which the contractual paradigm is deeply implicated in the common (and civil) law traditions imported into Canada but is inimical to the territory's Indigenous forms of law. This has dramatic implications for treaty interpretation; it also has significance for legal pluralist scholarship and our focus in this volume on the

[36] *R.* v. *Syliboy* [1929] 1 DLR 30.

[37] *R.* v. *Sioui* [1990] 1 SCR 1025, pp. 1068–9; *R.* v. *Badger* [1996] 1 SCR 771, pp. 52–4.

[38] See, for example, M. Asch, *On Being Here to Stay: Treaties and Aboriginal Rights in Canada* (University of Toronto Press, 2014); A. Craft, *Breathing Life into the Stone Fort Treaty: An Anishinabe Understanding of Treaty One* (Purich Publishing, 2013); J. S. Long, *Treaty No. 9: Making the Agreement to Share the Land in Far Northern Ontario* (McGill-Queen's University Press, 2010); R. T. Price (ed.), *The Spirit of the Alberta Indian Treaties*, 3rd ed. (University of Alberta Press, 1999); Treaty 7 Elders and Tribal Council with W. Hildebrandt, D. First Rider and S. Carter, *The True Spirit and Original Intent of Treaty 7* (McGill-Queen's University Press, 1996).

ways in which norms become entangled. Indeed, it is significant for what we see as being entangled.

One of the 'strategic pathways' taken up by the French, Dutch and British was the adoption of the metaphors and tropes of Indigenous diplomatic language. Kinship terms in treaty formalities abounded: the Haudenosaunee were addressed as 'brethren' in the eighteenth-century treaties collected by Benjamin Franklin, and the British were invited, through rituals of care and concern between parties ('wiping tears' and 'clearing the ground'), to eschew purely mercantile concerns in favour of human solidarity.[39] These treaties invoked the bodily gesture of 'linking arms' or the linkage metaphor of the Covenant Chain that had to be polished regularly, lest it tarnish.[40] In treaty negotiations following the Royal Proclamation, Kings George III and George IV were referred to as 'our Great Father', Queen Victoria the 'Great Mother',[41] while the newcomers were greeted as *Kiciwamanawak* or cousin by the Cree: elder Harold Johnson writes of the treaty his forebears signed as an adoption ceremony under Cree law.[42]

These kinship tropes are not mere flourish, but speak to an underlying 'worldview' or, as I have been taught, a legality. Kinship extended beyond the human, to animals, plants, water, rocks and spirits, which are often linguistically marked as 'animate' and attributed agency in North American Indigenous languages.[43] For Anishinaabe peoples, *Nindoodem* (totem) animals – representations of which were placed as signatures on the Great Peace of Montreal in 1701 – were not only symbolic ways to organize human groups and to structure identity but, as explained by Anishinaabe of the period, were taken as their apical ancestors in the Creation period.[44] Harold Johnson puts the connection of humans to non-humans in prosaic terms:

[39] Pomedli, 'Eighteenth-Century Treaties', 319.

[40] Williams Jr, 'Linking Arms Together'.

[41] M. Walters, '"Your Sovereign and Our Father": The Imperial Crown and the Idea of Legal-Ethnohistory', in S. Dorsett and I. Hunter (eds), *Law and Politics in British Colonial Thought: Transpositions of Empire* (Palgrave Macmillan, 2010).

[42] H. Johnson, *Two Families: Treaties and Government* (Purich Publishing, 2007), p. 82.

[43] R. W. Kimmerer, 'Learning the Grammar of Animacy' (2017) 28 *Anthropology of Consciousness* 128–34; J. Cruikshank, *Do Glaciers Listen? Local Knowledge, Colonial Encounters, and Social Imagination* (University of British Columbia Press, 2005).

[44] H. Bohaker, '"Nindoodemag": The Significance of Algonquian Kinship Networks in the Eastern Great Lakes Region, 1600–1701' (2006) 63 *The William and Mary Quarterly* 23–52.

> This is where my ancestors are buried, where their atoms are carried up by insects to become part of the forest, where the animals eat the plants of the forest, and where my ancestors' atoms are in the animals that I eat, in my turn. I am part of this place.[45]

The term 'worldview' undersells these connections, though, in that it suggests simply a way of seeing rather than an actual world in which people are engaged (similar to the difference between culture and ontology that worries Paul Nadasdy).[46]

These entanglements at the ontological level give rise to specific kinds of law. In her examination of documented accounts of Treaty 1 negotiations, Aimée Craft notes how identification with the land gave rise to an ethos of responsibility, in contrast to the British concept of property:

> Chief Ayee-ta-pe-pe-tung [. . .] spoke to the Queen's negotiators about his 'ownership' and his view that rather than owning it, he was *made of the land*. Other Chiefs relayed their view that they had a sacred responsibility towards the land and that the future of the land was intimately linked to the future of Anishinaabe children: 'The land cannot speak for itself. We have to speak for it.'[47]

Indeed, the treaties I have mentioned can be understood as modelled after more pervasive forms of interdependence in the 'natural' world. Heidi Stark argues that Anishinaabe stories demonstrate a continuity between human–human treaties and human–animal relationships, both of which are characterized by mutual respect and gift circulation – such as when the beaver agree to offer themselves as food and the Anishinaabe commit to returning their bones to the water and offering tobacco in thanksgiving.[48] Aaron Mills characterizes this as a form of 'rooted' constitutionalism which he calls 'mutual aid', rooted because the practices of gifting and interdependence are learned from, and continuous with, earthly relations. Earthly somethings – plants, animals, bacteria, fungus, rocks, air and light – provide natural constraints to human law, but more importantly, sustain it through a web of relations.[49]

45 Johnson, *Two Families: Treaties and Government*, p. 13.

46 P. Nadasdy, 'The Gift in the Animal: The Ontology of Hunting and Human–Animal Sociality' (2007) 34 *American Ethnologist* 25–43.

47 Craft, *Breathing Life into the Stone Fort Treaty*, p. 94.

48 H. Stark, 'Respect, Responsibility and Renewal: The Foundations of Anishinaabe Treaty Making with the United States and Canada' (2010) 34 *American Indian Culture and Research Journal* 145–64, at 146. See also Borrows, 'With or Without You'.

49 Mills, 'What Is a Treaty?' and Mills, 'Miinigowiziwin: All That Has Been Given for Living Well Together – One Vision of Anishinaabe Constitutionalism', PhD thesis, University of Victoria (2019), http://dspace.library.uvic.ca/handle/1828/10985.

Further, the somethings are not just in the material realm: Sákéj Henderson stresses that Indigenous law also emerges out of experiences with the spiritual realm – that is, with the affective forces of the ecosystem for which he borrows quantum physicist David Peat's term, the 'implicate order'.[50]

3.4 Logics of Contract, Logics of Kinship

If interdependence is a way of being in the world, this brings a particular inflection to our study of legalities. It is not so much that ecological relatedness creates a norm of responsibility or obligations of gift-giving. It is, as Mills so carefully lays out in his work, that kinship, interdependence and 'mutual aid' are logics that structure the way we think and act, including the specific laws we come up with in service of them;[51] they are law as a mode of being alive.[52] For this, the choice of the term 'legalities' rather than law or norm as the focus of this volume is inspired. Legality is the most adjectival or adverbial of nouns; it speaks to the *qualities* of being legal or acting in accordance with the law; it is modal rather than categorical or concrete. A focus on legality allows us to ask not only 'why such and such a normative proposition is or isn't good law, but also and more foundationally [. . .] how a community comes to have a concept of what law is and a view of its purposes',[53] to notice the ways in which 'law [is] so deeply embedded in the world that one can look anywhere and see its reflection'.[54]

Here I will return to a view of treaties as transactional contracts that is likely more familiar to most readers, in order to now shed light on the legality that informs *that* understanding. Agreements with Indigenous peoples were referred to in the language of contract in contemporary colonial communications;[55] the written documents themselves record quid pro quo agreements in which the 'Indians' promise collaboration

[50] J. Y. Henderson, '*Ayukpachi:* Empowering Aboriginal Thought', in M. Battiste, *Reclaiming Indigenous Voice and Vision* (University of British Columbia Press, 2000), p. 262. See also G. Cajete, *Native Science: Natural Laws of Interdependence* (Clear Light Publishers, 2000).

[51] Mills, 'Miinigowiziwin', p. 24.

[52] R. Macdonald, 'Everyday Lessons of Law Teaching – Le quotidien de l'enseignement juridique' (2012) 3 *Canadian Legal Education Annual Review* 3–37, at 12.

[53] Mills, 'Miinigowiziwin', p. 24.

[54] B. Mann, 'Afterward: The Death and Transfiguration of Early American Legal History', in C. Tomlins and B. Mann (eds), *The Many Legalities of Early America* (University of North Carolina Press, 2001), p. 447.

[55] See examples in Miller, *Compact, Contract, Covenant*, p. 13.

with the British,[56] grant that the King may 'hold, occupy, possess and enjoy' the land in question 'irrevocably' for 'consideration' or in light of 'presents',[57] or 'cede, release, surrender and yield up' territories in exchange for cash annuities and other benefits, for example.[58] We have already looked fleetingly at two ways in which these texts have come into question as being representative of the nature of the agreements reached between the parties. First, the wealth of research in the past few decades on the oral negotiations shows that Indigenous parties did not cede title to land (much less sovereignty) but were negotiating on the basis of consensual coexistence and the sharing of land and resources.[59] Second, images like the Covenant Chain emphasize that, from the perspective of Indigenous parties, treaties were relational – and thus involving a need for 'polishing' or renewal as parties revisit their commitments to one another and attend to evolving situations – rather than transactional, constituted by a discrete moment in time that fixed parties' rights with respect to one another.[60] These two points capture something of the contrast between Indigenous treaty jurisprudence and contract. However, the legality of interdependence that I introduced above allows us to see that the transactional character of contract is just the tip of the iceberg.

In exploring the broader ways of being that lie underneath contractarian logic, I am indebted to Mills' comparative analysis of constitutional logics in Canada/Turtle Island, one of the most thorough and clearheaded that I have yet seen.[61] Contracts, as we know, create obligations when two parties exercise their free will to make and accept binding promises, in a 'meeting of the minds'. Aside from these privately created bonds, we are subject to other obligations created by legitimate political authority – again, justified by the consent of the governed through the putative 'social contract'. The autonomous selves at the heart of this story

[56] Such as the Peace and Friendship Treaties from 1752 and 1760–1, www.rcaanc-cirnac.gc.ca/eng/1370373165583/1581292088522.

[57] The language typical of the Upper Canada Land Surrenders from the 1780s to 1862, ibid.

[58] The formula frequently used in the 'numbered' treaties of 1871–1921, ibid.

[59] See references cited at n. 38.

[60] J. Y. Henderson, 'Empowering Treaty Federalism' (1994) 58 *Saskatchewan Law Review* 241–329; M. Walters, 'Brightening the Covenant Chain: Aboriginal Treaty Meanings in Law and History After Marshall' (2001) 24 *Dalhousie Law Journal* 75–138.

[61] Mills, 'What Is a Treaty?' and Mills, 'Miinigowiziwin'; A. Mills, 'The Lifeworlds of Law: On Revitilizing Indigenous Legal Orders Today' (2016) 61 *McGill Law Journal* 847–84; A. Mills, 'Driving the Gift Home' (2016) 33 *Windsor Yearbook of Access to Justice* 167–86.

of obligations are of course deeply liberal ones, with capacities for self-direction and rational choice. The relationship between humans set up by the pattern of offer and acceptance is one of direct and strictly defined reciprocity. Without contract, in the liberal story, we are disconnected, even antagonistic, individuals;[62] only the social contract and its appointment of a sovereign stop us from descending into Hobbes' 'war of all against all'. Rights underwritten by the sovereign are also oppositional, a power over things or others because their compliance is compelled;[63] they secure negative liberty and freedom *from* our fellow humans; rights and obligations, and the autonomy and self-interest they protect, square up bilaterally in a zero-sum game.[64] The disconnection extends to humans' ecological contexts as liberal legality collaborates with the extractive 'mastery' of nature, and in turn underwrites the physical alienation of peoples from land through commodification of the commons and colonization.

In the logics of gift and mutual aid, Mills writes, treaty is not the means to bring into relation atomistic persons in order to secure their liberty, that is, their capacity to exercise their autonomy. Instead, persons are always and already interdependent – the sum of their relations – and treaties deepen their intentional participation in a complex circulation of gifts through specific kinship forms.[65] In place of the contractual structure offer/acceptance/consideration, where what is offered in response corresponds directly to the initial offer, the response to gift is gratitude that then moves us to reciprocate, although likely not directly, to the gift giver.[66] Alternatively, and this is a formulation seen often in treaty records, Mills explains that mutual aid might be initiated through the presentation of a need to one's relatives that then inculcates a sense of responsibility and initiates beneficent action: hence the language of petitioning the King for 'pity' or protection in treaties.[67] In this way, and whether they are initiated as gifts or petitions, treaties are offered not as a way for Indigenous peoples and non-Indigenous peoples to bind

[62] Mills notes that even communitarian theorists hold that our social embeddedness is simply a factor in how we are able to exercise individual autonomy rather than see it as grounding a different understanding of the self: see Mills, 'Miinigowiziwin', p. 52.

[63] Brian Tierney, *The Idea of Natural Rights: Studies on Natural Rights, Natural Law and Church Law 1150–1625* (William B. Eerdmans, 2001), p. 16.

[64] Mills, 'Miinigowiziwin', p. 101.

[65] Mills, 'What Is a Treaty?'

[66] Mills, 'Miinigowiziwin', p. 102.

[67] Ibid., p. 104.

themselves to their promises, but as an invitation to specific forms of kinship, a relationship governed by Indigenous legality.

This understanding of treaty has implications for Canada's reconciliation project. If, as the aphorism now goes, 'we are all treaty people' here in Canada, the possibility of reconciliation and respect for Indigenous law is undermined if contract – and the baggage of its legality – is taken as the framing device. It would constitute what Mills calls 'constitutional capture', that is, that Indigenous claims are worked out through common and civil law categories, and within the presumptive structure of Canada's liberal constitution.[68] Further, the logic of gifts and mutual aid does not presume, as does liberal legality, that human political and legal relational structures can be severed from those of the Earth. In the logic of mutual aid, the reconciliation question is not about securing space for Indigenous legal traditions and the exercise of autonomy for different legal orders, but about sustaining healthy relationships in our ecosystems.[69] The treaty invitation to non-Indigenous peoples is to root themselves in Canadian soil, quite literally.

Learning, as an outsider, about the legal traditions specific to particular places in Canada, and the life-worlds that inform them, is part of

[68] Mills, 'Miinigowiziwin', pp. 35–7, 212. This is a particular instance of a larger problem with political 'recognition': see P. Markell, *Bound by Recognition* (Princeton University Press, 2003); D. Turner, *This Is Not a Peace Pipe: Towards a Critical Indigenous Philosophy* (University of Toronto Press, 2006); Coulthard, *Red Skin, White Masks*.

[69] The Two-Row Wampum (*Kaswenta*), a beaded belt with two parallel purple lines on a white background and closely associated with colonial-era treaty-making, is often said to represent a principle of non-interference – the European ship and the Haudenosaunee canoe sail separately in the shared river. It thus looks at first glance like an Indigenous (or intercultural) endorsement of something akin to negative liberty. This wampum may well have emerged in an era during which the original covenant had been forgotten by British authorities (see D. Bonaparte, 'The Disputed Myth, Metaphor and Reality of Two Row Wampum' (8 September 2013), http://indiancountrytodaymedianetwork.com/2013/08/09/disputed-myth-metaphor-and-reality-two-row-wampum; and K. Muller, 'The Two "Mystery" Belts of Grand River: A Biography of the Two Row Wampum and the Friendship Belt' (2007) 31 *American Indian Quarterly* 129–64). Stepping back from efforts to quash and undermine Indigenous legal orders is a necessary redress of imperial relations. However, it is only an initial remedial step, and it would be a mistake to assume that non-interference as a liberal value of negative liberty is an end goal of treaty. A more fulsome reading of the Two-Row, which includes the three alternating white lines representing peace, friendship and respect (J. Borrows, *Recovering Canada: The Resurgence of Indigenous Law* (University of Toronto Press, 2002), p. 149), is consistent with the ethos of relationality found throughout Haudenosaunee thinking (see generally K. P. Williams, *Kayenerenkó:wa: The Great Law of Peace* (University of Manitoba Press, 2018)).

a process of decolonization. Supreme Court jurisprudence has underlined that the goal of reconciliation in s. 35 of the Canadian Constitution requires the inclusion of the 'Aboriginal perspective' on rights under s. 35,[70] and the Indian Residential School Truth and Reconciliation Commission report of 2015 calls on law schools to include courses on Indigenous legal traditions so that future judges and lawyers may be equipped to go beyond paying lip service to 'the Aboriginal perspective'.[71] Such cross-cultural projects inevitably raise issues of translation – who can do it and how, the problems of rendering living and highly contextualized traditions legible to outsiders and their institutions, and the risk of appropriating what little remains after centuries of destructive colonial policies. These dynamics are reconfigured by the framing of Mills and others of the issue as one of relatedness rather than recognition. Mills writes that Anishinaabe constitutionalism is not about ethnic identity but about a way of being in political community on Earth: 'Though your stories may be different and you and I may not read the earth the same way, this is a constitutional framework available to all.'[72] This is why my approach here and elsewhere is to explore ways in which the messages of Anishinaabe and Haudenosaunee jurisprudence (the two rooted traditions growing out of the place where I live) resonate with the knowledge from my own inherited traditions.[73]

This understanding of treaties also has consequences for expanding our consideration of the heuristic of entangled legalities itself. Conceiving of entangled legalities in terms of normative pluralism – borrowing or transplanting rules and principles, developing hybrids, instituting structures that deal with conflicting norms – presupposes the form that law takes and constitutes its own kind of capture. If an actor – like a judge or other decision-maker – can select from a range of norms, we would have to think about law as dismembered pieces, as abstract propositions to be

[70] *R* v. *Van Der Peet* [1996] 2 SCR 507, [49].

[71] Call to Action 28 in Truth and Reconciliation Commission of Canada, *Honouring the Truth, Reconciling for the Future: Summary of the Final Report of the Truth and Reconciliation Commission of Canada* (Truth and Reconciliation Commission of Canada, 2015), www.trc.ca/res-trc-finding.html. See K. Drake, 'Finding a Path to Reconciliation: Mandatory Indigenous Law, Anishinaabe Pedagogy, and Academic Freedom' (2017) 95 *Canadian Bar Review* 9–46.

[72] Mills, 'What Is a Treaty?', p. 245.

[73] See K. Anker, 'Law as Forest: Eco-Logics, Stories and Spirits in Indigenous Jurisprudence' (2017) 21 *Law Text Culture* 191–213.

'applied' rather than an integral part of the way we live.[74] In the case of Indigenous law, such a floating rule or principle would, as Gordon Christie argues, be disembedded from the landscape.[75] Sákéj Henderson's vivid metaphor is that understanding Indigenous law as rules would be trying to appreciate an opera by reading the flute score.[76] In fact, Mills argues that rooted legalities do not find their usual or ultimate expression as rules at all.[77] This is partly because rules require abstraction – the disembedding from relationships – and partly because the agency of beings is suppressed if they are subject to (even provisionally) determinate rules.[78] Our entanglements, our giving and receiving of gifts, are continually co-constituting the world and, if I have understood well, the law is learned as a way of being in those relationships, producing not generalizable rules but rather a capacity to exercise judgement in situ to foster those relationships.[79]

Many scholars working on law in the Anthropocene have noticed the dysfunctionality of the conventional notion of law as rules faced with the dynamic and integrated nature of ecological crises, largely because the rule of law is based on predictability and resistance to change.[80] Law needs, consequently, to mirror ecological systems, to become dynamic and adaptive.[81] It may be that models of adaptive management, in which decisions and regulations are provisional and adjustable in light of environmental feedback, have something in common with the indeterminacy of law-as-judgement of rooted legalities. This short foray into the

[74] See M. Constable's retelling of the Norman conquest as the origin of positive law in the move from implicit knowledge about how to act to the articulation of rules in propositional language: *The Law of the Other: The Mixed Jury and Changing Perceptions of Citizenship, Law, and Knowledge* (University of Chicago Press, 1994), chapter 4.

[75] G. Christie, 'Indigenous Legal Orders, Canadian Law and UNDRIP', in *UNDRIP Implementation: Braiding International, Domestic and Indigenous Laws* (Centre for International Governance Innovation, 2017), p. 49.

[76] J. S. Henderson, 'Comprehending First Nations Jurisprudence', unpublished paper, Indigenous Law and Legal Systems Conference (University of Toronto Faculty of Law, 27 January 2007).

[77] Mills, 'Miinigowiziwin', p. 135.

[78] See the story of Wiisakejak and the ducks discussed by Mills, 'Miinigowiziwin', p. 137.

[79] Ibid., t pp. 137–45.

[80] J. Stacey, *The Constitution of the Environmental Emergency* (Hart, 2018); C. Voigt, *Rule of Law for Nature: New Dimensions and Ideas in Environmental Law* (Cambridge University Press, 2013); J. Ebbesson, 'The Rule of Law in Governance of Complex Socio-ecological Changes' (2010) 20 *Global Environmental Change* 414–22.

[81] J. Ellis, 'Crisis, Resilience, and the Time of Law' (2019) 32 *Canadian Journal of Law and Jurisprudence* 305–20.

legalities of entanglement that inform treaty-making in North America gives insight into the ways in which the premises of ecological law – a rule of law grounded in the Earth, in which each of us has an 'ecological citizenship' calling on us to 'respect the workings of the Earth's life systems'[82] – can be more than just the means to the end of sustainability; those workings are more than simply a model to copy or calculate with, they are a set of relationships to live in.

3.5 Conclusion

But wait. How are we separate? This can also be enumerated. Being an individual and distinct organism is a dominant and recurring part of my existence. When I touch a boiling kettle, it is only my hand that recoils. My body mostly feels like a bounded unit with my 'self' located somewhere in my head. Although individualism is often decried as a mythological foundation for liberalism, it has a phenomenological and pragmatic reality – alongside entanglement, it is *also* part of the way the world thinks. Human symbolic thought has the property of permitting the experience of an interior or virtual world that can seem separate from the domain of the concrete, material world. This separation between mind and matter, and between culture and nature, has in part been actualized – and amplified – through agricultural practices, the construction of cities and states, and empirical science. As anthropologist Eduardo Kohn comments, the phenomenon we are calling the Anthropocene seems to be the apotheosis of the mind–matter dualism inherent in symbolic thinking.[83]

There is now a multitude of disciplines seeking to critique or find solutions to the ways in which the current legal and political paradigm ignores our ontology of entanglement, among them ecological jurisprudence, ecology of mind,[84] new materialisms[85] and

[82] UN GA, 'Sustainable Development: Harmony with Nature – Report of the Secretary General' (17 August 2012) UN Doc A/67/.

[83] E. Kohn, 'Anthropology as Cosmic Diplomacy: Toward an Ecological Ethic for the Anthropocene', unpublished paper, Yale Ethnography and Social Theory Colloquium Series (Yale University, 5 February 2018), https://fore.yale.edu/files/Kohn.pdf, p. 6.

[84] G. Bateson, *Mind and Nature: A Necessary Unity* (E. P. Dutton, 1979).

[85] J. Bennett, *Vibrant Matter: A Political Ecology of Things* (Duke University Press, 2010); A. Grear, 'Toward New Legal Futures? In Search of Renewing Foundations', in A. Grear and E. Grant (eds), *Thought, Law, Rights and Action in an Age of Environmental Crisis* (Edward Elgar, 2015).

cosmopolitics.[86] Many of their insights, like those I related in Section 3.1, may be useful, in the reconciliation project, for taking Indigenous law seriously, particularly in engaging elements – like spirits or animals as persons – that can sound fanciful because the idiom used to express them has become denigrated within a modern disenchanted approach to knowledge.[87]

But these disciplines addressing the ecological project also have much to learn from engaging with Indigenous perspectives. Zoe Todd, Kyle Powys Whyte and others have pointed out that discourses of the Anthropocene have tended to both overstate the extent to which the problem is a merely recent or impending dystopia, instead of the continuity of an apocalypse that for Indigenous peoples began with colonization, and ignore or erase the contributions of Indigenous activists and thinkers to our framing.[88] Many factors in anthropogenic climate change and ecocide relate to the genocides, land transformations, migrations and global trade wrought by colonialism, but the Anthropocene as a discursive trope also 'continues a logic of the universal which is structured to sever the relations between mind, body and land'.[89] What this study of treaty shows is that the exchange on entanglement cannot be simply an intellectual one, as Indigenous ontologies are part of legal orders through which those who share their territories are, like it or not, related.[90] And as we have seen, that legality – manifest in treaty – is centred on grounded practices of creating and sustaining kin.

Given that entanglement and separation are both 'in' the world, we desperately need to choose to amplify those aspects of the way the world thinks that foster connection and care. As philosopher of science Donna Haraway puts it in her book for these troubled times, *Staying with the*

[86] B. Latour, 'Whose Cosmos? Which Cosmopolitics? A Comment on Ulrich Beck's Peace Proposal' (2004) 10 *Common Knowledge* 450–62; I. Stengers, *Cosmopolitics I* (University of Minnesota Press, 2011).

[87] M. Berman, *The Reenchantment of the World* (Cornell University Press, 1981).

[88] Z. Todd, 'An Indigenous Feminist's Take on the Ontological Turn: "Ontology" Is Just Another Word for Colonialism' (2016) 24 *Journal of Historical Sociology* 4–22; K. P. White, 'Our Ancestors' Dystopia Now: Indigenous Conservation and the Anthropocene', in U. Heise, J. Christensen and M. Niemann (eds), *The Routledge Companion to the Environmental Humanities* (Routledge, 2017).

[89] H. Davis and Z. Todd, 'On the Importance of a Date, or Decolonizing the Anthropocene' (2017) 16 *ACME: An International Journal for Critical Geographies* 761–80, at 761.

[90] Todd, 'An Indigenous Feminist's Take on the Ontological Turn'.

Trouble, given the irreversible losses that we are facing, any renewed generative flourishing will need the kind of refuge spaces that are made by a mesh of symbiotic, sym*poetic*, collaborators.[91] The answer that both she and Indigenous treaty jurisprudence give to the question 'how are we related, how are we entangled'? Let us multiply the ways.

[91] D. Haraway, *Staying with the Trouble: Making Kin in the Cthulucene* (Duke University Press, 2016).

4

And an Algorithm to Entangle Them All?

Social Credit, Data-Driven Governance and Legal Entanglement in Post-law Legal Orders

LARRY CATÁ BACKER

> In the sixth month, Gabriel the angel was sent from God to a town in Galilee called Nazareth, to a virgin engaged to a man called Joseph, from the family of David. [. . .] 'Don't be afraid, Mary', said the angel to her. 'You're in favour with God. Listen: you will conceive in your womb and will have a son; and you shall call his name Jesus [. . .] The Lord God will give him the throne of David his father, and he shall reign over the house of Jacob for ever. His kingdom will never come to an end.'[1]

4.1 Introduction

The annunciation by Jessup[2] of the birth of what would become transnational law conceived within the womb of Western (and then global) jurisprudence imagined a transformed juridical order in which the notion of law was broadened beyond the state (at least with respect to a definable set of activities). These legalities, in turn, were to be *entangled*[3] to solve what before had been issues the resolution of which could be undertaken solely by reference to the law of a state.[4] But this

[1] Luke 26:31.

[2] P. C. Jessup, *Transnational Law* (Yale University Press, 1956).

[3] E.g., N. Krisch, 'The Open Architecture of European Human Rights Law' (2008) 71 *Modern Law Review* 183–216 ('we find different norms and actors competing for ultimate authority; and since they lack a common legal frame of reference, they compete, to a large extent, through politics rather than legal argument').

[4] L. C. Backer, 'The Cri de Jessup Sixty Years Later: Transnational Law's Intangible Objects and Abstracted Frameworks Beyond Nation, Enterprise, and Law', in P. Zumbansen (ed.), *The Many Lives of Transnational Law: Critical Engagements with Jessup's Bold Proposal* (Cambridge University Press, 2019), pp. 386–418.

'good news' did not immediately produce transformations in the halls of the priestly castes charged with the preservation of the jurisprudential order carefully nurtured in recognizable form from the time of Martin Luther and centred on the state as the principal expression of regulatory power through law.[5] For this caste and the states they served, the solution was, is and remains the law of conflicts and traditional private international law.[6] However, the twenty-first century has seen a reluctant acceptance in theory of the decentring of the state, and consequentially, of the recognition of the rise of multiple centres of governance with multiple forms of law.[7] That conceptual recognition comes at least a century behind early modern studies of its realities in some states.[8] The reluctance arises from the ideological consequences of such a conceptual acceptance. At its limit, the fear produces a modernist panic[9] about the state of the state, and of law as its official language. Despite the need expressed by some,[10] there remains a reluctance to give up 'the ultimately law-focused epistemological mechanism still at work',[11] and thus to forgo the post-1945 ambitions for a transformation of global politics based on the self-reflexive state as the highest legitimate form of communal political expression,[12] the expression of which could be made legitimate only when undertaken through the language of law.[13] Indeed, '[t]he main

[5] United Nations, *Guiding Principles for Business and Human Rights: Implementing the United Nations 'Protect, Respect and Remedy' Framework* (United Nations, 2011), p. 7 ('States individually are the primary duty-bearers under international human rights law, and collectively they are the trustees of the international human rights regime').

[6] C. A. Whytock, 'Conflict of Laws, Global Governance, and Transnational Legal Order' (2016) 1 *UC Irvine Journal of International, Transnational, and Comparative Law* 117–40.

[7] P. Zumbansen, 'Transnational Legal Pluralism' (2010) 1 *Transnational Legal Theory* 141–189; L. C. Backer, 'Governance without Government: An Overview', in G. Handl, J. Zekoll and P. Zumbansen (eds), *Beyond Territoriality: Transnational Legal Authority in an Age of Globalization* (Martinus Nijhoff, 2012), pp. 87–123.

[8] E. Patrignani, 'Legal Pluralism as a Theoretical Programme' (2016) 6 *Oñati Socio-legal Series* 707–25, at 711.

[9] A. D. Smith, *Nationalism and Modernism: A Critical Survey of Recent Theories of Nations and Nationalism* (Routledge, 1998), pp. 8–23, 221–8.

[10] G. Teubner, 'The Two Faces of Janus: Rethinking Legal Pluralism' (1991) 13 *Cardozo Law Review* 1443–62.

[11] T. Duve, 'European Legal History: Concepts, Methods, Challenges', in T. Duve (ed.), *Entanglements in Legal History: Conceptual Approaches* (Max Planck Institute for European Legal History, 2014), pp. 29–66, at p. 58.

[12] L. C. Backer, 'God(s) Over Constitutions: International and Religious Transnational Constitutionalism in the 21st Century' (2008) 27 *Mississippi College Law Review* 11–65.

[13] D. Dyzenhaus, 'Hobbes and the Legitimacy of Law' (2001) 20 *Law and Philosophy* 461–98.

shortcoming of the extended conception of law advocated by anthropological and sociological approaches is the one pointed at by the so-called pan-legalist objection: the problem of the distinctiveness of law from other social normative orderings has been haunting the theorists of legal pluralism until today'.[14] In short, what factions of the leader class feared most in the twenty-first century was precisely the consequences of legal entanglements that might bring down their tightly woven conceptual house.[15]

Yet that very rejection provides strong evidence not merely of its existence but also of its effects, principal of which are the ruptures that entanglement produces between these emerging centres of law/norms/governance,[16] both within and among the conventional nation state.[17] It is within these spaces that one might seek both the meaning and manner in which what Luhmann once described as structural coupling might occur.[18] These spaces without a space, these in-between spaces of law (and governance), these fragmented but entangled legalities, have assumed a spatial dimension.[19] It is now understood as both a connector (the *trames*[20] through which spaces connect and communicate) but also as its own normative territory within which those communications and connections are not merely mediated but managed through complex entanglements,[21] or dynamic processes of communicative irritations.[22]

14 Patrignani, 'Legal Pluralism as a Theoretical Programme', 713; M. Croce, 'All Law Is Plural: Legal Pluralism and the Distinctiveness of Law' (2012) 65 *Journal of Legal Pluralism and Unofficial Law* 1–30.

15 J. Crowe, 'The Limits of Legal Pluralism' (2015) 24 *Griffith Law Review* 314–31.

16 N. Krisch, *Beyond Constitutionalism: The Pluralist Structure of Postnational Law* (Oxford University Press, 2010); P. S. Berman, *Global Legal Pluralism: A Jurisprudence of Law beyond Borders* (Cambridge University Press, 2012).

17 M. Davies, 'Legal Pluralism', in P. Cane and H. M. Kritzer (eds), *The Oxford Handbook of Empirical Legal Research* (Oxford University Press, 2010).

18 N. Luhmann, *The Differentiation of Society* (Columbia University Press, 1982).

19 A. Bianchi, *International Law Theories: An Inquiry into Different Ways of Thinking* (Oxford University Press, 2016), pp. 227–31.

20 Here understood both as a side path (e.g. and ironically here, Sallust (*c.*40 BC) C. 57, 1: '*uti per tramites occulte perfugeret in Galliam Transalpinam*'; J. 48: '*per tramites occultos Metelli antevenit*') but also as a way of life or course or manner of engagement (e.g. Lucretius. (*c.*55 B.C.) 6, 27: '*ab aequitatis recto tramite deviare*').

21 G.-P. Calliess and P. Zumbansen, *Rough Consensus and Running Code: A Theory of Transnational Private Law* (Hart Publishing, 2010).

22 G. Teubner, 'Legal Irritants: Good Faith in British Law or How Unifying Law Ends Up in New Differences' (1998) 61 *Modern Law Review* 11–32.

The budding focus on the interspatial carries with it both promise and challenge. The promise: an interspatial gap filling in all of its complexities and theoretical possibilities. This has been the central exploration of entanglements among law, norms, rules and habits with coercive effect.[23] The challenge is centred on the risk of boundaries without end: of the permanent and quite dynamic cacophony of borders that is produced by the obsession with the interfaces between bodies of norms that themselves create borders within the space between norm systems for which other interfaces are necessary.[24] The problem of the never-ending spaces between spaces, where every law system defines its own inter-spaces, becomes self-entangling, and might itself be undergoing an extra-spatial transformation. That extra-spatial form of governance – in which space loses its centrality and law changes its forms and function – is the object of the exploration here.

More specifically, the chapter considers the emergence of data-driven analytics and the algorithmic techniques of imposing consequences (some of it machine driven, on the basis of artificial intelligence (AI))[25] as defining not just new modalities of governance but also reshaping the conception of spatiality within which entangled governance happens, national and transnational, public and private. So reshaped, these data-driven governance legalities entangle with traditional modes of governance through law in what may be new and interesting ways. These 'social credit' ratings, risk management, assessment, accountability or compliance systems have been established as a means to aid traditional governance;[26] yet they have the potential to displace the structures of governance they are meant to serve. But more than that, they may well change the landscape and language in which one encounters legal entanglements and its operational effects. The thesis of this chapter is simple: legal entanglement has moved beyond the two-dimensional space

[23] Berman, *Global Legal Pluralism*; G. Teubner, '"Global Bukowina": Legal Pluralism in the World Society', in G. Teubner (ed.), *Global Law without a State* (Ashgate, 1997).

[24] Cf. H. Nagendra and E. Ostrom, 'Polycentric Governance of Multifunctional Forested Landscapes' (2012) 6 *International Journal of the Commons* 104–33.

[25] People's Republic of China, 'Chinese State Council released the New Generation AI Development Plan (新一代人工智能发展规划的通知)' (July 2017), www.gov.cn/zhengce/content/2017-07/20/content_5211996.htm; see European Commission website on Digital Single Market, Policy, Artificial Intelligence (2019), https://ec.europa.eu/digital-single-market/en/artificial-intelligence.

[26] See, e.g., essays in K. E. Davis, A. Fisher, B. Kingsbury and S. E. Merry (eds), *Governance by Indicators: Global Power through Quantification and Rankings* (Oxford University Press, 2012).

for engagement envisioned by Jessup and his successor. Entanglement was once confined to states, other governance institutions and between them all. That engagement was built around and with the traditional language of law and jurisprudence. Increasingly, the emerging quantitative legalities built around AI and big data management systems (e.g. social credit initiatives) that are neither dependent on the forms and techniques of law nor on the bureaucratic apparatus of state entangle more decisively with conventional and plural law and norm systems. These add an additional layer of actor (the 'market', the analyst, the modeller, the systems engineer, the coder) and seek to displace the language of law and jurisprudence with the language of data-based analytics applied towards a comprehensive management of behaviour. The resulting entanglement may reshape the meaning and making of entanglement itself. At its limit, this reshaping will have a particular effect on the way in which conventional plural legalities, until now the singular feature of globalized law frameworks, may be assembled through dynamic and sometimes unstable entangled linkages and rationalized by a regulatory algorithm that may come to manage them all.[27]

This contribution, then, considers *governance* entanglement *between* the entangled legalities of law-norm systems and the legalities emerging from data-driven systems of behaviour management. The realities of emerging legalities that exceed the capacity of law to express their form require a three-dimensional analysis of entanglement and a broader view of legality, one that reconsiders data-driven, machine-administered regulatory systems more than an enhanced form of property.[28] One deals here not just with the flattened inter-legalities of the traditional structures of ordering power by rules. Instead, one must now understand the way those clusters of entanglement themselves are entangled with emerging modalities of law/regulation/norms which have come to form the centre of what is understood as plural legalities.

[27] J. R. R. Tolkien, *The Fellowship of the Ring* (Random House, 1954), chapter 2. That extra-spatiality is nicely captured through what is now a sadly hackneyed and often quoted passage from a well-known book which provides a rich metaphor for multidimensional entanglement, rings of power for all communities to each bind themselves and 'One Ring to rule them all, … to find them, … to … bind them.'

[28] E.g., OECD, 'OECD Council Recommendation on Artificial Intelligence' (adopted 21 May 2019) OECD/LEGAL/0449, https://legalinstruments.oecd.org/en/instruments/OECD-LEGAL-0449.

Section 4.2 briefly sketches the characteristics of emerging legalities that neither embrace the form nor the language of law. The two sections that follow examine the nature of inter-systemic entanglements which occur when data-driven governance legal orders[29] are thrown into the already plural mix of legalities. Two principal forms of data-driven governance have emerged that are increasingly linking to traditional legalities.[30] The first is the Chinese 'social credit' initiative, which emerged in its current form in 2014, and is an undertaking by the present administration of the Chinese government that is meant to produce an all-around approach to ensuring compliance with law and social responsibility under the guidance of the state. The second are US and Western private initiatives around emerging markets for data. These are framed around principles of governance, risk management and compliance. With respect to each, the nature and textures of entanglement that encounters between traditional plural legalities and data-driven governance systems produce is considered. These entanglements present a distinct challenge, the challenge of linguistic disjunction, for the management of human organization. While law- and norm-based systems speak the same language, data-driven governance does not. Communicative disjunction may have profound effects on the nature and quality of entanglement, producing a competition for the lingua franca that may affect the way in which law is expressed, and may threaten the plurality of law.[31] Each also exhibits quite distinct characteristics and therefore quite different forms and qualities of entanglement, suggesting a more complex fracture and interaction among ever more different systems of legalities that are emerging in fractured political systems arranged around global trade regimes.

4.2 The Construction of Data-Driven Operating Systems

The governance consequences of data-driven compliance and risk management systems, and of the informal systems of ratings and assessment, has only recently exploded into the popular imagination of academics

[29] T. C. Halliday and G. Shaffer (eds), *Transnational Legal Orders* (Cambridge University Press, 2015).

[30] At greater length in L. C. Backer, 'Next Generation Law: Data-Driven Governance and Accountability Based Regulatory Systems in the West and Social Credit Regimes in China' (2018) 28 *Southern California Interdisciplinary Law Journal* 123–72.

[31] E.g., J. House, 'English as Lingua Franca: A Threat to Multilingualism?' (2003) 7 *Journal of Sociolinguistics* 556–78.

and others.[32] What started as an effort to rationalize the emerging techniques of indicators,[33] as a *means* of governance, quickly became a study of these techniques, increasingly systematized, *as* governance.[34] The recognition of algorithmic governance appeared like a direct and hidden threat to the carefully constructed public structures of law and governance systems.[35] Just as it seemed that theory could come to grips with the possibility of law (governance) systems beyond the state, the entire framework of law systems themselves seemed to be sidelined by data-based algorithmic systems to which law and norms appeared to be a stranger. And these challenges have come to the West in forms that appear to conflate the operations of Marxist-Leninist *government* with Western democratic markets-driven polycentric (plural) *governance*.[36] Yet these judgements ought not to deter from considering the (inevitable it seems) rise of these systems in both China and the West, and the additional layer of entanglement they add to the emerging formal and public systems of governance that constitute global legal polycentric (pluralist) governance.[37] To that end, a brief exploration of the shape of social credit initiatives fuelled by AI and machine learning-enabled algorithms is worth considering.

The rise of social credit initiatives (ratings and data-driven governance in the West) and big data management systems (as a means to implement these governance frameworks) appears to further entangle legalities in perhaps unexpected ways. It takes as its starting point the significant drive towards accountability and measurement in governance incarnated through rankings and ratings. Administration of rankings and ratings then devolves to the institutions that administer and along with that devolution goes the power to determine what behaviours will be valued, and in what amount, to rank and rate. In effect, the indicator acquires

[32] F. Pasquale, *The Black Box Society: The Secret Algorithms That Control Money and Information* (Harvard University Press, 2016).

[33] S. E. Merry, *The Seductions of Quantification: Measuring Human Rights, Gender Violence, and Sex Trafficking* (University of Chicago Press, 2016) (measurement systems constitute a form of power).

[34] Backer, 'Next Generation Law'.

[35] Pasquale, *The Black Box Society*.

[36] M. Harris, 'The Moral Hazard of Big Data', *New Republic* (6 February 2015), https://newrepublic.com/article/120987/pasquales-black-box-challenges-digital-sphere-run-algorithms.

[37] E. Ostrom, 'Beyond Markets and States: Polycentric Governance of Complex Economic Systems' (2010) 100 *American Economic Review* 641–72.

regulatory autonomy. Thus characterized as a regulatory system, it is then entangled with traditional law-norm systems.[38] If law and norms – traditional governance – are grounded in the supremacy of space, of territory, then how is one to approach governance orders that might themselves be detached from traditional spatial limitations? That is the principal focus of this chapter. It considers the emergence of what might eventually be understood as a legal/normative order that has arisen not from the need to organize a territory, within which people and things are corralled, but generated from and centred on the objects of regulation themselves. The emerging systems that have been referenced in this chapter as 'social credit' initiatives offer a glimpse at a governance operating system quite distinct from the legal/normative systems that have served as the building blocks first of the Westphalian state system (in its domestic and international elements), and thereafter the poly-centric systems that mark this transnational age.[39]

In place of legal/normative systems driven through the construction of an apparatus of government within territories (physical or abstract) it fashions a system driven through data generated by people and things.[40]

[38] Consider the example of corruption, one well examined in the essays in S. E. Merry, K. E. Davis and B. Kingsbury (eds), *The Quiet Power of Indicators: Measuring Governance, Corruption, and Rule of Law* (Cambridge University Press, 2015). In this case trans-national measures inform international instruments that then inform national transpos-ition of corruption measures. These, in turn, are substantially affected by systems of analytics of performance built around proprietary assessments of corruption compliance that are framed around these legal principles and rules, but which are interpreted and quantified in ways that reflect the values and objectives of the analysts and coders preparing the analytical framework (and providing quantifiable values to identified actions). See, e.g., D. Kaufmann, A. Kraay and M. Mastruzzi, 'Measuring Corruption: Myths and Realities', World Bank (April 2007); Transparency International, 'Corruption Perceptions Index' (2019), www.transparency.org/research/cpi/overview; O. E. Hawthorne, 'Do International Corruption Metrics Matter? Assessing the Impact of Transparency International's Corruption Perceptions Index', PhD thesis, Old Dominion University (2012), https://digitalcommons.odu.edu/gpis_etds/50.

[39] M. Zürn, A. Nollkaemper and R, Peerenboom, 'Introduction: Rule of Law Dynamics in an Era of International and Transnational Governance', in M. Zürn, A. Nollkaemper and R, Peerenboom (eds), *Rule of Law Dynamics in an Era of International and Transnational Governance* (Cambridge University Press, 2012) pp. 1–18.

[40] L. C. Backer, 'Global Panopticism: Surveillance Lawmaking by Corporations, States, and Other Entities' (2008) 15 *Indiana Journal of Global Legal Studies* 101–48. These data-driven systems can be aligned with and enhance control over a territory/population in the manner of Foucault's bio-politics. See T. Lemke, '"The Birth of Bio-Politics": Michel Foucault's Lecture at the College de France on Neo-Liberal Governmentality' (2010) 30 *Economy and Society* 190–207; M. Foucault, *Society Must Be Defended: Lectures at the Collège de France, 1975–1976*, trans. D. Macey (St. Martin's Press, 1997). The notion of

Data substitute for custom and tradition; data-driven governance substitutes the language of counting for the more qualitative descriptive language of practice. Governing organs substitute, in place of custom and tradition, the quite precise data warehouse, one with a vocabulary and rule of normativity all of its own.[41] It can be filled constantly with the detritus of daily activity – at the market, on the web, in the car, on the street, in the store, etc.[42] These can be used for a variety of ends, some of them public, but in the process entangling the normative decisions about character of data for the content of norms.[43] In the place of policy and principle one encounters data analytics. Choice ceases to be politically potent only within the electoral field; all choices become political as they point behaviour managers to desires and habits of the masses producing data. In lieu of debate there is analytics. The framing of that analysis, that is the judgements and principles embedded in those analytics, is not subsumed within the algorithm. The algorithm itself is the expression of the sum of the objectives and perspectives of those for whose objectives the algorithm is deployed. In lieu of principles, then, there are presumptions and the self-created limitations of data fields that create the

population, however, has long breached the political borders of territorial states (see Backer, 'The Cri de Jessup Sixty Years Later'). Consider in this case the entanglements of public, private and data-driven systems in the operation of social media platforms like Facebook. Facebook's rules with respect to posts on its platform represent the uneasy and unstable product of collisions between public law (e.g. the EU General Data Protection Regulation (O. Solon, 'How Europe's "Breakthrough" Privacy Law Takes on Facebook and Google', *The Guardian*, 19 April 2018)), private regulation (Facebook's normative rules for acceptable content and procedural rules for content removal (J. C. Wong and O. Solon, 'Facebook Releases Content Moderation Guidelines—Rules Long Kept Secret', *The Guardian*, 24 April 2018)), Facebook's algorithms (how Facebook determines post views on newsfeeds, for example), and in 2020 a private quasi-judicial Oversight Board constituted by Facebook as its own internal judicial-administrative body, 'a 20-member independent panel that will rule on which posts can be blocked as false or as hate speech or harassment' (New York Post Editorial Board, 'Facebook's New "Supreme Court" Looks Like a License to Censor', *New York Post*, 7 May 2020).

[41] R. Kimball et al., *The Data Warehouse Lifecycle Toolkit*, 2nd ed. (Wiley, 2008); H. Edelstein and R. C. Barquin, *Planning and Designing the Data Warehouse* (Simon & Schuster, 1996).

[42] Cf., essays in J. Wang (ed.), *Data Warehousing and Mining: Concepts, Methodologies, Tools, and Applications* (IGI Global, 2008).

[43] This is particularly true in the West in the context of cyber criminality. Cf. I.-Y. Song et al., 'Designing a Data Warehouse for Cyber Crimes' (2006) 1 *Journal of Digital Forensics, Security and Law* 5–22; L. C. Backer, 'Chinese Strategies to Combat Corporate Corruption: From a "Two Thrust Approach" to a "Two Swords One Thrust Strategy" of Compliance, Prosecutorial Discretion, and Sovereign Investor Oversight in China' (2019) 152 *International Lawyer* 1–45.

boundaries within which choices are cabined. These are the structures of conventional governance, but now deployed in a quite different space.

But these are not normative orders in the traditional sense. That fundamental characteristic suggests the opportunities and challenges that these emerging systems represent. Social credit initiatives – data and algorithmic orders – change the relation among governance actors, decentring the judge, the regulator and the social actors, in favour of those who can manage, organize and apply metrics to some end or other (that is to the same ends of law). Yet they do not mediate relations among norms so much as absorb them all in furtherance of extra-spatial objectives – to focus on behaviours in a self-reflexive loop founded on behaviour-generated data, the vectors of which may be modified through systems of real-time rewards and punishments (of individuals and institutions, including governmental and economic institutions). These orders, then, are not so much enmeshed as they are ubiquitous – serving both as techniques of management, and as the primary structures of regulation themselves. Absorption does not mean elimination; it posits an entanglement of a different order – between conventional governmental orders, the entanglements of which continue to produce norms, but their interpretation and application, that is the way these norms are given meaning, entangle conventional legalities with the analytic legalities of the algorithm and the entanglement of choices made between techno-experts, coders and public or private officials. These characteristics became much more visible in the context of the Covid-19 pandemic where the entanglement of simulation and conventional political legalities became the central regulatory element of institutional responses to the virus.[44]

It follows then that the anticipated entanglements become more confused where one set of systems (law/regulation) continues to posit that metrics-based governance is merely technique, rather than a regulatory system in its own right. The interspatial, and its data-driven forms, produces a quite distinctive template for the conceptual construction of law/norms between law/norm systems; and it emerges with its own language and sensibilities in ways that are not yet completely clear. Every political culture approaches the emerging realities of 'artificial

[44] L. C. Backer, 'Simulating Politics in the Shadow of COVID-19: "Like the School Nurse Trying to Tell the Principal How to Run the School"', Law at the End of the Day blog (4 May 2020), https://lcbackerblog.blogspot.com/2020/05/simulating-politics-in-shadow-of-covid.html.

intelligence', machine learning and the data-driven governance that is sometimes its object, in ways that tend to affirm cultural expectations and points of view. Where cultures are obsessed with particular conceptions of privacy and property, the result is an engagement that is centred on political constraints against states and enterprises, on the management of markets for data and at the same time on an enhanced methodology of data-driven analytics to deepen cultures of compliance, assessment and accountability.

In liberal democratic states, that focus also has constitutional and political dimensions.[45] Thus, the regulatory machinery of the European Union has lately been tasked to manage data under the presumption of a hierarchy of authority that further presumes the normative nature of law and the mechanical nature of data and their analytics. Data and data processing 'should be designed to serve mankind. The right to the protection of personal data is not an absolute right; it must be considered in relation to its function in society and be balanced against other fundamental rights, in accordance with the principle of proportionality.'[46] There is a particular aversion to the forms of data-driven intrusions from the economic sector (the 'for hire' fields) on the formalities and rituals of exogenous democratic expression.[47] And, of course, there is an equal obsession with theft of information[48] and its misuse.[49] And yet, even as its elites offer the protection of law, it manages that data which itself manages behaviour.

> A tiny microchip inserted under the skin can replace the need to carry keys, credit cards and train tickets. [. . .] The small implants were first used in 2015 in Sweden – initially confidentially – and several other

[45] P. N. Howard, S. Woolley and R. Calo, 'Algorithms, Bots, and Political Communication in the US 2016 Election: The Challenge of Automated Political Communication for Election Law and Administration' (2018) 15 *Journal of Information Technology & Politics* 81–93.

[46] Regulation 2016/679 of 27 April 2016 on the protection of natural persons with regard to the processing of personal data and on the free movement of such data, and repealing Directive 95/46/EC (General Data Protection Regulation), OJ 2016 No L119, 4 May 2016 ('GDPR'), preamble, section 4.

[47] N. Statt, 'The Justice Department and FBI Are Reportedly Investigating Cambridge Analytica over Facebook Scandal', *The Verge* (15 May 2018), www.theverge.com/2018/5/15/17358802/facebook-cambridge-analytica-justice-department-fbi-investigation.

[48] A. Narayanan and V. Shmatkov, 'Robust De-anonymization of Large Sparse Datasets', Proceedings of the 2008 IEEE Symposium on Security and Privacy (2008), www.cs.utexas.edu/~shmat/shmat_oak08netflix.pdf, pp. 111–25.

[49] General Data Protection Regulation.

> countries. Swedes have gone on to be very active in microchipping, with scant debate about issues surrounding its use, in a country keen on new technology and where the sharing of personal information is held up as a sign of a transparent society.[50]

Thus combined, there is a tension between the centrality of the individual as the incarnation of data, and the utility of data in the production of economic goods with great disciplinary effects. This debate has been refined in the context of the Covid-19 pandemic, which has produced a substantial entanglement between data-driven indicator systems, national and international law and regulation in ways that will take some time to untangle.[51]

On the other hand, where cultures are obsessed with communal solidarity and the protection of stability around socio-political core values as the basis for legitimate social organization and operation, then the result is an engagement that is centred on issues of surveillance, of detection, and of management of behaviour around key societal principles. There is a particular aversion to antisocial behaviour as a politically destabilizing force.[52] Feng Xiang, a law professor at Tsinghua University, recently spoke about the end of markets: '[i]f AI rationally allocates resources through big data analysis, and if robust feedback loops can supplant the imperfections of "the invisible hand" while fairly sharing the vast wealth it creates, a planned economy that actually works could at last be achievable'.[53] He might not be wrong about AI and markets; even the Cubans have sought to turn their economic planning into the rudiments of complex algorithms.[54] Yet this culture shares with the other a mania for observation – and for punishment and reward based on that power to observe,[55] one which is incompatible with the

[50] AFP, 'Thousands of People in Sweden get Microchip Implants for a New Way of Life', *South China Morning Post*, 13 May 2015.

[51] UN CESCR, 'Statement on the Coronavirus Disease (COVID-19) Pandemic and Economic, Social and Cultural Rights' (adopted 17 April 2020) UN Doc. E/C.12/2020/1.

[52] D. Zhang, H. Peng, Y. Haibin and Y. Lu, 'Crowd Abnormal Behavior Detection based on Machine Learning' (2013) 12 *Information Technology Journal* 1199–205.

[53] F. Xiang, 'AI Will spell the End of Capitalism', *Washington Post*, 25 April 2018.

[54] L. C. Backer, 'The Algorithms of Ideology in Economic Planning: A Critical Look at Cuba's National Economic and Social Development Plan 2030' (2017) 27 *Cuba in Transition* 115–36.

[55] S. Leng, 'Big Data to Give China Edge over the West', *South China Morning Post*, 21 January 2018.

values of property and rights-based legal orderings.[56] And yet, even as there is a movement towards the overt management of behaviour through data, there is as well an obsession to ground that regulatory approach within the structures of regulation – in this case a regulation that protects the integrity of data and its use by the state and its delegees. Data and consequence (accountability for business, incentive to encourage preferred behaviours and punish violations of behaviour norms) thus combined, focus on stability and order in social development.

4.3 Chinese 'Social Credit' Systems: The State at the Centre

Social credit is a deeply entangled system; it is a system that will eventually apply to all legal actors, persons, institutions, officials and foreigners in or seeking to engage with China and Chinese actors.[57] It is more than that – it has been created as a nexus point between the constituting role of law (as well as the normative guides that are its rules) and the evaluative function of data-driven analytics.[58] It sits at the borderlands between a rating-evaluation system and systems of legal regulation. It is also entangled with the core political premises that drive Marxist-Leninist political economy in China under the leadership of the

[56] L. Fan, V. Das, N. Kostyuk and M. M. Hussain, 'Constructing a Data-Driven Society: China's Social Credit System as a State Surveillance Infrastructure' (2018) 10 *Policy & Internet* 415–53.

[57] Fan et al., 'Constructing a Data-Driven Society'.

[58] The Covid-19 pandemic has provided a powerful if simple illustration of how this works in China. In order to better manage responses to the Covid-19 pandemic, Chinese residents were each assigned a colour code representing a rating of contagion risk. That risk rating is administered through Alibaba, a private enterprise. It has developed the Alipay Health Code which adds a health colour code to each person's Alipay account (held by the vast majority of individuals). To access the rating each account holder downloads an app. The system of data-driven colour coding (the analytics of which remain opaque) are then used by other actors (state and private) to determine whether the individual will be required to quarantine, and whether the individual will be granted access to places of business or public spaces. The ranking data are shared with state authorities and aligned with the state's regulations and policies respecting Covid-19 mitigation measures. P. Mozur, R. Zhong and A. Krolik, 'In Coronavirus Fight, China Gives Citizens a Color Code, with Red Flags', *New York Times*, 1 March 2020; X. Wǎng, 'Zhīfùbǎo jiànkāng mǎ 7 tiān luòdì chāo 100 chéng shùzìhuà fángyì pǎo chū "zhōngguó sùdù' ('Alipay Health Code Implemented in 100 Cities in 7 Days: Digital Epidemic Prevention at China Speed'), *Xinhuanet*, 19 February 2020, www.xinhuanet.com/tech/2020–02/19/c_1125596647.htm.

Communist Party of China (CPC).[59] Its autonomous and systemic character was emphasized from the beginning:

> It is founded on laws, regulations, standards and charters, it is based on a complete network covering the credit records of members of society and credit infrastructure, it is supported by the lawful application of credit information and a credit services system, its inherent requirements are establishing the idea of an sincerity culture, and carrying forward sincerity and traditional virtues, it uses encouragement to keep trust and constraints against breaking trust as incentive mechanisms, and its objective is raising the honest mentality and credit levels of the entire society.[60]

Yet one notes the entanglement – the system is constituted through law, but is established as autonomous from the law system around which it operates. The object is to establish *a structure for managed entanglement within the state*. Each, in turn, requires the production of a self-reflexive legality whose operation is entangled with those of the normative political, societal and economic order. Its mechanism, machine learning and AI, the entanglement of a rule system for AI and AI as law itself was also elaborated by the State Council in 2017.[61] 'Social credit systems are centered on ratings. Ratings are derived, in turn, from data generated by what is being rated—individuals, businesses, public and private institutions, and eventually even [CPC] members. To that end, it is necessary to manage data production as it is to manage the analytics and consequences drawn from the data.'[62]

Social credit initiatives have as their object the development of a national reputation system, assigning a rating that reflects a qualitative judgement of relevant data gathered about the subject. Reputation, itself, embraces notions of sincerity, and of integrity and compliance, in accordance with the standards and objectives overseen by the state. Four areas are identified: 'sincerity in government affairs' (政务诚信), 'commercial sincerity' (商务诚信), 'societal sincerity' (社会诚信) and 'judicial credibility' (司法公信). AI and machine learning focus on the

[59] L. C. Backer, 'China's Social Credit System: Data-Driven Governance for a "New Era"' (2019) 118 *Current History: A Journal of Contemporary World Affairs* 209–14.

[60] People's Republic of China, 'State Council Notice Concerning Issuance of the Planning Outline for the Construction of a Social Credit System (2014–2020)' (2014), https://chinacopyrightandmedia.wordpress.com/2014/06/14/planning-outline-for-the-construction-of-a-social-credit-system-2014-2020/, p. 1.

[61] People's Republic of China, 'Chinese State Council Released the New Generation AI Development Plan'.

[62] Backer, 'China's Social Credit System', 211.

generation of mechanisms for the management and integrity of data and for its marketization.[63]

The objectives of both are grounded in economic and social development and support for national security.[64] The project of a comprehensive and nationally integrated programme of credit ratings of virtually all aspects of organized life in China, built pursuant to rules and laws, administered by public and private bodies and overseen by the CPC remains a work in progress, though one increasingly structured by the highest Chinese state organs.[65] It is self-consciously constructed as an alternative legality, both within China and against the forms of plural legalities in the West that the Chinese leadership increasingly find difficult to enmesh with their own.[66]

Nearly from its inception, social credit was understood as a new kind of law, separate from but entangled with traditional law systems, which had been themselves the product of the fusion of traditional approaches to law and Western concepts of law, rule of law and legal mechanics.[67] At the same time, social credit expressed a form of governance that also deeply entangled systems of social ordering through rules (laws) and the paramount authority of the CPC to guide such lawmaking and its application through its own political-economic model.[68] The determination to adopt a social credit initiative (and its operationalization through AI-enhanced algorithmic governance techniques) was itself a function of

63 E. Kania, 'China's AI Agenda Advances: As China Throws State Support behind AI Development, Major Chinese Technology Companies Will Remain Integral Players', *The Diplomat* (14 February 2018), https://thediplomat.com/2018/02/chinas-ai-agenda-advances/.

64 Kania, 'China's AI Agenda Advances'.

65 People's Republic of China, 'State Council 关于加快推进社会信用体系建设构建以信用为基础的新型监管机制的指导意见' ('Guiding Opinion on Accelerating the Advancement of the Establishment of the Social Credit System with New Forms of Credit-Based Regulatory Mechanisms'), translated by Jeremy Daum, China Law Translate (17 July 2019), www.chinalawtranslate.com. This document issued by the General Office of the State Council provided guiding opinions on the acceleration of the construction of the system. The document emphasized the centrality and importance of the social credit system as a separable form of legality, and served as a reminder of the determination of the current political leaders to move from a primary dependence on law to data-driven management of behaviour as a central element of ordering society. Backer, 'China's Social Credit System', 209.

66 Backer, 'China's Social Credit System', 210.

67 X. Dai, 'Toward a Reputation State: The Social Credit System Project of China' (10 June 2018), https://ssrn.com/abstract=3193577.

68 S. Jiang, 'Written and Unwritten Constitutions: A New Approach to the Study of Constitutional Government in China' (2010) 36 *Modern China* 12–46.

the determination that such data-driven governance would enhance the long-term Chinese political-economic objectives embedded in their concept of socialist modernization, a core policy of the Chinese state since the era of Deng Xiaoping. Social credit was to evidence the transformation of techniques that marked a new phase of the socialist market economy system and of the social governance system, one which received its more definitive political form after the announcement of the 'New Era' political line of the CPC in the wake of the 19th CPC Congress of October 2017.[69]

But its genesis also represented a practical response to a long-term problem that both state and private elements of society found increasingly burdensome.[70] These included a number of issues that threatened not merely the orderly progress of socialist modernization, but also inhibited the progressive advancement of social and cultural objectives. These included grave production safety accidents, food and drug security incidents, commercial swindles, the manufacture and sale of counterfeit products, tax evasion, fraudulent financial claims, academic impropriety and gaps between the extent of integrity in government affairs and judicial credibility and the expectations of the popular masses. If neither law nor regulation appeared to produce conformity, and if the transaction costs of deploying a vast enforcement network was counterproductive to the long-term goal of a self-regulating society that was efficient and productive in socially approved ways, then a different approach to the management of societal factors was necessary.

This ambitious set of objectives was to be guided by a set of core premises and constraints. Social credit initiatives must conform to and advance the objectives of the CPC Basic Line, including the development of economic forces for policy ends.[71] The Chinese social credit system also has a moral dimension, which deeply informs its regulatory and enforcement dimensions. Its object is to steer the culture and practices of people in virtually every aspect of their lives. To those ends, the Twelve

[69] J. Xi, 'Secure a Decisive Victory in Building a Moderately Prosperous Society in All Respects and Strive for the Great Success of Socialism with Chinese Characteristics for a New Era: Report Delivered to the 19th National Congress of the Communist Party of China', Xinhuanet, 18 October 2017, www.xinhuanet.com/english/download/Xi_Jinping's_report_at_19th_CPC_National_Congress.pdf.

[70] People's Republic of China, 'State Council Notice Concerning Issuance of the Planning Outline'.

[71] Constitution of the Communist Party of the People's Republic of China (General Program).

Core Socialist Values unveiled in 2012 play an important role.[72] Entanglement is meant to be conscious and coordinated rather than organic and serendipitous[73] – highlighting the difference between a central-planning (public and administrative) versus a markets-based (private and demand driven) political order.

The social credit initiative was comprehensive. It was envisioned that when completed, social credit systems would manage key operations in four sectors: government, commercial activities, social integrity and judicial credibility.[74] With respect to the role of social credit in government, the focus was on the use of data-driven analytics tied to algorithms that produced the basis for accountability to result in rewards or punishments around a variety of governmental actions. These included: administrative permissions, government procurement, tendering and bidding, labour and employment, social security, scientific research management, cadre promotion and appointment, management and supervision, application for government financial support and other such areas and fostering the development of a credit services market. Clearly, data-driven analytics and its resulting assessment system would produce an immediate effect on those whose conduct triggers measured responses. For those who met credit minima, access to benefits would be enhanced. Those assessed at a low enough level would be placed on an effective blacklist that would make functioning in a modern society substantially more difficult and costly, absent readjustment. Moreover, social credit was also to be used as a tool for intra-governmental accountability, and to monitor civil servants.

Social credit mechanisms were also directed towards a very broad range of commercial activities – whether by state-owned enterprises or the private sector. Private behaviour by individuals was also to be managed through social credit systems under the umbrella of enhancing 'Social Integrity'. An area of particular note for the application of data-driven analytics was that of the judicial system. The specific focus was on judicial creditability and on the integrity of the judicial function and the performance (and accountability) of judges for their work. The State

[72] L. C. Backer, 'Blacklists and Social Credit Regimes in China', interdisciplinary symposium Super-Scoring? Data-Driven Societal Technologies in China and Western-Style Democracies as a New Challenge for Education (Cologne, Germany, 11 October 2019), www.superscoring.de/2019/08/28/blacklists-and-social-credit-regimes-in-china/.

[73] Ibid.

[74] People's Republic of China, 'State Council Notice Concerning Issuance of the Planning Outline', II(1)–(4).

Council identified a number of areas: proceedings transparency, prosecutorial and public security services conduct, the operation of judicial administrative systems and law enforcement standardization. Here one notes the likelihood of a vertical entanglement. Judges are the objects of law and the agents of procedures reflected in the legalities of law and regulation. Yet the content of the way those functions are assessed (and consequentially the way that the implementation of legal duties is understood and measured, and thus interpreted) become a function of a distinct legality – that of the social credit system applied to the judge. Data-driven projects might well include the production of data-driven algorithms to guide judicial decision-making or to develop guidelines for charging and prosecution. Here one encounters an entanglement in which the discretionary scope of one system is constrained by the operation of the other.

The societal effects of social credit programmes were to be enhanced through the application of these mechanisms on education and culture projects. Social credit in the development of education system reform was to be tied to the construction of the socialist core value system. Education was to be a means for the socialization of social credit mentalities and its general acceptance.[75] Assessment would be built around parameters for judging the development and operation of 'moral' classrooms. These are to be built around the establishment of models of appropriate conduct.[76] Appropriate conduct, in turn, is to be assessed against the twelve socialist values that have been established after the CPC's 18th Congress: 'Core socialist values comprise a set of moral principles summarized by central authorities as prosperity, democracy, civility, harmony, freedom,

[75] People's Republic of China, 'State Council Notice Concerning Issuance of the Planning Outline'.

[76] See L. C. Backer, 'What Is the Fundamental Task of Education? Xi Jinping's Concept of 立德树人 [Cultivating People of Moral Character] and Its Implementation through Undergraduate University Reform in 教育部关于一流本科课程建设的实施意见 [Implementation Opinions of the Ministry of Education on the Construction of First-Class Undergraduate Courses]', Law at the End of the Day (1 November 2019), https://lcbpsusenate.blogspot.com/2019/11/what-s-fundamental-task-of-education-xi.html. The Ministry of Education's draft Measures for the Appointment and Management of Foreign Teachers [外籍教师聘任和管理办法] (www.moj.gov.cn/news/content/2020-07/21/zlk_3252777.html) establishes the parameters by which the Chinese social credit system is extended to foreign teachers including assessments relating to the foreign teacher's compliance with law, ethics and quality of teaching be included in a national foreign teacher comprehensive information service platform. Article 31 includes the list of activities that will permit dismissal and require listing on a social credit blacklist.

equality, justice, the rule of law, patriotism, dedication, integrity and friendliness.'[77] To that end, state organs are encouraged to oversee special campaigns in focus sectors, and to 'persist in correcting unhealthy trends and evil practices of abusing power for personal gain, lying and cheating, forgetting integrity when tempted by gains, benefiting oneself at others' expense, etc., and establish trends of sectoral sincerity and integrity'.[78]

All of this is to be accomplished by building social credit baseline systems[79] and their mechanisms.[80] These systems were then to be operationalized through blacklists. Blacklists – made up of the names of people whose social credit scores fall below certain thresholds – have already begun to have a substantial effect in everyday life. The system is manifested through ratings, and more importantly from the collection of blacklists produced as a function of ratings. Blacklists then affect the availability of goods and services.[81]

These, then, will serve as the systems through which entanglement will be coordinated. Baseline systems were identified as (1) sectoral credit information systems; (2) local information systems; (3) credit investigation systems; and (4) uniform credit investigation platforms in the financial sector. In addition, government in cooperation with the private sector were to develop credit information exchange and sharing. These shall provide the regulatory structures for the operationalization of data-driven assessment and punishment/reward systems. The forms of entanglement are also identified as (1) incentive structures and punishments for deviations; and (2) legal, regulatory and standards systems for credit.

The entanglements of social credit within the Chinese context are as comprehensive as its ambitions. Social credit is meant to provide a new language for law, at least as it is meant to serve to control behaviour. At the same time, the constitution of social credit is driven by law. That is, law serves as a constituting element of regulatory systems that themselves

[77] *China Daily*, 'Core Socialist Values' (2017), www.chinadaily.com.cn/china/19thcpcnationalcongress/2017-10/12/content_33160115.htm.

[78] People's Republic of China, 'State Council Notice Concerning Issuance of the Planning Outline'.

[79] Ibid., part IV.

[80] Ibid., part V.

[81] T. F. Chan, 'China's Social Credit System Has Blocked People from Taking 11 Million Flights and 4 Million Train Trips', *Business Insider* (21 May 2018), www.businessinsider.com/china-social-credit-system-blocked-people-taking-flights-train-trips-2018-5?r=UK&IR=T.

are grounded in forms and practices that are not law. At the same time, those forms and practices of social credit then drive law as it is applied. They do so by giving meaning to the objectives and expectations written into law by the way that social credit is administered through the process of identifying behaviour, analysing its meaning and attaching consequences. At the same time, social credit provides a bridge between law, compliance and assessment systems. In the process it also helps shape the cultures within which expectations are shaped and cultural habits formed, which then lend themselves to expression in the normative content of law. Here social credit moves entanglement into an ecology of interrelated subsystems all deployed to move forward the political project of the CPC.

4.4 'Social Credit' in the West: A Governmentalized Private Sector around Markets for Data

To speak of 'social credit initiatives' in the West is to consider an initiative that does not exist – as such. And yet, a more careful consideration reveals the outlines of the forms of social credit outside of the state. To speak to the development of social credit and its operationalization through machine learning and AI-enhanced algorithms, is to understand how the fracture and diffusion of power has produced something more than the aggregation of governance spaces and their 'in-between' spaces arranged in some manner or other. It evidences the organization of power beyond the orthodox space of law, in the sense that these new data-driven legalities use conventional polycentric governance spaces themselves as fuel for the generation of behaviour-managing 'incentives' or 'punishments' that function as regulation while avoiding anything like its traditional forms.

Social credit in the West is made possible not merely by the availability of spaces within spaces, but by the effective borderlessness of the market itself. Those extra-spatial zones have been enhanced through the governmentalization of the private sphere, the privatization of the public sphere and the migration from law and regulation to systems and systems management.[82] To speak about social credit in the West is to identify a host of fractured and market-driven projects by a large number of

[82] L. C. Backer, 'Theorizing Regulatory Governance within Its Ecology: The Structure of Management in an Age of Globalization' (2018) 24 *Contemporary Politics* 607–30.

actors.[83] These actors also exercise governance authority in traditional ways (through rules, laws and the exercise of political and economic power). But for them, increasingly, assessment and accountability regimes, born of compliance objectives within the spaces and inter-spaces of conventional law/normative systems,[84] provide incentives to manage populations above the multiple governance spaces to which they might have to account.

What emerges in the West are systems of 'governance, risk management, and compliance'.[85] Where in China the government (under the guidance of the CPC) pushes data-driven governance, in the West it is the market, and the delegation of managerial authority (compliance), that tends to drive these oversight and control systems – the literature highlighting this dynamic is by now well developed.[86] Anyone can rate and assess – but there are markets for rating as well; the most successful producers of rating enhance their profitability in markets for ratings. They focus on creating everything from hierarchies of value to assessment of conformity to a variety of corporate social responsibility obligations.[87] Less well developed is the conception of data, and the ratings that draw on them, as a system with regulatory effect. 'Simply put, because of big data, managers can measure, and hence know, radically more about their businesses, and directly translate that knowledge into improved decision making and performance.'[88] Data-driven governance is essential for a variety of private sphere activities, and has become a business in its own right.[89]

For both, data-driven analytics and the algorithms through which data-based judgements can be formed and consequences processed have

[83] L. C. Backer, 'The Structural Characteristics of Global Law for the 21st Century: Fracture, Fluidity, Permeability, and Polycentricity' (2017) 17 *Tilburg Law Review* 177–99.

[84] American Law Institute, *Principles of the Law: Compliance, Risk Management, and Enforcement*, Tentative Draft No. 1 (American Law Institute, 2019).

[85] Cf. R. M. Steinberg, *Governance, Risk Management, and Compliance: It Can't Happen to Us; Avoiding Corporate Disaster While Driving Success* (John Wiley & Sons, 2011).

[86] T. J. Sinclair, *The New Masters of Capital: American Bond Rating Agencies and the Politics of Creditworthiness* (Cornell University Press, 2014); L. J. White, 'Markets: The Credit Rating Agencies' (2010) 24 *Journal of Economic Perspectives* 211–26; E. I. Altman and H. A. Rijken, 'How Rating Agencies Achieve Rating Stability' (2004) 28 *Journal of Banking & Finance* 2679–714; see also essays in Davis et al., *Governance by Indicators.*

[87] Backer, 'Next Generation Law'.

[88] A. McAfee and E. Brynjolffon, 'Big Data: The Management Revolution', *Harvard Business Review* (October 2012), https://hbr.org/2012/10/big-data-the-management-revolution.

[89] C. Tang, *The Data Industry: The Business and Economics of Information and Big Data* (Wiley, 2016).

become important elements of risk and compliance systems in five critical areas. The first is *law enforcement* (state entities) and compliance (private entities). Data-driven analytics here is presented as a method for complying with legal duty or responsibility. Administrative regulation and law provide the objectives, but the implementation occurs within automized data-driven systems. Examples include regimes for the distribution of governmental funds through revenue sharing and other programmes.[90] The second is *transparency* regimes: 'It is used within an organization or community to enhance its operation and discipline its members; it is used externally to enhance legitimacy (norm) and accountability (technique) among stakeholders who have an interest in but not a direct participation in the operation of the enterprise.'[91] The third is in *controlling behaviour*. For economic enterprises this was driven in part by law,[92] and in part by changes in the way that administrative officials exercised authority.[93] Data-based analytics may be essential in the exercise of prosecutorial discretion in the USA[94] and the UK.[95] Businesses are increasingly using data-driven analytics to control behaviours through health and wellness programmes. The fourth, *shaping cultures*, is possible when monitoring (micro-surveillance) is tied to transparency and enforcement. Smoking campaigns are a well-known example.[96] Here one entangles moral value systems (about smoking) into political action (anti-smoking regulation) which is then entangled within medical and quantitative measures of harm which contribute to health

[90] *Department of Commerce* v. *New York*, Supreme Court No. 18–966, 588 US (2019).

[91] L. C. Backer, 'Transparency between Norm, Technique and Property in International Law and Governance: The Example of Corporate Disclosure Regimes and Environmental Impacts' (2013) 22 *Minnesota Journal of International Law* 1–70.

[92] Under the Delaware fiduciary duty law, *Stone* v. *Ritter*, 911 A.2d 362 (Del. 2006).

[93] J. Nassikas, J. Tan and L. Carson, 'New DOJ Compliance Program Guidance', Harvard Law School Forum on Corporate Governance (10 June 2019), https://corpgov.law.harvard.edu/2019/06/10/new-doj-compliance-program-guidance/ ('Compliance program effectiveness is a key variable DOJ takes into consideration when (1) making charging decisions and exercising prosecutorial discretion, (2) making sentencing recommendations, including calculating recommended fines, and (3) deciding whether to impose reporting requirements or appoint an outside compliance monitor as part of a corporate resolution').

[94] US Department of Justice, 'The Fraud Section's Foreign Corrupt Practices Act Enforcement Plan and Guidance' (5 April 2016), www.justice.gov/criminal-fraud/file/838416/download.

[95] See UK Criminal Finances Act 2017, chapter 22.

[96] T. Hu et al., 'The Impact of California Proposition 99, a Major Anti-smoking Law, on Cigarette Consumption' (1994) 15 *Journal of Public Health Policy* 26–36.

rankings that affect private markets for insurance, and rankings that may affect individual access to credit or education.[97] Fifth is *accountability* as assessment, self-assessment and accountability regimes at the individual and entity levels.[98] These entangle both legal systems through compliance regimes and markets-based systems through data-driven ratings systems.

Entanglements between data and conventional governance orders have only recently emerged more clearly. The recent controversy over the inclusion of questions about citizenship on the US census provides a case in point.[99] Inclusion of the question would generate data, a core operational principle of census taking. That generation is coupled with a host of conventional law which relied on the governance of census data generation for its own operation. But the generation of data has significant consequences precisely because the system of regulation into which those data are injected is itself based on the way data are curated. Here is the point of entanglement between census as a system of data generation, census as the jurisdiction of compiling a quantitative narrative image of the American population, and census as a necessary predicate for the operationalization of a number of conflicting political objectives expressed though the law of states and the federal government. It's no surprise to see census questions shifting with the times: 'Lots of questions go off the census when they're not very important anymore.'[100] The conflict within data governance became famously entangled with the legal regulation of the administrative state in a US Supreme Court opinion most notable for its recognition of conflict expressed in rules governing the exercise of political discretion within a web of legislation where the interests of secondary sovereigns are affected.[101]

[97] C. P. Guzalian, M. A. Stein and H. S. Akiskal, 'Credit Scores, Lending, and Psychological Disability' (2015) 95 *Boston University Law Review* 1807.

[98] L. C. Backer, 'Unpacking Accountability in Business and Human Rights: The Multinational Enterprise, the State, and the International Community', in L. Enneking, I. Giesen, A.-J. Schaap, C. Ryngaert, F. Kristen and L. Roorda (eds), *Accountability and International Business Operations: Providing Justice for Corporate Violations of Human Rights, Labor and Environmental Standards* (Routledge, 2019).

[99] *Department of Commerce* v. *New York* (2019).

[100] C. E. Shoichet, 'Why Putting a Citizenship Question on the Census Is a Big Deal', CNN (28 March 2018), https://edition.cnn.com/2018/03/27/politics/census-citizenship-question-explainer/index.html (quoting University of Wisconsin Professor Margo Anderson).

[101] *Department of Commerce* v. *New York* (2019).

Another important point of entanglement between data-driven and traditional legalities centres on the scope and principles through which data may be harvested. Most aggressive – again voluntary and on a bargained for basis – are chip implants for employees[102] by merchants (including the state). This is a system grounded in consent, in value added as an inducement for participation. Increasingly, however, states have sought to use their legislative authority to restrict, or at least manage, this essential feature of data-based rule systems, by legislating the legal effects (and limits) of consent, especially within an employment relationship.[103] More passive are the seamless systems of cameras, credit card transactions, turnstiles, passes for highway tolls, key stroke and internet tracking systems and the like that can effectively track individuals and record their activities on a continuous basis. Their regulatory effect is now well known.[104] Yet their entanglements with plural legal systems have only just invaded the consciousness of regulatory stakeholders. Emerging issues include privacy rights;[105] and rights to be forgotten.[106] But the focus has also turned to the application of issues of race, gender and other non-discrimination law and policy to the structures of data-driven governance bound up in the extraction of information for behaviour management ends.[107] Conversely, data-driven systems themselves have entangled with law systems in the area of discrimination law by providing a complementary system, the products

[102] M. Fox, 'Installing Microchips in Employees Is "the Right Thing to Do," CEO says', CNBC (24 July 2017), www.cnbc.com/2017/07/24/installing-microchips-in-employees-is-the-right-thing-to-do-ceo-says.html.

[103] A. Keshner, 'States Are Cracking Down on Companies Microchipping their Employees' *MarketWatch* (4 February 2020), www.marketwatch.com/story/states-are-cracking-down-on-companies-microchipping-their-employees-how-common-is-it-and-why-does-it-happen-2020-02-03.

[104] N. Just and M. Latzer, 'Governance by Algorithms: Reality Construction by Algorithmic Selection on the Internet' (2017) 39 *Media, Culture & Society* 238–58; P. Bergevin, 'Addicted to Ratings: The Case for Reducing Governments' Reliance on Credit Ratings' (May 2010) 130 *C. D. How Institute Backgrounder*; F. Partnoy, 'The Siskel and Ebert of Financial Markets: Two Thumbs Down for the Credit Rating Agencies' (1999) 77 *Washington University Law Quarterly* 619–712.

[105] W. Kerber, 'Digital Markets, Data, and Privacy: Competition Law, Consumer Law and Data Protection' (2016) 11 *Journal of Intellectual Property Law & Practice* 856–66; S. Spiekermann, A. Acquisti, R. Böhme and L. Hui, 'The Challenges of Data Markets and Privacy' (2015) 25 *Electronic Markets* 161–7.

[106] J. Rosen, 'The Right to Be Forgotten' (2012) 64 *Stanford Law Review* 88.

[107] E.g., S. U. Noble, *Algorithms of Oppression: How Search Engines Reinforce Racism* (New York University Press, 2018); V. Eubanks, *Automating Inequality: How High-Tech Tools Profile, Police, and Punish the Poor* (St Martin's Press, 2018).

of which are used by law systems as techniques of proof of discriminatory intent or in forming or assessing policy and regulations.[108]

Compliance itself is a data-driven exercise, but one in which the parameters are set by legal systems, administered through the actors onto which compliance is imposed, and assessed and disciplined either by the state or private actors.[109] Compliance is expressed as the private law internal governance systems that implement the delegation of responsibility (in part) from the state effected through law or regulatory directive. These include implementing administrative guidance,[110] to compliance systems built around disclosure and reporting systems, for example, the French Supply Chain Due Diligence Law[111] or the Australian Modern Slavery Law.[112] The second is crafted through data-driven assessment systems that take their objectives from the policies of private law internal governance and which rely heavily on markets for external disciplining.[113] These entanglements are clearest in the context of corporate governance.[114]

Of all of the forms of data-driven governance, perhaps the closest the West has to the emerging Chinese social credit initiative are credit rating agencies. Financial credit rating agencies, for example, become actors in the governance of financial markets through their production of a standardized rating of risk (creditworthiness), which is then used for making investment decisions, and consequently to make the regulation of financial markets dependent on the risk assessed.[115] These operate within a market

[108] E.g., J. Ringelheim, 'Collecting Racial or Ethnic Data for Anti-discrimination Policies: A U.S.–Europe Comparison' (2008) 10 *Rutgers Race and Law Review* 39; P. Simon, 'The Measurement of Racial Discrimination: The Policy Use of Statistics' (2005) 57 *International Social Science Journal* 9–25; M. Chamallas, 'Questioning the Use of Race-Specific and Gender-Specific Economic Data in Tort Litigation: A Constitutional Argument' (1994) 63 *Fordham Law Review* 73.

[109] American Law Institute, *Principles of the Law*.

[110] US Department of Justice, 'The Fraud Section's Foreign Corrupt Practices Act Enforcement Plan and Guidance'.

[111] F. Baddache, 'What to Learn from France's and UK's Human Rights Due Diligence Laws?', KSAPA (15 June 2019), https://ksapa.org/what-to-learn-from-france-and-uks-human-rights-due-diligence-laws/.

[112] See Australian Modern Slavery Act 2018, Act No. 153 of 2018.

[113] Backer, 'Theorizing Regulatory Governance Within Its Ecology'.

[114] P. Baxter, 'Corporate Governance Ratings and Financial Performance: Evidence from Australia' (2014) 5 *International Journal of Corporate Governance* 178–96.

[115] D. Kerwer, 'Standardizing as Governance: The Case of Credit Ratings Agencies', in A. Heritier (ed.), *Reinventing European and International Governance* (Rowman & Littlefield, 2002), pp. 293–316, at p. 294.

for services with a few big players rating business and public credit. Their profit derives from subscriptions or issuer-pays models of income. This produces a markets-driven model that mimics the effects of Chinese centralizing and public control models. These credit agencies' businesses are grounded in data-based analytics applied to objectives and their effect is to discipline behaviours through reward–punishment systems derived from their analytics. Their systems are functionally differentiated, and they exhibit only a necessary unification even within the same field. At the same time, their activities serve as the basis for regulation, and are, to some extent, regulated by the state whose finances they in turn rate.

4.5 Conclusion

The relationship between traditional governance orders, in a context of spatially distinct but intermeshed legal/normative orders, remains to be fully explored. This chapter suggested some points of entry and on fundamental approaches. First, the use of metrics and the quantification of accountability has moved beyond an increasingly sophisticated palette of rankings and inducement to become a regulatory space in its own right. Second, that regulatory space embeds politics and law within the construction of its analytics and the determination of the meaning of rankings. China is building a centralized system tied to its political organization. Most of the elements of social credit have already been developed in the West. But the unification of the various elements, and their seamless operation, would be a great innovation. While the West approaches data-driven governance entanglements through the lens of privatization and markets,[116] China inverts the trajectories of entanglement, focusing instead on recreating within the state the universe of data-driven governance in which law becomes the instruction manual for the operation of social ordering through data-driven analytics. Third, these systems pose a challenge for the conventional understanding of entanglement among systems all characterized by qualitative approaches to regulation. Perhaps most interesting of all the consequences of these social credit systems may be their ability to absorb traditional systems, and in that process of absorption to reduce the centrality of borderlands between systems.

[116] C. Cutler, 'The Privatization of Global Governance and the Modern Law Merchant', in A. Heritier (ed.), *Reinventing European and International Governance* (Rowman & Littlefield, 2002), pp. 127–58.

Hints of this trajectory are evident in the movement towards compliance and accountability. These increasingly data-driven exercises turn traditional governance systems, and the governance systems arising between and within them (conventional spatiality of governance), into the generators of data that themselves can be subject to management in accordance with principles and objectives. These objectives may themselves be drawn from the political-cultural assumptions of society or themselves may be dynamic expressions monitored through the aggregate conduct of data generators themselves. The multiplicity of legal regimes, then, is itself a source of data useful for data-driven analytics that can manage these as well as aid in the management of systems.[117] This suggests entanglement of a different order, between qualitative and quantitative regulatory measures which increasingly fold one into the other while retaining an element of autonomy based on the different regulatory spaces from which they are sourced.

What is clear is that entanglement can no longer ignore the legalities of data-driven governance even as it seeks to embed its language and structure its communication across systems that do not speak the same language. The entanglements of a law after modernity[118] become more complicated – not merely as between distinct and polycentric rule systems sharing common characteristics (the forms and functions of rules), but now between systems that do not speak the same language (words versus metrics, compliance versus assessment, etc.). Governance evolves from the language and conceptual universe of politics and principles to the language of the operating system grounded in systemic objectives. In a world of algorithms, those who would devise them will be king. And those who would be kings in Western democratic republics may well soon be scientists and not lawyers.[119] 'When you look at the most important issues facing our country, it is climate change or health-care policy or cyber security, the integrity of our elections. Who better to address these issues than a scientist?'[120] Who better indeed, when the

[117] E. Finn, *What Algorithms Want: Imagination in the Age of Computing* (MIT Press, 2017).

[118] S. Douglas-Scott, *Law after Modernity* (Hart Publishing, 2013).

[119] M. Dhar, 'Hey, Congress: Scientists Are Coming for Your Seats', LiveScience (26 April 2018), www.livescience.com/62411-scientists-running-for-congress.html.

[120] K. Karson, '"The Year that Science Strikes Back": Historic Number of Scientists Taking Over Ballots in 2018', ABC News (9 February 2018), https://abcnews.go.com/Politics/year-science-strikes-back-historic-number-scientists-taking/story?id=52959780 (quoting Shaughnessy Naughton president of 314 Action organization).

state is a container for accountability systems through data-driven algorithms? That, ultimately, suggests the great challenge for legalities and their entanglements where society continues to move beyond the problems of entangling legal systems to those for which the econometrician, the statistician and the *moralist*[121] may have as great a voice as the lawyer or the judge, and the politician or administrator.[122]

[121] F. Nietzsche, *On the Genealogy of Morals: A Polemic,* trans. W. Kaufmann and R. J. Hollindale (Vintage Books, 1967), pp. 58–9.

[122] J. Cheney-Lippold, *We Are Data: Algorithms and the Making of Our Digital Selves* (New York University Press, 2017).

5

Belt, Road and (Legal) Suspenders

Entangled Legalities on the 'New Silk Road'

TOMER BROUDE

5.1 Introduction

This chapter aims to make three main descriptive and implicitly critical points of varying importance regarding the phenomenon of 'entangled legalities',[1] using China's 'Belt and Road Initiative' (BRI) as a platform for discussion.

The first point, deceptively the simplest, is that legal entanglement is not necessarily an outcome of chance, anarchy or disorder, but can rather be produced and augmented by centralized (albeit not necessarily structurally hierarchical) political aims and ideas, that create legal and regulatory ripple effects, in ways both intended and unintended. Thus, for example, BRI, also previously known as the 'One Belt, One Road' (OBOR) and more romantically as the 'New Silk Road', is a central controlling idea in the People's Republic of China's (PRC) thirteenth five-year plan (2016–20) and beyond,[2] clearly guided from above within

Thanks to Yael Berda, Marcia Harpaz, Nico Krisch and Heng Wang for comments on earlier drafts, and to the participants in the May, 2018 workshop on 'Entangled Legalities' at the Graduate Institute Geneva. The cut-off date for factual discussion in this chapter is 15 September 2019, and all websites referred to were accessible then.

[1] As identified in this project's framing piece, see Chapter 1.

[2] See Chapter 51, 'The 13th Five-Year Plan for Economic and Social Development of the People's Republic of China' (official translation https://en.ndrc.gov.cn/newsrelease_8232/201612/P020191101481868235378.pdf); and National Development and Reform Commission, Ministry of Foreign Affairs and Ministry of Commerce of the People's Republic of China, 'Vision and Actions on Jointly Building Silk Road Economic Belt and 21st-Century Maritime Silk Road' (March 2015), https://en.ndrc.gov.cn/newsrelease_8232/201612/P020191101481868235378.pdf. For comprehensive analysis, see J. Chaisse and J. Górski (eds), *The Belt and Road Initiative: Law Economics and Politics* (Brill Nijhoff, 2018); and H. Wang, 'China's Approach to the Belt and Road Initiative: Scope, Character and Sustainability' (2019) 22(1) *Journal of International Economic Law* 29–55.

PRC political hierarchies.[3] Nevertheless, its local and international legal implications are in many respects non-hierarchical, diffuse and decentralized, touching upon a very broad and diverse range of distinctive, though not entirely discrete, norms, systems and especially actors. The interaction between the presumptively hierarchical and the miscellany of interacting parts, so to speak, produces a high level of legal entanglement. In other words, legal entanglement, or entangled legalities, can be the outcome of strategic thinking and intent, a type of deliberate order of governance, applied to a diversity of actors that serve as nodes or bridges of entanglement between otherwise disparate legal systems. These ideas are expanded on in Section 5.2, using BRI as a case study.

The second point is that, a priori, entangled legalities cannot exist without high degrees of separateness or compartmentalization between norms, systems and actors, even as they constantly interact with each other. This is not merely a trite dialectical observation – that is, just like threads in a ball of string, there must be separate strands of legality for them to become entangled – but a statement related to the structures of legal and law-relevant practice. A global or multi-regional governance project – if that is indeed what it is[4] – as massive and largely opaque but increasingly familiar as BRI, is obviously overwhelming in its scope and implications to individuals and indeed to organizations (both public and private, governmental and non-governmental). Arguably, most legal practitioners and/or private/public economic operators and government officials in the multitude of relevant jurisdictions do not consider their everyday work to be part of the overall project of BRI or related to it, or at least it's not the primary way in which they understand their work. Many

[3] On BRI/OBOR as a global geopolitical and economic strategy, see U. W. Chohan, 'The Political Economy of OBOR and the Global Economic Center of Gravity', in J. Chaisse and J. Górski (eds), *The Belt and Road Initiative: Law Economics and Politics* (Brill Nijhoff, 2018), pp. 59–82, at p. 59. A much harder line, that envisions China's strategy for global supremacy, is taken in M. Pillsbury, *The Hundred-Year Marathon: China's Secret to Replace America as the Global Superpower* (St. Martin's Griffin, 2015), p. 244, mentioning BRI/OBOR only as a means to an end.

[4] Many contend that it is, and China does not seem to conceal this; see W. Zhou and M. Esteban, 'Beyond Balancing: China's Approach towards the Belt and Road Initiative' (2018) 27 *Journal of Contemporary China* 487–501; W. A. Callahan, 'China's "Asia Dream": The Belt Road Initiative and the New Regional Order' (2016) 1 *Asian Journal of Comparative Politics* 226–43. A fascinating though clearly propagandist exposé of BRI as a global governance project, including rhetoric on 'the construction of a community with a shared future for mankind', can be found in H. Liang and Y. Zhang, *The Theoretical System of Belt and Road Initiative* (People's Publishing House and Springer Nature, 2019).

might not even know what BRI actually is, if only because it does not conform to more standardized international economic legal structures and conventions. They are just 'doing their job' within much more limited, object specific, cognitively manageable and often jurisdictionally divided (*ratione loci* or *ratione materiae*), a.k.a. 'siloed', strands of an overarching legal entanglement to which they might be largely oblivious in practice. This is demonstrated through a stylized and imagined ethnography (which is nevertheless well grounded in realistic scenarios), undertaken in Section 5.3, the heart of this chapter, in which I trace the different legal practices and local perspectives of particular individual actors, legal and other,[5] engaging in this era, in different ways, with BRI. These actors are the contact points of entanglement, each of them representing a normative and/or legal system that is entangled with BRI and with other systems. These actors include, for example, an investment protection lawyer at MOFCOM[6] in Beijing, a public procurement regulator in Greece, an associate or partner at (insert big law firm name) in Kazakhstan, insurgents in Balochistan and judges in national constitutional courts and indeed regional courts such as the Court of Justice of the European Union and the European Court of Human Rights.

Taking note of their separateness, the distinctive and representative existence of these individual narratives should not be taken to imply

[5] The focus here is deliberately on individual actors and agents engaged with different levels and dimensions of law; the role of the individual in international legality is increasingly acknowledged, from a variety of perspectives. See, e.g., A. Peters, *Beyond Human Rights: The Legal Status of the Individual in International Law* (Cambridge University Press, 2016); T. Megiddo, 'Methodological Individualism' (2019) 60 *Harvard Journal of International Law* 219–80; and T. Broude and I. Levy, 'Outcome Bias and Expertise in Investigations under International Humanitarian Law' (2020) 30(4) *European Journal of International Law*, 1303–18.

[6] MOFCOM is China's Ministry of Commerce. As international trade and governance scholars Gao and Shaffer have recently put it, 'MOFCOM has a Janus-faced role of looking inward and outward', in the sense that it regulates both domestic and international commercial affairs – see G. Shaffer and H. Gao, 'China's Rise: How it took on the U.S. at the WTO' (2018) 1 *University of Illinois Law Review* 115–84, at 138. As in trade, the MOFCOM mandate covers both outgoing and incoming foreign investment, including International Investment Agreements; see K. P. Sauvant and V. Z. Chen, 'China's Regulatory Framework for Outward Foreign Direct Investment' (2014) 7 *China Economic Journal* 141–63; and A. C. Dai, 'The International Investment Agreement Network under the "Belt and Road" Initiative', in J. Chaisse and J. Górski (eds), *The Belt and Road Initiative: Law Economics and Politics* (Brill Nijhoff, 2018), pp. 220–49, at p. 220.

*dis*entanglement in any way. Rather, the opposite is true; this separateness establishes a pattern of a set of different systems, approaches and perspectives that coexist with normative entanglement. Put differently, this is not simple, straightforward self-containment or 'fragmentation' of international law.[7] Rather, to my mind the main contribution of the concept of international or transnational legal entanglement is its emphasis on querying how different legal norms and systems, with heterogeneous yet often shared legal foundations, engage with each other in unanticipated circumstances. Thus, Section 5.4 demonstrates how the seemingly separate worlds of law and practice can come together, and indeed are already conjoined in an actual case – the Belgrade–Budapest railway project – emphasizing their interdependencies, some of them unexpected and counterintuitive, but in any case, deeply legally entangled.

The third point, discussed in the concluding Section 5.5, builds on the first two, and is well demonstrated by BRI, namely that entangled legalities may be strongly and positively associated with the gradual, messy and piecemeal process of empire-building, or at least empire-bidding. The combination of top-down and bottom-up forces of legal entanglement create flexibilities and benefits for hegemonic contenders, such as in the present case, China, that well acknowledge their own political constraints.

5.2 Between Centralized Goals and Localized Effects: Entanglement, from above

Perhaps counterintuitively, entangled legalities are not necessarily (or at all) a chance or accidental occurrence, disrupting an otherwise settled and logically well-organized legal order. Entangled legalities clearly defy

[7] The fragmentation of international law has been a central feature in both the practice and theorization of international law since the rise of distinct regimes and institutions in the 1990s, exacerbating the decentralized and anarchic nature of international law (see, e.g., M. Koskenniemi and P. Leino, 'Fragmentation of International Law? Postmodern Anxieties' (2002) 15 *Leiden Journal of International Law* 553–79; Report of the Study Group of the International Law Commission, 'Fragmentation of International Law: Difficulties Arising from the Diversification and Expansion of International Law' (13 April 2006) UN Doc A/CN.4/L.682, as corrected (11 August 2006) UN Doc A/CN.4/L.682/Corr.1 (finalized by Martti Koskenniemi). It remains a fixture of international legal debate to this day (e.g. T. Megiddo, 'Beyond Fragmentation: On International Law's Integrationist Forces' (2019) 44 *Yale Journal of International Law* 115–48).

the neat analytics of the Kelsenian idea of a 'hierarchical structure' or *stufenbau*[8] – in the absence of any clear pyramid between the enmeshed norms involved – or any pretence of distinguishing, in a Hohfeldian sense, between rights, liberties, powers and immunities.[9] Entangled legalities plainly lie in the theoretical and practical realms of legal pluralism,[10] characterized as 'complex intertwined networks'.[11] Add to these the substantively contested but formally accepted public and private law distinction,[12] and further dimensions of entanglement emerge. It is not, however, always that difficult to 'fix the own point of departure' of entanglement,[13] if one accepts that entangled legalities can actually be a preference, 'from above'. They may express a preference for legal plurality that serves centralized and powerful interests and ideas – even hegemonic aspirations – better and more flexibly than a clearly defined hierarchy. This is to say that entanglement can be an established mode of legal and regulatory governance, at both macro (centralized) and micro (localized) levels. Regarding public (and private) international law it is not merely a phenomenon of the famous international 'anarchical society'[14] – it is not necessarily a form of anarchy at all, even if it defies the suffix '-archy'. Thus, in terms of 'pathways' to its emergence, there is a type of legal entanglement that is inevitably a combination of mutual benefit, appeal and coercion,[15] or alternatively, imperfectly close to

[8] H. Kelsen, 'The Concept of the Legal Order' (1982) 27 *The American Journal of Jurisprudence* 64–84.

[9] W. N. Hohfeld, 'Fundamental Legal Conceptions as Applied in Judicial Reasoning' (1917) 26 *The Yale Law Journal* 710–70.

[10] See Section 1.1 in Chapter 1.

[11] T. Duve, 'Entanglements in Legal History: Introductory Remarks', in T. Duve (ed.), *Entanglements in Legal History: Conceptual Approaches* (Max Planck Institute for Legal History, 2014), pp. 3–25, at p. 8.

[12] M. Rosenfeld, 'Rethinking the Boundaries between Public Law and Private Law for the Twenty First Century: An Introduction' (2013) 11 *International Journal of Constitutional Law* 125–28 and subsequent contributions in the same issue of the journal: A. Supiot, 'The Public–Private Relation in the Context of Today's Refeudalization' (2013) 11 *International Journal of Constitutional Law* 129–45; P. Goodrich, 'The Political Theology of Private Law' (2013) 11 *International Journal of Constitutional Law* 146–61; and J. Resnik, 'Globalization(s), Privatization(s), Constitutionalization, and Statization: Icons and Experiences of Sovereignty in the 21st Century' (2013) 11 *International Journal of Constitutional Law* 162–99.

[13] Duve, 'Entanglements in Legal History', p. 8.

[14] H. Bull, *The Anarchical Society: A Study of Order in World Politics* (Macmillan, 1977).

[15] Krisch identifies these three 'pathways' to entanglement, see Section 1.4.2 in Chapter 1.

coercion, the outcome of a fourth pathway – through implicit dominance or disguised hegemony.

In other words, whether by default or by design, a central actor, which has the authority and perhaps even the real power to create a structured, hierarchical legal system, may refrain from doing so or even prefer not to if this conduct better serves its goals, and if the costs of hierarchical regulation outweigh its benefits. Moreover, grand ideas can be both centralized as guiding elements – *telos* or *teloi* – and in this respect can be very effective in creating localized effects through legal entanglement. The BRI is, arguably, a case in point. I return to this, in brief, in Section 5.5.

But what is BRI or the 'New Silk Road', actually? BRI defies definition, yet cannot be ignored. At its rawest, it can be understood straightforwardly as an ambitious programme of infrastructure project finance within China (primarily in the less developed western provinces)[16] and in dozens of other countries, spreading to the south and mainly outward to the west of China, all to the tune of US$1 trillion to be invested over twenty years. BRI, which has been often been analogized to the post-World War II 'Marshall Plan',[17] can transform the living conditions of hundreds of millions throughout the nether lands of South and Central Asia, reaching into Africa and, more discreetly, into Europe.

Indeed, Europe seems to be very much a crucial economic objective of BRI, presenting a 'pivot to Europe' in response to the Obama administration's now all but forgotten 'Pivot to Asia' which included US leadership in negotiations over the Trans-Pacific Partnership (TPP),[18] a policy

[16] See A. Chatzky and J. McBride, 'China's Massive Belt and Road Initiative', Council on Foreign Relations Backgrounder (21 May 2019), www.cfr.org/backgrounder/chinas-massive-belt-and-road-initiative.

[17] Quite recently: 'Will China's Belt and Road Initiative Outdo the Marshall Plan?', *The Economist* (8 March 2018), www.economist.com/finance-and-economics/2018/03/08/will-chinas-belt-and-road-initiative-outdo-the-marshall-plan.

[18] The TPP was envisioned as a 'mega-regional' trade and investment agreement encompassing most of the economies of the Pacific Rim. One of President Trump's first decisions upon entering office was to withdraw from the TPP, with significant regional implications (see S. Narine, 'US Domestic Politics and America's Withdrawal from the Trans-Pacific Partnership: Implications for Southeast Asia' (2018) 40 *Contemporary Southeast Asia* 50–76). All other parties to the negotiations continued to discuss a revised regional trade agreement without the USA, the Comprehensive and Progressive Agreement for Trans-Pacific Partnership, which entered into force for the first six ratifying states in December 2018; for comparison, see H. Wang, 'The Future of Deep Trade Agreements: The Convergence of TPP (and CPTPP) and CETA)?' (2019) 53 *Journal of World Trade* 317–42.

obliterated by President Trump but not considered a great success even beforehand.[19] Chinese investments in European ports and rail systems are transforming market access and distribution in the EU much more positively than the legal conundrums of Brexit will.[20] Reportedly, China now controls – in current terms – one-tenth of all European port capacity, with gateways in Piraeus, Zeebrugge and elsewhere.[21] This can only be expected to expand, as China invests in rail infrastructures through the Balkans to central Europe.[22] Thus, BRI is not only important in simple economic terms. The historical Silk Road had two sides; from a Eurocentric perspective, it was a road to China, from a Chinese perspective it was a road to Europe. BRI is more of the latter than the former. Europeans have only recently started to grasp this,[23] as more states in the EU sign on to the programme (e.g. Greece, Hungary, Italy) – literally through 'non-binding' BRI Memoranda;[24] attend BRI diplomatic forums; and grant Chinese firms infrastructure projects and accept their loans. This has created an intra-EU tension between member states and the EU Commission, which is explicitly more reserved regarding China and BRI,[25] due to concerns about foreign investment approval and

[19] M. J. Green, 'The Legacy of Obama's 'Pivot' to Asia', *Foreign Policy* (3 September 2016), https://foreignpolicy.com/2016/09/03/the-legacy-of-obamas-pivot-to-asia/.

[20] Indeed, some see the possible strengthening of the United Kingdom's bilateral economic relations with China as a remedy to problems arising from Brexit, while others see it as a threat to the UK's sovereignty; see K. Brown, 'How Brexit Britain Can Gain from China's Belt and Road', *This Week in Asia* (12 May 2017), www.scmp.com/week-asia/opinion/article/2094166/what-brexit-britain-has-gain-chinas-belt-and-road; and M. Auslin, 'Brexit Britain Is Eager for a Sweet Deal with Beijing: But at What Price?', *The Spectator* (4 August 2018), www.spectator.co.uk/2018/08/making-china-great-again/. As of the time of this writing, there is no United Kingdom–China trade arrangement outside of the WTO.

[21] See K. Johnson, 'Why Is China Buying up Europe's Ports?', *Foreign Policy* (2 February 2018).

[22] 'Serbia Starts Construction of Chinese-Funded Railway to Budapest', Reuters (28 November 2017), www.reuters.com/article/serbia-china-railway/serbia-starts-construction-of-chinese-funded-railway-to-budapest-idUSL8N1NY4RR.

[23] AFP, 'Europe Casts a Wary Eye on China's Silk Road Plans', *Straits Times* (7 January 2018), www.straitstimes.com/world/europe/europe-casts-a-wary-eye-on-chinas-silk-road-plans.

[24] See *Memorandum of Understanding between the Government of the Republic of Italy and the Government of the People's Republic of China on Cooperation within the Framework of the Silk Road Economic Belt and the 21st Century Maritime Silk Road Initiative* (March 2019), www.governo.it/sites/governo.it/files/Memorandum_Italia-Cina_EN.pdf.

[25] See European Commission and High Representative of the Union for Foreign Affairs and Security Policy, 'Joint Communication to the European Parliament, the European Council and the Council, *EU-China – A Strategic Outlook*' (12 March 2019) JOIN

debt-entrapment,[26] and prompted the EU Commission to develop closer economic relations with Japan, including a very recent bilateral agreement on infrastructure connectivity, depicted as a counter to BRI.[27]

Moreover, it would be naïve to think that BRI is not indeed also a governance project, potentially the greatest geopolitical transformation since the end of the first Cold War, aiming to create a Eurasian economic and political space under Chinese dominance. It brings to mind George Kennan's 'Long Telegram' regarding Soviet influence after World War II, in that it 'involves questions so intricate, so delicate, so strange to our form of thought, and so important to analysis of our international environment that I cannot compress answers into single brief message without yielding to what I feel would be a dangerous degree of oversimplification'.[28] The EU Commission *EU-China: Strategic Outlook* document from 2019,[29] is of course a public document and hence much more cautious in its drafting; notably, however, it does not mention BRI by any of its names, while the word security appears, in a variety of contexts, much more than the words trade or investment. In other words, the EU has become acutely aware of the geopolitical/economic gauntlet that China has thrown down through BRI.

But again, *what* is BRI, in legal governance terms? It has been noted that locating the 'formal legal sources, either domestic or international' of

(2019) 5 final, https://ec.europa.eu/commission/sites/beta-political/files/communication-eu-china-a-strategic-outlook.pdf. Belgian/EU politician and EU Parliament Brexit coordinator Guy Verhofstadt has said that Italy's endorsement of BRI is 'antithetical' to the interests of the EU and its member states (see G. Verhofstadt, 'Europe Must Unite on China', ING THINK Outside (29 March 2019), https://think.ing.com/opinions/guy-verhofstadt-europe-must-unite-on-china/.

[26] 'Debt trap diplomacy' concerns – the idea that high financial indebtedness to China will cause political dependence – has also been raised in Asia, in particular following the leasing of the Hambantota Port to a Chinese corporation for ninety-nine years, following loan non-performance; see T. H. Shih, 'China Risks Imperial Image With Belt and Road Initiative', *Asia Sentinel* (8 October 2019), www.asiasentinel.com/econ-business/china-imperial-image-belt-and-road-initiative/.

[27] See European Commission, 'EU Charts New Ground in Global Connectivity – Looks to Boost Strategic Ties with Asia', Press Release IP/19/5851 (26 September 2019), https://europa.eu/rapid/press-release_IP-19-5851_en.htm.

[28] George Kennan (22 February 1946), https://digitalarchive.wilsoncenter.org/document/116178.pdf.

[29] See European Commission and High Representative of the Union for Foreign Affairs and Security Policy, *EU-China: A Strategic Outlook* (12 March 2019), JOIN (2019) 5, https://ec.europa.eu/info/sites/default/files/communication-eu-china-a-strategic-outlook.pdf.

BRI is a difficult task.[30] Heng Wang has called the Chinese approach to BRI 'less institutional', presumably in comparison with Western approaches that have relied on institutions in the architecture of international law and regimes. Within this Chinese approach he notes two layers or categories of non-domestic law relevant to BRI: first, 'BRI-specific' documents, such as the increasing number of non-binding or binding Memoranda of Understanding (MOUs) between China and states and international organizations;[31] and second, 'BRI-related' rules that can apply to BRI economic activity, such as World Trade Organization (WTO) law, regional trade agreements and international investment agreements.[32] To these one might add a variety of international legal rules and norms that are also BRI-related, such as human rights instruments, and environmental, maritime and other standards and private law. Seeking further for historical and institutional analogies, one can clutch on to the Asian Infrastructure Investment Bank, established by China supposedly as an alternative to longstanding multilateral development banks, a competitor to the World Bank Group and an essential political and economic instrument for BRI.[33] One can also look to the Silk Road Fund, a multi-million dollar investment fund, wholly controlled by China.[34] But as China scholar Maria Adele Carrai has written, these financial branches do not provide BRI with a rigid legal structure.[35] BRI does not have a 'membership', an 'institution', a 'decision-making' process. It does not fit easily into any boxes of conventional international legal order. This does not mean, however, that it does not have many significant implications for law in its spheres of influence, creating entangled legalities at many levels, down to the most localized.

[30] L. Zeng, 'Conceptual Analysis of China's Belt and Road Initiative: A Road towards a Regional Community of Common Destiny' (2016) 15 *Chinese Journal of International Law* 517–41, at 539.

[31] Such as the 2017 MOU between China's National Development and Reform Commission (NDRC) and the United Nations Economic Commission for Europe (UNECE) (UNECE-NDRC MOU), www.unece.org/fileadmin/DAM/MoU_between_UNECE___the_NDRC_in_China_2017-05-14.pdf; and AFP, 'Europe Casts a Wary Eye on China's Silk Road Plans'.

[32] Wang, 'China's Approach to the Belt and Road Initiative', section II.

[33] M. Callaghan and P. Hubbard, 'The Asian Infrastructure Investment Bank: Multilateralism on the Silk Road' (2016) 9 *China Economic Journal* 116–39.

[34] See www.silkroadfund.com.cn/.

[35] M. A. Carrai, 'It Is Not the End of History: The Financing Institutions of the Belt and Road Initiative and the Bretton Woods System' (2017) 14 *Transnational Dispute Management* 1–14, at 2–3.

To be sure, the present section of this chapter does not aspire to provide a comprehensive descriptive analysis of BRI. Indeed, the nature of the beast, as already stylized above, as well as the current flux in international 'geoeconomics',[36] would seem to preclude this.[37] Rather, the point to be made is that while BRI evidently constitutes a complex system of entangled legalities, it would appear to have been deliberately *conceived* as such, 'top down', by its initiator, not by chance or oversight, and in lieu of attempting to establish a less entangled, more structured (if not hierarchical) form of governance.

One possible point of departure towards understanding this and its implications for entangled legalities, is the top-down definition of the BRI goals, as set out quite innocuously in Chapter 51 of the PRC's thirteenth five-year plan,[38] which reads as follows:

> *We* will uphold amity, sincerity, mutual benefit, and inclusiveness as well as the principle of joint discussion, common development, and shared growth as we look to undertake practical and mutually-beneficial cooperation in multiple sectors with countries and regions *involved in* the Belt and Road Initiative, with the *aim* of developing *a new picture* of all-around opening up in which China is opened to the world through eastward and westward links and across land and sea [emphases added].[39]

Compare to this unexpected source, Article 2 of the 1957 Treaty of Rome establishing the European Economic Community:

> *The Community* shall have *as its task*, by establishing a common market and progressively approximating the economic policies of Member States, to promote throughout the Community a harmonious development of economic activities, continuous and balanced expansion, an increase in stability, an accelerated raising of the standard of living and closer relations between the States belonging to it [emphases added].[40]

These passages are fascinating, when read side by side, in both their similarities and their differences. The similarities of mutual benefit,

[36] See A. Roberts, H. C. Moraes and V. Ferguson, 'The Geoeconomic World Order', *Lawfare* (19 November 2018), www.lawfareblog.com/geoeconomic-world-order, arguing that at this time 'We appear to be entering into a new geoeconomic world order, characterized by great power rivalry between the United States and China and the clear use of economic tools to achieve strategic goals'.

[37] The sources in n. 2 provide the most comprehensive surveys to date, especially Wang.

[38] Ibid.

[39] See n. 2.

[40] See Art. 2 of EEC, 'Treaty of Rome: Treaty Establishing the European Economic Community' (25 March 1957) 298 U.N.T.S. 3, 4 Eur. Y.B. 412.

economic development amity and harmony are clear (although also worthy of deeper theoretical analysis in other contexts). The differences relate to the conceptual mindset of governance. 'The Community' contrasts with 'We', 'task' may be opposed to 'aim'. China's five-year plan sets out goals and aspirations for BRI, leaving open the institutional technology for their achievement, while placing China firmly as *primus inter pares* in a decentralized project. Elsewhere one can find that BRI has a driving concept of a 'community of common destiny',[41] but the terms in which it is couched only enhance the difference in institutional (or non-institutional) design – China at the centre of a decentralized system (oxymoron intended). In contrast, the corollary in the Treaty of Rome sought to establish an orderly structure of institutional governance, which will have as its task the achievement of its common goals.

We know how dramatic the Treaty of Rome has been for the peoples of Europe over the last six decades, for its governance and for its legalities, which are often entangled but nevertheless structured upon formal principles such as direct effect, supremacy and subsidiarity. We do not know how dramatic the vision of BRI, posed in its own terms, will be over the next decades. But it can be said that it is a politically centralized vision that can have manifold unintended consequences in many established legal systems – in any state or territory that BRI relates to, directly or indirectly, in any international legal system that it relates to, and indeed in any issue area of regulation or legal domain. Perhaps the key phrase in the paragraph quoted from the five-year plan is 'a new picture'. Let us try to hypothesize what this picture could be – indeed, already is – for a variety of entangled legal actors.

5.3 Between Separateness and Entanglement: Vignettes of Entangled Legal Practice on the New Silk Road

A comprehensive study of the different legal practices and local perspectives of particular individual actors, legal and otherwise, with BRI, is well beyond the scope of this chapter. Nevertheless, I wish to demonstrate that these actors are the very contact points of entanglement, each of them representing a normative and/or legal system that is entangled with BRI and with other systems. The following are constructed vignettes of professionals and other agents interacting with BRI and other related

[41] D. Zhang, 'The Concept of "Community of Common Destiny" in China's Diplomacy: Meaning, Motives and Implications', *Asia and the Pacific Policy Studies* (16 April 2018).

legal systems in recent history, from variegated legal and geographical perspectives. The reader can consider this as a narrative or as an imagined or hypothetical ethnography,[42] but the section does not aspire to methodological insight, rather aiming at illustrating one end of the spectrum of legal entanglement, namely, the relative separateness of legal actors, actions and environments and their interconnections. The names, characters and incidents portrayed can be thought of as fiction, but they are all based on or derived from real situations. Thankfully, there are social scientists and legal scholars conducting actual field research in this area. The contribution here is aimed towards the theory of entangled legalities, not to legal sociology or anthropology or to the empirical study of BRI, at least not directly.

The main point to be made here is that entangled legalities exist on a regular basis, first and foremost because of separateness and compartmentalization derived from structures of legal and law-relevant practice, as well as overarching cognitive limits, that constrain these actors to a focus on their particular environments, backgrounds and objectives. In Section 5.4 I show, through a more detailed real-life example, how this separateness is only part of the story of legal entanglement, as the distinct fields of legal practice inevitably, though sometimes unexpectedly, have points of contact and interdependence.

Let us start where it all begins, in China itself, with an initial ethnographical vignette. *A* is a very senior lawyer at the investment law division of MOFCOM, the PRC's Ministry of Commerce.[43] *A*, in his late thirties, works in Beijing, which is no less than the centre of the real-world universe for him (forget about Manhattan or Berlin, unless you are thinking of Leonard Cohen). Born in a prefecture-level city in Hubei province in central China, he has been predominantly trained and groomed in the PRC, from a very young age, for public service, through its system of

[42] Ethnography is a (not uncontroversial) anthropological/sociological qualitative methodology of describing people or cultures through observation; it has become accepted also in socio-legal studies (see, e.g., J. Starr and M. Goodale (eds), *Practicing Ethnography in Law: New Dialogues, Enduring Methods* (Palgrave Macmillan, 2002)) entailing interviews, field research and other qualitative social science methods. An excellent example of ethnographical research in the field of international economic law is G. A. Sarfaty, *Values in Translation: Human Rights and the Culture of the World Bank* (Stanford University Press, 2012). The vignettes in this section are not based on such systematic research, so they cannot claim to be a true ethnography, and don't wish to be, hence the qualifiers 'imagined' or 'hypothetical'.

[43] See references in n. 6.

'meritocracy'.[44] He is, however, distinctly a 'man of the world'. He holds an LLM degree from a leading law school in the USA, speaks excellent English, and has travelled – in his professional capacity, of course, primarily as an advisor to trade and investment agreement negotiations, perish the thought of corruption – several times to Brussels, Singapore, Kuala Lumpur, Johannesburg, Dubai and Canberra, and has previously worked at a junior level in the Chinese delegation in Geneva. Despite his worldliness, his sights are always set on promotion within the Chinese system. He cautiously hopes to hold high office in the Party and government someday.[45] To him, BRI is very significant. It will project and extend China's economic and political power and prowess to the world, and *A* is both confident and proud that he is part of this project, in particular because it will, on balance, bring wealth, welfare and Chinese values to other cultures.[46] Law is an important instrument to this end, utilizing formats developed by Western powers (such as International Investment Agreements (IIAs), which he negotiates)[47] that are now fundamental for facilitating and establishing China's trade and investment policies, which can promote BRI as a significant global public good.[48] Entangled legality is de rigueur, it comes naturally, so long as the overarching goals are promoted and ideally achieved. *A* is not concerned at all with the formal problem posed by parallel or even contradictory legal systems, such as international investment agreements and commercial obligations,[49] so long as they serve the greater purposes of BRI.

44 For a survey on competing views regarding Chinese meritocracy, and a comparison with promotion systems in Western democracies (at the ministerial level), see D. S. Lee and P. J. Schuler, 'Testing the "China Model" of Meritocratic Promotions: Do Democracies Reward Less Competent Ministers than Autocracies?' (2020) 53 *Comparative Political Studies* 531–66.

45 The Communist Party plays a crucial role in Chinese governance, and according to some analysis, over the last few years, administrative power is shifting in the direction of the Party; see L. L. P. Gore, 'The Communist Party-Dominated Governance Model of China: Legitimacy, Accountability, and Meritocracy' (2019) 51 *Polity* 161–94.

46 In line with Part 16 of the five-year plan (see n. 2), which addresses socialist values and ethics as well as Chinese cultural heritage.

47 On China's BRI IIA policy, see Dai, 'The International Investment Agreement Network under the "Belt and Road" Initiative'; and Sauvant and Chen, 'China's Regulatory Framework for Outward Foreign Direct Investment'.

48 Similarly, see C. He, 'The Belt and Road Initiative as Global Public Good: Implications for International Law', in W. Shan, K. Nuotio and K. Zhang (eds), *Normative Readings of the Belt and Road Initiative: Road to New Paradigms* (Springer, 2018), pp. 85–104.

49 As an example, China has at least two co-existing agreements with South Korea, which include investment protection provisions – a Bilateral Investment Agreement from 2007 and a Trade Agreement from 2012.

For *A*, 'law' is technically public international law, that needs to be upheld as an overarching order that serves China's interests in general and BRI in particular; but in practice much of it is commercial law. This need not be enforced through traditional Western dispute settlement systems, but through combinations of legal argumentation and diplomacy, and alternative dispute resolution procedures, such as mediation.[50]

Moving on to another entangled and entangling actor at the European portal representing the other end of BRI, *B* is a mid-level legal counsel in the Greek Ministry of Infrastructure, Transport and Networks in the Athens suburb of Cholargos. At the age of thirty-two, *B*'s worldview is inevitably coloured by the financial and government debt crises of the 2000s that began when she was a law student at the Kapodistrian University of Athens, and the scepticism that it has brought in Greece towards international institutions, both at the EU level[51] and beyond. *B* aspires to attain an internationally recognized graduate law degree, perhaps in the UK (though this is becoming less attractive because of Brexit, making the Netherlands her new first choice), but she first needs to establish herself economically and in her professional career, and perhaps start a family. *B* is a formalist, she follows the book, even when the book is blurred. But she also patriotically understands her state's strengths and weaknesses, and that an opportunity for foreign investment and increased employment should not be passed up. In her eyes, austerity, imposed by international neoliberal forces, pales in the face of the riches offered by a powerful and trustworthy economic good faith partner from China. The Chinese state-operated enterprises that offer lucrative terms for infrastructure projects that place Greece at a crucial juncture between China and the rest of Europe are a breath of fresh air. Yes, the Chinese can be

[50] China has been involved in only a handful of disputes under its IIAs. There is a trend towards constructing and viewing BRI projects and potential disputes related to them as private, commercial law issues, and within that framing to encourage resolution through mediation; see, e.g., the MOU reportedly signed by the Singapore International Mediation Centre and the China Council for the Promotion of International Trade in January 2019, setting up a BRI-focused panel of mediators (T. D. Wei, 'Singapore, China to Set Up Mediators' Panel for Belt and Road Projects', *Straits Times* (25 January 2019), www.straitstimes.com/asia/east-asia/singapore-china-to-set-up-mediators-panel-for-belt-and-road-projects).

[51] Greece was traditionally a Europeanist state, but public opinion towards the EU and its major member states has declined, although not to the level of 'Grexit'; see B. Clements, K. Nanou and S. Verney, '"We No Longer Love You, But We Don't Want to Leave You": The Eurozone Crisis and Popular Euroscepticism in Greece' (2014) 36 *Journal of European Integration* 247–65.

difficult to deal with, but they don't have the arrogance of the Western Europeans or Americans.[52] They know what civil law means and are willing to negotiate flexibly and pragmatically. *B* is not really sure what BRI is – she's heard of it, after all she reads the Greek economic press and *The Economist* from time to time. Over the last few years, however, she has been much more focused on settling the terms of the corporate franchise of a shipping container terminal in the port of Piraeus, and the sale of a majority share in the port authority, with a huge Chinese state-owned shipping company. As time goes by, she takes pride in her small professional contribution to the major increase in shipping container traffic through Piraeus (about ten times the 2008 volume),[53] as well as the increase in the number of Chinese tourists visiting Greece, all of which have helped the Greek economy. She was delighted when, in August 2018, the Tsipras government signed a BRI MOU with China, and is pleased that the current government is continuing to expand the relationship, while cognizant of US and EU concerns.[54]

For *B*, law is mainly Greek administrative and corporate law, in the shadow of EU law; *A*'s world of law is entirely foreign to her.

In-between *A* and *B*, *C* is a partner in the Almaty office of *X, Y and Z* LLP, a global 'big law' firm. He is only aged twenty-eight, actually born on the day that Kazakhstan declared sovereignty on its territory just before the dissolution of the Soviet Union. He is considered something of a maverick in the Kazakh energy and infrastructure law scene. Fluent in Kazakh, Russian and English, his legal education is exclusively from law schools in Kazakhstan. He is a deal-maker, building on his excellent family connections. His legal specialty is project finance, and he sees BRI as the future – breaking away from Russia, disengaging from the USA (with which he has become personally disillusioned), China is the way forward to Kazakhstan's prosperity and international recognition.[55]

[52] According to public opinion polls (2017), between 50 and 60 per cent of the Greek population considers China favourably; see P. Le Corre, 'China's Rise as a Geoeconomic Influencer: Four European Case Studies', Carnegie Endowment for International Peace Working Paper (2018), p. 20, https://carnegieendowment.org/files/WP_LeCorre_China_Final_Web.pdf.

[53] For more details of COSCO's Piraeus deals, see ibid. at 15.

[54] See S. Lau, 'Amid Headwinds, Greece Gives Cosco Green Light for Partial Piraeus Port Upgrade', *South China Morning Post* (11 October 2019), www.scmp.com/news/china/diplomacy/article/3032618/amid-headwinds-greece-gives-cosco-green-light-partial-piraeus.

[55] See N. Kassenova, 'China's Silk Road and Kazakhstan's Bright Path: Linking Dreams of Prosperity' (2017) 24 *Asia Policy* 110–16.

He has worked with US and EU companies on energy projects, but prefers to work with China – far less red-tape, no social and environmental risk assessments through the Equator Principles or Global Compact,[56] no EU regulations. This is not to say that he is not concerned with these issues, but they can be addressed through Kazakhstan's laws and regulations. He is particularly proud of his involvement with the massive Khorgos 'Dry Port' project, with its potential for regional transformation.[57]

To *C*, law is a somewhat blurry (if not shady) area of Kazakhstani business and corporate law,[58] transnational financial law and energy law. From the perspective of legal practice, his work is quite similar to that of *B*, but the legal environment is very, very different. As an ambitious young commercial lawyer, he is driven not only by his clients' interests but also by his own – knowing that he and his partners stand to gain a lot from the Chinese presence in Kazakhstan.[59] He considers himself no less a businessman than a lawyer, and is contemplating entering politics. He is happy to take Chinese dictates and stay within the bounds of Kazakh legality, so long as the project gets done.

D is a Baloch nationalist and insurgent separatist in Balochistan, the most destitute province in Pakistan, despite being extremely rich in natural gas and minerals – and hence, of great interest to the PRC. Balochistan is also a key building block in BRI, in the form of the 'China–Pakistan Economic Corridor', in which reportedly some US$60 billion have been invested or pledged by China, not least in the port of Gwadar on the Arabian Sea, now wholly run by a Chinese corporation,

[56] See http://equator-principles.com/ and www.unglobalcompact.org/ respectively.

[57] A. Higgins, 'China's Ambitious New "Port": Landlocked Kazakhstan', *New York Times* (1 January 2018), www.nytimes.com/2018/01/01/world/asia/china-kazakhstan-silk-road.html; and H. Ruehl, 'The Khorgos Hype on the Belt and Road', *The Diplomat* (27 September 2019), https://thediplomat.com/2019/09/the-khorgos-hype-on-the-belt-and-road/.

[58] Kazakhstan is highly ranked in the World Bank's 'Ease of Doing Business' index (see https://data.worldbank.org/indicator/IC.BUS.EASE.XQ), but its business and corporate law is a patchwork of different legal foundations and practices, itself a legal entanglement; see F. Karagussov, 'Development of Company Law in Kazakhstan: Main Issues and Trends' (2016) 24 *Juridica International* 84–95; and Baker and McKenzie, 'Doing Business in Kazakhstan 2019' (2019), www.bakermckenzie.com/-/media/files/insight/guides/2019/doing-business-in-kazakhstan-2019.pdf?la=en.

[59] Consider T. Yu, 'China's "One Belt, One Road Initiative": What's in It for Law Firms and Lawyers?' (2017) 5 *The Chinese Journal of Comparative Law* 1–21. The article deals primarily with gains to lawyers in China, but clearly the same question is asked by lawyers around the world.

with a lease until 2059. At twenty-four, he was extremely disappointed with the 2018 surrender of the leadership of the Baloch Liberation Army (BLA), which seems to him connected to China's increased involvement in the region.[60] He is very concerned that Chinese control in his homeland will benefit elites and not trickle down to his people. Weighing his steps carefully, he is not excluding the possibility of joining militant factions and insurgents that advocate taking armed action against the Chinese presence and have even attacked Chinese engineers under the name of the BLA, if only to gain more political traction, even independence, by raising political risk to BRI operations.[61]

For *D*, law, in general, is not very relevant. There is tribal law, there are social norms, but he is not concerned with Pakistani law or with contracts beyond a handshake (that is to say, legality can be entangled with an absence of legality too). *A*'s, *B*'s and *C*'s worlds of legality are as distant from him as are their air-conditioned offices.

Even more distant, occupying her own tempered chambers, *E* is a western European Judge in the European Court of Human Rights. Trained in the best law schools of Europe, a well-respected professor of law in her country and with several honorary doctorates around the world, for her, Strasbourg is no less than the centre of the normative universe (forget about Geneva, Washington, DC or Karlsruhe, let alone San Jose or Beijing), and the European Convention for the Protection of Human Rights and Fundamental Freedoms is her moral compass. It is of course the law, and even more so, it is a constitution. Yes, it can get messy sometimes with the overburdened caseload, and the unclear effectiveness and the constitutional orders of the Council of Europe members, such as Georgia and Azerbaijan. These are BRI states, but now also Greece, Italy, Hungary, Serbia and fourteen other Central and Eastern European states are. BRI is not remotely on her judicial radar, though if something relevant comes up in the

[60] F. Bokhari and K. Stacey, 'China Woos Pakistan Militants to Secure Belt and Road Projects', *Financial Times* (19 February 2018), www.ft.com/content/063ce350-1099-11e8-8cb6-b9ccc4c4dbbb.

[61] See D. R. Chaudhury, 'Baloch Liberation Army Attacks Chinese Assets for 3rd Time Since Aug 2018', *Economic Times* (1 April 2019), https://economictimes.indiatimes.com/news/defence/baloch-liberation-army-attacks-chinese-assets-for-3rd-time-since-aug-2018/articleshow/68664144.cms?from=mdr; and M. A. Notezai, 'Will Balochistan Blow up China's Belt and Road?', *Foreign Policy* (30 May 2019), https://foreignpolicy.com/2019/05/30/will-balochistan-blow-up-chinas-belt-and-road/.

Caucasus, or anywhere in Europe for that matter, the European Convention and Court will surely kick in.

For *E*, law is Western, European human rights law, and her legal practice, originally one of scholarship and court-watching, is now firmly the practice of judging.

The list, this cast of characters, can easily go on, but the point should be clear. Each and every one of these legal actors is a constitutive part of BRI, even if they are barely aware of it. They seem to occupy separate universes in which each of their representative narratives does not imply disentanglement, but rather separateness, a separateness that is both necessary for entanglement and coexists with it. They occupy legal silos across national and substantive lines. They are entangled without really knowing it, as they are cognitively limited and object oriented and, above all, practice focused. In Section 5.4 I briefly relate one recent, actual case in which both the separateness and connectedness dimensions of entanglement have been brought to bear.

5.4 Between Entanglement and Interdependence: Bringing Separate Strands Together

In light of the extreme plurality of law and viewpoints of practice – entangled legalities along the New Silk Road – as described only indicatively in Section 5.3, many questions may arise regarding their interdependence, especially as I have so far emphasized their separateness. For example, how might Chinese officials like *A* link their efforts and rules with the legalities found in the places where they are doing business and seeking influence, when they come into contact with people like *B* and *C*? How would the last two and their corollaries along the BRI navigate potential tensions between Chinese expectations and their own laws and norms? How should Chinese actors engage with normative sensibilities they may risk offending, such as those of *E* – and also of *D*? To be sure, these questions are worthy of real rather than hypothetical research, whether through doctrinal legal analysis or through political, sociological and anthropological field research. Instead, within the bounds of this chapter, we can look at a brief case study, to appreciate the interdependence of separate entangled strands of legality in action. The following is a brief descriptive analysis of such a case, based on mainly secondary sources.

The case relates to the ongoing project for the modernization of the train line between Belgrade and Budapest, the capitals of Serbia and

Hungary respectively, and the entanglement of BRI project-related law with EU law. The project, which will include high-speed trains, fits in with the broader vision of modernized train lines from Piraeus/Athens into the heart of central Europe,[62] and indeed with its engagement strategy with Central and Eastern European countries, which preceded BRI – the so-called '16+1 initiative' informally launched in 2011,[63] now often referred to as '17+1', including Greece. Our focus here is on the segment that lies in Hungarian territory and the project's interaction with EU law (Serbia not being an EU member state). Hungary was the first EU member state to sign a BRI MOU with China, in 2015.[64] In November of the same year, China, Hungary and Serbia signed a US$1.9 billion government-to-government (G2G) agreement regarding the Belgrade–Budapest line, and the project's main contractor was named – a consortium between the Hungarian State Railways corporation and two Chinese railway companies. This legal relationship – the China–Hungary MOU and the infrastructure construction and financing agreement – constitute one strand in this story of entangled legality. The second strand emerged and entangled with the first once the EU launched a preliminary infringement procedure against Hungary in May 2017, based on concerns that the absence of a competitive tender for the huge contract violated EU competition and procurement law; and that the role of the Hungarian corporation, with only 15 per cent of the deal (and 85 per cent of the project to be funded through twenty-year loans from China) was unclear. Reportedly, the Hungarian government was of the position that since the infrastructure agreement was not within the commercial competence of the EU, it was 'none of Brussels' business'.[65]

Even at this early stage of the story – the plot is soon to thicken, though the general setup is the same – one can think of the sources of both separateness and interdependence in this case of entangled legality, at least on a speculative basis. If one is charitable, at least regarding intent

[62] For external analysis, see 'The Potential for Growth through Chinese Infrastructure Investments in Central and South-Eastern Europe along the "Balkan Silk Road"', report prepared by Dr Jens Bastian for the European Bank for Reconstruction and Development (July 2017), www.ebrd.com/documents/policy/the-balkan-silk-road.pdf.

[63] See T. Matura, 'The Belt and Road Initiative Depicted in Hungary and Slovakia' (2018) 7 (2) *Journal of Contemporary East Asia Studies* 174–89, section 4.

[64] Ibid., section 5.1.2.

[65] J. Spike, 'EC Launches Infringement Proceeding Concerning Budapest–Belgrade Railway Project', *Budapest Beacon* (16 September 2016), https://budapestbeacon.com/ec-launches-infringement-proceeding-concerning-budapest-belgrade-railway-project/.

rather than legal capacity, perhaps the Hungarian public and most likely also private lawyers (think of variations of *B* and *C*) involved in the rail infrastructure agreement truly thought that it had nothing to do with EU law, having been signed between three governments in an area that generally is (so Hungary claims) not within EU competence. Perhaps they just didn't think of it, being so cognitively focused on making the deal on the legal separateness of this kind of agreement. Or, less charitably, maybe they were aware of possible problems, but took the chance in order to make progress with China, and with the hope that the EU would back down for political reasons. Least charitably, they had other incentives that perhaps justified EU scrutiny.

China's lawyers – *A*'s colleagues in a different department of a different ministry and their counterparts in the Chinese corporations – were either oblivious to EU law and/or did not consider the possibility that a governmental party to a G2G agreement would make representations of this nature with any real legal (or political) risk, or perhaps thought that if there were a problem it would be handled as it would have been in China, or were so self-motivated that they chose to ignore all of these issues, or deliberately took this chance in order to signal to the EU their determination to engage with EU member states and corporations directly.

What about the EU Commission lawyers, whom we can to some extent analogize to *E*? For them, there is no question that EU law on competition, procurement, corporations and more are applicable, answerable and supreme. To them, the infrastructure agreement is no different than any of the multitude of structurally similar agreements that are subject to EU law. Maybe this one required additional scrutiny due to its size and mainly because of its role in bringing Chinese influence into the heart of Europe.[66]

Apparently, conceding interdependence, Hungary issued a tender for the project later in 2017,[67] and a new one in late 2018, which was won in April 2019 by a similar Chinese–Hungarian consortium, with a similar financial structure,[68] but for the fact that the Hungarian partner would be

[66] See J. Kynge, A. Beesley and A. Byrne, 'EU Sets Collision Course with China over "Silk Road" Rail Project', *Financial Times* (20 February 2017), www.ft.com/content/003bad14-f52f-11e6-95ee-f14e55513608.

[67] 'Hungary to Launch Tender on Budapest–Belgrade Rail Project', *RailPro* (5 October 2017), www.railwaypro.com/wp/hungary-launch-tender-budapest-belgrade-rail-project/.

[68] 'Hungarian–Chinese Consortium Wins Budapest–Belgrade Rail Contract', *IE – Industry Europe* (29 April 2019), https://industryeurope.com/hungarian-chinese-consortium-wins-budapest-belgrade-rail-contract/.

a company controlled by Lőrinc Mészáros, reportedly 'a key ally' of Prime Minister Viktor Orbán,[69] a strong proponent of the project and of strong relations with China – among his many other well-known political views.

This is not the place to reflect in-depth on either the economic and political undercurrents of this episode, or on its actual outcomes, or on the effectiveness of the different legal actors and legalities involved. What can be said is that in this case, separate strands of legality – international law in the form of the Hungary–China BRI MOU, international G2G commercial law and EU law – started off as separate, with actors even in denial of their entanglement, and ended up in a state that may be called 'interdependent accommodation'. At least for now, EU law and institutions have been placated, and the Belgrade–Budapest project is projected to go ahead.

5.5 Between Entanglement, State and Empire: Beyond a Conclusion

In Sections 5.3 and 5.4, we saw that entangled legalities entail both separateness and interdependence of legal systems. In Section 5.1, we saw that legal entanglement need not be the result of chance or accident, but can be a deliberately preferred form of international governance. We can now add to this a final observation: that entangled legalities as a form of governance can be a preference of empire builders and empire bidders (though not exclusively so), and an aggregation of the preferences and attitudes of actors at a variety of levels of action.

In the realm of modern public international law, a similar point has been made with respect to institutional and normative fragmentation by Eyal Benvenisti and the late George Downs: powerful states thrive in fragmented legal environments and encourage them because they divide and rule along functional lines. These environments create high transaction costs for normative integration, and cause ambiguity that deflects accountability despite the existence of power.[70] In a less positivistic mode, however, sociologists have suggested that we should 'look at empire as a set of

69 See 'Talks on Budapest–Belgrade Rail Financing to be Accelerated', *Budapest Business Journal* (24 September 2019), https://bbj.hu/economy/talks-on-budapest-belgrade-rail-financing-to-be-accelerated_171667.

70 E. Benvenisti and G. W. Downs, 'The Empire's New Clothes: Political Economy and the Fragmentation of International Law' (2010) 60 *Stanford Law Review* 595–631.

slow-moving, temporally based, entrenched, yet also changing political formations that need to be studied to understand how they change, adapt and move on to maintain themselves, partly through reproduction and partly through innovation of their institutional structures'.[71] Histories of the British and other European empires,[72] and of the American 'non-empire',[73] confirm the relationship between legal pluralism and the creation of imperial domination over extended periods of time. It is no coincidence that Queen Elizabeth included the statement that 'Rome was not built in a day', albeit in different circumstances, in an address at the University of Cambridge in 1564.[74] No empire, new or old, is so built.

This 'set of slow moving [. . .] political formations' would seem to inevitably lead to 'entangled legalities', or in other words, to a set of separate, but enmeshed, legal and governance constructs. Although these constructs may seem to lack a hierarchy or 'centre', they nevertheless constitute a system of non-national power allocation, however vague it may be, for example globalization as empire, *selon* Hardt and Negri.[75] Alternatively, in a more historified manner, empires may be built on entangled legalities as 'transnational organizations that aim[ed] to mobilize the resources available not only within their areas, but outside them as well' that '[w]hatever their origins, [. . .] ow[ed] their existence and their unity to the broad network of connections that they manage[d] to establish'.[76]

These understandings of empire are not, of course, without controversy or critique, as fitting to the topic itself.[77] They are brought out here to accentuate – once again, descriptively but implicitly critically – that BRI, with its attributes and character of entangled legalities, shares similarities with other imperialist projects, representing a shift 'beyond the state' and perhaps postnational or transnational trends, at a time that

[71] K. Barkey, *Empire of Difference: The Ottomans in Comparative Perspective* (Cambridge University Press, 2008), p. 5.

[72] L. Benton and R. J. Ross (eds), *Legal Pluralism and Empires, 1500–1850* (New York University Press, 2013).

[73] D. Immerwahr, *How to Hide an Empire: A History of the Greater United States* (Farrar, Straus and Giroux, 2019).

[74] J. Nichols, *The Progresses and Public Processions of Queen Elizabeth*, Vol. 1 (John Nichols and Son, 1823), p. 176.

[75] M. Hardt and A. Negri, *Empire* (Harvard University Press, 2000).

[76] H. Kamen, *Empire: How Spain Became a World Power, 1492–1763* (Harper Collins, 2003).

[77] F. Cooper, 'Empire Multiplied: A Review Essay' (2004) 46 *Comparative Studies in Society and History* 247–72.

seems to be marked by heightened statism, nationalism and perceived disrespect for international law.

All of this is manifested in BRI, which combines both a non-national, ultimately global vision with localized segments that can be recognized and comprehended along national, territorial and object-oriented lines. Pre-national, postnational – perhaps the only way to understand entangled legalities is through the lens of empire: 'a new and all-pervasive system of power, based on networks and amorphous connections, rooted nowhere in particular'.[78] 'Nowhere in particular' is not necessarily a geographical statement. Communism was 'rooted' in Moscow, 'globalization' in Washington; both were empires by this definition, both built upon nationalism and created and encouraged 'entangled legalities' (with separateness) in multiple ways. BRI might be thought of in a similar fashion.

[78] Ibid., 248, describing Hardt and Negri.

PART II

International Law and Its Interfaces

6

Giving Due Consideration

A Normative Pathway between UN Human Rights Treaty-Monitoring Bodies and Domestic Courts

MACHIKO KANETAKE

6.1 Introduction

Human rights law is one of the fields of law that creates the subject matter overlap between international and domestic law. Human rights treaties purport to regulate the governmental authority exercised over individuals, which is, in parallel, regulated by domestic constitutional and administrative law. This overlap creates the deliberative space between human rights treaty-monitoring bodies and national authorities, including domestic courts. In fact, judicial decisions can be at times 'entangled' with the findings of UN human rights treaty-monitoring bodies. Domestic courts take note, discuss, accept or resist decisions, comments or observations of UN human rights treaty-monitoring bodies. The quality of such a deliberative space is crucial for the effectiveness of the treaty-monitoring bodies, whose findings ultimately aim at bringing about change to domestic legal frameworks and practices, including those of the judiciary.

Against this background, this chapter engages in the analysis of pathways that guide the deliberative space involving UN human rights treaty-monitoring bodies and domestic courts. Such pathways can be pragmatic or sociological in nature. For instance, the unavailability of treaty body findings in local languages significantly limits public knowledge about them and the likelihood that litigant parties rely on general comments and other treaty body findings. Interactions can be facilitated if judges periodically receive training regarding the work of the monitoring bodies. At the same time, domestic judges' interactions with treaty body findings have also been guided by *normative* pathways. They can originate in both international and national law. In limited circumstances, such pathways exhibit a formalistic character that Views, one of the categories of the documents produced by treaty bodies, have legal binding force. Yet it is usually the case that normative pathways are much less dichotomous.

This chapter examines one of such normative pathways, namely that state parties ought to give due consideration to the findings of UN human rights treaty-monitoring bodies. The legal basis of such a duty to consider remains contested. Furthermore, the duty to consider is necessarily precarious, inasmuch as its effectiveness depends on how precisely consideration is given by judges in a particular case. Nevertheless, the duty to consider – and its normative variations, as will be discussed in this chapter – occasionally appears in the reasoning of domestic courts whose narrative is entangled with treaty interpretation by UN human rights-monitoring bodies.

The chapter starts by outlining the different types of the findings of the monitoring bodies (Section 6.2). Domestic courts' engagement varies depending on states, courts and judges. The limited research I have conducted[1] demonstrates a great deal of variance with regard to domestic courts' explicit engagement with the monitoring bodies. Domestic judges may not be aware of the relevant documents; and even if they are, they may reject the judicial relevance of such documents (Section 6.3). At the same time, there are a number of domestic court decisions that have explicitly invoked treaty body findings (Section 6.4). What matters for the sake of this chapter is that judicial engagement can be guided by the duty to consider and its variations (Sections 6.4 and 6.5). These pathways serve as 'interface norms' that facilitate ties yet preserve discretion on the part of domestic courts.[2] Under limited circumstances, the duty to consider may even be understood as entailing an obligation to give effect to Views (Section 6.6). The duty to consider may not be a robust normative path. Yet it can still pave the way for a sustainable and forward-looking deliberative space, by creating the opportunities for learning and self-reflection for domestic courts and the international guardians.

[1] The chapter's analysis is based on my previous publication: M. Kanetake, 'UN Human Rights Treaty Monitoring Bodies before Domestic Courts' (2018) 67 *International & Comparative Law Quarterly* 201–32. For the sake of the previous publication, I have collected and analysed 150 domestic court decisions (decided from 1982 to 2016) across forty-one jurisdictions. For the sake of the present chapter, I have additionally collected and analysed forty other domestic court decisions (decided between 1992 and 2018) across twenty-one jurisdictions, based on my own research, existing literature, the Oxford Reports on International Law in Domestic Courts (ILDC) and the International Law Reports (ILR).

[2] See Chapter 1.

6.2 Measuring the Domestic Relevance of the 'Jurisprudence' of the Monitoring Bodies

UN human rights treaty-monitoring bodies are part of the institutional arrangements at the international level that assist states' implementation of nine core human rights treaties. There are ten bodies tasked with monitoring the implementation of the treaties, namely: (1) Human Rights Committee (HRC), (2) Committee on Economic, Social and Cultural Rights (CESCR), (3) Committee on the Elimination of Racial Discrimination (CERD), (4) Committee on the Elimination of Discrimination against Women (CEDAW), (5) Committee Against Torture (CAT), (6) Subcommittee on Prevention of Torture, (7) Committee on the Rights of the Child (CRC), (8) Committee on Migrant Workers (CMW), (9) Committee on the Rights of Persons with Disabilities (CRPD), and (10) Committee on Enforced Disappearances (CED). These committees have been adjusting their working methods towards better harmonization, particularly in response to the UN General Assembly's resolution 68/268 of 2014.[3]

The ten bodies issue a wide range of documents (which are generally termed 'findings' in this chapter). They can be categorized into three types:[4] (1) General Comments and Recommendations, which are addressed to all state parties; (2) Concluding Observations and Concluding Comments, which are addressed to a particular state party; and (3) Views (or Decisions) and Suggestions and Recommendations, which pertain to individual communications or petitions.[5] There are eight treaty bodies that are competent to receive and consider petitions from individuals.[6] By mobilizing the limited staff resources, the committees adopted 250 decisions on individual communications per year during 2018–19, for instance.[7] In some of those decisions, the committees found breaches of treaty obligations. Between 1977 and March 2019,

[3] UN General Assembly, 'Strengthening and Enhancing the Effective Functioning of the Human Rights Treaty Body System' (21 April 2014) UN Doc. A/RES/68/268, para. 38.

[4] See N. Ando, 'General Comments/Recommendations', in R. Wolfrum (ed.), *The Max Planck Encyclopedia of Public International Law* (Oxford University Press, 2008), para. 2.

[5] This chapter consistently uses the term 'Views' to describe the types of findings regarding individual communications or petitions, even if the findings can also be entitled as 'Decisions', etc.

[6] These eight bodies are: HRC, CESCR, CERD, CEDAW, CAT, CRC, CRPD, and CED. The CMW also anticipates the petition mechanism.

[7] Report of the Secretary-General, 'Status of the Human Rights Treaty Body System' (10 January 2020) UN Doc. A/74/643, para. 18.

the HRC found violations of the International Covenant on Civil and Political Rights (ICCPR) in 1,157 Views.[8] The adoption of Views is in addition to thirty-six General Comments adopted by the HRC between 1981 and 2018, accompanied by numerous state-specific observations.

The crux is that these different types of findings are cross-referenced with one another, which internally strengthens each body's treaty interpretation.[9] Just to provide one specific example, in its Concluding Observations addressed to the Netherlands in 2016, the CEDAW urged the state party to implement its earlier Views, by further indicating that the state's non-implementation of the Views is inconsistent with the CEDAW's General Recommendation No. 33 on women's access to justice.[10] By cross-referencing its own documents, each treaty body creates what the International Court of Justice (ICJ) termed 'jurisprudence' in para. 66 of the *Diallo* case (2010)[11] – although, I must add, the use of such a juridical vocabulary depends on how one appreciates the functions of the treaty-monitoring bodies.

Para. 66 of the *Diallo* case is crucial in that the ICJ commented on the normative relevance of the HRC's treaty interpretation. The court observed that the HRC has 'built up a considerable body of interpretive case law' through Views and General Comments.[12] Having reiterated the formalistic starting point that the court is 'in no way obliged' to follow the interpretation of the HRC, the court continued by saying that it '*should ascribe great weight* to the interpretation' of the HRC.[13] The *Diallo* case was not the first occasion on which the ICJ had resorted to the position of the HRC.[14] Yet the remark of the court in *Diallo* was noteworthy, in that the court elucidated the normative 'weight' to be

[8] UNHRC, 'Report of the Human Rights Committee, 123rd Session (2–27 July 2018), 124th Session (8 October–2 November 2018), 125th Session (4–29 March 2019)' (2019) UN Doc. A/74/40, para. 25.

[9] See, on the CERD's work, R. Wolfrum, 'The Committee on the Elimination of Racial Discrimination' (1999) 3 *Max Planck Yearbook of United Nations Law Online* 489–519, at 509.

[10] CEDAW, 'Concluding Observations on the Sixth Periodic Report of the Netherlands' (24 November 2016) CEDAW/C/NLD/CO/6, para. 14.

[11] *Ahmadou Sadio Diallo (Republic of Guinea* v. *Democratic Republic of the Congo)*, Merits, Judgment of 30 November 2010, [2010] ICJ Reports 639, para. 66.

[12] Ibid., para. 66.

[13] Ibid., para. 66 (emphasis added).

[14] E.g., *Legal Consequences of the Construction of a Wall in the Occupied Palestinian Territory*, Advisory Opinion of 9 July 2004, [2004] ICJ Reports 136, paras 109–10. See L. Crema, 'The Interpretive Work of Treaty Bodies: How They Look at Evolutionary Interpretation, and How Other Courts Look at Them', in G. Abi-Saab et al. (eds),

given to the HRC's interpretation. This does not mean that the ICJ is consistent in terms of its willingness to substantively engage with UN human rights treaty-monitoring bodies. In the *Obligation to Prosecute or Extradite (Belgium* v. *Senegal)* case (2012), the ICJ took a rather dismissive attitude towards the CAT's treaty interpretation.[15]

Methodologically, it is hard to assess the extent to which treaty body findings alter domestic legal practices. The international bodies' interpretation can influence legal discourse indirectly and over a long period of time. That said, one form of assessment is to measure the level of compliance. Some treaty-monitoring bodies indicate the level of satisfactory follow-up by states parties to the outcomes of individual communications. For example, the CAT's report of May 2017 shows that 42 per cent of its communications (55 out of 131), in which the CAT found violations, resulted in satisfactory or partially satisfactory outcomes.[16]

Yet this chapter's focus is not on assessing general rates of compliance. Instead, the chapter analyses the explicit reference to treaty body findings in judicial reasoning. The cases I examine are therefore inclusive of, but not limited to, the case-specific responses to Views. This wider coverage is appropriate and necessary, precisely because the chapter's focus is on the judiciary, as opposed to other branches of the government. As I further explain in Section 6.3, domestic courts play a relatively limited role in providing case-specific responses to Views. The principle of *res judicata* often prevents judges from reopening cases at the domestic level. National courts may be able to give effect to Views if there are any relevant pieces of domestic law that allow judges to reopen a case.[17] Illustrative in this regard is a Norwegian example. By the Act of 15 June 2001 No. 63 which amended the Criminal Procedure and the Civil Procedure Acts, Norway allowed the reopening of cases following the

Evolutionary Interpretation and International Law (Hart Publishing, 2019) p. 77–90, at p. 84.

15 *Obligation to Prosecute or Extradite (Belgium* v. *Senegal)*, Judgment of 20 July 2012, [2012] ICJ Reports 422, para. 101. Cf. separate opinion of Judge Cançado Trindade at 551–2, paras 161–5.

16 CAT, 'Report of the Committee against Torture, Fifty-eighth session (25 July–12 August 2016), Fifty-ninth session (7 November–7 December 2016), Sixtieth session (18 April–12 May 2017)' (2017) UN Doc. A/72/44, para. 87.

17 See R. van Alebeek and A. Nollkaemper, 'The Legal Status of Decisions by Human Rights Treaty Bodies in National Law', in H. Keller and G. Ulfstein (eds), *UN Human Rights Treaty Bodies: Law and Legitimacy* (Cambridge University Press, 2012) pp. 356–413, at pp. 360–82.

findings of the monitoring body.[18] While the Norwegian initiatives have been welcomed by the HRC,[19] few countries seem to have followed the same path that systematically allows the reopening of proceedings. This means that the case-specific responses to Views primarily depend on the willingness of the executive and legislative branches of the government.[20]

6.3 Judicial Non-engagement

6.3.1 Domestic Courts' Practices

As noted in Section 6.2, while the monitoring bodies adopt a number of general and country-specific findings, their practical relevance ultimately relies upon domestic acceptance. While it is methodologically challenging to have an overview of the practices of national courts' engagement with the monitoring bodies, the analysis of judicial decisions I have conducted[21] provides some ideas about the patterns of engagement. To begin with, the pronouncement of the monitoring bodies has not been used as an independent and free-standing basis for the final decisions of domestic courts. Namely, Views, and much less General Comments and Concluding Observations, do not serve as the basis on which domestic courts decide the wrongfulness of acts or the legality of law.

In light of this, attempts to construe Views as an autonomous legal basis for judicial decisions have met with rejection.[22] Illustrative in this regard is the Irish Supreme Court's decision in *Kavanagh* v. *Governor of Mountjoy Prison* (2002),[23] forming a part of the case-specific response to the HRC's Views in which Ireland was found in breach of Article 26 of

[18] UNHRC, 'Consideration of Reports Submitted by States Parties under the Covenant, Fifth Periodic Report, Norway' (3 December 2004) CPR/C/NOR/2004/5, para. 157. See also para. 158 (establishment of the Criminal Cases Review Commission to assist petitioners).

[19] UNHRC, 'Concluding Observation of the Human Rights Committee, Norway' (25 April 2006) CCPR/C/NOR/CO/5, para. 3(b) (establishment of the Commission to assist petitioners).

[20] See, e.g., *X* v. *Council of Ministers*, Appeal judgment ILDC 2520 (ES 2015), ROJ: STS 507/2015, ECLI: ES:TS:2015:507 (Spain, Supreme Court, Administrative Chamber, 6 February 2015) paras 41–5 (OUP page numbers).

[21] See n. 1 above.

[22] See nn. 17–19 and accompanying text on the principle of *res judicata* and the need for specific pieces of legislation.

[23] *Kavanagh* v. *Governor of Mountjoy Prison* [2002] 3 IR 97; 132 ILR 380 (Ireland, Supreme Court, 1 March 2002) 404.

the ICCPR on equality before the law.[24] While the Irish Supreme Court's rejection was based on the constitutional ground that justice ought to be administered by properly constituted courts,[25] the court also commented on the absence of international legal grounds. According to the Irish court, '[n]either the Covenant nor the Protocol at any point purports to give any binding effect to the views expressed by the Committee' which, as the Supreme Court reiterated, 'does not formulate any form of judgment or declare any entitlement to relief'.[26]

In a similar vein, another noteworthy case is *Wilson* v. *Ermita* (2016) before the Supreme Court of the Philippines.[27] In 1998, Wilson, a British national, was convicted of the crime of rape and sentenced to death. Before his conviction was set aside by the Supreme Court in 1999,[28] Wilson submitted the communication to the HRC, which eventually rendered its Views in 2003.[29] According to the HRC, the conditions under which Wilson was arrested, detained and imprisoned infringed several provisions of the ICCPR, including Article 7 on the prohibition of torture, or other cruel, inhuman or degrading treatment or punishment.[30] The HRC observed that the Philippines should provide compensation for Wilson.[31] He then filed a petition for mandamus before the Supreme Court of the Philippines, arguing that the government is obliged to enforce the Views as part of its duties under international law.[32] The Supreme Court dismissed Wilson's claim. While the court's rejection was based primarily on the lack of domestic effect of treaties,[33] the Supreme Court made remarks on the characteristics of Views. According to the court, nowhere in the ICCPR does it state that Views formed part of the treaty.[34]

[24] UNHRC, *Kavanagh* v. *Ireland (No.1)*, Views, Communication No. 819/1998, CCPR/C/71/D/819/1998, adopted 4 April 2001, paras 10.3 and 11.

[25] *Kavanagh* v. *Governor of Mountjoy Prison*, 404 (referring to Article 34.1 of the Irish Constitution).

[26] Ibid.

[27] *Wilson* v. *Ermita and ors*, Petition for mandamus, GR No 189220, ILDC 3005 (PH 2016) (Philippines, Supreme Court, 7 December 2016).

[28] Ibid., paras 3–6 (paragraph numbers added by Oxford University Press (OUP)).

[29] UNHRC, *Albert Wilson* v. *The Philippines*, Views, Communication No. 868/1999, CCPR/C/79/D/868/1999 (11 November 2003).

[30] Ibid., paras 7.3–8 (violations of Articles 7, 9(1)–(3), 10(1)–(2)).

[31] Ibid., para. 9.

[32] *Wilson* v. *Ermita*, para. 17 (OUP numbers).

[33] Ibid., paras 32–3 (OUP numbers). The Court's view on the domestic effect of the ICCPR seems inconsistent with the Court's own jurisprudence: see E. K. P. Aguilan, 'Analysis: ILDC 3005 (PH 2016)' (2019), para. A3.

[34] *Wilson* v. *Ermita*, para. 34 (OUP numbers).

The court's conclusion in *Wilson* v. *Ermita* is nothing new. Noteworthy still, however, is that the Supreme Court of the Philippines invoked the HRC's General Comment No. 33 in the course of denying the applicability of Views to case-specific judicial responses. In General Comment No. 33 (advanced unedited version of November 2008), the HRC regarded its Views as exhibiting 'some important characteristics of a judicial decision'.[35] The Supreme Court quoted this phrase, observing that the HRC's Views '*only* displays "important characteristics of a judicial decision"'.[36] According to the court, the Views are thus '*mere* recommendations to guide the State it is issued against'.[37] While the Supreme Court of the Philippines at least engaged with the narrative of General Comment No. 33, the court's use of the finding was rather ironic. Judges used it in order to dismiss, as opposed to augment, the judicial relevance of the Views of the HRC.

These examples again remind us of the structurally limited role of the judiciary in providing case-specific follow-up.[38] Yet even outside case-specific circumstances, some domestic courts have much more 'distanced relations'[39] with UN treaty-monitoring bodies and have taken a dismissive attitude towards the relevance of their treaty interpretation.[40] In some countries, judicial narrative accommodates little or no reference to treaty body findings. While the International Law Association's (ILA) Committee on International Human Rights Law and Practice (1997–2008) conducted extensive studies on judicial practices, the study could not specifically identify judicial references to the monitoring bodies in, among others, the countries of Francophone Africa or the Arab region. According to the 2004 Berlin report of the ILA Committee, there were no identifiable judicial practices in Bulgaria, Jordan, Egypt, Saudi Arabia, Colombia, Ecuador, Chile, Argentina, Malaysia, Singapore or Brunei.[41] The absence

[35] UNHRC, 'General Comment No. 33: The Obligations of States Parties under the Optional Protocol' (Advance unedited version, 5 November 2008) CCPR/C/GC/33, para. 11.

[36] *Wilson* v. *Ermita*, para. 35 (OUP numbers) (emphasis added).

[37] Ibid. Any responses to such recommendations are a matter to be determined by the legislative and executive branches of the government, the Supreme Court added – see para. 36 (OUP numbers).

[38] See nn. 17–19 and accompanying text.

[39] See Chapter 1.

[40] Kanetake, 'UN Human Rights Treaty Monitoring Bodies before Domestic Courts', 226–7.

[41] ILA, Committee on International Human Rights Law and Practice, 'Final Report on the Impact of Findings of the United Nations Human Rights Treaty Bodies' (2004) para. 29, ft 28.

of explicit reference is also evident in French courts. A study of French courts' practices suggests that not only judges, but also the litigants themselves rarely refer to the monitoring bodies' findings.[42]

6.3.2 *International Legal Justification for Non-engagement*

There are, no doubt, country-specific backgrounds that sustain and justify no or very limited judicial engagement with the findings of the monitoring bodies.[43] Judges' strong loyalty to the separation of powers, for instance, may sustain distanced relations with formally non-binding international documents.[44] What should be remembered, however, is that non-engagement can be explained and justified, not only by domestic specificities, but also by international law. A regularly invoked ground in this regard is the formalistic narrative that treaty body findings lack legal binding force. As a matter of formal status, it is hard to deny that Views themselves are not binding under international law.[45] States generally consider that the HRC's Views, as well as interim measures, are non-binding under international law.[46] The lack of binding force is even more evident with regard to General Comments and Concluding Observations.

The legal status of the findings themselves does not speak of the status of the *content* of the committees' findings. States, and indirectly their courts, are obliged to give effect to the substance of the findings of the treaty-monitoring bodies, if it reflects established treaty obligations. The content of General Comments and Views may reflect 'subsequent practice in the application of the treaty which establishes the agreement of the

[42] S. El Boudouhi and G. Dannenberg, 'France: Implementation of International Human Rights Decisions in France', in S. Kadelbach, T. Rensmann and E. Rieter (eds), *Judging International Human Rights* (Springer International Publishing, 2019) pp. 453–70, at p. 466.

[43] Kanetake, 'UN Human Rights Treaty Monitoring Bodies before Domestic Courts', 228–30.

[44] Ibid., 229–30.

[45] See, e.g., 'Report of the International Law Commission, Seventieth Session (30 April–1 June and 2 July–10 August 2018)' (2018) UN GAOR, 73rd Sess., Supp. No. 10, UN Doc. A/73/10, 109, para. 7, fn 614; C. Tomuschat, 'Human Rights Committee', in R. Wolfrum (ed.), *The Max Planck Encyclopedia of Public International Law* (Oxford University Press, 2010), para. 14.

[46] See van Alebeek and Nollkaemper, 'The Legal Status of Decisions by Human Rights Treaty Bodies', pp. 372–3, pp. 385–90.

parties regarding its interpretation'.[47] While, in principle, 'subsequent practice' is not equated with the institutional practices of the monitoring bodies themselves, the monitoring bodies' findings can facilitate an interpretation accepted by states parties which may support or acquiesce to the observations of the monitoring bodies,[48] even though caution should be exercised.

Despite the content-based obligation on the part of states parties, the rule of treaty interpretation is so flexible that domestic courts can readily argue that the monitoring bodies' interpretation does not reflect 'subsequent practice'. The flexibility is preserved by the International Law Commission (ILC), which adopted, in 2018, a set of draft conclusions on 'subsequent agreements and subsequent practice in relation to the interpretation of treaties'.[49] In the draft conclusions, the ILC reiterated that a pronouncement of 'expert treaty bodies', such as UN human rights treaty-monitoring bodies,[50] 'may' give rise to, or refer to, a 'subsequent agreement or subsequent practice by parties' under Article 31(3) of the Vienna Convention on the Law of Treaties.[51] The draft conclusions, however, warned that '[s]ilence by a party shall not be presumed to constitute subsequent practice' under Article 31(3)(b) of the Vienna Convention.[52] As the ILC acknowledges, 'it cannot usually be expected that States parties take a position with respect to every pronouncement by an expert treaty body, be it addressed to another State or to all States generally'.[53] While this caution against the misinterpretation of silence by states parties makes pragmatic sense, the ILC's work did not elaborate upon possible indicators with which to assess whether the pronouncement of UN human rights treaty-monitoring bodies reflects established treaty interpretation. Overall, the ILC's work preserved the

[47] Vienna Convention on the Law of Treaties, 23 May 1969, in force 27 January 1980, 1155 UNTS 311, Article 31(3)(b).

[48] ILA, 'Final Report on the Impact of Findings' (2004), para. 21; G. Ulfstein, 'Individual Complaints', in H. Keller, G. Ulfstein and L. Grover (eds), *UN Human Rights Treaty Bodies: Law and Legitimacy* (Cambridge University Press, 2012) pp. 73–115, at pp. 97–100.

[49] 'Text of the Draft Conclusions on Subsequent Agreements and Subsequent Practice in Relation to the Interpretation of Treaties', see 'Report of the International Law Commission, Seventieth Session', 12–16.

[50] 'Report of the International Law Commission, Seventieth Session' above, 106 (Conclusion 13).

[51] Ibid., 106 (Conclusion 13.3).

[52] Ibid., 106 (Conclusion 13.2).

[53] Ibid., 113, para. 19 (commentary regarding Conclusion 13.3).

flexibility – and associated uncertainty – inherent in Article 31(3)(b) of the Vienna Convention on the Law of Treaties, which, in the context of the theme of this chapter, effectively leaves ample space for domestic courts to reject the obligatory nature of the specific content of the findings.

6.4 Judicial Engagement

6.4.1 Domestic Courts' Practices

While the lack of legally binding force may serve as a justification for non-engagement, some other domestic courts have shown greater willingness to refer explicitly to treaty body findings. General Comments, Concluding Observations and Views can be invoked to interpret the terms of relevant human rights treaties, which may ultimately be used to inform the construction of domestic (constitutional) provisions regarding fundamental rights. Admittedly, judges tend to be less hesitant in referring to treaty body findings in such countries as Canada, the UK, New Zealand and possibly some other common law countries.[54] Yet judicial proximity to treaty body findings is by no means limited to jurisdictions with common law traditions.

There are abundant examples of judicial interpretive engagement.[55] Among many others, for instance, the Israeli Supreme Court in *Kav Laoved* v. *Interior Ministry* (2011), in denying the constitutionality of the country's work permit procedure designed for female migrant workers, consulted the CEDAW's General Recommendations 21 (on equality in marriage and family relations) and 26 (on women migrant workers), as well as the CERD's General Recommendation 30 (on discrimination against non-citizens).[56] Likewise, the Israeli Supreme Court in *Adam* v. *Knesset* (2014) invoked the Views of the HRC in order to

[54] Kanetake, 'UN Human Rights Treaty Monitoring Bodies before Domestic Courts', 226.

[55] Ibid.

[56] *'Kav LaOved' – Worker's Hotline and ors* v. *Ministry of Interior and ors*, Original petition to the High Court of Justice, HCJ 11437/05, ILDC 2181 (IL 2011) (13 April 2011) (Israel, Supreme Court as High Court of Justice), paras H3–H4 (ILDC paragraph numbers). See CEDAW, 'General Recommendation No. 21: Equality in Marriage and Family Relations' (1994) UN Doc. A/49/38; CEDAW, 'General Recommendation No. 26 on Women Migrant Workers' (5 December 2008) CEDAW/C/2009/WP.1/R; CERD, 'General Recommendation 30 on Discrimination against Non-citizens' (2004) UN Doc. A/59/18, 93.

interpret the scope of arbitrary arrest and detention under the ICCPR, which served ultimately to decide upon the constitutionality of domestic legislation.[57]

In a similar vein, the Federal Court of Australia in *Iliafi* v. *The Church of Jesus Christ and the Latter-Day Saints Australia* (2014) resorted to several findings of the monitoring bodies: General Recommendation No. 20 of the CERD,[58] the HRC's General Comments Nos. 22 (on the right to freedom of thought, conscience and religion) and 23 (on the rights of minorities),[59] and the jurisprudence of the HRC formulated through its Views.[60] These documents were mentioned by the Australian court in order to interpret the Racial Discrimination Convention and the ICCPR,[61] and, ultimately, to construe the Racial Discrimination Act 1975 of Australia.[62] Interestingly, the Federal Court of Australia cited para. 66 of the ICJ's decision in *Diallo*, as well as Article 38(1)(d) of the ICJ Statute, in consulting the CERD's General Recommendation No. 20.[63] Yet the court did not specify whether it intended to ascribe, as the ICJ did in paragraph 66 of *Diallo*, 'great weight' to the interpretation of the monitoring bodies.[64]

While there are abundant examples of judicial reference, the extent of *substantive engagement* varies depending on courts and judges. Illustrative in this regard is the comparison between UK and Canadian courts in a series of decisions concerning the interpretation of Article 14(1) of the

[57] *HCJ Infiltrators Case, Adam and Ors* v. *The Knesset and Ors*, Original petition to the High Court of Justice, HCJ 7146/12, ILDC 2078 (IL 2013), 16 September 2013 (Israel, Supreme Court), paras H5–H6 (ILDC report by Nita Benoliel); Y. Shany, 'Israel', in F. M. Palombino (ed.), *Duelling for Supremacy: International Law vs. National Fundamental Principles* (Cambridge University Press, 2019) p. 167–83, at pp. 177–8.

[58] *Iliafi and Others* v. *The Church of Jesus Christ of Latter-Day Saints Australia* [2014] FCAFC 26 (19 March 2014) (Federal Court of Australia), paras 62–4; CERD, 'General Recommendation 20: The Guarantee of Human Rights Free from Racial Discrimination' (1996) UN Doc. A/51/18 (1996), annex VIII, 124.

[59] *Iliafi*, paras 66–7, 85, 96–9, 103; HRC, 'General Comment No. 22 (Art. 18)' (27 September 1993) CCPR/C/21/Rev.1/Add.4; HRC, 'General Comment No. 23: The Rights of Minorities (Article 27)' (26 April 1994) CCPR/C/21/Rev.1/Add.5.

[60] E.g., *Iliafi*, paras 100–1.

[61] International Convention on the Elimination of All Forms of Racial Discrimination, 21 December 1965, 660 UNTS 195, Art 5; International Covenant on Civil and Political Rights, 16 December 1966, 999 UNTS 171, Articles 18, 27.

[62] Racial Discrimination Act 1975 (Australia), Act No. 52 of 1975 (11 June 1975), section 9.

[63] *Iliafi*, para. 62.

[64] *Diallo*, para. 66.

Torture Convention.[65] Both UK and Canadian courts disagreed with the CAT's interpretation of the provision that a civil remedy ought to be made available for all acts of torture, including those committed outside the forum state,[66] by limiting the scope of state immunity.[67]

While both UK and Canadian courts disagreed with the CAT's treaty interpretation, there were differences in terms of the extent to which courts substantively engaged with the CAT's position. In the House of Lords, judges rather summarily dismissed the relevance the CAT in *Jones* v. *Saudi Arabia* (2006).[68] Lord Bingham noted that '[w]hatever its value in influencing the trend of international thinking, the legal authority of the Committee's recommendation is slight'.[69] In a similar vein, Lord Hoffmann found 'no value' in the Committee's position.[70] The disagreement of UK judges in *Jones* was referred to by the Canadian Supreme Court in *Kazemi (Estate)* v. *Iran* (2014).[71] The Canadian court, however, while disagreeing with the CAT's interpretation, took a few more steps to provide substantive explanations as to why judges did not agree with the CAT's interpretation.

In *Kazemi*, the Canadian Supreme Court admitted that 'the Committee's comments may be helpful for purposes of interpretation',[72] by referring to its earlier decision in *Suresh* (2002) where the Supreme Court had consulted the CAT's position.[73] Yet the majority of the Canadian Supreme Court noted that the Committee's

[65] Convention against Torture and Other Cruel, Inhuman or Degrading Treatment or Punishment, 10 December 1984, 1465 UNTS 85, Art. 14(1). See Kanetake, 'UN Human Rights Treaty Monitoring Bodies before Domestic Courts', 212–13.

[66] See, e.g., CAT, 'General Comment No. 3 (2012): Implementation of Article 14 by States Parties' (13 December 2012) CAT/C/GC/3, para. 22.

[67] The CAT made it clear in its Concluding Observations addressed to Canada: CAT, 'Concluding Observations of the Committee against Torture: Canada' (25 June 2012) CAT/C/CAN/CO/6, para. 15; CAT, 'Concluding Observations on the Seventh Periodic Report of Canada' (21 December 2018) CAT/C/CAN/CO/7, para. 41.

[68] *Jones* v. *Saudi Arabia* [2006] UKHL 26; (2007) 1 AC 270 (UK, House of Lords, 14 June 2006).

[69] Ibid., para. 23 (Lord Bingham).

[70] Ibid., para. 57 (Lord Hoffmann). See also *Jones and Others* v. *The United Kingdom*, App. Nos. 34356/06 and 40528/06, Judgment of 14 January 2014, para. 208 (disagreeing with the CAT's interpretation).

[71] *Kazemi (Estate)* v. *Islamic Republic of Iran* 2014 SCC 62, [2014] 3 S.C.R. 176 (Canada, Supreme Court, Judgment of 10 October 2014), para. 148.

[72] Ibid., para. 148.

[73] *Suresh* v. *Canada, (2002) 208 DLR (4th) 1* (2002) 124 ILR 343 (Canada, Supreme Court, 11 January 2002), para. 73; Kanetake, 'UN Human Rights Treaty Monitoring Bodies before Domestic Courts', 211.

comments, 'despite their importance', 'should not be given greater weight than the pronouncements of states parties and judicial authorities'.[74] The court observed that the CAT's comments 'do not override adjudicative interpretations', such as those seen in *Jones*.[75] 'At best', according to the highest court of Canada, the CAT's comments 'form part of a dialogue within the international community where no consensus has yet developed' on treaty interpretation.[76] The majority's treatment of the CAT's remarks is contrasted with the narrative of Justice Abella in dissent. She observed that the CAT's 'expertise lends support to the weight of its interpretation',[77] referring to the fact that the Committee had made critical remarks on Canadian legal practices.[78] The narrative of the Canadian court was noteworthy in that the court explained how much weight it should give to the CAT's treaty interpretation. While judges in the majority substantively engaged with the CAT's position, the Supreme Court, at least in this specific case, regarded it as merely one of the opinions that the court may take into account.

6.4.2 *Normative Pathway: Authorization to Consider*

Domestic courts' discretionary reference to treaty body findings is no doubt conditioned by domestic sociological and legal contexts. At the same time, it must be once again noted that international law also explains and justifies domestic courts' discretionary engagement. Namely, states, and indirectly their courts, may consider the findings of UN human rights treaty-monitoring bodies as part of 'supplementary means of interpretation' under Article 32 of the Vienna Convention on the Law of Treaties.[79]

In fact, Article 32 of the Vienna Convention on the Law of Treaties has been mentioned by domestic courts in consulting treaty body findings. For example, in *Minister for Immigration and Citizenship* v. *Anochie*

[74] *Kazemi* (2014), para. 147.
[75] Ibid., para. 148.
[76] Ibid.
[77] Ibid., para. 224 (Justice Abella in dissent, agreeing with the Canadian Bar Association's remark).
[78] Ibid., para. 226 (Justice Abella in dissent).
[79] E.g., Y. Iwasawa, 'Domestic Application of International Law' (2016) 378 *Recueil des Cours* 236–7 (regarding Japanese courts' practices); Kanetake, 'UN Human Rights Treaty Monitoring Bodies Before Domestic Courts', 220–1.

(2012)[80] before the Federal Court of Australia, the judge consulted the HRC's Views and General Comments Nos. 15 (on the position of aliens) and 31 (on the nature of the general obligation)[81] in the process of interpreting Australia's non-refoulement obligations. The Federal Court explicitly elaborated upon the question of what materials the court may consult in interpreting the ICCPR.[82] The judge accepted, 'upon reflection', that 'the Committee's interpretation of the ICCPR is admissible' in court for the interpretation of the treaty.[83] The Federal Court suggested that its recourse to the HRC's interpretation was justified by Article 40(4) of the ICCPR and Article 1 of the Optional Protocol.[84] Article 40(4) serves as a legal basis for the HRC to issue General Comments,[85] while Article 1 of the Optional Protocol empowers the Committee to receive and consider individual communications.[86] On this basis, according to the Federal Court, the Committee's Views and General Comments form part of 'supplementary means of interpretation' (under Article 32 of the Vienna Convention on the Law of Treaties).[87] Equally, the Views and General Comments serve as 'subsidiary means for the determination of rules of law' (under Article 38(1)(d) of the Statute of the International Court of Justice).[88]

The characterization of treaty body findings as part of supplementary means leaves states (and their courts) to decide whether to consider a particular finding of the committees and how much weight states give to

[80] *Minister for Immigration and Citizenship* v. *Anochie and Another* [2012] FCA 1440, (2012) 209 FCR 497 (Australia, Federal Court, 18 December 2012). The subsequent decision did not refer to the Committee's findings: *Anochie* v. *Minister for Immigration and Citizenship* [2013] AATA 391 (Australia, Administrative Appeals Tribunal, 12 June 2013).

[81] UNHRC, 'General Comment No. 15: The Position of Aliens under the Covenant' (11 April 1986) HRI/GEN/1/Rev.9 (Vol. I); HRC, 'General Comment No. 31: Nature of the General Legal Obligation Imposed on States Parties to the Covenant' (29 March 2004) CCPR/C/21/Rev.1/Add.13.

[82] *Anochie*, paras 40–50.

[83] Ibid., para. 45.

[84] Ibid., paras 45–6.

[85] ICCPR, Article 40(4).

[86] Optional Protocol to the International Covenant on Civil and Political Rights, 16 December 1966, 999 UNTS 302, Article 1. The Federal Court also noted the fact that the HRC's Views are forwarded to the individual and the state party concerned, according to Article 5(4) of the Optional Protocol.

[87] *Anochie*, para. 48. This is based on the Federal Court's earlier case: *Minister for Immigration and Multicultural and Indigenous Affairs* v. *Al Masri* (2003) 126 FCR 54, para. 148.

[88] Ibid., para. 49.

the committees' interpretation. In the aforementioned *Anochie*, the Australian court noted that, given that the members of the HRC were supposed to be 'persons of high moral character and recognized competence in the field of human rights',[89] the HRC's output may form part of the 'teachings of the most highly qualified publicists' under Article 38(1)(d) of the ICJ Statute.[90] On this basis, the Federal Court quoted para. 66 of the ICJ's judgement in *Diallo*, in which the ICJ found that it 'should ascribe great weight' to the interpretation of the Committee.[91]

6.5 Beyond Discretionary Judicial Engagement

6.5.1 Domestic Courts' Practices

As noted in Section 6.4, states, and indirectly their courts, are authorized under international law to consider the findings of UN human rights treaty-monitoring bodies. At the same time, the survey of domestic court decisions[92] indicates the existence of normative expectations beyond mere discretionary consideration. Some courts referred to a normative expectation to consider, both in and outside the context of case-specific responses to Views on individual communications.

For instance, in the Jamaican case of *Lewis* (2000),[93] the Judicial Committee of the Privy Council observed that the HRC's Views should be considered in case-specific contexts. The *Lewis* case involved appellants who had been sentenced to death by the Jamaican courts and had petitioned the HRC. According to the Privy Council, '[w]hen the report of the international human rights bodies is available that should be considered and if the Jamaican Privy Council do [*sic*] not accept it [then] they should explain why'.[94] This observation is significant, in that the Privy Council found it necessary, not merely to consider Views, but also to provide explanation in case of disagreement. The Dutch Administrative High Court in its decision of July 2006 seems to have given an even stronger assertion in favour of Views. The Court regarded

89 ICCPR, Article 28(2).

90 *Anochie*, para. 49.

91 Ibid. See n. 64 and accompanying text.

92 See n. 1 on the scope of the research on which the chapter is based.

93 *Lewis* v. *Attorney General of Jamaica* (2000) 134 ILR 615 (Jamaica, Judicial Committee of the Privy Council, 12 September 2000).

94 Ibid., 635.

the Views of the HRC as non-binding, yet still 'authoritative', and noted that national courts could only deviate from the Views if justified by 'compelling reasons'.[95]

These instances of judicial respect for Views do not alter the fact that domestic courts have a limited role in taking case-specific follow-up measures.[96] In this sense, it is much more relevant to see how domestic courts navigate their pathways to the monitoring bodies *outside* case-specific contexts. Some judges were willing to indicate the existence of normative expectations – if not a strict obligation – for domestic courts to engage with the monitoring bodies' interpretation when the courts interpret relevant treaty provisions. For instance, the Colombian Constitutional Court in 2004 characterized the CESCR as an 'authorized interpreter' of the Covenant.[97] In the *Test Trial Fund Clara Wichmann* case of 2005, the Dutch court noted that the CEDAW is empowered to issue General Recommendations and that such Recommendations should be taken into account in the context of interpreting the Convention.[98] In 2007, the Belize Supreme Court in the case of *Cal* noted that, given Belize's commitments under the Racial Discrimination Convention, the government 'should take this communication [country-specific Correspondence] seriously and respond accordingly'.[99]

Another noteworthy example is the German Federal Constitutional Court's engagement with the CRPD's Concluding Observations and General Comments in the Order of 26 July 2016.[100] The case involved the provision of medical treatment to a woman against her natural will in circumstances where she suffered from mental and physical illnesses and was deemed unable to provide consent. The Federal Constitutional Court

[95] *Appellante* v. *de Raad van Bestuur van de Sociale Verzekeringsbank*, 21 July 2006, LJN: AY5560 (the Netherlands, Central Appeals Tribunal); cited in van Alebeek and Nollkaemper, 'The Legal Status of Decisions by Human Rights Treaty Bodies', p. 402, fn 199.

[96] See nn. 17–19 and accompanying text on the principle of *res judicata*. In this vein, see, e.g., *X* v. *Council of Ministers*, paras 41, 43 (OUP numbers).

[97] *Decision No T-025 of 2004* (2004) (Constitutional Court, Colombia, 22 January 2004, English translation www.brookings.edu), para. 8.3.2 ('como intérprete autorizado del Pacto sobre la materia').

[98] *Test Trial Fund Clara Wichmann (Stichting Proefprocessenfonds Clara Wichmann) and Ors* v. *Netherlands*, First instance decision (2005) HA ZA 03/3395, LJN: AU2088, ILDC 221 (NL 2005) (the Netherlands, District Court, 7 September 2005), para. 3.18.

[99] *Cal* v. *Attorney-General* (2007) 71 WIR 110; 135 ILR 77 (Belize, Supreme Court, 18 October 2007), para. 125.

[100] *German Federal Constitutional Court (BVerfG), Order of the First Senate of 26 July 2016, 1 BvL 8/15* (English translation www.bverfg.de/e/ls20160726_1bvl000815en.html).

obliged the legislature to enact laws to allow coercive medical treatment in such cases. In holding that coercive treatment was compatible with the Convention on the Rights of Persons with Disabilities, the German court effectively disagreed with the CRPD's General Comment No. 1, Concluding Observations on Germany, and Guidelines on Article 14, in which the CRPD had criticized the practices of custodianship and forced treatment for failing to respect disabled persons' autonomy and will.[101] According to the Constitutional Court, these CRPD documents do not address the critical scenario involving persons who cannot form a free will.[102] While the German Federal Constitutional Court took a critical look at the CRPD's observations, the court substantively engaged with the Committee's position. Furthermore, the court notably observed that a national court, although it is not obliged to follow the CRPD,[103] should deal with the CRPD's opinions 'in an argumentative way and in good faith'[104] – as the German court seems to have done in this specific instance.

6.5.2 Normative Pathway: An Obligation to Consider and Its Variations

The aforementioned judicial narratives – such as those in *Test Trial Fund Clara Wichmann* in the Netherlands, *Cal* in Belize and the Order of 26 July 2016 in Germany – are nuanced. By no means do they elucidate an obligation to consider or give due consideration to certain types of findings. Yet the courts' nuanced position ought to be understood in light of some of the limitations extant at the national level for domestic courts vis-à-vis legislative and executive bodies.[105] Normative expectations expressed by judges cannot be separate from a contested obligation to consider, incumbent on states parties themselves. In discussing such an obligation, it is necessary to distinguish different types of treaty body findings.

[101] CRPD, 'General Comment No. 1 (2014), Article 12: Equal Recognition Before the Law' (19 May 2014) CRPD/C/GC/1, para. 26; CRPD, 'Concluding Observations on the Initial Report of Germany' (13 May 2015) CRPD/C/DEU/CO/1, paras 25–6; CRPD, 'Guidelines on Article 14 of the Convention on the Rights of Persons with Disabilities: The Right to Liberty and Security of Persons with Disabilities' (September 2015), paras 11–12.

[102] *German Federal Constitutional Court, 1 BvL 8/15*, para. 91.

[103] Ibid., para. 90.

[104] Ibid., para. 90.

[105] See nn. 17–19 and accompanying text.

6.5.2.1 Case-Specific Responses to Views

With regard to the case-specific responses to Views, it is hard to deny the existence, under international law, of such an obligation to consider. In fact, some treaties explicitly provide such an obligation. With regard to the CEDAW, Article 7(4) of the Optional Protocol obliges a state party to 'give due consideration to the views of the Committee' and to submit within six months the state's follow-up action.[106] These dual obligations (to give due consideration and to provide information on follow-up action) are also explicitly laid down in regard to the Views of the CESCR[107] and the CRC.[108]

The language is less explicit when it comes to the HRC. Yet the ICCPR's Optional Protocol, adopted in 1966, at least obliges a state party to submit information in response to the Views.[109] On top of the explicit requirement, there is an obligation to cooperate with a committee, which is applicable to all the monitoring bodies, including the HRC. Such an obligation is based on the general obligation to perform a treaty in good faith, under Article 26 of the Vienna Convention on the Law of Treaties,[110] accompanied by states parties' recognition of the competence of the committees under relevant human rights treaties. While the meaning of 'good faith' is no doubt contextual,[111] the good faith obligation has been understood as an obligation to cooperate with the committees, as the HRC remarked in General Comment No. 33.[112] Cooperation does not amount to require compliance; yet a state party may be acting in bad faith towards its treaty commitment if frequent non-compliance is combined with the failure to attempt to seriously engage with Views.[113]

[106] Optional Protocol to the Convention on the Elimination of All Forms of Discrimination against Women, 6 October 1999, 2131 UNTS 83, Article 7(4).

[107] Optional Protocol to the International Covenant on Economic, Social and Cultural Rights, 10 December 2008, UN Doc. A/63/435, Article 9(2).

[108] Optional Protocol to the Convention on the Rights of the Child on a communications procedure, 19 December 2011, UN Doc. A/RES/66/138, Article 11(1).

[109] Optional Protocol to the ICCPR (n 86).

[110] VCLT, Article 26.

[111] See R. Kolb, *Good Faith in International Law* (Hart Publishing, 2017), pp. 166–9.

[112] UNHRC, 'General Comment No. 33: The Obligations of States Parties under the Optional Protocol' (25 June 2009) CCPR/C/GC/33, para. 15. Cf. UNHRC, 'Draft General Comment No 33 (Second Revised Version as of 18 August 2008)' (25 August 2008) CCPR/C/GC/33/CRP.3, para. 16.

[113] S. Joseph, 'Committees: Human Rights Bodies', in R. Wolfrum (ed.), *The Max Planck Encyclopedia of Public International Law* (Oxford University Press, 2010), para. 9.

It is readily possible to find statements by states parties that they owe an obligation to take into account the Views addressed to them.[114] Iceland, for instance, expressed its position in a series of actions following the HRC's Views in *Haraldsson et al.* v. *Iceland* in October 2007 regarding the fisheries management system.[115] According to the Icelandic government, Iceland 'elected to become a party' to the Optional Protocol to the ICCPR, 'thereby recognising the competence of the Human Rights Committee to decide whether there has been a violation of the provisions of the Covenant or not'.[116] On this basis, Iceland noted that it is 'therefore required by international law to address the conclusions of the Committee'.[117] Not surprisingly, the government still preserved the space for discretion, adding that the Views in question were not detailed enough. According to Iceland, the Views 'do not include a summarized conclusion in the form of an adjudication, but a general discussion' without 'detailed guidance as to the precise measures required'.[118] In short, Iceland is acknowledging an obligation to consider and respond to Views, while, at the same time, characterizing them as 'a general discussion'.[119]

There are also some influential academic writings that support the existence of the obligation to consider with regard to states parties' case-specific responses to Views. Tomuschat articulated that 'States Parties cannot simply ignore' the Views of the HRC, despite the fact that they

[114] See van Alebeek and Nollkaemper, 'The Legal Status of Decisions by Human Rights Treaty Bodies', p. 386.

[115] UNHRC, *Erlingur Sveinn Haraldsson and Örn Snævar Sveinsson* v. *Iceland*, Communication No. 1306/2004, CCPR/C/91/D/1306/2004 (14 December 2007). The communication concerned discrimination in the business of commercial fishing quotas. See G. Gauksdottir and T. Ingadottir, 'Compliance with the Views of the UN Human Rights Committee and the Judgments of the European Court of Human Rights in Iceland', in A. Eide, J. T. Möller and I. Ziemele (eds), *Making Peoples Heard: Essays on Human Rights in Honour of Gudmundur Alfredsson* (Nijhoff, 2011) pp. 511–36, at pp. 526–9.

[116] Letter from the government of Iceland concerning the Views adopted by the Human Rights Committee on 24 October 2007, cited in Gauksdottir and Ingadottir, 'Compliance with the Views of the UN Human Rights Committee', pp. 530–1.

[117] Ibid., p. 531.

[118] Ibid., p. 531.

[119] Ibid. Iceland's readiness to review its system has led the HRC to close the follow-up examination of the case: 'Report of the Human Rights Committee, Volume I, 103rd Session (17 October–4 November 2011), 104th Session (12–30 March 2012)', (2012) UN Doc. A/67/40 (Vol. I), at 114–15 (with a finding of a partly satisfactory implementation of the recommendation).

lack legally binding force.[120] States parties 'have to consider' the Views 'in good faith (bona fide)'.[121] Tomuschat observes that states' lack of reaction 'would appear to amount to a violation of the obligations under the ICCPR'.[122] By quoting Tomuschat's remarks, the Venice Commission reiterated that 'member states are under the obligation to take the HRC's final views into consideration in good faith'.[123]

A main point of contestation remains the extent to which the obligation to consider in good faith requires states parties, and indirectly their courts, to favour the monitoring bodies' treaty interpretation. According to Tomuschat, states parties have to 'carefully examine' the Views addressed to them, and that 'there exists a presumption in favour of substantive correctness of such views'.[124] In case of disagreement, a state party 'must present detailed observations specifying its counter-arguments'.[125] An observation of a similar nature to the one by Tomuschat was relied upon by the Privy Council, in the New Zealand case of *Tangiora* in 1999, which found the HRC's Views hard to dismiss despite the lack of binding force.[126] According to the Privy Council, the Views of the HRC acquire 'authority from the standing of its members and their judicial qualities of impartiality, objectivity and restraint'.[127] Moreover, the Privy Council suggested that the functions of the Committee are 'adjudicative', as it makes a definitive and final ruling which is determinative of an issue that has been referred to it.[128] Despite these statements, however, the basis of the presumption of substantive correctness remains unclear.

6.5.2.2 Outside Case-Specific Responses

It has been further argued that the obligation to consider is not limited to states' case-specific follow-up to the Views addressed to them. In the

120 Tomuschat, 'Human Rights Committee', para. 14.
121 Ibid.
122 Ibid.
123 European Commission for Democracy through Law (Venice Commission), 'Report on the Implementation of International Human Rights Treaties in Domestic Law and the Role of Courts' adopted by the Venice Commission at its 100th plenary session (Rome, 10–11 October 2014), CDL-AD(2014)036 (8 December 2014), para. 78.
124 Christian Tomuschat, *Human Rights: Between Idealism and Realism* (Oxford University Press, 2014), p. 267.
125 Ibid.
126 *Tangiora* v. *Wellington District Legal Services Committee* (1999) [2000] 1 WLR 240; 124 ILR 570 (New Zealand, Judicial Committee of the Privy Council, 4 October 1999).
127 Ibid., 575.
128 Ibid.

commentary to its draft conclusions adopted in 2018, the ILC acknowledge that 'State parties may have an obligation, under a duty to cooperate under certain treaties, to *take into account* and to *react to* a pronouncement of an expert treaty body'[129] where the pronouncement is '*specifically addressed to them* or to individual communications regarding their own conduct'.[130] The ILC's commentary signals that the dual obligations to consider and react may be applicable, not only to Views, but also to Concluding Observations addressed to a specific state party. The 2016 Final Report of the ILA International Human Rights Law Committee may have even gone beyond the ILC's suggestion. According to the Final Report, the 'jurisprudence' developed by human rights bodies 'constitutes *res interpretata* within the treaty system accepted by the state'.[131] On this basis, the ILA's Final Report observed that domestic courts implement the good faith obligation by 'giving serious consideration' to the decisions of human rights bodies.[132] The ILA's Final Report indicated that the treaty bodies' 'jurisprudence' – and not necessarily limited to Views in case-specific follow-up – ought to be considered seriously.

It seems plausible to argue that states parties' obligation to cooperate with the committees, based on the obligation to perform a treaty in good faith,[133] is applicable to Concluding Observations as they are addressed to specific states. One cannot be certain, however, whether this obligation is applicable to General Comments. Further contested is whether the presumption of substantive correctness applies to findings outside case-specific follow-up to Views. In para. 66 of *Diallo*, the ICJ was prepared to accord 'great weight' to the HRC's 'interpretation' or 'jurisprudence' in general.[134] Interestingly, the ICJ's justification for doing so was not only because the Committee is the 'independent body that was established specifically to supervise the application of that treaty [i.e. the ICCPR]'.[135]

[129] 'Report of the International Law Commission, Seventieth Session' above, p. 113, para. 19 (commentary regarding Conclusion 13.3) (emphasis added).

[130] Ibid. (emphasis added).

[131] S. Kadelbach, 'The Domestic Implementation of Judgments/Decisions of Courts and Other International Bodies That Involve International Human Rights Law: Final Report of the ILA International Human Rights Law Committee (Part 2)', in S. Kadelbach, T. Rensmann and E. Rieter (eds), *Judging International Human Rights* (Springer International Publishing, 2019) pp. 51–100, at pp. 70–1.

[132] Ibid., p. 71.

[133] See nn. 110–113 and accompanying text.

[134] See *Diallo*, para. 66.

[135] See ibid.

The ICJ ascribed great weight to the HRC's interpretation, also because of the wider interests at stake in achieving 'the necessary clarity and the essential consistency of international law, as well as legal security' necessary for the rights holders and duty bearers.[136] The reasoning of the ICJ shows that the degree of normative weight to be given to treaty body findings relies not only on one's understanding of the characteristics of the monitoring bodies, but also the wider role that one wishes to ascribe to the bodies within the international legal order.

6.6 Engagement and Acceptance

6.6.1 Domestic Courts' Practices

In contrast with the nuanced engagement of domestic courts with UN human rights treaty-monitoring bodies, the Spanish Supreme Court in its judgement of July 2018 (Judgment No. 1263/2018) has taken a different and dichotomous path.[137] In this exceptional yet significant case, the Spanish highest court established the binding character of the Views of the CEDAW at the domestic level. The Supreme Court's decision came after many years of legal battles by the appellant, González Carreño.[138] Having been subject to physical and psychological violence by her partner, González Carreño filed a number of complaints in order to bring the abuses to the attention of the Spanish authorities.[139] While local courts took some measures to protect the appellant, they did not fully take into account the risks that her partner could pose, not only to the appellant, but also to her daughter, Andrea.[140] In May 2002, a Spanish local court allowed the partner, with respect to whom the appellant had obtained an order of marital separation, to visit their daughter Andrea without supervision.[141] In April 2003, during the scheduled visit, the daughter was shot by her father who eventually killed himself.

[136] See ibid.

[137] Judgment No. 1263/2018 of 17 July 2018, ROJ: STS 2747/2018, ECLI: ES:TS:2018:2747 (Tribunal Supremo [Supreme Court], Sala de lo Contencioso-Administrativo [Contentious-Administrative Chamber]) (Spain). For detailed analysis, see M. Kanetake, 'María de los Ángeles González Carreño v. Ministry of Justice' (2019) 113 *American Journal of International Law* 586–92.

[138] For facts, see CEDAW, *Angela González Carreño* v. *Spain*, Communication No. 47/2012 (16 July 2014), paras 2.1–2.21.

[139] Ibid., para. 2.5.

[140] See, e.g., ibid., para. 2.12.

[141] Ibid., para. 2.13.

After the tragic incident, González Carreño went through a series of domestic court proceedings, trying to prove the pecuniary liability of the state which failed to protect her and her late daughter. From April 2004 to October 2010, her liability claims met rejection four times before Spanish courts.[142] Her constitutional claim was likewise rejected by the Constitutional Court in April 2011.[143] Having exhausted domestic remedies, on 19 September 2012, González Carreño brought her petition to the CEDAW. The Committee rendered its Views on 16 July 2014, finding the Spanish government in violation of her Conventional rights.[144] Having found a violation of the state's obligations under the Convention,[145] the Committee recommended Spain to provide compensation and conduct an exhaustive and impartial investigation.[146] At the domestic level, however, the CEDAW's recommendations in July 2014 did not result in any changes to the situation of the appellant. A year later, in July 2015, the CEDAW still expressed its concern about the 'lack of follow-up to the Committee's views' on the part of the state party regarding González Carreño.[147] Meanwhile, she launched a series of new administrative and judicial proceedings, ultimately before the Supreme Court, requesting the government to give effect to the CEDAW's Views.[148]

In its judgement of 17 July 2018, the Spanish Supreme Court regarded the Views of the CEDAW as binding at the domestic level, ordering the government to pay €600,000 for moral damages suffered by the appellant.[149] The Supreme Court reached such a conclusion on the basis of both international and domestic laws. With regard to the international legal basis, the Spanish court held that the Views of the CEDAW have a 'binding/obligatory' character.[150] The court ascribed such a character to Views, despite its acknowledgement that the CEDAW Convention does not oblige states parties to adopt any specific procedures in order to give

[142] Ibid., paras 2.18–2.20.
[143] Ibid., para. 2.21.
[144] Ibid., para. 10.
[145] CEDAW, *Angela González Carreño*, para. 10 (Articles 2(a–f), 5(a) and 16(1)(d) of the CEDAW Convention).
[146] Ibid., para. 11(a).
[147] CEDAW, 'Concluding Observations on the Combined Seventh and Eighth Periodic Reports of Spain' (29 July 2015) CEDAW/C/ESP/CO/7–8, paras 10–11.
[148] See further Kanetake, 'María de los Ángeles González Carreño', 588–9.
[149] Judgment No. 1263/2018 of 17 July 2018, 14.
[150] Ibid., 12.

effect to Views.[151] The court derived the 'binding/obligatory' character on the basis of Article 24 of the CEDAW Convention and Articles 7(4) and 1 of the Optional Protocol.[152]

The Supreme Court's reasoning was further supported by domestic law. The court reiterated that the CEDAW Convention, on which the Committee and its Views are based, forms part of the domestic legal order under Article 96 of the Spanish Constitution.[153] Pursuant to Article 10(2) of the Constitution, fundamental rights shall be interpreted in accordance with human rights treaties ratified by Spain.[154] An important aspect of the court's reasoning was the manner in which the court invoked Article 9(3) of the Spanish Constitution. The provision guarantees 'the principle of legality and the normative hierarchy', according to which international obligations relating to the execution of the decisions of the CEDAW form part of the Spanish internal order and enjoy a hierarchical position above ordinary domestic law.[155] On this basis, the Supreme Court observed that the Convention and the Views 'can and should be a decisive element' in proving the possible infringement of the fundamental rights of the appellant.[156] While the Supreme Court emphasized the particularities of the appellant's case, the court took the position that the CEDAW's Views must be considered as a 'valid basis' for bringing a claim concerning the pecuniary liability of the state.[157] Otherwise, as articulated by the Supreme Court, the 'absence of a specific procedure for executing' the Views of the Committee constitutes 'in itself a breach of a legal and constitutional mandate by Spain'.[158]

The Spanish Supreme Court's reasoning pertains only to the CEDAW's Views on individual communications, and not to other types of findings. Yet it would be good to reiterate once again that each monitoring body engages with its own previous findings. In the CEDAW's Views in *Angela González Carreño* v. *Spain*, the Committee's

[151] Ibid., 12.
[152] Ibid., 12.
[153] See ibid., 12.
[154] Ibid., 12.
[155] Ibid., 12. It must be noted that international obligations are superior to ordinary domestic law – but not above the Constitution – based on Articles 95 and 96 of the Constitution, instead of Article 9(3) itself.
[156] Ibid., 12.
[157] Judgment No. 1263/2018 of 17 July 2018., 13.
[158] Ibid., 13.

reasoning built on its General Recommendation No. 19 (1992),[159] in which the CEDAW had made it clear that states ought to act with due diligence to prevent violations involving the acts of private persons.[160] In *Angela González Carreño* v. *Spain*, the Committee found the violations of the Convention, 'read jointly with . . . general recommendation No. 19 of the Committee'.[161] In other words, by according legal binding effect to Views, the Spanish Supreme Court in the judgement of July 2018 augmented the normative relevance of other CEDAW findings at the domestic level.

6.6.2 *Normative Pathway: An Obligation to Comply*

The Spanish Supreme Court's identification of the binding character of the Views of the CEDAW resembles the draft version of the HRC's General Comment No. 33 concerning the general obligations of states parties. In an early draft of what became the HRC's General Comment No. 33, the HRC characterized its role as an 'authentic interpreter' of the Covenant[162] and regarded its Views as exhibiting 'most of the characteristics of a judicial decision'.[163] Also, in the draft version, the HRC translated the obligation to cooperate with the Committee as entailing 'an obligation to respect the views of the Committee in the given case'.[164] The HRC is not the only body that attempted to put forward an imperative tone. Within the CAT, one of its members observed that, '[w]hile the Committee's decisions were not strictly mandatory, States parties had *an obligation to comply with them in good faith*', which also justifies the CAT's follow-up mechanism.[165]

159 CEDAW, 'General Recommendation No. 19: Violence against Women' (1992).

160 Ibid., para. 9.

161 CEDAW, *Angela González Carreño*, para. 10.

162 UNHRC, 'Draft General Comment No 33', para. 14 ('the [an] authentic interpreter'). See, further, Kanetake, 'UN Human Rights Treaty Monitoring Bodies Before Domestic Courts', 205–6.

163 UNHRC, 'Draft General Comment No 33', para. 11. On differences between the adoption of Views and judicial decision making, see, e.g., L. S. Borlini and L. Crema, 'The Legal Status of Decisions by Human Rights Treaty Bodies: International Supervision, Authoritative Interpretations or *Mission Éducatrice*?' (2019) 18 *Global Community Yearbook of International Law and Jurisprudence*, section III C.

164 Ibid., 'Draft General Comment No 33', para. 16.

165 CAT, 'Thirty-Sixth Session, Summary Record of the 717th Meeting' (1 June 2006) CAT/C/SR.717, para. 65 (Mr. Mariño Menéndez, emphasis added). The remarks were also endorsed by the chairperson: see para. 66 (Mr. Mavrommatis).

The imperative vocabularies used in the draft version of General Comment No. 33 met with criticisms from several states parties.[166] In the end, the wording of the final version of General Comment No. 33 was revised, including the critical phrase 'authentic interpreter'.[167] The draft version of General Comment No. 33 was an attempt to creatively translate a procedural duty to cooperate with the Committee, based on the good faith obligation, into the substantive obligation to respect the Views of the HRC.[168] Such an attempt was not successful in 2008, at least in the context of the HRC.

In the judgement of July 2018, the Spanish Supreme Court by no means characterized the CEDAW as an authentic interpreter. In fact, the Spanish Constitutional Court reiterated in 2002 that the HRC was not a judicial organ and that the Views of the HRC could not represent the 'authentic interpretation' of the ICCPR.[169] The crux, however, is that the Spanish Supreme Court's reasoning in 2018 was in part based on the state party's obligation to take Views seriously. The Spanish court referred to not only Article 24 of the Convention, according to which states parties 'undertake to adopt all necessary measures at the national level aimed at achieving the full realization of the rights recognized in the present Convention'.[170] The Court also relied on Article 7(4) of the Optional Protocol, according to which the state party has dual obligations. Namely, the party 'shall give due consideration to the views of the Committee, together with its recommendations' and 'shall submit to the Committee, within six months, a written response'.[171] As noted in Section 6.5.2.1, these dual obligations are enunciated for the CESCR and the CRC as well.[172] Overall, the reasoning of the Spanish highest

[166] Kanetake, 'UN Human Rights Treaty Monitoring Bodies before Domestic Courts', 205–6.

[167] UNHRC, 'Draft General Comment No 33', para. 14; UNHRC, 'General Comment No. 33', para. 13. Regarding the distinction between authentic and authoritative interpretation, see Iwasawa, 'Domestic Application of International Law', 239–41.

[168] UNHRC, 'Draft General Comment No 33', para. 16.

[169] *PM* v. *Criminal Chamber of the Supreme Court*, Constitutional Appeal (recurso de amparo), ILDC 1794 (ES 2002), STC 70/2002, para. 7 of the section on legal foundations (Spain, Constitutional Court, 3 April 2002) ('Dictámenes no pueden constituir la interpretación auténtica del Pacto'). The Constitutional Court's narrative was reproduced by the Spanish Supreme Court in its judgment of 8 June 2015: Judgment of the Supreme Court of 8 June 2015 (Spain, Supreme Court, Third Chamber, Contentious-Administrative), https://supremo.vlex.es/vid/575807258.

[170] Judgment No. 1263/2018 of 17 July 2018, 12; CEDAW Convention, Article 24.

[171] Optional Protocol CEDAW, Article 7(4).

[172] See nn. 107–108.

court demonstrates the breadth of what can be offered through the obligation to consider. After the lengthy administrative and judicial proceedings involving the victim of the state's neglect, the obligation to consider has reached the point where no further deliberation may be welcome.

6.7 Conclusion

The shortcomings of human rights protection at the domestic level have sustained the need for institutional mechanisms at the international level that monitor and assist states' implementation of human rights treaties. The ten human rights treaty-monitoring bodies, within their significantly limited resources, actively adopt general and specific findings. Each treaty-monitoring body generates and reiterates its own interpretation of relevant treaty obligations by cross-referencing previous findings. Despite the accumulation of instruments adopted, the effectiveness of treaty body findings ultimately relies on the degree to which their treaty interpretation becomes entangled with the practice of states parties, including their judiciary.

As illustrated by some examples discussed in this chapter, the treaty interpretation built by UN human rights treaty-monitoring bodies has been intertwined with the discourse of domestic court decisions. Various courts have shown their willingness to take into account General Comments, Concluding Observations and Views in the course of interpreting applicable human rights treaties and relevant domestic legal provisions. Judges' proximity to the international monitoring bodies varies, depending on sociological contexts in which judges have been situated. If UN treaty-monitoring bodies are not integrated in judges' legal training, it may be unrealistic to expect them to see the relevance of treaty body findings.

At the same time, a connecting point between UN treaty-monitoring bodies and domestic courts can also be normative, at least in part. One such normative pathway which generates 'discursive entanglement'[173] is the obligation to consider. As illustrated in the present chapter, there are a number of variations surrounding such an obligation, from mere encouragement to take into account to an obligation to implement. While normative expectations may be limited to certain types of treaty

[173] See Chapter 1.

body findings, the monitoring bodies regularly refer back to General Comments in drafting Concluding Observations or Views, reminding a state party of the monitoring bodies' earlier remarks on which specific observations are built. In other words, the consideration of Views would substantively involve a state party's reflection of General Comments or Concluding Observations.

Pathways built around the obligation to consider are not single routes. There are multiple normative variations: ranging from a cursory look, to substantive and reasoned engagement, to legally obliged acceptance. Due to the fact that there are multiple possibilities, judges' willingness to substantively engage with the treaty body's interpretation can be altered, for instance, by the initiatives to better ensure independence and impartiality of UN treaty-monitoring bodies.[174] Substantive engagement on the part of domestic courts creates further opportunities for the treaty bodies to tailor their approaches to states parties. Deliberative space involving domestic courts and the monitoring bodies may be multifaceted and changeable, in that it allows various degrees of entanglement on the part of domestic courts. Yet it is precisely because of its precariousness that there arises the need for constant attempts to augment the quality of engagement, both on the part of domestic courts and UN treaty-monitoring bodies.

[174] E.g., 'Guidelines on the Independence and Impartiality of Members of the Human Rights Treaty Bodies ("the Addis Ababa Guidelines")' (2 August 2012) UN Doc. A/67/222 Annex I.

7

The Social Life of Entanglements

International Investment and Human Rights Norms in and beyond ISDS

FRANCESCO CORRADINI

7.1 Introduction

Metaphors may be helpful tools to think about law. They may also help us to imagine what happens when law makes its actual appearance in the plural rather than in the singular. Consider the following statement:

> [W]estbrook's intriguing metaphor of cream poured into coffee, swirling and billowing before blending into a homogenized liquid, is suggestive. But this only captures part of what we should be concerned with. The cream comes from a single outside source, it is poured from above, the flow is in one direction, and the blending is relatively harmonious; but many of our stories of diffusion of law are more complex often involving two or more reciprocally interacting change agents, crossing of levels, and repression, resistance, or avoidance.[1]

A former judge of the International Court of Justice (ICJ) employed a similar rhetorical device as he imagined how investment protection and human rights norms could be brought in relation. He observed:

> [O]il and water do not mix, at least not readily. Is this also true of human rights and the protection of foreign investment-here also in the sense that they ought to be kept apart? Some observers, or rather stakeholders, might think so. There is, of course a way to overcome this separation: science

I am grateful to Nico Krisch for his constructive comments and criticism on earlier versions of this work. I also thank Tomáš Morochovič for his careful editing and helpful suggestions on this text. I gratefully acknowledge financial support by the Swiss National Science Foundation, which made this research possible.

[1] W. Twining, 'Diffusion and Globalization Discourse Symposium: Diffusion of Law in the 21st Century: Interaction and Influence' (2006) 47 *Harvard International Law Journal* 507–16.

> and industry employ some sort of mediators between the water and the oil (so-called 'emulgators') to achieve this.[2]

From a legal theory perspective, the observation of contemporary phenomena akin to the interactions captured by these metaphors has led to the hypothesis that, particularly in contexts of societal disagreement and institutional pluralization, law has become 'entangled'.[3] International legal scholarship has diagnosed similar dynamics in disputes over the relationship between global economic governance and human rights.[4] From this perspective, efforts to establish human rights obligations for multinational corporations in 2003, followed by the UN Guiding Principles in 2011 and leading to current discussions at the UN about a new international instrument on transnational corporations,[5] may be seen as fragments belonging to a common dynamic process of defining relations between business and human rights norms.[6]

To illustrate this process, this chapter investigates forms of interaction between international investment and human rights law. As these forms depend on the contexts in which they are construed, I focus on governance sites where actors have disagreed about the best way to order the encounter of multiple legalities. Examining the 'social life' of this encounter, I seek to understand when and how 'entangled legalities'[7] emerge – where, how and by whom have they been produced? Drawing upon the conceptual framework of the volume, I analyse competing claims of actors and institutions through which investment protection and human rights norms have been brought in relation over time.

The chapter has three sections, in addition to an introduction and a conclusion. Section 7.2 identifies the rational and ideational parameters

[2] B. Simma, 'Foreign Investment Arbitration: A Place for Human Rights?' (2011) 60 *International & Comparative Law Quarterly* 573–96.

[3] See Chapter 1.

[4] P. Alston, 'Resisting the Merger and Acquisition of Human Rights by Trade Law: A Reply to Petersman' (2002) 13 *European Journal of International Law* 815–44; see also, in the context of the interface between trade and environment, Chapter 8.

[5] OEIGWG Chairmanship, 'Second Revised Draft, Legally Binding Instrument to Regulate, in International Human Rights Law, the Activities of Transnational Corporations and Other Business Enterprises' (6 August 2020) www.ohchr.org/Documents/HRBodies/HRCouncil/WGTransCorp/Session6/OEIGWG_Chair-Rapporteur_second_revised_draft_LBI_on_TNCs_and_OBEs_with_respect_to_Human_Rights.pdf.

[6] N. Krisch, F. Corradini and L. Lu Reimers, 'Order at the Margins: The Legal Construction of Interface Conflicts Over Time' (2020) 9 *Global Constitutionalism* 343–63.

[7] See Chapter 1.

that are likely to affect whether and how 'forms of entanglement'[8] in international investment law have come about and developed. On the one hand, these forms may be an effect of competing interests of actors with unequal access to resources and knowledge to shape and organize them. Rational actors' attitudes towards what they represent as 'other' legalities may depend upon the potential gains involved in that determination. On the other hand, actors' mindsets and the cultural setting of investment arbitration are bound to have repercussions on how the boundaries of international investment law and its relations with competing legalities are shaped. Against this background, Section 7.3 examines how actors have actually dealt with multiple legalities, in particular with human rights norms, in the context of investor–state dispute settlement (ISDS) and analyses the various forms that they have generated there. As actors' responses to multiplicity have varied considerably in practice, the emerging picture is not coherent. When interpreting investment treaty standards, investment adjudicators have disregarded human rights norms in some cases, while in other cases they accorded them some weight, but always doing so from the perspective of their own legality. Actors' strategic interests and ideational context may partly account for the diversity of interpretive practices observed. As the institutions of international investment protection face growing challenges from national governments, academics and non-governmental actors, linkages with human rights may be beneficial to their cause.

Section 7.4 examines similar dynamics of convergence and divergence between legalities in contexts of international investment law reform, where the norm of ISDS itself has become the object of acute contestation. Human rights experts have articulated a mode of ordering multiplicity that is similar to the dominant forms of relationing observed in foreign investment litigation. Associated as they are to a systemic vision of order, human rights lawyers have also relied on norms of internal hierarchy according to which different legalities have to be 'consistent' with human rights and the rule of law. Some of these experts went so far as to claim that human rights norms have priority over conflicting legalities.

[8] See Chapter 1. For the purpose of this chapter, I use 'entanglement' and 'enmeshment' interchangeably.

7.2 Pathways to Entanglement in International Investment Governance Sites

Legal scholars have emphasized the pluralist, decentralized and incrementally evolving character of international investment law.[9] Indeed, in contexts of investment treaty disputes, often this law makes its appearance more in the plural than in the singular.[10] For example, bilateral investment treaties (BITs), multilateral or regional trade and investment agreements often interplay with domestic laws, contractual frameworks and other rules of international law and therefore it becomes crucial to define their relations.[11] At sites of foreign investment governance, entanglements do not build themselves but are defined by the interplay of situated actors with competing stakes and normative orientations.[12] Such diversity of actors and 'bodies of norms'[13] makes this arena of global economic governance, and investment treaty arbitration in particular,[14] an ideal setting to analyse how entangled legalities are formed and operate. The purpose of this chapter is to get closer to the social life of relations built in and around this law. To do so, I consider how actors' attitudes towards human rights norms in investor–state arbitration may respond to competing interests and the ideational background in which they are formed.

7.2.1 Competing Interests

Societal actors' interests are a first potential determinant of entangled legalities.[15] From a rational choice perspective, international investment

[9] J. Pauwelyn, 'Rational Design or Accidental Evolution? The Emergence of International Investment Law', in Z. Douglas, J. Pauwelyn and J. E. Viñuales (eds), *The Foundations of International Investment Law: Bringing Theory into Practice* (Oxford University Press, 2014), pp. 11–43; A. Roberts, 'Clash of Paradigms: Actors and Analogies Shaping the Investment Treaty System' (2013) 107 *The American Journal of International Law* 45–94.

[10] Z. Douglas, 'The Hybrid Foundations of Investment Treaty Arbitration' (2003) 74 *British Yearbook of International Law* 151–289, referring to the 'laws applicable to an investment dispute' at 194.

[11] J. Viñuales, 'Sources of International Investment Law: Conceptual Foundations of Unruly Practices', in S. Besson and J. d'Aspremont (eds), *Oxford Handbook on the Sources of International Law* (Oxford University Press, 2017).

[12] See Chapter 1, Section 1.4.1.

[13] On this notion, see Chapter 1, Section 1.2.

[14] On ISDS as a mechanism and form of global governance, see S. Schill, 'W(h)ither Fragmentation? On the Literature and Sociology of International Investment Law' (2011) 22 *European Journal of International Law* 875–908.

[15] See Chapter 1, Section 1.4.1.

arbitration participants – foreign investors, host governments, investment arbitrators, lawyers and non-governmental organizations (NGOs) – act rationally to maximize their self-interest.[16] Given the competition of interests and concerns involved, conflicting demands and priorities are bound to condition whether and how norms will be brought together or kept apart.[17] This outcome may depend on actors' 'prudential reasons-for-action' – different actors will shape forms of relation depending on their own expected gains.[18]

Since 'states, investors, and NGOs often favour different paradigms in light of their divergent normative interests and agendas',[19] these interests and agendas will also determine what weight they will give to the legalities at play. I assume that the interest of the two disputing parties – foreign investor and responding state – is to win the dispute. As investors argue 'for broad investor rights',[20] we can expect them to defend their own interests from the potentially disruptive effects of human rights protecting the interests of other individuals or groups. Empirical findings suggest that foreign investors have benefited from investment litigation. Particularly since the second half of 1990s, they have gained from using investment claims against poor and rich governments.[21] The stability and predictability of international investment protection – legally sanctioned through international arbitration – has been economically beneficial to international investors. It seems that the status quo has protected foreign investors' interests against the preferences of other societal actors.[22] Given the beneficial environment in which investors bring their claims, couplings with bodies of norms of different origin may open unpredictable scenarios. As rational actors, foreign investors will seek to resist this

[16] J. Bonnitcha, L. N. S. Poulsen and M. Waibel, *The Political Economy of the Investment Treaty Regime* (Oxford University Press, 2017), at 127.

[17] On the competition of interests involved, see M. Sornarajah, *The International Law on Foreign Investment* (Cambridge University Press, 2017), 'Introduction'.

[18] T. Schultz, *Transnational Legality: Stateless Law and International Arbitration* (Oxford University Press, 2014), pp. 26–30.

[19] Roberts, 'Clash of Paradigms', 48.

[20] J. Pauwelyn, 'The Rule of Law without the Rule of Lawyers? Why Investment Arbitrators Are from Mars, Trade Adjudicators from Venus' (2015) 109 *American Journal of International Law* 761–805, at 782.

[21] T. Schultz and C. Dupont, 'Investment Arbitration: Promoting the Rule of Law or Over-empowering Investors? A Quantitative Empirical Study' (2015) 25 *European Journal of International Law* 1147–68.

[22] N. Tzouvala, 'The Academic Debate about Mega-Regionals and International Lawyers: Legalism as Critique?' (2018) 6 *London Review of International Law* 189–209, at 200.

outcome.[23] However, in cases in which it is convenient to them, they may also entangle their rights with human rights norms, perhaps to enhance the persuasiveness of their claims against the host government.[24] States, too, may expect gains from these types of connections. Frequently, and especially in times of economic crises, linkages with human rights might strengthen their defences against investor's claims. Countries with limited financial resources may use these linkages as a rhetorical strategy to expand their 'regulatory authority'[25] and avoid costly liability or reduce the amount of compensation due to the investor. Finally, NGOs (other than business associations) and human rights experts may entangle international investment and human rights law to advance the interests of affected outsiders like local communities and human rights holders.

Investment arbitration insiders' decision-making may also respond to constraints and incentives.[26] Previous empirical analysis has concluded that arbitrators of the International Centre for Settlement of Investment Disputes (ICSID) form a 'network' that 'reinforces prevailing norms and behaviours and insulates its most important members from outside influence'.[27] Beyond international arbitrators, legal counsel, expert witnesses and tribunal secretaries have also become particularly influential actors.[28] In conditions of professional competition, the members of the investment arbitration industry may have professional incentives to distance human rights. As co-operators of the system, they will have material incentives to defend their legal specialization and their role as the masters of its law. From their perspective, investment arbitration may be a specialized profession with its own 'ethos' and associated relevant

[23] '[I]nvestors will not invoke the kind of international law that may weaken their legal position', A. van Aaken, 'Fragmentation of International Law: The Case of International Investment Protection' (2008) 17 *Finnish Yearbook of International Law* 91–130, at 93.

[24] On the 'strategic function of human rights references in investment arbitration', see S. Steininger, 'What's Human Rights Got To Do With It? An Empirical Analysis of Human Rights References in Investment Arbitration' (2018) 31 *Leiden Journal of International Law* 33–58, at 45–9.

[25] Pauwelyn, 'The Rule of Law', at 782.

[26] T. Schultz, 'Arbitral Decision-Making: Legal Realism and Law and Economics' (2015) 6 *Journal of International Dispute Settlement* 231–51.

[27] S. Puig, 'Social Capital in the Arbitration Market' (2014) 25 *European Journal of International Law* 387–424, at 390.

[28] M. Langford, D. Behn and R. H. Lie, 'The Revolving Door in International Investment Arbitration' (2017) 20 *Journal of International Economic Law* 301–32.

frameworks and practices.[29] Therefore, distancing human rights may be needed to secure reputation from other members of their community of practice and to continue their practice as usual.[30] Yet empirical work has found that over time there have been incentives for these legal experts to be reflexively open to societal demands. As investor–state arbitration faces a legitimacy crisis, some arbitrators may act strategically to 'manage consciously or unconsciously the legitimacy of arbitration' by showing 'greater deference to respondent states'.[31] To do so, they might seek to adjust their decision-making in response to the claims and interests of dominant states like the European Union, the United States and China, but also to those of some Latin America countries that have been vocal against investment arbitration. In this context, investment arbitration officials might benefit from linkages with norms with strong social backing like human rights law to strengthen their own legitimacy.[32]

7.2.2 Ideational Contexts

A second possible cause of entanglements is the ideational context in which they come about. In investment arbitration, this context is shaped by multiple factors, including actors' 'shared understandings' of international investment law and their role in the 'community of practice' they form a part of.[33] 'Epistemic communities – that is, social groups of professionals and academics that shape the discursive policies'[34] in investment arbitration have played a role in the formation of those understandings,[35] with possible implications for the 'interface norms' and practices emerging from the inside of that community of practice and its discourse. From this perspective, situations of enmeshment may

[29] T. Schultz, 'The Ethos of Arbitration', in T. Schultz and F. Ortino (eds), *Oxford Handbook of International Arbitration* (Oxford University Press, 2020).

[30] Schultz, 'Arbitral Decision-Making'.

[31] M. Langford and D. Behn, 'Managing Backlash: The Evolving Investment Treaty Arbitrator?' (2018) 29 *European Journal of International Law* 551–80.

[32] See Chapter 1, Section 1.2. See also Steininger, 'What's Human Rights', at 49–50.

[33] See Chapter 1, Section 1.2. On the concepts of 'shared understanding' and 'communities of practice', see J. Brunnée and S. Toope, 'Interactional International Law: An Introduction' (2011) 3 *International Theory* 307–18.

[34] A. Bianchi, 'Epistemic Communities in International Arbitration', in T. Schultz and F. Ortino (eds), *The Oxford Handbook of International Arbitration* (Oxford University Press, 2020).

[35] Roberts, 'Clash of Paradigms'; E. Gaillard, 'Sociology of International Arbitration' (2015) 1 *Arbitration International* 1–17.

be driven by how different actors regard international investment law, for example by adopting primarily an international public law, commercial arbitration or public law approach.[36]

Investment tribunals will often understand their role as strictly confined to the determination of whether foreign investors' rights have been violated or not. In that determination, arbitrators will see themselves primarily as interpreters of the legal basis creating those rights (e.g. a treaty), with implications for their room for manoeuvre to create relations with bodies of norms perceived as external. ISDS participants' choice of 'conceptual maps'[37] is likely to impact whether and how legalities are brought together or kept apart and with which effects. This choice may depend upon actors' background and projects. For instance, investment arbitrators with knowledge in public international law have drawn on the judgements of the ICJ, while others with experience in trade law have relied on the World Trade Organization (WTO) jurisprudence.[38] The same holds true for arbitrators emphasizing a 'universalistic' versus 'particularistic' perspective of the interaction between 'general international law' and other 'special regimes'. For example, a former ICJ judge has situated 'international investment law' within 'general international law' in keeping with his vision about the relationship between 'special regimes' within the wider 'universe of international law'.[39] Similarly, lawyers believing in a unified 'international legal system' as opposed to a 'fragmented' one will consider linkages between international investment and human rights law with less hesitancy.[40]

However, previous sociological analysis of the 'investment arbitration culture' has concluded that lawyers with a strong background in public international law are the minority in investment arbitration settings while the 'commercial arbitration paradigm' appears as the dominant

[36] Roberts, 'Clash of Paradigms'.

[37] Ibid.

[38] Ibid., at 55.

[39] Simma, 'Foreign Investment Arbitration'. B. Simma and J. Kill, 'Harmonizing Investment Protection and International Human Rights: First Steps Towards a Methodology', in C. Binder, U. Kriebaum, A. Reinisch and S. Wittich (eds), *International Investment Law for the 21st Century: Essays in Honour of Christoph Schreurer* (Oxford University Press, 2009), pp. 679–707.

[40] P.-M. Dupuy, 'Unification Rather than Fragmentation of International Law? The Case of International Investment Law and Human Rights Law', in P.-M. Dupuy, E.-U. Petersmann and F. Francioni (eds), *Human Rights in International Investment Law and Arbitration* (Oxford University Press, 2009), pp. 45–62.

one.[41] Empirical work on the composition of investor–state arbitral tribunals at ICSID has found that these tribunals comprise individuals – mostly men from the USA and Europe – whose conception of law reflects their particular training and professional background.[42] Here, international 'business lawyers' with competence in 'commerce, industry or finance' appear as the dominant players.[43] The investment arbitration community seems to have little knowledge of human rights law due to the particular 'sociocultural features' and processes of socialization of that community.[44] Indeed, 'culture influences how people think, communicate, behave',[45] including how they situate themselves in relation to different constituencies and their legalities. However, legal culture and socio-psychological influences[46] are not the only elements of the ideational context in which arbitrators' decision-making is situated. Empirical work has found that arbitrators' 'policy preferences', including their ideology, also shape their decisions.[47] As a consequence of the 'set of values and beliefs'[48] that seem dominant in investment arbitration we might expect resistance to tight linkages with human rights,[49] although it is possible that investment arbitrators' 'background preferences'[50] might begin to change.

7.3 Navigating Multiplicity in ISDS Practice

7.3.1 Varying Forms of Relation

As claims about human rights have begun to be heard in investment arbitration, ISDS participants have faced the challenge of 'navigating'

[41] M. Hirsch, 'The Sociological Dimension of International Arbitration: The Investment Arbitration Culture', in T. Schultz and F. Ortino (eds), *Oxford Handbook of International Arbitration* (Oxford University Press, 2020).
[42] Pauwelyn, 'The Rule of Law'.
[43] Puig, 'Social Capital', 402.
[44] M. Hirsch, *Invitation to the Sociology of International Law* (Oxford University Press, 2015), pp. 129–55.
[45] Ibid., p. 131.
[46] M. Gicquello, 'The Reform of Investor–State Dispute Settlement: Bringing the Findings of Social Psychology into the Debate' (2019) 10 *Journal of International Dispute Settlement* 561–81.
[47] M. Waibel and Y. Wu, 'Are Arbitrators Political? Evidence from International Investment Arbitration?' (2017) www.yanhuiwu.com/documents/arbitrator.pdf.
[48] Gaillard, 'Sociology of International Arbitration'.
[49] Hirsch, *Invitation to the Sociology*.
[50] Langford and Behn, 'Managing Backlash'.

between multiple bodies of norms.[51] Influenced by the discourse of institutions like the World Bank-based ICSID, the Permanent Court of Arbitration (PCA) or the United Nations Commission on International Trade Law (UNCITRAL), ISDS has become one among many governance sites where 'horizontal' and 'vertical' interactions between legal orders have been articulated over time. At this site, ad hoc investment arbitrators have become key decision-makers in setting the boundaries of 'international investment law'.[52] While scholars have observed an increase in the number of actors' statements referring to human rights norms in investment litigation,[53] we know less about the forms of relation constructed through those claims. In Section 7.3.2, I draw on a selection of statements to analyse the ways in which different actors have brought bodies of norms in relation in ISDS.

7.3.2 *Hierarchies and Separation*

Foreign investors and states have dealt with multiplicity by relying on hierarchies, as exemplified in the *CMS Gas Transmission Company* case.[54] The dispute arose after Argentina adopted measures to protect the welfare of the population, including by guaranteeing access to public services, amid an economic crisis at the end of the 1990s. At the time, CMS, a US corporation with an investment in the gas transportation sector of Argentina, claimed it suffered financial losses as a result of those exceptional measures and invoked its rights under the Argentina–United States BIT to protect its interests through ICSID arbitration. While Argentina and CMS disagreed over the ultimate source of authority to decide their dispute, they both referred to norms about hierarchy to order the relation between bodies of norms. Particularly contentious

[51] See Chapter 1.

[52] J. E. Alvarez, *Boundaries of Investment Arbitration: The Use of Trade and European Human Rights Law in Investor-State Disputes* (Juris, 2018). Already in 1990, the *AAPL* tribunal stated that an investment treaty 'is not a self-contained closed legal system limited to provide for substantive material rules of direct applicability, but it has to be envisaged within a wider juridical context in which rules from other sources are integrated through implied incorporation methods, or by direct reference to certain supplementary rules, whether of international character or of domestic law nature'. *Asian Agricultural Products Ltd* v. *Republic of Sri Lanka*, ICSID Case No ARB/87//3, Award, 27 June 1990, 21.

[53] Steininger, 'What's Human Rights'; Alvarez, *Boundaries of Investment Arbitration.*

[54] *CMS Gas Transmission Co* v. *Argentine Republic,* ICSID Case No. ARB/01/8, Award, 12 May 2005.

was the question of the 'applicable law'.[55] While the investor regarded the BIT and international law as *lex specialis*, Argentina not only considered its constitutional order relevant but also superior to the BIT. Drawing on its constitution, public law and international customary rules on state of necessity, Argentina said that obligations to safeguard constitutional rights prevailed over its BIT commitments, including investor's fair and equitable treatment (FET) claims.[56] Argentina situated and construed the relation between the legalities at play within an order where constitutional public law and human rights had primacy over investment treaties.

Drawing on a 'more pragmatic and less doctrinaire' approach and 'taking the facts of the case and the arguments of the parties into account',[57] the tribunal concurred with Argentina that both the international and the domestic legal orders applied to the dispute. It found 'a close interaction between the legislation and the regulations governing the gas privatization, the Licence and international law, as embodied both in the Treaty and in customary international law'.[58] While the tribunal emphasized that the multiple legalities were 'inseparable', it also specified that they were to be applied 'to the extent justified'.[59] As a consequence, the tribunal decided against Argentina that 'while treaties in theory could collide with the Constitution, in practice this is not very likely'[60] and 'in this case, the tribunal does not find any such collision' partly because 'there is no question of affecting fundamental human rights when considering the issues disputed by the parties'.[61] The tribunal highlighted that 'the specific domestic legislation of Argentina and rules of international law applied by the Tribunal will be discussed in connection with the issues contended'.[62] By assigning a specific 'role' to domestic and international law in relation to the 'facts' of the dispute, the tribunal created distance between these legal orders. It insisted on regarding the two laws as separate legal orders that could simultaneously apply in the circumstances of the case, rather than creating a hierarchical

[55] Ibid., para. 109.
[56] Ibid., para. 114.
[57] 'It is no longer the case of one prevailing over the other and excluding it altogether. Rather both sources have a role to play'. Ibid., para. 116–18.
[58] *CMS Gas Transmission.*, above, para. 117.
[59] Ibid., para. 117.
[60] Ibid., para. 120.
[61] Ibid., para. 121.
[62] Ibid., para. 122.

relation between them, as if the obligations owed to the investor and to the Argentinian population could run in parallel.

7.3.3 Proximity and Distance

NGOs have played an important role in tying human rights and ISDS. For example, they have highlighted conflicts between human rights and investment protection norms, as reflected in the *Glamis* dispute.[63] The case was initiated by a Canadian mining company, investing in the United States, claiming that the mandatory backfilling requirements adopted by California violated its right of FET and of protection from 'expropriation without compensation', under chapter 11 of the North American Free Trade Agreement (NAFTA).[64] Indigenous communities inhabiting the surrounding areas were affected by the investment project.

Although the United States remained silent on the relation between NAFTA chapter 11 and Indigenous rights, representatives from the Quechan Indian Nation situated the dispute within a wider juridical context including the international legal framework for the protection of Indigenous cultural heritage rights.[65] They argued that the tribunal ought to 'be guided by' Indigenous people's norms when interpreting investors' rights to avoid an 'arbitrary and discriminatory decision' that would violate 'international law'.[66] They employed the flexible interface norm of 'taking into account', expressed in article 31(3)(c) of the Vienna Convention on the Law of Treaties (VCLT), through which they weaved together article 1105 (minimum standard of treatment), article 1110 (compensation for expropriation) of NAFTA and the rights of Indigenous people. They also referred to the need of ensuring consistency with 'public international law' within which they situated the multiple legalities. Yet the tribunal's interpretation of its mandate had the effect of narrowing down the relevant laws at play, thereby creating distance from other bodies of norms.[67] Based on the understanding that its task was to undertake a 'case-specific arbitration with awareness of the NAFTA

[63] *Glamis Gold, Ltd.* v. *United States of America*, ICSID, Award, 8 June 2009.

[64] Ibid., para. 353.

[65] *Glamis Gold, Ltd.* v. *United States of America*, ICSID, Non-party supplemental submission of the Quechan Indian Nation, 16 October 2006.

[66] *Glamis Gold, Ltd.* v. *United States of America*, ICSID, Non-party supplemental submission.

[67] On the implications of this interpretative practice for the construction of relations with human rights norms, see Hirsch, *Invitation to the Sociology*, p. 148.

Chapter 11 system',[68] the tribunal refused to 'decide many of the most controversial issues raised in this proceeding'[69] and therefore did not consider the multiplicity of laws that the Quechan people invoked. Eventually, the tribunal dismissed the claims of the investor but also disregarded the claims by the Quechan people by placing emphasis on its 'case-specific mandate' and on the 'issues presented' by the parties to the dispute.[70] The interpretation of investment treaty standards in the 'context' of human rights norms was on display in the *Suez* case,[71] in which foreign investors brought claims against Argentina under three BITs.[72] In this case, investors' rights to 'full protection and security' and 'fair and equitable treatment' were pitched against Argentina's human rights obligations. While the investors deemed human rights 'irrelevant' to the determination of whether the obligations under the BITs had been breached,[73] five NGOs brought the right to water and to life to bear in the definition of the 'applicable law' for the 'proper adjudication of the dispute' and for the 'proper application' of fair and equitable treatment and indirect expropriation.[74] They maintained that the case involved a conflict between the state's duty to protect the right to water and its obligations to the investor[75] and that the former norm prevailed over the latter.[76] They ordered the conflicting norms by invoking the requirement 'not to interpret certain rules in isolation from other parts of the legal order'.[77] According to the NGOs, the interpretation of the BIT had to take human rights law 'into account'. Similarly, Argentina framed human rights law as the 'context' in which the BIT standards had to be interpreted.[78] The tribunal's determination of the relative weight of the bodies

[68] *Glamis Gold, Ltd.*, Award, para. 3.

[69] Ibid., para. 8.

[70] Ibid., para. 8.

[71] *Suez, Sociedad General de Aguas de Barcelona S.A., and Vivendi Universal S.A.* v. *The Argentine Republic*, ICSID Case No. ARB/03/19, Decision on Liability, 30 July 2010.

[72] These were the Argentine–France BIT, the Argentine–Spain BIT and the Argentine–UK BIT.

[73] *Suez*, Decision on Liability, para. 255.

[74] Centro de Estudios Legales y Sociales ('CELS') et al., '*Amicus Curiae* Submission in ICSID Case No. ARB/03/19' (2007).

[75] On the background of the dispute see J. Calvert, 'Civil Society and Investor–State Dispute Settlement: Assessing the Social Dimensions of Investment Disputes in Latin America' (2018) 23 *New Political Economy* 46–65.

[76] Centro de Estudios Legales y Sociales ('CELS') et al., '*Amicus Curiae*'.

[77] On this requirement as a type of overarching norm, see Chapter 1.

[78] '[I]n order to judge whether a treaty provision has been violated, for example the provision on fair and equitable treatment', the 'Tribunal must take account of the context

of norms at play was different from that of Argentina and the NGO. In contrast to the *Glamis* tribunal, which had chosen to ignore the multiplicity of laws, the *Suez* tribunal interpreted them as separate layers moving in parallel directions and simultaneously applicable to the factual circumstances of the case.[79] As a result, it insisted on keeping a great distance between bodies of norms, which it perceived as separate and independent legal units. This particular way of ordering bodies of norms may indeed be read as a 'general reluctance [. . .] to openly decide potential conflicts between investment protection and public policy objectives'.[80]

7.3.4 *Taking into Account*

A selected integrationist perspective on the relation between investment treaty norms and human rights was articulated in the *Al-Warraq* case.[81] The dispute originated from criminal proceedings *in absentia* by Indonesian authorities against an investor from Saudi Arabia holding shares in an Indonesian bank. The investor brought claims against Indonesia under a multilateral investment treaty (OIC Agreement)[82] and used international human rights law to interpret its provisions. Drawing on the 'principle of systematic integration of international law norms',[83] the investor brought the right to a fair trial under article 14(2) of the International Covenant on Civil and Political Rights (ICCPR), the UN Human Rights Committee's General Comment 13, regional human rights institutions' pronouncements on 'presumption of innocence',[84] the

in which Argentina acted and that the human right to water informs that context'. See *Suez*, Decision on Liability, para. 252.

79 '[A]rgentina is subject to both international obligations, *i.e.* human rights *and* treaty obligation, and must respect both of them equally'. *Suez*, Decision on Liability, para. 262.

80 J. E. Viñuales, *Foreign Investment and the Environment in International Law* (Cambridge University Press, 2012), p. 155.

81 *Hesham T. M. Al Warraq* v. *Republic of Indonesia*, ICSID, Award, 15 December 2014. For a commentary, see L. Cotula, 'Human Rights and Investor Obligations in Investor-State Arbitration: Hesham Talaat M. Al-Warraq v The Republic of Indonesia, UNCITRAL Arbitration, Final Award, 15 December 2014 (Bernardo M. Cremades, Michael Hwang, Fali S. Nariman)' (2016) 17 *The Journal of World Investment & Trade* 148–57.

82 Agreement for the Promotion, Protection and Guarantee of Investment among Member States of The Organization of the Islamic Conference.

83 *Al-Warraq*, Award, para. 519.

84 The European Convention on Human Rights (ECHR), the African Commission on Human and People's Rights and the Inter-American Court of Human Rights.

'basic rights' and the fair and equitable treatment standard under the OIC Agreement into relation.[85]

The tribunal concurred with the investor that certain civil and political rights were part of investment protection norms, but it distanced the notion of 'basic rights' under the OIC Agreement from human rights norms by highlighting the particular 'object and purpose' of the former (i.e. investment promotion and protection).[86] However, the tribunal construed greater proximity between the FET standard and the norm against 'denial of justice' under various human rights instruments, in particular article 14(3) of the ICCPR. Eventually, the tribunal decided that 'denial of justice constitutes a clear violation of the FET standard'.[87] The tribunal brought ICCPR norms and the FET standard in relation after claiming that 'the ICCPR is now regarded as a part of "general international law"', which suggests that 'general international law' was used as an 'overarching norm' to connect ICCPR norms to the investment legal order.[88] The *Urbaser* dispute[89] between foreign investors and Argentina, related to a concession for water and sewage services under the terms of the Spain–Argentina BIT, partly redefined the openness of ISDS to human rights. The question of the relation between international investment agreements and human rights emerged in the context of a counterclaim by Argentina seeking compensation for damages from the investor, which affected basic human rights.[90] In contrast to the *Suez* dispute, investors did not consider human rights 'irrelevant' but distanced them through interpretive practices. The investors claimed that human rights were duties of the state rather than of private companies and said that Argentina was under the 'obligations regarding the population's right to water, and its obligations towards international investors', which ought to be fulfilled 'simultaneously',[91] reflecting the approach of the *CMS* and *Suez* awards. The investors also drew on the precedent of the *Biloune* v. *Ghana* dispute, in which the tribunal decided that 'a ruling on human rights violations is outside the scope of its

[85] *Al-Warraq*, Award, paras 177–82.
[86] Ibid., paras 519–22.
[87] Ibid., para. 621.
[88] On this type of interface norm, see Chapter 1. For a similar observation in the context of international trade law, see Chapter 8.
[89] *Urbaser S.A. and Consorcio de Aguas Bilbao Bizkaia, Bilbao Biskaia Ur Partzuergoa* v. *The Argentine Republic,* ICSID Case No. ARB/07/26, Award, 8 December 2016.
[90] Ibid., para. 1156.
[91] Ibid., para. 694.

jurisdiction'.[92] While the investors emphasized the BIT, claiming that its 'provisions, principles and rights' were 'essential to resolve the dispute', Argentina maintained that the 'applicable law' consisted of the 'BIT, Argentine law and general international law' and that they ought to be applied 'jointly and harmoniously'.[93] According to Argentina, the BIT was not 'a set of self-contained rules' and therefore 'international law in general' had to be applied, including 'imperative international law', which trumped standards of investment protection.[94] The *Urbaser* tribunal responded to this situation of multiplicity by situating the legalities at play within an overarching structure. It found that 'the BIT does not represent, in the view of the Contracting Parties and its clear text, a set of rules defined in isolation without consideration given to rules of international law external to its own rules'.[95] Drawing on the *Tulip* annulment decision,[96] the tribunal listed various international human rights instruments followed by article 31(3)(c) of the VCLT and decided that 'the BIT cannot be interpreted and applied in a vacuum' and that, while it ought to be 'mindful of the BIT's special purpose as a Treaty promoting foreign investments', 'it cannot do so without taking the relevant rules of international law into account. The BIT has to be construed in harmony with other rules of international law of which it forms part, including those relating to human rights'.[97] Reliance on 'overarching norms', which the tribunal implicitly construed by interpreting the provisions on applicable

[92] '[W]hile the acts alleged to violate the international human rights of Mr Biloune may be relevant in considering the investment dispute under arbitration, this Tribunal lacks jurisdiction to address, as an independent cause of action, a claim of violation of human rights'. *Antoine Biloune and Marine Drive Complex Ltd.* v. *Ghana Investment Centre and the Government of Ghana*, Awards of 27 October 1989 and 30 June 1990, Yearbook Commercial Arbitration XIX (1994) p.11 (CUL-207). Cited in *Urbaser.*, Award, para. 1129.

[93] *Urbaser.*, Award, para. 548.

[94] Ibid., para. 555.

[95] Ibid., para. 1192.

[96] In the *Tulip* case, the investor invoked art. 6 of the ECHR on the right to a fair trial. Turkey, the respondent state, argued that the invoked provision was irrelevant in the context of the dispute as the ECHR and the ICSID Convention belonged to two 'different regimes'. In the view of the Annulment Committee, human rights were relevant and 'shall be taken into account' in light of Article 31(3)(c) of the 'VCLT'. *Tulip Real Estate and Development Netherlands B.V.* v. *Republic of Turkey*, ICSID Case no. ARB/11/28, Decisions on Annulment, 30 December 2015, paras 86–92, where the ad hoc Committee refers to the 'principle of systemic integration', stating that resort to authorities stemming from the field of human rights is a 'legitimate method of treaty interpretation'.

[97] *Urbaser*, Award, para. 1200.

law under article X(5) of the BIT and article 42 of ICSID Convention, enabled the tribunal to place the BIT in 'the overall system of international law'.[98] Conflicting statements about the relation between international investment and human rights norms were brought forward in the *Bear Creek* dispute,[99] involving claims by a Canadian mining company investing in a mining project in Peru under the investment chapter of the Canada–Peru Free Trade Agreement (FTA). The investment project generated acute protests by affected Indigenous communities, including the Aymara population, inhabiting the surrounding area and demanding respect for their human rights. With regard to the applicable law to the dispute, the investor and the state focused on the FTA and applicable rules of international law.[100] However, two civil society organizations presented a description of the facts and of the law which highlighted connections between the Aymara population's Indigenous rights and the FTA provisions.[101] The two organizations argued that Indigenous rights had to be taken into account when interpreting the FTA.[102] In his dissenting opinion, co-arbitrator Sands drew on the *Urbaser* award to argue that consultation requirements in article 15 of the International Labour Organization (ILO) Convention 169 were part of the 'applicable rules of international law' which the tribunal could 'take into account'.[103] By failing to carry out its obligations vis-à-vis the Aymara peoples' 'rights under international law', the investor contributed to the demise of the investment. Consequently, the amount of damages to be awarded was to be reduced by half.[104] Although co-arbitrator Sands' dissenting opinion in *Bear Creek* and the award in *Urbaser* placed a different degree of emphasis on human rights,[105]

[98] Ibid., para. 1201.

[99] *Bear Creek Mining Corporation* v. *Republic of Peru*, ICSID Case No. ARB/14/2, Award, 30 November 2017.

[100] Ibid., paras 267–9.

[101] The two organizations were the Association of Human Rights and the Environment-Puno together with Mr. Carlos Lopez, and the Columbia Center on Sustainable Investment (CCSI). Eventually, only the former organization was allowed to participate as 'other persons' under the FTA whereas the latter's application was rejected by the tribunal.

[102] The CCSI placed strong emphasis on legal relationships and on the relevance of the legal context to the interpretation of the FTA. See CCSI, 'Application to File a Written Submission as an "Other Person" Pursuant to Article 836 and Annex 836'.

[103] *Bear Creek Mining Corporation* v. *Republic of Peru*, ICSID Case No. ARB/14/2, Partial Dissenting Opinion of Professor P. Sands, 30 November 2017, at 11.

[104] Ibid., pp. 38–40.

[105] I am indebted to Tomáš Morochovič for this observation.

both statements strengthened the expectation that international investment agreements cannot be interpreted in isolation from other parts of the legal order.[106] Claims about the primacy of human rights over investment protection norms were formulated by the state in the *South American Silver* dispute, related to an investment in mining activities in Bolivia under the terms of the United Kingdom–Bolivia BIT. The dispute stemmed from measures adopted by Bolivia to protect Indigenous communities inhabiting the areas surrounding the investment project. The parties to the dispute disagreed over the relation between the BIT and international law and between the BIT and the Bolivian national legal system. The investor deemed the BIT to be the 'primary source of law and *lex specialis*, as supplemented by general principles of law, as needed'.[107] It distanced domestic law, arguing that it did not form part of the 'law applicable to the merits of the arbitration proceeding'[108] and contended that recourse to supplementary means to interpret the BIT was 'unnecessary'.[109] By contrast, Bolivia demanded that a wider body of norms be taken 'in consideration' when interpreting the applicable law.[110] The state said that its constitution and international norms on the protection of Indigenous rights[111] were 'supplementary' to the BIT and prevailed over norms in investment treaties in case of conflict.[112] The investor contested this representation, arguing that the invoked rights could not be taken into consideration by the tribunal since they were not binding on the United Kingdom and did not constitute customary international law or general principles of law.[113] Having identified the BIT as 'the principal instrument'[114] for resolving the dispute, the tribunal found that the tool of 'systemic interpretation' under article 31(3)(c) of the VCLT is not limitless and must be applied

[106] On this type of overarching norm, see Chapter 1.

[107] *South American Silver Limited* v. *Plurinational State of Bolivia*, PCA Case No. 2013-15, Award, 22 November 2018, para. 187.

[108] Ibid., para.193.

[109] Ibid., para. 261.

[110] Ibid., para. 200.

[111] Bolivia referred to the 1969 American Convention on Human Rights, the 1994 Inter-American Convention on the Prevention, Punishment and Eradication of Violence against Women, ILO Convention No.169, the 2007 United Nations Declaration on the Rights of Indigenous Peoples and the Political Constitution of the Plurinational State of Bolivia. Ibid., para. 199.

[112] Ibid., para. 196.

[113] Ibid., para. 190.

[114] Ibid., para. 208.

with caution.[115] According to the tribunal, 'this principle must be applied in harmony with the rest of the provisions of the same article and cautiously, in order to prevent the tribunal from exceeding its jurisdiction and applying rules to the dispute which the Parties have not agreed to'.[116] Eventually, the tribunal concluded that Bolivia had to pay compensation and compound interests to the investor but dismissed all other claims of the investor.

7.3.5 *Constrained Entanglements*

The previous analysis of ISDS cases suggests that strategic, institutional and cultural factors impacted the way actors brought international investment law and 'other' legalities in relation. In a context with high institutional barriers to access and with an unequal representation of the interests involved, certain claims were accorded greater weight than other, competing ones. In particular, investment arbitrators and lawyers representing investors and states played a dominant role, whereas the voice of other affected polities was silenced.

The 'tension between proximity and distance'[117] in investment treaty disputes was shaped by the interplay of a limited number of actors. Understandably, with the exception of the *Al-Warraq* dispute, investors had clear incentives to keep human rights law at bay in investment disputes. By contrast, states had stronger incentives to draw on that law to formulate their defences. Non-disputing parties and actors not represented in ISDS – workers, Indigenous groups, poor communities – had limited access to inform investment arbitrators' decisions. In the *Bear Creek* dispute, arbitrators denied a request for participation as *amicus curiae* by one academic institution, showing little consideration for actors other than the parties to the dispute, including disputes generating 'public interest'.[118]

As a consequence, entangled legalities in ISDS have mainly reflected the preferences of foreign investors, states and investment arbitrators. From this perspective, greater participation from affected outsiders[119]

115 Ibid., para. 212.

116 Ibid., para. 216.

117 See Chapter 1, Section 1.4.

118 Langford and Behn, 'Managing Backlash'.

119 E. Benvenisti, 'Democracy Captured: The Mega-Regional Agreements and the Future of Global Public Law' (2016) 23 *Constellations: An International Journal of Critical and Democratic Theory* 58–70.

may lead to a greater variety of claims and forms of relation than the status quo allows. Yet this is unlikely to lead to entanglements that would be independent from the institutional and ideational structures of investment arbitration – enhanced participation would still operate within structural constraints.

Indeed, the analysis of ISDS cases has also shown that the multiplicity of laws was framed from the perspective of the dominant interpretive and legal frames of reference in the investment arbitration context and in conformity with the interface norms recognized within the ISDS 'community of practice'.[120] In particular, investment tribunals approached multiplicity from the standpoint of international investment law by relying on the principle of 'systemic integration' in article 31(3)(c) of the VCLT.[121] This principle was used to tie bodies of formal international law that were recognized by actors as the relevant law. Through this integrating principle of treaty interpretation, lawyers and arbitrators connected international investment and human rights norms by situating them within the 'system' of general international law as opposed to framing them as two separate legal systems[122] and ordering them through 'reception norms'.[123] The dominant structures of relation observed reflect the institutional background in which ISDS lawyers have been trained and work.[124] ISDS professionals' mindsets and the 'discursive policies'[125] in which they are situated may contribute to explaining the particular modes of ordering multiplicity in ISDS. These situated jurists seem to share a particular 'way of thinking' about the law of foreign investment arbitration, which shapes the way they practice it in relation to 'foreign' legalities.[126] These actors operate in a professional

[120] Brunnée and Toope, 'Interactional International Law'.

[121] J. Alvarez, '"Beware: Boundary Crossings" – A Critical Appraisal of Public Law Approaches to International Investment Law' (2016) 17 *The Journal of World Investment & Trade* 171–228.

[122] R. Michaels and J. Pauwelyn, 'Conflict of Norms or Conflict of Laws: Different Techniques in the Fragmentation of Public International Law' (2012) 22 *Duke Journal of Comparative & International Law* 349–76.

[123] On reception norms, see Chapter 1; Michaels and Pauwelyn, 'Conflict of Norms or Conflict of Laws'.

[124] On the institutional context of ICSID, see Pauwelyn, 'The Rule of Law'. On the 'investment arbitration culture', see Hirsch, 'The Sociological Dimension'.

[125] Bianchi, 'Epistemic Communities', 588.

[126] On how different ways of thinking about law impact legal practice, see A. Bianchi, *International Law Theories: An Inquiry into Different Ways of Thinking* (Oxford University Press, 2016). On the implications of actors' situatedness for the construction of entanglements, see Chapter 1.

environment that does not create strong incentives to question the dominant schemes for thinking and practising law, much less to depart from them. For example, these specialists have to behave in conformity with the rules of the game of the institutional site in which they operate[127] in order to pursue or maintain reputation.[128] These rules include shared presuppositions about the nature of 'international investment law', its 'sources', institutional circumstances and the 'rituals'[129] of international arbitration. According to the recognized norms of investment arbitration, the rules on jurisdiction, applicable laws and consent of the parties have narrowed the space for linking bodies of norms in practice.[130] For example, the doctrine of the limitation of tribunals' jurisdiction[131] to 'investment disputes' has enabled adjudicators to create distance between bodies of norms and strengthen the autonomy of their legal order from the interference of competing legalities. Similarly, international investment lawyers perceive that there must be 'legal grounds' for tribunals to consider human rights norms.[132] ISDS insiders may benefit from the dominant mode of ordering legalities in this setting – therefore there seem to be fewer incentives to change the status quo than to maintain it.

In summary, the dominant interests, institutional structures and 'legal culture'[133] in ISDS seem to have influenced the way situated actors have ordered multiplicity in that setting. However, ultimate conclusions on the implications of actors' ideational context and strategic interests for the particular forms of enmeshment observed seem premature. For example, it is not clear whether investment arbitrators' background had more influence than the material incentives associated with the international investment dispute settlement culture.[134] Not only did arbitrators with expertise in public international law decide in favour of foreign investors in some cases, they also kept investment protection and human rights

[127] Pauwelyn, 'The Rule of Law'.
[128] Schultz, 'Arbitral Decision-Making'.
[129] Gaillard, 'Sociology of International Arbitration'.
[130] On these rules, see Sornarajah, *The International Law*.
[131] F. Balcerzak, 'Jurisdiction of Tribunals in Investor–State Arbitration and the Issue of Human Rights' (2014) 29 *ICSID Review* 216–30.
[132] F. G. Santacroce, 'The Applicability of Human Rights Law in International Investment Disputes' (2019) 34 *ICSID Review – Foreign Investment Law Journal* 136–55.
[133] Hirsch, *Invitation to the Sociology*, p. 146.
[134] R. Howse, 'Venus, Mars, and Brussels: Legitimacy and Dispute Settlement Culture in Investment Law and WTO Law: A Response to Joost Pauwelyn' (2015) 109 *AJIL Unbound* 309–15.

norms at a great distance from each other, against our expectations.[135] This finding suggests that arbitrators' proficiency in public international law and human rights law would not automatically translate into an outcome where the distance between bodies of norms is reduced, as other factors may be simultaneously at play. For example, arbitrators' interests, including reappointment as arbitrator, may have had greater impact in shaping arbitrators' decision-making. They may have created proximity or distance between bodies of norms to pursue their own goals. In this respect, the potentially 'addictive'[136] practice of investment arbitration and the high financial stakes involved in it may have played a greater role than, or at least interplayed with, the legal background of its participants in the formation of relations between bodies of norms. From this perspective, to 'properly train' the future operators of ISDS[137] may indeed be necessary but perhaps not enough.

7.4 Entangled Legalities at the Margins

7.4.1 Beyond ISDS

Thus far, I have contextualized interpretative practices through which international investment and human rights norms have been brought in relation in investment adjudication settings. The statements of investment arbitrators and of the lawyers representing foreign investors and states have been given greater weight than those of other stakeholders, partly due to the dominant interests and ideational context of investment treaty arbitration. Civil society input has remained limited and only a few legal specialists have been authorized to determine the relative weight of legalities at play at that site. Yet ISDS is not, and should not be, the only global governance site for determining relations between these legalities. Rather, the claims of institutions and affected actors 'at the margins' of that context and its discourse should also be accounted for when appraising the enmeshment of the overall order. Against the background of the so-called 'legitimacy crisis' of international investment law,[138] expressions of contestation have encouraged a reform of investment agreements

[135] For example, in the *CMS* dispute.
[136] Howse, 'Venus, Mars, and Brussels'.
[137] J. Viñuales, 'Foreign Investment and the Environment in International Law: Current Trends', in K. Miles (ed.), *Research Handbook on Environment and Investment Law* (Edward Elgar, 2019), pp. 12–37.
[138] Langford and Behn, 'Managing Backlash', 554–8.

and investment dispute settlement. The reform process could pave the way for greater civil society input than the status quo allows, thereby creating room for closer proximity with other legalities. In this context, struggles for change within and from international investment law are situated at multiple sites and involve different actors with competing interests and approaches to reform.

7.4.2 Reforming Investment Agreements

At sites of treaty negotiation, states have responded to the legitimacy crisis of international investment law by rearticulating their relation with it through different lawmaking practices. While countries like Ecuador, Venezuela, Argentina and Bolivia have withdrawn or intended to withdraw from the ICSID Convention and BITs, others have amended existing investment treaties.[139] The wording of these texts indicates that state parties have given human rights some consideration.[140] Similar references have appeared in 'new generation international investment agreements', originally championed by the United States and Canada and subsequently adopted by the EU.[141] The concept of 'governments' right to regulate', included in the 2017 Colombia model BIT as well as in the 2019 Dutch Model BIT,[142] has opened a space to construe connections with states' obligations under international human rights law.[143]

139 M. Langford, D. Behn and O. Fauchald, 'Backlash and State Strategies in International Investment Law', in T. Aalberts and T. Gammeltoft-Hansen (eds), *The Changing Practices of International Law* (Cambridge University Press, 2018), pp. 70–102.

140 The 2012 US Model BIT mentions in a relatively open-ended way the interface between 'investment and the environment' (art. 12) and 'investment and labor' (art. 13); the New Zealand–Australia BIT, refers to the Treaty of Waitangi; the 2015 Norwegian Model BIT refers to the Universal Declaration of Human Rights; the 2016 BIT between Morocco and Nigeria imposes human rights obligations on investors too (art. 18). N. Zugliani, 'Human Rights in International Investment Law: The 2016 Morocco–Nigeria Bilateral Investment Treaty' (2019) 68 *International and Comparative Law Quarterly* 761–70.

141 C. Titi, 'International Investment Law and the European Union: Towards a New Generation of International Investment Agreements' (2015) 26 *European Journal of International Law* 639–61.

142 Article 7(5) states: '[t]he Contracting Parties express their commitment to the international framework on Business and Human Rights, such as the United Nations Guiding Principles on Business and Human Rights and the OECD Guidelines for Multinational Enterprises, and commit to strengthen this framework'. For a commentary, see K. Duggal and L. van de Ven, 'The 2019 Netherlands Model BIT: Riding the New Investment Treaty Waves' (2019) 35 *Arbitration International* 343–74.

143 L. W. Mouyal, *International Investment Law and the Right to Regulate: A Human Rights Perspective* (Routledge, 2016).

The Comprehensive Economic Trade Agreement (CETA) between the EU and Canada has brought together investment protection, trade and sustainable development and labour and environmental protection norms, and article 8.9 of its investment protection chapter reaffirms state parties' 'right to regulate'.[144] Similar lawmaking practices, driven in particular by the interests of economically powerful countries, include 'mega-regulation' instruments like the Trans-Pacific Partnership that has incorporated environmental and labour norms, perhaps to address demands by civil society actors concerned with the impact of ISDS on social and environmental protection within domestic legal systems.[145] Therefore, processes of investment treaty negotiations, especially if transparent and open to the participation of affected stakeholders,[146] are potentially effective arenas for reshaping entanglements through textual references.

Yet, we should not read too much into these references as they tell us little about how relations with other, competing polities and their legal orders ought to be ordered.[147] On the one hand, their relationship remains formally open and its shape will be determined only through political processes and the practice of societal actors. On the other hand, those references do not reflect the more contestatory claims of actors who challenge the very existence of international investment protection. While those provisions may enable linkages with 'community interests',[148] it remains to be seen how the relevant decision-makers will weigh bodies of norms in practice. Under current structural circumstances in ISDS,

[144] Joint Interpretative Instrument on the Comprehensive Economic and Trade Agreement (CETA) between Canada and the European Union and Its Member States, 2017.

[145] E. Meidinger, 'TPP and Environmental Regulation', in B. Kingsbury et al. (eds), *Megaregulation Contested* (Oxford University Press, 2019), pp. 175–95.

[146] Benvenisti, 'Democracy Captured'.

[147] Similarly, references to international investment law in human rights instruments provide little guidance in this respect. Principle 9 of the UN Guiding Principles on Business and Human Rights expects state parties to investment agreements to 'maintain adequate domestic policy space to meet their human rights obligations'. The Commentary to this article is not very helpful either in its explanation that: 'States should ensure that they retain adequate policy and regulatory ability to protect human rights under the terms of such agreements, while providing the necessary investor protection.' OHCHR, 'Guiding Principles on Business and Human Rights: Implementing the United Nations "Protect, Respect and Remedy" Framework' (United Nations, 2011).

[148] S. Schill and V. Djanic, 'International Investment Law and Community Interests', in E. Benvenisti and G. Nolte (eds), *Community Interests Across International Law* (Oxford University Press, 2018), pp. 122–48.

characterized by a substantial preference for 'stronger rather than weaker investor protection'[149] and under-inclusiveness of relevant actors, a concrete change from dominant ways of dealing with multiplicity seems unlikely. Future practice might tell us more about the interface norms at play, and much is likely to depend on who the actors construing them will be. However, efforts at rewriting investment treaties may be seen as attempts to respond to growing voices of contestation stemming from other sites in the overall order.

7.4.3 Human Rights Claims

Similarly to the main type of interface norms construed in investment adjudication contexts, human rights experts have approached investment protection norms through overarching norms, which might be explained by taking account of the ideational and institutional context in which they operate. For example, in the *Sawhoyamaxa* case,[150] involving a dispute over human rights of Indigenous communities in Paraguay, the Inter-American Court of Human Rights articulated its view of the relationship between international investment law and the Inter-American Convention on Human Rights. Paraguay sought to justify non-enforcement of the Indigenous people's property rights by arguing that the land, which had been bought by a German investor, was protected under an investment treaty between Paraguay and Germany.[151] Yet the court regarded the Inter-American Convention as the ultimate frame of reference and accorded it more weight than investment agreements. It ruled that 'the enforcement of bilateral commercial treaties [...] should always be compatible with the American Convention, which is a multilateral treaty on human rights that stands in a class of its own and that generates rights for individual human beings and does not depend entirely on reciprocity among States'.[152] Under the presidency of Judge

149 Mattias Kumm has argued that one general presupposition of these actors is to favour 'stronger, rather than weaker investor protection'. See 'An Empire of Capital? Transatlantic Investment Protection as the Institutionalization of Unjustified Privilege', Verfassungsblog (27 May 2015), https://verfassungsblog.de/an-empire-of-capital-transatlantic-investment-protection-as-the-institutionalization-of-unjustified-privilege/.

150 *Sawhoyamaxa Indigenous Community* v. *Paraguay*, Judgment (Merits, Reparations and Costs), 29 March 2006.

151 Ibid., para. 115.

152 Ibid., para. 140.

Cançado Trindade, the court's interpretation reflected a strong commitment to human rights law.

Similarly, the Office of the United Nations High Commissioner for Human Rights (OHCHR) has approached investment agreements through 'overarching norms', reflecting a conception of order under international law where human rights are accorded primacy.[153] For example, the former independent expert on the promotion of a democratic and equitable international order has claimed that 'in case of conflict, only the highest public courts can decide in the light of the totality of international law. Until amended by States Members, the Charter of the United Nations remains the principal treaty that determines the structure and functioning of the international order.'[154] Therefore '[s]tates must ensure that all trade and investment agreements recognize the primacy of human rights and specify that, in case of conflict, human rights obligations prevail'.[155] In the eyes of the independent expert, international investment norms and human rights were to be integrated within a hierarchical form ordered through the principle of binding character of treaties, good faith and in conformity with article 103 of the United Nations Charter.[156]

In its General Comment 24, the UN Committee on Economic, Social and Cultural Rights articulated a similar hierarchical conception of order between competing legalities.[157] The Committee claimed that: '[s]tates parties should identify any potential conflict between their obligations under the Covenant and under trade or investment treaties, and refrain from entering into such treaties where such conflicts are found to exist, as required under the principle of the binding character of treaties'.[158] The group of experts distinguished 'investment treaties currently in force' from 'future treaties'. In the first case, interpretation 'should take into

[153] See Chapter 1.

[154] OHCHR, 'Report of the Independent Expert on the Promotion of a Democratic and Equitable International Order, Alfred-Maurice de Zayas' (2015) UN Doc. A/HRC/30/44.

[155] OHCHR, 'Report of the Independent Expert', 20.

[156] '[P]acta *sunt servanda* requires States to fulfil their human rights treaty obligations in good faith and prohibits them from entering into agreements that would delay, circumvent, undermine or make impossible the fulfilment of their human rights treaty obligations'. OHCHR, 'Report of the Independent Expert', para. 18.

[157] Committee on Economic, Social and Cultural Rights (CESCR), 'General Comment No. 24 (2017) on State Obligations under the International Covenant on Economic, Social and Cultural Rights in the Context of Business Activities' (2017), UN Doc E/C.12/GC/24.

[158] CESCR, 'General Comment No. 24'.

account the human rights obligations of the state, consistent with Article 103 of the Charter of the United Nations and with the specific nature of human rights obligations'.[159] In the second case, '[states parties] are encouraged to insert, in future treaties, a provision explicitly referring to their human rights obligations, and to ensure that mechanisms for the settlement of investor–state disputes take human rights into account in the interpretation of investment treaties or of investment chapters in trade agreements'.[160] The Committee's stance towards the investment protection suborder reproduced the Inter-American Court of Human Rights' approach discussed in Section 7.4.3.

Over time, human rights specialists have combined 'overarching norms' with less imposing practices aimed at persuading states to take account of their human rights obligations when making new investment agreements. One example is the 2018 initiative 'Crowd-Drafting: Designing a Human Rights-Compatible International Investment Agreement'.[161] Its promoters referred to a 'human rights-based approach' to international investment treaty-making.[162] Attempts at crafting a 'human rights impact assessment' norm, addressed both at states parties to international investment agreements[163] as well as companies as part of their due diligence obligations, fall within these accommodation strategies.[164] The United Nations Conference on Trade and Development's (UNCTAD) initiatives to investment law reform have adopted a similar approach, seeking to promote greater convergence with human rights and sustainable development norms, as exemplified by the UNCTAD's Investment Policy Framework for Sustainable Development.[165] Most recently, overarching norms seem to

159 Ibid.

160 Ibid.

161 See www.ohchr.org/Documents/Issues/Business/Forum2018CrowdDrafting.pdf.

162 '[A] human rights-based approach to trade and investment entails considering how States' obligations under trade/investment law agreements might impact on their ability to fulfil their human rights obligations', see further at: www.ohchr.org/EN/Issues/Globalization/Pages/GlobalizationIndex.aspx.

163 UNHRC, 'Report of the Special Rapporteur on the Right to Food, Olivier De Schutter. Addendum, Guiding Principles on Human Rights Impact Assessments of Trade and Investment Agreements' (2011) UN Doc. A/HRC/19/59/Add.5.

164 Columbia Center on Sustainable Development and OHCHR, 'Impacts of the International Investment Regime on Access to Justice' (Roundtable outcome document, September 2018).

165 P. Muchlinski, 'Negotiating New Generation International Investment Agreements: New Sustainable Development Oriented Initiatives', in S. Hindelang and M. Krajewski (eds), *Shifting Paradigms in International Investment Law* (Oxford University Press, 2016), pp. 41–64.

have informed the ongoing struggle for a new international 'instrument' on global business and human rights, as reflected in particular in article 14 of its second revised draft, which demands that investment agreements be consistent 'with international law principles and instruments'.[166]

7.4.4 *Reforming Investment Adjudication*

The effects of entangled legalities have often been located in the Global South, in places where foreign investments affect local communities. At these sites, often characterized by a multilayered and scattered legal landscape where transnational and domestic bodies of norms contradict each other,[167] local populations have mobilized human rights against the state and global capital.[168] Local communities have contested the proximity of investment protection norms to their domestic legal order,[169] but their claims have received little consideration in investment jurisprudence.[170] In recent years, struggles against investment protection have become visible in the Global North, too. Particularly in Europe, citizens, environmental activists and other political actors have used contestatory mechanisms to distance investment treaties from their domestic legal orders. Protests and claims of political parties and NGOs against the intrusion of the Transatlantic Trade and Investment Partnership (TTIP), CETA and the ISDS norm into the European legal order and the constitutional order of EU member states have been one manifestation of this practice of resistance.[171] In this context, European institutions and courts, too, have become important actors. The European Commission's

[166] OEIGWG Chairmanship 'Second Revised Draft, Legally Binding Instrument'.

[167] S. Randeria, 'The State of Globalization: Legal Plurality, Overlapping Sovereignties and Ambiguous Alliances between Civil Society and the Cunning State in India' (2007) 24 *Theory, Culture & Society* 1–33.

[168] B. Rajagopal, 'The Role of Law in Counter-Hegemonic Globalization and Global Legal Pluralism: Lessons from the Narmada Valley Struggle in India' (2005) 18 *Leiden Journal of International Law* 345–87.

[169] B. Rajagopal, 'Counter-Hegemonic International Law: Rethinking Human Rights and Development as a Third World Strategy' (2006) 27 *Third World Quarterly* 767–83.

[170] There have been calls to give more attention to these 'invisible' actors. See N. Perrone, 'The "Invisible" Local Communities: Foreign Investor Obligations, Inclusiveness, and the International Investment Regime' (2019) 113 *AJIL Unbound* 16–21.

[171] J. Rone, 'Contested International Agreements, Contested National Politics: How the Radical Left and the Radical Right Opposed TTIP in Four European Countries' (2018) 6 *London Review of International Law* 233–53. See also M. Kumm, 'An Empire of Capital?'; Legal Statement on Investment Protection and Investor–State Dispute Settlement Mechanisms in TTIP and CETA, 2016.

proposal to replace ISDS with a multilateral investment court might open a space for a wider number of actors to create different forms of relations with human rights.[172] The Court of Justice of the European Union (CJEU) has recently shown a sign of resistance to investor–state arbitration by ruling that the ISDS provision in BITs between EU member states is 'not compatible' with EU law.[173] By contrast, in its recent 'CETA Opinion', the CJEU has shown more openness to the prospect of an investment court system.[174]

In the context of ISDS reform, currently under the auspices of UNCITRAL Working Group III, the debate has focused on procedural and institutional design issues rather than on questions about the relations between investment protection and other substantive norms.[175] However, some states and international institutions have emphasized connections with human rights, too. For example, in a letter addressed to participants in the ISDS reform process, human rights experts have highlighted that international investment agreements are often incompatible with international human rights law and the rule of law.[176] They called for a 'fundamental systemic change' of ISDS, beyond procedural reform, and towards a 'multilateral system' that 'takes into account the rights and obligations of investors and states, in line with all applicable international laws and standards concerning human rights'.[177] They also claimed that greater proximity to human rights and the Sustainable Development Goals would enhance the legitimacy and effectiveness of

[172] Robert Howse has concluded that 'a multilateral court system is best suited to offering standing or intervention to a wide range of actors who have concerns of international justice that relate to foreign investment'. See R. Howse, 'International Investment Law and Arbitration: A Conceptual Framework' (2017) *IILJ Working Paper 2017/1 MegaReg Series* 69.

[173] The Court ruled that EU law precludes: 'a provision in an international agreement concluded between Member States [. . .] under which an investor from one of those Member States may, in the event of a dispute concerning investments in the other Member State, bring proceedings against the latter Member State before an arbitral tribunal whose jurisdiction that Member State has undertaken to accept'. Judgment in *Slovak Republic* v. *Achmea B.V.* (Case C-284/16).

[174] The Court found that the international investment system is compatible with EU law. See Opinion 1/17 of the Court (Full Court) (*CETA Opinion*), 30 April 2019.

[175] On different states' approaches to ISDS reform, see A. Roberts, 'Incremental, Systemic, and Paradigmatic Reform of Investor–State Arbitration' (2018) 112 *American Journal of International Law* 410–32.

[176] OHCHR, 'Letter to the UNCITRAL Working Group III on ISDS Reform, Urging Systemic Changes to the ISDS System' (7 March 2019).

[177] Ibid.

the UNCITRAL process.[178] The government of South Africa has also strongly advocated to take account of human rights and the principle of sustainable development.[179]

7.5 Conclusion

This chapter has analysed how relations between international investment and human rights norms have been construed in multiple global governance sites. Investment treaty arbitration has remained a central arena where foreign investors, states, investment adjudicators and NGOs have supplied competing forms of relation between bodies of norms, especially when defining the law applicable to the dispute. These relations have reflected the preferences and the ideational context of the actors involved in their construction.

In the majority of cases examined, the claims of investment arbitrators, investors and states have been given greater consideration than the claims by NGOs and the public at large, limiting room for contestation. Foreign investors have sought to narrow the scope of relevant bodies of norms whereas states and NGOs have aimed at expanding it. Over time, ISDS participants, and investment adjudicators in particular, have tended to regard relations with human rights norms with less hesitancy. Although the decisions of investment tribunals affect many constituencies, possibilities for these affected outsiders to make their claims heard in investment arbitration have been limited. Their priorities have often been silenced in sites of investment treaty negotiation too.

The analysis has observed an evolution in the way actors have dealt with human rights in ISDS over time, although dialectic tendencies of proximity and distancing persist. Initially, foreign investors adopted a clear rhetoric against the relevance of human rights in ISDS. In a second phase, they recognized their relevance but they kept them at a distance to downplay any potential conflict with investment protection standards. As states began to refer to human rights norms in their defences, investment tribunals had to find ways to articulate relations with them. The current phase seems marked by a very limited reliance on human rights on the part of investors and tribunals and more frequent linkages construed by

[178] Ibid.

[179] United Nations Commission on International Trade Law et al., 'Possible Reform of Investor–State Dispute Settlement (ISDS) Submission from the Government of South Africa' (2019) UN Doc A/CN.9/WG.III/WP.176.

states and NGOs, thereby creating entanglement on a rhetorical level but one constantly undercut by using other tools to create distance. In most of the cases examined, ISDS participants have used 'overarching norms' to order legal pluralism within international law, which may be explained by reference to the cultural and institutional context of ISDS. However, the dominant use of this 'interface norm' has not led to a new, fully integrated system as considerable contestation persists in other parts of the legal order. Indeed, forms and dynamics of entanglement have become observable in struggles 'at the margins' of and beyond the bounds of ISDS. These forms of contestation have led to a process of reform of international investment agreements and investment adjudication that may create room for shaping new forms of relations with human rights. However, only the future practice of actors will tell us how they will be construed. In the different contexts examined, the practice of taking other norms 'into account' has been one of the main tools for ordering multiplicity, yet without determining the substantive outcome of the practice of giving regard to other bodies of norms. Even when using this interface norm, ISDS participants have had discretion to determine the relative weight of the legalities brought together. Human rights actors have also had recourse to a similar interface norm when articulating their views of the relation with investment agreement, but their vision of legal order differs from the one put forward in the practice of investment arbitration.

8

International Trade Law

Legal Entanglement on the WTO's Own Terms

LUCY LU REIMERS

8.1 Introduction

Ever since the inception of the contemporary globalized trade regime, environmental concerns found their way into the regulatory system framed by international trade law. The interaction (and tension) between trade and environmental interests further intensified with the development of international environmental law, and global trade was placed under the scrutiny of two overlapping regulatory regimes which are commonly perceived as having diverging aims and rationales. A pronounced outlet for this relationship was found within the World Trade Organization (WTO) system, particularly in trade disputes in which WTO rules interacted with public policies seeking to address environmental externalities. This chapter explores the way in which the relationship between international trade law and norms governing environmental protection are construed from within the WTO dispute settlement system. The findings shine a light on evolving forms of *legal entanglement* that challenge the dominant perception of the WTO as an insular regime prima facie hostile to international environmental law. Surprisingly, the analysis shows that even in controversial trade environment disputes (e.g. infamously *Tuna Dolphin I*), all parties to the dispute routinely refer to norms of international environmental law to make their respective claims. With respect to the Panels and the Appellate Body, the findings indicate that external environmental norms are allowed to penetrate WTO law more often than commonly assumed, although such linkages do not necessarily result in more 'environmentally friendly' interpretations/applications of trade law. Moreover, without centralized coordination, WTO judicial bodies tend to construe the relationship with outside norms in an ad hoc and discretionary way, relying on 'interface norms' to invoke external rules of international environmental law on a case-by-case basis, while keeping them formally at bay. Although the mechanisms of relationing employed by the WTO judicial bodies may seem unprincipled at first glance, an analysis over time reveals how the Panels and the Appellate Body repeatedly emphasize certain attributes in their treatment of outside norms (such as multilateralism, inclusiveness and consensus), and have allowed for more progressive interpretations to evolve over time (through so-called irritative norm conflict).

8.2 Trade and Environment: Resetting the Stage for an Age-Old Debate

8.2.1 Trade and Environment: Unresolved Tensions and Emerging Forms of Entanglement

The General Agreement on Tariffs and Trade (GATT) was signed in 1947 on the cusp of what has been dubbed the 'Great Acceleration', a period of intensified human impact on the Earth that over the latter half of the twentieth century significantly contributed to the global environmental challenges we face today.[1] International environmental law was still in its 'early glimmers'.[2] Nevertheless, the 1947 GATT already 'recognized environmental concerns in its Article XX(b) and (g) exceptions'.[3] By 1994, and the founding of the WTO, the extent of human-wrought environmental degradation had become increasingly apparent, and international environmental law had developed and matured into its modern incarnation of a sprawling global governance complex. Two years prior, the United Nations Conference on Environment and Development had taken place in Rio de Janeiro, and produced a number of instruments, including the Rio Declaration, Agenda 21, the United Nations Framework Convention on Climate Change (UNFCCC) and the Convention on Biodiversity (CBD).

Notably, modern international environmental law evolved within an international legal environment in which international trade rules were already long established and could not be ignored. The drafters in Rio took these existing legal structures into account by explicitly integrating international trade norms into the new instruments. Principle 12 of the

[1] W. Steffen, W. Broadgate, L. Deutsch, O. Gaffney and C. Ludwig, 'The Trajectory of the Anthropocene: The Great Acceleration' (2015) 2 *The Anthropocene Review* 81–98.

[2] E. B. Weiss, 'The Evolution of International Environmental Law' (2011) 54 *Japanese Yearbook of International Law* 1–27, at 2.

[3] Ibid., 12.

Rio Declaration, for example, emphasizes the importance of 'an open international economic system' and states that '[t]rade policy measures for environmental purposes should not constitute a means of arbitrary or unjustifiable discrimination or a disguised restriction on international trade', which is almost a word-for-word copy of the *chapeau* of GATT Article XX.[4] Notably, the same wording is reproduced in Article 3(5) of the UNFCCC.[5] Thus, international environmental law was actively *entangled* with the body of norms that governs the multilateral trading system.

From within the trade law sphere, efforts at legal entanglement with international environmental law were more tentative. While a reference to sustainable development was included in the preamble to the Marrakesh Agreement establishing the WTO (1994), the 1947 GATT was incorporated wholesale into the new WTO Agreement, with no changes or additions to the environmental provisions of the original text indicating how WTO law should relate to international environmental law. This was problematic because a host of new multilateral environmental agreements (MEAs) had sprung up since 1947, some of which explicitly relied on potentially GATT-inconsistent trade measures for their implementation (e.g. the Basel Convention and the Montreal Protocol).[6] Further, the extent to which WTO rules restricted national environmental policy space also remained unclear, particularly in relation to environmental measures targeting processing and production methods (PPMs) and the applicability of the precautionary principle.[7]

The lack of relationing can be explained by GATT signatories' diverging interests with regard to trade and environment concerns at the time (and still prevailing today). While developed countries supported the integration of environmental standards into international trade policy to counter 'environmental dumping', developing countries resisted, fearing market access restrictions due to 'green protectionism'.[8] Thus, a meaningful debate for greater integration of environmental concerns *within* the trade regime was 'out of the question'. Politically, the

[4] United Nations Conference on Environment and Development, 'Rio Declaration on Environment and Development' (New York, 1992), Principle 12.

[5] UNEP, 'United Nations Framework Convention on Climate Change (UNFCCC)' (1992).

[6] A. Tancredi, 'Trade and Inter-Legality', in J. Klabbers and G. Palombella (eds), *The Challenge of Inter-legality* (Cambridge University Press, 2019), pp. 158–87, at p. 159.

[7] T. Santarius, H. Dalkmann, M. Steigenberger and K. Vogelpohl, 'Balancing Trade and Environment: An Ecological Reform of the WTO', Wuppertal Papers (2004), p. 63.

[8] Ibid., p. 10.

'environmental critique [also] came at an awkward time for GATT signatories since the Uruguay Round entered a deep crisis in the early 1990s, and the agricultural dispute between the USA and the EU threatened to scupper talks'.[9] Thus, an opportunity for entanglement – or at least clarification – between the two bodies of norms was missed. This state of affairs was supposed to be remedied in the subsequent Doha Round of trade negotiations, which gave members a mandate to negotiate the relationship between WTO rules and specific trade obligations set out in MEAs.[10] The talks failed however (they were finally abandoned in 2015),[11] and thus a second opportunity for 'enhancing mutual supportiveness' was missed. Instead, it became incumbent upon the dispute settlement bodies to mediate the relationship between free trade and environmental protection (and, by extension, the 'clash of interests' between developed and developing countries).

8.2.2 The Question of Insularity

According to the provisions of the Dispute Settlement Understanding (DSU) the WTO dispute settlement mechanism 'has exclusive [as well as compulsory and quasi-automatic] jurisdiction to resolve disputes arising from violations of the WTO covered agreements'.[12] The WTO Dispute Settlement Body (DSB) in particular has 'the authority to establish panels, adopt panel and Appellate Body reports, maintain surveillance of implementation of rulings and recommendations, and authorize suspension of concessions and other obligations under the covered agreements'.[13] Without a centralized mechanism for resolving international trade and environment conflicts, nor a specialized environmental court, the DSB has become central to coordinating the relationship between WTO law and international environmental law. The Panels' and the Appellate Body's (unanticipated and unofficial) role in mediating the

[9] Ibid., p. 10.

[10] WTO, 'WTO Ministerial Declaration Adopted on 14 November 2001' (20 November 2001) WT/MIN(01)/DEC/1, para. 31.

[11] R. Howse, 'The World Trade Organization 20 Years on: Global Governance by Judiciary' (2016) 27 *European Journal of International Law* 9–77.

[12] G. Marceau, 'The Primacy of the WTO Dispute Settlement Mechanism' (2015) 23 *Questions of International Law* 3–13, at 4.

[13] Article 2(1) of the WTO DSU on Rules and Procedures Governing the Settlement of Disputes, Marrakesh Agreement Establishing the World Trade Organization, Annex 2, 1869 U.N.T.S. 401, 33 I.L.M. 1226 (1994).

relationship between WTO law and external norms raises the question of whether (and to what extent) international law not contained in the covered agreements is applicable in WTO dispute settlement.

While the majority of scholars maintain a restrictive view regarding the extent to which other norms of international law may influence the interpretation and application of WTO law,[14] others have pointed out that the DSU does not contain an explicit limitation with regard to the applicable law.[15] The distinction between the *jurisdiction* of the WTO DSB and *applicable law* in WTO dispute settlement is relevant here.[16] While the *jurisdiction* of the WTO DSB is restricted to *disputes arising out of the covered agreements*,[17] WTO law contains no explicit provision which identifies or restricts the *law that should apply* to the disputes.[18] Thus, international law from *all sources* is potentially applicable as WTO law. Such a reading seems to be supported by the Panel in *Korea-Government Procurement*, which held that 'Customary international law applies generally to the economic relations between the WTO Members [...] to the extent that the WTO treaty agreements do not "contract out" from it.'[19] The Panel saw no basis 'for arguing that the terms of reference [set out in the DSU] are meant to exclude reference to

14 G. Z. Marceau, 'A Call for Coherence in International Law' (1999) 33 *Journal of World Trade* 87–152; J. P. Trachtman, 'The Domain of WTO Dispute Resolution' (1999) 40 *Harvard International Law Journal* 333–77; G. Z. Marceau, 'Conflicts of Norms and Conflicts of Jurisdictions, the Relationship between the WTO Agreement and Meas and Other Treaties' (2001) 35 *Journal of World Trade* 1081–131, at 1116.

15 J. Pauwelyn, *Conflict of Norms in Public International Law: How WTO Law Relates to Other Rules of International Law* (Cambridge University Press, 2003), p. 460. Pauwelyn argues that the applicable law before a WTO panel is limited only by four factors: the claims that can be brought to a WTO panel; the defences invoked by the defending party; the scope of the relevant rules *ratione materiae, ratione personae* and *ratione temporis*; and any conflict rules in the WTO treaty, general international law and other non-WTO treaties.

16 Ibid., p. 460.

17 Articles 1(1), 3(2), 7(1) and 11 of the DSU.

18 L. Bartels, 'Applicable Law in WTO Dispute Settlement Proceedings' (2001) 35 *Journal of World Trade* 499–519, at 504 *et seq*. Article 7 of the DSU, for example, has been used to justify both closed and open positions with regard to the applicable law in WTO dispute settlement procedures – although the provision itself is rather ambiguous. Indeed, while Article 7 requires Panels to examine disputes 'in light of' relevant provisions in the covered agreements, and to address relevant provisions in any covered agreement cited by the parties to the dispute, it does not prevent Panels from addressing other sources of law in the course of deciding the dispute.

19 Korea – Measures Affecting Government Procurement (2000) WTO Doc. WT/DS163/R, para. 7.96.

the broader rules of customary international law'.[20] There is no reason to assume why the same logic should not also apply with regard to the external rules of treaty law (applicable between the parties).

The degree to which 'external' international law has a bearing on WTO law is thus largely up to the discretion of the WTO dispute settlement bodies. However, the Panels and the Appellate Body are viewed as having made insufficient use of this flexibility,[21] and have been criticized for creating 'a value hierarchy that [favours] trade over environmental concerns and [operates] as a barrier to the integration of environmental considerations into the law of the GATT/WTO'.[22] Thus, the dominant perception of international trade law is of a distinct legal system that is bounded, rigid and hostile to environmental norms and considerations. The following account of irritative norm conflict complicates this picture.

8.3 Irritative Norm Conflict and Contingent Forms of Entanglement over Time

The debate about whether trade liberalization and environmental protection are in conflict with one another is not new and does not need to be rehashed in detail here.[23] Suffice to say that many environmentalists and scholars have long criticized the legal framework established by the GATT and the WTO as 'inherently biased against environmental protection and towards economic growth'.[24] GATT jurisprudence, beginning with the *Tuna Dolphin I*, seemed to confirm the prioritization of international trade obligations vis-à-vis environmental protection.[25] However, a close reading of the trade and environment disputes *over time* reveals subtle shifts in the relationship between the WTO and environmental norms and a modicum of responsiveness of the GATT – and later the WTO – dispute settlement bodies towards evolving social context and external pressures, most prominently in *Shrimp-Turtle*.

[20] Ibid., para. 7.101.

[21] Tancredi, 'Trade and Inter-Legality'.

[22] O. Perez, *Ecological Sensitivity and Global Legal Pluralism: Rethinking the Trade and Environment Conflict* (Hart Publishing, 2004), p. 51.

[23] Trachtman, 'The Domain of WTO Dispute Resolution'.

[24] M. Jeffery, 'Environmental Imperatives in a Globalized World: The Ecological Impact of Liberalizing Trade' (2007) 7 *Macquarie Law Journal* 25–52, at 29.

[25] J. P. Trachtman, 'WTO Trade and Environment Jurisprudence: Avoiding Environmental Catastrophe' (2017) 58 *Harvard International Law Journal* 273–310.

Disputes brought before the WTO DSB constitute important historical 'flashpoints' for the study of legal entanglement, as they galvanize actors to formulate claims about the relationship between international trade law and other bodies of norms in legal terms.

8.3.1 Tuna Dolphin I

8.3.1.1 Overview

Tuna Dolphin I was a highly controversial trade and environment case brought to the GATT dispute settlement mechanism by Mexico in 1991.[26] The dispute concerned US measures aimed at reducing dolphin mortality incidental to tuna fishing, a practice common in the Eastern Tropical Pacific (ETP) region. The measures comprised an embargo on yellowfin tuna caught with purse seine nets in the ETP, certification requirements for imported tuna and a prohibition on marking tuna products harvested in the ETP with purse seine nets as 'dolphin safe'. While the dispute became notorious for the Panel's hard-line position on environmental trade measures, it is notable from the perspective of legal entanglement as – contrary to expectations – both parties to the dispute referred to international environmental law to support their respective claims. *Tuna Dolphin I* was closely followed by the filing of a second dispute in 1992 – known as *Tuna Dolphin II* – in which the European Communities (EC) challenged the United States' secondary embargo against countries that re-exported tuna from countries under the primary embargo.[27]

8.3.1.2 Legal Entanglement

Notably, both the United States and Mexico implicitly accepted the relevance of international environmental treaty law to the dispute at hand (in addition to relevant GATT provisions). The United States, invoking the Convention on International Trade in Endangered Species (CITES), argued that countries should not be forced to allow access to their markets as an incentive to depleting the populations of species that are vital components of the ecosystem.[28] Mexico countered by stating

[26] United States – Restrictions on Imports of Tuna – Report of the GATT Panel, (3 September 1991) DS21/R (unadopted) ('Tuna Dolphin I').

[27] United States – Restrictions on Imports of Tuna – Report of the GATT Panel, (16 June 1994), DS29/R (unadopted) ('Tuna Dolphin II').

[28] *Tuna Dolphin I* Panel report, para. 3.49.

that CITES 'did not include in its Appendix I list of species in danger of extinction any of the species of dolphins which the United States was claiming to protect'.[29]

The Panel, finding a violation of the GATT's substantive provisions (relating to quantitative restrictions and non-discrimination), turned to the environmental exceptions contained in GATT Article XX. In a fateful decision, the Panel interpreted a purely domestic scope to Article XX and ruled that its exceptions could not be invoked to justify extraterritorial measures.[30] Trade restrictions in response to other countries' environmental policies or practices were per se inconsistent with the GATT.[31] However, the Panel proceeded to argue that even if the GATT permitted extraterritorial protection of life and health, the United States had to first exhaust all GATT-consistent measures available to it, in particular through the negotiation of international cooperative agreements.[32] This reasoning already hints at a general (though still implicit) understanding that environmental measures should be based on multilateral consensus in order to be taken into account by the WTO DSB/within the GATT framework, a notion that was further developed in subsequent case law.

Ultimately, the Panel ruled in favour of Mexico, concluding that the US trade embargo was inconsistent with the GATT and not justified under Article XX. Crucially, the Panel also set up the 'infamous product/process distinction' – prompting a debate that continues to this day – by ruling that the US was not allowed to embargo tuna products from Mexico based on the way tuna was *produced*.[33] The Panel took a more environmentally favourable stance with regard to the 'dolphin-safe' label, ruling that it did not violate the GATT 'because the labelling regulations governing the tuna caught in the ETP [. . .] applied to all countries whose vessels fished in this geographical area and thus did not distinguish between products originating in Mexico and products originating in other countries'.[34] Notably, this measure became subject to a subsequent

[29] Ibid., para. 3.44.

[30] *Tuna Dolphin I* Panel report, para. 5.28.

[31] Howse, 'The World Trade Organization 20 Years On', 36. The rulings in *Tuna Dolphin I* and *II* are widely regarded as having no textual basis in the GATT but to have been informed instead by 'some intuitive notion that allowing trade measures to address global environmental externalities was somehow countenancing the slippery slope towards unconstrained green protectionism'.

[32] *Tuna Dolphin I* Panel report, para. 5.28.

[33] Ibid., para. 5.12 – 5.15. Also see Howse, 'The World Trade Organization 20 Years On', 37.

[34] *Tuna Dolphin I* Panel report, para. 5.43–5.44.

dispute brought by Mexico in 2008, in *US-Tuna II*. The Panel reports in *Tuna Dolphin I (1991)* and *II* (1994) were never adopted due to the consensus requirement under old GATT dispute settlement rules.[35]

8.3.1.3 Aftermath

Although the report remained unadopted, the Panel's reasoning in *Tuna Dolphin I* generated widespread 'controversy over the capacity of the multilateral trading system to accommodate legitimate environmental concerns'.[36] The United States, arguably one of the most powerful 'shapers' of the GATT/WTO legal regime, threatened to push for amendments to the GATT in light of international environmental objectives.[37] Proposals made towards this endeavour included a new 'Environmental Code' as a side agreement to the GATT and establishing an international tradeable pollution allowance system (similar to what was later instituted in the Kyoto Protocol) under the auspices of the GATT.[38] Although neither of the *Tuna Dolphin I and II* Panels' reports were ever adopted and they retained little to no legal value following subsequent Appellate Body rulings, they significantly contributed to the perception of WTO insularity in relation to global environmental concerns.[39]

8.3.2 *Shrimp-Turtle*

8.3.2.1 Overview

The legal outcome of the *Shrimp-Turtle* dispute was seen by many environmentalists as a breakthrough in the trade environment debate, indicating a more environmentally friendly interpretation of WTO law

35 The new WTO dispute settlement mechanism instituted a reverse consensus rule, making the adoption of post 1994 panel reports virtually automatic.

36 World Trade Organization, *CITES and the WTO: Enhancing Cooperation for Sustainable Development* (WTO, 2015) p. 3.

37 T. E. Skilton, 'GATT and the Environment in Conflict: The Tuna-Dolphin Dispute and the Quest for an International Conservation Strategy' (1993) 26 *Cornell International Law Journal* 455–94. The US House of Representatives promptly passed a resolution mandating the US representative to actively seek GATT reform in order to make international trade rules more amenable to national and international environmental laws and to secure a working party on trade and environment within the GATT as soon as possible.

38 Ibid., 192.

39 G. M. Duran, 'NTBs and the WTO Agreement on Technical Barriers to Trade: The Case of PPM-Based Measures Following US – Tuna II and EC – Seal Products' (2015) 6 *European Yearbook of International Economic Law* 87–136, at 109.

by the DSB. The dispute was brought jointly by India, Malaysia, Pakistan and Thailand, challenging a US environmental measure prohibiting the import of shrimp harvested without the use of Turtle Excluder Devices (TEDs). Not using TEDs during shrimp harvesting was linked to a high number of deaths of endangered species of sea turtles. The measures in *Shrimp-Turtle* 'were thus closely analogous' to those in *Tuna Dolphin* with the crucial difference that sea turtles were listed as endangered species in CITES.[40]

8.3.2.2 Legal Entanglement

Like in *Tuna Dolphin I*, both the complainants and the defendant state invoked outside environmental norms – especially treaty law – to support their respective claims. The United States referred to the CITES Appendix I, implying that CITES provided a legal basis for its environmental trade measure.[41] The USA further claimed that the use of TEDs had evolved into an international standard, invoking Agenda 21[42] as well as the UN Fish Stocks Agreement to support its claim.[43] The complainants, on the other hand, argued that the US measure was not only in violation of the GATT but also inconsistent with CITES: while CITES did prohibit trade in sea turtles, it did not sanction restrictions on *shrimp* imports as shrimp were not an endangered species listed in any of CITES's annexes.[44]

The reference to sustainable development in the Preamble of the WTO Agreement significantly altered the 'backdrop' against which substantive WTO obligations were to be interpreted. The USA noted that the WTO Agreement was the first multilateral trade agreement concluded after the Rio Conference, and argued that trade rules should now operate 'in a manner that [respected] the principle of sustainable development and [protected] and [preserved] the environment'.[45] The complainants,

[40] Howse, 'The World Trade Organization 20 Years On', 37.

[41] United States – Import prohibition of certain shrimp and shrimp products – Panel Report (15 May 1998) WT/DS58/R ('*Shrimp-Turtle*'), para. 3.94 Additionally, the USA also invoked the UN Convention on the Law of the Sea (UNCLOS) Articles 61(2), (4) and 119(1)(b), and Agenda 21 in support of this claim.

[42] *Shrimp-Turtle* Panel report, para. 7.57. Specifically, the USA referred to paragraph 17.46 (c) of Agenda 21, which promotes 'the development and use of selective fishing gear and practices that minimize [. . .] the bycatch of non-target species' as a 'multilateral environmental standard to minimize bycatch'.

[43] *Shrimp-Turtle* Panel report, para. 3.95.

[44] Ibid., paras 3.5 and 3.98 (India); para. 3.221 (Malaysia).

[45] Ibid., para. 3.146.

however, were quick to qualify of the reference to sustainable development by reading it in light of the principle of sovereignty and the special rights of developing countries under the WTO framework.[46]

The dispute forced the Panel to revisit the question of extraterritoriality in relation to Article XX of the GATT. Although both the United States and the complainants had put forward arguments relating to how Article XX should be interpreted in light of outside norms (inter alia UNCLOS[47] and general principles of international law[48]), the Panel restricted itself to interpreting Article XX within the object and purpose of WTO law and relevant jurisprudence. Echoing the GATT Panel's reasoning in *Tuna Dolphin I*, it found that Article XX could not justify measures conditioning market access upon the adoption of certain environmental policies by exporting members as that would threaten the security and predictability of the multilateral framework for trade.[49]

The Panel did not completely ignore international environmental law, however. It drew on the Rio Declaration to interpret the reference to sustainable development in the WTO Agreement, but used it to emphasize the right of each state to design its own environmental policies on the basis of its particular environmental and developmental situations.[50] The Panel further emphasized the principle of international cooperation by reference to inter alia Article 5 of the CBD (despite the USA not being a party to the CBD).[51] The Panel found that instead of resorting to unilateral measures the USA should have entered into negotiations to develop internationally accepted conservation methods.[52]

The Panel proceeded to examine whether international environmental law provided a justification for the WTO-inconsistent measure.[53]

46 Pakistan, for example, referred to the concept of sustainable development as an environmental norm to be taken into consideration *while Pakistan exercises its sovereignty to decide on the conservation measures to be taken within its jurisdiction* (ibid., para. 3.54). Pakistan also noted that the preamble required members to enhance their means for protecting and preserving the environment *in a manner consistent with the member's respective needs and concerns at different levels of economic development* (para. 3.85).

47 Ibid., para. 3.95; para. 3.41; and para. 3.157.

48 Ibid., para. 3.274.

49 Ibid., para. 7.45.

50 *Shrimp-Turtle* Panel report, para. 7.52.

51 Article 5 of the CBD promotes the principle of international cooperation when it comes to matters of mutual interest for the conservation and sustainable use of biological diversity.

52 *Shrimp-Turtle* Panel report, para. 7.53.

53 Ibid., para. 7.58 et seq.

The Panel concluded that CITES 'neither authorized nor prohibited' the US import prohibition as it was directed at shrimp and not listed species of sea turtles.[54] Furthermore, while acknowledging that UNCLOS and Agenda 21 addressed the objective of limiting by-catches of non-target species in trawling operations, the Panel noted that these instruments do not require the application of specific methods.[55]

Even though the Panel's finding in *Shrimp-Turtle* is generally regarded as an environmental setback (primarily due to its restrictive interpretation of Article XX), it is remarkable from the standpoint of legal entanglement as all parties involved in the dispute *frequently and directly* referred to external environmental norms/instruments to support their claims. Notably, international environmental law was invoked both to support a flexible (i.e. environmentally friendly) as well as a more restrictive (i.e. trade-friendly) interpretation of GATT Article XX.

8.3.2.3 Appeal

On appeal, the Appellate Body acknowledged the right of WTO members to legislate for the protection of natural resources extraterritorially, overruling the Panel's finding.[56] Accordingly, Article XX *could* justify measures conditioning market access on the adoption of certain conservation policies by exporting members.[57] Contrary to the Panel, the Appellate Body proceeded to take full advantage of the reference to sustainable development in the WTO Agreement in order to interpret the environmental exceptions of Article XX. It noted that the preamble gives 'colour, texture and shading' to the substantive obligations in the WTO agreements.[58] In particular, the Appellate Body held that because migratory sea turtles were listed under CITES as being in danger of extinction, they constituted 'exhaustible natural resources' within the

[54] Ibid., para. 7.58.

[55] Ibid., para. 7.59.

[56] United States – Import Prohibition of Certain Shrimp and Shrimp Products – Appellate Body Report (12 October 1998) WT/DS58/AB/R, paras 121–2.

[57] Duran, 'NTBs and the WTO Agreement on Technical Barriers to Trade', 110. See also *Shrimp-Turtle* Appellate Body Report, para. 121: 'It is not necessary to assume that requiring from exporting countries compliance with, or adoption of, certain policies (although covered in principle by one or another of the exceptions) prescribed by the importing country, renders a measure a priori incapable of justification under Article XX. Such an interpretation renders most, if not all, of the specific exceptions of Article XX inutile, a result abhorrent to the principles of interpretation we are bound to apply.'

[58] D. A. Wirth, 'Some Reflections on Turtles, Tuna, Dolphin, and Shrimp' (1998) 9 *Yearbook of International Environmental Law* 40–7, at 42.

meaning of Article XX(g) of the GATT.[59] The Appellate Body further stated that '[t]he words of Article XX(g) "exhaustible natural resources" [. . .] must be read by a treaty interpreter in the light of *contemporary concerns of the community of nations* about the protection and conservation of the environment [. . .] From the perspective embodied in the Preamble of the WTO Agreement, the generic term of "natural resources" in Article XX(g) is not "static" in its content or reference but is rather, "by definition evolutionary"'.[60]

Ultimately, however, the Appellate Body found that while 'the overall approach of the US shrimp ban was acceptable under the WTO', the USA had failed to do justice to the requirements of the *chapeau* of Article XX.[61] The Appellate Body held that in its application, the US measure had 'intended an actual coercive effect on the specific policy decisions made by foreign governments' since the application of the measure required other WTO members to demonstrate that a regulatory scheme was in place, which was essentially the same as in the USA.[62] In addition, the Appellate Body also faulted the United States for having negotiated seriously with some but not other members about arrangements for sea turtle protection (as an alternative to the embargo), which had a discriminatory effect.[63] To determine whether the discrimination was also 'unjustifiable' in relation to the stated objective of protecting sea turtles, the Appellate Body turned to international environmental law.[64] Invoking the Rio Declaration (Principle 12), Agenda 21 and the CBD (Article 5), the Appellate Body found that the protection and conservation of highly migratory species of sea turtles demanded 'concerted and co-operative efforts',[65] and that, in general, transboundary/global environmental problems should be dealt with through cooperation and consensus to the greatest extent possible.[66]

59 *Shrimp-Turtle* Appellate Body Report, paras 128–31.
60 *Shrimp-Turtle* Appellate Body Report, paras 129–30.
61 Howse, 'The World Trade Organization 20 Years On', 42.
62 M. Bowman, P. Davies and C. Redgwell, *Lyster's International Wildlife Law* (Cambridge University Press, 2010), p. 664.
63 P. Sands, J. Peel and R. MacKenzie, *Principles of International Environmental Law* (Cambridge University Press, 2012), p. 970.
64 R. Howse, 'The Appellate Body Rulings in the Shrimp/Turtle Case: A New Legal Baseline for the Trade and Environment Debate' (2002) 27 *Columbia Journal of Environmental Law* 491–521, at 506.
65 *Shrimp-Turtle* Appellate Body Report, para. 168.
66 Sands, Peel and MacKenzie, *Principles of International Environmental Law*, p. 970.

8.3.2.4 Aftermath

Following the Appellate Body's ruling, which concerned the discriminatory *application* of the US measure, the United States made modifications in order comply with the ruling. Nevertheless, one of the original complainants, Malaysia, brought a compliance action under Article 21.5 of the DSU, 'where it sought to reintroduce arguments about the *per se* unacceptability of trade measures to target other countries' environmental policy'.[67] However, the Appellate Body 'held its ground', '[pronouncing] itself fully satisfied that the USA had addressed its concerns under the chapeau', while '[expressing] surprise that Malaysia would, in effect, challenge the authority of the Appellate Body's original ruling with arguments apparently inconsistent with it'.[68] The rulings in *Shrimp-Turtle* and the subsequent compliance proceedings thus represent a significant departure from the way the *Tuna Dolphin* cases had been handled by the GATT Panels. The Appellate Body corrected previous rulings with regard to PPM-based measures and extraterritorial environmental trade measures, while signalling a larger degree of deference towards members' environmental objectives.

8.3.3 EC-Hormones

8.3.3.1 Overview

The *EC-Hormones* dispute before the WTO illustrates how the Agreement on Sanitary and Phytosanitary Measures (SPS Agreement) operates in relation to international standards and in relation to other norms of international law, specifically the precautionary principle.[69] Like the Agreement on Technical Barriers to Trade (TBT Agreement) (see *US-Tuna II*), the SPS Agreement goes beyond the non-discrimination principles enshrined in the GATT by promoting 'global regulatory harmonization through the application of international standards'.[70] By requiring WTO members to base their measures on either international standards or on science and risk assessment (Articles 3.1

[67] Howse, 'The World Trade Organization 20 Years On', 41.

[68] Ibid., 42.

[69] European Communities – Measures Concerning Meat and Meat Products (Hormones) (Canada) – Panel report (19 August 1997) WT/DS48/R/CAN; European Communities – Measures Concerning Meat and Meat Products (Homones) (US) – Panel report, (18 August 1997) WT/DS26/R/USA ('EC Hormones').

[70] Tancredi, 'Trade and Inter-Legality', p. 171.

and 3.2), the SPS Agreement actively encourages legal entanglement in the area of sanitary and phytosanitary measures. The SPS Agreement explicitly recognizes specific international standardizing bodies as points of reference for compliance, including the Codex Alimentarius Commission (CAC').[71] Conformity with Codex standards implies conformity with WTO law,[72] whereas a member's decision to set standards higher than Codex standards is subject to a higher burden of proof to defend its own measures.

From the perspective of legal entanglement, the implications of this active coupling mechanism between the SPS Agreement and international standards versus the way WTO law relates to other norms of international law is significant. The WTO's contrasting approaches to entanglement are best demonstrated in the *EC-Hormones* case. In the 1990s, following widespread public concern, the European Council introduced a set of measures prohibiting the placing on the market of hormone-injected meat. In 1996, the United States challenged these measures and brought the dispute before the WTO alleging violations of inter alia the SPS Agreement.[73]

8.3.3.2 Legal Entanglement

The CAC had already developed standards for some of the hormonal substances concerned. The USA therefore contested the EC's measures on the grounds that they *were not based on the relevant international standards, guidelines or recommendations* and that this departure from international standards could not be scientifically justified. The EC countered that WTO members had the right to choose their own levels of protection, which may be higher than those recommended by international standards, invoking the *precautionary principle* as a justification for a higher protection level.[74] While the SPS Agreement requires

[71] Annex A.3 SPS.

[72] Article 3.2 SPS.

[73] *EC Hormones* Panel Report (US), para. 3.2 With regard to the SPS Agreement, the USA claimed inter alia that the measures were not based on an assessment of risk and therefore inconsistent with Article 5.1, that they lacked sufficient scientific evidence in contravention of Article 2.2, that they were not justified as a provisional measure under Article 5.7 and that they were not based on scientific principles thereby breaching Articles 2.2 and 5.6, that they were applied beyond the extent necessary to protect human life or health, and that they were more trade restrictive than required to achieve the appropriate level of sanitary protection.

[74] Ibid., para. 4.203.

members to base their measures on risk assessments and available scientific data, the precautionary principle allows countries to take measures in the face of scientific uncertainty. Notably, the EC did not invoke Article 5.7 of the SPS Agreement which permits members to take *interim measures* in the face of insufficient scientific evidence and is generally viewed as reflecting the precautionary principle in the context of the SPS Agreement. The EC reasoned that this decision was deliberate because the measures were considered definitive and not provisional.[75] The EC also pointed out that the Codex standards had been adopted by a very slim margin in what was ordinarily a consensus-based system. By questioning the level of support for the Codex standards the EC expressed expectations about the *substantive dimensions of the interface norm contained in the SPS Agreement*: international standards should only be taken into account if they are considered legitimate, as indicated by widespread to universal acceptance during adoption.[76] The Panel rejected the need to consider by what margin any relevant standard was adopted,[77] and found that the EC measure violated the SPS Agreement by deviating from the relevant international standard (in the sense that it afforded a higher level of protection) without sufficient justification.[78] Further, the Panel found that the precautionary principle (to the extent that it could be considered as part of customary international law) 'would not override the explicit wording' of SPS provisions relating to risk assessment techniques (and scientific evidence), 'in particular since the precautionary principle [had] been incorporated and given specific meaning in Article 5.7 of the SPS Agreement'.[79] The harmonization logic of the SPS Agreement thus contributed to lowering a member's chosen protection threshold – in accordance with international standards adopted with only tenuous international support – while a

[75] *EC Hormones* Panel Report (US), para. 4.239.

[76] P. Delimatsis, *The Law, Economics and Politics of International Standardisation* (Cambridge University Press, 2015), p. 90. The EU and other countries have repeatedly expressed this claim that the Codex should respect consensus-based decision-making as one of the fundamental principles of the organisation; see a recent example: Codex Alimentarius Commission (35th Session) Rome, 2–7 July 2012, EU Statement on ractopamine 'for standards to be universally applicable, they also need to be universally accepted'.

[77] *EC Hormones* Panel Report (US), para. 8.69.

[78] Ibid., paras 8.75–8.77.

[79] Ibid., para. 8.157.

relevant norm of *international law* (the precautionary principle) was dismissed in the process.

8.3.3.3 Appeal

The EC appealed the ruling, arguing that the precautionary principle's applicability extended beyond Article 5.7 to influence risk assessment (and risk management) under Article 5.1 of the SPS Agreement, and thus operated to justify higher protection thresholds.[80] Notably the EC did not refer to the precautionary principle in the context of international *environmental* law but in the context of *general and customary international* law. The Appellate Body, siding with the Panel, found that while the precautionary principle may have crystallized in the field of international *environmental* law, its status as *customary* international law or a *general principle* of law was less certain. By relegating the principle to the confines of international environmental law, the Appellate Body downplayed its relevance for the dispute at hand. Further, the Appellate Body stated that 'the precautionary principle does not, by itself, and without a clear textual directive to that effect, relieve a panel from the duty of applying the normal (i.e. customary international law) principles of treaty interpretation in reading the provisions of the SPS Agreement'.[81] In effect, the Appellate Body communicated that *whatever* the state of the precautionary principle in international law was, 'the principle could not override the explicit obligations contained in the SPS Agreement and it could not be used to justify measures otherwise inconsistent with the SPS Agreement'.[82] The EC ultimately 'lost' the case as its measures were found not to have been based on appropriate risk assessment: the EC could neither prove 'laboratory scientific evidence' nor 'real-world risk' (misuse in the administration of hormones to animals).[83] This ruling flies in the face of the precautionary principle (as codified for example in Principle 15 of the Rio Declaration), the purpose of which is precisely to empower governments in the face of scientific *uncertainty*.

[80] European Communities – Measures Concerning Meat and Meat Products (Hormones) – Report of the Appellate Body (16 January 1998), WT/DS26/AB/R and WT/DS48/AB/R, para. 16.

[81] *EC Hormones* Appellate Body Report, paras 124–5.

[82] M. L. Maier and C. Gerstetter, 'Risk Regulation, Trade and International Law: Debating the Precautionary Principle in and around the WTO', TranState working papers (2005), 12.

[83] Howse, 'The World Trade Organization 20 Years On', 58.

Nevertheless, the Appellate Body did point out that 'a panel charged with determining for instance, whether "sufficient scientific evidence" exists to warrant the maintenance by a Member of a particular SPS measure may [. . .] bear in mind that responsible, representative governments commonly act from the perspectives of prudence and precaution where risks of irreversible, e.g., life-terminating, damage to human health are concerned'.[84] This statement implies a greater degree of flexibility where the future application of Article 5 is concerned; the implication is that in cases of grave potential damage, Panels are to content themselves with a lower evidentiary standard for assessing a measure's SPS consistency.[85]

8.3.3.4 Aftermath

Following the *EC-Hormones* disputes, the EC made a concerted push for strengthening the precautionary principle in international law. After having unsuccessfully advocated for a renegotiation of relevant provisions within the SPS Agreement, the EC turned its attention to multilateral fora outside the WTO.[86] In 2000, the Cartagena Protocol on Biosafety to the Convention on Biological Diversity (the 'Biosafety Protocol') was agreed upon, which regulates risks associated with the transboundary movement of living modified organisms. The Biosafety Protocol '[reaffirms] the precautionary approach contained in Principle 15 of the Rio Declaration on Environment and Development'[87] and grants importing states the right to make decisions that would avoid or reduce potential adverse effects in the face of scientific uncertainty.[88] The Biosafety Protocol thus '*multilateralizes* the EU regulatory approach' towards sanitary measures, opening the door to other countries to adopt restrictive, EU-style market access rules.[89] Unsurprisingly, one of the

84 *EC Hormones* Appellate Body Report, para. 172.

85 Maier and Gerstetter, 'Risk Regulation, Trade and International Law', 16.

86 Santarius et al., 'Balancing Trade and Environment'. Notably, environmental organizations/groups – such as the Forum Umwelt und Entwicklung – and states had long been pushing for the precautionary principle to be incorporated into WTO law in more unrestricted form.

87 UNEP, Preamble, 'Cartagena Protocol on Biosafety to the Convention on Biological Diversity (the Biosafety Protocol)' (2000).

88 This is in the context of the 'advanced informed agreement' procedure which applies to the first transboundary movement of a living modified organism that is intended to be released into the environment of an importing party.

89 G. E. Isaac and W. A. Kerr, 'The Biosafety Protocol and the WTO: Concert or Conflict?', in R. Falkner (ed.), *The International Politics of Genetically Modified Food: Diplomacy, Trade and Law* (Palgrave Macmillan, 2006), pp. 195–212, at p. 196.

most contentious issues during the negotiation process was the Protocol's relationship with international trade law.[90] In this regard, the preamble '[recognizes] that trade and environment agreements should be mutually supportive with a view to achieving sustainable development' and '[emphasizes] that [the] Protocol shall not be interpreted as implying a change in the rights and obligations of a Party under any existing international agreements' (while also 'understanding that the above recital [was] not intended to *subordinate* [the] Protocol to other international agreements'). The EC also successfully campaigned for the inclusion of the precautionary principle in the risk assessment techniques developed by the Codex Alimentarius Commission.[91] As a result, two newly negotiated documents, the 2003 and 2007 Working Principles for Risk Analysis for Food Safety for Application by Governments, recognize precaution as an inherent element of risk assessment.[92]

After several years of keeping its genetically modified organism (GMO) measures in place while accepting the punitive tariffs imposed by the USA and Canada in return, the EC was able to produce scientific evidence to prove risk from synthetic growth hormones. The EC subsequently amended its law to bring them into compliance with the Appellate Body's ruling.[93] Nevertheless, the USA and Canada continued to retaliate, prompting the EC to challenge the legality of continued retaliatory measures in 2005. This 'follow-up dispute' *Canada/US – Continued Suspension (2008)*, gave the Appellate Body the opportunity to revisit its previous ruling (in light of the new normative developments that had occurred outside the WTO). In *Canada/US – Continued Suspension*, the Appellate Body developed the concepts of 'risk assessment' and 'sufficiency of scientific evidence' as 'relational concepts' implying that issues such as 'the appropriate level of protection' chosen by a government could shape the methodology and questions studied in

[90] P. E. Hagen and J. B. Weiner, 'The Cartagena Protocol on Biosafety: New Rules for International Trade in Living Modified Organisms' (2000) 12 *The Georgetown International Environmental Law Review* 697–717, at 702.

[91] Maier and Gerstetter, 'Risk Regulation, Trade and International Law'.

[92] FAO, Principle 11, 'Working Principles for Risk Analysis for Application in the Framework of the Codex Alimentarius' (Risk Analysis Principles Applied by the Codex Committee on Food Additives and Contaminants) (2003); FAO, Principle 12, 'Working Principles for Risk Analysis for Food Safety for Application by Governments (CAC/GL 62-2007)' (2007).

[93] Delimatsis, *The Law, Economics and Politics of International Standardisation*, p. 97.

risk assessment.[94] The Appellate Body also *relativized* the centrality of international standards and conceded that scientific evidence could be sufficient for one member but not for another.[95] This more deferential approach towards members' right to regulate on the basis of precaution significantly departed from the Appellate Body's initial reasoning in *EC-Hormones*.[96]

8.3.4 *EC-Biotech*

8.3.4.1 Overview

The *EC-Biotech* dispute represents another deliberation on the extent to which the precautionary principle is applicable in relation to the SPS Agreement. In 2003, three exporters of agricultural products containing GMOs – the United States, Canada and Argentina – challenged the EC on some of its measures relating to GMOs. The EC had instituted a moratorium on the approval of GMOs during the period of October 1998 and August 2003 and, in addition, some EC member states had put in place national restrictions on GMOs and genetically modified foods. Notably, the EC's regulatory regime for GMOs was (and is) significantly informed by the precautionary principle.

The dispute came on the heels of the adoption of the Biosafety Protocol, which was not only substantively relevant to the dispute at hand (namely GMO-related measures) but also incorporated a more robust version of the precautionary principle than the SPS Agreement.[97] Indeed, the complaint has been viewed as implicitly targeting the Biosafety Protocol in order to weaken its relevance for the SPS Agreement.[98] With regard to the trade–environment interface, the Panel's reasoning in *EC-Biotech* is widely viewed as a setback for a mutually supportive relationship as the Panel prima facie dismissed the relevance of the Biosafety Protocol to the dispute.

[94] Ibid., p. 97 *et seq*.
[95] Ibid., p. 98.
[96] Howse, 'The World Trade Organization 20 Years On', 58.
[97] J. Zhao, 'The Role of International Organizations in Preventing Conflicts between the SPS Agreement and the Cartagena Protocol on Biosafety' (2020) 29(2) *Review of European, Comparative & International Environmental Law* 1–11.
[98] Isaac and Kerr, 'The Biosafety Protocol and the WTO', p. 196.

8.3.4.2 Legal Entanglement

The EC justified some of the EC members' national bans by invoking the precautionary principle as codified in the Biosafety Protocol. The EC argued that the SPS Agreement and the Biosafety Protocol were 'so closely connected that they should be interpreted and applied consistently with each other, to the extent that is possible'; the two agreements were 'complimentary' and therefore 'the Protocol's provisions on precaution and risk assessment inform the meaning and effect of the relevant provisions of the WTO agreements'.[99] The complainants were not parties to the Protocol and rejected its application to the dispute. They argued that the Protocol did not constitute a 'relevant rule of international law applicable in the relations between the parties' and should therefore not be taken into account in the interpretation of the obligations under the WTO Agreement.[100]

An *amicus curiae* brief is of note in the context of *EC-Biotech* as it makes additional claims about how the interface between trade law and environmental concerns/precaution should be managed. In its submission, the Centre for International Environmental Law (CIEL) noted that the Appellate Body had emphasized the importance, in certain circumstances, of interpreting terms in the WTO agreements in light of 'the contemporary concerns of the community of nations' (see *Shrimp-Turtle*).[101] CIEL argued that 'interpreting bodies' consequently had a responsibility 'to take into account [external treaties not ratified by all parties to the treaty being interpreted], especially when they address issues of global concern where the interests of the international community were involved'.[102]

8.3.4.3 Aftermath

The EC decided not to appeal the ruling of the Panel and instead pursued a 'Mutually Agreed Solution', decided between Canada and the EU in 2009, which established 'a bilateral dialogue on agricultural biotech

[99] European Communities – Measures Affecting the Approval and Marketing of Biotech Products – Panel report (29 September 2006) WT/DS291/292/293/R ('EC-Biotech'), para. 7.55.

[100] *EC-Biotech* Panel report, para. 4.600.

[101] CIEL, 'EC-Biotech: Overview and Analysis of the Panel's Interim Report' (Mach 2006), p. 46.

[102] Ibid., p. 49.

market access issues of mutual interest'.[103] This cooperation agreement was subsequently reaffirmed in the EU–Canada Comprehensive Economic and Trade Agreement (CETA), which largely reproduced the text of the Mutually Agreed Solution in Article 25.2(1). Thus, CETA institutionalizes international cooperation on biotech market access and inter alia sets out the shared objective of promoting 'efficient *science-based* approval processes for biotechnology products [emphasis added]'. This provision was criticized as running counter to the EC's strict regulation of GMOs as informed by the precautionary approach and has generated concerns around the weakening of GMO protections in the EU.[104] Arcuri points out that while 'international cooperation' may sound innocuous and indeterminate, the fact that an international body of norms on low-level presence of GMOs already exists (the Global Low-Level Presence Initiative) and given that *most state members of this framework are GMO producers with a clear interest in lowering GMO protections*, the requirement of international cooperation may in fact further skew international standards on GMO protections, to the detriment of the EC's precautionary 'zero tolerance' approach.[105] At the same time, however, the preamble of the Joint Interpretative Instrument on the CETA 'reaffirms the commitments made with respect to precaution that [the European Union and its members states and Canada] have undertaken in international agreements', hence relativizing the provisions requiring science-based evaluations. Reading the relevant CETA provisions in the context of the 2003 and 2007 Codex Working Principles for Risk Analysis – which recognize precaution as an inherent element of risk analysis – further neutralizes their potential to weaken the precautionary principle.

8.3.5 *US-Tuna II*

8.3.5.1 Overview

Following the GATT Panels' rulings in *Tuna Dolphin I and II*, 'the United States eventually allowed all tuna, no matter how it had been

[103] European Communities – Measures Affecting the Approval and Marketing of Biotech Products – Mutually Agreed Solution between Canada and the European Communities (15 July 2009) WT/DS292/40, G/L/628/Add.1.

[104] A. Arcuri, 'Is CETA Keeping up with the Promise? Interpreting Certain Provisions Relating to Biotechnology' (2017) 41 *Questions of International Law, Zoom-Out* 35–58.

[105] Ibid., 47 *et seq.*

harvested, to be sold in its market' while reserving the 'dolphin-safe' label for tuna harvested in a particular manner.[106] In 2008, Mexico requested consultations with the United States with regard to its 'dolphin-safe' labelling requirements, initiating the next phase of the long-running tuna dolphin dispute. This section will focus primarily on how the Appellate Body in *US-Tuna II (Mexico)* (not to be confused with *Tuna Dolphin II*, the 1994 dispute initiated by the EC against the USA concerning its secondary embargo against re-exported tuna) shed light on how the relationship between the TBT Agreement and international standards should be construed. Like the SPS Agreement, the TBT Agreement requires the harmonization of national regulations on the basis of international standards (Article 2.4). However, unlike the SPS Agreement, which provides a list of international standard-setting organizations (such as the Codex Alimentarius Commission), the TBT Agreement does not list any institutional/authoritative *sources* of international standards. The question of what counts as an international standardizing body is important as such a classification automatically triggers the harmonization obligation (i.e. pressure for entanglement) established in Article 2.4 of the TBT.[107]

Mexico challenged the 'dolphin-safe' labelling requirements as inconsistent with inter alia the TBT Agreement.[108] Notably, the (state-administered) *voluntary* labelling scheme was considered to be a *mandatory* technical regulation, thus falling within the remit of the TBT Agreement.[109] As such, Mexico claimed that the US measure should have been based on the relevant international standard (according to Article 2.4), specifically the labelling scheme established under the Agreement on the International Dolphin Conservation Program (AIDCP). Notably, the AIDCP is only a regional organization to which only a subset of WTO members adheres. The Panel and the Appellate Body were tasked with determining whether the AIDCP labelling scheme

[106] P. C. Mavroidis, 'Last Mile for Tuna (to a Safe Harbour): What Is the TBT Agreement All About?' (2019) 30 *European Journal of International Law* 279–301, at 280.

[107] TBT 2.4 requires national technical regulations, standards and conformity assessments to be based on relevant international standards except where such standards would be an ineffective or inappropriate means for the fulfilment of the legitimate objectives pursued.

[108] M. A. Crowley and R. Howse, 'Tuna–Dolphin II: A Legal and Economic Analysis of the Appellate Body Report' (2014) 13 *World Trade Review* 321–55, at 321.

[109] Both the Panel and the Appellate Body in *Tuna Dolphin II* found that the US measure constituted a mandatory technical regulation because it *prescribed by law* minimum requirements for accessing the 'dolphin-safe' labelling scheme in the USA.

constituted an international standard within the meaning of the TBT Agreement. Section 8.3.5.2 focuses on the Appellate Body's rulings as the Panel's findings are of little relevance to the question of legal entanglement.

8.3.5.2 Legal Entanglement/Appeal

For the purposes of the TBT Agreement, 'international standards are those adopted by international standardizing bodies, meaning those with *recognized activities* in standardization that are *open* on a non-discriminatory basis to relevant bodies of at least all WTO Members'.[110] While the Panel agreed with Mexico that the AIDCP was an international standardizing body,[111] the Appellate Body found that it did not fulfil the requirement of 'openness' because countries could only accede to the AIDCP by invitation.[112] As a result, the 'AIDCP dolphin-safe definition and certification' scheme did not constitute an international standard within the meaning of the TBT Agreement, and the USA was not required to base its domestic 'dolphin-safe' regulation upon it.

However, the Appellate Body did not stop there, clarifying further the meaning of 'recognized' activities in standardization. Considering that the resulting standards would apply to all WTO members, the Appellate Body found that recognition of international standardization activities had to go beyond the subset of WTO members participating in the standard-setting process, therefore 'the larger the number of countries that participate in the development of a standard, the more likely it can be said that the respective body's activities in standardization are "recognized"'.[113] Moreover, '[e]vidence of a body's compliance with procedural and substantive safeguards formulated by WTO Members would be relevant for the question of whether its standardizing activities are "recognized" for the purposes of the TBT Agreement'.[114] In this context, the Appellate Body referred to a TBT Committee Decision from the

[110] P. V. den Bossche and D. Prévost, *Essentials of WTO Law* (Cambridge University Press, 2016), p. 190.

[111] United States – Measures Concerning the Importation, Marketing and Sale of Tuna and Tuna Products – Panel report (15 September 2011) WT/DS381/R ('US-Tuna II'), para. 7.691.

[112] United States – Measures Concerning the Importation, Marketing and Sale of Tuna and Tuna Products – Report by Appellate Body (16 May 2012) WT/DS381/AB/R, para. 399.

[113] *US-Tuna II* Appellate Body Report, para. 390.

[114] Ibid., para. 377.

year 2000 ('the Decision'), which sets out guiding principles and procedures that standardizing bodies should observe when developing international standards, inter alia *transparency, openness, impartiality and consensus.*[115] The Decision is significant as it spells these principles out in some detail, thus defining a relatively precise guidance for the entanglement of WTO law with standards from other sources. In an early case under the TBT Agreement, *EC-Sardines*, the Panel had dismissed the Decision as 'a [mere] *policy statement of preference* and not the controlling provision in interpreting the expression "relevant international standard" as set out in Article 2.4 of the TBT Agreement'.[116] In *Tuna Dolphin II*, the Appellate Body reversed this finding, stating that the Decision constituted a *subsequent agreement of the parties* in the meaning of Article 31(3)(a) VCLT and should be read together with the TBT.[117]

The weight that the Appellate Body gave to the Decision is significant because it directly clarifies several points of contention with regard to interpreting the TBT and how it relates to international standards. Principle three, for example, explicitly emphasizes *consensus* as a requirement for international standards in the TBT Agreement, even though an explanatory note to TBT Annex I.2 states that the TBT also covers documents not based on consensus. Notably, the Appellate Body in *EC-Sardines* had rejected the consensus requirement.[118] The Appellate Body's ruling in *EC-Sardines* had also implied a large measure of regulatory harmonization and 'a very close fit or relationship between any technical regulation and the international standard, providing very little flexibility for regulatory diversity'.[119] By contrast, the Appellate Body in *US-Tuna II* resisted 'demands for regulatory harmonization through Article 2.4' by emphasizing the criteria contained in the Decision relating to transparency and meaningful participation.[120] Thus, the Appellate Body effectively transformed the Decision into 'a code of administrative

[115] TBT Committee, 'Decision on Principles for the Development of International Standards, Guides and Recommendations' (13 November 2000) G/TBT/9, Annex 4.
[116] European Communities – Trade Description of Sardines – Panel report (29 May 2002) WT/DS231/R, para. 7.91.
[117] *US-Tuna II* Appellate Body Report, para. 372.
[118] European Communities – Trade Description of Sardines – Report by Appellate Body (26 September 2002) WT/DS231/AB/R, para. 224.
[119] Howse, 'The World Trade Organization 20 Years On', 56.
[120] Ibid., 56.

procedure and practice for international standardization' in the vein of global administrative law.[121]

Ultimately, the Appellate Body found that while the 'dolphin-safe' labelling provisions did not violate Article 2.4 of the TBT, they were inconsistent with Article 2.1 of the TBT because of a lack of even-handedness in the manner in which risks from different fishing techniques in different areas of the ocean were addressed.

8.3.5.3 Aftermath

In response to the Panel and the Appellate Body reports, the United States modified its dolphin-safe labelling requirements to comply with the Appellate Body's ruling. However, the US measure continued to impose different certification and tracking and verification requirements depending on the fishery where the tuna was caught, with more burdensome requirements for tuna caught in the ETP. After several rounds of compliance proceedings, in which Mexico continued to challenge the United States' measure due to discriminatory effects and with both parties repeatedly appealing, the Panel found that the US measure was not discriminatory and exonerated the USA from responsibility, a finding that the Appellate Body confirmed. The distinctions made in the United States' measure (i.e. its discriminatory elements) were found to be calibrated to the different levels of risk posed by the practice of 'setting' on dolphins vis-à-vis other fishing methods. Thus, the detrimental impact caused by the US measure stemmed exclusively from a legitimate regulatory distinction and did not result in 'treatment less favourable than that accorded to like products from the United States and other countries' (consistency with Article 2.1 as well as with the chapeau of GATT Article XX).[122] The final compliance report (with no finding of non-compliance) was circulated to members in December 2018, and adopted in January 2019, thereby concluding a dispute that had run on for almost thirty years.

[121] Crowley and Howse, 'Tuna–Dolphin II', 342.

[122] United States – Measures Concerning the Importation, Marketing and Sale of Tuna and Tuna Products – Recourse to Article 21.5 of the DSU by the United States; United States – Measures Concerning the Importation, Marketing and Sale of Tuna and Tuna Products – Recourse to Article 21.5 of the DSU by Mexico, Report by Appellate Body (14 December 2018) WT/DS381/AB/RW/USA; WT/DS381/AB/RW2, paras 7.1–7.14.

8.4 Main Findings

8.4.1 *Irritative Norm Conflict Over Time*

The unadopted Panel report in *Tuna Dolphin I* set the stage for an antagonistic relationship between the GATT-based multilateral trading system and environmental trade measures for the achievement of global environmental objectives. Through repeated 'irritations' of trade law by environmental norms (through litigation in the WTO combined with external pressure), subsequent rulings by Panels and the WTO Appellate Body significantly corrected/recalibrated controversial aspects of the trade and environment interface, a process that is referred to here as *irritative norm conflict over time.*[123]

The 'Tuna Dolphin saga' (in which *Shrimp-Turtle* constitutes a crucial building block) illustrates how irritative norm conflict over a period of almost thirty years allowed WTO judicial bodies to adjust elements of previous jurisprudence that had 'gone too far' in asserting trade objectives over members' right to regulate. Although *Tuna Dolphin I* had found unilateral environmental trade measures with extraterritorial effects prima facie incapable of justification under the GATT, the Appellate Body in *Shrimp-Turtle* reversed this finding and clarified that GATT Article XX could, in fact, justify measures conditioning market access on environmental policies/PPMs abroad – as long as the measures do not amount to arbitrary or unjustifiable discrimination.[124] As a result, the ruling of the Appellate Body in *Shrimp-Turtle* was widely perceived as 'a bold attempt to construct a broader societal vision of the WTO [...] more sensitive to environmental concerns'.[125] Both the *Shrimp-Turtle* import requirements and the *Tuna Dolphin/US-Tuna II* labelling provisions were ultimately found to be consistent with WTO law; however, this was only after the United States had been subjected to several (costly) rounds of litigation and revisions of the law. Thus, while environmental norms have gained clout in the WTO, the fundamental objective of the WTO system – an open international economic system – is preserved through the meticulous enforcement of non-discrimination principles.

[123] On irritative norm conflicts, see N. Krisch, F. Corradini and L. L. Reimers, 'Order at the Margins: The Legal Construction of Interface Conflicts over Time' (2020) 9 *Global Constitutionalism* 343–63.

[124] J. Pauwelyn, 'Recent Books on Trade and Environment: GATT Phantoms Still Haunt the WTO' (2004) 15 *European Journal of International Law* 575–92.

[125] Perez, *Ecological Sensitivity and Global Legal Pluralism*, p. 65.

In *EC-Hormones*, *EC-Biotech*, and *Canada/US-Continued Suspension* – a series of distinct but interrelated disputes – what was being negotiated was inter alia the scope/applicability of the precautionary principle in the WTO context. Repeated irritations of international trade rules (and pressure from both within and outside of the WTO) led to a shift in the Appellate Body's construction of precaution in the WTO and SPS context (*Canada/US-Continued Suspension*). While the tension between the precautionary principle (as codified in international environmental law) and the emphasis on scientific evidence and risk assessment in the SPS Agreement is not completely resolved, the role of precaution has been significantly strengthened (both in WTO law and outside of it – e.g. in the Codex Alimentarius Commission and in the Biosafety Protocol). The compromise around the role of precaution versus scientific risk assessment in CETA shows how WTO dispute settlement is not the only arena in which actors negotiate and navigate irritative norm conflict.

Finally, it is of note that the appeals mechanism in the WTO serves to process – and to accelerate – irritative norm conflict, allowing the Appellate Body to make (rapid) adjustments in the wake of contentious Panel findings, member state pressure and public protest. 'Follow-up' disputes prompted by issues around compliance or continued retaliation also provide the opportunity for rebalancing or 'fine-tuning' previous findings (e.g. *Canada/US-Continued Suspension*).

8.4.2 Legal Entanglement (and Mechanisms of Distancing)

The narrative of competing objectives between international trade law and international environmental law obscures the way in which the two bodies of norms are already *entangled*, going as far back as *Tuna Dolphin I* (in which both parties made legal claims relating to international environmental law). All participants in the GATT/WTO dispute settlement system regularly invoke outside bodies of norms to justify their claims. The judicial bodies themselves have on several occasions inquired into possible legal bases/defences for WTO-inconsistent measures, grounded in international environmental law (e.g. the Panel in *Shrimp-Turtle*), and routinely draw on international environmental norms in their legal reasoning. Notably, this is not always done to advance 'trade-friendly' arguments. WTO disciplines on non-discrimination are often brought into relation with international environmental norms that emphasize international cooperation (e.g. the Panel and Appellate Body in *Shrimp-Turtle*). Consequently, a closer relationship between international trade law and international environmental law will not necessarily result in more 'environmentally friendly' rulings. In this vein, some of the foundational critiques directed at the multilateral trading system can also be levelled against the international environmental regime, which has incorporated into its body of norms a bias against unilateral trade measures and has embraced the objective of liberalized trade (e.g. Principle 12 of the Rio Declaration). The two bodies of norms have always been more entangled (and mutually reinforcing) than generally assumed.

The reference to sustainable development in the Preamble of the WTO Agreement plays a central 'entangling' function at the interface between trade and environment, opening the door for outside environmental norms to enter WTO law through GATT Article XX (e.g. in *Shrimp-Turtle*). However, such forms of relationing between international trade law and outside bodies of norms are tenuous and remain contingent on the Panels' and Appellate Body's willingness to take outside norms into consideration on a case-by-case basis – essentially at their discretion. For instance, while the Appellate Body in *Shrimp-Turtle* had referred to outside treaty law not binding on all the disputing parties (the CBD), the Panel in *EC-Biotech* rejected the applicability of the Biosafety Protocol because the United States was not a party to it, and it could therefore not be considered 'applicable' in the relations between the parties according to Article 31(3)(c) of the Vienna Convention.

Resistance to *legal entanglement* comes in the form of strategies for *distancing*. In *EC-Hormones*, various techniques for creating *distancing* between the precautionary principle and obligations under the SPS Agreement were employed by the disputants, the Panel and the Appellate Body, including (1) relegating the precautionary principle to the realm of international environmental law while calling into question the status of the precautionary principle as a general principle of international law or a rule of customary international law; (2) restricting the applicability of the precautionary principle to its (partial) reflection in the SPS Agreement (Article 5.7) but rejecting its general applicability with regard to other provisions (namely Articles 5.1 and 5.2); and (3) pointing to the absence of a 'clear textual directive' that would allow an external norm to affect the interpretation of a provision in a WTO Agreement. Article 3.2 of the DSU requires treaty interpreters to refer to any relevant rules of international law applicable in the relations between the parties (according to Article 31(3)(c) of the Vienna Convention). As customary and general international law is always applicable between all parties to a dispute, relevant customary norms or general principles of international law will more likely be brought into relation with WTO law than external treaty norms which may not have been ratified by all WTO members/ parties in a given dispute. It is therefore unsurprising that emphasizing the customary or general international law nature of an external norm *or lack thereof* is a dominant mechanism for creating either entanglement or distancing between WTO law and other bodies of norms.

8.4.3 *Interface Norms in the GATT/WTO Context*

Although the relationship between WTO law and international environmental law is not centrally regulated, both bodies of norms contain 'interface norms' that guide forms of relationing to the other 'from the inside out'. In the WTO context, Article XX of the GATT can be viewed as a *reception norm*, allowing external norms to enter into GATT law. The specific environmental terms mentioned in GATT Article XX serve as 'docking points' for environmental norms to connect to. Once made, such linkages endure even as external legal orders change over time, in turn influencing the interpretation of 'coupled' WTO norms. Notably, the *chapeau* of GATT Article XX sets out *substantive criteria* for the *application of environmental measures* by conditioning 'entry' on non-discrimination/even-handedness and multilateralism/international consensus (see Section 8.4.4).

Not all reception norms are textually explicit, however. The concept of 'legitimate regulatory distinction' to justify discriminatory treatment was read into Article 2.1 of the TBT Agreement by the Appellate Body through successive case law (including *US-Tuna II*). It allows for balancing TBT non-discrimination objectives/obligations with legitimate regulatory interventions (such as for environmental protection) and thus fulfils the same purpose as GATT Article XX, including – conceivably – as a reception norm. Similarly, even though Article 5.7 of the SPS Agreement does not mention the term 'precaution' as such, the provision is generally viewed as a reflection of the precautionary principle and thus allows for external bodies of norms related to the precautionary principle to enter into WTO law.

The reference to sustainable development in the Preamble of the WTO Agreement *connects* trade rules to the vast body of international environmental law (and the emerging field of 'international sustainable development law'). As a *connecting norm*, somewhat akin to the multi-sourced equivalent norms identified by some,[126] the reference to sustainable development provides a linkage function and enhances the discretion of Panels and the Appellate Body to interpret the environmental exceptions of Article XX expansively (e.g. the Appellate Body in *Shrimp-Turtle* construed a close relationship between WTO rules and international environmental norms according to preambular directive). In this way, interface norms can be mutually supportive.

While the WTO, on the whole, keeps substantive norms from other areas of *international law* at bay, it actively seeks entanglement with *international standards*. International standards attract linkages with WTO law more readily due to the WTO's inherent harmonization dynamic. This is done through the TBT and SPS Agreements, which coordinate the relationship between international standards and WTO harmonization obligations through Articles 2.4 and 3.1 respectively. The contrasting approaches to entanglement are best illustrated in *EC-Hormones*, where the Panel and the Appellate Body interpreted the SPS Agreement in a way as to promote entanglement with Codex norms, while creating *distancing* with an external substantive norm originally developed in the context of international environmental law, namely the precautionary principle.

8.4.4 *Substantive Dimensions for Interface Norms*

An important factor influencing the porosity of WTO law is whether the external norm is of multilateral origin or constitutes an international standard. Environmental measures based on multilateral consensus have a higher likelihood of being taken into account in the WTO context than unilateral measures with little international support (although this is not guaranteed, see the Panel's dismissal of the Biosafety Protocol in *EC-Biotech*). This way of reasoning is in line with the notion that the interface between international trade law and other norms of international law is governed primarily by the customary rules on treaty interpretation (as codified in the Vienna Convention) that require any relevant rules of international law applicable in the relations between the parties to be taken into account together with context. As opposed to external treaty norms, customary international law binds all states and will always be binding on parties in a given trade dispute (no matter the

[126] See T. Broude and Y. Shany (eds), *Multi-sourced Equivalent Norms in International Law* (Bloomsbury Publishing, 2011).

constellation). It follows that linkages with external norms are more easily produced if the latter are considered general or customary international law (see Section 8.4.2), as well as when there are 'docking norms' in the text that can provide the Panel or the Appellate Body with a 'textual directive' – that is, a mandate – for linkage.

Further, entanglement between WTO law and international standards is explicitly encouraged through the TBT Agreement and the SPS Agreement, which promote the harmonization of national regulations on the basis of *international standards*. The substantive dimensions of entanglement between WTO law and international standards is gradually being 'fleshed out' with additional (still contested) criteria such as the level of international support for the adoption of the norm in question (consensus, broad membership, inclusiveness/participation). For example, in *EC-Hormones* the EC did not recognize a specific set of Codex standards as being 'international standards' due to the narrow margin by which it was adopted. The EC thus expressed expectations about the *substantive dimensions* of the interface norm contained in the SPS Agreement: international standards should only be taken into account if they are considered legitimate, as indicated by broad acceptance during adoption (see Section 8.3.3.2). While the Panel in *EC-Hormones* rejected the EC's reasoning, the Appellate Body in *US-Tuna II* gave significant weight to a 2000 TBT Committee Decision, which contains a set of substantive criteria that qualify the appropriateness of international standards from the perspective of the WTO (specifically the TBT Agreement), including transparency, openness, consensus and effectiveness. In this regard, the Appellate Body also indicated that the number of countries participating in a standard-setting process relative to the total number of WTO members is relevant for the entry of international standards into WTO law via TBT Article 2.4.

8.5 Conclusion

This chapter addressed horizontal ways of relationing between international trade law and international environmental law, and explored how these different legalities respond to each other and manage tensions without subordination. The findings show how repeated 'irritations' of trade law through environmental norms, expressed in WTO dispute settlement and combined with external political pressure (including by building and harnessing pressure in other multilateral fora), can prompt 'recalibrations' at the interface of WTO law and encourage the clarification of the relationship over time. What emerges from this analysis is a kind of modified 'island' view of the WTO in relation to other bodies of norms. Interface norms allow for the contingent adaptation of 'foreign' rules into WTO law while broader systemic connections are resisted through mechanisms of distancing. Thereby new developments in international law can be reflected in jurisprudential interpretations without compromising the stated objective of ensuring the 'security and predictability of the multilateral framework for trade'. To this end, the WTO regime actively *encourages* legal entanglement with international standards because harmonization helps facilitate trade. Ultimately, this chapter demonstrates how the WTO has successfully negotiated legal entanglement *on its own terms* and in service to the regime's overarching goal of free trade.

PART III

Weaving Transnational Legalities

9

Targeting Bad Apples or the Whole Barrel?

The Legal Entanglements between Targeted and Comprehensive Logics in Counter-Proliferation Sanctions

GRÉGOIRE MALLARD AND AUREL NIEDERBERGER

9.1 Introduction

Jurists and legal historians have increasingly come to the realization that the story of their discipline is not, in fact, that of the gradual diffusion of Western concepts to the rest of the world. The emergence of new norms of global governance and the history of international law more generally are made up of multiple stories that have no single point of departure.[1] The history of legal concepts, imaginaries and fields of practice is full of examples of such 'legal entanglements' between various systems of law, located at different scales, and generated according to different temporalities and historicities.[2] The new historiography on colonialism and empires, for instance, has insisted on the two-way transport of legal concepts and practices and the plurality of legal orders that were constituted over time during the Spanish, British, French and even German empires.[3] In many cases, scholars of colonial law have demonstrated that

This chapter is directly based on a project headed by Grégoire Mallard that received funding from the European Research Council under the European Union's Horizon 2020 research and innovation program (Grant Agreement PROSANCT, 'Bombs, Banks and Sanctions', Project 716216). The authors thank all the interviewees who participated in the research.

[1] T. Duve, 'Entanglements in Legal History. Introductory Remarks', in T. Duve, *Entanglements in Legal History: Conceptual Approaches* (Max Planck Institute for European Legal History, 2014), pp. 3–25.

[2] B. S. Chimni, *International Law and World Order: A Critique of Contemporary Approaches* (Cambridge University Press, 2017).

[3] L. Benton, *Law and Colonial Cultures: Legal Regimes in World History, 1400–1900* (Cambridge University Press, 2001); G. Steinmetz, *The Devil's Handwriting: Precoloniality and the German Colonial State in Qingdao, Samoa, and Southwest Africa* (University of Chicago Press, 2008); Duve, *Entanglements in Legal History*; J. Go, 'Global

the colonizers' rule was far from being the sole source of authority and legitimacy in disputes between colonizers and colonial subjects.[4] The resulting 'legal entanglements' may have looked contradictory in principle but were effective in practice.[5]

Similarly, political scientists have looked at the co-constitution of normative and/or rules-based regimes, which has grown increasingly more complex through practices of interlinkages. Experts often push the boundaries of technical fields of governance by claiming jurisdiction over the regulation of innovations in adjacent fields. Such practices promote an ever tighter entanglement between expert knowledge and policy domains, leading to either conflict, cooperation or free-riding by transnational policy networks, private companies and states.[6] Political sociologists and socio-legal scholars have also recently paid attention to the circulation of various kinds of capital (economic, cultural, political or even colonial) and their transmission across entangled national and international regulatory fields. These scholars conclude that the distribution of such forms of capital does not follow a purely national logic, such that we need a transnational perspective on the workings of the state in the age of globalization.[7]

Although these various disciplines differ in methods and findings, we find, across fields, a number of scholars who seek to explain the evolution of complex forms of transnational legal rules as 'legal entanglements'. These scholars converge on some epistemic principles. They hold that history originates from many parts of the world; that asymmetries of

Fields and Imperial Forms: Field Theory and the British and American Empires' (2008) 26 *Sociological Theory* 201–29; G. Mallard, *Gift Exchange: The Transnational History of a Political Idea* (Cambridge University Press, 2019).

4 S. E. Merry, 'Legal Pluralism' (1988) 22 *Law & Society Review* 869–96; see also S. E. Merry, *Human Rights and Gender Violence: Translating International Law into Local Justice* (University of Chicago Press, 2009).

5 Colonial legal entanglements were not tightly tied together, and the multiple actors who circulated from one imperial order to another well tolerated multiplicity and contradiction in the interpretation of plural legal orders (see Benton, *Law and Colonial Cultures*).

6 S. C. Hofmann, 'Overlapping Institutions in the Realm of International Security: The Case of NATO and ESDP' (2009) 7 *Perspectives on Politics* 45–52; K. J. Alter and K. Raustiala, 'The Rise of International Regime Complexity' (2018) 14 *Annual Review of Law and Social Science* 329–49.

7 Y. Dezalay and B. Garth, *The Internationalization of Palace Wars: Lawyers, Economists and the Struggle to Transform Latin American States* (Chicago University Press, 2002); Y. Dezalay and B. Garth, *Asian Legal Revivals: Lawyers in the Shadow of Empire* (Chicago University Press, 2010); Steinmetz, *The Devil's Handwriting*; Go, 'Global Fields and Imperial Forms'; Mallard, *Gift Exchange*.

power are inscribed in norms but that it is mostly in practice where power actually manifests itself – most often, through practices of knowing, classifying and reifying certain visions of the world.[8] They also tend to agree that although some hidden path dependency may well explain the overall direction of history, the continued existence of normative contradictions within any given 'regime complex'[9] leaves room for contingencies and even sudden reversals. Importantly, scholars who use the notion of 'legal entanglement' accept that normative contradictions do *not* necessarily threaten the working and stability of a transnational legal order.[10] This position departs from the traditional rationalistic view that a normative system can only be stable if it is based on clear, self-reinforcing and non-contradictory principles, such that one can derive from it rules of conduct and agreed-upon punishments in case of violations. The notion of 'legal entanglement' therefore introduces a 'post-modern' perspective[11] to modernity's rationalist project of building universal rules beyond the nation state based on clear and quasi-constitutional foundations.

In this chapter, we adopt a similar perspective on 'legal entanglements' to explain contemporary dynamics in transnational legal orderings in the field of security. In particular, we want to explain the normative order by which states adopt international sanctions against individuals and/or states which have threatened international security and/or violated agreed-upon rules. We start from the assumption that sanctions are better thought of as bodies of norms and practices, also known as 'sanctions regimes'.[12] These sanctions regimes have long been elaborated at the intersection of various bodies of law, both at the domestic and international levels, which define principles related to the responsibility of states and/or norms ensuring the protection of human rights. For

[8] M. Foucault, *Discipline and Punish: The Birth of the Prison* (Vintage, 1995).

[9] Alter and Raustiala, 'The Rise of International Regime Complexity'.

[10] T. C. Halliday and G. Shaffer, *Transnational Legal Orders* (Cambridge University Press, 2015); D. Halberstam and E. Stein, 'The United Nations, the European Union, and the King of Sweden: Economic Sanctions and Individual Rights in a Plural World Order' (2009) 46 *Common Market Law Review* 13–72.

[11] M. Koskenniemi and P. Leino, 'Fragmentation of International Law? Postmodern Anxieties' (2002) 15 *Leiden Journal of International Law* 553–79.

[12] T. J. Biersteker, S. E. Eckert and M. Tourinho, 'Thinking about United Nations Targeted Sanctions', in T. J. Biersteker, S. E. Eckert and M. Tourinho (eds), *Targeted Sanctions: The Impacts and Effectiveness of United Nations Action* (Cambridge University Press, 2016), pp. 11–37.

instance, the notion that innocent civilians should not suffer from the application of sanctions was translated in the United Nations Security Council (UNSC) sanctions regimes that were once 'comprehensive' and showed little respect to the human rights of populations in sanctioned areas, and that have become more targeted – or, in other words, 'smarter'.[13] This 'miniaturization' of UN sanctions began with various sanctions against conflict actors in Africa in the late 1990s and early 2000s, and it was further developed with the well-known sanctions regimes against Iran and North Korea, at least in their earlier stages in the 2000s. These processes occurred according to different temporalities and scales depending on where they were located.

This chapter argues that, on the one hand, the developments that have affected the sanctions regime have strengthened the normative coherence of the UN system of norms and rules, giving it more legitimacy and unity. The new UNSC sanctions regime was indeed greeted as a reconciliation of the UNSC's main responsibility to safeguard international peace and security with better respect for other pillars of international law and the UN, namely human rights, which include the right to access vital goods such as food or medical care.[14] On the other hand, it remains to be seen whether new contradictions have not also spurred from some of the latest developments in the broader 'sanctions regime', which not only includes the UNSC sanctions but also multiple domestic sanctions regimes, in particular in the United States and Europe. In contrast to the story of a clear paradigmatic shift characterized by the emergence of a new 'targeted sanctions' paradigm, relegating to the dustbin of history all previous forms of comprehensive sanctions that clashed with other UN norms, we explain how, particularly in counter-proliferation sanctions, contradictions persisted in the legal entanglements between targeted and comprehensive logics and in overlapping multilateral and domestic legal sources of sanctions. We further explain why the presence of such contradictions in counter-proliferation regimes has gone largely unnoticed by 'targeted sanctions' designers and advocates who do not use the notion of 'legal entanglement'.[15]

[13] D. W. Drezner, 'How Smart Are Smart Sanctions?' (2003) 5 *International Studies Review* 107–10.

[14] E.g., Article 25 of the Universal Declaration of Human Rights.

[15] J. J. Lew and R. Nephew, 'The Use and Misuse of Economic Statecraft: How Washington Is Abusing Its Financial Might' *Foreign Affairs* (November/December 2018), 139–49.

In this chapter, we will thus show the heuristic power of the notion of 'legal entanglement' when applied to the evolution of global sanctions regimes in the last thirty years. To demonstrate how targeted sanctions regimes in the field of counter-proliferation are best analysed as 'legal entanglements' between targeted and comprehensive logics, as well as between multilateral and unilateral regimes, the chapter proceeds in three parts. In Section 9.2, we show how a discourse on the 'targetedness' of sanctions was promoted by sanctions entrepreneurs, policy experts and international governmental and non-governmental organizations in the context of the 'War on Terror' during which sanctions increasingly targeted specific individuals listed by states for their association with non-state networks of terrorists, namely Al Qaeda, the Taliban and later ISIS. In Section 9.3, we show how the multilateral machinery that was created in the context of counter-terrorism initiatives, especially under the aegis of the UNSC, extended its reach to the field of counter-proliferation, when specific sanctions committees modelled after the Al Qaeda Sanctions Committee were created in the UNSC to monitor UN member states' compliance with new UNSC Resolutions (UNSCRs) that targeted the Democratic People's Republic of Korea (DPRK) and Iran's sanctioned nuclear activities. In Section 9.4, we show how, during the early 2010s, the targeted sanctions that the UNSC imposed on the DPRK and Iran were 'comprehensivized'. This process of comprehensivization, we show, followed different pathways: the comprehensivization of UNSC sanctions occurred either directly at the level of the UNSC (as in the case of the DPRK), or indirectly (as in the case of Iran), because of the entanglement between UNSC sanctions with the comprehensive logic of domestic sanctions adopted in a unilateral fashion by the United States and the European Union. This was the case regardless of claims by the USA, and especially by the EU, that their 'multilateral restrictive measures' (as sanctions are called in EU parlance) did not amount to comprehensive measures.

Our analysis shows that the legal entanglements between targeted and comprehensive logics that traverse the global sanctions regimes rest on a few core mechanisms. These mechanisms include the assertion of judicial authority by US regulators over the world's financial transactions denominated in US dollars; the use of instruments that designated central actors within designated jurisdictions (in particular, the central banks of sanctioned states); and the ambiguity of the concept of 'risk' held by global financial actors, which allowed financial institutions to adopt a 'zero-risk' approach when it came to the implementation of financial sanctions.[16] The ambiguity of this concept of risk, which circulated through a network of cross-references across regulatory documents,[17] led financial institutions to massively cut their operations in the targeted economy while remaining, on the face of it, within the bounds of the targeted logic of 'risk-based approaches'. We conclude by highlighting key normative reflections that derive from the realization that such entanglements between targeted and comprehensive logics are central to the operation of counter-proliferation sanctions.

9.2 The Creation of the UNSC Counter-Terrorist Sanctions Regime and Its Extension to the Field of Counter-Proliferation: A Case of Isomorphism?

The application of sanctions is not new, as states have long agreed upon historically specific appropriate responses against threats to peace and security as well as violations of international norms and rules.[18] However, the move towards targetedness appears to be a more recent phenomenon, spurred by the UNSC's efforts to respond to recent crises, taking advantage of equally recent phenomena, such as the new information technologies that facilitate the identification of individual targets,[19] the acceptability of designating non-state actors as subjects of international law and the desire of the international community to protect innocent civilians during responses against state and non-state perpetrators.

The global push towards more coherence in the UN system of norms that affected the design and monitoring of sanctions at the UNSC came with the realization that, after the Cold War, comprehensive sanctions

[16] G. Mallard, 'Governing Proliferation Finance: Multilateralism, Transgovernmentalism and Hegemony in the Case of Sanctions against Iran', in E. Brousseau, J.-M. Glachant and J. Sgard (eds), *Oxford Handbook of Institutions of International Economic Governance and Market Regulation* (Oxford University Press, 2019).

[17] A. Riles, 'Models and Documents: Artifacts of International Legal Knowledge' (1999) 48 *International and Comparative Law Quarterly* 805–25.

[18] M. Finnemore, *The Purpose of Intervention: Changing Beliefs about the Use of Force* (Cornell University Press, 2004).

[19] M. de Goede and G. Sullivan, 'Introduction: The Politics of the List' (2016) 34 *Environment and Planning D: Society and Space* 3–13; for a comprehensive review of the legal and technical developments in the UNSC counter-terrorism sanction regime, see G. Sullivan. *The Law of the List: UN Counterterrorism Sanctions and the Politics of Global Security Law* (Cambridge University Press, 2020).

proved too devastating in a less divided world. From 1945 until 1989, the world was divided into trading blocs; thus, a country that was excluded by one bloc could still trade with the other bloc. Therefore, 'sanctions' in the sense of trading restrictions applied by the West for instance may have been comprehensive in design, but never fully sealed off a country. Furthermore, the UNSC sanctions that were adopted in 1966 against Rhodesia, and in 1977 against South Africa, were limited to arms embargoes. This changed with the end of the Cold War. In 1990, the UNSC unanimously imposed comprehensive sanctions on Iraq after Saddam Hussein's invasion of Kuwait. While these sanctions were modelled on the initiative of the West, in particular the USA, they were backed by universal condemnation of the Iraqi act of aggression. These sanctions initially consisted of an embargo against all Iraqi imports and exports and were to be applied by all UN member states. Their effects were drastic and counterproductive: even though exemptions on food and medical supplies were gradually introduced, the impact on the civilian population was devastating, while hardly hurting – or, by some accounts, even strengthening – Saddam Hussein's regime.[20] This paradigmatic case of comprehensive sanctions convinced the international community to move towards a targeted design of sanctions to avoid hurting civilians in sanctioned territories.[21]

In the following years (i.e. the late 1990s and early 2000s), a 'transnational policy network' of diplomats, national politicians and academics promoted these targeted sanctions, consisting of tools such as assets freezes, travel bans, sectoral economic restrictions and arms embargoes.[22] These targeted sanctions became the only type of sanctions imposed by the UNSC since, with early applications responding to internal armed

[20] D. Cortright and G. A. Lopez, *The Sanctions Decade: Assessing UN Strategies in the 1990s* (Lynne Rienner, 2000); J. Gordon. *Invisible War: The United States and the Iraq Sanctions* (Harvard University Press, 2012).

[21] M. W. Reisman and D. L. Stevick, 'The Applicability of International Law Standards to United Nations Economic Sanctions Programmes' (1998) 9 *European Journal of International Law* 86–141.

[22] T. J. Biersteker, 'Scholarly Participation in Transnational Policy Networks: The Case of Targeted Sanctions', in M. E. Bertucci and A. F. Lowenthal (eds), *Narrowing the Gap: Scholars, Policy-Makers and International Affairs* (Johns Hopkins University Press, 2014), pp. 137–54.

conflicts in Angola, Sierra Leone, and Liberia in the late 1990s and early 2000s.[23] Since then, as a sign of the normative appeal of targeted sanctions, human rights organizations – staunch critics of the comprehensive sanctions against Iraq – have repeatedly called for the imposition of targeted sanctions in the context of various civil wars.[24] Consequently, academic literature on sanctions has usually spoken of a clear break between the comprehensive Iraq sanctions and the post-Iraq era of 'targeted sanctions',[25] whose coherence with the broader system of UN norms is emphasized by many.[26]

In the late 1990s and early 2000s, a series of large-scale terrorist attacks – most prominently 9/11 – pushed states to confront transnational non-state groups as significant threats to their security. The ensuing War on Terror involved UN targeted sanctions that were similar in their formal setup to the peacebuilding sanctions put in place in response to African civil wars, but came with longer lists of targeted individuals and entities. As a further difference, while early peacebuilding sanctions included sectoral trade embargoes (such as diamonds), the targets of counter-terrorism sanctions were too amorphous for such measures. Instead, these sanctions regimes relied chiefly on financial measures and travel bans. During the 2000s, under the stimulus of the UNSC, the financial sector thus became heavily mobilized in the quest for more efficiency and more targetedness in the fight against individual terrorists linked to Al Qaeda.[27] The range of measures imposed on those individuals who were added to the list of identified terrorists were (and continue to be) forceful, including asset freezes and the systematic screening of all cross-border transactions. Immediately after 9/11, the United States – and then the UNSC – asked the financial sector to help them with implementing this targeted logic with measures to counter the

[23] D. Cortright and G. A. Lopez, 'Introduction: Assessing Smart Sanctions: Lessons from the 1990s', in D. Cortright and G. A. Lopez (eds), *Smart Sanctions: Targeting Economic Statecraft* (Rowman & Littlefield Publishers, 2002), pp. 1–22.

[24] A. Niederberger, 'Expert Networks and the Emergence of Practice in UN Arms Embargo Monitoring', Paper presented at EISA PEC 2019 (2019).

[25] Biersteker, Eckert and Tourinho, 'Thinking about United Nations Targeted Sanctions'; E. Solingen, *Sanctions, Statecraft, and Nuclear Proliferation* (Cambridge University Press, 2012).

[26] R. Nephew, *The Art of Sanctions: A View from the Field* (Columbia University Press, 2017).

[27] J. Zarate, *Treasury's War: The Unleashing of a New Era of Financial Warfare* (Hachette, 2013).

financing of terrorism (CFT). This request inspired new conceptions, practices and technologies.[28] For instance, before 9/11, banks conceived of financial fraud as a problem of organized crime and corruption and used almost no digital technology to detect such fraud among their clients; after 9/11, however, financial watchdogs and software companies offered their techniques as weapons in the War on Terror, enabling identification and blocking of specific transactions, as well as automatic freezing of the money held in suspicious accounts.[29] It was, therefore, as part of the War on Terror that targeted financial measures were devised and implemented on a large scale.[30]

Thus, after targeted sanctions were initially designed as a response to the costly impact of comprehensive sanctions against Iraq (as explained earlier in this section), the War on Terror played an important role in further developing and promoting this tool. Throughout the years, the UNSC made a consistent effort to keep the sanctions directed at the right targets and not to harm innocent civilians by constantly improving the technical characteristics of its mode of designation. For instance, the UNSC sought to specify the identities of targeted terrorists with enough detail to prevent banks from unintentionally applying the penalties against 'false positives' (i.e. entities or individuals who are mistakenly identified as sanctioned actors because their names coincide with names on the sanctions list). After international pressure and legal conflicts in European countries, the UNSC also created the office of the 'Ombudsperson' which gives listed individuals the possibility to appeal for delisting by demonstrating that they no longer meet the listing criteria.[31] The 'politics of lists'[32] and financial surveillance thus became intrinsic parts of the logic of targetedness that was developed in the new War on Terror, first within the Bush administration and later by the international community at the UNSC level.

[28] See Sullivan, *The Law of the List*.

[29] G. Mallard and A. Hanson, 'Embedded Extra-Territoriality: US Judicial Litigation and the Global Banking Surveillance of Digital Money Flows', in C. Beaucillon (ed.), *Research Handbook on Unilateral and Extraterritorial Sanctions* (Edward Elgar, 2021), pp. 269–86.

[30] M. S. Navias, 'Finance Warfare as a Response to International Terrorism' (2002) 73 *The Political Quarterly* 57–79.

[31] M. de Goede and G. Sullivan, 'Between Law and the Exception: The UN 1267 Ombudsperson as a Hybrid Model of Legal Expertise' (2013) 26 *Leiden Journal of International Law* 833–54.

[32] De Goede and Sullivan, 'Introduction: The Politics of the List'.

New actors entered the domain of CFT, as counter-terrorism sanctions incited new cooperation (or intensified existing cooperation) between member states' bureaucracies (notably intelligence agencies and treasury departments), private companies (especially airline companies and global banks) and international organizations.[33] Prominent among the last of these was the Financial Action Task Force (FATF): an international organization of like-minded states that was established at a G7 summit in 1989 with the mandate to 'examine and develop measures to combat money laundering'.[34] In October 2001 – in the aftermath of 9/11 – the FATF mandate was then extended from anti-money laundering (AML) to CFT, leading to FATF's entry into the field of international security; as we show in Section 9.3, the mandate was later expanded to include counter-proliferation finance (CPF). It wasn't so much the FATF staff which lobbied to be entrusted with these security-related tasks, as at that time it possessed little expertise and credentials in international security. However, according to policy insiders we interviewed, the member states deemed it preferable to entrust a small organization, largely dependent upon member state intel, with the tasks of improving CFT strategies and helping the UNSC enrol the banking sector in its fight against terrorists.

The FATF worked hard to empower member states with 'better' legislation through the diffusion of best practices or model law in AML, CFT or CPF fields, as well as to provide private financial institutions with knowledge about typical money-laundering and terrorism-financing schemes.[35] As such, the UNSC and the FATF have cooperated in the elaboration of a logic of targetedness in the design of counter-terrorism sanctions. In parallel, in the UNSCRs against Iran (for instance, in UNSCR 1803),[36] the UNSC started to make explicit references to and praise the work of the FATF, and called on all governments to push legislation addressing financial sector reform that would enable banks

[33] See Mallard, 'Governing Proliferation Finance'.

[34] The FATF is an organization with strong expert authority and little legal authority as it only counts thirty-seven state members (as of 2020, up from thirty-four in 2008) and two regional organizations (the European Commission and the Gulf Co-operation Council) among its members. Monitoring and enforcement mechanisms are restricted to its member states, on the basis of the yearly questionnaire that FATF member states conduct as *self*-evaluations of their implementation of the FATF's core principles (namely its forty general recommendations and its nine recommendations to counter the financing of terrorism), and on the basis of periodic mutual evaluations, see J. Johnson, 'Is the Global Financial System AML/CFT Prepared?' (2008) 15 *Journal of Financial Crime* 7–21.

[35] FATF, 'Typologies Report on Proliferation Financing' (18 June 2008).

[36] UNSC Res 1803 (3 March 2008) UN Doc S/RES/1803.

and other private financial operators to fully cooperate with the creation of the new system of targeted sanctions. All international organizations with a stake in the global sanctions regimes have thus seemed to converge towards the same goals, well in line with broader UN norms.

When applied against 'pariah' states designated by the Bush administration in 2003 – in this case, Iran and the DPRK – the same logic of targetedness that shaped the design of counter-terrorism sanctions meant that new counter-proliferation sanctions would also avoid hurting the civilian populations who were not responsible for the undeclared nuclear programmes.[37] After Iran's file was sent from the International Atomic Energy Agency (IAEA) Board of Governors to the UNSC in 2006, as well as after the UNSC passed sanctions against the DPRK in the wake of its first nuclear test in 2006, the UNSC adopted successive rounds of sanctions against both countries that were targeted rather than comprehensive in scope, and discriminatory rather than non-discriminatory in nature.[38] Their targeted nature was exemplified by the specific designation of companies and individuals allegedly associated with Iran's or the DPRK's nuclear programmes. These entities were systematically listed in the appendices of each of the UNSCRs targeting the two countries – just like the UNSC Al Qaeda sanctions listed scores of names associated with the terrorist network.

In the case of Iran, for instance, UNSCR 1737, passed in December 2006, banned the supply of specific goods (e.g. nuclear-related material) to Iran and froze the assets of specific individuals and companies associated with Iran's hidden centrifuge programme.[39] Similarly, UNSCR 1929, passed in June 2010, only called upon states to exercise vigilance over the transactions of the assets of entities associated with the procurement of illicit goods, such as members of the Iranian Revolutionary Guard Corps listed in its Annex II.[40] The same logic of targetedness characterized UN sanctions against the DPRK, at least until the end of the Obama presidency, whose focus was on negotiations with Iran rather than the DPRK. Therefore, the UN counter-proliferation sanctions were indeed initially devised as targeted sanctions.

[37] G. Mallard, 'Antagonistic Recursivities and Successive Cover-Ups: The Case of Private Nuclear Proliferation' (2018) 69 *The British Journal of Sociology* 1007–30.

[38] Zarate, *Treasury's War*.

[39] UNSC Res 1737 (23 December 2006) UN Doc S/RES/1737.

[40] UNSC Res 1929 (9 June 2010) UN Doc S/RES/1929.

The institutionalization of the logic of targetedness in the domain of counter-proliferation was facilitated by the UNSC's cooperation with other international organizations and by intertextuality and cross-referencing across various actors. As with the counter-terrorism sanctions, the UNSC worked in tandem with other organizations, again notably with the FATF.[41]

The UNSC passed UNSCR 1803 in 2008, which commended the guidelines issued by the FATF that same year with regard to the detection of suspicious activities in proliferation finance.[42] UNSCR 1803 'called upon' all states to exercise 'vigilance' regarding activities of financial institutions in their territory with banks domiciled in Iran 'in order to avoid such financial support contributing to the proliferation sensitive nuclear activities' (para. 10), and to report to the UNSC's Sanctions Committee on Iran the steps undertaken to this end.

The UNSC and the FATF thus incentivized states and banks to work towards a decentralized and autonomously targeting financial system, in which private and public financial institutions are individually responsible for establishing mechanisms to ensure compliance with sanctions regimes. In principle, these institutions remained committed to the same logic of targetedness: both FATF documents and UNSCRs promoted specific measures (like 'enhanced due diligence' protocols) that global banks could adopt in order to conduct proper calculations of the risk of certain activities of their clients being related to Iran's sanctioned nuclear activities. Banks should only prevent those activities if the risk was substantial. As described in interviews we conducted with US sanctions specialists, such intertextuality and cross-referencing were strengthened due to the fact that the same experts (largely Western experts, in particular those working on sanctions in the US State and Treasury

[41] The first important FATF report on counter-proliferation financing was published in 2008, although according to its website, it was only in 2012 that combating proliferation finance was added to the FATF's mandate (www.fatf-gafi.org/about/whatwedo/).

[42] In the context of the DPRK, it was only in 2013 that UNSCR 2094 referred to the FATF, when it 'welcomed' the FATF's recommendation 7 and the interpretative note along with that recommendation, which was newly added to the list of FATF recommendation in 2012. The recommendation simply calls upon states to implement targeted sanctions in compliance with UNSCRs. As the UNSC 'urged' states to apply this recommendation (more precisely, the FATF's interpretive note on the recommendation), it did so only in the preamble of the UNSCR, that is, not as a binding Chapter VII measure. The UNSC reinforced this call three years later, in 2016, and now in the decision part of the resolution (UNSCR 2270 from 2016, para. 38), still referring, however, only to recommendation 7 and using the less binding expression to 'call upon' states.

Departments) contributed to the activities of both institutions (the UNSC and FATF).

Still, some other trends in the sanctions against Iran and the DPRK force us to rethink the narrative of a clear break with the comprehensive logic of sanctions. Considering the increasing difficulties that countries under sanctions (like Iran or DPRK) meet when they have to respond to the humanitarian needs of their populations,[43] does that mean that the paradigmatic shift towards targeted sanctions has been reverted? Or has that paradigmatic shift in fact never fully happened, as a comprehensive logic (or a process of comprehensivization) continued to be produced as a result of the entanglement between various sanctions regimes, some at the unilateral level, others at the multilateral level? As UNSC sanctions haven't operated in a vacuum since the turn to 'targeted sanctions', and as they have consistently been complemented by domestic sanctions unilaterally adopted by UNSC permanent member states (especially the P3 – the USA, the UK and France), has the UNSC relinquished its duty of ensuring the coherence of its actions vis-à-vis the broader UN normative system? These questions are especially urgent to ask since the legality and normative coherence of unilateral sanctions adopted by the P3 with other UN principles, such as the protection of human rights, has increasingly been the object of criticism, even from within the UN system, as illustrated for instance by the many reports published by the office of the UN Special Rapporteur on the Negative Impact of Unilateral Coercive Measures on the Enjoyment of Human Rights.[44]

9.3 The Internal Dynamics Driving the Gradual Comprehensivization of Sanctions: The Role of Panels of Experts

Some analysts may argue that counter-terrorism sanctions, and most notably the financial measures they entailed, buttressed the normative

[43] G. Mallard, F. Sabet and J. Sun, 'The Humanitarian Gap in the Global Sanctions Regime: Assessing Causes, Effects and Solutions' (2020) 26 *Global Governance: A Review of Multilateralism and International Organizations* 1–33.

[44] OHCHR, 'Research-Based Progress Report of the Human Rights Council Advisory Committee Containing Recommendations on Mechanisms to Assess the Negative Impact of Unilateral Coercive Measures on the Enjoyment of Human Rights and to Promote Accountability' (10 February 2015) UN Doc A/HRC/28/74; OHCHR, 'Report on the Negative Impact of Unilateral Coercive Measures on the Enjoyment of Human Rights' (30 August 2018) UN Doc A/HRC/39/54.

standard of hitting those responsible while avoiding costs for innocent civilians.[45] However, we argue that those sanctions also entailed a redirection of intervention practices, new types of expertise, technologies and cooperative engagements that amounted to a loss of control in how UNSC sanctions were to be implemented by the private parties (global banks especially) in charge of blocking financial transactions on the basis of suspicion rather than a demonstrated relation to the nuclear programmes of Iran or North Korea. In this section, we want to show how the logic of targetedness that the UNSC and FATF inscribed in the regulation of counter-proliferation finance was gradually entangled with a logic of comprehensiveness.

The UNSC's innovative approach to targeted sanctions went well beyond the publicization of lists of names of suspected terrorists and nuclear proliferators, and the description of their financial practices, found in the documents voted upon by fifteen UNSC and thirty-seven FATF member states. The powerful states behind the edification of the new sanctions regimes called for implementation by *all* states and for cooperation by private actors around the world (such as global banks and airline companies), asking them to deeply reform their compliance systems in order to catch suspicious transactions. It is thus important to understand UN sanctions and FATF recommendations not simply as an attempt by the UNSC or FATF to reign in one specific actor (Al Qaeda and its individual affiliates, or the individual companies and persons related to the nuclear programmes of Iran and the DPRK), but as an attempt to govern *states* – all of them – and to convince them to reform their banking sectors so as to ensure that they can detect suspicious transactions and freeze the assets of terrorists and suspected nuclear proliferators in seconds, without hurting the rest of their population.

Here is, thus, a particular *mélange* of international and transnational logics inherent to targeted sanctions, as they target non-state actors *through* addressing state jurisdictions. States were furthermore not just asked to inhibit certain flows of finances, goods and people, but to change their domestic financial regulations more broadly. This focus on broader financial regulations was likely promoted by the FATF, as the FATF is less concerned with individual security threats such as those emanating from Al Qaeda, Iran or the DPRK, and more with systematic patterns and risks of abusing the financial system. These more systematic

[45] Zarate, *Treasury's War*.

concerns were increasingly integrated into UNSC resolutions, asking all UN member states to change their domestic jurisdictions.

These demands contain the seed of a 'comprehensivization' of supposedly targeted sanctions, as banks worldwide were pushed by the UNSC and FATF (through the pressure these two international organizations placed on governments) to become part of a larger governance infrastructure, whose algorithms automatically hooked the compliance departments of global banks to the listing decisions of the UNSC and other entities. Even though the UNSC itself remained rather conservative with regards to listing individuals (its list of targeted terrorists containing about 350 individuals/entities), its regulations contributed to a dynamic of ever-growing lists and their almost automatic adoption by global banks: the targeting is supposed to become decentralized and automatized at a systematic level, a far cry from the few handpicked, high-profile targets of the early peacebuilding sanctions whose evolution remained heavily centralized in the hands of the UNSC.

The banking reforms adopted by the UNSC and FATF have led to the creation of a system of private 'algorithmic governance'[46] which led to eternally growing lists that were supposed to capture a fluid enemy. Given the fluidity of this non-state enemy, the asset-freezing measures could never be called 'comprehensive': soon, private companies such as World-Check proactively identified targets on their own and sold these listings to global banks.[47] As many compliance officers working in the banking sector told us in the context of a large-scale interviewing campaign conducted between 2017 and 2019, once individuals are on a list sold by compliance software companies to banks, they will remain black-listed by some banks for the rest of their lives, even if their name is later removed from listings due to the decision of a court or the UNSC ombudsperson. The exclusion of individuals has also become maximalist because private companies have tended to pile up names from not only UNSC listings, but also all the domestic lists that states from all over the world publicize, rarely having the means of checking in which jurisdictions any given individual is listed and therefore just applying all lists globally.

[46] F. Pasquale, *The Black Box Society* (Harvard University Press, 2015); M. Ziewitz, 'Governing Algorithms: Myth, Mess, and Methods' (2016) 41 *Science, Technology & Human Values* 3–16; S. U. Noble, *Algorithms of Oppression: How Search Engines Reinforce Racism* (New York University Press, 2018); C. Katzenbach and L. Ulbricht, 'Algorithmic Governance' (2019) 8 *Internet Policy Review*, https://doi.org/10.14763/2019.4.1424.

[47] De Goede and Sullivan, 'Introduction: The Politics of the List'.

The demands for domestic regulatory change that the UNSC made on behalf of international security concerns have had other important implications. Existing literature has analysed it as an indication of the UNSC becoming a 'global legislator'.[48] Here, however, we want to point out a different implication, namely the creation of new institutions and monitoring mechanisms that would contribute to a network of cross-referencing reports and regulatory guidelines. As the UNSC set up new sanctions regimes, it instituted new Sanctions Committees, to which it appended specific Panels of Experts (PoEs), which participated in the expansion of lists of designated individuals and which changed the relationship between political negotiation and the rule by experts. PoEs are mandated to 'gather, examine and analyze information from States, relevant United Nations bodies and other interested parties regarding the implementation of the measures imposed in [the respective resolutions]' and to 'make recommendations on actions the Council, or the Committee or Member States, may consider to improve implementation of the measures' in their annual or biannual reports.[49] PoEs are supposed to have the necessary independence from UN member states to scrutinize the national implementation of specific UNSCRs, like those targeting Al Qaeda, Iran or the DPRK.

It is necessary to point out that the setup of these PoEs has been very political, as the nationalities of their members mirror the five permanent members of the UNSC plus the composition of member states involved in the broader negotiation with, respectively, Iran and the DPRK.[50] This political dimension of their work goes largely unacknowledged, even though some observers of the UN sanctions machinery acknowledge in interviews a divide between PoE members

[48] E. Rosand, 'The Security Council as Global Legislator: Ultra Vires or Ultra Innovative United Nations and the Law of War' (2004) 28 *Fordham International Law Journal* 542–90; K. L. Scheppele, 'The Migration of Anti-Constitutional Ideas: The Post-9/11 Globalization of Public Law and the International State of Emergency', in S. Choudhry (ed.), *The Migration of Constitutional Ideas* (Cambridge University Press, 2007), pp. 347–73; N. Krisch, 'International Law in Times of Hegemony: Unequal Power and the Shaping of the International Legal Order' (2005) 16 *European Journal of International Law* 369–408; N. Krisch, 'Decay of Consent: International Law in an Age of Global Public Goods' (2014) 108 *American Journal of International Law* 1–40.

[49] UNSC Res 1874 (12 June 2009) UN Doc S/RES/1874, para. 26.

[50] For Iran, each of the E3+3 (or, in the language of the UN, the P5+1) sends one expert; for the DPRK, each of the member states involved in the Six Party talks sends one expert, plus one further member. In addition, one panel member from a non-aligned country is added to both panels.

who adopt a maximalist interpretation of the UNSCRs, which come closer to the views of the P3, and others who take a minimalist interpretation closer to the *souverainism* of Russia and China. It should be noted that, despite their formal independence, many PoE members hold a background in national ministries or agencies and sometime maintain close contacts with their country representatives in New York or even with their capital throughout the mandate, and interpret sanctions violations in accordance with their capital's view.[51] As for PoE members from P3 countries, this also entails closer direct or indirect ties to other multilateral institutions which hold similar views, like the FATF, or with like-minded think tanks specialized in the monitoring of the global arms trade or illicit finance, like the Stockholm International Peace Research Institute or the International Crisis Group. In their daily practice as PoE members, they are entitled to escape the logic of pure diplomatic negotiation by checking information that they obtain through personal networks and then pushing for factual consensus on such sensitive issues as sanctions implementation, enforcement, and redress.[52]

In the field of CPF, PoEs and the FATF have reinforced each other, mutually 'enhanc[ing] their own position by linking up with bodies of norms produced by other, reputed institutions'.[53] In so doing, they elaborated and universally promoted a set of financial rules that originated in Western states and was diffused by the P3 to the rest of the world. To begin with, PoE reports – which are submitted to the UNSC and made public – regularly refer to FATF reports: for example, the section on financial sanctions in the first report of the DPRK PoE mostly just reprinted the heuristics on money laundering from a 2008 FATF report. Already in its first report on the DPRK sanctions, the PoE recommended that '[a]ll Member States should be encouraged to adopt and implement the non-proliferation and anti-money-laundering/combating the financing of terrorism guidelines published by FATF' (DPRK S/2010/571,

[51] This accounts for the DPRK PoE and the Iran PoE (prior to the JCPOA), rather than the PoEs responsible for African regimes, see: A. Niederberger, 'Independent Experts with Political Mandates: "Role Distance" in the Production of Political Knowledge' (2020) 5(3) *European Journal of International Security* 350–71.

[52] A. Niederberger, 'Investigative Ignorance in International Investigations: How United Nations Panels of Experts Create New Relations of Power by Seeking Information' (2018) 69 *The British Journal of Sociology* 984–1006; Niederberger, 'Independent Experts with Political Mandates'.

[53] See Chapter 1.

recommendation 15).[54] We should assume that the term 'member states' refers to UN member states here (as it usually does in PoE reports), not to FATF member states, meaning that the PoE recommended that states adopt FATF guidelines even if they are not a member of the organization.

Another illustrative example concerns measures against front companies, which have frequently been used to circumvent sanctions: front companies have been repeatedly problematized in FATF reports,[55] but remained largely ignored by UNSCRs, with the minor exception of a few designations of front companies in UNSCR 1803 on Iran.[56] However, after the DPRK PoE recommended more systematic measures be forcefully undertaken against front companies (S/2015/131, recommendation B7),[57] the issue was addressed more systematically in UNSCRs (from UNSCR 2270/2016).[58] This process of cross-citation shows how UNSC permanent member states, like the United States, the United Kingdom or France, who place a lot of attention on the work of the FATF, can leverage the work of PoEs to raise the relevance of certain issues related to sanctions implementation, CFT or CPF in the global international security agenda; and how they can use the UNSC and its complex institutional architecture to commend FATF recommendations at multiple levels.

PoEs have played another important role by increasing the frequency of the monitoring and evaluation of national financial sanctions adopted by the UNSC. PoEs have sometimes gone beyond the FATF, which has a relatively thorough monitoring mandate involving eighteen-months of mutual evaluations, but at distant intervals – every five years or so. In contrast, PoEs conduct all-year-long, more or less independent investigations of any UNSC sanctions breaches reported by states, and issue up to two reports per year. Through their monitoring activities, the FATF and the PoEs participate in strengthening the expert belief that new 'targeted' sanctions always need to be added to past rounds of sanctions, according to a logic of a continuous progress in the detection of new

[54] UNSC, 'Letter Dated 12 May 2010 from the Panel of Experts Established Pursuant to Resolution 1874 (2009) Addressed to the President of the Security Council' (5 November 2010) UN Doc S/2010/571.

[55] FATF, 'Typologies Report on Proliferation Financing'.

[56] See UNSC Res 1803.

[57] UNSC, 'Letter Dated 23 February 2015 from the Panel of Experts Established Pursuant to Resolution 1874 (2009) addressed to the President of the Security Council' (23 February 2015) UN Doc S/2015/131.

[58] UNSC Res 2270 (2 March 2016) UN Doc S/RES/2270.

types of practices and actors associated with illicit finance and sanctions violations. Whereas new measures are usually only added to an existing sanctions regime in response to actions that threatened international security and/or constitute a serious breach of the existing sanctions regime, PoE reports are routinely suggesting new targets to existing sanctions, based on the discovery of new methods or actors of sanctions evasion. With the precise enumeration of verified violation cases by PoEs, and the submission of their documentation to the scrutiny of the UNSC and its Sanctions Committees, the PoEs diffuse the view that new sanctions designations shall always improve the system of 'targetedness' and perfect the sanctions regimes already in place. Typical demands in PoE reports on the DPRK, for instance, are to close down new shell companies and new circuits of exchange (from cash economies to *hawalas* or networks exchanging digital currencies), which are created by proliferators in response to past rounds of targeted sanctions. PoEs not only seek to verify the validity of leaked intelligence and public information on new sanctions evasion techniques, but also lobby the UNSC member states to pass new rounds of sanctions meant to close the observed loopholes. Whether such an accumulation of targets leads to the progressive comprehensivization of sanctions or whether they can remain targeted in scope and discriminatory in nature is the question that we assess in Section 9.4.

Some examples illustrate how PoEs have encouraged states to go beyond the explicit requirements of UNSCRs and leave the ethos of diplomatic prudence in favour of a more expert-based justification for independent monitoring and forceful implementation of all of the UNSCRs' obligations and recommendations by UN member states. For instance, the UNSC decided in 2013 that member states shall prevent transfer of bulk cash through/to/from their territories if it '*could* contribute to the DPRK's nuclear or ballistic missile programmes, or other activities prohibited by resolutions' (2094/2013 para. 11, emphasis added; UNSCR 2270 subjected gold transports to the same measures).[59] The term 'could' is ambiguous and may invite very broad interpretations, but, if interpreted along a logic of targetedness, the measures should refer to cases with a credible risk that the gold/cash is being used for prohibited purposes. However, the wording suggests a broader interpretation, recommending that smuggled bulk cash or gold by DPRK nationals should

[59] UNSC Res 2094 (7 March 2013) UN Doc S/RES/2094, para. 11.

be frozen and that member states 'ensure that [frozen gold/cash amounts] *cannot* be used for prohibited activities or evasion of sanctions before releasing them' (S/2017/150, para. 253).[60] Ensuring that assets *cannot* be used for prohibited tasks is a higher threshold pertaining to an eventual future that goes beyond the threshold of a credible risk that was more likely implied by the UNSCR.

To add another example, in UNSCR 2321,[61] the UNSC decided that 'all States shall take steps to limit the number of bank accounts to one per DPRK diplomatic mission and consular post, and one per accredited DPRK diplomat and consular officer, at banks in their territory'. The PoE repeatedly asked member states to go beyond these measures; in the following year, it passed the recommendation that member states 'must ensure that additional accounts are not established in the names of family members' (S/2017/742 recommendation C 5).[62] Yet another year later, the PoE also recommended that member states apply the restrictions to *all* embassy personnel,[63] as opposed to only the 'accredited DPRK diplomat and consular officers' mentioned in the UNSCR.[64] A year later, the PoE recommended that states provide banks with a list of names of all family members of DPRK diplomats, to ensure that diplomats cannot open bank accounts in their names[65] and that only one bank within each country be allowed to hold accounts of DPRK diplomats.[66] Furthermore, the PoE recommended that 'Member States advise their financial

[60] PoE reports gave extensive evidence of sanctions evasions through the smuggling of cash and gold and that the PoE should thus feel a responsibility to propose counter-measures; likewise, the same report containing those recommendations stated that such contraband is frozen only exceptionally by states anyways; see UNSC, 'Letter Dated 17 February 2017 from the Panel of Experts Established Pursuant to Resolution 1874 (2009) Addressed to the President of the Security Council' (27 February 2017) UN Doc S/2017/150.

[61] UNSC Res 2321 (30 November 2016) UN Doc S/RES/2321, para. 16.

[62] UNSC, 'Letter Dated 28 August 2017 from the Panel of Experts Established Pursuant to Resolution 1874 (2009) Addressed to the President of the Security Council' (5 September 2017) UN Doc S/2017/742.

[63] UNSC, 'Letter Dated 1 March 2018 from the Panel of Experts Established Pursuant to Resolution 1874 (2009) Addressed to the President of the Security Council' (5 March 2018) UN Doc. S/2018/171, para. 210, recommendation 3.

[64] Ibid.

[65] UNSC, 'Letter Dated 21 February 2019 from the Panel of Experts Established Pursuant to Resolution 1874 (2009) Addressed to the President of the Security Council' (5 March 2019) UN Doc S/2019/171, para. 161.

[66] UNSC, 'Letter Dated 21 February 2019 from the Panel of Experts', para. 162.

institutions not to open accounts for diplomats of the Democratic People's Republic of Korea who are not accredited to their country',[67] based on the finding that North Korean embassies have served as traditional conduits of illicit financing. Still, if DPRK diplomats are prohibited, per UNSCRs, from holding more than one bank account, it lies in the discretion of the UNSC and its Sanctions Committee to designate any third-party individual assisting in the violation of this rule and there is, as of now, no UNSCR demanding that banks target family members of diplomats or that diplomats should not be allowed to choose a bank of their preference. The PoE thus recommends states to prevent sanctions evasions by recommending *additional* sanctioning measures that are *not* asked for by the UNSC. This is the very logic of illicit finance expertise that PoE members have endorsed.

A last example shows how private financial actors, too, can respond to the recommendations of the PoEs. In its 2017 report, the PoE on DPRK sanctions remarked that the Society for Worldwide Interbank Financial Telecommunication (SWIFT) maintained in its system North Korean banks that were designated for special attention by the UNSC.[68] As SWIFT is (only) the messenger between banks exchanging value through its system, and to the extent that banks are supposed to conduct the risk analysis related to specific payments (depending on a range of criteria), SWIFT's decision to keep these banks in its system may not have appeared a case of violation of the new UNSCR to its managers. Indeed, SWIFT provides the infrastructure that allows money to flow between accounts, and it leaves to those using that messaging infrastructure and ordering the money movements (e.g. banks sending messages through SWIFT) the responsibility to comply with the rules of UNSC, EU and US sanctions, and any other local systems of sanctions that may apply. This view of SWIFT's neutrality, however, was strongly challenged in the run-up to the Iran nuclear deal, when the P3 repeatedly asked SWIFT to disconnect some Iranian banks from its system between 2012 and 2015, and yet again after the USA left the Joint Comprehensive Plan of Action (JCPOA) after 2018. After the publication of this 2017 DPRK PoE report, SWIFT cut off the last North Korean banks from its messaging networks, thus cutting the whole North Korean formal financial

[67] Ibid., para. 163.
[68] UNSC, 'Letter Dated 28 August 2017 from the Panel of Experts'.

system from the global network.[69] In so doing, the Belgian-based financial organization implemented what looks like comprehensive rather than targeted sanctions against North Korea's financial system. It may have responded to the pressure due to the publication of the PoE report, or it may also have been retaliating due to the fact that the DPRK had manipulated its system by hacking the financial software that SWIFT sells to banks in order to initiate transfers of funds from one bank to another. In fact, in the last five years, it is estimated that the DPRK made more than US$1 billion in this way,[70] a huge sum compared to the income that the DPRK regime generated over the same period from arms sale in certain African countries, like Namibia or Ethiopia.[71] These hacks may have convinced SWIFT that it needed the protection of the long arm of US judicial authorities to chase the hackers, bring them to justice and thus obtain a deterrent against other hacks in order to re-establish its credibility in the market of financial data management equipment.[72] Whatever the reason, the publication of the PoE report was likely factored into its calculation

[69] T. Bergin, 'SWIFT Messaging System Cuts Off Remaining North Korean Banks', Reuters (14 March 2017), www.reuters.com/article/us-northkorea-banks/swift-messaging-system-cuts-off-remaining-north-korean-banks-idUSKBN16N2SZ.

[70] Bloomberg, 'U.S. Sanctions North Korean Hackers for Swift Hack, Wannacry and Other Cyberattacks that Fund Its Weapons Programs', *Japan Times* (14 September 2019), www.japantimes.co.jp/news/2019/09/14/asia-pacific/u-s-sanctions-north-korean-hackers-swift-hack-wannacry-cyberattacks-fund-weapons-programs/#.XibZ1L97nq1.

[71] Notorious victims include the Bangladesh Bank, whose money (to the amount of US$80 million) held in accounts at the New York Fed, was ordered in 2015 and 2016 to be transferred to the benefit of DPRK-controlled entities elsewhere (see FireEye, 'North Korean Hackers Used Swift Network to Steal More Than $100m – Fireeye' Finextra (5 October 2018), www.finextra.com/newsarticle/32742/north-korean-hackers-used-swift-network-to-steal-more-than-100m—fireeye). The fake money orders sent through SWIFT were impossible to distinguish from real money orders, which exposed vulnerabilities in the global SWIFT messaging system prior to the release of the 2017 PoE report. See also S. Pham, 'North Korea Still Making Millions from Small Arms Exports' CNN (14 September 2017), https://money.cnn.com/2017/09/14/news/north-korea-small-arms-trade/index.html.

[72] The US judicial authorities are the only ones with such sweeping powers thanks to the International Emergency Economic Powers Act, which lets them indict persons for comparably small offenses like giving a conference on Blockchain technology in the DPRK as an attempt to 'conspire' to violate the Act (See J. Brett, 'Internet Man of Mystery Virgil Griffith Indicted for Crypto Trip to North Korea', Forbes (11 January 2020), www.forbes.com/sites/jasonbrett/2020/01/11/internet-man-of-mystery-virgil-griffith-indicted-for-crypto-trip-to-north-korea/#2514738d18b0).

when SWIFT decided to cut off the whole financial system of the DPRK regime from its messaging system.

It is understandable that PoEs would come up with strict interpretations of sanctions implementation, given that they are supposed to conduct monitoring and see themselves confronted with numerous violations. What matters in our context, however, is that the PoE recommends to member states that they take a maximalist interpretation of measures in UNSCRs that is mutually reinforcing with FATF recommendations and the comprehensive sanctions favoured by the USA in its campaign for 'maximum pressure' against states like Iran and the DPRK. It is worth emphasizing that the PoEs also formulate recommendations to the UNSC Sanctions Committees, which the UNSC Committees then discuss and vote upon. And even if Sanctions Committees do not act upon these recommendations, today, public and private authorities use the biannual PoE reports as interpretation guidelines for UNSCRs. As a consequence, PoE reports have shaped the expectations of the financial industry and their willingness to take risks, as each exchange in goods or financial transaction carries a remaining risk of inadvertently violating sanctions, should one, for instance, fall victim to deception or incomplete information. Just like the FATF, PoEs have continuously stressed that both private and public actors must be made aware of the importance of adopting a 'risk-based culture'.[73] But this call for a 'risk-based culture' can be interpreted very differently: either that you should accept that every decision comes with the risk of making the wrong decision, and that risks are part of life; or that you should take no risk of making a mistake by authorizing suspicious payments, especially when the penalty for making the wrong decision is too high. Clearly, the latter became the dominant interpretation, and this extension of the domain of what can be considered a 'risky activity' plays a role in the comprehensivization of sanctions, so we argue.

[73] UNSC, 'Letter Dated 1 March 2018 from the Panel of Experts', para. 210 (recommendation 2): 'The Panel recommends that Member States, as part of their implementation of the financial provisions of the resolutions, ensure that their financial institutions implement a risk-based approach to identifying sanctions violations in their "know-your-customer" and compliance programmes . . . To that end, Member States should provide their financial institutions with more detailed and regular information on sanctions evasion risks.'

9.4 The External Dynamics in the Comprehensivization of Sanctions: Legal Entanglements between Multilateral and Domestic Sanctions

If the institutional innovations of the 2000s may give the impression of a general, sudden and unbeatable adoption of the targeted sanctions paradigm, and a stark contrast to the comprehensive sanctions against Iraq, some other trends already highlighted point to the entanglements between targeted and comprehensive logics as well as multilateral and unilateral sanctions regimes. One reason for this is that targeted sanctions were embedded in a broader decentralized network of comprehensive domestic prohibitions on any type of trade with certain countries under UNSC sanctions, especially Iran. We have already identified various facilitating dynamics in the entanglement of targeted and comprehensive logics at the level of the UNSC, which were most prevalent in the case of the DPRK, where the 'maximum pressure' campaign has been steered by the UNSC itself.

However, in cases like Iran, the UNSCRs only served to give a legal basis for sanctions that were otherwise mostly adopted in a unilateral manner, supposedly to 'complement' 'soft' UNSCRs that only 'called upon' states to adopt certain financial restrictions. In this case, the decentralization of targeting practices at the level of the P3, and the 'deputization' of sanctions implementation to Western-led global banks in charge of enforcing financial sanctions, as well as the inherent tendency of lists to grow[74] under the proactive efforts of private sector vendors of sanctions lists, were much more influential processes explaining the comprehensivization of UNSC sanctions than efforts by PoEs and other international organizations like FATF. In what follows, we focus on a key driver of the entanglement between comprehensive (domestic) and targeted (UN-based multilateral) logics: a change in the notion of risk that was particularly fostered by US regulators.

While this section further works out the role of the USA as a key actor in fostering this entanglement, it also shows how 'the scope of relevant actors goes well beyond the governmental [or intergovernmental] sphere'[75] by pointing out the important role of private financial institutions. As the history of the last ten years of US judicial prosecution of financial crime shows,[76]

[74] De Goede and Sullivan, 'Introduction: The Politics of the List'.

[75] See Chapter 1.

[76] G. Mallard and J. Sun, 'Viral Governance: How the US Unilateral Sanctions against Iran Changed the Rules of Financial Capitalism' *American Journal of Sociology*, under review.

financial institutions have come to adopt a strategy of complete risk aversion with regards to sanctions under the influence of two important mechanisms: the adoption of comprehensive sanctions by the United States against Iran and the DPRK, and the extraterritorial effect of such unilateral sanctions on multinational companies – even outside the USA. These multinational companies were thus forced to choose between applying those sanctions to their *global* activities or facing the risk of exclusion from the US financial sector. Hence, when considering the risk of imposing comprehensive sanctions on civilian populations in Iran, global banks weighted another risk: that of being excluded from the leading world market and losing all of their US revenues. Furthermore, many of the UNSC sanctions against Iranian businesses involved prohibitions related to trade finance, and when they were framed by additional sanctions adopted by the USA and then by the EU (with the prohibition, after 2011, of oil import and export as well as of investment, insurance and credit related to the oil trade), it became easy for the US government to use the UNSCRs against Iran as a lever to police the activities of the world's leading banks in general, and the field of trade finance in particular.

For two decades, domestic US legislative acts slowly built up a comprehensive net that was supposed to catch any activity involving Iranian oil and the import/export of other commodities, with pretensions of legal extraterritoriality. At the domestic level, beginning in 1994 the USA passed the Nuclear Proliferation Prevention Act and Executive Order (EO) 12938 instituting a ban on US procurement from any person who, on or after 30 June 1994, knowingly and materially contributes, through the export of nuclear-related goods or technology, to the efforts of any individual, group or non-nuclear weapon state to acquire a nuclear explosive device or unsafeguarded special nuclear material. Through EO 12938, President Clinton declared a 'state of emergency' with respect to the proliferation of weapons of mass destruction. Then, the Export-Import Bank Act of 1996 instituted a ban on access to credit to any person who, after 23 September 1996, knowingly aided or abetted a non-nuclear weapon state to acquire a nuclear explosive device or unsafeguarded material, like Iran's enriched uranium not currently placed under IAEA safeguards. In the 2000s, a number of EOs complemented this legal basis, leading up to EO 13622, and EO 13645, which was adopted in 2013 and which prevented European and Japanese car companies present in Iran from continuing to sell cars and spare parts to the Iranian market. In parallel, the US Congress also passed a wide range of acts which banned trade with Iran and claimed extraterritorial competence: from the Helms–Burton Act to the 2011 Comprehensive Iran Sanctions, Accountability, and Divestment Act to the Iran Freedom and Counter-Proliferation Act and the Nuclear Iran Prevention Act of 2013 as well as various Defense Appropriation Acts in the early 2010s. During this period, reports abound of US pressure exerted directly by the US Treasury on foreign banks without going through national finance ministries, to directly push them 'to stop dealing with Iran'.[77]

Taken together, these US 'emergency' measures with extraterritorial ambitions banned credit, guarantees or insurance in support of exports to Iranian sanctioned individuals; forbade US imports from sanctioned entities; and froze the assets of Iranian sanctioned entities within US jurisdiction even before a trial could be held. From 2008 until 2015, wholesale sectoral prohibitions (especially targeting Iran's financial sector), which had been opposed – and specifically vetoed – by the Russian and Chinese governments in the UNSC, were unilaterally added post hoc by EU and US governments in the form of domestic instruments. For private actors like global banks, applying only the targeted sanctions of the UNSCRs against Iran would thus have meant ignoring US and EU sanctions, and exposing themselves to the 'risk' of committing sanctions violations in the two largest economies of the world, even if the transactions concerned didn't take place in the USA or Europe.

Some banks originally contemplated such action, but they were convinced to change strategy and take maximal measures to avoid any kind of financial contact with individuals and entities targeted by the US Treasury – and not only with them, but also with entities that may be suspected of carrying a second or third degree of relationship with such targeted entities, as interviewees in Washington told us. In a few years, from 2005 to 2015, the US government levied fines against global banks that handled transactions to Iran and Sudan which were prohibited under US law (but not under UNSC resolutions or even EU law) if these transactions were denominated in US dollars. These fines amounted to billions of dollars, as in the case of the fine that BNP-Paribas had to pay to US authorities for clearing transactions in its New York branch related

[77] S. Fayazmanesh, *The United States and Iran: Sanctions, Wars and the Policy of Dual Containment* (Routledge, 2008), p. 198; see also S. Fayazmanesh, 'The Politics of the US Economic Sanctions against Iran' (2003) 35 *Review of Radical Political Economics* 221–40.

to Iranian oil proceeds coming from or going to Iran and Iranian entities that were denominated in US dollars.[78]

Our interviewees, who worked as compliance officers in private financial institutions before the signing of the JCPOA, insisted that it was impossible to apply the logic of targeted sanctions to Iran during this period: for them, the potential benefits of admitting Iranian clients or carrying out transactions from/to Iran were not worth the intense vetting procedures that would have been required each time; furthermore, the remaining risk of unwittingly admitting prohibited transactions despite such vetting procedures was even less acceptable. While it is true that entities linked to either Iran's or now North Korea's nuclear programmes have taken many covert identities and used many masks to hide their links to these programmes, with this amount of suspicion in these cases, banks and their compliance departments that were asked by the UNSC to adopt 'vigilance' and its associated concepts of 'enhanced due diligence' in fact stopped calculating the risks associated with every transaction and rather engaged in wholesale practices of derisking.[79]

The signing of the JCPOA didn't change that situation, as it left in place many US domestic sanctions based on the US designation of many Iranian entities as linked to groups (like Hezbollah) that the US government designated as terrorists, which meant that global banks were still wary of too quickly changing their regulation with regard to Iran. After the JCPOA was signed, the logic of targetedness should have meant that, with the lifting of the comprehensive EU and US trade sanctions that targeted the oil trade and investment activities in Iran, the financial sanctions would have been lifted at the same time as sectoral restrictions. This is not what happened. The post-JCPOA situation in Iran suggests that sanctions against Iran followed the logic of comprehensive sanctions.[80] According

[78] For instance, see Department of Justice, 'Standard Chartered Deferred Prosecution Agreement' (2012), www.justice.gov/opa/pr/standard-chartered-bank-agrees-forfeit-227-million-illegal-transactions-iran-sudan-libya-and; OFAC (Office of Foreign Assets Control, U.S. Treasury Dept.), 'BNP Paribas Deferred Prosecution Agreement' (2014), www.treasury.gov/resource-center/sanctions/CivPen/Documents/20140630_bnp_settlement.pdf.

[79] P.-E. Dupont, 'Compliance with Treaties in the Context of Nuclear Non-proliferation: Assessing Claims in the Case of Iran' (2013) 19 *Journal of Conflict and Security Law* 161–210; Mallard, Sabet and Sun, 'The Humanitarian Gap in the Global Sanctions Regime'; Department of Justice, 'Standard Chartered Deferred Prosecution Agreement'; OFAC (Office of Foreign Assets Control, U.S. Treasury Dept.), 'BNP Paribas Deferred Prosecution Agreement'.

[80] P. Clawson, 'Sanctions as Punishment, Enforcement, and Prelude to Further Action' (1993) 7 *Ethics & International Affairs* 17–37.

to the logic of comprehensive sanctions (and, as previously illustrated in the case of sanctioned individuals whose names are likely to stay on the financial sector's blacklists forever, even if they have been delisted by the UNSC), once a country has been labelled as a 'cause of money laundering concern' by the organizations in charge of issuing such statements (e.g. the FATF, or the US Treasury and its Office of Foreign Assets Control (OFAC)), it becomes almost impossible for that country and its economy to be brought back into the community of global banks.

It is therefore not a surprise that, after the Iran nuclear deal of 2015, the first law that Iran contemplated was the so-called 'FATF bill' – heatedly debated in the Iranian Parliament – which required that Iranian banks adopt AML and CFT measures promoted by the FATF in order to convince the FATF to change its designation of Iran as a country of money-laundering concern. But even as this legislative effort was pursued in Iran, it was clear that the efforts would hardly bring a change in the FATF's assessment of Iran's political economy, not to speak of OFAC's assessment, and that the reinclusion of Iranian financial institutions (after years of exclusion) was next to impossible, even if the JCPOA explicitly called on European private companies and banks to work towards Iran's economic recovery by investing massively in its oil sector.

This path dependency illustrated the comprehensive logic of CPF sanctions. It was reinforced, in the specific case of Iran, by the decision made by the US president to pull out of the JCPOA, despite the fact that UNSCR 2231 gives it the force of law. After 2018, banks faced for the first time a stark option: either follow the logic of targeted sanction, by applying only the prohibitions contained in the UNSCRs, or to follow US domestic changes in their worldwide activities. Their over-cautious behaviour, and their refusal to touch any oil-financing schemes in Iran clearly shows which direction they have chosen to follow since 2018. It is unlikely that, even with the change in the US administration, the contradictions between US and multilateral sanctions will be eliminated and that the logic of targetedness will be strictly followed in the counter-proliferation field.

9.5 Conclusion

Today, many international organizations, including the World Bank[81] or the International Monetary Fund (IMF), have issued warnings after

[81] World Bank, 'De-risking in the Financial Sector' (7 October 2016) www.worldbank.org/en/topic/financialsector/brief/de-risking-in-the-financial-sector.

realizing that global banks and other financial actors have massively pulled out of sanctioned jurisdictions as they applied sanctions in a comprehensive manner rather than by implementing narrow sanctions exclusively targeting the culprits responsible for a country's wrong policy course.[82] International organizations such as the IMF or the World Bank see such cases of overcompliance as illegitimate in an age when comprehensive sanctions are no longer deemed appropriate under new norms of 'civilized' state conduct. Still, global banks and other financial actors are not solely responsible for that 'comprehensivization' of sanctions: the movement is spurred by the entanglements between targeted and comprehensive logics, especially in the field of counter-proliferation sanctions. These legal entanglements have been patiently weaved together by a proliferation of other international organizations, including the FATF and the Panel of Experts created by the UNSC Sanctions Committees, particularly those verifying the implementation of sanctions against Iran and the DPRK. Together, these organizations have participated in the creation of a fiction which implies that 'targetedness' would necessarily rhyme with 'narrowness', when in fact 'targetedness' is not necessarily incompatible with 'comprehensiveness': if the list of 'targets' is gradually or suddenly extended to become all-encompassing, then targeted sanctions could be both targeted and comprehensive in principle.

If we observe a general trend towards the 'comprehensivization' of so-called 'targeted' sanctions, then why do all these institutions still claim to design, monitor and enforce 'targeted' sanctions? In fact, we claim that the logic of targetedness is no longer an empirical fact, or even a policy goal, which would be shared by UNSC member states, but it has become a functional assumption that is necessary for the system to continue operating. By implicitly accepting that states are compartmentalized and cannot be assumed to be in full control of their many state agencies nor private actors, all the organizations which claim that the system operates under the logic of targetedness enact a useful charade or 'fiction'[83] that allows all governments to distance themselves from the entities suspected of breaching US, EU or UNSC sanctions: if parts of a government are blamed by a PoE or by a foreign government branch (the US Department of Justice or OFAC in particular) for sanctions violation, the central authorities can always claim that such entities couldn't have

82 Mallard, Sabet and Sun, 'The Humanitarian Gap in the Global Sanctions Regime'.

83 A. Riles, *Collateral Knowledge: Legal Reasoning in the Global Financial Markets* (University of Chicago Press, 2011).

acted on behalf of the state, and that they weren't responsible for such failings. Here, the logic of 'targetedness' – with its separation between states and individual perpetrators – protects member states and thus makes their consent to sanctions, including sanction enforcement and monitoring, more likely.

We not only see this protective mechanism functioning in the cases of US sanctions enforcement against Europe's major banks (from BNP-Paribas to HSBC), in which European governments have largely turned their eyes away from the settlements, but also during PoE investigations, as in the case of the DPRK. It is standard practice for most UNSC PoEs that PoE members would never publish information in their report without first giving the monitored state (for instance, Russia, Vietnam or Ethiopia) the chance to either deny and disprove accusations or work to solve problems. Thus, where PoEs uncover sanctions violations in a given country, they tend *not* to link violations to governments as a whole but only to specific actors or entities within a country (even if the actors in question are state agencies). For instance, as reported by the DPRK PoE in 2018 in the case of Russia, Russian companies that forged joint ventures with DPRK state companies in violation of UNSC sanctions needed to be investigated, and the PoE members could gain Russia's support for their investigations by allowing the government to claim that such entities had violated the government's will if they did create such joint ventures. By operating under the assumption that states are not complicit in sanctions violations before having been alerted of the existence of these violations by PoEs or by OFAC investigations, multilateral and domestic investigatory bodies give them the benefit of the doubt, and strengthen the belief that a few bad apples within the state may have covered up such illegal behaviours, or that miscommunication problems within complex administrations may have prevented such information from surfacing. Investigatory bodies in the field of sanctions enforcement normally use this assumption as a public script when interacting with states or private actors, even where they may find it hard to believe it themselves.

In this chapter, we have also identified several reasons why UNSC member states (especially the P3) have preferred to entangle a comprehensive set of interventions with a targeted sanction regime, rather than imposing comprehensive sanctions in the first place: first, the lack of legitimacy of blatantly comprehensive regimes, at least since the Iraq case; second, the fact that within the UNSC, Russia and China, and sometimes European states, would not agree to adopt comprehensive sanctions against a UN member state, as they are rather critical of sanctions; and third, because the fiction that enforcement actions against sanctions violations should also be targeted helps protect UN member states from being accused of having been complicit in sanction violations, which means, in turn, that sanctions violators are likely to opt more often for cooperation rather than conflict when accused of misdeeds.

Sanctions experts and policy-makers who pursue an interest in upholding peace and the rule of international law through sanctions (rather than war) as well as a concern for human rights may be convinced of the necessity to fight the trend towards comprehensivization, as it risks creating the same human rights disasters in Iran, Venezuela or Syria today that were witnessed in Iraq in the 1990s. They may see this trend as a distortion of their original intent and a misuse of the instruments of algorithmic governance that they collectively created. However, we argue that the financialization of the sanctions regimes bore in its premises an inherent dynamic towards comprehensivization, which could only reveal itself after the first wave of sanctions were adopted and implemented, when contradictions between comprehensive domestic sanctions regimes and narrower multilateral sanctions regimes were partially solved to the benefit of the former, with one reason being the private financial sector's changing notion of 'risk'.

To that extent, we believe that the concept of legal entanglement, which places the focus of socio-legal scholars and international organizations specialists at the intersection between these domestic, transnational and multilateral dynamics, is particularly useful to social scientists who are dissatisfied with the old notion of 'international regime', even reworked through the use of the updated notion of 'regime complexity', as well as to policy-makers who are interested in reconciling sanctions with a concern with human rights. Its use suggests that although efforts to arrive at a more coherent system of rules are welcome, they rarely achieve complete success, and that regimes traversed by a plurality of contradictory rules are not inherently unstable: to the contrary, such legal entanglements can be quite stable over time.

10

Seamstress of Transnational Law

How the Court of Arbitration for Sport Weaves the *Lex Sportiva*

ANTOINE DUVAL

Lex mercatoria, *lex petrolea*, *lex electronica* and *lex sportiva* have gradually entered the mainstream vocabulary of legal scholarship as phenomena highlighting the functionalization and privatization of law in a globalizing world.[1] They embody what are often qualified as distinct legal orders or systems arising out of transnational communities segregated along functional lines.[2] This chapter aims to show that the work of the Court of Arbitration for Sport (CAS), which is often identified as the institutional centre of the *lex sportiva*,[3] can be understood as that of a seamstress weaving a plurality of legal inputs into authoritative awards. In other words, the CAS panels are assembling legal material to produce (almost) final decisions that, alongside the administrative practices of sports governing bodies (SGBs), govern international sports. It is argued that, instead of purity and autonomy, the CAS's judicial practice is best characterized by assemblage and hybridity. This argument will be supported by an empirical study of the use of different legal materials, in particular pertaining to Swiss law, EU law and the European Convention

[1] Gunther Teubner has been a precursor in charting this transformation, see G. Teubner, 'Global Bukowina: Legal Pluralism in the World-Society', in G. Teubner (ed.), *Global Law without a State* (Dartmouth, 1996), pp. 3–28 and G. Teubner, 'Breaking Frames: Economic Globalization and the Emergence of Lex Mercatoria' (2002) 5 *European Journal of Social Theory* 199–217. For a general overview of the by now extremely vast literature, see R. Michaels, 'Global Legal Pluralism' (2009) 5 *Annual Review of Law and Social Science* 243–62.

[2] Specifically, on the role of transnational communities, see R. Cotterrell, 'Transnational Communities and the Concept of Law' (2008) 21 *Ratio Juris* 1–18.

[3] See F. Latty, *La lex sportiva: Recherche sur le droit transnational* (Brill, Nijhof, 2007) and L. Casini, 'The Making of a Lex Sportiva by the Court of Arbitration for Sport' (2011) 12 *German Law Journal* 1317–40.

on Human Rights (ECHR), within the case law of the CAS. The view advanced here should not be confused with one arguing that the CAS is fully integrated into the Swiss legal order, the EU legal order or into a monistic international legal order. Its main claim is that the judicial practice of the CAS can be captured as the work of a seamstress weaving 'different bodies of norms with one another'[4] and that *lex sportiva* can 'no longer be understood without an account of the ways in which its different parts are entangled'.[5]

The CAS plays a central role in the governance of international sports as the main judicial body to which athletes, clubs or federations can turn to challenge the decisions of international SGBs.[6] Its core function in global sports governance is to act as a review mechanism through its appeal procedure which is regulated by the Code of Sports-Related Arbitration (CAS Code).[7] Thus, the CAS is dealing with almost all the high-profile disputes that occupy the sports pages (and sometimes beyond) of our newspapers. It decided whether Caster Semenya or Oscar Pistorius can participate in athletics competitions,[8] it determined whether Michel Platini or Sepp Blatter can be banned from football for violating FIFA's (Fédération Internationale de Football Association) ethics rules[9] and it assessed whether Maria Sharapova or Alejandro Valverde have committed a violation of the World Anti-Doping Code (WADC).[10] In short, very few of the fundamental decisions that shape the way we experience international sports escape the CAS. While there is no doubt that international sports are being ruled by a transnational

[4] See Chapter 1.

[5] Ibid.

[6] The latest CAS statistics available indicate that 458 appeals procedures were initiated in 2016. See www.tas-cas.org/fileadmin/user_upload/CAS_statistics_2016_.pdf.

[7] On the appeal procedure, see Articles R47 to R59 of the CAS, *Code of Sports-Related Arbitration 2019* (entered into force 1 January 2019) ('CAS Code'). For a detailed commentary of these provisions, see A. Rigozzi and E. Hasler, 'Commentary on the CAS Procedural Rules', in M. Arroyo (ed.), *Arbitration in Switzerland: The Practitioner's Guide* (Kluwer Law International, 2013), pp. 982–1060.

[8] CAS 2018/O/5794, *Mokgadi Caster Semenya* v. *International Association of Athletics Federations*, award of 30 April 2019 and CAS 2008/A/1480 *Pistorius* v. *IAAF*, award of 16 May 2008.

[9] TAS 2016/A/4474, *Michel Platini* v. *FIFA*, award of 9 May 2016 and CAS 2016/A/4501 *Joseph S. Blatter* v. *FIFA*, award of 5 December 2016.

[10] CAS 2016/A/4643, *Maria Sharapova* v. *International Tennis Federation (ITF)*, award of 30 September 2016 and CAS 2009/A/1879 *Alejandro Valverde Belmonte* v. *Comitato Olimpico Nazionale Italiano*, award of 16 March 2010.

regime in which private associations play a fundamental role and dispose of considerable regulatory powers, this regime also provides an interesting terrain to study transnational legal entanglements.[11]

To this end, I focus on the way the CAS produces its awards. I aim to show that the *lex sportiva* is not an isolated set of norms produced by an autonomous community but results from the blending of different laws assembled through discursive weaving by CAS panels. In this regard, not all national laws are equal at the CAS and, as we will see in Section 10.1, Swiss law is more equal than the others. In practice, the CAS panels draw heavily on Swiss law, its actors, doctrines, rules and decisions.[12] Despite being a global court, the CAS remains anchored (physically, sociologically and legally) in a local context. In addition to Swiss law, Sections 10.2 and 10.3 highlight how CAS arbitrators are also weaving references to EU law and the ECHR into their awards. This chapter is a first attempt at looking at the hermeneutic practice of the CAS from the perspective of a transnational legal pluralism that goes beyond the identification of a plurality of autonomous orders to turn its sights towards the enmeshment and entanglement characterizing contemporary legal practice.[13]

10.1 The Ubiquity of Swiss Law in CAS Awards

In its awards, the CAS refers to many different national laws. However, one is clearly more present than the others: Swiss law.[14] The centrality of Swiss law at the CAS can be linked to three factors: the sociology of the CAS practitioners, the shadow of the Swiss Federal Tribunal (SFT) and the localization of the seats of the SGBs. To start with the last of these, the majority of the international SGBs, which are the primary purveyors of CAS appeals, are located in Switzerland. This means that in most appeal

[11] For another attempt, see A. Duval, 'What Lex Sportiva Tells You about Transnational Law', in P. Zumbansen (ed.), *The Many Lives of Transnational Law: Critical Engagements with Jessup's Bold Proposal* (Cambridge University Press 2019), pp. 269–93.

[12] A. Rigozzi, 'L'importance du droit suisse de l'arbitrage dans la résolution des litiges sportifs internationaux' (2013) 1 *ZSR* 301–25.

[13] See P. Zumbansen, 'Transnational Legal Pluralism' (2010) 1 *Transnational Legal Theory* 141–89 and J. Klabbers and G. Palombella (eds), *The Challenge of Inter-Legality* (Cambridge University Press, 2019).

[14] A full text search (in the CAS appeal awards) of 'Swiss law' in the CAS database yields hits in 1031 CAS awards (out of 1,636 appeal awards included in the database). A comparable search of 'German law', 'Italian law' and 'French law' yields exactly the same number of awards: nineteen. These searches were all conducted on the same date (11 December 2019).

cases Swiss law will be subsidiarily applicable under R58 CAS Code which determines the applicable law and acts very much as a 'reception norm' in the sense outlined in Chapter 1.[15] Furthermore, the appeals are often based on CAS arbitration clauses enshrined in the statutes of the SGBs which can expressly provide for the application of Swiss law.[16] Second, the legal seat of the CAS is Lausanne. Hence, its awards can only be appealed at the SFT where they are reviewed, relatively leniently, on the basis of Article 190(2) of the Swiss Private International Law Act.[17] The CAS panels are naturally aware of the need for their awards to pass this (relatively low) bar and therefore pay specific attention to Swiss law in their decisions. Finally, arbitrators, lawyers or administrators active at the CAS often have a Swiss background.[18] In this section, I aim to substantiate the depth of the entanglement between Swiss law and CAS awards through a case study focused specifically on appeals against FIFA decisions.

10.1.1 Swiss Law as Applicable Law in FIFA Cases

Appeals against FIFA decisions constitute an important share of the caseload of the CAS appeal division. In particular, cases involving transfer disputes and the application of the FIFA Regulations on the Status and Transfer of Players (FIFA RSTP) are numerous and CAS panels have repeatedly been asked to determine the law applicable in these cases. In principle, as FIFA is seated in Zürich, Swiss law is subsidiarily applicable in the absence of any other choice of law as provided under R58 CAS Code. Moreover, CAS panels have regularly pointed out that the parties are, at least indirectly, affiliated to FIFA (i.e. 'members of the FIFA

[15] R58 CAS Code (2019 version) provides: The Panel shall decide the dispute according to the applicable regulations and, subsidiarily, to the rules of law chosen by the parties or, in the absence of such a choice, according to the law of the country in which the federation, association or sports-related body which has issued the challenged decision is domiciled or according to the rules of law the Panel deems appropriate. In the latter case, the Panel shall give reasons for its decision.

[16] See, for example, the Article 57(2) FIFA Statutes 2019 discussed further in Section 10.1.1.

[17] On the limited scope of this review, see A. Rigozzi, 'Challenging Awards of the Court of Arbitration for Sport' (2010) 1 *Journal of International Dispute Settlement* 217–65.

[18] Lindholm in a recent empirical study of the CAS identified a high number of Swiss parties and arbitrators active at the CAS, see J. Lindholm, *The Court of Arbitration for Sport and Its Jurisprudence: An Empirical Inquiry into Lex Sportiva* (T.M.C. Asser Press, 2019), pp. 270–4.

family')[19] and therefore bound by the choice of Swiss law enshrined in Article 57(2) FIFA Statutes 2019.[20]

Yet, the applicability of Swiss law is not only justified by the parties' contractual choice but also on functional grounds, that is, in order to 'level the playing the field' in football disputes. For example, a CAS panel concluded in 2005 that the 'indispensable need for the uniform and coherent application worldwide of the rules regulating international football' is secured '[o]nly if the same terms and conditions apply to everyone who participates in organized sport'.[21] Similarly, another panel concluded, 'if the desired uniformity is to be achieved, also the interpretation of the FIFA rules and regulations cannot be affected by the peculiarities of the domestic legal system in which they are called to apply'.[22] Thus, appeals against FIFA decisions will necessarily trigger the application of Swiss law 'for all the questions that are not directly regulated by the FIFA Regulations'.[23] In this context, 'there is no place for the application of the rules of another national law, except in the case where these rules would have to be considered as mandatory according to the law of the seat of the arbitration, i.e. Swiss law'.[24]

Nevertheless, based on the wording of R58 CAS Code, Swiss law should not prevail over the express choice of law of the parties.[25] Even

[19] CAS 2013/A/3165, *FC Volyn* v. *Issa Ndoye*, award of 14 January 2014, para. 68.

[20] CAS 2008/A/1517, *Ionikos FC* v. *C.*, award of 23 February 2009, paras 7 and 17; CAS 2006/A/1180, *Galatasaray SK* v. *Frank Ribéry* and *Olympique de Marseille*, award of 24 April 2007, para. 13. See also CAS 2008/A/1482, *Genoa Cricket and Football Club S.p. A.* v. *Club Deportivo Maldonado*, award of 9 February 2009, para. 18.

[21] TAS 2005/A/983 and 984, *Club Atlético Peñarol* v. *Carlos Heber Bueno Suarez, Cristian Gabriel Rodriguez Barrotti and Paris Saint-Germain*, award of 12 July 2006, para. 24. See also in CAS 2006/A/1180, para. 13; CAS 2006/A/1123, *Al-Gharafa Sports Club* v. *Paulo Cesar Wanchope Watson* and CAS 2006/A/1124, *Paulo Cesar Wanchope Watson* v. *Al-Gharafa Sports Club*, award of 18 December 2006, para. 12; CAS 2008/A/1517; CAS 2011/A/2375, *FK Dac 1904 a.s.* v. *Zoltan Vasas*, award of 31 October 2011; CAS 2013/A/3165, para. 67; TAS 2014/A/3505, *Al Khor SC* v. *C.*, award of 3 December 2014, para. 85; CAS 2014/A/3742, *US Città di Palermo S.p.A.* v. *Goran Veljkovic*, award of 7 April 2015, para. 47.

[22] CAS 2006/A/1123, para. 13. Similarly, see CAS 2013/A/3383–3385, *Volga Nizhniy Novgorod* v. *Levan Silagadze*, award of 13 November 2014, para. 48 and TAS 2016/A/4569, *Abdelkarim Elmorabet* v. *Olympic Club Safi and Fédération Royale Marocaine de Football (FRMF)*, award of 20 September 2016, para. 5.8.

[23] CAS 2005/A/871, *FC Rodopa* v. *Markovitch*, award of 19 September 2006, para. 4.15. Or 'if there is a gap in the FIFA regulations', CAS 2013/A/3165, para. 69.

[24] CAS 2009/A/1956, *Club Tofta Itróttarfelag, B68* v. *R.*, award of 16 February 2010, para. 15.

[25] CAS 2006/A/1024, *FC Metallurg Donetsk* v. *Leo Lerinc*, para. 27.

then, recent awards determined that such cases give 'rise to a co-existence of the applicable regulations, Swiss law and the law chosen by the Parties', in which 'Swiss law is confined to ensuring uniform application of the [FIFA] Regulations'.[26] In other words, in order to protect the uniform interpretation of FIFA Regulations, Swiss law is deemed to supersede the parties' choice of law.[27] This view, first advanced by Professor Ulrich Haas, was subsequently endorsed as the 'Haas doctrine' by a series of CAS panels.[28] Finally, if FIFA Regulations are considered sufficiently clear and comprehensive by the CAS panels, Swiss law does not come into play, as it 'does not supersede or supplant all aspects of the regulations of FIFA'.[29] Yet in practice, as Section 10.1.2 shows, the FIFA Regulations are often ambiguous and in need of interpretation.

10.1.2 How Swiss Law Shapes CAS Awards in FIFA Cases

The recognition of the (exclusive) applicability of Swiss law to interpretative questions related to the FIFA Regulations would, however, remain meaningless if it were not relied upon in practice. While it is in theory possible to construct the FIFA Regulations as sufficiently clear and comprehensive, in practice Swiss law plays a crucial interpretative role in CAS appeals against FIFA decisions. Indeed, many concepts that are at the heart of the FIFA Regulations have been defined and concretized with references to Swiss law, Swiss doctrine and Swiss precedents. This includes questions related to:

26 CAS 2016/A/4605, *Al-Arabi Sports Club Co. For Football* v. *Matthew Spiranovic*, award of 22 February 2017, para. 5.6. See also CAS 2017/A/5341, *CJSC Football Club Lokomotiv* v. *Slaven Bilic*, para. 59.

27 See CAS 2010/A/2316, *Stoke City FC* v. *Brescia Calcio S.p.A.*, award of 6 December 2011, para. 20.

28 See U. Haas, 'Applicable Law in Football-Related Disputes: The Relationship between the CAS Code, the FIFA Statutes and the Agreement of the Parties on the Application of National Law' (2015) *Bulletin TAS/CAS Bulletin* 7. CAS 2016/A/4605, para. 5.6; CAS 2017/A/5341, paras 57 and 59; CAS 2017/A/5465, *Békéscsaba 1912 Futball* v. *George Koroudjiev*, award of 20 September 2018, paras 74 and 76; CAS 2017/A/5402, *Club Al-Taawoun* v. *Darije Kalezic*, award of 7 June 2018, para. 89; CAS 2016/A/4471, *Abel Aguilar Tapias* v. *Hércules de Alicante FC*, award of 2 February 2017, paras 69–70; CAS 2016/A/4859, *Hong Kong Pegasus FC* v. *Niko Tokic*, award of 30 June 2017, paras 60–1; TAS 2016/A/4569, paras 5.8 and 5.9.

29 CAS 2012/A/2919, *FC Seoul* v. *Newcastle Jets FC*, award of 24 September 2013. In other words, FIFA regulations apply in 'priority', TAS 2005/A/983 and 984, para. 49.

- the method to be followed to interpret the FIFA Regulations;[30]
- the applicability of mandatory rules, such as EU law;[31]
- whether a party has standing to sue or to be sued;[32]
- who bears the burden of proof;[33]
- the calculation of time limits;[34]
- whether there is a contract or an offer 'in writing';[35]
- whether an offer has been received;[36]
- whether there is 'just cause' for one of the parties to terminate an employment contract between a player and a club;[37]

30 CAS 2008/A/1521, *VfB Admira Wacker Modling* v. *A.C. Pistoiese s.p.A.*, award of 12 December 2008; CAS 2010/A/2316; CAS 2013/A/3365, *Juventus Football Club S.p.A.* v. *Chelsea Football Club Ltd* and CAS 2013/A/3366, *A.S. Livorno Calcio* v. *Chelsea Football Club Ltd*, award of 21 January 2015.

31 CAS 2008/A/1485, *FC Midtjylland A/S* v. *Fédération Internationale de Football Association (FIFA)*, award of 6 March 2009 and TAS 2016/A/4490, *RFC Seraing* v. *Fédération Internationale de Football Association (FIFA)*, award of 9 March 2017.

32 CAS 2006/A/1206, *Milan Zivadinovic* v. *Iraqi Football Association (IFA)*, award of 2 April 2007; CAS 2006/A/1192, *Chelsea Football Club Limited* v. *Adrian Mutu*, award of 21 May 2007; CAS 2007/A/1329, *Chiapas F.C.* v. *Cricuma Esporte Clube* and CAS 2007/A/1330, *Chiapas F.C.* v. *R.*, awards of 5 December 2007; CAS 2008/A/1518, *Ionikos FC* v. *L.*, award of 23 February 2009; CAS 2012/A/2906, *Alain Geiger* v. *Egyptian Football Association (EFA) and Al Masry Club*, award of 12 February 2013; TAS 2013/A/3351, *Fédération de Football de la République Islamique de Mauritanie (FFRIM) and ASAC Concorde* v. *CS Hammam-Lif and Fédération Tunisienne de Football (FTF) and Fédération Internationale de Football Association (FIFA)*, award of 24 January 2014; CAS 2013/A/3278, *Maritimo de Madeira – Futebol SAD* v. *Desportivo Brasil Participacoes LTDA*, award of 2 June 2014; CAS 2017/A/5227, *Sporting Clube de Braga* v. *Club Dynamo Kyiv and Gerson Alencar de Lima Junior*, award of 8 March 2018; CAS 2017/A/5352, *FK Sileks* v. *GFK Dubočica Leskovac*, award of 24 April 2018.

33 CAS 2009/A/1909, *RCD Mallorca SAD and A.* v. *Fédération Internationale de Football Association (FIFA) and UMM Salal SC*, award of 25 January 2010; CAS 2009/A/1956; CAS 2013/A/3444, *S.C. FC Brasov S.A* v. *Renato Ferreira Da Silva Alberto*, award of 29 October 2015.

34 CAS 2011/A/2354, *E.* v. *Fédération Internationale de Football Association (FIFA)*, award of 24 August 2011; CAS 2015/A/3883, *Al Nassr Saudi Club* v. *Jaimen Javier Ayovi Corozo*, award of 26 August 2015.

35 CAS 2008/A/1521; CAS 2010/A/2316; CAS 2013/A/3207, *Tout Puissant Mazembe* v. *Alain Kaluyituka Dioko and Al Ahli SC*, award of 31 March 2014.

36 CAS 2016/A/4720, *Royal Standard de Liège* v. *FC Porto (Player T.)*, award of 19 May 2017 and CAS 2016/A/4721, *Royal Standard de Liège* v. *FC Porto (Player C.)*, award of 19 May 2017.

37 CAS 2006/A/1100, *E.* v. *Club Gaziantepspor*, award of 15 November 2006; CAS 2007/A/1210, *Ittihad Club* v. *Sergio Dario Herrera*, award of 3 July 2007; TAS 2007/A/1233, *FC Universitatea Craiova* v. *Marcos Honorio Da Silva* and TAS 2007/A/1234, *FC Universitatea Craiova* v. *Eduardo Magri*, awards of 19 December 2007; CAS 2008/A/1447, *E.*

- the amount of damages that a party is entitled to in case of a contractual breach;[38]
- the conditions that must be met for a renunciation by a player of his outstanding wage to be valid;[39]
- the validity and amount of a penalty clause;[40]
- the validity of a waiver to the right to receive a training compensation;[41]
- the validity of a dual pricing method for a transfer fee;[42] and
- the interest rate applicable in case of payment default.[43]

These examples are a large but certainly incomplete sample of the many instances in which Swiss law has been relied on to support a specific interpretation of the FIFA Regulations. These interpretative decisions are not trivial. They affect, for example, whether a party will have standing to appeal a decision before the CAS, whether a party will be deemed to have broken an employment contract or the amount of damages a party will be able to obtain in case of breach. For each of these questions, the CAS panels have leaned on Swiss law to justify their interpretative (and therefore distributive) choices. This use of Swiss law is not limited to

v. *Diyarbakirspor*, award of 29 August 2008; CAS 2008/A/1518; CAS 2009/A/1956; CAS 2013/A/3216, *Anorthosis Famagusta FC* v. *Sinisa Dobrasinovic*, award of 14 May 2014; CAS 2013/A/3407, *Green Gully Soccer Club* v. *Pedro Henrique Coelho de Oliveira*, award of 20 June 2014; CAS 2014/A/3626, *Carmelo Enrique Valencia Chaverra* v. *Ulsan Hyundai Football Club*, award of 23 April 2015; TAS 2016/A/4569; CAS 2016/A/4588, *FC Internazionale Milano* v. *Sunderland AFC* and CAS 2016/A/4589, *Sunderland AFC* v. *FC Internazionale Milano*, awards of 15 June 2017; CAS 2017/A/5242, *Esteghlal Football Club* v. *Pero Pejic*, award of 16 April 2018; CAS 2017/A/5465.

[38] TAS 2005/A/902, *Mexès and AS Roma* v. *AJ Auxerre* and TAS 2005/A/903, *AJ Auxerre* v. *Mexès and AS Roma*, awards of 5 December 2005; CAS 2006/A/1024; CAS 2006/A/1100; TAS 2007/A/1315, *Hassan El Mouataz and Sporting Lokeren Oost-Vlaanderen* v. *Association Sportive des Forces Armées Royales (ASFAR)*, awards of 31 January 2008; CAS 2008/A/1447; CAS 2008/A/1518; TAS 2014/A/3505; CAS 2013/A/3216; CAS 2014/A/3626; TAS 2016/A/4569; CAS 2016/A/4588; CAS 2017/A/5242.

[39] TAS 2018/A/5896, *Yves Diba Ilunga* v. *Al Shoullah Club*, award of 15 April 2019.

[40] CAS 2012/A/2847, *Hammarby Fotboll AB* v. *Besiktas Futbol Yatirimlari Sanayi ve Ticaret A.S.*, award of 22 March 2013; CAS 2014/A/3555, *FC Vojvodina* v. *Almami Samori Da Silva Moreira*, award of 18 December 2014; CAS 2017/A/5242.

[41] CAS 2017/A/5277, *FK Sarajevo* v. *KVC Westerlo*, award of 16 April 2018.

[42] CAS 2006/A/1196, *Sociedade Esportiva Palmeiras* v. *Clube Desportivo Nacional*, award of 19 July 2007.

[43] CAS 2008/A/1482; CAS 2013/A/3443, *Ginés Carvajal Seller* v. *FC Dnipro Dnipropetrovsk*, award of 6 October 2014; CAS 2016/A/4567, *Al Jazira FSC* v. *FC Lokomotiv*, award of 9 November 2016; TAS 2016/A/4569; CAS 2017/A/5374, *Jaroslaw Kolakowski* v. *Daniel Quintana Sosa*, award of 10 April 2018.

cases involving FIFA decisions. It is relevant to a majority of appeals against the decisions rendered by international SGBs. It shows that the CAS is not engaging in the production of denationalized awards with little connection to state law. Instead, it is weaving the local and the global, as the transnational private rules of the SGBs are being entangled with norms, case law and doctrinal authorities grounded in Swiss law. What might, from a distance, appear like a sort of global law without a state is actually intimately linked to, and reliant on, the law of the Swiss state.

The fact that Swiss law has a prominent position at the CAS is not an original claim. Scholars and practitioners had emphasized it before.[44] Yet, it raises interesting questions connected to the theme of this volume, which have so far been widely ignored. How are the CAS panels applying Swiss law? What is the purpose and effect of this entanglement between Swiss law and the private regulations of the SGBs? What is the responsibility of Switzerland with regard to the shape of the transnational sporting regime? How can Swiss law be leveraged to change the shape of this regime in one way or another? These questions can become relevant only once we perceive the *lex sportiva* as a transnational assemblage and see the fundamental role of Swiss law in it. This intertwining of normative material at the CAS extends, in much more limited fashion, to other types of legal filaments, such as EU law or the ECHR.

10.2 The Limited Entanglement of EU Law in CAS Awards

EU law and the private regulations of the SGBs have a long history of 'war and peace'.[45] The famous *Bosman*[46] ruling of the Court of Justice of the European Union (CJEU) constitutes the high point, in terms of public visibility, of this encounter. Despite the intense relationship between the private regulations of the SGBs and EU law, the latter was

44 A. Rigozzi, 'L'importance du droit suisse de l'arbitrage'.

45 A. Duval, 'La Lex Sportiva face au droit de l'Union européenne: guerre et paix dans l'espace juridique transnational', PhD thesis, EUI (2015). On the interaction between EU law and sport, see S. Weatherill, *Principles and Practice in EU Sports Law* (Oxford University Press, 2017).

46 Case C-415/93, *Union royale belge des sociétés de football association ASBL* v. *Jean-Marc Bosman, Royal club liégeois SA* v. *Jean-Marc Bosman and others and Union des associations européennes de football (UEFA)* v. *Jean-Marc Bosman* [1995] ECR I-04921.

until recently quite absent from the CAS.[47] Nevertheless, in an important award dating back to 1999, a CAS panel already recognized the applicability of EU law. It found:

> With regard to EC competition law, the Panel holds that, even if the parties had not validly agreed on its applicability to this case, it should be taken into account anyway. Indeed, in accordance with Article 19 of the LDIP, an arbitration tribunal sitting in Switzerland must take into consideration also foreign mandatory rules, even of a law different from the one determined through the choice-of-law process, provided that three conditions are met:
>
> (a) such rules must belong to that special category of norms which need to be applied irrespective of the law applicable to the merits of the case (so-called lois d'application immédiate);
> (b) there must be a close connection between the subject matter of the dispute and the territory where the mandatory rules are in force;
> (c) from the point of view of Swiss legal theory and practice, the mandatory rules must aim to protect legitimate interests and crucial values and their application must allow an appropriate decision.[48]

Thus, arguments grounded in Swiss private international law played a pivotal role in opening the possibility for the application and entanglement of EU law at the CAS. Yet, before 2010, only a few (published) CAS awards referred to EU law and even fewer were engaging with it in detail.[49] This has changed in recent years, with a couple of awards

[47] A. Duval, 'The Court of Arbitration for Sport and EU Law: Chronicle of an Encounter' (2015) 22 *Maastricht Journal of European and Comparative Law* 224–55.

[48] CAS 98/200, *AEK Athens and SK Slavia Prague* v. *Union of European Football Associations (UEFA)*, award of 20 August 1999, para. 10.

[49] Before 2010, we find mentions of EU law in the following CAS awards publicly available in the CAS database (on 1 September 2019): TAS 92/80, *B.* v. *Fédération Internationale de Basketball (FIBA)*, award of 25 March 1993; CAS 98/200; TAS 2000/A/290, *Abel Xavier and Everton FC* v. *Union des Associations Européennes de Football (UEFA)*, award of 2 February 2001; TAS 2002/A/423, *PSV Eindhoven* v. *Union des Associations Européennes de Football (UEFA)*, award of 3 June 2003; TAS 2004/A/708, *Philippe Mexès* v. *Fédération Internationale de Football Association (FIFA)* and TAS 2004/A/709, *AS Roma* v. *FIFA* and TAS 2004/A/713, *AJ Auxerre* c. *AS Roma and Philippe Mexès*, awards of 11 March 2005; CAS 2005/A/951, *Guillermo Cañas* v. *ATP Tour*, revised award of 23 May 2007; CAS 2006/A/1125, *Hertha BSC Berlin* v. *Stade Lavallois Mayenne FC*, award of 1 December 2006; CAS 2007/A/1272, *Cork City FC* v. *FIFA (Healy)*, award of 15 October 2007; CAS 2007/A/1287, *Danubio FC* v. *Fédération Internationale de Football Association (FIFA) and FC Internazionale Milano S.p.A.*, award of 28 November 2007; CAS 2008/A/1485; CAS 2008/A/1644, *M.* v. *Chelsea Football Club Ltd.*, award of 31 July 2009; CAS 2009/A/

addressing at length EU law questions.[50] Such a development is potentially related to the greater sensitivity of legal counsels to EU law and to the arbitrators' growing awareness of the considerable risk that the cases would *in fine* reach the European Commission or the CJEU. In general, EU law has found two main applications at the CAS: it has been mobilized to challenge the legality (even constitutionality) of the SGBs' regulations and it has been constructed as part and parcel of the SGBs' regulations.

10.2.1 EU Law as Constitutional Check at the CAS

EU law does not regulate transnational sports through the imposition of detailed primary rules. Instead, it imposes a duty of justification on the SGBs.[51] EU law forces, through the strength of its internal market rules, the SGBs to advance legitimate objectives for their regulations and to argue why their rules or decisions are to be deemed proportionate means to attain the set objectives. In other words, it functions analogously to a constitutional review of the rules and decisions of the SGBs. This duty of justification has been formally imported in a number of cases submitted to the CAS, in which the panels have conducted proportionality assessments of the rules and decisions challenged. In many cases, the CAS does not conduct a deep appraisal of the proportionality of a disputed measure.[52] It has, for example, regularly considered that the fact that the FIFA RSTP are based on an agreement with the European Commission suffices to guarantee their compatibility with EU law.[53] Nevertheless, in a range

1757, *MTK Budapest* v. *FC Internazionale Milano S.p.A.*, award of 30 July 2009; CAS 2009/A/1788, *UMMC Ekaterinburg* v. *FIBA Europe e. V.*, award of 29 October 2009.

50 For deep engagements with EU law, see, for example: TAS 2016/A/4490 and CAS 2016/A/4492, *Galatasaray* v. *UEFA*, award of 3 October 2016.

51 The centrality of the idea of justification in the European integration process has been theorised by J. Neyer, *The Justification of Europe: A Political Theory of Supranational Integration* (Oxford University Press, 2012).

52 See TAS 2000/A/290, para. 17.7; CAS 2005/A/951, para. 29; CAS 2008/A/1644, para. 44.

53 CAS 2007/A/1272, para. 32; CAS 2007/A/1287, paras 37–40; CAS 2009/A/1757, paras 29–30; CAS 2009/A/1810 and 1811, *SV Wilhelmshaven* v. *Club Atlético Excursionistas and Club Atlético River Plate*, award of 5 October 2009, paras 48–9; CAS 2009/A/1957, *Fédération Française de Natation (FFN)* v. *Ligue Européenne de Natation (LEN)*, award of 5 July 2010, paras 37–40; CAS 2013/A/3119, *Dundee United FC* v. *Club Atlético Vélez Sarsfield*, award of 20 November 2013, paras 70–1; CAS 2014/A/3710, *Bologna FC 1909 S.p.A.* v. *FC Barcelona*, award of 22 April 2015, para. 81.

of recent cases, the CAS panels quite comprehensively engaged in a proportionality assessment of the reviewed regulations.[54]

More precisely, in the *Galatasaray*[55] and *Seraing*[56] awards, delivered in 2016 and 2017, the CAS was asked to review the compatibility of two controversial rules introduced respectively by the Union of European Football Associations (UEFA) and FIFA. It is interesting to note that Jean-Louis Dupont, who represented Jean-Marc Bosman, was acting for the claimants in both cases. The *Galatasaray* case involved the UEFA Club Licensing and Financial Fair Play Regulations (UEFA FFP Regulations) and their compatibility with EU law. It is not the right place to revisit the debate on the compatibility of the UEFA FFP Regulations with EU law, but it is interesting to note that the CAS panel decided to conduct a comprehensive proportionality analysis relatively similar to the one that would have been conducted by the European Commission or the CJEU if they were asked a similar question. Likewise, the *Seraing* case, in which the Belgian club was challenging the validity under EU law of FIFA's 2015 ban on third-party ownership, also led to the integration of a proportionality analysis grounded in EU law into the CAS award.[57] In both cases, the CAS concluded that the regulations were pursuing a legitimate objective and represented necessary and proportionate means to attain that objective.

It is uncertain whether the CJEU or the European Commission would reach the same conclusion, but the above awards highlight that the two CAS panels were in the position of decentralized EU law enforcers, not unlike national courts but without the obligation or capacity to refer a preliminary question to the CJEU. The question whether the CAS is applying EU law properly, for example as the CJEU would, is almost impossible to settle until a case reaches Luxembourg. A review of the CAS awards involving EU law shows that the SGBs' regulations are very

54 CAS 98/200; CAS 2009/A/1788, paras 22–47; CAS 2012/A/2852, *S.C.S. Fotbal Club CFR 1907 Cluj S.A. and Manuel Ferreira de Sousa Ricardo and Mario Jorge Quintas Felgueiras* v. *Romanian Football Federation (FRF)*, award of 28 June 2013; CAS 2014/A/3561 and 3614, *International Association of Athletics Federation (IAAF) and World Anti-Doping Agency (WADA)* v. *Marta Domínguez Azpeleta and Real Federación Española de Atletismo (RFEA)*, award of 19 November 2015, paras 172–91; TAS 2016/A/4490; CAS 2016/A/4492.

55 CAS 2016/A/4492. See my commentary in A. Duval, 'CAS 2016/A/4492, Galatasaray v. UEFA, Award of 3 October 2016', in A. Duval and A. Rigozzi (eds), *Yearbook of International Sports Arbitration 2016* (T.M.C. Asser Press, 2017), pp. 377–91.

56 TAS 2016/A/4490.

57 TAS 2016/A/4490, paras 90–144.

rarely deemed in contravention of EU law. In fact, there is only one example in which a CAS panel struck down an SGB regulation on this basis.[58] It involved the Romanian Football Federation (FRF) and its home-grown players regulations, which imposed a fixed quota of locally trained players in the teams of Romanian clubs participating in national competitions. The panel was not convinced that the FRF had demonstrated that its regulations were necessary and proportionate. In any event, the use of EU law as a vehicle to conduct a constitutional check of the SGBs' regulations constitutes another (rare) form of legal entanglement at the CAS. Additionally, beyond this constitutional role, EU law is also directly interwoven in the genome of the FIFA RSTP.

10.2.2 Interpreting the FIFA RSTP with a Little Help from EU Law

After the Bosman ruling, FIFA devised a new transfer system regulating the transnational movement of football players between clubs.[59] This new system, however, was quickly challenged at the European Commission on the basis of EU competition law and a protracted negotiation started between the European Commission, FIFA, the players' union FIFPro, the European Club Association and UEFA.[60] It concluded with the adoption of the general principles upon which the FIFA RSTP is officially grounded.[61] This peculiar transnational genealogy of the RSTP became relevant at the CAS because panels have considered that, insofar as the statutes of large entities are concerned, 'it may be more appropriate to have recourse to the method of interpretation applicable to the law' and therefore adopt a 'contextual approach' that entails reviewing the legislative history and purpose.[62]

[58] See CAS 2012/A/2852.

[59] On the FIFA RSTP and its interpretation by the FIFA Dispute Resolution Chamber in general, see F. De Weger, *The Jurisprudence of the FIFA Dispute Resolution Chamber* (T.M.C. Asser Press, 2016).

[60] For a detailed history of this episode of transnational law-making, see A. Duval, 'The FIFA Regulations on the Status and Transfer of Players: Transnational Law-Making in the Shadow of Bosman', in A. Duval and B. Van Rompuy (eds), *The Legacy of Bosman: Revisiting the Relationship Between EU Law and Sport* (T.M.C. Asser Press, 2016), pp. 81–116.

[61] European Commission, 'Outcome of Discussions between the Commission and FIFA/UEFA on FIFA Regulations on International Football Transfers' (press release IP/01/314, 5 March 2001).

[62] CAS 2013/A/3365 and 3366, para. 143.

The first case involving an interpretive use of EU law was the *Mexès* case which concerned the interpretation of Articles 21(1) and 23(1) FIFA RSTP 2001 edition.[63] The key question was whether the prolongation of the contract of a professional football player would trigger an extension of the stability period – a period during which the player could not leave the club without risking a sporting sanction. To answer this question, the Panel analysed the question in light of EU law as it decided to go back to the *ratio legis* of the provisions to determine their concrete meaning.[64] The text of the award refers to the *Bosman* ruling as well as to the decision of the European Commission in the competition law case opened against FIFA.[65] Hence, to support its decision, the CAS panel felt that it had to grapple with EU law requirements, although whether it did so in an orthodox fashion is another matter. This first example of recourse to EU law as part of the relevant context for a proper interpretation of the RSTP was endorsed in following awards.[66] Most prominently, in a case pitching the Italian football clubs Juventus F.C. and A.S. Livorno Calcio against the English club Chelsea F.C., the CAS provided an extensive analysis of this interpretive link between EU law and the RSTP.[67] The case was related to the legal saga surrounding Chelsea's 2005 dismissal of Adrian Mutu over his consumption of cocaine. The CAS panel considered it necessary to do an in-depth review of the legislative history of the FIFA RSTP in order to determine whether Article 14(3) FIFA RSTP 2001 edition applied, and therefore whether Juventus and Livorno jointly owed a considerable transfer fee to Chelsea. In doing so, it carefully scrutinized the case law of the CJEU and the decisions of the European Commission.[68] This led the arbitrators to reject the interpretation advanced by Chelsea as contrary to the EU law

63 TAS 2004/A/708 and 709 and 713.

64 Ibid., paras 24–30.

65 Ibid., paras 25–6.

66 See CAS 2006/A/1125, paras 43–7; CAS 2010/A/2316, para. 37; CAS 2016/A/4903, *Club Atlético Vélez Sarsfield* v. *The Football Association Ltd., Manchester City FC and Fédération Internationale de Football Association (FIFA)*, award of 16 April 2018, paras 91–105.

67 CAS 2013/A/3365 and 3366. See A. Duval, 'CAS 2013/A/3365 Juventus FC v. Chelsea FC and CAS 2013/A/3366 A.S. Livorno Calcio S.p.A. v. Chelsea FC, Award of 21 January 2015', in A. Duval and A. Rigozzi (eds), *Yearbook of International Sports Arbitration 2015* (T.M.C. Asser Press, 2016), pp. 155–68.

68 CAS 2013/A/3365 and 3366, paras 149–57.

foundations of the RSTP and to conclude that Livorno and Juventus were free to recruit Adrian Mutu without compensation after his dismissal.[69]

As demonstrated, EU law finds its relatively narrow way at the CAS. This limited enmeshing of EU law in CAS awards is most likely driven by external challenges to the SGBs' regulations and decisions in national courts or before EU institutions. In fact, EU law's capacity to disrupt the authority of CAS is certainly a (rational) pathway to drive the entanglement of EU law into its awards.[70] However, by harnessing EU law, the CAS panels might also be betraying it. The CAS is not referring questions to the CJEU and CAS awards are, for reasons of costs and time, rarely challenged in national courts on EU law basis. In the absence of systematic control of CAS awards, the panels' approach to EU law escapes the possibility of direct oversight by EU institutions. In other words, CAS might be speaking an EU law dialect that is primarily fitted to the needs and power structure of its social context, while at the same time formally proximate to and at a substantial distance from the EU law of the EU institutions.[71]

10.3 The Influential Use of the ECHR in CAS Awards

While EU law has been dancing a slow-moving tango with the SGBs' regulations since the 1970s, the ECHR was, until very recently, almost entirely foreign to the world of sport.[72] The European Court of Human Rights (ECtHR) only started to indirectly scrutinize the practice of the CAS and the world anti-doping regime in 2018 and has done so in a relatively restrained fashion.[73] In spite of this, the ECHR has been

[69] Ibid., paras 161–3.

[70] Most recently in the ISU decision of the European Commission, see Case AT.40208 – International Skating Union's Eligibility rules, 8 December 2017.

[71] On the dialectic between proximity and distance in the context of legal entanglements, see Chapter 1, Section 1.4.3.

[72] For a general summary of the ECtHR cases applying to sport, see ECtHR, 'Sport and the European Convention on Human Rights, Factsheet' (October 2019), www.echr.coe.int/Documents/FS_Sport_ENG.pdf. However, few of the cases mentioned are directly related to the regulations or decisions of SGBs.

[73] See *Mutu and Pechstein* v. *Switzerland*, app. no. 40575/10 and 67474/10, judgment of 2 October 2018; *Fédération Nationale des Syndicats Sportifs (FNASS) and Others* v. *France*, app. no. 48151/11 and 77769/13, judgment of 18 January 2018; *Platini* v. *Switzerland*, app. no. 526/18, judgment of 11 February 2020.

regularly mentioned in CAS awards.[74] Even though some panels expressed 'serious doubts'[75] regarding the applicability of the ECHR to the SGBs' private regulations or even sometimes squarely denied it,[76] when confronted with claimants invoking the ECHR most CAS awards at least considered its application. This inconsistency can be traced back to the unstable composition of CAS panels and non-binding nature of CAS precedents. In any event, most panels at least emphasized the need to respect the procedural rights enshrined in Article 6(1) ECHR.[77] Indeed, a panel 'should nevertheless account for their [the provisions of the ECHR] content within the framework of procedural public policy'.[78] In a more direct language, a sole arbitrator found 'rather obvious' that 'a federation cannot opt out from an interpretation of its rules and regulations in light of principles of "human rights" just by omitting any references in its rules and regulations to human rights'.[79] In this latter version, the ECHR seems to be even assimilated to an 'overarching norm'.[80]

10.3.1 CAS Jurisdiction and the ECHR

Among the many legal questions that have triggered references to the ECHR, some are connected to the jurisdiction of the CAS. For example, the CAS faced a case in which an athlete was challenging the validity of

[74] See for a general overview U. Haas, 'Role and Application of Article 6 of the European Convention on Human Rights in CAS Procedures' (2012) 3 *International Sports Law Review* 43–60.

[75] CAS 2008/A/1513, *Emil Hoch* v. *Fédération Internationale de Ski (FIS) and International Olympic Committee (IOC)*, award of 29 January 2009, para. 9.

[76] See CAS 2009/A/1957, para. 14; TAS 2011/A/2433, *Amadou Diakite* v. *Fédération Internationale de Football Association (FIFA)*, award of 8 March 2012, para. 23; TAS 2012/A/2862, *FC Girondins de Bordeaux* v. *Fédération Internationale de Football Association (FIFA)*, award of 11 January 2013, paras 106–7.

[77] The first award in this regard is TAS 2000/A/290, para. 10. The ECHR is seen as 'indirectly applicable' (TAS 2011/A/2433, para. 24) and CAS Panels as 'indirectly bound' (CAS 2015/A/4304, *Tatyana Andrianova* v. *All Russia Athletic Federation (ARAF)*, award of 14 April 2016, para. 46). See also CAS 2013/A/3139, *Fenerbahçe SK* v. *Union des Associations Européennes de Football (UEFA)*, award of 5 December 2013, para. 93.

[78] CAS 2011/A/2384, *Union Cycliste Internationale (UCI)* v. *Alberto Contador Velasco and Real Federación Española de Ciclismo (RFEC)* and CAS 2011/A/2386, *World AntiDoping Agency (WADA)* v. *Alberto Contador Velasco and RFEC*, award of 6 February 2012, para. 22.

[79] CAS 2015/A/4304, para. 45.

[80] See Chapter 1.

the arbitration clause on the basis of the ECHR.[81] In order to allow the case to proceed, the CAS had to determine whether the clause was compatible with the ECHR. The main argument advanced by the claimant was that the unequal bargaining power between the parties to the arbitration (i.e. the athlete and the SGB) threatened the validity of the arbitration agreement. The panel considered that '[i]f – according to this jurisprudence of the ECtHR – the right of access to the courts enshrined in Art. 6.1 ECHR can be subject to a weighing up in the event that arbitral jurisdiction is prescribed by statute, then the same must apply also in a case of unequal bargaining power'.[82] Therefore, it concluded: 'only if there were no reasons in terms of "good administration of justice" in favour of arbitration a violation of article 6.1 ECHR could be acknowledged'.[83] As the panel, maybe unsurprisingly, identified some reasons which justified that CAS arbitration was linked to the 'good administration of justice', it decided that the arbitration agreement was valid under the ECHR.[84]

Furthermore, the CAS jurisdiction in appeal cases is dependent on the conditions enshrined in statutory arbitration clauses enshrined in the SGBs' regulations. This has led in particular to challenges, on the basis of the ECHR, against a ten-day time limit to request a decision from FIFA's dispute resolution bodies in order to lodge a CAS appeal. While the CAS panel recognized 'that the time limit of ten days is short', it concluded: 'the provision serves a legitimate purpose i.e. to cope with the heavy caseload of FIFA and contributes to the goal of an efficient administration of justice'.[85] To support this conclusion, the panel invoked the fact that 'even' the ECtHR 'has all along allowed the right of access to the

[81] CAS 2010/A/2311 and 2312, *Stichting Anti-Doping Autoriteit Nederland (NADO) and the Koninklijke Nederlandsche Schaatsenrijders Bond (KNSB)* v. *W*, awards of 22 August 2011, paras 14–18.

[82] Ibid., para. 18, referring to *Lithgow and others* v. *The United Kingdom*, app. nos. 9006/80, 9262/81, 9263/81, 9265/81, 9266/81, 9313/81, 9405/81, judgment of 8 July 1986.

[83] Ibid.

[84] Ibid., para. 19. For a more sceptical view, see J. Lukomski, 'Arbitration Clauses in Sport Governing Bodies' Statutes: Consent or Constraint? Analysis from the Perspective of Article 6(1) of the European Convention on Human Rights' (2013) 13 *The International Sports Law Journal* 60–70.

[85] CAS 2008/A/1708, *Football Federation Islamic Republic of Iran (IRIFF)* v. *Fédération Internationale de Football Association (FIFA)*, award of 4 November 2009, para. 21; CAS 2008/A/1705, *Neue Grasshopper Fussball AG Zurich* v. *Club Alianza de Lima*, award of 18 June 2009, para. 23; see also CAS 2011/A/2439, *Football Association of Thailand* v. *Fédération Internationale de Football Association (FIFA)*, award of 17 June 2011, para. 16.

courts to be limited "in the interests of the good administration of justice"'.[86] However, this does not extend automatically to any other statutory limitation to the scope of the review of the CAS.[87] Indeed, the CAS also invoked the ECHR to remind that '[r]estrictions to the fundamental right of access to justice should not be accepted easily, but only where such restrictions are justified both in the interest of good administration of justice and proportionality'.[88] In this latter case, the sole arbitrator failed 'to see why a restriction of his mandate – contrary to the clear wording of the Art. R57 of the CAS Code – would be in the interest of good administration of justice'.[89]

As one can gather from these examples, the ECHR and its interpretations by the ECtHR are used by CAS panels to justify fundamental choices regarding their scope of jurisdiction. The entanglement is complex as the ECHR is both used against an athlete, who is challenging the validity of a CAS arbitration clause, and SGBs, who are trying to reduce the scope of the CAS review of their decisions. It highlights the importance of references to the ECHR as legitimating devices to support the CAS's interpretation of its jurisdictional space.

10.3.2 *Challenging the Compatibility of the SGBs' Regulations with the ECHR*

Like EU law, the ECHR can also be used to impose a form of constitutional review upon the rules and decisions of the international SGBs. In that framework, it operates as a kind of cosmopolitan constitution that would extend beyond the state parties to private entities engaging in transnational regulation. Yet, in practice, such a use of the ECHR as a constitutional check remains relatively rare at the CAS.

10.3.2.1 The ECHR Compatibility of the WADC

One of the vexing questions of international sports law is whether the current world anti-doping regime based on the WADC is infringing on the human rights of athletes subjected to it.[90] Many commentators have

86 CAS 2011/A/2439.
87 CAS 2013/A/3274, *Mads Glasner* v. *Fédération Internationale de Natation (FINA)*, award of 31 January 2014, para. 65.
88 Ibid.
89 Ibid.
90 J. Soek, *The Strict Liability Principle and the Human Rights of the Athlete in Doping Cases* (T.M.C. Asser Press, 2006). See also C. Tamburrini, 'WADA's Anti-doping Policy and

raised this issue and it is therefore unsurprising to see the validity of the WADC being tested on the basis of the ECHR.[91] As a consequence, the World Anti-Doping Agency (WADA) has along the years requested a number of opinions from respected scholars and practitioners to certify the compatibility of the WADC with human rights, and the ECHR in particular.[92] Numerous CAS panels have religiously invoked these opinions as authoritative material supporting the compatibility of the WADC with the ECHR.[93] Jean-Paul Costa, the former president of the ECtHR, concluded in his 2013 expert opinion that the WADC is 'in harmony'

Athletes' Right to Privacy' (2013) 1 *Revista de Filosofía, Ética y Derecho del Deporte* 84–96; A. J. Schneider, 'Privacy, Confidentiality and Human Rights in Sport' (2004) 7 *Sport in Society* 438–56; M. Hard, 'Caught in the Net: Athletes' Rights and the World Anti-Doping Agency' (2010) 19 *Southern California Interdisciplinary Law Journal* 533–64.

91 The ECtHR has recently decided two cases related to anti-doping, see *Fédération Nationale des Syndicats Sportifs (FNASS) and Others* v. *France* and *Bakker* v. *Switzerland*, app. no. 7198/07, judgment of 3 September 2019.

92 G. Kaufmann-Kohler, G. Malinverni and A. Rigozzi, 'Conformity of Certain Provisions of the Draft WADC with Commonly Accepted Principles of International Law' (February 2003), www.wada-ama.org/en/resources/legal/conformity-with-international-law; G. Kaufmann-Kohler and A. Rigozzi, 'Conformity of Art. 10.6 with Fundamental Rights of Athletes' (November 2007), www.wada-ama.org/en/resources/world-anti-doping-program/conformity-with-fundamental-rights-of-athletes; J.-P. Costa, 'Legal Opinion Regarding the Draft World Anti-doping Code' (June 2013), www.wada-ama.org/en/resources/legal/legal-opinion-on-the-draft-2015-world-anti-doping-code; and J-P. Costa, 'Legal Opinion on the 2021 Code' (October 2019), www.wada-ama.org/en/resources/the-code/legal-opinion-on-the-2021-code-by-judge-jean-paul-costa.

93 The opinion by G. Kaufmann-Kohler, G. Malinverni and A. Rigozzi is cited in CAS 2004/A/690, *H.* v. *Association of Tennis Professionals (ATP)*, award of 24 March 2005, para. 54; CAS 2005/A/830, *S.* v. *FINA*, award of 15 July 2005, para. 41; CAS 2006/A/1025, *Mariano Puerta* v. *International Tennis Federation (ITF)*, award of 12 July 2006, para. 78; CAS 2009/A/2012, *Doping Authority Netherlands* v. *Mr Nick Zuijkerbuijk*, award of 11 June 2010, para. 50; CAS 2009/A/1915, *World Anti-Doping Agency (WADA)* v. *Polish Wrestling Federation (PWF), Kamil Blonski and Wojciech Zieziulewicz*, award of 12 August 2010, para. 17; CAS 2010/A/2307, *WADA* v. *Jobson Leandro Pereira de Oliveira, CBF and STJD*, award of 14 September 2011, paras 45 and 99. While the Costa opinion is referred to in CAS 2016/A/4534, *Maurico Fiol Villanueva* v. *Fédération Internationale de Natation (FINA)*, award of 16 March 2017, para. 52; CAS 2017/A/4927, *Misha Aloyan* v. *International Olympic Committee (IOC)*, award of 16 June 2017, para. 82; CAS 2017/A/5099, *Artur Taymazov* v. *International Olympic Committee (IOC)*, award of 4 December 2017, para. 82; CAS 2018/A/5546, *José Paolo Guerrero* v. *FIFA* and CAS 2018/A/5571, *WADA* v. *FIFA and José Paolo Guerrero*, awards of 30 July 2018, para. 87; CAS 2018/A/5581, *Filip Radojevic* v. *Fédération Internationale de Natation (FINA)*, award of 10 July 2018, para. 85; and CAS 2018/A/5739, *Levi Cadogan* v. *National Anti-Doping Commission of Barbados (NADCB)*, award of 20 February 2019, para. 81.

with 'the accepted principles of international law and human rights'.[94] Based on this conclusion, one Panel noted that 'the previous President of the European Court of Human Rights' had 'vouched for' the proportionality of the WADC.[95] More broadly, with regard to the fixed minimum sanctions in doping cases, a CAS panel concluded 'that legal scholars, CAS panels and the Swiss Federal Tribunal seem to concur that the current sanctioning system based on the WADA Code does not conflict with fundamental human rights'.[96] Finally, an award endorsed the compatibility with Article 8 ECHR of the long-term storage of samples (for up to eight years).[97] In all these cases, the panels did not engage in deep proportionality assessments of the compatibility of the WADC with the ECHR but merely invoked the (scholarly or professional) authority of expert opinions to reject the challenges.

10.3.2.2 The ECHR Compatibility of Other Disciplinary Rules and Decisions of the SGBs

The ECHR could naturally also find an application with regard to other types of disciplinary proceedings in the sporting context. In fact, CAS panels have recognized that SGBs must comply with the *nulla poena sine lege* principle enshrined in Article 7 ECHR.[98] In other words, 'before a person can be found guilty of a disciplinary offence, the relevant disciplinary code must proscribe the misconduct with which he is charged'.[99] However, challenges on the basis of Article 6(2) ECHR to the widespread use of strict liability in sports regulations have not been successful.[100] More specifically, clubs and athletes argued that strict liability runs contrary to the presumption of innocence guaranteed in Article 6(2)

94 CAS 2017/A/4927, para. 82 and CAS 2017/A/5099, para. 82.
95 CAS 2018/A/5546 and 5571, para. 87 and CAS 2018/A/5739, para. 81.
96 CAS 2015/A/4184, *Jobson Leandro Pereira de Oliveira* v. *Fédération Internationale de Football Association (FIFA)*, award of 25 April 2016 (operative part of 24 March 2016), para. 188. Or that 'CAS case law and various legal opinions confirm that the WADC mechanisms are not contrary to human rights legislation' in CAS 2009/A/2012, para. 47.
97 TAS 2009/A/1879, para. 81.
98 CAS 2014/A/3516, *George Yerolimpos* v. *World Karate Federation*, award of 6 October 2014, para. 104 and CAS 2016/A/4921 and 4922, *Maria Dzhumadzuk, Irina Shulga and Equestrian Federation of Ukraine* v. *Federation Equestre Internationale (FEI)*, award of 30 May 2017, para. 62.
99 CAS 2014/A/3516, para. 104.
100 Strict liability foresees that a disciplinary violation, such as a violation of anti-doping rules, can be constituted even without fault of the accused. See CAS 2013/A/3139 above and CAS 2014/A/3628, *Eskişehirspor Kulübü* v. *Union of European Football Association (UEFA)*, award of 2 September 2014 (operative part of 7 July 2014).

ECHR. One award referred to ECtHR case law to support the claim that the recourse to strict liability is not per se contrary to the ECHR.[101] In another more recent case, the panel rejected Article 6(2)'s applicability to the disciplinary sanctions of SGBs 'as Article 6(2) is only applicable to criminal proceedings and the present proceedings are not of a criminal nature'.[102] Furthermore, the CAS also touched upon whether disciplinary proceedings run counter to the privilege against self-incrimination recognized by the ECtHR,[103] rejected on the basis of the ECHR the retroactive application of a longer statute of limitation to a case that was already time-barred at the time of the entry into force of the new provision[104] and invoked the *lex mitior* principle and its interpretation by the ECtHR.[105] In short, while disciplinary sanctions have a direct and profound effect on those subjected to them, the CAS has been quite reluctant to engage in a constitutional review of the SGBs' decisions on the basis of the ECHR.

10.3.3 The CAS and the Procedural Guarantees of Article 6(1) ECHR

The procedural rights guaranteed by Article 6(1) ECHR, and in particular their interpretation by the ECtHR, are more present in CAS awards. The ECtHR's case law plays a fundamental role in defining the intensity of procedural review exercised by the CAS with regard to the decisions of the SGBs, as well as in justifying the key procedural constraints applicable to the CAS itself.

10.3.3.1 The ECHR and Due Process Inside the SGBs

The internal disciplinary bodies of the international SGBs are taking most of the disciplinary decisions affecting international sports. *In fine*,

[101] See CAS 2009/A/1768, *Hansen* v. *Fédération Equestre Internationale (FEI)*, award of 4 December 2009, para. 21 referring to *Salabiaku* v. *France*, app. no. 10519/83, judgment of 7 October 1988, paras 28–9.

[102] CAS 2013/A/3139, para. 91.

[103] CAS 2018/A/5769, *Worawi Makudi* v. *Fédération Internationale de Football Association (FIFA)*, award of 11 February 2019, paras 135–6.

[104] CAS 2015/A/4304, para. 48. Referencing decision dated *Oleksandr Volkov* v. *Ukraine*, app. no. 21722/11, judgment of 9 January 2013, marg. no. 137.

[105] The reference to the ECtHR decision *Scoppola* v. *Italy*, app. no. 10249/03, judgment of 17 September 2009 is found in CAS 2012/A/2817, *Fenerbahçe Spor Kulübü* v. *Fédération Internationale de Football Association (FIFA) and Roberto Carlos Da Silva Rocha*, award of 21 June 2013, para. 122 and CAS 2010/A/2083, *UCI* v. *Jan Ullrich and Swiss Olympic*, award of 9 February 2012, para. 63.

only a small share of these decisions is subsequently appealed at the CAS. Yet, the CAS has consistently refused to assess the compatibility of these first instance proceedings with Article 6(1) ECHR, relying instead on the curative quality of an appeal before the CAS.

Sometimes awards simply exclude the applicability of the ECHR to internal proceedings of the SGBs, such as when a panel noted that it 'does not see any reason in the present case to depart from the line established in earlier jurisprudence, namely that the ECHR is not applicable to disciplinary proceedings before a Sport association's jurisdictional bodies'.[106] In other words, 'procedural fundamental rights protect citizens against violations of such rights by the State and its organs and are therefore only applicable to a jurisdiction established by a State and not to legal relationships between private entities such as associations and their members'.[107] The panel would only consider otherwise if the SGB had 'inserted into its Constitutional Rules and Regulations procedural rights based on the ECHR or if it had referred to the ECHR as applicable to disciplinary proceedings before its jurisdictional bodies'.[108]

Many panels, however, do not share this view. Contrariwise, another panel recognized that 'there are more and more authorities in legal literature advocating that the ECHR also applies directly to sports associations'.[109] Yet, CAS panels have also long held that 'if the hearing in a given case was insufficient in the first instance [. . .] the fact is that, as long as there is a possibility of full appeal to the Court of Arbitration for Sport, the deficiency may be cured'.[110] This curative ability has been supported with references to the case law of the ECtHR.[111] Awards claim

[106] CAS 2009/A/1957, para. 14. In particular, the award referenced previous decisions such as CAS 2000/A/290 above and CAS 2005/A/895, *Al-Hilal Al-Saudi Club* v. *Fédération Internationale de Football Association (FIFA)*, order of 12 December 2008.

[107] Ibid., para. 15.

[108] Ibid., para. 20.

[109] CAS 2008/A/1513, para. 9.

[110] CAS 94/129, *USA Shooting and Q.* v. *Union Internationale de Tir (UIT)*, award of 23 May 1995 para. 59. For similar conclusions, see CAS 2009/A/1957, para. 21; CAS 2009/A/1985, *Franchon Crews* v. *International Boxing Association (AIBA)*, award of 10 June 2010; para. 24. For a hint of a different direction, see CAS 2015/A/4095, *Bernardo Rezende and Mario da Silva Pedreira Junior* v. *Fédération International de Volleyball (FIVB)*, award of 6 October 2015, paras 74–7.

[111] The *Wickramsinghe* v. *The United Kingdom*, app. no. 31503/96, decision of 9 December 1997 is referenced in CAS 2007/A/1396 and 1402, *World Anti-Doping Agency (WADA) and Union Cycliste Internationale (UCI)* v. *Alejandro Valverde and Real Federación Española de Ciclismo (RFEC)*, award of 31 May 2010, para. 43; CAS 2009/A/1920, *FK Pobeda, Aleksandar Zabrcanec, Nikolce Zdraveski* v. *UEFA*, award of 15 April 2010,

that this jurisprudence is 'in line'[112] with the *Bryan* v. *The United Kingdom* ruling of the ECtHR and the *Wickramsinghe* decision of the European Commission of Human Rights. The latter held, citing the former, that 'even where an adjudicatory body determining disputes over civil rights and obligations does not comply with Article 6(1) [ECHR] in some respect, no violation of the Convention will be found if the proceedings before that body are subject to subsequent control by a judicial body that has full jurisdiction and does provide the guarantees of Article 6 (1)'.[113]

This position of the CAS has fundamental consequences for those going through the internal judicial systems of the SGBs, as it basically endorses, with the (alleged) blessing of the ECtHR, any type of procedural wrongs at the level of the internal adjudicative bodies of the SGBs.

10.3.3.2 The ECHR and Evidence at the CAS

The CAS has also leveraged references to the ECtHR case law to justify allowing certain types of evidence in CAS proceedings. First, the CAS has had to decide whether recourse to anonymous witnesses infringes the right to be heard under Article 6(1) ECHR.[114] In particular, the CAS referred to the jurisprudence of the SFT drawing on the case law of the ECtHR which allowed the recourse to anonymous witnesses if necessary for the personal safety of the witness.[115] Nevertheless, the Panel also relied on the ECtHR's jurisprudence to nuance this conclusion by

para. 28; CAS 2009/A/1985, para. 24; CAS 2011/A/2430, *Football Club Apollonia* v. *Albanian Football Federation (AFF) and Sulejman Hoxha*, award of 18 October 2012, para. 9.24; CAS 2013/A/3262, *Joel Melchor Sánchez Alegría* v. *Fédération Internationale de Football Association (FIFA)*, award of 30 September 2014 (operative part of 18 June 2014), para. 83; CAS 2016/A/4871, *Vladimir Sakotic* v. *FIDE World Chess Federation (FIDE)*, award of 2 August 2017, para. 120. The ECtHR's *A. Menarini Diagnostics S.r.l.* v. *Italy*, app. no. 43509/08, judgment of 27 September 2011, paras 58–9 is cited in CAS 2011/A/2362, *Mohammad Asif* v. *International Cricket Council*, award of 17 April 2013, para. 41. Finally, the *Bryan* v. *The United Kingdom*, app. no. 19178/91, judgment of 22 November 1995 is referred to in CAS 2008/A/1513, para. 9.

112 CAS 2009/A/1985, para. 24; CAS 2011/A/2430, para. 9.24; CAS 2013/A/3262, para. 83.

113 *Wickramsinghe* v. *The United Kingdom*, para. 41.

114 CAS 2009/A/1920, para. 13. See as well CAS 2011/A/2384 and 2386, paras 167–86.

115 Ibid. However, in CAS 2011/A/2384 and 2386, para. 184, the CAS refused to allow a witness to testify anonymously because the Panel considered that 'it was insufficiently demonstrated that the interests of the witness worthy of protection were threatened to an extent that could justify a complete protection of the witness' identity from disclosure to the Respondents'.

highlighting that the right to be heard must be guaranteed by other means such as 'by cross examination through "audiovisual protection" and by an in-depth check of the identity and the reputation of the anonymous witness by the court'.[116]

Second, the CAS has had to decide whether the use of illegally obtained evidence in disciplinary proceedings is contrary to the ECHR.[117] For example, a panel refused to draw an analogy between the *Texeira de Castro* decision of the ECtHR, which found that Portugal contravened the ECHR in a case in which the police had gathered evidence through illegal means, and the reliance by FIFA on evidence gathered illegally by an English newspaper.[118] This led the arbitrators to deny the claimant the right to rely on the ECtHR's case law to challenge the admissibility of evidence obtained indirectly through unlawful wiretapping by the press. In support of this conclusion, the panel referenced the ECtHR's case law on freedom of expression insofar as it protects the intrusion of the press in a person's private life.[119] In a subsequent award, the CAS panel went further by invoking the ECtHR's finding that 'the courts shall balance the interest in protecting the right that was infringed by obtaining the evidence against the interest in establishing the truth'.[120] While another panel concluded that 'the interest underlying the fight against doping can be preponderant over the individual's interest, whether an athlete or athlete support personnel, in not having an illicitly obtained evidence admitted in an arbitral procedure concerning an alleged anti-doping rule violation'.[121] The arbitrators insisted that this balancing test is 'in line'[122] with the jurisprudence of the ECtHR.

[116] CAS 2009/A/1920.

[117] TAS 2011/A/2433. On the use of the secret recordings that led to the recent Russian anti-doping scandal, see CAS 2016/A/4480, *International Association of Athletics Federations (IAAF)* v. *All Russia Athletics Federation (ARAF) and Vladimir Kazarin*, award of 7 April 2017, paras 76–7; CAS 2016/A/4486, *International Association of Athletics Federations (IAAF)* v. *Ekaterina Poistogova*, award of 7 April 2017, paras 104–6; and CAS 2016/A/4487, *International Association of Athletics Federations (IAAF)* v. *Alexey Melnikov*, award of 7 April 2017, paras 104–6.

[118] Ibid., para. 27. Referring to *Teixeira de Castro* v. *Portugal*, app. no. 25829/94, judgment of 9 June 1998.

[119] Ibid., paras 31–2.

[120] CAS 2016/A/4480, para. 76.

[121] CAS 2016/A/4486, para. 105.

[122] Ibid., para. 106. In particular the award refers to *K.S and M.S* v. *Germany*, app. no. 33969/11, judgment of 6 October 2016.

The question of the admissibility of evidence is crucial in determining the outcome of any judicial process. Instead of relying on self-made principles, it is interesting to note that the CAS has borrowed from the ECtHR's jurisprudence to support its relatively liberal view regarding the admissibility of evidence. The latter can be traced back to the difficult position in which SGBs are placed when enforcing their regulations, as they do not enjoy the police powers (or the capacity) to conduct typical investigatory measures and are mostly reliant on indirectly (and often illegally) obtained information.

10.3.3.3 The ECHR and Due Process at the CAS

Lastly, one case has led the CAS to evaluate the compliance of its own procedures with Article 6(1) ECHR, with the panel concluding, perhaps unsurprisingly, that the CAS Code was compliant.[123] Based on a number of ECtHR decisions, the panel held that 'in compliance with the constant jurisprudence of the ECtHR' the athlete had freely consented to the jurisdiction of the CAS and that, therefore, 'the guarantees required by Article 6 para. 1 ECHR do not have to be fulfilled by the CAS'.[124] In spite of this preliminary conclusion, the CAS Panel went on to argue that, in any case, it was fully compliant with Article 6(1) ECHR.[125] In particular, the need for both parties to agree for a hearing to be held in public was deemed to 'not constitute a violation of Article 6 para. 1 of the ECHR as this provision allows, in its second sentence, restrictions with regards to the publicity of the hearing'.[126] More precisely, it held that disputes 'relating to doping controls very often give rise to numerous questions concerning, on the one hand, the private life of the parties involved and, on the other hand, sophisticated technical mechanisms and data especially developed in order to establish anti-doping rule offences', and, therefore, it found that 'publicity of the hearing would have prejudiced the interests of justice'.[127] In addition, it insisted that 'confidentiality of hearings is very common in private arbitration and no judicial precedent has to date stated that such confidentiality would violate Article 6 para.1 ECHR'.[128] Ironically, a few years later, the ECtHR itself would reach the

[123] CAS 2014/A/3561 and 3614.
[124] CAS 2014/A/3561 and 3614, para. 196.
[125] Ibid., para. 197–207.
[126] Ibid., para. 207.
[127] Ibid.
[128] Ibid.

exact opposite conclusion on both the free consent of athletes to CAS arbitration and the need for the publicity of CAS hearings in doping cases.[129] This fundamental divergence highlights the potential gap between the CAS's application of the ECHR (or Swiss law and EU law) and the ECtHR's own interpretation (or the SFT's and the CJEU's interpretation). This situation of interpretive pluralism is not dissimilar to the interaction between national courts and the CJEU or the ECtHR. Thus, this entanglement opens up a field of dialectical play between textual proximity and interpretative distance which will never be entirely bridged.

In different ways, and for different purposes, CAS arbitrators have weaved the ECHR into their judicial reasoning. Such intertwinement is never anodyne, however. It supports important substantial and procedural choices with clear distributive consequences for the parties to CAS arbitration.

10.4 Conclusion

The CAS is a special place. It is not really an arbitral tribunal, nor is it a proper international court, but it stands as a living embodiment of the 'unidentified legal objects'[130] that proliferate in transnational legal practice. It is often presented as necessary to the transnational governance (and mere existence) of international sports. Important CAS decisions, such as the recent *Semenya* award, are subjected to global attention and intense scrutiny. This chapter portrays the CAS as a judicial site where awards are being produced through a process of legal weaving that enmeshes different types of legal material. Its practice is not a solipsistic work based only on the denationalized law of an autonomous transnational community but rather an artistic mélange of styles producing a textual assemblage that is tailored to each case. In the context of the *lex*

[129] *Mutu and Pechstein* v. *Switzerland* above. See A. Duval, 'Time to Go Public? Transparency at the Court of Arbitration for Sport after the Pechstein Decision of the European Court of Human Rights', in A. Duval and A. Rigozzi (eds), *Yearbook of International Sports Arbitration 2017* (T.M.C. Asser Press, 2020), pp. 3–28.

[130] In reference to what Benoît Frydman calls 'objets juridiques non ou mal identifiés', in B. Frydman, 'Comment penser le droit global?' (2012) *Working Papers du Centre Perelman de Philosophie du Droit*, www.philodroit.be/IMG/pdf/comment_penser_le_droit_global_2011.pdf, p. 5.

sportiva, entanglement is undoubtedly the 'normal state of the law'[131] and the CAS represents a striving 'Inter-Legality Hub'.[132]

Nevertheless, it is true that not all legal texts are equally present in CAS awards. As we have seen, Swiss law is much more present than, say, French law (or any other national law for that matter). Similarly, EU law and the ECHR are regularly invoked while there are very few mentions of other sources of international law. One should not lose sight of the fact that the CAS is not an a-national construct hovering above our heads, but is embedded (like many international SGBs) in the territorial and legal context of Switzerland. Furthermore, entanglements cannot be severed from the actors.[133] Many of the professionals active before the CAS as arbitrators or lawyers are Europeans or even Swiss. Finally, the main avenue to challenge CAS awards is the SFT (and, to a much lesser extent, other European courts and administrative bodies). It is thus quite logical that when CAS panels are called to assemble an award, they draw on both what they know and what they want to assuage. Thus, the CAS works not so much as an autarkic judicial machinery reliant on its own supply of power and inputs but rather as a transnational legal assembly line importing various parts of its awards from different suppliers on a case-by-case basis. Hence, the judicial practice of the CAS can help us move beyond the billiard ball model of autonomous transnational legal orders or systems in order to perceive the hybridity of transnational legal practice.[134] At the CAS, Swiss law, EU law and the ECHR are not so much clashing with the *lex sportiva* as they are entangled within it. They become an integral part of the *lex sportiva*. This conclusion does not imply that the ECtHR or the CJEU should defer to the CAS, to the contrary. It means that they should scrutinize closely the way it speaks 'their' language, like they assess the way national courts are speaking it. In a world where nobody is in a position to impose top down a single set of global rules applied in a uniform way, transnational legal practice is bound to be the result of strange loops and contextual assemblages.

The complex beauty of these rhetorical entanglements should not hide the fact that the CAS is taking distributive decisions which are very hard (i.e. costly) to challenge. This chapter has not focused on the politics

131 Chapter 1.

132 Y. Shany, 'International Courts as Inter-legality Hubs', in J. Klabbers and G. Palombella (eds), *The Challenge of Inter-legality* (Cambridge University Press, 2019), pp. 319–38.

133 Chapter 1, Section 1.4.1.

134 See A. Duval, 'What Lex Sportiva Tells You about Transnational Law'.

lurking behind these entanglements. In other words, what are their underlying drivers or unspoken purposes? In order to answer this question, one would need to carefully investigate who does the entangling and why. There is no reason to believe that these entanglements are per se fair or just. Therefore, the ethics of those producing legal entanglements must be subjected to strict scrutiny.[135] In fact, the dark face of the ubiquity of transnational legal entanglements might be that ultimate political accountability becomes difficult to locate as decisions are enmeshed in a plurality of political and legal contexts. Who should be blamed for a particular interpretation of the FIFA RSTP? Is it the responsibility of FIFA, the European Commission, the CAS or the SFT? Where can we ask to change it and how? The risk is that entanglements lead to a form of organized irresponsibility, as if the legal assemblages of the CAS were not the result of deliberate choices but natural reflections of what a patchwork of laws say. Hence, the age of entanglements calls for a relentless critique of the politics lurking behind the textual assemblages. If legislators are found simultaneously in multiple places and levels, inside the SGBs, at the Swiss parliament or in Brussels, we need to think about how to recreate a transnational democratic space (and process) adapted to this multiplicity. Similarly, if the CAS is in a position to assemble its awards relatively freely, in light of the extremely limited control exercised by the SFT and the high costs of challenging a CAS award elsewhere, then we must seriously consider those who are doing the assembling. Who are they? How is their legitimacy and authority justified? Are they sufficiently impartial and independent from the SGBs? How are they selected? What are the mechanisms in place to prevent the rise of conflicts of interests? Once we recognize that the assembling or entangling of transnational law is the new normal, we must urgently grapple with these questions. The hybridization and pluralization of transnational legal practice might be a necessary consequence of the liquefaction of our transnational lives, but it raises fundamental problems for the way in which political agency is exercised and decision-makers are held accountable. One answer to this conundrum could be to move towards entangling our politics and accountability mechanisms, meaning that the citizenry has to exercise agency at multiple levels (e.g. through social movements, consumer boycotts or simply voting at the European Parliament elections) and to move strategically between different accountability fora (e.g. the

[135] J. Klabbers, 'Judging Inter-legality', in J. Klabbers and G. Palombella (eds), *The Challenge of Inter-legality* (Cambridge University Press, 2019), pp. 339–62.

European Commission, national competition authorities, national courts, Organisation for Economic Co-operation and Development contact points or the ECtHR).[136] In the context of the CAS and the *lex sportiva*, Claudia Pechstein has shown the way, even though it came at great personal costs,[137] by challenging her doping ban before the SFT, the German courts and the ECtHR. To initiate these critical shifts in the way we engage in politics and law, it is first essential to grasp the ubiquity of legal entanglements in the operation of transnational law. The aim of this chapter was to contribute to this *prise de conscience* by exposing how the CAS transforms transnational sporting disputes into legal gold: authoritative awards.

[136] This shift in the exercise of power is theorised by U. Beck, *Power in the Global Age* (Polity, 2005).

[137] 'Pleite zwingt Pechstein zu dramatischem Hilferuf' *Die Welt* (1 July 2015), www.welt.de/sport/article143390802/Pleite-zwingt-Pechstein-zu-dramatischem-Hilferuf.html.

11

The Struggle for International Financial Standards

An Historical Analysis of Entangling Legalities in Finance

FRANCESCO CORRADINI

11.1 Introduction

The global financial order is key to our economy but highly fragile. And the norms and institutions to stabilize it are themselves plural and fragmented – in fact, a prime example of multiple bodies of norms coexisting in global governance. This order is characterized by a multiplicity of norms and institutions with various claims to authority, reflecting different priorities and normative orientations. How have actors dealt with the tensions that this plurality generates and where has this left the multiple legalities and their relations?

To answer this question, this chapter examines the recent history of the global administration of financial stability. In the last two decades, this area of financial regulation has been shaped by responses to the perceived risks associated with multiplicity of norms and institutions. The contemporary administration of financial and monetary affairs seems to be surrounded by 'mystery'[1] and 'ambiguity about the relationship between all of the various sources of international regulatory standards'.[2] This complexity may partly depend on our limited

I am particularly grateful to Professor Nico Krisch for his generous support and comments on earlier versions of this chapter. I wish to thank the participants in the workshop 'Entangled Legalities', in May 2018, where a first draft of this text was presented, and Tomáš Morochovič for his careful editing of this text. I also gratefully acknowledge the financial support by the SNF, which made this research possible.

[1] D. Kennedy, 'The Mystery of Global Governance', in J. L. Dunoff and J. P. Trachtman (eds), *Ruling the World? Constitutionalism, International Law, and Global Governance* (Cambridge University Press, 2009), pp. 37–68.

[2] A. Riles, 'Managing Regulatory Arbitrage: A Conflict of Laws Approach' (2014) 47 *Cornell International Law Journal* 63–119, at 80–1.

understanding of the organizational structures of these relationships and the drivers behind them.

In various contexts of global financial governance, characterized by a significant degree of informality, regulatory decentralization and dynamic institutional interactions, societal actors have shaped different ordering projects in opposition to 'chaos' over time. From a macro perspective, previous studies have helpfully analysed the broad historical and political contexts in which these ordering projects have come about by placing emphasis on 'the power and interests of leading financial powers, domestic political dynamics, and the role of transnational actors'.[3] Yet we do not quite know the forms through which institutional multiplicity has been organized and with what effects for the overall order. Drawing upon the concepts of this volume, this chapter analyses different forms of entanglements in contexts of global financial regulation, focusing on some of the sites, actor constellations and dynamics behind them.[4] This chapter uses the term bodies of norms to connect the variety of recommendations, standards, best practices and codes recognized by regulators as factors of financial stability. At various decision-making settings, financial regulators, legal professionals and economic experts disagreed over the identification of the relevant sources of authority and their organizational structures. For example, the prevailing regulatory response that followed the global financial crisis of 2008 was a call for a more or less centralized institutional framework for 'a global banking and financial system'. Some lawyers imagined a new field of international financial law or *lex financiera*.[5] Many argued that the International Monetary Fund (IMF) should have institutional primacy, while others regarded the Financial Stability Board (FSB) as the appropriate locus of authority, and yet others suggested that the function of a new World Financial Authority should be allocated. However, opposing views defended a more modest reform through a pluralist approach to ordering.[6] This chapter questions ambitious attempts at structuring

[3] E. Helleiner, 'Regulating the Regulators: The Emergence and Limits of the Transnational Financial Legal Order', in T. C. Halliday and G. Shaffer (eds), *Transnational Legal Orders* (Cambridge University Press, 2015), pp. 231–57, p. 235.

[4] See Chapter 1. Throughout the text, I use 'entanglement' and 'enmeshment' interchangeably.

[5] See, for example, R. M. Lastra, 'Do We Need a World Financial Organization?' (2014) 17 *Journal of International Economic Law* 787–805.

[6] C. Brummer, *Minilateralism: How Trade Alliances, Soft Law, and Financial Engineering Are Redefining Economic Statecraft* (Cambridge University Press, 2014).

and controlling multiplicity through one 'common frame of reference'[7] such as legalization in finance. I contrast this dominant view with the perspective of 'entangled legality'[8] as an alternative way of thinking about relations between multiple kinds of laws populating global finance. From this perspective, the project of legalization is only one among a variety of ways of ordering multiplicity, which may equally contribute to dynamics of enmeshment. While these relations are embedded in a mosaic of interactions between multiple orders, elements of this wider environment form the background of the analysis.

The analysis proceeds as follows. Following this introduction, Section 11.2 describes international financial standards as interrelated bodies of norms and foregrounds how they became entangled in regulatory settings over time. Drawing on public documents from the Bank for International Settlements (BIS), the United Nations (UN) and the IMF, I examine the forms in which these bodies of norms were brought into relation by different actors. In the wake of the Asian financial crisis of 1997, officials at the IMF, UN and BIS made claims ordering institutional fragmentation. In this context, the Financial Stability Forum (FSF) emerged as a 'site of entanglement' and the drafters and users of its Compendium of Standards came to play a central role in organizing relations between norms that were identified as 'international standards'. Against this historical backdrop, Section 11.3 identifies different interface norms and examines how they were used by actors in norm-making and norm-implementation settings. Within the debate on the reform of the international financial architecture, regulatory harmonization and overarching institutions have been dominant responses to the perceived risks of institutional multiplicity. Yet, while there seems to be no consensus over the content of these overarching institutions, competing forms of ordering persist.

11.2 Contexts of Entanglement in Global Financial Governance over Time

From the perspective of international legal theory, the actors and structures characterizing global financial regulation differ from those encountered in traditional fields of international law. Three striking features of

[7] N. Krisch, 'Pluralism', in J. d'Aspremont and S. Singh (eds), *Concepts for International Law* (Edward Elgar, 2019), pp. 691–707.

[8] See Chapter 1.

this area of global governance are the informality, multiplicity and dynamic interactions of its norms, institutions and sites of decision-making.[9] In many of these settings, state officials, international organizations, financial institutions and other private actors have recognized norms that often take the form of best practices and standards rather than more established categories of international law.[10] Equally striking, these norms have often made their appearance in groups, resembling a relatively loose assemblage of 'clusters' of norms. In this respect, the term bodies of norms seems apt to underline their interrelatedness.[11] Institutional players in global financial regulation have often highlighted this particular feature of international standards by placing emphasis on their interconnectedness and interdependence as commonsensical, just the 'normal' thing to do,[12] and in doing so they have not found it problematic to blur their boundaries, for example by referring to their own previous work or work done by others.

An early manifestation of the discursive formation of these associations could be observed circa 1995 at the 'Tripartite Group of Banks, Securities and Insurance Regulators'. An informal working group created by the Basel Committee on Banking Supervision, the Tripartite Group facilitated the encounter of national bank, securities and insurance regulators[13] to exchange information and perform 'intensive cooperation' to address regulatory problems related to 'financial conglomerates'. A senior official from the US Treasury reported that states' competing interests made it challenging to agree on one single supranational institution to provide a solution to these problems.[14] It is worth mentioning what this

[9] C. Brummer, *Soft Law and the Global Financial System: Rule Making in the 21st Century* (Cambridge University Press, 2015), see in particular chapter 2. Annelise Riles has described 'global financial regulation' as a 'global system that is inherently pluralistic'. A. Riles, 'Is New Governance the Ideal Architecture for Global Financial Regulation?', in C. Goodhart, D. Gabor, J. Vestergaard and I. Ertürk (eds), *Central Banking at a Crossroads: Europe and Beyond* (Anthem Press, 2014), pp. 245–64.

[10] According to Brummer, the three forms of soft financial law are: best practices, data and information sharing agreements. Brummer, *Minilateralism*, pp. 96–8.

[11] See Chapter 1.

[12] 'The recognition of authority can flow from many sources: it can result from rational calculus, normative internalization or a mere acceptance as "normal".' N. Krisch, 'Liquid Authority in Global Governance' (2017) 9 *International Theory* 237–60, at 242.

[13] For the list of members, see Basel Committee, 'The Supervision of Financial Conglomerates: A Report by the Tripartite Group of Bank, Securities and Insurance Regulators' (July 1995), at 67–8.

[14] 'Since a single global financial regulator is not a feasible idea from our point of view due to sovereignty concerns, we had to look at the problem in terms of promoting regulatory

informal working group aimed at innovating against. Until then, challenges associated with 'financial conglomerates', in particular the 'regulatory arbitrage' problem, had been dealt with from the perspective of different 'regulatory groups'.[15] In contrast, the Tripartite Group responded to pluralism 'from a joint perspective'. The making of this 'joint perspective' in opposition to the 'different approaches adopted by supervisors' enabled national financial regulators to 'synthetize' the work that had previously been done.

This synthesis was recognized by members of the Basel Committee on Banking Supervision (BCBS), the Technical Committee of the International Organization of Securities Commission (IOSCO) and the International Association of Insurance Supervisors (IAIS) as a 'sound basis for further collaborative efforts'[16] which led to the creation, in 1996, of a 'Joint Forum on Financial Conglomerates'.[17] The Joint Forum was an informal setting where senior bank, insurance and securities supervisors from thirteen countries[18] assembled to 'exchange information' and practice 'supervisory coordination'. The Basel Committee's Minimum Standards for the Supervision of International Banking Groups and their Cross-border Establishments, IOSCO's Principles for Memoranda of Understanding and IAIS 'Insurance Concordat' – Principles Applicable to the Supervision of International Insurers and Insurance Groups and their Cross-border Establishments – were jointly recognized by members of the Joint Forum as 'a common set of principles' to practice exchange of information among supervisors.[19]

cooperation and information exchange among regulators'. W. Murden, 'Banking Supervision and Government Policy: The Role of Regulators in International Financial Reform' (1999) 4 *Fordham Journal of Corporate & Financial Law* 35–40.

15 These actors were 'the Basle Committee on Banking Supervision, the Working Group of the Conference of Insurance Supervisors of the European Economic Community, the Technical Committee of the International Organization of Securities Commissions (IOSCO), the Banking Advisory Committee of the Commission of the European Communities and the Insurance Committee of the Commission of the European Communities'. Basel Committee, 'The Supervision of Financial Conglomerates', 11.

16 Ibid., ii.

17 Basel Committee, 'Supervision of Financial Conglomerates: Papers Prepared by the Joint Forum on Financial Conglomerates' (February 1998).

18 In 1998, these countries were: Australia, Belgium, Canada, France, Germany, Italy, Japan, the Netherlands, Spain, Sweden, Switzerland, the United Kingdom and the United States. The EU Commission participated as an observer. See also Brummer, *Soft Law and the Global Financial System*, p. 82.

19 Consultation documents released by the Basle Committee on Banking Supervision, see Basel Committee, 'Supervision of Financial Conglomerates'.

Another informal site of interaction between ministers of finance, central bankers from 'industrial countries'[20] and 'emerging markets'[21] and representatives from international institutions and international standards organizations[22] was the Working Party on Financial Stability in Emerging Market Economies. In 1997, under the chairmanship of Mario Draghi, the Working Party issued a report on the banking sector in emerging markets, referring to 'a corpus of sound principles and practices'[23] by which they brought norms produced by 'international groupings' into relation.[24]

11.2.1 Ordering Bodies of Norms after Financial Crises

The anecdotal evidence just presented suggests that informal settings of interaction between institutional players have also been 'sites of entanglement' where bodies of norms have been pieced together through social 'practices of recognition and deference'.[25] This section takes a closer look at similar statements pronounced by situated actors at three different regulatory sites: the IMF, the UN and the BIS, to examine whether and how, in the aftermath of financial crises, dynamics of entanglement played out there.[26] Financial crises have often been moments of change

[20] France, Germany, Japan, the Netherlands, Sweden, the United Kingdom and the United States.

[21] Argentina, Hong Kong, Singapore, Indonesia, Korea, Mexico, Poland, Singapore, Thailand.

[22] These actors were Representatives of the Basel Committee on Banking Supervision, the International Accounting Standards Committee (IASC) and the International Organization of Securities Commissions (IOSCO) and staff members of the Bank for International Settlements (BIS), the European Commission, the International Monetary Fund (IMF), the Organization for Economic Co-operation and Development (OECD) and the International Bank for Reconstruction and Development (World Bank).

[23] Working Party on Financial Stability in Emerging Market Economies, 'Report on Financial Stability in Emerging Market Economies, a Strategy for the Formulation, Adoption and Implementation of Sound Principles and Practices to Strengthen Financial Systems' (April 1997). The members of the Working Party are listed on pp. 101–2 of the report.

[24] These actors were: the IASC, IOSCO, the Basel Committee on Banking Supervision of the Group of Ten (G10) central banks, the Committee on Payment and Settlement Systems of the G10 central banks, International Association of Insurance Supervisors.

[25] Krisch, 'Liquid Authority in Global Governance', 249.

[26] We might expect to observe different or similar forms of ordering plurality in other settings, too. See Chapter 1.

in the historical development of the global financial order.[27] They have also been key historical contexts in which regulatory actors formulated reform efforts to reorder institutional multiplicity. For example, in response to the Asian financial crisis of 1997, IMF jurists and economists placed emphasis on 'international standards and codes' against the different domestic laws that some IMF officials saw as problematic for financial stability.[28] However, the definition of these bodies of norms and the articulation of their relations were neither uncontroversial nor necessary decisions but occurred in multiple and incremental steps.

In 1997, Morris Goldstein,[29] an IMF economist, published a book entitled *The Case for an International Banking Standard*[30] which strengthened the project of international harmonization in the banking area. Goldstein argued for the creation of a new international banking standard (IBS) through the combination of existing norms and practices. The envisaged standard had to be shaped through 'vigorous cross-agency cooperation' rather than by one single decision-maker, and be comprehensive and broad in scope and design. The Basel Committee 'should not be the only group working on an IBS'[31] – instead, the new norm should draw not only on the expertise and norms of good banking supervision by the Basel Committee but also on those of international accounting and transparency, traditionally considered to fall under the jurisdiction of the International Accounting Standards Committee (IASC) and IMF respectively.[32] Goldstein's approach straddled boundaries between standards traditionally considered to be confined to well-defined domains. The IBS would only aim at 'partial' as opposed to 'full' international harmonization of banking standards, leaving 'room for states to maintain their

[27] Helleiner, 'Regulating the Regulators'. See also C. Brummer and M. Smallcomb, 'Institutional Design: The International Architecture', in N. Moloney, E. Ferran and J. Payne (eds), *The Oxford Handbook of Financial Regulation* (Oxford University Press, 2015).

[28] On the historical background of the trajectory towards international standards, see R. P Delonis, 'International Financial Standards and Codes: Mandatory Regulation without Representation' (2004) 36 *New York University Journal of International Law and Politics* 563–604.

[29] Deputy Director of the IMF Research Department (1987–94).

[30] M. Goldstein, *The Case for an International Banking Standard* (Peterson Institute for International Economics, 1997).

[31] Ibid., at 53.

[32] Ibid., at 35.

national preferences towards risk, as well as to maintain some of their institutional diversity'.[33]

Actors associated with the Bretton Woods institutions began referring to 'internationally accepted best practices' and 'international standards' to bring together select bodies of norms that they recognized as central features of the new international financial architecture.[34] IMF officials referred to 'international financial standards' to link multiple bodies of norms deemed relevant to 'the soundness of the financial system'.[35]

An international consensus on how standards relate to each other and with domestic legal orders was shaped through various tools, including monitoring practices performed by international financial institutions. Through these practices, IMF and World Bank officials connected norms produced by the IMF itself, the World Bank or other international standard-setting organizations and associated them with domestic legal orders in developed and developing economies.[36] In particular, the

[33] Ibid.

[34] Michel Camdessus, former managing director of the IMF, referred to 'internationally accepted best practices' to bind together the Basel Adequacy standards, internationally accepted accounting standards and disclosure rules. M. Camdessus, 'The Role of the IMF: Past, Present, and Future – Speech' (13 February 1998). He further stated: 'the Fund has been working to help disseminate a set of "best practices" in the banking area – as developed by the Basle Committee – so that standards and practices that have worked well in some countries can be adapted and applied in others. These efforts will now be stepped up.' See address by M. Camdessus to the Parliamentary Assembly of the Council of Europe, 'From the Asian Crisis toward a New Global Architecture' (23 June 1998). Stanley Fisher, first deputy managing director of the IMF (1994–2001) expressed similar ideas: 'As we help countries strengthen their financial systems, we need guideposts to judge what has been achieved and what remains to be done. This requires international standards against which to assess the soundness and stability of financial systems. There are many players in the international community with a keen interest in such standards, and their development requires the active participation of both private and official bodies, domestic and international [. . .] But there has been a growing recognition of the links between their work and the consequent need for collaboration [. . .] the main contribution of the Fund is in encouraging the implementation of standards that have been determined by others and then using them in our work on the assessment of financial systems [. . .] Standards cannot be written in stone. They are bound to evolve in the light of experience.' S. Fischer, 'The IMF and the Financial Sector – Introductory Remarks' (5 June 2000).

[35] These bodies of norms were on: data dissemination, fiscal transparency, monetary and fiscal policies, banking supervision, securities market regulation, insurance regulation, accounting, auditing, bankruptcy and corporate governance. See IMF Policy Development and Review Department, 'Progress Report Developing International Standards' (1999).

[36] T. Halliday, 'Legal Yardsticks: International Financial Institutions as Diagnosticians and Designers of the Law of Nations', in K. Davis, A. Fisher, B. Kingsbury and S. E. Merry

creation of the Financial Sector Assessment Program (FSAP) authorized IMF officials to link standards that they recognized as relevant for a safe international financial system and bring them into relation with domestic legal orders.[37] One important outcome of monitoring practices performed in the context of FSAP is the production of a report on 'Financial System Stability Assessment'. This report is subsequently taken into account when the IMF conducts 'bilateral surveillance' and performs 'consultations' with domestic authorities being assessed, under Article IV of the IMF Articles of Agreement.[38] Through these monitoring practices, IMF officials have deferred to the authority of twelve international standards setters[39] they consider to be 'relevant' in the context of their work.[40] The report resulting from these monitoring practices verifies and strengthens the recognition of standards but their recommendations also provide 'feedback' to the standard-setting organizations that produce standards.[41]

Previous historical analyses of international financial institutions have argued that the IMF's monitoring practices have normative power and

(eds), *Governance by Indicators: Global Power through Quantification and Rankings* (Oxford University Press, 2012), pp. 180–216, at pp. 200–2; A. Feibelman, 'Law in the Global Order: The IMF and Financial Regulation' (2017) 49 *New York University Journal of International Law and Politics* 687–746.

37 FSAPs Reports consist of three 'Volumes'. Volume III is titled 'Assessment of Observance of International Standards and Codes'. On the operation of FSAP and Reports on the Observance of Standards and Codes, see the perspective of François Gianviti, former General Counsel of the IMF, in F. Gianviti, 'Legal Aspects of the Financial Sector Assessment Program' (2005) 3 *Current Developments in Monetary and Financial Law* 219.

38 Gianviti, 'Legal Aspects of the Financial Sector Assessment Program'.

39 'The IMF has recognized 12 areas and associated standards as useful for the operational work of the Fund and the World Bank. These comprise accounting; auditing; anti-money laundering and countering the financing of terrorism (AML/CFT); banking supervision; corporate governance; data dissemination; fiscal transparency; insolvency and creditor rights; insurance supervision; monetary and financial policy transparency; payments systems; and securities regulation; AML/CFT was added in November 2002.' See www.imf.org/external/NP/rosc/rosc.aspx.

40 'An FSAP assessment will look at the financial sector's legislative underpinnings to evaluate regulatory capacity and practice. This will include a systematic assessment of compliance with the Basel Core Principles for Effective Banking Supervision, transparency practices in monetary and financial policies, and – if relevant – standards for securities markets, insurance, and payment systems. Other legal and institutional issues that bear on the financial sector may also be reviewed.' P. Hilbers, 'The IMF/World Bank Financial Sector Assessment Program', *IMF*, February 2001.

41 IMF and World Bank, 'Financial Sector Assessment Program – Review, Lessons, and Issues Going Forward' (24 February 2005).

'hegemonic' features. In particular, IMF conditionality has discursively reinforced colonial relations of domination reinscribing the North–South divide.[42] Indeed, 'globalization [...] requires the replacement of numerous national laws and jurisdictions by uniform global standards in order to remove the barriers to capital accumulation at the global level'.[43] From these perspectives, conditionality operates as a 'path to entanglement' based on coercion,[44] which is often made invisible by taking the form of 'incentives'. For example, according to the IMF, it is 'in countries' own interest to adopt and implement internationally recognized standards and codes'.[45] For borrowing countries, highlighting linkages with international standards becomes crucial to persuade institutional creditors of their creditworthiness. These linkages appeared for example in the 'letters of intent' of Korea, Indonesia and Thailand as they requested institutional creditors' support to recover from an economic crisis.[46] Similarly, the government of Turkey deferred to the authority of international standards[47] and officials from Colombia gave weight to international standards on auditing, the Basel core principles and codes of conduct on money laundering and terrorism financing.[48] From the perspective of states seeking financial support there have been incentives and constraints to tie their domestic legal orders to international financial standards, although the latter are formally non-binding.[49] In this context, entanglement was driven by both states' rational interests and the

[42] S. Pahuja, 'Technologies of Empire: IMF Conditionality and the Reinscription of the North/South Divide' (2000) 13 *Leiden Journal of International Law* 749–813.

[43] B. S. Chimni, 'Marxism and International Law: A Contemporary Analysis' (1999) 34 *Economic and Political Weekly* 337–49; B. S. Chimni, 'International Institutions Today: An Imperial Global State in the Making' (2004) 15 *European Journal of International Law* 1–37.

[44] Brummer and Smallcomb, 'Institutional Design'.

[45] See www.imf.org/en/About/Factsheets/Sheets/2016/08/01/16/25/Standards-and-Codes.

[46] Camdessus, 'The Role of the IMF'.

[47] Letter of Intent of the government of Turkey (2001), www.imf.org/external/np/loi/2001/tur/02/.

[48] Letter of Intent, Memorandum of Economic and Financial Policies, and Technical Memorandum of Understanding of Colombia (2002), www.imf.org/external/np/loi/2002/col/01/index.htm.

[49] On the idea of conditioning the disbursement of funds to the adherence to such standards, see B. J. Eichengreen, *Toward a New International Financial Architecture: A Practical Post-Asia Agenda* (Peterson Institute for International Economics, 1999). Giovanoli has called these determinants 'official incentives' (FSAP) and 'unofficial incentives' (market expectations). See M. Giovanoli, 'The Reform of the International Financial Architecture after the Global Crisis' (2009) 42 *New York University Journal of International Law and Politics* 81–123, at 118–19.

realization of their position in a relation of economic dependency, close to a material condition of coercion.[50] In the UN context, officials represented the 'international financial architecture' as a 'system'. For example, a UN Task-Force led by José Antonio Ocampo[51] argued that 'the international financial system is an organic whole and requires a comprehensive approach'.[52] From this systemic perspective, the UN Task-Force articulated a vision of the international financial architecture in close connection with human rights laws and UN institutions. UN officials did not invoke the UN Charter but relied instead on the provisions of the Covenant on Economic, Social and Cultural Rights to create normative expectations for all the subsystems constituting the international financial architecture.

At the BIS, 'international standards' were also invoked against institutional pluralism.[53] Here, Hans Tietmeyer[54] criticized the 'fragmented supervisory structures' characterizing the status quo and suggested improve 'international cooperation and coordination' by 'bringing together the major international institutions and key national authorities involved in financial sector stability' and to include 'emerging market economies'.[55] Arguing that the model of the Joint Forum[56] had to be applied 'in a comprehensive manner', Tietmeyer referred to 'accepted best practices' to bind the 'Core Principles issued by both the BCBS and IOSCO, and those being developed by other international groupings' together.[57] Based on Tietmeyer's report, the Group of Seven (G7) created the Financial Stability Forum.[58] The new organization enabled the encounter of a large number of actors, mainly 'public' but also 'private'

50 On these different paths to entanglement, see Chapter 1.

51 Report of the Task-Force of the Executive Committee on Economic and Social Affairs of the United Nations, 'Towards a New International Financial Architecture' (21 January 1999), 14–15.

52 Ibid., 7.

53 Institutional pluralism seems the only form of pluralism considered by participants in international financial regulation reform. This form of pluralism is different from 'systemic pluralism'. On this conceptual distinction, see Krisch, 'Pluralism', pp. 695–8.

54 Economist and former president of the Deutsche Bundesbank (1993–9).

55 H. Tietmeyer, 'Report on International Cooperation and Coordination in the Area of Financial Market Supervision and Surveillance' (11 February 1999).

56 On the Joint Forum, see Section 11.2.

57 Tietmeyer, 'Report on international cooperation and coordination'.

58 On the creation of the Financial Stability Forum, see Brummer, *Soft Law and the Global Financial System*, p. 74. See also Helleiner, 'Regulating the Regulators'.

ones.[59] Andrew Crockett[60] was appointed as first chairman for a three-year term.[61] A member of the Board of Trustees of the International Accounting Standards Board (2000–3), an organization with the mission to create a global financial reporting standard,[62] Crockett was in favour of global approaches to ordering multiplicity[63] and regarded international financial standards as 'interrelated'.[64]

11.2.1.1 Competing Ordering Projects

At their second meeting, FSF members introduced a 'Compendium of Standards', describing it as 'a common reference for the various economic and financial guidelines, principles, and codes of good practices that are internationally accepted as relevant to sound, stable and well-functioning financial systems'.[65]

[59] These actors were: 'the finance minister, central bank governor, and a supervisory authority from each of the G-7 countries, as well as representatives from the IMF, World Bank, Bank for International Settlements ("BIS"), Organization for Economic Cooperation and Development ("OECD"), Basel Committee on Banking Supervision ("BCBS"), International Accounting Standards Board ("IASB"), International Association of Insurance Supervisors ("IAIS"), International Organization of Securities Commissions ("IOSCO"), Committee on Payment and Settlements Systems ("CPSS"), and Committee on the Global Financial System ("CGFS"). After its creation, the FSF added the European Central Bank, and additional national members Australia, Hong Kong, the Netherlands, and Switzerland.' E. Carrasco, 'The Global Financial Crisis and the Financial Stability Forum: The Awakening and Transformation of an International Body Global Financial and Economic Crisis Symposium' (2010) 19 *Transnational Law & Contemporary Problems* 203–20, at 206.

[60] Andrew Crockett worked at the IMF (1972–89), was executive director of the Bank of England (1989–93) and worked as general manager of the BIS (1994–2003).

[61] Communiqué of G7 Finance Ministers and Central Bank Governors, 20 February 1999, Petersberg, Bonn. On the role of Tietmeyer and the BIS in the creation of the FSF, see C. Brummer, 'A Theory of Everything: A Historically Grounded Understanding of Soft Law and the BIS', in C. Borio, S. Claessens, P. Clement, R. McCauley and H. Shin (eds), *Promoting Global Monetary and Financial Stability: The Bank for International Settlements after Bretton Woods, 1973–2020* (Cambridge University Press, 2020), pp. 112–33.

[62] K. Camfferman and S. A. Zeff, *Aiming for Global Accounting Standards: The International Accounting Standards Board, 2001–2011* (Oxford University Press, 2015).

[63] '[A] set of global financial reporting standards that is accepted and, equally importantly, widely and effectively implemented is a critical missing pillar in the emerging international financial architecture.' A. Crockett, 'Towards Global Financial Reporting Standards: A Critical Pillar in the International Financial Architecture' (BIS, 2002).

[64] A. Crockett, 'International Financial Arrangements: Architecture and Plumbing' (BIS, 15 November 1999).

[65] 'The *Compendium* is a joint product of the various standard-setting bodies represented on the Forum. It will be reviewed and updated on an ongoing basis and is envisaged to cover a range of areas relevant to sound and stable financial systems: (a) transparency of

Yet the FSF's response to institutional pluralism was not uncontroversial. Born in the midst of controversies over a new 'international financial architecture',[66] the Compendium triggered opposing reactions. Some interpreted it as 'a single global rule book' providing 'reference rules' for the operation of financial markets.[67] BIS officials supported the 'pragmatic multitherapy' approach to ordering provided by the Compendium in contrast to an institutional framework.[68] However, some lawyers sought to embed its prescriptions within an institutional structure, in particular within the jurisdiction of the rule of law.[69] For example, Mario Giovanoli[70] invoked the rule of 'international law' as the frame of reference to govern institutional multiplicity.[71] The legalization project was similar to the idea of 'international regulation' under a new 'World Financial Authority' advocated by economists Barry Eichengreen, Lance Taylor and John Eatwell.[72] Two institutional innovations provoked by the 2008 financial crisis had implications for reorganizing multiplicity. The Group of Twenty (G20) replaced the G7 as a central forum of economic diplomacy and transformed the FSF in the Financial Stability Board, enabling participation of state representatives from the

fiscal, monetary, and financial policies; (b) dissemination of economic and financial data; (c) regulation and supervision of banking, securities, and insurance; (d) disclosure, transparency, and risk management practices of financial institutions; (e) corporate governance, accounting, auditing, and bankruptcy; and (f) payment and settlement systems.' Background brief made available to the press at the second meeting of the Financial Stability Forum, 15 September 1999.

66 J. Eatwell and L. Taylor, *Global Finance at Risk: The Case for International Regulation* (Polity Press, 2000); Eichengreen, *Toward a New International Financial Architecture*; M. Giovanoli (ed.), *International Monetary Law: Issues for the New Millennium* (Oxford University Press, 2000).

67 G. Walker, 'A New International Architecture and the Financial Stability Forum', in R. M. Lastra (ed.), *The Reform of the International Financial Architecture* (Kluwer Law International, 2000).

68 A. Icard, 'Strengthening Financial Stability: Institutional Approach or Pragmatic Multitherapy?' (BIS, 1999).

69 On law as a variant of jurisdiction, see S. Pahuja, 'Laws of Encounter: A Jurisdictional Account of International Law' (2013) 1 *London Review of International Law* 63–98.

70 General Counsel of the BIS from 1989 to 2005.

71 '[I]t is therefore important to examine all the possibilities which might strengthen international financial standards by granting them an appropriate legal status in international law.' Giovanoli, *International Monetary Law*, p. 59.

72 Eatwell's and Taylor's project was to construct 'a framework within which a coherent international policy can be worked out at implemented'. Eatwell and Taylor, *Global Finance at Risk*. For a similar perspective, see A. Kern, R. Dhumale and J. Eatwell, *Global Governance of Financial Systems: The International Regulation of Systemic Risk* (Oxford University Press, 2006), at xiii.

G20.[73] These institutional rearrangements meant that a larger group of actors was able to assemble and shape the Compendium by recognizing new standards. However, the majority of FSB members were (and still are) public regulators, and regulators from the Global North seem to have greater influence than those from other regions. Furthermore, interactions with market participants and other private actors have remained limited.[74]

While the G20 and the FSB provided a limited 'vertically integrated' structure of economic decision-making,[75] the two organizations also sidelined ambitious efforts to create overarching institutions, including through a reform of the IMF. Calls for 'international harmonization' and attempts to 'reset' the 'international financial (non-) system'[76] became the dominant responses to institutional heterogeneity.[77] The project to bring multiplicity within the jurisdiction of international law and international lawyers has been one manifestation of this trajectory towards legalization.[78] Finding a contradiction between a 'global' financial system and the lack of a coherent institutional framework, many lawyers called for a global 'ruler' in international finance. In keeping with a professional sensibility shared by many jurists, the legalization project has sought to conceptualize 'international financial law' as the frame of reference to contain the panoply of norms and practices in finance. From the standpoint of the legalization project, sometimes this heterogeneity is framed

[73] On the transformation of the FSF into the FSB, see E. Carrasco, 'The Global Financial Crisis and the Financial Stability Forum'; S. Gadinis, 'The Financial Stability Board: The New Politics of International Financial Regulation' (2013) 48 *Texas International Law Journal* 158–75.

[74] As Annelise Riles has observed: 'the FSB process has mainly engaged representatives of governments and international bureaucracies, with private parties participating only through more attenuated opportunities for public comment'. Riles, 'Is New Governance the Ideal Architecture for Global Financial Regulation?', 257.

[75] Brummer, 'A Theory of Everything'.

[76] J. A. Ocampo, *Resetting the International Monetary (Non)System: A Study Prepared by the United Nations University World Institute for Development Economics Research* (UNU-WIDER, 2017).

[77] For an analysis and critique of approaches to harmonization, see Riles, 'Managing Regulatory Arbitrage', 77–87.

[78] T. Cottier et al., *The Rule of Law in Monetary Affairs: World Trade Forum* (Cambridge University Press, 2014); for a critique of this tendency in international economic interactions, see A. Lang, 'Rule of Law in International Economic Relations', in T. Cottier and K. N. Schefer (eds), *Elgar Encyclopedia of International Economic Law* (Edward Elgar, 2017).

as a 'black hole'.[79] This expression refers to an absence of traditional frames of international law, and the contrast is often made with more established fields of international economic law, such as international trade and investment law.

The rationale underlying this approach is that 'international solutions are needed for international problems'.[80] Under this view, the IMF should become the institutional centre of the international monetary and financial system. Proponents of this way of thinking have regarded international trade law as a model to design a rule of law-based system in international financial and monetary interactions. The envisaged system would provide for a 'World Financial Authority' and an international dispute settlement mechanism to fill the 'black hole' in international law and finance.

Others have seen the FSB as a more suitable site and actor to promote the movement of international financial law 'from a heterarchical setting to a more centralized and coordinated pattern'.[81] When articulating their position in relation to multiple bodies of norms, FSB members have described themselves as providers of a 'framework for strengthening adherence to international standards'.[82] They have called for 'international coordination' through practices of 'international harmonization' among domestic regulators. Another approach has sought to articulate a vision of the global financial order against institutional pluralism through the notion of 'multilayered governance'. This perspective seeks to identify 'common core values shared by the international community' as guiding principles for the allocation of regulatory power among the various layers of governance.[83] Similar to the legalization project, advocates of this mode of ordering start from an intra-systemic perspective from which

[79] 'In finance, we have a "black hole" with few formal international rules and no adequate system to deal with cross-border crisis or conflicts.' Lastra, 'Do We Need a World Financial Organization?', 797.

[80] Ibid., 804.

[81] C. de Stefano, 'Reforming the Governance of International Financial Law in the Era of Post-Globalization' (2017) 20 *Journal of International Economic Law* 509–33. See also M. De Bellis, 'Relative Authority in Global and EU Financial Regulation: Linking the Legitimacy Debates', in J. Mendes and I. Venzke (eds), *Allocating Authority: Who Should Do What in European and International Law?* (Hart Publishing, 2018), pp. 241–70.

[82] See FSB, 'Promoting Global Adherence to International Cooperation and Information Exchange Standards' (2010).

[83] R. Weber, 'Multilayered Governance in International Financial Regulation and Supervision', in T. Cottier, J. H. Jackson and R. M. Lastra (eds), *International Law in Financial Regulation and Monetary Affairs* (Oxford University Press, 2012), pp. 151–70, at 158–69. For a similar perspective, see P. E. Avgouleas, *Governance of Global Financial*

they formulate a global regulatory framework to construct full coherence among the different parts of the overall system.

Yet competing visions have been sceptical of legalization as a workable way of organizing diversity in global financial governance. Critics have contended that the idea of one overarching institution – a 'global sheriff'[84] of sorts – seems out of touch with the heterogeneity and competition of national concerns and interests driving global business firms operating in modern global finance.[85] For an environment characterized by 'increasing multipolarity' and 'dispersed economic power and interests', a model of pragmatic 'minilateralism' may be a better fit than an institutional grand design.[86] The project of harmonization sought to provide a centre of gravity – a new 'architecture' – against or irrespective of the autonomous norms and practices of legal technique and self-regulation that market actors, including private organizations such as the International Swaps and Derivatives Association, use in their financial business operations on over-the-counter derivatives but that fly under the radar of overarching institutions.[87]

11.3 Responding to Multiplicity in Global Financial Governance

Against the historical and doctrinal background of some of the projects of reordering global financial regulation discussed so far, this section looks more closely at the interface norms associated with projects to respond to multiplicity in the different institutional settings examined.

11.3.1 The Project of Harmonization: Overarching Norms and Reception Norms

The historical process of associating bodies of norms after the Asian financial crisis and global financial crisis was partly defined by competing

Markets: The Law, the Economics, the Politics (Cambridge University Press, 2012), chapter 8.

84 R. M. Lastra, *International Financial and Monetary Law* (Oxford University Press, 2015).

85 Brummer argues that the idea of a single global authority is impractical because 'states are unlikely to cede power to a global financial regulator', Brummer, *Soft Law and the Global Financial System*, p. 328. See also L. Baxter, 'Understanding the Global in Global Finance and Regulation', in R. Buckley, E. Avgouleas and D. Arner (eds), *Reconceptualising Global Finance and Its Regulation* (Cambridge University Press, 2016), pp. 28–48.

86 Brummer, *Minilateralism*.

87 A. Riles, *Collateral Knowledge: Legal Reasoning in the Global Financial Markets* (University of Chicago Press, 2011).

efforts to reimagine the global financial order. Two manifestations here were the projects of 'international regulation' and 'legalization' advocated by actors associated with the IMF institutional context. Though the two projects had different nuances, they adopted an intra-systemic perspective to govern institutional relations from a central vantage point. Indeed, they both imagined a common integrating principle – 'international regulation' or 'international law' – at the apex of the 'international financial architecture'. Thus, the philosophy of overarching norms informed both reform projects.[88] In the UN context, the approach to ordering followed a somewhat similar logic. Relying on a similar form but a different content of interface norms, the UN Task-Force referred to 'sustainable human development' and 'democracy'[89] as principles governing the decision-making process within the envisaged international financial architecture. The UN Task-Force interpreted 'International codes of conduct, improved information, and enhanced financial supervision and regulation' as an overarching framework governing the system. However, they went so far as to argue that the framework would 'include international standards to combat money and asset laundering as well as corruption and tax evasion' but also ensure 'consistency' with human rights, particularly those in the International Covenant on Economic, Social and Cultural Rights.[90] Moreover, the UN Task-Force went beyond a purely intra-systemic perspective to take into view relationships between the international financial system and different domestic legal systems. While emphasizing the 'global' character of 'financial regulation and supervision', the UN Task-Force also gave weight to domestic legal orders and their 'different national financial structure and traditions as regards financial regulation and supervision'.[91]

[88] On 'overarching norms', see Chapter 1.

[89] 'We must emphasize that any reform of the international financial system ought to be based on a broad discussion, involving all countries, and a clear agenda, including all key issues. The process must ensure that the interests of all groups of developing and transition economies, including poor and small countries, are adequately represented. The United Nations, as a universal and the most democratic international forum, should play an important role in these discussions and in the design of the new system.' Task-Force of the Executive Committee on Economic and Social Affairs of the United Nations, 'Towards a New International Financial Architecture', 9.

[90] Ibid., 15.

[91] Task-Force of the Executive Committee on Economic and Social Affairs of the United Nations, 'Towards a New International Financial Architecture', 15.

While it is not obvious that UN officials perceived domestic legal systems as integrated parts within the 'international financial system', it seems more plausible that they relied on the more flexible interface norm of 'taking into account' to connect 'domestic' and 'international' systems.[92] When bringing these legal orders into a mutual relation, the UN body of experts relied on reception norms in so far as they required that 'due account should be taken' of local circumstances in domestic legal systems.[93] The project of international harmonization was never uncontroversial and provoked tensions with domestic sites of governance, as evidenced by the attitudes of some national authorities creating resistance to international standards. For instance, the deputy governor of the Reserve Bank of India articulated a 'national law perspective' highlighting the 'discretion' and 'considerable flexibility' that officials in India had while interpreting 'general principles' in international standards and bringing them in relation to the domestic legal order.[94] This language is similar to reception norms in its effect of creating distance between international standards and the Indian domestic legal system.

After the 2008 financial crisis, the reform of the international financial architecture emerged as a new site of struggle between lawyers, economists and policy-makers to redefine interactions between bodies of norms.[95] In this context, forms of entanglement mirrored the dominant response to multiplicity, in particular at the IMF, that followed the Asian financial crisis of 1997. Seeking more centralization and unity than diversity and collaboration, many actors sought to frame multiplicity from a systemic perspective, adopting a functional analysis. They have often done so by deploying interface norms such as the 'rule of law'.[96] Particularly in Europe, a similar reliance on overarching norms characterized most responses to institutional diversity,[97] placing emphasis on

[92] Chapter 1.

[93] Task-Force of the Executive Committee on Economic and Social Affairs of the United Nations, 'Towards a New International Financial Architecture', 15.

[94] '[T]here are several reasons to be circumspect about the role of standards and codes as primary instruments of enhancing international financial stability.' See Y. V. Reddy, 'Legal Aspects of International Financial Standards – National Law Perspective' (BIS Review, 2002).

[95] The financial press also promoted the idea of a formal amendment of Articles of Agreement to transform the IMF in the new 'guardian of the global financial system'. See 'Wanted: A Guardian of the World's Financial System', *Financial Times* (April 2007).

[96] Cottier et al., *The Rule of Law in Monetary Affairs*.

[97] C. Reinhart and K. Rogoff, 'Regulation Should Be International', *Financial Times* (November 2008).

regulatory coherence and centralization of authority.[98] For example, the 'de Larosière Report'[99] proposed an integrated approach to financial regulation in Europe and at the international level.[100] Noting the 'evident lack of a coherent framework', the authors of the report recommended that a 'reformed FSF would be in the best position for coordinating the work of the various international standard-setters in achieving international regulatory consistency'.[101] They envisaged a treaty establishing a 'full international standard-setting authority' creating binding obligations for states and monitored by the IMF through its Article IV Consultations powers.[102] At a more general level, this argumentative structure reflects the imagery suggested by proponents of constitutionalism in controversies over the shape of postnational law and politics. Sharing a similar ambition, many theorists of international financial regulation have sought to construe a legal system to 'contain' the plurality of sources characterizing global financial governance.[103]

11.3.2 Making the Compendium of Standards: Straddling Practices and Reception Norms

As a 'joint product', the Compendium was produced by an ad hoc Task-Force on Implementation of Standards (Task-Force), a group of specialists[104] that had been assembled by the FSF with the aim of developing a 'strategy' to strengthen 'international consensus on key standards' for financial stability. To shape the form and content of the Compendium, the Task-Force drew upon 'prior work' by the IMF, World Bank and standard-setting bodies in 'promulgating and assessing observance of standards'.[105] Given the plurality of 'economic and financial standards'

[98] M. Giovanoli and D. Devos (eds), *International Monetary and Financial Law: The Global Crisis* (Oxford University Press, 2011).

[99] Report by the High-Level Group on Financial Supervision in the EU (Chaired by Jacques de Larosière), 2009, at 59. See chapter 4 of the report (Global Repair, Promoting Financial Stability at the Global Level), 2009.

[100] The financial press appreciated the 'step-by-step' approach advocated by the de Larosière group. See, 'A Single Rulebook', *Financial Times* (February 2009).

[101] Report by the High-Level Group on Financial Supervision in the EU.

[102] Ibid.

[103] N. Krisch, *Beyond Constitutionalism: The Pluralist Structure of Postnational Law* (Oxford University Press, 2010), chapter 2.

[104] For the full list of members of the Task-Force, see FSF, 'Issue Paper of the Task-Force on Implementation of Standards' (March 2000), 29–30.

[105] Ibid., 3.

recognized as relevant for 'sound financial systems', the Task-Force highlighted a 'subset' of twelve standards that were 'likely to make the greatest contribution to reducing vulnerabilities and strengthening the resilience of financial systems'.[106] This group of experts recommended that 'policy-makers' should focus on a 'list of standards' with 'priority implementation depending on countries' circumstances'.

In a footnote of its report, the Task-Force articulated the rationale of its decision-making by claiming that 'while a broad range of political, social, legal, and institutional factors impinge on financial stability, the focus of the FSF is on economic and financial standards which are generally accepted by the international community as being objective and relatively free of national biases'.[107] It is worth analysing how the Task-Force simultaneously distanced a group of norms from the list and brought other bodies of norms together. Indeed, it seems that the Task-Force had recourse to a 'knowledge practice'[108] when it distinguished between, on the one hand 'political', 'social', 'legal' and 'institutional' norms, and on the other hand 'economic and financial standards for sound financial systems'. This practice of boundary-drawing enabled the Task-Force to carve out what it termed 'internationally accepted standards for economic, financial and market activities', creating distance from norms that did not fit in that category.[109] This technique contrasts with straddling practices, that is, 'practices that straddle different bodies of norms without being seen to belong to either, thus blurring the boundaries between them'.[110] However, straddling practices were also at play in the making of the Compendium. After distancing 'political', 'social', 'legal' and 'institutional' norms from the scope of its work, the Task-Force assembled 'the set of standards it considers the most relevant to strengthening financial systems'. By 'drawing on prior work'[111] the Task-Force connected twelve standards to create something new out of this assemblage, namely a consolidated list of 'key standards for sound financial systems'[112]

[106] Ibid., 3.
[107] FSF, 'Issue Paper of the Task-Force on Implementation of Standards', 7.
[108] On 'knowledge practices' and their effects, see Riles, *Collateral Knowledge*.
[109] FSF, 'Issue Paper of the Task-Force on Implementation of Standards', 7.
[110] Chapter 1.
[111] FSF, 'Issue Paper of the Task-Force on Implementation of Standards', 18.
[112] Code of Good Practices on Transparency in Monetary and Financial Policies, Code of Good Practices in Fiscal Transparency, Special Data Dissemination Standard/General Data Dissemination System, Principles of Corporate Governance, International

around which 'international consensus' had to be forged. This list of 'twelve key standards' then was the effect of a straddling practice, blurring the boundaries between the bodies of norms that were assembled in it. From the perspective of the Task-Force, the definition of this select group of bodies of norms as 'key international standards' was crucial to achieve international consensus. In this assessment, the Task-Force placed emphasis on those standards that were 'endorsed' by the 'international community', by which the Task-Force meant in particular national regulators, the IMF, the World Bank and international standard-setting bodies. In this way, the Task-Force brought into a mutual relation the standards that had been recognized as authoritative by the official sector of which the Task-Force itself was a part. As a creation of the FSF, the Task-Force included representatives of national governments, the IMF, the World Bank and the Basel Committee on Banking Supervision. By bringing together and giving weight to the standards that had been recognized by FSF members, international financial institutions and international standard-setting organizations, the Task-Force manifested a certain degree of self-referentiality.[113]

The choice of focusing on standards produced and used by the 'official sector' (i.e. public actors)[114] created distance from norms of private origin, with the exception of standards developed by the IASC and the International Federation of Accountants. The Task-Force framed the Compendium as a 'one-stop reference' to forge international consensus on 'key standards', limiting disagreement on their definition and with the aim of accommodating 'a large number of standards' that users could easily refer to.[115] For the internal organization of the Compendium, the Task-Force preferred a 'web-based' structure to a hierarchical form to create linkages with a corpus of other 'relevant standards' that were 'not less important than the 12 key standards [...] but [were] complementary' to them.[116] These complementary standards ought to be 'organized

Accounting Standards, International Standards on Auditing, Core Principles for Systemically Important Payment Systems, the Forty Recommendations of the Financial Action Task-Force, Core Principles for Effective Banking Supervision, Objectives and Principles of Securities Regulation, Insurance Supervisory Principles.

113 FSF, 'Issue Paper of the Task-Force on Implementation of Standards', 21.

114 IMF, World Bank, OECD, CPSS, FATF, BCBS, IOSCO, IAIS. Ibid., 19.

115 Ibid., 21.

116 Ibid., 20.

separately' under three different categories.[117] The Task-Force also envisaged that additional standards could be added to the Compendium as long as they were approved by relevant standard-setting bodies and FSF members.[118]

After the financial crisis of 2008, the creation by the G20 of the FSB as the successor of the FSF confirmed the forms of enmeshment construed when the Compendium was still in the making. The number of standards included in the Compendium grew considerably after the institutionalization of the FSB. As FSB members recognized new standards for 'sound financial systems', the boundaries of the Compendium expanded akin to the pages of a rule book, positing a distance between standards included in the Compendium and other bodies of norms that were kept *outside*. The incremental growth of the Compendium also strengthened the position of the FSB as an actor in the organization of standards recognized by the 'official sector'.

At the FSB, structures and dynamics of entanglement may depend on the actors involved in its decision-making.[119] Here, the forms and content of interface norms may reflect the composition of the FSB but also the set of relations that the FSB has with other actors and institutions in the social and political environment in which it operates. With respect to membership, existing analyses have placed emphasis on the interactions between FSB members as central factors driving the activities of the FSB. Characterized by a broader membership than the FSF, the FSB has been portrayed as 'a nexus point' enabling interaction and communication between 'communities of private actors' and 'communities of states'.[120] Stavros Gadinis has described it as 'an umbrella organization that brings together [. . .] networks of ministry executives, national regulators, and private professionals',[121] placing emphasis on its strong ministry component. As such analyses have shown, state officials from the G20 and experts from standard-setting organizations have been the dominant

[117] The categories that the Task-Force construed were: 'broad headings' (including macroeconomic fundamentals, institutional and market infrastructures, and financial regulation and supervision), 'policy areas' and 'functional areas'. Ibid., 21.

[118] Ibid., 21.

[119] On the centrality of actors in the construction of entanglements, see Chapter 1.

[120] L. C. Backer, 'Private Actors and Public Governance beyond the State: The Multinational Corporation, the Financial Stability Board, and the Global Governance Order' (2011) 18 *Indiana Journal of Global Legal Studies* 751–802.

[121] S. Gadinis, 'Three Pathways to Global Standards: Private, Regulator, and Ministry Networks' (2015) 109 *American Journal of International Law* 1–57, at 56.

players shaping the agenda of the FSB. This dominance is reflected for example in the fact that there is a higher number of members from countries which are a part of the European Union than from other economies.[122]

On the other hand, participation from market actors and public–private collaboration appear to be limited. According to the FSB's self-representation, the degree of recognition of actors and norms of private origin seems rather limited. For example, the International Accounting Standards Board, formally a private organization, is a member of the FSB, and the International Financial Reporting Standards that they produce have been included in the Compendium of Standards. However, according to Annelise Riles, the FSB 'fails to recognize the practical authority of organizations such as the International Swaps and Derivatives Association in constructing their own forms of international financial governance beyond the state'.[123] Thus, the interface norms construed within the Compendium are likely to be shaped by the convergence or competition of interests of the dominant public actors that have access to the FSB and by the wider institutional environment (i.e. the 'international financial architecture') in which the FSB itself is situated. For example, interactions between the FSB and the G20 may have consequences for the types of norms that are brought in relation in this context.

In the FSB context, straddling practices were not the only form of entanglement. Rather, conditional recognition practices originally performed by the Task-Force were also instrumental in organizing relations between 'key standards', the 'complementary standards' included in the Compendium and those yet to be included. Over time, FSB members have relied on a set of 'criteria for inclusion' to give weight only to standards deemed to be 'relevant', 'implementable', 'internationally recognized' and 'widely applicable'.[124] However, the combined application of these criteria also consolidated a distinction between standards perceived to meet these criteria and standards which failed to do so. The interpretation of these requirements then had a rejection effect because it

[122] D. Arner and M. Taylor, 'The Financial Stability Board and the Future of International Financial Regulation', in R. Buckley, E. Avgouleas and D. Arner (eds), *Reconceptualising Global Finance and Its Regulation* (Cambridge University Press, 2016), pp. 51–66.

[123] Riles, 'Is New Governance the Ideal Architecture', 257.

[124] These criteria of recognition have been published on the website of the FSB. See www.fsb.org/work-of-the-fsb/about-the-compendium-of-standards/.

distanced laws of private origin, which many actors use in their practices. For example, norms produced by the financial industry do not seem to be considered as relevant by FSB members, hence their absence from the Compendium. From this perspective, the 'criteria for inclusion of standards in the Compendium' may be seen as the content of an interface norm governing interactions between internal and external bodies of norms. In particular, the reproduction of this inside/outside distinction was performed by a reception norm whose content was a specific set of requirements defining 'the ways in which outside norms enter a given body of norms'.[125] In sum, it seems that straddling practices and reception norms played a more prominent role than overarching norms in the institutional site in which the Compendium took shape. The Compendium was the outcome of a work of composition that consisted of selecting, assembling and distancing bodies of norms. As the Compendium was still in the making, the Task-Force relied less on overarching norms than on straddling practices to perform this task. Such a form of entanglement makes sense because the task at hand was the creation of a new regulatory arrangement, in a context relatively free from pre-existing systemic constraints. Indeed, the project of a Compendium was in the first place the key innovation of the Task-Force and therefore its boundaries were still in flux. The effect of using this type of interface norm was closer to an assemblage type of order than to a system with clear institutional boundaries. However, the Task-Force also generated rules for the inclusion of 'international standards' and these criteria of recognition form the content of the reception norm that continues to order relations between the Compendium and external bodies of norms.

11.3.3 Connecting International Financial Standards

Financial regulators have also written reports containing recommendations that draw on previous reports or on documents written by other actors. The practice of drawing on other actors' bodies of norms have often had the effect of blurring their boundaries to create something new. Forms of entanglement have also been shaped in the context of institutional interactions between the FSB and international financial institutions. For example, FSB member jurisdictions have decided 'to undergo

[125] See definition of 'reception norms' in Chapter 1.

FSAP assessments every five years'.[126] FSB members have practised thematic and country-based peer reviews to assess compliance with international financial standards through a 'holistic approach'.[127] These practices have followed the FSB Handbook for Peer Review and taken the FSAP's and Reports on the Observance of Standards and Codes' recommendations into account.[128] In the context of these monitoring practices and 'peer reviews', acts of referring to the prescriptions of 'the other' have also blurred the boundaries between bodies of norms and enabled a mutual strengthening of their relations.

The straddling practice of compiling lists of international standards was not unique to the FSF/FSB as other actors and institutions beyond the FSB had recourse to similar techniques.[129] Indeed, global governance practices through the creation of lists have also been common in other issue areas of global administration, for example international security.[130] The Basel Committee on Banking Supervision issued a 'Compendium of Basel Committee documents', which was subsequently updated in 2001.[131] In December 2019, the Committee published its 'Consolidated Framework' (referred to as 'Basel Framework') which embodies all fourteen standards it produced since its creation.[132] Beyond its own norms, the chapter on 'Core Principles for Effective Banking Supervision' refers to other standards and practices, such as the recommendations by the IMF formulated in its FSAPs.[133] These

[126] See www.fsb.org/about/leading-by-example/participation/.

[127] Gadinis, 'The Financial Stability Board', 161.

[128] The Handbook for FSB Peer Review specifies that 'Country Reviews [. . .] examine the steps taken or planned by national/regional authorities to address IMF-World Bank Financial Sector Assessment Program (FSAP) and Reports on the Observance of Standards and Codes (ROSCs) recommendations on financial regulation and supervision.' See Standing Committee on Standards Implementation, 'Handbook for FSB Peer Reviews' (2017).

[129] M. De Bellis, 'Global Standards for Domestic Financial Regulations: Concourse, Competition and Mutual Reinforcement between Different Types of Global Administration' (2006) 6 *Global Jurist Advances*, https://doi.org/10.2202/1535-1661.1184.

[130] See, for example, G. Sullivan, *The Law of the List: UN Counterterrorism Sanctions and the Politics of Global Security Law* (Cambridge University Press, 2020).

[131] Basel Committee on Banking Supervision, 'Compendium of Documents Produced by the Basel Committee on Banking Supervision' (May 2001).

[132] Basel Committee on Banking Supervision, 'The Basel Framework' (December 2019).

[133] 'The regular reports by the IMF and the World Bank on the lessons drawn from assessment experiences as part of FSAP exercises constitute a useful source of information which has been used as an input to improve the Principles'. Footnote 40 at p. 28 of the chapter on Core Principles.

practices have allowed shaping an entanglement between international financial standards and between these bodies of norms and domestic legal orders.

Basel Committee members encouraged taking account of anti-money laundering recommendations by the Financial Action Task Force (FATF).[134] IOSCO, the Basel Committee and IAIS have blurred boundaries between their recommendations on combating money laundering and the financing of terrorism. In a joint statement, the three institutions claimed that the FATF 40 Recommendations provided a basis that would allow them to 'take account' of their respective standards in future work.[135] The FATF, on the other hand, also took account of Basel Committee recommendations when it linked the 'customer due diligence' norm for banks originally crafted in 2001 by the Committee[136] to its recommendations to combat money laundering.[137] The language of 'taking into account' other standards reappeared in another statement, but this time the norms referred to were those of the FATF itself.[138] Similarly, the interconnected structure of international standards has

[134] '[S]upervisors should encourage the adoption of those recommendations of the Financial Action Task-Force on Money Laundering (FATF) that apply to financial institutions.' Basel Committee on Banking Supervision, 'Core Principles on Banking Supervision' (1997).

[135] 'The revised 40 FATF Recommendations will provide an opportunity for the standard-setting organizations to review their standards and guidance taking account of each other's work in this respect with the aim of preventing as far as possible inconsistencies between their standards and guidance where this is unwarranted from a risk-based approach.' The Joint Forum Basel Committee on Banking Supervision, International Organization of Securities Commissions, International Association of Insurance Supervisors, 'Initiatives by the BCBS, IAIS and IOSCO to Combat Money Laundering and the Financing of Terrorism – Joint Statement' (3 June 2003).

[136] Basel Committee on Banking Supervision, 'Customer Due Diligence for Banks' (October 2001).

[137] Following this, the BCBS stated that it was 'pleased to note the extent to which its publication Customer Due Diligence for Banks [...], has been reflected in the FATF's recommendations concerning customer due diligence. In all substantive respects, the spirit of the Committee's paper has been incorporated within the FATF approach.' Basel Committee on Banking Supervision, 'Basel Committee Welcomes Revised FATF Recommendations' (2003).

[138] '[T]he IAIS adopted a Guidance paper on anti-money laundering and combating the financing of terrorism [...] The new guidance paper takes into account the revised FATF 40 Recommendations of June 2003 and the Methodology for Assessing compliance with the FATF 40 recommendations and the 8 special recommendations issued in February 2004, as well as the 8 Special Recommendations on Terrorist Financing of October 2001.' The Joint Forum: Basel Committee on Banking Supervision, International Organization of Securities Commissions, International Association of

been emphasized by private norm addressees in financial markets.[139] These statements have been subtle conduits in the discursive enmeshment of financial standards. Financial regulators and producers of those standards have often construed standards in connection with other standards, which suggests that these norms have become entangled in an interconnected 'web' of norms.[140] As we have seen, the web-like shape of the Compendium equipped with hyperlinks to enable users to connect to the webpages of the different standard producers (and their standards) was indeed foreseen by the Task-Force on Implementation of Standards. This particular feature enabled users of the Compendium to create loose, ad hoc connections between standards through their statements and practices. It may be that this particular way of constructing relations between bodies of norms was done for strategic reasons, perhaps to strengthen the authority of the technical bodies that make those standards, including standard-setting organizations that are members of the FSB itself.[141]

11.4 Conclusion

This chapter has focused on forms, locations and practices in which relations between bodies of norms in global financial governance have been defined in the aftermath of the Asian financial crisis and the global financial crisis. Drawing on official pronouncements connected to the IMF, the UN and the BIS, it has observed the different contexts in which these relations have come about. The institutional memory examined has provided traces of ad hoc but not uncontroversial construction of entanglements and the participants and factors behind them. In many of the sites of governance examined, different forms were articulated through dynamic and informal interactions of a multiplicity of

Insurance Supervisors, 'Initiatives by the BCBS, IAIS and IOSCO to Combat Money Laundering and the Financing of Terrorism Update – Joint Statement' (2005).

139 The European Banking Federation has referred to the plurality of norms contained in the document 'Basel III: Finalising Post-Crisis Reform', which they call Basel IV, as a 'package'. See EBF, 'Summary on Basel IV in Europe' (2019).

140 Chapter 1.

141 Previous work has suggested that international standards might be 'mutually reinforcing' through practices of cross-referencing and incorporation. See De Bellis, 'Global Standards for Domestic Financial Regulation'. On this 'strategic' path to entanglement, see Chapter 1.

regulators, international institutions and international standard-setting organizations involved in the global governance of financial stability.

Competing ordering projects have emerged in different contexts in the theory and practice of global financial governance over time. These projects were also sites in which actors imagined different ways of shaping 'international standards' and their relations, with implications for the forms of entanglement that came about through their claims. Since the second half of 1990s, the multiplication of standards deemed to be relevant by financial regulators has triggered efforts to define their relations, and regulators have relied on different interface norms at different sites of governance to create order. International lawyers have often imagined the global financial order from an intra-systemic perspective and sought to organize institutional pluralism through overarching norms such as the rule of law.

Although many of the actors analysed imagine a global financial system, there is a lack of general agreement on the implications for the relations between different bodies of norms. Differently situated actors defined their relative weight in different ways by placing emphasis on different norms and sites of authority. For example, in their respective ordering projects in response to multiplicity, officials at the UN, the IMF and at the BIS have come up with conflicting views on the position of the relevant sites of authority. From this perspective, the emerging overall order remains pluralistic.

Drawing on the history of the Compendium of Standards, differences between forms of entanglement connected with the Financial Stability Forum and those linked to the IMF and UN contexts could be observed. Standards included in the Compendium were ordered through an interplay of straddling practices and reception norms. When the Compendium was still in the making, the former type of interface norm appeared in the work of the Task-Force on Implementation of Standards. In this context, boundary-drawing practices, too, were used to create distance from norms that actors assembled at the FSF did not identify as relevant. By contrast, other bodies of norms were connected to form an official list of international financial standards, around which an international consensus had to be built. The making of a list of 'twelve key standards' was the outcome of a straddling practice by the Task-Force, which had the effect of blurring the boundaries between the bodies of norms that were brought within this new list. However, the increasing institutionalization of the FSB has been coupled with a greater emphasis on practices of regulatory uniformity and centralization. Through the

Compendium of Standards, regulators assembled at the FSB sought to provide a common frame to respond to the dilemmas of proximity and difference of bodies of norms in global financial governance. Over time, the FSB has sought to bring together multiple monitoring practices and their bodies of norms within a single overarching 'framework'.[142] From this perspective, it seems that a hierarchical ambition has also been at play.

However, institutional pluralism provoked similar responses in other settings, too, which triggered further forms of entanglement through the production of further compendia, lists, and rule books to order relations between bodies of norms for global financial stability. The emerging picture is heterogeneous, as evidenced by the absence of a single global decision-maker, the coexistence of different plans for reform and different visions of the relevant sites of decision-making and forms of authority.

[142] FSB, 'Framework for Strengthening Adherence to International Standards' (January 2010); FSB, 'A Coordination Framework for Monitoring the Implementation of Agreed G-20/FSB Financial Reforms' (2011).

12

Hidden in the Shades

Patterns of Entanglement within the Web of Corporate Social Responsibility Law

TOMÁŠ MOROCHOVIČ AND LUCY LU REIMERS

12.1 Introduction

The field of corporate social responsibility (CSR) is a rapidly growing area of transnational regulation that is characterized by a multiplicity of norm-making processes in a variety of institutions and different forums. These processes are reflexive, engaging in mutual interaction through mirroring, distancing or complementing existing normative frameworks. The resulting landscape of CSR is defined by contestation and entanglement as CSR instruments of different origin coexist side by side, sometimes with competing claims to compliance. As a result, CSR is a particularly fertile ground for studying how the relations between different bodies of norms are construed.

This chapter sets out to understand how actors entangle CSR norms and, in doing so, create an interlinked web of normative systems, both formal and informal, operating within the state as well as without it. Section 12.2 serves as a brief orientation within the complex world of CSR, identifying the main discourses and categorizations. Out of the multitude of collections of norms which come under the umbrella of CSR, the chapter draws focus to meta-regulatory CSR norms, and in particular the Organisation for Economic Co-operation and Development (OECD) Guidelines for Multinational Enterprises (the Guidelines).[1] Being positioned at the intersection of traditional international law, soft law initiatives developed within international organizations, and private standards and codes, the Guidelines provide a focal

[1] OECD, *Declaration on International Investment and Multinational Enterprises Annex I: Guidelines for Multinational Enterprises* (adopted 21 June 1976, last amended 25 May 2011) OECD/LEGAL/0144.

point for CSR entanglement. Section 12.3 looks at how the structural features of the Guidelines have contributed to the coordinated legal entanglement between various bodies of norms, which should be understood as the creation of stable, systemic and lasting connections and points of interaction. Coordinated legal entanglement can also create space for ad hoc entanglement, which is analysed in Section 12.4. The idea of ad hoc entanglement refers to more fluid and contingent interactions which might deepen the ties between bodies of norms but also sever them. The turn to ad hoc entanglement also involves a change of the subject of enquiry, moving from the systemic features of the OECD Guidelines to focus on actual instances of disputes around CSR, crystallized in the case law arising out of OECD National Contact Points (NCPs) – the Guidelines' implementation mechanism. As indicated, the picture here is more diverse, and interactions between various frameworks are analysed on a scale ranging from distancing to proximity.

By exploring forms of legal entanglement in the field of CSR, the aim is to glean more insight into the evolving shape of this global legal order, which has expanded to include a range of new subjects, norm-making institutions and regulatory tools. To this end, Section 12.5 draws attention to some of the dynamics which appear to be emerging through the interaction of the Guidelines with other bodies of norms. These types of structuring disrupt the traditional notion of a horizontal international legal order. What we see instead is something more akin to a three-dimensional and polycentric web created through new and irreverent forms of linkage and accommodation over time.

12.2 The Contours of Corporate Social Responsibility

There is no single, accepted definition of CSR or its scope. Many definitions exist, each highlighting different aspects of CSR according to the interests of the defining actor. Business groups, for example, tend to adopt definitions of CSR that highlight voluntariness, reinforcing the distinction often made between law and CSR.[2] Capital-exporting states similarly emphasize the voluntary aspect of CSR. The EU, for instance, defines CSR as 'a concept whereby companies integrate social and environmental concerns in their business operations [...] on a voluntary

[2] J. A. Zerk, *Multinationals and Corporate Social Responsibility: Limitations and Opportunities in International Law* (Cambridge University Press 2006), p. 30.

basis'.[3] On the opposite end of the spectrum, non-governmental organizations (NGOs) – confronted with the reality of human rights abuses and environmental harms associated with the activities of global corporations – often prefer not to use the term CSR at all, rejecting the way it has been framed and operationalized by businesses. For example, the Amnesty International homepage on 'corporations' does not mention the term 'corporate social responsibility' once. Instead, Amnesty International calls for corporate accountability, thus bringing it closer to the notion of accountability under law.[4]

The dichotomy about CSR being either intrinsically voluntary or binding is somewhat misleading, however. As Zerk notes, the regulatory impact of CSR provisions does not necessarily correlate to their formal binding power.[5] More neutral definitions of CSR thus avoid references to the mandatory/voluntary distinction, emphasizing instead the social and environmental embeddedness of corporate activities and focusing on the corporate responsibility to address negative impacts while maximizing positive contributions. In this vein, Aguinis and Glavas define CSR as 'context-specific organizational actions and policies that take into account stakeholders' expectations and the triple bottom line of economic, social, and environmental performance'.[6] Similarly, Zerk defines CSR as 'the notion, that each business enterprise, as a member of society, has a responsibility to operate ethically and in accordance with its legal obligations and to strive to minimise any adverse effects of its operations and activities on the environment, society, and human health'.[7]

In sum, CSR can encompass adherence to both voluntary commitments and legal obligations with regard to corporations' impacts on society in the broad sense of the term. CSR norms can be codified in many different forms and may be produced by a host of different actors. Individual companies produce 'codes of conduct' containing general principles for 'ethical business conduct', often applicable in relation to suppliers/subcontractors, and occasionally linked to specific monitoring

[3] EU Commission, 'Green Paper: Promoting a European Framework for Corporate Social Responsibility' (adopted 18 July 2001) COM (2001) 366.

[4] Amnesty International, *Everything You Need to Know about Human Rights and Corporate Accountability*, www.amnesty.org/en/what-we-do/corporate-accountability/.

[5] Zerk, *Multinationals and Corporate Social Responsibility*, p. 32 *et seq.*

[6] H. Aguinis and A. Glavas, 'What We Know and Don't Know about Corporate Social Responsibility: A Review and Research Agenda' (2012) 38 *Journal of Management* 932–68, at 933.

[7] Zerk, *Multinationals and Corporate Social Responsibility*, p. 32.

(and even complaints) mechanisms, and with sanctions in case of non-compliance. Codes of conduct are also produced at the sectoral level by industry associations, or in the context of multi-stakeholder groups (e.g. the Fair Labour Organization). NGOs and civil society actors have also produced a wide-ranging set of CSR norms, including labelling initiatives (e.g. Fairtrade), sectoral principles or certification schemes (e.g. the Fairmined Standard for Gold from Artisanal and Small-Scale Mining), multi-stakeholder initiatives (e.g. the Ethical Trading Initiative) and guidelines (e.g. the Voluntary Principles on Security and Human Rights). In many instances, governments have organized, facilitated, funded or participated in the drafting of CSR codes, sometimes even establishing their own labelling schemes (such as the EU's Ecolabel).

A category of CSR norms which is of particular interest to this chapter is the so-called 'meta-regulatory' instruments. These can be broadly described as CSR norms produced by international organizations and standard-setting organizations which are directed at multinational corporations (e.g. the International Labour Organization (ILO) Tripartite Declaration containing minimum labour standards). Some of these instruments cover a broad range of areas (e.g. the OECD Guidelines) and are linked to non-judicial complaints mechanisms, while others are directed at specific sectors (e.g. the OECD-Food and Agriculture Organization Guidance for Responsible Agricultural Supply Chains) or cover only specific areas of impact (e.g. the UN Guiding Principles on Business and Human Rights). Positioning themselves above other CSR norms, they often attract entanglement and serve as focal points for interaction.

12.3 Coordinated Interaction at the Meta-regulatory Level: CSR Systems and Their Linkages

The uninhibited increase in the number of CSR systems and their ensuing plurality makes them an excellent target for the study of legal entanglement. The proliferation of CSR initiatives creates a veritable 'market' in which regulatory systems mutually interact, with cooperation and competition representing merely the pinnacle of their diverse interactions.[8] This section focuses on meta-regulatory instruments which

[8] Marx and Wouters map the dynamics of cooperation and competition in the more narrowly construed space of voluntary sustainability standards – see A. Marx and J. Wouters, 'Competition and Cooperation in the Market of Voluntary Sustainability

inherently 'regulate regulation'[9] and, as a result of this, have a higher propensity for *coordinated* entanglement – that is, creating lasting and relatively stable regime interactions which contribute to an interlinked web of normative bodies of norms. Among these CSR frameworks, the OECD Guidelines stand out in particular due to their comprehensive coverage of corporate behaviour and structural openness towards other frameworks. As Backer notes, the Guidelines 'are beginning to serve as the focal point for the construction of an autonomous transnational governance system that is meant to serve as the touchstone for corporate behaviour in multinational economic relationships'.[10]

The history of the Guidelines dates back to 1976 when the document was born as an annex to the OECD's Ministerial Declaration on International Investment and Multinational Enterprises. Other authors have written comprehensively about the development of the Guidelines;[11] here it suffices to say that they are a soft law document containing recommendations to multinational enterprises in relation to

Standards', in P. Delimatsis (ed.), *The Law, Economics and Politics of International Standardisation* (Cambridge University Press, 2015), pp. 215–41; see also S. Wood, K. W. Abbott, J. Black, B. Eberlein and E. Meidinger, 'The Interactive Dynamics of Transnational Business Governance: A Challenge for Transnational Legal Theory' (2015) 6 *Transnational Legal Theory* 333–69 for a more comprehensive study of dynamics of interaction.

9 Although note that there is divergence on what meta-regulation means – Marx and Wouters, 'Competition and Cooperation in the Market of Voluntary Sustainability Standards', 37; cf. L. C. Backer, 'From Guiding Principles to Interpretive Organizations: Developing a Framework for Applying the UNGPs to Disputes That Institutionalizes the Advocacy Role of Civil Society', in C. Rodriguez-Garavito (ed.), *Business and Human Rights: Beyond the End of the Beginning* (Cambridge University Press, 2017), pp. 97–110; A. Loconto and E. Fouilleux, 'Politics of Private Regulation: ISEAL and the Shaping of Transnational Sustainability Governance – Politics of Private Regulation' (2014) 8 *Regulation & Governance* 166–85; C. Parker, 'Meta-Regulation: Legal Accountability for Corporate Social Responsibility', in D. McBarnet, A. Voiculescu and T. Campbell (eds), *The New Corporate Accountability: Corporate Social Responsibility and the Law* (Cambridge University Press, 2007), pp. 207–37.

10 L. C. Backer, 'Rights and Accountability in Development (Raid) v. Das Air and Global Witness v. Afrimex: Small Steps towards an Autonomous Transnational Legal System for the Regulation of Multinational Corporations Case Notes' (2009) 10 *Melbourne Journal of International Law* 258–307, at 284.

11 See e.g. J. Murray, 'A New Phase in the Regulation of Multinational Enterprises: The Role of the OECD' (2001) 30 *Industrial Law Journal* 255–70; S. Tully, 'The 2000 Review of the OECD Guidelines for Multinational Enterprises' (2001) 50 *The International and Comparative Law Quarterly* 394–404; J. L. Cernic, 'Corporate Responsibility for Human Rights: A Critical Analysis of the OECD Guidelines for Multinational Enterprises International Law' (2008) 4 *Hanse Law Review* 71–102.

the adverse impacts which arise as part of their business activities. While the recommendations themselves are not binding on corporations, adhering countries (including some non-OECD countries) have an obligation to promote the Guidelines.[12] Over the years, the Guidelines have undergone multiple revisions which have significantly expanded both their subject scope and geographical reach, with the major revisions happening in 2000 and 2011. From a legal entanglement perspective, the earlier versions of the Guidelines were uninspiring as they 'made no reference to standards other than those created in the national sphere'.[13] Despite the existence of reservations about the merits of 'cross-pollination' with other bodies of norms,[14] however, the 2000 revision of the Guidelines embraced coordinated entanglement through a number of provisions in the updated text. First, the scope of regulation applicable to corporate behaviour was extended beyond domestic norms to include all 'applicable law',[15] clarified through the OECD's commentary to the Guidelines' chapter on labour standards as referring to the idea that enterprises can be subject to 'national, sub-national, as well as supranational levels of regulation'.[16] A similarly broad wording was adopted in relation to the chapter on environment, which refers to 'relevant international agreements, principles, objectives, and standards'.[17] The wording created an opening through which the Guidelines could be entangled with other bodies of norms, at first being mainly restricted to more traditional international law norms, but this continuously expanded. Second, the 2000 version of the Guidelines explicitly identified a number of instruments which were considered as a relevant resource to determine the scope of obligations, or which the Guidelines were aligned with. Out of those, the various ILO documents cited[18] and the International Organization for Standardization (ISO) Standard on Environmental Management Systems stand out, as they can be seen as directly competing with the Guidelines in the 'market' of transnational

[12] OECD, 'Decision of the Council on the OECD Guidelines for Multinational Enterprises' (adopted 27 June 2000) OECD/LEGAL/0307. See also R. Nieuwenkamp, 'The OECD Guidelines for Multinational Enterprises on Responsible Business Conduct' (2013) *Dovenschmidt Quarterly* 171–5, at 172.

[13] Murray, 'A New Phase in the Regulation of Multinational Enterprises', 258.

[14] Tully, 'The 2000 Review of the OECD Guidelines for Multinational Enterprises', 397.

[15] See 2000 edition of the OECD Guidelines, chapters I and IV.

[16] Ibid., chapter IV commentary.

[17] Ibid., chapter V.

[18] Ibid., chapter IV.

regulation of corporate conduct. By including such references in the text, and predominantly in the Commentary which forms an integral part of the Guidelines, the OECD began to create the sort of lasting, systemic connections between bodies of norms which characterize coordinated entanglement and enmeshment, and realize the benefits resulting from cooperation between systems.[19]

The 2011 revision of the Guidelines further developed this trend. 'Applicable law' became 'applicable laws and internationally recognized standards',[20] providing a basis for entanglement with bodies of norms which might not be considered law under doctrinal interpretations. The collection of explicitly entangled frameworks grew as well. The undeniably biggest contribution came from the inclusion of a new, standalone chapter on human rights, inspired by the UN Guiding Principles on Business and Human Rights (UNGPs).[21] The alignment of the Guidelines with the UNGPs significantly expanded the normative CSR web, creating direct and indirect linkages with a multitude of bodies of norms. The UNGPs are framed as a 'conceptual and policy framework' for business and human rights, elaborated through extensive multi-stakeholder consultations led by Special Representative (SR) John Ruggie. Having been adopted by the UN Human Rights Council,[22] they operationalize the three-pillar 'Protect, Respect and Remedy' Framework[23] developed by SR Ruggie. While they perform a number of complex roles vis-à-vis a multitude of actors, for the purposes of this chapter we can classify them as a global soft law CSR framework, albeit acknowledging their multifaceted nature. An important element of the UNGPs is that their implementation takes place through 'influence on or integration into other transnational business governance instruments'.[24]

[19] Such as mutually enhancing legitimacy and the prevention of a race to the bottom between standards – Marx and Wouters, 'Competition and Cooperation in the Market of Voluntary Sustainability Standards', 232.

[20] See 2011 edition of the OECD Guidelines, chapter I [1].

[21] Special Representative of the Secretary-General, 'Guiding Principles on Business and Human Rights: Implementing the United Nations "Protect, Respect and Remedy" Framework' (21 March 2011) UN Doc A/HRC/17/31.

[22] UNHRC, 'Human Rights and Transnational Corporations and Other Business Enterprises' (6 July 2011) UN Doc A/HRC/RES/17/4.

[23] Special Representative of the Secretary-General, 'Protect, Respect and Remedy: A Framework for Business and Human Rights' (7 April 2008) UN Doc A/HRC/8/5.

[24] K. Buhmann, 'Business and Human Rights: Understanding the UN Guiding Principles from the Perspective of Transnational Business Governance Interactions' (2015) 6 *Transnational Legal Theory* 399–434, at 426.

Among these, the Guidelines take pride of place, evidenced by SR Ruggie's assertions that in parallel to preparing the UNGPs he worked closely with the OECD to ensure consistency between the two bodies of norms.[25] Beyond the Guidelines, the most recent amendment of the ILO MNE Declaration[26] takes into account normative developments within the UNGPs, directly transposing some parts of the UNGPs with only minor clarificatory changes in their wording; and both the International Finance Corporation (IFC) Performance Standards and ISO 26000 Sustainability Standard have been coordinated so as to ensure compliance of their respective human rights provisions with the UNGPs.[27] Buhmann describes this as 'mutual piggybacking' between corporate governance schemes, providing implementation mechanisms for the UNGPs, and the UNGPs in turn imbuing other bodies with legitimacy.[28] Using the categorization suggested by Krisch in Chapter 1, the UNGPs are performing the role of 'overarching norms', characterized by the intra-systemic and overarching nature which they display in regard to the regulation of multiple bodies of norms within a single system.[29] Thus, the UNGPs enable the weaving together of international human rights law provisions across different normative bodies and, in doing so, indirectly entangling the Guidelines in an intricate normative web.

A further major feature of the 2000 and 2011 revisions of the Guidelines is the development of straddling practices – 'norms and practices that straddle different bodies of norms without being seen to belong to either'[30] – and again, the UNGPs are prominent in this regard, with their introduction of the concept of human rights due diligence. Although the notion of due diligence is not uncommon within

[25] J. G. Ruggie, 'Hierarchy or Ecosystem? Regulating Human Rights Risks of Multinational Enterprises', in C. Rodriguez-Garavito (ed.), *Business and Human Rights: Beyond the End of the Beginning* (Cambridge University Press, 2017), pp. 46–61, at p. 49; J. G. Ruggie and T. Nelson, 'Human Rights and the OECD Guidelines for Multinational Enterprises: Normative Innovations and Implementation Challenges' Corporate Social Responsibility Initiative Working Paper No. 66 (2015) 426.

[26] ILO, *Tripartite Declaration of Principles Concerning Multinational Enterprises and Social Policy* (adopted November 1977, last amended 17 March 2017).

[27] Ruggie, 'Hierarchy or Ecosystem?', 49–50.

[28] Buhmann, 'Business and Human Rights', 427.

[29] See Chapter 1, Section 1.5.1.

[30] The effect of such straddling is that boundaries between bodies of norms are blurred. Straddling practices are thus closest to what we would understand as trans-systemic norms which find applicability across multiple systems and have the ability to 'weave' linkages between them. See Chapter 1, Section 1.5.1.

international law, particularly in international environmental law,[31] the decision by SR Ruggie to reconceptualize it in the context of human rights obligations of corporations, that is non-state actors, was novel. Yet, when the human rights due diligence principle was incorporated into the Guidelines, it was not restricted to the human rights chapter – the OECD took the decision to make it applicable to all areas covered by the Guidelines. A similar thing happened to the concept of Environmental Impact Assessments (EIAs), introduced in the earlier versions of the Guidelines. The fundamentals of the concept, which originated within international environmental law, found application also in relation to non-environmental impacts of corporate behaviour, morphing into Environmental and Social Impact Assessments (ESIAs) and Social Impact Assessments. As will become clear from Section 12.4, the implementation mechanisms of the Guidelines have steadily portrayed these concepts as true straddling practices, being irreverent about their origins and treating them as inherent to the Guidelines.

12.4 Focal Points for CSR Interaction: NCPs as Sites of Ad Hoc Legal Entanglement

One of the distinguishing features of the OECD Guidelines is their implementation framework, based primarily on the practice of mediating complaints (called 'specific instances') by NCPs established domestically in countries adhering to the Guidelines. The geographic spread of NCPs, significant differences in their inner organization and the flexible and open-ended nature of the specific instance procedure create an inherently diverse system which has proved to be a suitable breeding ground for ad hoc legal entanglement. At present, there are forty-eight NCPs, distributed both in the home and host countries of multinational enterprises. The Guidelines provide adhering countries with significant leeway when it comes to setting up NCPs, with different organizational forms being envisaged and with room for the involvement of a variety of stakeholders.[32] As the most recent annual report on the Guidelines shows, NCPs appear to be operating with four decision-making structures with varying

[31] H. Cullen, 'The Irresistible Rise of Human Rights Due Diligence: Conflict Minerals and beyond' (2015) 48 *George Washington International Law Review* 743–80, at 745–49.

[32] See 2011 edition OECD Guidelines, Procedural Guidance, Chapter I (A).

degrees of interministerial integration and stakeholder engagement.[33] The diversity of actors already involved at the organizational level creates space for a variety of perspectives, and bodies of norms, to be brought to the table. The inclusion of external CSR norms is further facilitated by the open-endedness of the provisions on specific instances. The mandate for specific instances is defined vaguely – essentially, it 'is intended to provide a consensual, non-adversarial, "forum for discussion"'.[34] What this means in practice, however, is open to interpretation by NCPs, and as this section shows, NCPs do diverge significantly in the way they understand this mandate.

At its simplest, the procedure is supposed to bring together interested parties to discuss issues arising in relation to activities of multinational enterprises which potentially impact on the implementation of the Guidelines. The term 'interested parties' is important, as it denotes the open-ended definition of who can trigger a specific instance. Complaints are generally brought by NGOs supporting the claims of affected communities but can also be initiated by trade unions, directly by concerned individuals, multi-stakeholder initiatives, local communities, businesses and even the NCPs themselves, showing that the potential range of actors who can initiate procedures is extensive.[35] There is similar flexibility when it comes to the determination of relevant CSR norms, with the Guidelines simply stating that specific instance proceedings should be carried out 'in accordance with applicable law'.[36] In interpreting the rather vaguely formulated provisions of the Guidelines, parties to the NCP process can thus refer to external bodies of norms, including international soft law. As neither the Guidelines nor the Procedural Guidance set out how external norms should be brought to bear on the Guidelines, normative relationing between bodies of norms in the NCP process often has an ad hoc, even haphazard quality to it, relying on the discursive contributions of the various actors involved in specific instances. NCP case law thus provides a window into the still fuzzy, emerging structures of the postnational world of law in which actors

[33] OECD, 'Annual Report on the OECD Guidelines for Multinational Enterprises 2018' (2019) 35–6. For example, some NCPs are organised within a single ministry, others can involve multiple ministries or governmental agencies, and the most unusual ones could involve a multitude of stakeholders or be led by external experts.

[34] OECD, 'Guide for National Contact Points on Coordination When Handling Specific Instances' (2019), 4; 2011 edition OECD Guidelines, Procedural Guidance, Chapter I (C).

[35] OECD, 'Annual Report 2018', 34.

[36] 2011 edition OECD Guidelines, Procedural Guidance, Chapter I (C).

irreverently weave loose ties between non-hierarchically situated bodies of norms in new governance spaces.

The case studies in Sections 12.4.1–12.4.3 allow us to look through the window and see whether patterns and common dynamics can be identified. The study provides an overview of over 130 concluded NCP cases dating back to 2011 when the second revision of the Guidelines took place. The study also includes a number of pre-2011 cases which provide perspective on how the NCP system dealt with entanglement before the revision. It is important to note that the majority of submitted complaints are not resolved (a small number are withdrawn, many are rejected and a significant number of cases are concluded without a mediated agreement due to withdrawal by one of the parties).[37] Moreover, only in rare cases are NCPs willing to make assessments of non-compliance with the Guidelines in the absence of a joint/mediated agreement. The present study only focuses on those specific instances concluded by the NCPs (whether with or without a mediated agreement), thus excluding cases which were not accepted or are still pending.

The picture which emerges shows a nuanced approach to normative entanglement. While most complaints are concluded without references to external norms, interaction with other bodies of norms is not uncommon – some form of relationing was identified in around a quarter of the cases studied. A dominant feature apparent from the cases is the notion of different 'shades of entanglement', with NCP-specific instances which demonstrate distancing and proximity occupying opposite ends of the spectrum. Some of the examples cannot be clearly categorized as either but nevertheless prove informative regarding how participants in the NCP process construct the responsibilities of corporations under the Guidelines by reference to other bodies of norms and thus fall into a grey area somewhere in-between. However, even specific instances falling into a single category show different intensities of each dynamic and variation as to the 'commitment' by an NCP to distancing or proximity between bodies of norms. Thus, while the three main categories are useful from an analytical perspective, entanglement within the system of the OECD Guidelines is best understood as operating on a spectrum with different shades being present both between and within the two opposite ends of the distancing–proximity dichotomy.

[37] This is also true for this study – in the relevant period, only about half of the submitted specific instances were formally concluded.

12.4.1 Distancing

While distancing can be understood as a dynamic of interaction between bodies of norms and thus as a category of entanglement, it is a mechanism of relationing which is closest to the notion of separation. However, it does not solely perform the role of division. As Krisch notes in Chapter 1, distancing creates space between bodies of norms but it can also be strategically deployed to horizontalize the relationship between them and prevent the emergence of hierarchies.[38] It is necessary to keep this in mind when analysing distancing within the NCP system, as the overall approach adopted by NCPs is very subtle and indicates only limited attempts to distance other CSR frameworks. Notably, none of the cases studied here featured what could be classified as a clear effort at separation, that is, an explicit rejection by an NCP of another normative system as manifestly inapplicable or irrelevant in certain circumstances. This indicates straight away that the Guidelines are a relatively open system. However, it also means that we need to rely on implicit or hidden forms of distancing which can create ambiguous interpretations of the intentions behind them.

Arguably the strongest example of distancing is silence by an NCP in the face of claims by another party in a specific instance as to the applicability of a normative system.[39] Such a situation occurred in the *Salini Impregilo S.p.A.* (2016)[40] specific instance handled by the Italian NCP, in which the NGO Survival International Italia complained about the alleged human rights violations caused by the Gibe III dam construction, carried out by Salini in Ethiopia. The complaint, brought on behalf of affected Indigenous communities in Ethiopia and Kenya, relied on provisions of the African Charter on Human and People's Rights (ACHPR)[41] in apportioning blame on Salini for its failure to respect

[38] See Chapter 1, Section 1.4.3.

[39] In general, the research found only a handful of examples of distancing within the analysed cases but this may be a result of the methodology adopted which focuses only on final statements within the specific instance procedure. Thus, if a body of norms was identified as relevant within the earlier stages of a specific instance and the NCP subsequently remained silent on its interaction with the Guidelines in the final statement, it would fall outside of the scope of this research. This limitation means that the number of examples of distancing may be underrepresented.

[40] Italy NCP, *Survival International Italia* v. *Salini Impregilo S.p.A. (Final statement)* (8 June 2017).

[41] OAU, *African Charter on Human and Peoples' Rights* (adopted 27 June 1981, entered into force 21 October 1986) OAU Doc CAB/LEG/67/3 rev. 5.

human rights. In response to this, the company highlighted its membership of the UN Global Compact and adherence to a number of ISO standards and sustainability policies. However, none of these found its way into the examination carried out by the NCP nor into its final recommendations. By remaining silent on their relevance to the specific instance, the NCP can be seen as engaging in distancing and asserting the dominance of the Guidelines. Another example of distancing through silence occurred in *Triumph International* (2009).[42] In this specific instance, a coalition of labour unions and NGOs alleged that Triumph, a Swiss company, had not complied with the Guidelines' provisions concerning employment. Unable to successfully initiate mediation between the complainants and the company, the Swiss NCP concluded the specific instance. Although the complaint referred to various bodies of norms beyond the Guidelines, including the company's own CSR code of conduct and ILO documents, the NCP limited its analysis to the Guidelines in the final statement. The silence of the Swiss NCP with regard to assessing compliance with the OECD Guidelines in relation to external bodies of norms can thus be interpreted as a form of distancing.

Interestingly, both of these specific instances related to conduct which happened before 2011 and thus were decided on the basis of the pre-2011 Guidelines which contained only rudimentary human rights provisions. The NCPs' hesitant approach towards analysing compliance with regard to human rights – as evidenced by the Italian NCP's reluctance to engage with external norms, including the ACHPR, in *Salini* – was indicative of the uncertainty surrounding business and human rights at the time. Sticking to the status quo position might have represented the conservative choice for NCPs unsure of where and how to position the 2000 version of the Guidelines within the emerging business and human rights 'galaxy of norms'.[43]

12.4.2 The Grey Area

With the next category of cases, the approach taken by NCPs is even more ambiguous and moves away from efforts at distancing. The analysed cases can be seen as straddling a grey area between distancing and

[42] Switzerland NCP, *Specific Instance regarding Triumph in the Philippines and in Thailand (Final Statement)* (14 January 2011).

[43] E. Diggs, M. Regan and B. Parance, 'Business and Human Rights as a Galaxy of Norms' (2019) 50 *Georgetown Journal of International Law* 309–62.

proximity. Silence still plays a role here, but it has both an integrative and exclusionary function. The dynamic in these cases can be described as 'silent entanglement' – NCPs rely on particular norms (as opposed to bodies of norms) which are not clearly featured within the OECD Guidelines without referring to the framework in which the norm originated. This has been the approach adopted by the German NCP in the *NORDEX SE* (2014)[44] specific instance, which concerned a complaint by an individual against a German wind turbine supplier involved in a wind park energy project in Izmir, Turkey. The complainant pointed to general failures in the respondent's risk management, including insufficient due diligence and failure to carry out an environmental impact assessment – both concepts which can be found in the Guidelines. However, the measures recommended by the NCP and accepted by the respondent through the mediation procedure were more extensive. They included, among other things, the carrying out of environmental and social impact assessments which are distinct from EIAs and external to the Guidelines.[45] Despite recommending the use of a measure external to the OECD system, the NCP did not provide any indication as to its origin or contents, at least not publicly.

A similar process has occurred in relation to the concept of free, prior and informed consent (FPIC) under the auspices of the Swiss NCP, which utilized it on a couple of occasions without giving due consideration to its integration into the Guidelines. FPIC is not mentioned within the Guidelines, yet it was utilized in the *World Wildlife Fund for Nature International (WWF)* (2016)[46] specific instance. In 2016, Survival International filed a landmark complaint against WWF for adverse human rights impacts, including the establishment of protected areas without the free, prior and informed consent of the Baka, an Indigenous tribe in Cameroon. While mediation efforts failed, with the complainant withdrawing from the process, the NCP nevertheless issued a final statement and recommended to WWF 'to help ensure open and transparent FPIC processes in Cameroon'.[47] As with ESIAs in *NORDEX SE*, the NCP did not give any consideration to the pedigree of FPIC, again

[44] Germany NCP, *Dominic Whiting* v. *NORDEX SE (Final statement)* (31 August 2016).

[45] IFC Performance Standards are an example of a normative body which works with the concept of ESIAs.

[46] Switzerland NCP, *Survival International* v. *World Wide Fund for Nature International (Final statement)* (21 November 2017).

[47] *WWF*, p. 6.

engaging in silent entanglement. The Swiss NCP repeated this in the *Credit Suisse* (2017)[48] specific instance, brought in respect of the respondent's business relations with companies involved in the construction of the Dakota Access Pipeline. The mediation ended successfully, with a joint statement in which the respondent committed to incorporating FPIC within its sector-specific policies. While the NCP simply welcomed the respondent's adoption of FPIC, it is notable that there was not complete silence – Credit Suisse, quoting its modified internal policies, traced FPIC to the IFC Performance Standards and the UN Declaration on the Rights of Indigenous Peoples (UNDRIP).[49] If anything, however, this creates further confusion, as the silence by the NCP stands in contrast with the acknowledgement by the corporation. There are other plausible sources for the norm, notably ILO Convention 169[50] which, in contrast to the UNDRIP, is legally binding. Moreover, there is considerable disagreement as to whether FPIC represents a standalone right or should be treated more as an overarching principle, with differences in interpretation existing depending on the norm-system within which FPIC is being deployed.[51] In such circumstances, the potential problems caused by silent entanglement are further accentuated.

There is one more group of cases falling within the grey zone category, representing instances where an NCP acknowledged the relevance of other bodies of norms but does not say which ones it is referring to. In the *Atradius Dutch State Business* (2015)[52] specific instance, the NCP noted that the respondent had a duty to 'comply not only with national and regional laws and regulations, but also with relevant international norms and standards, including – but not limited to – the Guidelines', without specifying which norms and standards it considers as relevant.[53]

[48] Switzerland NCP, *Society for Threatened Peoples Switzerland (Final statement)* (16 October 2019).

[49] UNGA, *United Nations Declaration on the Rights of Indigenous Peoples* (adopted 2 October 2007) UN Doc A/RES/61/295.

[50] ILO, *Convention Concerning Indigenous and Tribal Peoples in Independent Countries* (adopted 27 June 1989, entered into force 5 September 1991) C169, Art. 16.

[51] B. O. Giupponi, 'Free, Prior and Informed Consent (FPIC) of Indigenous Peoples before Human Rights Courts and International Investment Tribunals: Two Sides of the Same Coin?' (2018) 25 *International Journal on Minority and Group Rights* 485–529.

[52] Netherlands NCP, *Both ENDS et al.* v. *Atradius Dutch State Business (Final statement)* (30 November 2016).

[53] Although in light of the mediation process, the details of which were mentioned in the final statement, it can be implied that 'relevant standards' referred to the UNGPs and IFC Performance standards.

Similarly, the UK NCP in the *ENRC* (2013)[54] specific instance noted that, in preparing its assessment, it 'consulted open sources for information on relevant international standards (including IFC performance standards and UN conventions and reports on human rights)'. Yet, when assessing the behaviour of the company, it only vaguely notes that '[i]nternational standards (including the OECD Guidelines) oblige companies to consider environmental and social aspects of projects throughout their life cycle'.[55] What standards other than the Guidelines the NCP is referring to remains unclear. The most sensible interpretation of what NCPs are doing here is interpreting the Guidelines as a system inherently open to entanglement, which is in line with the analysis of the development of the instrument in relation to other CSR norms in Section 12.3. This links us back again to the idea of resonance, with NCPs situating the Guidelines into a more extensive project of human rights protection which in turn can be understood as providing legitimacy.

12.4.3 Proximity

The specific instances just covered show that the analysis is steadily moving towards proximity between bodies of norms. Here, the existence of varying shades of entanglement is particularly pronounced. It can range from paying mere lip service to another framework by mentioning it in passing, all the way to a thorough analysis of another system's approach to an issue and the intricate weaving together of norms. The starting point here is those instances where entanglement is arguably unsurprising because the external body of norms referred to is 'integrated' or 'enmeshed' with the OECD Guidelines. The research then turns towards the arguably most interesting examples of entanglement: bodies of norms which are wholly external to the Guidelines.

12.4.3.1 Integrated Normative Systems

As noted earlier, some normative systems enjoy a privileged position in terms of their relationship with the Guidelines as they are explicitly mentioned in the text. The UN Guiding Principles as well as the ILO Tripartite Declaration on Multinational Enterprises stand out in this regard. However, just as with distancing and the intermediate category,

[54] UK NCP, *Rights and Accountability in Development (RAID)* v. *ENRC (Final statement)* (February 2017).

[55] *ENRC*, p. 15.

proximity also appears in shades. In some specific instances, NCPs simply note the alignment between the Guidelines and the other body of norms, as the French NCP did in *Michelin Group* (2012) where the UNGPs were mentioned as inspiration for the 2011 revision of the Guidelines.[56] On other occasions, alignment between the two standards is noted in the context of applying a particular rule. This can be seen in relation to the due diligence requirement of the UNGPs in the Danish *PWT Group* (2014).[57] Moreover, NCPs are not always the main drivers behind proximity and the relevance of other bodies of norms is raised by the parties to the complaint. This occurred in the Dutch NCP *Bralima and Heineken* (2015)[58] specific instance. Bralima, Heineken's Congolese subsidiary, was accused of labour misconduct in relation to the departure of a group of employees from its Bukavu brewery in the period between 1999–2003, when an open conflict was ongoing in the Democratic Republic of Congo. Given the historic nature of the complaint, the NCP only played a restricted role and facilitated discussions between the parties. With Heineken already having a human rights policy in place by the time of the specific instance, the NCP encouraged 'Heineken's commitment to continue working on an internal analysis of Heineken's existing policies and processes in the light of the Guidelines and the [UNGPs]'.[59] Another example is the *Norconsult AS* (2015) specific instance, which was resolved through mediation and via a joint statement between the complainants and respondent, endorsed by the Norwegian NCP. In the statement, the respondent committed to respect Indigenous peoples' rights in accordance with ILO Convention 169 and acknowledged the relevance of UNDRIP and the Universal Declaration of Human Rights (UDHR) for its internal human rights policies. It is interesting to see that parties to proceedings also push for proximity through the specific instance procedure – it highlights that the intertwined nature of CSR norms is not only something imposed from above.

Efforts at creating proximity can also take a much stronger form, such as an NCP extensively engaging with the substantive content of other bodies of norms. One example is the Dutch specific instance *VEON*

[56] France NCP, *Tamil Nadu Land Rights Federation* v. *Michelin (Final statement)* (29 February 2016).

[57] Denmark NCP, *Clean Clothes Campaign Denmark and Active Consumers* v. *PWT Group (Final Statement)* (17 October 2016).

[58] Netherlands NCP, *Former employees of Bralima* v. *Bralima and Heineken (Final statement)* (18 August 2017).

[59] *Bralima and Heineken*, p. 5.

(2016),[60] which focused on a labour dispute between VEON, its Bangladeshi subsidiary, and a trade union established at the Bangladeshi operations. The complainants claimed that VEON tried to suppress the employees' attempts to unionize. However, the respondents challenged this by stating that the trade union was illegitimate as it lacked registration with the Bangladeshi authorities – a mandatory requirement under the laws of Bangladesh, but in direct violation of the OECD Guidelines and ILO regulations. The NCP recognized the ILO's competence in this area, noting that 'the ILO has stated on many occasions that the stringent procedural conditions for the registration of trade unions in Bangladesh are not in line with international legislation and necessitate amendment of local legislation'.[61] It suggested to VEON 'to comply with international labour law standards to the fullest extent possible'.[62] In essence, entanglement was utilized here strategically by the NCP in order to assert the authority of a desirable outcome which might be seen as contrary to the requirements of domestic law. Another example of reliance on the substantive provisions is the Dutch *Bresser* (2017)[63] specific instance. The company, a specialist in object relocation, was responsible for the relocation of a fifteenth-century tomb as part of the construction of the Ilisu Dam in Turkey. The complainants claimed that Bresser failed to adequately consult the local population before moving the tomb, violating their right to culture. With the NCP noting that this was the first instance in which the right to culture has been the subject of an NCP procedure, it had to decide whether the matter comes under the scope of the Guidelines. It affirmatively did so, but only through reliance on Principle 12 of the UNGPs and its commentary, as well as Art. 15 of the International Covenant on Economic, Social and Cultural Rights and the UNESCO Declaration concerning the Intentional Destruction of Cultural Heritage.[64] The unexpected reliance on other bodies of norms in determining whether an issue comes within the ambit of the Guidelines underlines the strong proximity between the Guidelines and the integrated normative systems, in particular the UNGPs.

[60] Netherlands NCP, *UNI Global Union* v. *VEON (Final statement)* (11 February 2020).
[61] Ibid., p. 5.
[62] Ibid., p. 6.
[63] Netherlands NCP, *FIVAS, the Initiative to Keep Hasankeyf Alive and Hasankeyf Matters* v. *Bresser (Final statement)* (20 August 2018).
[64] *Bresser*, p. 4.

Moreover, the case also shows the tendency of NCPs to reach for norms depending on their suitability to the subject matter of the specific instance. This dynamic of 'specialization' is particularly common in instances of entanglement with more traditional normative systems, such as environmental or human rights law.[65] It also stands somewhat in contrast to how proximity is construed between the Guidelines and the UNGPs, with those interactions occurring pretty much universally regardless of the content of the proceedings. The UNGPs are usually utilized to provide detail to norms of a more procedural nature, such as due diligence or the concept of leverage, which find applicability regardless of the subject matter of a specific instance. In contrast, more traditional international law documents (but also ILO standards and, as will be seen, other external bodies of norms) are used more as precision tools to provide details on substantive issues which may relate to a particular right or a particular norm. For example, in the Danish *Greenpeas Enterprise ApS* (2013)[66] specific instance, Art. 8 of the International Covenant on Civil and Political Rights (ICCPR) (prohibition on forced and compulsory labour) was invoked by the NCP in a case addressing the retention of workers' passports against their will, creating 'conditions that can be associated with slavery'.[67] Similarly, in *Mercer PR* (2016),[68] the Australian NCP identified the right to privacy, as contained in Art. 12 of the UDHR and Art. 17 of the ICCPR, as relevant in a specific instance in which a small Australian company distributed personal information concerning an alleged sexual assault.

12.4.3.2 Wholly External Bodies of Norms

Instances of creating proximity between bodies of norms are not only restricted to those standards which are explicitly featured within the OECD Guidelines – entanglement between the Guidelines and wholly external bodies of norms is common. As the following cases show, NCPs adopt a very flexible interpretation of relevant frameworks, treating as

[65] As far as 'traditional' human rights norms are concerned, the specialisation dynamic can lead to the entanglement of norms which are not explicitly mentioned within the Guidelines. This is as a feature of the text of the Guidelines which allows for the consideration of additional human rights standards depending on the subject matter which they address – see 2011 edition of the Guidelines, Chapter IV commentary at [40].

[66] Denmark NCP, *3F* v. *Greenpeas Enterprise APS (Final Statement)* (14 August 2014).

[67] Ibid., p. 6.

[68] Australian NCP, *Australian Women Without Borders* v. *Mercer PR (Final statement)* (9 July 2019).

'applicable law' not only international soft law, but also private agreements and regulatory initiatives of a completely private nature. In addition to having the consequence of 'lumping together' typologically different bodies of norms with little nuance as to their bindingness, such entanglement can have a major legitimizing effect for the external systems due to the meta-regulatory stature of the Guidelines. In some ways, this category of specific instances most closely demonstrates the notion of entanglement as the cases often work with multiple bodies of norms and create linkages between them in an unexpected, even irreverent manner, weaving together a multidimensional web of CSR regulation.

Arguably a more doctrinally conservative collection of cases is represented by those specific instances displaying proximity between the Guidelines and international normative systems developed within international organizations or as a result of agreement between states, and such a dynamic predates the 2011 revision of the Guidelines. In *Vedanta Resources PLC* (2008), Survival International submitted a complaint with the UK NCP concerning Vedanta's planned construction of a bauxite mine in Orissa, India.[69] Survival alleged that Vedanta's operations were inconsistent with the Guidelines and drew on international environmental law and human rights law to substantiate the claims. In coming to its conclusions that the company had indeed breached the Guidelines, the NCP emphasized the rights of Indigenous peoples under international law, 'including the [ICCPR], the UN Convention on the Elimination of All Forms of Racial Discrimination, the Convention on Biological Diversity and the UN Declaration on the Rights of Indigenous People'.[70] The NCP also found that Vedanta had not engaged in adequate community consultation, interpreting the provision in light of the 2004 Akwé Kon Guidelines produced by the Secretariat of the Convention on Biological Diversity.[71] Thus, the NCP found that the company had breached the Guidelines by reference to an international soft law produced by the secretariat of a multilateral environmental agreement with no formal linkage to them. A post-2011 example is the Dutch *ING* (2017)[72] specific instance, which represented a broad challenge to the respondent's overall climate policy. The claimants

[69] UK NCP, *Survival International* v. *Vedanta Resources plc (Final statement)* (25 September 2009).

[70] Ibid., p. 1.

[71] Ibid., pp. 17–19.

[72] Netherlands NCP, *Oxfam Novib et al.* v. *ING (Final statement)* (19 April 2019).

specifically required ING to report its indirect carbon emissions, accrued through its loans and investments. Despite the broadly framed complaint, the NCP managed to secure cooperation from the respondent and, in doing so, entangled the freshly negotiated Paris international climate agreement into the Guidelines.[73] Not only was the Paris Agreement identified as relevant, but ING agreed to utilize the methodologies of the Paris Agreement in 'measuring, target setting and steering the bank's climate impact'.[74] This indicates another layer to the 'specialization' dynamic, as the international norm might have been chosen not only because of its closeness to the subject matter, but also because it provides effective and appropriate methodologies and solutions which the respondent could incorporate within its CSR policies.

However, coupling also happens with bodies of norms which are not normally considered law or which might originate outside of a state-centric environment, and again this is not limited only to the post-2011 version of the Guidelines. In *Intex Resources ASA and the Mindoro Nickel Project* (2009),[75] the complaint concerned alleged violations of the human and environmental rights of Indigenous peoples that would be affected by Intex Resources' planned nickel mine and factory in the Philippines. The Norwegian NCP concluded that the company had, inter alia, failed to properly consult the affected groups, thus breaching the Guidelines. As Intex had previously declared its adherence to the IFC Social and Environmental Performance standards and the Equator Principles, the Norwegian NCP repeatedly drew on the content of those standards when determining whether the company had complied with the Guidelines' recommendation 'to consider the views of other stakeholders'. In addition, the NCP referred to the UNDRIP, ILO Convention 169 in order to interpret and 'flesh out' the recommendations of the Guidelines.[76] In this instance, the NCP made full use of the in-text references to other bodies of norms in the Guidelines, as well as the fact that the company itself had proclaimed adherence to the IFC Performance standards.

[73] Ibid., p. 3.

[74] Ibid., p. 4.

[75] Norway NCP, *Future in Our Hands (FIOH)* v. *Intex Resources ASA* (*Final Statement*) (28 November 2011).

[76] Ibid., p. 21 *et seq*.

In the *KiK Textilien und Non-Food GmbH, C&A Mode GmbH & Co., and Karl Rieker GmbH & Co. KG* (2013)[77] specific instance, the German NCP provided an illustration of how private agreements can be entangled. The case concerned a fire at the Tazreen Fashion factory in Dhaka, Bangladesh, in November 2012. The complainant asserted that the respondent companies were jointly responsible for the fire because they continued to produce clothing at the site, even though an independent safety assessment carried out in 2011 found that safety measures were inadequate. All three enterprises were producing clothes in the factory indirectly through subcontractors. While the complaint against C&A was forwarded to the Brazilian NCP,[78] the German NCP did investigate the allegations against KiK and Karl Rieker. It did not consider the two respondents' direct liability for the fire to be substantiated, however, as both companies proved that they discontinued production at Tazreen Fashion over six months before the fire.[79] The NCP did initiate mediation proceedings for the part of the claim which concerned breaches of the duty of care in relation to the safety measures within the factory. As part of the mediation, the NCP and the parties relied upon the Bangladesh Safety Accord to which KiK and Karl Rieker were both signatories. While all parties were supportive of the measures taken as part of the Accord, it is interesting that these were not deemed to be sufficient and the NCP recommended other supplementary measures.[80] The dialectic deployed in the mediation shows that entanglement in a single case can be nuanced, with efforts to increase proximity but also to distance norms and create hierarchy. Entanglement can thus be used to further both legitimization and delegitimization. The parties and the NCP embraced the measures of the Accord, recognizing it as relevant. Yet, at the same time, the NCP limited its legitimacy by stating that the Guidelines require supplementary measures to be taken. In doing so, it reinforced the meta-regulatory status of the Guidelines and provided a hint as to the emergence of a hierarchy between the two bodies of norms.

A very similar dynamic can be seen in the *Rabobank* (2014)[81] specific instance, in which the Dutch NCP considered the respondent's provision

[77] Germany NCP, *Uwe Kekeritz* v. *KiK Textilien und Non-Food GmbH, C&A Mode GmbH & Co., and Karl Rieker GmbH & Co. KG (Final statement)* (November 2014).

[78] As a result of the legal structures of C&A's operations in Bangladesh at the time, the entity responsible in this case was the Brazilian subsidiary of C&A.

[79] *KiK Textilien*, pp. 3–4.

[80] *KiK Textilien*, p. 6.

[81] Netherlands NCP, *Friends of the Earth* v. *Rabobank (Final statement)* (15 January 2016).

of loans to the Indonesian palm oil company Bumitama. Interestingly, a central part of the complaint became obsolete during the proceedings, as Bumitama terminated the contract for the plantation which formed the primary subject of the complaint. Nevertheless, the Dutch NCP considered that some parts of the complaint still merited further consideration, allowing it to analyse more generally Rabobank's policy in relation to palm oil supply chains. A core part of this assessment was devoted to Rabobank's membership of the Roundtable for Sustainable Palm Oil (RSPO), which is a global multi-stakeholder sustainability initiative. A company wishing to become a member of the RSPO (and thus be able to use the RSPO trademark ecolabel) has to undergo a certification process, which itself is based on another set of private principles for sustainability standards – the International Social and Environmental Accreditation and Labelling (ISEAL) Alliance Credibility Principles, which perform a meta-regulatory role within the sustainability standards sector. By engaging the RSPO, the Dutch NCP is, possibly unknowingly, entangling the Guidelines with two layers of normative systems. Proximity within this specific instance takes the form of the NCP's cautious optimism about the RSPO in stating that its grievance mechanism and commitment to a multi-stakeholder approach can be seen as good practice within the palm oil production sector.[82] However, the NCP also notes the need for the respondent to develop its own practices beyond the RSPO, even suggesting disengagement as an option of last resort.

Thus, just as in the previous specific instance, we can identify a dual dynamic of both proximity and distancing with an external standard. On one hand, the NCP legitimizes the body of norms as a good practice, on the other, it delegitimizes it by encouraging the respondent to look beyond. The sense of hierarchy emerging between the Guidelines and the RSPO is further reinforced by the fact that in *RSPO* (2018),[83] a complaint was brought directly against the Roundtable before the Swiss NCP for the alleged failures of its complaint mechanism in dealing with a land dispute between local communities in Indonesia and one of its member companies. While the NCP was limited to the role of a mediator and did not directly draw upon an external standard, the specific instance is notable for the way in which it interacts with the RSPO as an external

[82] Ibid., p. 4.

[83] Switzerland NCP, *TuK Indonesia* v. *Roundtable for Sustainable Palm Oil (Final statement)* (5 June 2019).

system. The NCP carries out a somewhat supervisory role, relying on its own leverage over the RSPO to push the sustainability standard itself towards compatibility with the Guidelines. Thus, proximity and distancing both seem to be present, drawing the bodies of norms closer but also alluding to a hierarchy between them and, in doing so, demonstrating another shade of the complexity of entanglement.

The *Bresser* specific instance and a number of others have already shown NCPs drawing on multiple bodies of norms in one proceeding. The final part of this section focuses on three specific instances featuring this dynamic which were brought within the UK NCP system. These arguably represent the strongest examples of proximity, invoking multiple normative systems and showing extensive interaction by the NCP. The first specific instance is *GCM Resources plc* (2012),[84] concerning plans by the respondent to develop a mine in Bangladesh. The complaint dates back to 2004 when GCM Resources began the planning and consultation process for the mine. However, the company's activities were still effectively incomplete and on hold at the time of the complaint. Thus, parts of the specific instance were handled under the 2000 version as well as the 2011 version of the Guidelines. The respondent had undertaken an ESIA as part of its planning and consultation process which the NCP considered in light of the standards applied by the World Bank and the IFC. While the NCP acknowledged that the self-regulatory practices adopted by GCM Resources and based on the IFC standards were sufficient, it pointed out inadequacies in relation to the respondent's communication of its plans to affected communities.[85] In relation to adverse human rights impacts before September 2011, the NCP noted that the UNGPs were available to businesses from 2010 and also that human rights concerns were incorporated in the IFC standards. The NCP also noted the 'company's plans recognise the ILO standard on Indigenous Peoples'.[86] When considering activities happening after September 2011, the NCP reiterated the relevance of the UNGPs and highlighted the applicability a new set of IFC Performance Standards, issued in 2012. The NCP also noted that the respondent's updated plans will have to consider the right to FPIC, as contained within UNDRIP.[87]

[84] UK NCP, *International Accountability Project and World Development Movement v. GCM Resources plc (Final statement)* (November 2014).

[85] Ibid., p. 13.

[86] Ibid., p. 15.

[87] Ibid., p. 18.

The *GCM Resources plc* specific instance underscores that engagement with human rights norms intensified in the post-2011 Guidelines, but also shows that human rights considerations were clearly present even before. Interestingly, the NCP indicated that the IFC Performance Standards played a major role in this regard. The way in which the concepts of ESIA and FPIC were treated is also notable – in contrast to the examples of silent entanglement in *NORDEX SE*, *WWF* or *Credit Suisse*, the UK NCP in *GCM Resources plc* was very explicit about connecting ESIA with the IFC Performance standards and FPIC with UNDRIP. This again shows that entanglement is nuanced, with proximity being a more dominant dynamic in the UK context.

The second UK-specific instance to consider is *G4S plc* (2013),[88] which also concerned actions spanning both the 2000 and 2011 versions of the Guidelines. The complaint was addressed against the respondent's provision and maintenance of security equipment (CCTV, baggage scanners) at Israeli checkpoints within the Palestinian occupied territory and within Israeli prisons. At the outset of its fact-finding, the NCP noted the relevance of the 2004 International Court of Justice (ICJ) *Israeli Wall Advisory Opinion*[89] and the UK's acceptance of the advisory opinion.[90] In contrast to *GCM Resources plc*, the NCP predominantly focused on the respondent's human rights obligations after 2011, putting the UNGPs under the spotlight and drawing extensively on their provisions, especially those in regard to the termination of a business relationship.[91] Private standards were also engaged – the NCP recognized the relevance of the International Code of Conduct for Private Security Providers, 'of which G4S was a founder signatory in 2010'.[92] However, the NCP also explicitly dismissed another private initiative suggested by G4S (Voluntary Principles on Security and Human rights) as it was principally relevant to the sectors of mining and energy.[93] Showcasing both proximity and distancing, the approach in *G4S plc* is another good example of the specialization dynamic mentioned earlier.

[88] UK NCP, *Lawyers for Palestinian Human Rights (LPHR)* v. *G4s plc (Final statement)* (March 2015).

[89] *Legal Consequences of the Construction of a Wall in the Occupied Palestinian Territory (Advisory Opinion)* [2004] ICJ Rep 136.

[90] Such as the FCO Overseas Business Risk and FCO Human Rights and Democracy reports. *G4S plc*, p. 11.

[91] Ibid., p. 13.

[92] Ibid., p. 14.

[93] Ibid.

Finally, the *KPO Consortium* (2013)[94] instance involved a consortium of companies from three OECD member countries (Italy, the UK and the USA) operating an oil and gas production facility in Kazakhstan. After mutual agreement between the relevant NCPs, the UK NCP took care of handling the complaint and engaged KPO as a single entity. The adverse human rights impacts arose in relation to two households located within a protective zone around KPO's facility and who were consequently entitled to resettlement and compensation. Just as before, the issues were of a long-term nature, dating back to the 1990s and potentially involving three different versions of the Guidelines. The UK NCP changed tack from the previous specific instances by ingeniously applying the extensive human rights provisions of the 2011 Guidelines even to situations where the adverse impact arose before 1 September 2011 but was still ongoing.[95] This enabled the UK NCP to draw on the UNGPs and their predecessor, the UN Protect, Respect and Remedy Framework.[96] The IFC Performance Standards were also considered relevant, as KPO received a loan from the IFC, making their provisions directly applicable to the project.[97] The UK NCP went into some detail in considering how the IFC's standard for involuntary resettlement applied to the situation, noting that the situation wasn't a typical case for the IFC standard but that KPO should have nevertheless applied it as good practice.[98]

The three specific instances show that the UK NCP's approach is closest in resemblance to a more traditional, adversarial method of adjudication.[99] Maheandiran suggests that the nature of the approach adopted by an NPC can have an impact on the objectives and structure of the specific instance procedure.[100] It can be argued that this is also true for the dynamics of entanglement, with the UK approach showing the most extensive entanglement with multiple bodies of norms. As a consequence of establishing liability within its approach, the UK NCP necessarily considers the applicability of particular norms and systems in

[94] UK NCP, *Crude Accountability* v *KPO Consortium (Final statement)* (November 2017).

[95] Ibid., p. 9.

[96] *KPO Consortium*, p. 16.

[97] Ibid., p. 16. In fact, the complainant NGO even utilized the IFC's complaints system before resorting to the NCP procedure.

[98] Ibid., p. 18.

[99] B. Maheandiran, 'Calling for Clarity: How Uncertainty Undermines the Legitimacy of the Dispute Resolution System under the OECD Guidelines for Multinational Enterprises' (2015) 20 *Harvard Negotiation Law Review* 205–44.

[100] Ibid., pp. 227–37.

detailed fashion. This can seem counterintuitive, as a more traditional adjudication mechanism would probably draw clear lines between bodies of norms in an effort to determine the applicable law, thus moving closer towards distancing and possibly separation of systems. Yet the same dynamic within the open system of the Guidelines appears to go in the opposite direction and increase proximity between bodies of norms.

12.5 Implications and Observations

The open formulation of the OECD Guidelines gives ample room for NCPs to resort to external bodies of norms and to position themselves in the context of a broader and evolving discourse around CSR. As shown in Sections 12.3 and 12.4, the openness of the Guidelines has increased over time, creating structural opportunities for entanglement. However, as demonstrated by the specific instances covered, the NCP procedures are incredibly varied and have the effect of producing a web of entanglement. An NCP's understanding of its own role or its organizational structure and available resources can affect the degree to which it is willing to promote entanglement with external norms. The more restricted an NCP's understanding of the scope of the Guidelines and its role in the complaints process, the more reluctant it will be to make a compliance assessment. In contrast, as has been demonstrated in the last three UK-specific instances, an NCP that perceives its role as more than being a simple mediator will be more inclined to take a proactive approach in assessing the validity of a complaint which can increase the likelihood of entanglement.

Variety is not limited to NCPs only, as the parties to the proceedings have also been shown to drive entanglement. The broad formulation of who can initiate a specific instance procedure and the diverse range of entities which have found themselves in the position of respondents[101] means that an extensive group of actors can bring their perspective (and the bodies of norms to which they adhere) to the table. And, as the specific instances of *Bralima and Heineken* or *Norconsult AS* highlight, NCPs are often willing to endorse entanglement driven by the parties. Additionally, the form and substance of (external) norms also affect the likelihood of entanglement. For example, the World Heritage Convention as a 'list-based treaty' invites entanglement more readily

[101] Corporations, but also state-owned enterprises, state ministries, institutional investors and even sustainability standard bodies and NGOs.

than framework conventions such as the Convention on Biological Diversity, which does not have a clearly defined scope and contains only general provisions.[102]

Indeed, the categorization of specific instances adopted within this chapter can be deceptive, as it simplifies a very nuanced picture of entanglement in which multiple dynamics can be present in a single case. Even examples of the same dynamic can take various forms and can be framed in different terms, with different language corresponding to the different shades of entanglement. The UK-specific instances are again informative in this regard. In *GCM Resources* and *G4S*, when the NCP considered a particular norm or standard as applicable, it would often (but not exclusively) use the phrase 'the NCP notes' and then refer to the relevant provision in question, possibly engaging with it in more detail. The *KPO* instance stands in contrast to this, with the wording of 'notes' and a particular norm being much less used, and has been largely replaced by two separate subsections within the specific instance ('Applicable Standards' and 'Guidance Available on Human Rights') which include the majority (but, again, not all) of the standards referred to. Given that *KPO* represents a more recent instance, the change might indicate a move towards more systematization in engagement with norms external to the Guidelines. Another NCP to draw upon is the Dutch one, which has also utilized the combination 'note'/'notice' and a particular norm on occasions,[103] but has also relied on other formulations such as 'in light of'[104] a particular system, especially when it makes recommendations as to the conduct expected of a respondent. In general, some formulations are becoming standardized but the shades of entanglement are really characterized by diversity, mirroring the Guidelines' system, and maybe some indifference by the NCPs as to the language they use.

This indifference is also visible in the way in which NCPs treat bodies of norms with different legal status. Across the specific instances, one can see a strong tendency to 'lump together' systems and standards with little consideration for their legal authority or the manner in which they apply to a respondent in NCP proceedings. The issue seems to be partly structural. While the Guidelines in their chapter on concepts and

[102] N. Affolder, 'The Market for Treaties' (2010) 11 *Chicago Journal of International Law* 159–96, at 185.

[103] See e.g. *VEON*, *ING*.

[104] See e.g. *Heineken*.

principles differentiate between 'applicable laws' on the one hand and 'internationally recognised standards' on the other,[105] thus prima facie recognizing the distinction between law in the strict sense of the word and other bodies of norms, in other parts of the Guidelines the distinction is much more fluid. For example, the chapter on human rights lumps together binding treaties and non-binding declarations without differentiating between them. It is thus unsurprising to see NCPs being indifferent in this regard, such as in *Norconsult AS* or *Vedanta Resources PLC*, where the NCPs drew on the non-binding UNDRIP and Akwé Kon Guidelines. This is particularly problematic when the NCP works with a number of bodies of norms with different levels of bindingness. A similar concern is the application of norms which are not addressed to corporations in the first place, but rather to states. Of course, the Guidelines do provide a sort of transpositionary function in this regard, yet it is still surprising to see that NCPs pay very little consideration as to how normative systems developed for application in a state-centric (and thus very different) context can be applied to corporations. Thus, while instances of entanglement between transnational CSR norms and international law may strengthen the coherence of global law through active coordination by the Guidelines, this may also lead to adverse effects as to the integrity and normative force of international law. In this regard, Affolder has drawn attention to how 'corporate adoption and translation of treaty norms' may 'ultimately undermine a treaty's goals' as companies 'cherry-pick among treaty provisions, interpret treaty commitments in their least onerous forms, and obscure the ways in which corporate activities impede treaty implementation by selectively reporting on instances where corporate policies and actions advance treaty norms'.[106] From the evidence, it seems that NCPs might be complicit in allowing corporations to do so through a mere lack of diligence within the specific instance procedure.

The laxness in the NCPs' approach might be partially attributed to the perceived lack of enforceability and compliance with the specific instance procedure.[107] As the Guidelines are soft law and the specific instances do not create legal obligations or benefit from formalized enforceability,

[105] 2011 edition of the Guidelines, chapter I [1].
[106] Affolder, 'The Market for Treaties', 162.
[107] A. Marx and J. Wouters, 'Rule Intermediaries in Global Labor Governance' (2017) 670 *The ANNALS of the American Academy of Political and Social Science* 189–206, at 195.

NCPs can feel induced to be 'generous' with the application of bodies of norms to a particular context. However, they would be well advised to exercise caution in this regard as the decisions reached within a specific instance are hardly inconsequential. As Nieuwenkamp highlights, the exercise of pressure by civil society, making diplomatic protection conditional upon compliance, or the consideration of specific instances in decisions on the availability of export credits are only some of the ways in which the Guidelines can have a major impact on corporate behaviour.[108] In fact, some elements of the Guidelines are already undergoing a process of 'hardening' by being transposed into domestic legislation, such as in the case of the due diligence obligation within the US Dodd–Frank Act which uses the Guidelines' provisions as a reference point.[109]

Finally, it is notable what a prominent role has been assumed by straddling practices within NCP proceedings, and in particular the concept of due diligence. In the post-2011 specific instances analysed in this chapter, the due diligence obligation of the respondent has been invoked in the vast majority of cases. In the NCP system, due diligence has outgrown the image of an import from the UNGPs and it is being construed as inherent to the Guidelines. Such blurring of the origins of the norm, coupled with its application in non-human rights-specific contexts, provides attestation to its quality as a straddling practice which distorts the boundaries of individual normative systems. The OECD system doesn't only apply the due diligence principle, it also develops it further, going as far as producing a number of guiding documents for the carrying out of due diligence.[110] A similar dynamic can be identified in relation to ESIAs and the concept of FPIC, with the examples of silent entanglement identified showing that the norms are being interpreted as cross-cutting norms and not necessarily 'belonging' to a single normative system. Thus, straddling practices are emerging as one of the tools of entanglement within the system of the Guidelines.

[108] Nieuwenkamp, 'The OECD Guidelines for Multinational Enterprises on Responsible Business Conduct', 174.

[109] Ibid., 175; Cullen, 'The Irresistible Rise of Human Rights Due Diligence', 744.

[110] E.g. OECD, 'OECD Due Diligence Guidance for Responsible Business Conduct' (2018); or OECD, 'OECD Due Diligence Guidance for Responsible Supply Chains in the Garment and Footwear Sector' (2017).

12.6 Conclusion

At the outset of this chapter, the inherent pluralism within the regime of CSR regulation of business conduct was noted as a dominant feature. Even though the analysis zoomed in on one particular focal point for entanglement, the OECD Guidelines, multiplicity and variation did not leave the picture. Instead, the system of the Guidelines can be still characterized by a plurality of bodies of norms which are the target of engagement and a plurality of shades of entanglement. Thus, in a sense the OECD Guidelines are reflective of the dynamic which exists in the wider world of CSR normativity. As the section dealing with coordinated legal entanglement has shown, the openness of the Guidelines can be attributed to the structural features of the system which provide the necessary flexibility for the interaction with other bodies of norms. Moreover, the manner in which the UNGPs were integrated into the Guidelines shows that these structural features are not accidental – rather, they represent deliberate decisions to create linkages between CSR systems, arguably motivated by the potential benefits which accrue from cooperation between bodies of norms within the field of CSR.

If the provisions of the Guidelines lay the groundwork for extensive entanglement, the implementation mechanism of NCPs does a very good job in building up the rest of the structure. It is in Section 12.4 where the true scope of entanglement within the system of the Guidelines is demonstrated. Although the dialectic of distancing and proximity is utilized in order to frame the discussion, Section 12.4 illustrates that the identified shades of entanglement are often not easily subsumed within either of the main categories mentioned. This is exacerbated by the fact that entanglement often happens with multiple bodies of norms at once. Overall, NCPs appear to be more likely to engage other bodies of norms in ways which enhance proximity between them, often creating irreverent linkages with both public and private frameworks. While some bodies of norms are relied upon in general contexts, other external norms are used as specialized precision tools when their provisions are closely related to the subject matter of a specific instance. The use of certain norms is characterized by silence as to the normative system in which they originate, underlining their status as straddling practices which can span across multiple bodies of norms. On the distancing end of the spectrum, we saw only limited efforts at drawing borders between systems – instead, efforts at distancing were utilized to hierarchically position the Guidelines against other bodies of norms or as instances of the specialization dynamic. Despite such efforts, however, the picture of CSR which emerges is certainly not of a top-down, integrated system, but rather one which is best defined as a polycentric and multilayered web of bodies of norms.

PART IV

Situating Entanglements

13

Entangled Legalities beyond the (Byzantine) State

Towards a User Theory of Jurisdiction

CAROLINE HUMFRESS

13.1 Introduction

> At the outset, I ask the historian to look upon Indian America as a Middle Ages which was missing its Rome: a confused mass that emerged from an ancient syncretism, which was without doubt very loosely textured, that had contained within itself at one and the same time, for many centuries, centres of advanced civilisation and savage peoples, centralizing tendencies and disruptive forces.[1]

In 1964, the French social anthropologist and exponent of structuralism, Claude Lévi-Strauss, published volume one of his celebrated series *Mythologiques: Le Cru et le Cuit*, translated into English in 1969 as *The Raw and the Cooked.* In the volume's introductory chapter, Lévi-Strauss offered an explanation of the group nature of the Amerindian myths analysed in the volume. With his arresting image of Indian America before the ages of European conquest as 'a Middle Ages which was missing its Rome', Lévi-Strauss invoked a – seemingly eternal – idea of 'Rome' as a source of order and normativity. For Lévi-Strauss, the structure of Amerindian mythologies differed from those of medieval Europe because there was no 'Rome' – neither empire nor Church – to act as a centralizing, structuring, unifying force. Nonetheless, as Lévi-Strauss' *Mythologiques* set out to prove, there *was* structure to the

[1] C. Lévi-Strauss, *Mythologiques: Le Cru et le Cuit* (Plon, 1964), p. 16 (own translation): 'On commencera donc par inviter l'historien à voir, dans l'Amérique indienne, un Moyen âge auquel aurait manqué sa Rome: masse confuse, elle-même issue d'un vieux synrétisme dont la texture fut sans doute très lâche, et au sein de lacquelle subsistèrent çà et là, pendant plusiers siècles, des foyers de haute civilisation et des peuples barbares, des tendances centralisatrices et des forces de morcellement.'

seemingly 'confused mass' of Amerindian myth.[2] I begin with Lévi-Strauss and his vision of 'a Middle Ages which was missing its Rome' in order to problematize the idea of centralized authority itself. More specifically, this chapter challenges the seemingly natural idea, typified here by Lévi-Strauss, that the presence of a Rome – or a Brussels, or a United Nations, or even a UNIDROIT – implies the development of a centralized, hierarchical model through which various, heteronomous, normative orders politely interact.

'Rome' here performs as shorthand for the deceptively complex idea that law and governance should be understood primarily in the context of *imperium*: the power to command. As Karen Alter states: 'Most people presume that law is only meaningful when backed by a central enforcer.'[3] Hence for much of the twentieth century, in the absence of a 'world state', international relations could be conceptualized as operating outside the domain of law. Since 1989 the number of international courts has more than quadrupled in number from six to over twenty-four – resulting in the collective issuing of over 37,000 binding legal rulings in individual contentious cases.[4] Yet even this intensified judicialization of the international arena still tends to be framed by a persistent 'image of law beyond the nation state as a weak ordering and regulatory system, rather than a constitutive element in the ongoing tumble of transnational life'.[5] The field of private international law – 'the legal discipline that determines in which cases a court must apply a foreign law' – also rests on a paradigm of Westphalian state governance.[6] Private international law 'does not lay out substantive rules for such situations, but merely resolves

[2] Ibid., p. 11: 'Des filaments épars se soudent, des lacunes se comblent, des connexions s'établissent, quelque chose qui ressemble à un ordre transparait derrière le chaos. Comme autour d'une molécule germinale, des séquences rangées en groupes de transformations viennent s'agréger au groupe intial, reproduisant sa structure et ses déterminations. Un corps multi-dimensionnel nâit, dont les parties centrales dévoilent l'organisation alors que l'incercitude et la confusion règnent encore au portour.'

[3] K. J. Alter, *The New Terrain of International Law: Courts, Politics, Rights* (Princeton University Press, 2014), p. 3.

[4] Ibid., p. 3.

[5] D. Kennedy, 'Law in Global Political Economy: Now You See It, Now You Don't', in P. F. Kjaer (ed.), *The Law of Political Economy: Transformation in the Function of Law* (Cambridge University Press, 2020), pp. 127–51, at p. 128.

[6] Quotation from R. Michaels, 'What Is Non-state Law? A Primer', in M. A. Helfand (ed.), *Negotiating State and Non-state Law: The Challenge of Global and Local Legal Pluralism* (Cambridge University Press, 2015), pp. 41–58, at p. 55. On 'the peace of Westphalia' (1648) and the emergence of the modern state as 'an international subject' see A. Cassese, 'States: Rise and Decline of the Primary Subjects of the International Community', in

conflicts between the legal orders themselves', relying on relevant domestic choice-of-law principles and rules in order to resolve legal disputes with a foreign element.[7] As Neil Walker notes, choice-of-law rules 'and the interpretative aids of transnational law do not "stand above" the domestic systems in which they are applied. Rather, they are formulated or interpreted each in the context of their own system – in deference to and under the self-validating terms prescribed by each domestic legal order's sovereign authority.'[8] Notwithstanding the 'equality' between different domestic legal orders, the system of private international law prioritizes national sovereignty and is grounded within a hierarchical – in a Kelsenian sense – approach to international governance.

In contrast, the 'postnational' approach, as defined by Nico Krisch in his 2010 *Beyond Constitutionalism: The Pluralist Structure of Postnational Law* and further developed by the 'Entangled Legalities' project underlying this volume, argues that 'national' and 'international' law are interwoven to such an extent within the supranational legal order that norms and principles from both spheres interact heterarchically: 'operating side-by-side without the presumptive authority of one over the other'.[9] Like Lévi-Strauss' pre-conquest Amerindian myths, there is no centre or hierarchy (no 'Rome') to structure postnational law. Nonetheless, again like Lévi-Strauss' account of Amerindian myth-making, there is a structure at work: 'the nation-state itself shares ultimate authority with multiple regional and international legal orders with which it interacts without a common normative framework – hence a post-national law within a pluralist structure'.[10] Instead of mapping the contours of an emerging global constitutional framework in which

B. Fassbender and A. Peters (eds), *The Oxford Handbook of the History of International Law* (Oxford University Press, 2012), pp. 49–69.

[7] R. Michaels, 'A Symmetry of Asymmetries? A Private-International-Law Reconstruction of Lindahl's Work on Boundaries' (2019) 29 *Duke Journal of Comparative and International Law* 405–22, at 410.

[8] N. Walker, 'Beyond Boundary Disputes and Basic Grids: Mapping the Global Disorder of Normative Orders' (2008) 6 (3–4) *International Journal of Constitutional Law* 373–96, at 377.

[9] C. Mac Amlaigh, 'Pluralising Constitutional Pluralism', in N. Roughan and A. Halpin (eds), *In Pursuit of Pluralist Jurisprudence* (Cambridge University Press, 2017), pp. 64–89, at p. 68.

[10] G. Shaffer, 'A Transnational Take on Krisch's Pluralist Postnational Law' (2012) 23 *The European Journal of International Law* 565–82, at 566 (review of N. Krisch, *Beyond Constitutionalism: The Pluralist Structure of Postnational Law* (Oxford University Press, 2010)).

overarching principles govern relations between different normative orders, this volume's project seeks to reimagine the global legal order 'through the paradigm of entangled legalities':

> In short, we advance a view of global legal order that dissociates itself from the idea of law as a hierarchical system. In its place, we envision global law as having a fluid, network-like structure [. . .] the Interface Law Project proposes the concept of *interface norms* that structure *fluid and shifting* relations between different bodies of norms. Interface law (or law at the interfaces) allows us to isolate and describe the form and substance of these interactions through which the global legal order is being negotiated, constructed and contested, as well as enabling us to catch glimpses of the social practices shaping these processes.[11]

We shall return to the idea of interface norms structuring 'fluid and shifting relations between different bodies of norms' in greater detail in Section 13.2. For the moment, we should simply note that the 'postnational space seems to demand new, different, answers to the question of how to structure governance'.[12]

Rafael Domingo has recently argued, in the context of 'global constitutionalism', that if the future of the supranational legal order is post-sovereigntist, postnationalist and postpositivist, 'Roman law was, so to speak, *pre* all of them: presovereigntist, prenationalist, and prepositivist'.[13] Most legal historians would agree, however, that there was something akin to 'international law' in Greco-Roman antiquity (and in earlier antiquity too): a rule of law that governed relations between states, alongside the use of brute force.[14] Historians of Greco-Roman 'international law' tend to focus predominately on the laws of war and

11 L. L. Reimers and F. Corradini, 'The Entanglement of Global Legal Order', *The Global* (9 July 2018), https://theglobal.blog/2018/07/09/the-entanglement-of-global-legal-order/.

12 Krisch, *Beyond Constitutionalism*, 69.

13 R. Domingo, 'Roman Law and Global Constitutionalism' (2019) 21 *San Diego International Law Journal* 217–40, at 218. See also T. Duve, 'Entanglements in Legal History. Introductory Remarks', in T. Duve (ed.), *Entanglements in Legal History: Conceptual Approaches* (Max Planck Institute for European Legal History, 2014), pp. 3–25, at p. 3: 'In large part, legal historical research is dedicated to times and spaces in which the notion of the "modern state" did not exist, or to historical situations of limited statehood.'

14 D. J. Bederman, *International Law in Antiquity* (Cambridge University Press, 2001). For further discussion see R. Lesaffer, 'Roman Law and the Early Historiography of International Law: Ward, Wheaton, Hosack and Walker', in T. Marauhn and H. Steiger (eds), *Universality and Continuity in International Law* (Eleven International Publishing, 2011), pp. 149–84, at pp. 149–52.

diplomacy, including interstate peace treaties. Beyond the political and economic ordering of interstate relations, guaranteed by mutual oath-taking and divine invocation, Greco-Roman peace treaties also included clauses providing for the resolution of on-the-ground disputes that might otherwise threaten the newly agreed order. For example, the treaty concluded in 562 CE between the (Eastern) Roman Emperor Justinian I and the Sasanian King of Kings Xusro I set out – in both Greek and Persian languages – the terms of a fifty-year peace agreed between Rome and Sasanian Iran.[15] This 562 CE treaty contains two articles that could be compared loosely with modern 'private international law' provisions. Article 7 specifies that individuals who 'have suffered some hurt *at the hands of subjects of the other state*' should settle the dispute according to law: 'either those who have suffered harm themselves, or their representatives, shall meet on the frontier before the officials of both states, and in this manner the aggressor shall make amends for the damage'.[16] Article 11, on the other hand, specifies the procedure to be followed in the case of intercity disputes that fall outside the 'rules of war':

> If one city damages another or in any way destroys its property not in accordance with the rules of war and with a regular military force, but by guile and theft (for there are such godless men who do these things so that there might be a pretext for war), it was agreed that the judges stationed on the frontiers of both states should make a thorough investigation of such acts and remedy them.[17]

There follow various provisions outlining what should happen if the judges from the frontier zone are unable to resolve a dispute, culminating in a referral to the relevant ruler and a one-year delay before the peace treaty is held to have been broken. The fact that the provisions of the 562 CE treaty itself were negotiated and concluded on the frontier between the Roman and Sasanian Empires, at the border city of Dara, is a further reminder of what the plural constitutionalist theorist Neil Walker terms the 'centrality of the margins'.[18] Articles 7 and 11 of the 562 CE treatise, moreover, provide concrete examples of how action at the margins can

[15] The Greek text is included in a sixth-century CE history written by 'Menander Protector', *Fragment* 6.1. 314–97. English translation from G. Greatrex and S. Lieu, *The Roman Eastern Frontier and the Persian Wars: Part II AD 363–630* (Routledge, 2002), pp. 132–3 (revised *Menander Protector, The History of Menander Protector*, ed. and trans. R. Blockley (F. Cairns, 1985).

[16] Greatrex and Lieu, *The Roman Eastern Frontier*, p. 133 (my emphasis).

[17] Ibid., p. 133.

[18] Walker, 'Beyond Boundary Disputes and Basic Grids', 376–85 and 394–5.

be seen to structure an overall order. We shall return to this idea of the 'centrality of the margins' in Sections 13.2 and 13.3.

Whether there is anything in Classical or Postclassical Roman legal sources that could be mapped accurately onto the modern concept of 'private international law' is doubtful at best.[19] In fact, as we shall see in Section 13.3, the coordination of legal sources within the Roman Empire has more in common with the heterarchical approach of 'postnational law' than with the state sovereignty model of private international law. As Ulrike Babusiaux argues in a 2020 article comparing the legal ordering of imperial Rome with the legal ordering of the European Union, the question of 'how to coordinate different legal sources *without abstract hierarchy*' is an ancient one.[20] During the late Roman Republic, practical and concrete jurisdictional questions arose in the context of Roman imperial expansion and the creation of the provincial system.[21] Contact between Roman citizens and 'foreigners' (*peregrini*, free citizens of any political community besides the Roman) was unavoidable, especially in relation to commerce and business dealings more generally.[22] Roman magistrates, legal experts (*iurisperiti*), the emperors and their officials were thus well aware of a world of private legal transactions involving 'non-citizens' of various different types and recognized the need to regulate those transactions from within the Roman legal system. At Rome, from at least the time of the first Emperor Augustus, the *praetor peregrinus* handled litigation between 'foreigners' and also cases between 'foreigners' and Roman citizens.[23] The activity of the *praetor peregrinus* (and the *praetor urbanus*) at Rome may, to some extent, explain the origins of the Roman *ius gentium*: 'those legal habits which were accepted

[19] For further discussion see H. Cotton, 'Private International Law or Conflicts of Laws: Reflections on Roman Provincial Jurisdiction', in R. Haensch and J. Heinrichs (eds), *Herrschen und Verwalten. Der Alltag der römischen Administration in der Hohen Kaiserzeit* (Böhlau, 2007), pp. 235–55.

[20] U. Babusiaux, 'Coordination of Different Layers of Law in the Roman Empire and in the European Union', in U. Babusiaux and M. Igimi, *Messages from Antiquity: Roman Law and Current Legal Debates* (Böhlau Publishers, 2020), pp. 131–67, at p. 131 (my emphasis).

[21] Famous examples include Cicero's discussion of Roman jurisdiction in Sicily, 70 BCE (*Against Verres II*, 2.32) and the Cyrene edicts of the Emperor Augustus, 7–4 BCE. See further J. Richardson, 'Roman Law in the Provinces', in D. Johnston (ed.), *The Cambridge Companion to Roman Law* (Cambridge University Press, 2015), pp. 45–58.

[22] G. Minaud, *Les gens du commerce et le droit à Rome: Essai d'histoire juridique et social du commerce dans le monde antique romain* (Presses universitaires d'Aix-Marseille, 2011).

[23] D. Daube, 'The Peregrine Praetor' (1951) 41 *The Journal of Roman Studies* 66–70.

by the Roman law as applying to, and being used by, all the people they met, whether Roman citizens or not'.[24] The elaboration of this concept enabled Roman jurists to define certain private law interactions between *peregrini*, 'Latins' (who had some of the rights and privileges of Roman citizenship via Roman grants of the *ius Latii*) and Roman citizens, as falling under Roman jurisdiction. For example, *peregrini* could acquire ownership through 'natural' modes of acquisition (*traditio*, *occupatio*, *accessio*) and certain contracts of buying, selling and letting were also understood to be part of the *ius gentium*; slavery was *iure gentium*, all peoples had it although there were aspects of the (Roman) law of slavery that were peculiar to the Roman *ius civile* alone; and in certain Roman law actions a legal fiction even enabled foreigners to sue or be sued 'as if' they were Roman citizens.[25] The important point to note here is that while Roman jurists and magistrates worked within a conceptual framework that acknowledged different 'layers of law' (*Rechtsschichten*), including the *ius gentium*, their start and end point was the resolution of cases – hypothetical and real – in accordance with the citizen-law of Rome itself.[26] The opening of Gaius' *Institutes*, a mid-second-century CE introduction to Roman law, famously refers to 'all peoples who are governed by laws and customs' as having their own bodies of citizen-law – yet there are no extended discussions of clashes between national laws, nor 'cases [in which] a court must apply a foreign law', in Classical Roman juristic texts.[27] There is, however, an explicit discourse in both extra-legal and legal Roman texts acknowledging 'overlapping spheres' and entangled norms *within* Roman private law.[28]

[24] J. Crook, *Law and Life in Ancient Rome* (Cornell University Press, 1967), p. 29.

[25] C. Humfress, 'Law's Empire: Roman Universalism and Legal Practice', in P. du Plessis (ed.), *New Frontiers: Law and Society in the Roman World* (Edinburgh University Press, 2013), pp. 73–101.

[26] On the concept of *Rechtsschichten*, see Babusiaux, 'Coordination of Different Layers of Law', 131–2.

[27] Cf. J. Waldon, *'Partly Laws Common to All Mankind': Foreign Law in American Courts* (Yale University Press, 2012), pp. 33–5, which makes use of the same Gaius passage in its title: Gaius, *Institutes* 1.1.1 (*The Institutes of Gaius*, trans. W. Gordon and O. Robinson (Duckworth, 1988), p. 19).

[28] K. Tuori, 'The Reception of Ancient Legal Thought in Early Modern International Law', in B. Fassbender and A. Peters (eds), *The Oxford Handbook of the History of International Law* (Oxford University Press, 2012), pp. 1012–33, at pp. 1016–18, citing Cicero, *On Duties* 3.17.69 and 3.5.23, *Tusculan Disputations* 1.13.30 and *The Divisions of Oratory* 37.130; Gaius, *Institutes* 1.1; Aulus Gellius, *Attic Nights* 6.3.45; and Justinian *Digest*, 1.1.1.2, 1.1.4, 1.1.6 (Ulpian).

Alongside the *ius gentium* (discussed by some Classical Roman jurists in relation to 'natural law'), Babusiaux identifies three layers of Roman private law: the *ius civile* narrowly understood (the law of the citizen-body of Rome); the *ius praetorium* or *ius honorarium* (the law of the urban praetor – the praetor with jurisdiction between Roman citizens); and 'imperial law' (law enacted by or on behalf of the Roman emperors).[29] Through a series of detailed case studies, Babusiaux convincingly demonstrates how the application of these different layers of law to specific legal questions could seemingly create clashes, requiring conflicting legal outcomes. The Roman jurist's solution was not to rank the layers of law within an abstract hierarchy of precedence, but rather to reason out their application case by case:

> It must therefore be underlined that the Roman jurists were very well aware of the different requirements in the *ius civile* and *ius praetorium*, on the one hand, and the imperial law on the other hand. But neither did they coin a general principle in order to overcome these differences nor did they see a general conflict between these requirements. In fact, they seem to stick to a case by case view, in which the different layers had to be harmonised according to the individual circumstances.[30]

The structuring of the different layers of (Roman) law was thus case-specific and dependent on the specialized reasoning techniques of the jurists themselves. In one sense, then, these Roman layers of law can be said to have operated heterarchically: side by side without the presumptive authority of one over the other. Yet the crucial point here is that it was the Roman jurists, the expert legal actors, who provided the overall structure by reasoning out potential overlaps, entanglements and clashes casuistically.[31]

As I argue in Section 13.2, 'postnational' law's focus on legal norms and principles is itself influenced by a modern (Western) tradition: a tradition that links normative-conceptual approaches to 'defining what law is' with territorial approaches to defining nation state sovereignty.[32] Rather than locating multiplicity and plurality in different bodies of

[29] Babusiaux, 'Coordination of Different Layers of Law', 132–43.

[30] Ibid., 142–3.

[31] Babusiaux, ibid., suggests that the relevant Roman juristic techniques were developed from Roman rhetorical theory and practice. The article goes on to suggest the potential of applying a similar approach to the 'coordination of different layers of law' within the European Union.

[32] See further M. Madero, 'Penser la tradition juridique occidentale' (2012) 67(1) *Annales. Histoire, Sciences Sociales* 103–32, at 109–10 on the 'fundamental link between the

overlapping and entangled *norms* and then positing 'a set of new types of norms at the interfaces between different legal sub-orders', Babusiaux's analysis suggests that we should look to legal actors – in this case the Roman jurists – as structuring agents in their own right. As I suggest in Section 13.3 through a case study of the record of a protracted sixth-century CE dispute, this focus on legal actors as structuring agents is not simply a question of how different individuals and groups *apply* legal norms and principles in different times, places and contexts. Rather than adopting a modern 'law in action' or 'law in practice' perspective, Section 13.3 aims to develop an approach to norms and legal actors that is more akin to Lévi-Strauss' disentanglements of Amerindian myths: 'We thus do not pretend to show how men think in myths, but how myths are thought in men, and without their knowledge.'[33]

13.2 Beyond 'Norms' and the Nation State

> As the territorial argument ceases to be the decisive factor for the frontiers of legal orders, a picture unfolds in which the normative-conceptual dimension becomes increasingly important in defining what law is.[34]

From the later twentieth century onwards, jurisprudential attempts to define 'what law is' have become increasingly concerned with the normative-conceptual boundaries of legal 'systems', as opposed to the territorial boundaries of sovereign (nation) states.[35] As Michael Guidice stated in his 'think piece' for the Geneva 2019 meeting, with reference to H. L. A. Hart, Hans Kelsen and Joseph Raz: 'The concept of a legal system makes it possible to conceive of the membership of all norms within some domain.' Defining a legal system primarily in terms of the norms that it 'contains', in turn, enables the idea of 'norm interaction' across all levels of ordering. Defining the boundaries of legal systems in terms of norms and rules thus opens up space to identify pluralist legal orderings, operating within and beyond the 'conventional, and

political stakes of theories of the state and the role of law in the Western political tradition'.

33 Lévi-Strauss, *Mythologiques*, p. 20: 'Nous ne prétendons donc pas montrer comment les hommes pensant dans les mythes, mais comment les mythes se pensent dans les hommes, et à leur insu.'

34 D. Roth-Isigkeit, *The Plurality Trilemma: A Geometry of Global Legal Thought* (Springer International Publishing, 2018), p. 66.

35 Walker, 'Beyond Boundary Disputes and Basic Grids', especially 373.

conventionally separate, structures of constitutional law (considered as the law *of* the Keynesian-Westphalian state) and international law (considered as the law *between* Keynesian-Westphalian states)'.[36] According to Nico Krisch, 'The resulting "postnational law" is thus a frame comprised of different orders *and their norms*.'[37] Norms which, as we saw in Section 13.1, exist in heterarchical – rather than hierarchical – relation to each other. Hence one of the central claims of Krisch's 'postnational law' paradigm: 'that global law fares better if it embraces plurality, rather than trying to tame it in an institutional model'.[38]

To a historian whose research interests lie mainly within the presovereigntist, prenationalist and prepositivist world, the centrality of norms within 'postnational law' and the 'Entangled Legalities' project seems striking. Not only is the 'frame' of postnational law made up of orders which in turn are made up of norms, but the mechanism through which norm interaction is seen to take place is defined as a set of new types of norms, operating at the interfaces between different legal suborders. This set of new types of norms includes 'reception norms': 'the typical form through which a legal system deals with norms from the outside; they reproduce the inside/outside distinction and define the ways in which outside norms enter a given body of norms' (also referred to as between systems/conflict-of-law norms); 'overarching norms' which 'regulate relations centrally and with binding character for the different bodies of norms involved' (also referred to as within system/intra-systemic norms); and 'connecting norms' and 'straddling pactices', the 'norms and practices that straddle different bodies of norms without being seen to belong to either, thus blurring the boundaries between them' ('straddling boundaries').[39] Norms have a 'travelling content' through which they perform their operations, becoming entangled within a broader discursive context:

> Actors – litigants, judges, dispute settlers, observers, addressees – make claims about the relation of norms from different backgrounds, and they thus define and redefine the relative weights and interconnection between the norms at play. They also define the extent to which norms are perceived to form part of broader assemblages – in the relatively stable and firm mode of modern state legal orders, or in more porous ways, with a more open interplay of norms and characterized more through their

[36] Walker, 'Beyond Boundary Disputes and Basic Grids', 374.
[37] Krisch, *Beyond Constitutionalism*, p. 12 (my emphasis).
[38] Roth-Isigkeit, *The Plurality Trilemma*, p. 158.
[39] Chapter 1, Section 1.5.1.

> linkages across boundaries than any strong form of belonging to an order as such [. . .] When we focus on legal entanglement here, we mean such discursive entanglement: the universe of statements that link different bodies of norms with one another. This is similar to the 'relational' (as opposed to 'material') entanglement in cultural studies: an entanglement in which the difference in origin remains visible even if the object is embedded in a different practice.[40]

The explicit focus here is on postnational governance structures and dispute resolution; nonetheless, using norms (and rules) as the primary tools for identifying and framing legal systems is very much part of a modern, 'Keynesian-Westphalian', state-sovereigntist, framework. As Roth-Isigkeit states: 'the *legitimacy* of norm creation seems one of the most important achievements of the national state'.[41] What might appear (to 'us') as natural and timeless features of 'strong' legal norms and rules – their binding quality, their normativity, their legitimacy – have in fact been created through modern processes of nation state formation. With its main focus on legal norms – even entangled ones – the 'Entangled Legalities' project does not move us much beyond the (national) state. The fact that the project also includes some analysis of 'weaker' ('informal, unenforced') entangled norms, however, does potentially open up the field to much broader, legal pluralist, perspectives.

The idea that 'strong' legal norms have a jurisdictional aspect is central to both the state-sovereigntist and the postnational-pluralist 'normativisation' (*Durchnormierung*) of law:

> In addition, all rules have a *jurisdictional* aspect, or an aspect of *distribution of power*. This is an aspect of legal rules that is sometime overlooked. A legal rule, as we use the term here, attaches consequences to facts. But consequences do not attach to conduct by themselves; someone must manipulate the strings. Each rule, to be a meaningful rule, must carry with it a ticket to some person, agency, or institution, authorizing, permitting, forbidding, or allowing some action to take place. Each rule has its institutional and distributive side as well as its formal and substantive side. It distributes, or redistributes, power within the legal system or within the social order.[42]

The modern (Western) idea that every legal rule carries with it a 'ticket' to institutionalized enforcement links back to the presumption, discussed

[40] Chapter 1, Section 1.2.

[41] Roth-Isigkeit, *The Plurality Trilemma*, p. 60 (my emphasis).

[42] L. M. Friedman, 'Legal Rules and the Process of Social Change' (1967) 19 *Stanford Law Review* 786–840, at 788.

in Section 13.1, that law is only meaningful when backed by state power or – to phrase it more loosely – when structured by a Lévi-Straussian 'Rome'.

'Law in action' and 'law in practice' approaches tend to rely on this modern, Western, idea of legal norms and rules carrying a jurisprudential aspect. It is inherent, for example, in Neil MacCormick's call for a 'user-orientated understanding of norms' and also in the wider context of his definition of law itself as an 'institutional normative order'.[43] It is implied in Lon Fuller's 'interaction theory of law' which ascribes an active role to individuals within the 'legal system' through an analysis of their 'interactional expectancies' when engaging with 'enacted law' (i.e. law that is accompanied by an explicit ticket to institutionalized enforcement).[44] In terms of the international legal sphere, the 'Transnational Legal Process model' relies on norms having a jurisdictional aspect, enabling it to move beyond a formalist concept of rules, in order to stress the role of 'internalized obedience' in developing 'sets of normative practices'.[45] Finally, the 'Entangled Legalities' project's account of 'norm entanglement' – I would suggest – also relies on the idea of 'strong' legal norms from different origins carrying different jurisdictional 'tickets'. It is precisely this jurisdictional aspect which prevents individual norms from becoming integrated – rather than entangled – through the (repeated, dynamic) 'social interplay of actors':

> Norms from different origins become relevant in the same situation, and they often come with divergent prescriptions or at least orientations. Their relations are not predefined but remain to be determined through the social interplay of actors. A common state of affairs in the law – and likely a more common one than legal 'systems' with aspirations of hierarchy, order and coherence, as depicted in the standard image of law in the context of the modern, Western nation state.

Nonetheless, the claim that norm entanglement is 'a common state of affairs in the law' downplays the fact that the 'normativisation' of law is itself the product of a Keynesian-Westphalian, state-sovereigntist,

[43] N. MacCormick, *Institutions of Law: Essay in Legal Theory* (Oxford University Press, 2007), p. 287.

[44] S. Taekema, 'The Many Uses of Law: Interactional Law as a Bridge between Instrumentalism and Law's Values', in N. Roughan and A. Halpin (eds), *In Pursuit of Pluralist Jurisprudence* (Cambridge University Press, 2017), pp. 116–35, at p. 121.

[45] Roth-Isigkeit, *The Plurality Trilemma*, p. 181.

'political' framework.[46] Classical Roman jurists did not understand law (or legal order) as a system of binding, imperative norms. As the Roman legal historian José Luis Alonso Rodriguez states: 'Legal positivism not only means identifying law with legislation tout court [. . .] It means also the thorough normativisation ("Durchnormierung") of the law, the construction of the entire legal system as a system of imperative, binding norms. Nothing can be more remote from the Roman legal experience in the late Republic and early Empire.'[47]

We saw in Section 13.1 that relations between the different layers of Roman law were dynamic and heterarchical: they depended on the skill of Roman jurists to reason out potential overlaps, entanglements and clashes on a case-by-case basis. Alonso Rodriguez continues: 'Legal Positivism [. . .] stems from the normative monopoly of the sovereign and the subjection of the jurisdiction to the law, as theorized in modern political thinking from Hobbes onwards. Such normative monopoly and jurisdictional subjection are alien to the Roman political theory and practice of the late Republic and early Empire.'[48] In other words, Roman legal norms, rules and principles did not carry with them an automatic jurisprudential aspect: 'a ticket to some person, agency, or institution'. Roman jurisdiction was not subjected to the law, but was accorded to specific individuals and groups. These individuals and groups ranged from the formal *iurisdictio cum imperio* of Roman magistrates and provincial governors, to the legal authority granted to arbitrators by contractual Roman arbitration agreements, to the *auctoritas* exercised by jurists on account of their technical expertise, to the authority of a Christian bishop, a freelancing 'holy man', an Arab tribal leader, or any other local 'big man', recognized by two parties jointly seeking a (negotiated, mediated or adjudicated) resolution to a dispute.

Legal norms, then, did not define a Roman legal system any more than they defined a Late Antique Talmudic or early Christian legal order. My argument in Section 13.3 is not that legal norms, rules and principles were irrelevant to entangled legalities in Late Antiquity. Rather, I am suggesting that if we place the emphasis on Roman legal norms, we risk

[46] Chapter 1, Section 1.1. On the Keynesian-Westphalian frame as an 'at root [. . .] political settlement' see Walker, 'Beyond Boundary Disputes and Basic Grids', 393.

[47] J. L. Alonso Rodriguez, 'Customary Law and Legal Pluralism in the Roman Empire: The Status of Peregrine Law in Egypt' (2013) 43 *The Journal of Juristic Papyrology* 351–404, at 391.

[48] Ibid., 391.

importing a modern jurisprudential aspect to them; and this would be at the expense of neglecting the plurality of entangled legalities that operated, in practice, through concrete appeals to multiple, different, types of power. Section 13.3 thus emphasizes the construction of legalities – plural – on the ground and, more specifically, the juris(dictional)-generative practices revealed in one sixth-century CE document: *P. Petra* IV.39, a report of proceedings before arbitrators from the Eastern (Byzantine) Roman Empire.[49]

13.3 Entangled Legalities: Beyond the (Byzantine) State

> Where actors understand law as a web rather than a hierarchical system, we can expect them to turn away from the ambition of principled solutions – valid throughout the system – and shift towards forms of practical, localized and perhaps provisional accommodation.[50]

There is a history of Late Antique entangled legalities and juris(dictional)-generative practices yet to be written in which what went on in late Roman provinces is not simply labelled 'provincial law' or 'provincial practice' and seen to exist in a hierarchical relationship with laws and practices laid down by the imperial centre, but is instead conceptualized as a kind of heterarchical ordering in its own right. Most legal historians working today on the early Roman Empire (before 212 CE) would accept that its legal order was pluralistic: that there were multiple normative orders in operation on the ground, some of which were permitted, even encouraged, by the Roman state and some of which operated beyond it.[51] Whether this kind of legal pluralism persisted much beyond 212 CE – the date of the Emperor Caracalla's grant of Roman citizenship to almost all (free) inhabitants of the Roman Empire – is more fiercely contested.[52] For our purposes, however, the interesting question is not whether legal

[49] *P. Petra* IV.39 – see M. Kaimio (ed. and trans.), 'Settlement of a Dispute by Arbitration', in A. Arjava, M. Buchholz, T. Gagos and M. Kaimio (eds), *The Petra Papyri IV* (American Centre of Oriental Research, 2011), pp. 41–120.

[50] See Chapter 1, Section 1.6.2.

[51] K. Tuori, 'Legal Pluralism and the Roman Empire', in J. W. Cairns and P. J. du Plessis (eds), *Beyond Dogmatics: Law and Society in the Roman World* (Edinburgh University Press, 2007), pp. 39–52; and C. Ando, 'Legal Pluralism in Practice', in P. J. du Plessis, C. Ando and K. Tuori (eds), *The Oxford Handbook of Roman Law and Society* (Oxford University Press, 2016), pp. 283–93.

[52] C. Humfress, 'Laws' Empire: Roman Universalism and Legal Practice', in P. J. du Plessis (ed.), *New Frontiers: Law and Society in the Roman World* (Edinburgh University Press, 2013), pp. 73–101; and G. Kantor, 'Local Law in Asia Minor after the Constitutio

pluralism existed within the Roman Empire between the fourth and early seventh centuries – it did – but rather what *kinds* of legal plurality and hybridity we are talking about.[53] There is no reference in *P. Petra* IV.39 to formal Roman court proceedings or imperial bureaucratic legal officials.[54] Instead, the legal actors mentioned in the document seem to have understood justice-seeking as an interconnected web of possibilities – making use of practical, localized and provisional (at least when viewed from beyond the relevant immediate time frame) – accommodations. As we shall see in the case of the multiple dispute settlements recorded in *P. Petra* IV.39, Late Antique legal entanglements could stretch across jurisdictional, religious and ethnic boundaries. Through an analysis of *P. Petra* IV.39 we thus move from pluralism 'as a way an observer might see things from without – to pluralities: to seeing the world as experienced by those who inhabited it'.[55]

Since the 1950s, a wealth of new sixth- and early seventh-century documentary evidence has opened up the field of Late Antique juristic papyrology – the study of law through mainly documentary evidence recorded on papyri – beyond the large mass of texts recovered from Egypt.[56] The American Center of Oriental Research in Amman, Jordan, has recently coordinated the publication of a remarkable five-volume set of papyri from sixth-century Petra, the remotely located metropolis of

Antoniniana', in C. Ando (ed.), *Citizenship and Empire in Europe 200–1900* (Franz Steiner Verlag, 2016), pp. 45–62.

[53] On legal pluralism in the Late Roman East, see Y. Monnickendam, 'Late Antique Christian Law in the Eastern Roman Empire: Toward a New Paradigm' (2018) 2 *Studies in Late Antiquity* 40–83; on later, post-Islamic conquest legal entanglements, see U. Simonsohn, *A Common Justice: The Legal Allegiances of Christians and Jews under Early Islam* (University of Pennsylvania, 2011); and M. Tillier (ed.), 'Le Pluralisme judiciaire dans l'Islam prémoderne' (2014) special issue of the *Bulletin d'Études Orientales* 63.

[54] M. Wojtczak, 'Legal Aspects of Dispute Resolution in Late Antiquity: The Case of *P. Mich.* XIII 659' (2016) 46 *The Journal of Juristic Papyrology* 275–308, at 307, discusses two Late Antique papyri which explicitly state why disputes were settled 'privately': the distress connected with the court proceedings, the danger of losing a case in public proceedings and the costs of the trial, in particular the judges' fees.

[55] Phrase adapted from P. D. Halliday, 'Laws' Histories', in L. Benton and R. J. Ross (eds), *Legal Pluralism and Empires 1500–1850* (New York University Press, 2013), pp. 261–77, at p. 273.

[56] J. L. Alonso Rodriguez, 'Juristic Papyrology and Roman Law', in P. J. du Plessis, C. Ando and K. Tuori (eds), *The Oxford Handbook of Roman Law and Society* (Oxford University Press, 2016), pp. 56–66.

the Roman border province *Palaestina Tertia*.[57] The papyri were found in December 1993, as part of ongoing excavations of the Byzantine Church of the Virgin Mary in Petra led by the American Center of Oriental Research. Two teams of papyrologists – an American team from Michigan University and a Finnish team from Helsinki – worked with around 140 carbonized rolls, reconstructing the private papers of a certain Theodoros, son of Obodianos (born 514 CE and died 591 CE), a property owner, deacon and later archdeacon of the Christian Church of the Virgin Mary in Petra (the location where the papyrus rolls were found).[58] Taken as a whole, the Petra archive provides evidence for the persistence of Roman forms and structures in the city of Petra and its surrounding localities: there was a continued Roman military presence and the centralized land-tax system of the Byzantine Empire was still being implemented up to at least the period of the Arab conquests (*c*.634–8 CE).[59] Yet when read together with Late Antique papyri from Egypt, in addition to other papyri from the Near East, the Petra archive does not reveal an Eastern Provincial law: 'a hybrid, indigenous law of the Near East'.[60] Instead, we see a series of concrete situations in which individuals and groups around and beyond the Late Antique eastern Mediterranean – Syria, Palestine, the Arabian Peninsula and Egypt – made use of numerous, entangled, legal practices, forms of argument and juris(dictional)-generative situations in order to get things done.

P. Petra IV.39 is a complex and incomplete text, reconstructed from around 3,000 fragments of papyri by its editor Maarit Kaimio and others. The document is a report of proceedings before arbitrators (*dikastai*), probably drawn up on 8 August 574 CE by an official notary from the *Kastron Zadakathon* (Sadaqa), a garrisoned, fortified settlement 20 km south of Petra on the margins of the Eastern Roman Empire. The reconstituted papyrus' extant length is a remarkable *c*.6.2–6.5 metres,

57 J. Frösen, A. Arjava and M. Lehtinen (eds), *The Petra Papyri I* (American Centre of Oriental Research, 2002); L. Koenen, J. Kaimio, M. Kaimio and R. W. Daniel (eds), *The Petra Papyri II* (American Centre of Oriental Research, 2013); A. Arjava, M. Buchholz and T. Gagos (eds), *The Petra Papyri III* (American Centre of Oriental Research, 2007); Arjava et al., *Petra Papyri IV*; and A. Arjava, J. Frösén and J. Kaimio (eds), *The Petra Papyri V* (American Centre of Oriental Research, 2018).

58 L. Koenen, 'The Decipherment and Edition of the Petra Papyri: Preliminary Observations', in L. H. Schiffman (ed.), *Semitic Papyrology in Context: A Climate of Creativity* (Brill, 2003), pp. 201–26, at p. 202.

59 See ibid., p. 212, on the centralised land-tax system in operation at Petra.

60 P. Crone, *Roman, Provincial, and Islamic Law* (Cambridge University Press, 1987), p. 99.

with 523 lines of text surviving. Nine different hands can be distinguished in the document, with one clear cursive hand indicating a trained scribe.[61] The document itself is written in Greek, but its contents reveal a multilingual environment. At certain points the papyrus refers to two languages being used simultaneously: Greek and 'Syriac' (probably an Aramaic dialect).[62] Both of the parties involved in the 574 CE dispute – Theodoros, son of Obodianos, and Stephanos, son of Leontius – are clergymen; as is Heiros, son of Thomallos, who drafted the arbitration agreement's stipulation of penalty, and one of the arbitrators, Theodoros, son of Alpheios who is identified in the document as an archdeacon. The other arbitrator, Flavius Thomas, son of Boethos, was a senior officer in the local military unit garrisoned at Sadaqa.[63] As discussed in more detail later in this section, the record of the 574 CE arbitration settlement refers to two previously negotiated settlements: one probably from the 530s, decided by an Arab tribal leader and a further settlement from sometime before 574 CE that had been mediated by a Christian cleric from a neighbouring rural area. In addition to arbitration and mediation proceedings, *P. Petra* IV.39 also refers to other forms of justice-seeking, which include trips to the 'sacred shrine of the holy and glorious martyr Kerykos' (in Sadaqa) in order to swear oaths of innocence on the Christian Holy Scriptures.[64]

The report of proceedings given in *P. Petra* IV.39 touches upon numerous points of dispute, all related to the fact that Theodoros son of Obodianos and Stephanos son of Leontius owned neighbouring properties in Sadaqa, as had their fathers before them. Theodoros and his father, however, seem to have been absentee property owners; at line 103 in the text Theodoros responds indignantly to an accusation that he does not 'care for local matters'. Stephanos, on the other hand, seems to have taken advantage of Theodoros' absence from Sadaqa in order to build new physical structures and make alterations to the flow of the

[61] Arjava et al., *Petra Papyri IV*, p. 45.

[62] Arjava et al., *Petra Papyri IV*, p. 72, lines 475–85, mentions documents being presented in both Greek and Syriac letters.

[63] Ibid., p. 45. Further discussion in Z. T. Fiema, 'The Byzantine Military in the Petra Papyri: A Summary', in A. Lewin, P. Pellegrini, Z. T. Fiema and S. Janniard (eds), *The Late Roman Army in the Near East from Diocletian to the Arab Conquest* (Archaeopress, 2007), pp. 313–19.

[64] Arjava et al., *Petra Papyri IV*, pp. 72–3, lines 475–85 and 485–95.

water supply without Theodoros' approval.[65] This led to disputes over Stephanos' and Theodoros' rights to the water that drained from a roof-spout, which had originally been constructed by Theodoros and was the subject of an earlier dispute mediated by the 'country bishop' Sergios.[66] Who owned which parts of the adjacent properties was also at issue, including rights of access across a central courtyard and rights of ownership relating to a refuse pit and an outbuilding.[67] Theodoros claimed that the outbuilding was his by right of inheritance, producing a written deed of sale made for his father seventy years ago.[68] He also seems to claim that he had been sold the outbuilding by two other individuals (Kassisaios and Gregoria), but could not produce any supporting written documents. Stephanos, meanwhile, counter-claimed that his father had bought the outbuilding and surrounding courtyard fifty-three years ago, apparently from Theodoros' father. Stephanos produced two deeds of sale, but Theodoros responded that the outbuilding and surrounding land had not been included in the transaction. Added to this complex situation, *P. Petra* IV.39 also includes accusations of encroachment and theft of building materials – timber, blocks of stone and doors – by local soldiers, possibly under the command of one of the 574 CE arbitrators: Flavius Thomas.[69] In addition, the document records a further, rather murky, claim for two *solidi* (gold coins) related to an earlier dispute between the families over a vineyard.[70] Perhaps unsurprisingly, the hostilities between the two families spilled out into the local community, with Stephanos accusing Theodoros of deliberately stirring things up with the neighbours – who, we are told, made many 'unwritten accusations'.[71] *P. Petra* IV.39 thus records a longstanding series of disputes between two local families, spanning several decades. There is obviously a complex backstory to the 574 CE arbitration. As a 546/7 CE papyrus from the Egyptian city of Antinoe put it, 'many words

[65] Ibid., p. 51, and M. Wojczak, 'Settlements of Claims as a Way of Dispute Resolution in the Light of P. Petra IV 39: A Legal Commentary' (2012) 42 *The Journal of Juristic Papyrology* 353–80 at 359.

[66] Arjava et al., *Petra Papyri IV*, p. 54.

[67] Ibid., p. 53. The refuse pit, in particular, seems to have been the object of a longstanding feud.

[68] Ibid., pp. 52 and 69, lines 69–79.

[69] Arjava et al., *Petra Papyri IV*, p. 55.

[70] Ibid., p. 55.

[71] Ibid., p. 71, lines 305–19.

have been said and many moves have been made' before the parties brought their case before the arbitrators.[72]

Arbitration (and mediation), in contrast to judicial settlement by a standing tribunal, is designed by the parties to the dispute. The basic modern 'principle of party autonomy' – that the parties agree which issue(s) to submit to arbitration, that is, the issues to be decided upon; the choice of arbitrator(s); and the 'applicable law', that is, the law applicable to the dispute, including soft law and 'non-binding' law – can also be seen in operation in Roman arbitration proceedings. Similarly, the modern distinction between 'ad hoc arbitration' and 'institutional arbitration' (where the parties rely on the procedural rules of an arbitral institution determined by the relevant institution) can also be seen in Late Antique contexts. Arbitrations and other negotiation settlements before Late Antique Christian bishops and clerics, for example, developed institutionally specific norms and practices. Records of proceedings held before arbitrators and formal arbitration agreements survive on papyri from both the Late Antique Near East and the West. These include an Egyptian record of a dispute settled by arbitration in 647 CE and recorded in Coptic, which the editor of *P. Petra* IV.39, Maarit Kaimio, notes as the closest parallel to our 574 CE text. *P. Petra* IV.39, however, is unique in that it refers to the submission of written pleas and documents at an early stage of the proceedings, but records the parties' oral pleas before the arbitrators in direct speech: 'the speech flows in personal style, often becoming agitated and even insulting'.[73] In other words, aside from the opening and concluding formalities of the arbitration procedure and the stipulation of penalty, the language used by the parties is not formulaic. What we see recorded in *P. Petra* IV.39 is a localized culture of argumentation.

Chronologically, the earliest negotiated settlement mentioned in *P. Petra* IV.39 relates to the vineyard and the claim for two *solidi*. This dispute, the papyrus states, occurred sometime in the past – Kaimio suggests the late 520s or 530s – between Theodoros, son of Obodianos and Leontius, the father of Stephanos. It was resolved before a mediator referred to in the document as 'Abou Cherebos'. This is probably Abu Karib ibn Jabala, part of the Jafnid dynasty that acted as power brokers between Rome and the Bedouin.[74] Abu Karib ibn Jabala was granted the

[72] Wojtczak, 'Legal Aspects of Dispute Resolution', 36.

[73] Arjava et al., *Petra Papyri IV*, p. 48.

[74] Ibid., pp. 55 and 90 (commenting on lines 163–87 of the text).

Phylarcate of Palestine (including southern Jordan and Petra) by the Roman Emperor Justinian sometime in the 530s.[75] Thus we have a relatively minor dispute over a vineyard, involving two landowners of middling means, mediated by an Arab tribal leader with a network of contacts that stretched all the way from (present-day) Jordan to the Emperor in Constantinople.[76] In choosing Abu Karib as the mediator of their dispute, Theodoros and Leontius deliberately exploited local and imperial networks. The second negotiated settlement mentioned in *P. Petra* IV.39 took place sometime before 574 and was concluded between Theodoros, son of Obodianos, and the individual whom he claimed to have bought the disputed outbuilding from: a certain Kassisaios. The memorandum of this agreement, included in the documents submitted to the 574 CE arbitrators, states that it was made through 'Sergios, priest and "country-bishop" (*chorepiscopos*)'.[77] Here we have the parties appealing to a Christian cleric from a neighbouring rural area, perhaps either exploiting a personal network or, conversely, attempting to remove the dispute from its immediate, urban, context. We also see the use of a Christian cleric as arbitrator in the 574 CE settlement itself, alongside a high-ranking military officer who may have been directly implicated in the circumstances of the case. *P. Petra* IV.39 thus presents us with multiple justice-seeking attempts, before multiple individuals of different types. The crucial point to note here is that each of the different venues for dispute resolution were put into relation with each other *by the parties to the disputes themselves*. The interlinkage here is literally created through the parties' own juris(dictional)-generative practices.

We turn, finally, to the legal norms and principles that the parties rely upon in their justice-seeking activities. In common with other papyri in the Petra and Nessana archives, the protocol of *P. Petra* IV.39 seems to make use of procedural terms and concepts derived from Roman

[75] Procopius, *History of the Wars I.xix.10–13*, states that Justinian received a gift of 'the palmtrees' from Abu Karim, 'who now guarded the land from plunder'. In a brilliant example of Late Antique realpolitik, however, Procopius goes on to explain that, 'In formal terms the emperor holds the Palmtrees, but for him [Justinian] to possess himself of any of the country is in practice utterly impossible [...] The Palmtrees themselves are worth nothing and Abocharabos [Abu Karib ibn Jabala] only gave the form of a gift, and the emperor accepted it with full knowledge of the fact.'

[76] E. K. Fowden, *The Barbarian Plain: Saint Sergius between Rome and Iran* (University of California Press, 1999), pp. 167–70, notes that the Jafnid family constructed an 'audience hall' south of the town of Resafa which functioned as a Church and a place for dispute settlement for people coming on pilgrimage to the shrine of St Sergius.

[77] Arjava et al., *Petra Papyri IV*, pp. 50, 54 and 69.

law: 'Instances of such terms in the text demonstrate beyond doubt that the parties and arbitrators had some, considerable, specific legal knowledge.'[78] Marzena Wojtczak's careful and cautious reconstruction of the substantive Roman rules and concepts that can be pieced together from *P. Petra* IV.39 also suggests the use of legal norms and concepts derived from Roman law, while at the same time highlighting the specificity of localized practices.[79] According to Wojtczak, *P. Petra* IV.39 'gives an impression that we are actually dealing with a sequence of debts and securities between the two families', involving 'a sequence of fiduciary or fictitious sales' with multiple ownership changes over a relatively short period of time (what a modern lawyer might refer to as a situation of relational contracting).[80] As Wojtczak's article concludes: 'It should be considered that ordinary people, not acquainted with dogmatic legal patterns, sought solutions which would appear to protect their rights in [the] best possible manner. Transfer of ownership treated as a security for credit seems to be in accord with this idea.'[81]

The use of a technical Roman legal register in *P. Petra* IV.39 thus needs to be understood within the context of local relations and localized practices. Evidence for these localized practices can be difficult to pinpoint in Late Antique legal and documentary source material, nonetheless, as Wojtczak's example of the creative, 'localized' use of multiple fiduciary or fictitious sales suggests, Roman legal concepts and practices were put to work differently, by different networks of individuals, families and groups, operating within different localities around the empire. Moreover, the fact that this creative use of Roman legal norms in *P. Petra* IV.39 is apparent across a succession of settlements, decided in turn by Christian clerics, a Roman military official and an Arab tribal leader, underscores the fact that the Roman legal norms themselves were considered 'portable'. Once again, there may be modern parallels to be teased out here in terms of exploring the relationship between entangled legalities on the ground and 'strategic legal argumentation'. For example, Adam Bower stresses the role played by 'strategic legal argumentation' in contemporary multilateral settings: 'First, in multilateral settings actors will tend to invoke justifications based in legal principles, norms, and rules – potentially in conjunction with coercive efforts – in pursuing

78 Wojtczak, 'Settlements of Claims as a Way of Dispute Resolution', 357–8.
79 Ibid., 360–80.
80 Ibid., 377–9.
81 Ibid., 379–80.

policy goals. This strategy is preferable even when the actor making a claim does not fully endorse the standards it employs.'[82] Strategic legal argumentation, I would suggest, is at least as important as ('travelling') legal norms when it comes to the construction of entangled legalities past and present.

While it may be tempting to interpret *P. Petra* IV.39, and the Petra archive more generally, as evidence for the persistence of Roman forms and structures (the Roman military, the Roman land ownership and taxation system, Roman legal norms and principles), this would risk sidelining the situated, entangled web of practices that I discuss in this chapter. The fact that Roman legal norms underpin some of the parties' direct speech as recorded in *P. Petra* IV.39 is an important point, but Roman law should not be understood as 'the' centralizing, organizing, principle at work across the life of these disputes. What *P. Petra* IV.39 suggests instead is a complex picture of connected localisms: Roman military networks are enmeshed within civilian, urban, life; Arab tribal leaders mediate property disputes between Christian clerics; and urban clerical networks intersect with wider rural connections. To reduce this connectivity to a static (Roman) provincial law would in fact sideline the extent to which Roman legal norms *were* put to work, by the parties themselves, in concrete situations and contexts. *P. Petra* IV.39 shows us sixth-century legal actors operating at the margins of empire, mobilizing multiple networks and regimes – local, regional, trans-regional, imperial – and in the process creating connected, but crucially not integrated, legal orderings of their own.

13.4 Conclusion

With our analysis of the presovereigntist, prenationalist and prepositivist world of *P. Petra* IV.39 we have moved far beyond a modern, state-sovereigntist, court-centric framework. *P. Petra* IV.39, in contrast, underscores the central role of legal actors in creating localized and entangled legalities on the ground; entangled legalities within which arguments from – portable – Roman legal norms and principles play a significant, but not determinate, role. One of the central questions posed by the 'Entangled Legalities' project is how to reimagine the global legal order

82 A. Bower, 'Arguing with Law: Strategic Legal Argumentation, US Diplomacy, and Debates over the International Criminal Court' (2015) 41 *Review of international Studies* 337–60, at 339.

through the paradigm of entangled legalities. I would argue that one answer involves reframing the analysis so that it shifts from a predominate concern with legal norms towards a 'user theory of jurisdiction': an analysis of the ways in which different legal actors shape themselves to the jurisdictional claims made by state, non-state and extra-state authorities and, in turn, work to shape the concept of jurisdiction itself. As Nico Krisch states: 'the systemic, hierarchical and exclusive [image of law] may well constitute the exception rather than the rule'.[83]

[83] See Chapter 1, Section 1.6.2.

14

Entanglement of State and Indigenous Legal Orders in Canada

KEITH CULVER AND MICHAEL GIUDICE

The concept of entangled legality faces an uphill battle for respectability, as powerful human forces weigh against it from the first mention of its terms. We are all familiar with the reductionist impulse in legal theory, which seeks to reduce apparent novelty to ready explanation within extant concepts and categories. Assertions of legal entanglement, on this view, are mistaken ascriptions of something else – perhaps conflicts between sovereign states, or unsettled internal constitutional matters as federal and state authorities contest the boundaries between them. And even if the ontological credibility of entangled legality might be established, a familiar meliorist impulse may emerge, presuming that what is entangled is better off disentangled, leaving entangled legality a concept less seen in practice than spoken of when practice goes awry. Entanglement, after all, is rarely a good thing. We generally seek to keep marine life from becoming entangled in fishing gear, we often try to help friends out of romantic entanglements and we certainly do not want our political representatives to be entangled in scandal. Here we push back against these impulses, arguing first that entangled legality is not reducible to some familiar other concept or category, and second, that entangled legality can be both durable and a force for political good, even while its durable presence raises challenges to state-centred approaches to legal theory. Contrary to intuition and impulse, then, we argue that entangled legality is here to stay in both legal practice and in legal theory, and that both may be better off embracing entanglement.

The context of our argument is the rapidly evolving relations between state and Indigenous[1] legal orders in Canada. As we argue at length, the emergence of entanglement between these legal orders offers a clear instance of entanglement unlikely to be better explained by reduction

[1] A note on terminology: for the purposes of this chapter, we use as interchangeable 'Indigenous peoples', 'Aboriginal peoples' and 'First Nations'.

to existing relations and explanations, and moreover, this entanglement presents what may over time become the replacement of Canada's foundational unitary constitution by an equally durable pluriform foundation.

A brief foreshadowing of the context of our argument together with an explanation of its structure will serve as a helpful beginning. Canada was created in 1867 with the Constitution Act, 1867 (also known as the British North America Act, 1867, an act of the United Kingdom Parliament). Sections 91 and 92 of the Constitution Act, 1867 divide the powers and authority of the Canadian state, without remainder, between the federal and provincial governments. No constitutional power or authority is allocated to Indigenous peoples. Indigenous rights and claims have nonetheless been recognized in diverse ways since 1867. The Indian Act, 1876, a constitutional amendment in 1982 and several Supreme Court of Canada decisions have acknowledged the existence of Indigenous legal orders, albeit always through the particular lens of the Canadian legal institution undertaking an act of recognition – viewing claims of Indigenous law from the perspective and authority of the Canadian legal system and subject to the limitations set by Crown sovereignty and associated doctrines. Until very recently, this interaction was readily explained by what we have called elsewhere a state-centred approach to legal theory, taking the legal system of the sovereign state as the central instance and object of legal theory as a consequence of the sovereign state's centrality to legal order in the post-Westphalian era.[2]

The bulk of our argument presents evidence for the claim that practically and theoretically significant changes are occurring in the way Canadian legal institutions are engaging with Indigenous peoples' legal claims rooted in the assertion of the existence of Indigenous legal orders existing without recourse to Canadian recognition as a condition of their existence. We demonstrate a gradual yet unmistakably foundational change as institutions of the Canadian legal system embrace a different approach to recognizing Indigenous peoples' rights, claims and legal orders, through various letters of understanding, framework agreements and protocols. This new approach suggests a reconception of the basic terms of what this volume refers to as entangled legalities, from a supremacy-claiming systematicity view to one

[2] See K. Culver and M. Giudice, *Legality's Borders: An Essay in General Jurisprudence* (Oxford University Press, 2010); and K. Culver and M. Giudice, *The Unsteady State: General Jurisprudence for Dynamic Social Phenomena* (Cambridge University Press, 2017).

of 'government-to-government' partnership between state (federal and provincial) governments and Indigenous governments.

We proceed as follows. In Section 14.1, we show how claims to supreme authority made by Canada's legal institutions have exemplified the descriptive-explanatory picture of law offered by state-centred analytical legal theory, while noting along the way the beginnings of recognition of the limitations or inaptness of such claims in the context of Canada's changing relation with Indigenous peoples and their legal orders. In Section 14.2, we provide historical and recent Canadian evidence for the contingency of the relation between systemic claims of supremacy and the presence of durable legal order. Legal order, we argue, can and does exist in conditions of entanglement where there are no overarching legal systems claiming and enjoying some degree of supreme authority. In Section 14.3, we suggest an alternative to the system-centred view and the insistence on the necessity of a supremacy-claiming authority to the existence of durable legal order. That alternative was introduced in previous work, and is developed further here in the context of state–Indigenous entangled legality in Canada.

14.1 Supremacy Claims and Legal System

Generations of students of law and legal theory are familiar with the simple yet powerful characterization of the nature of law developed by H. L. A. Hart and those following in the analytical legal theory tradition to which he gave fresh life. According to Hart's famous formulation in *The Concept of Law*, for a legal system to exist there must be a union of primary rules of obligation, which direct norm-subjects in what they must and must not do, and secondary rules, primarily addressed to and operated by legal officials, authorizing the creation, application and enforcement of primary rules as well as setting in general terms how the primary rules are to be identified or recognized in the first place.[3] Many institutions have such a union of primary and secondary rules, such as hospitals, schools and sports associations, so what makes legal systems – especially of the sovereign state kind – distinctive is that, unlike other institutions, a legal system makes a general claim to supremacy over all other types of normative systems. In the 'Postscript', first included in the second edition of *The Concept of Law*, Hart writes: 'the

[3] H. L. A. Hart, *The Concept of Law*, 3rd ed. (Oxford University Press, 2012).

distinctive features of law are the provision it makes by secondary rules for the identification, change, and enforcement of its standards *and the general claim it makes to priority over other standards*'.[4] While Hart left the notion of supremacy or 'priority' with little further development of its content, the idea became central to Joseph Raz's largely complementary explanation of the concept of legal system. As Raz explains, in addition to comprehensiveness and openness, a general claim to supremacy is one of the unique and distinguishing characteristics of legal systems:

> The condition means that every legal system claims authority to regulate the setting up and application of other institutionalized systems by its subject-community. In other words, it claims authority to prohibit, permit, or impose conditions on the institution and operation of all the normative organizations to which members of its subject-community belong.[5]

Raz offers this observation in the context of discussion about the necessary features 'of all the intuitively clear instances of municipal legal systems'.[6] Raz's claim is carefully delimited, announcing a focus on obvious central instances of state systems of law, leaving unexamined what might be regarded as borderline cases, and forms of legal order beyond the state, as may be found in international law. Yet even Raz's delimited claim is subject to doubt, as critics argue that it may not be necessary to the nature of law that it claims supremacy, whether in state systems or other legal orders.[7] Here we leave this debate to one side, while observing that our argument regarding entangled legality in Canada supports the view that the relation between law and claims to supremacy is a contingent relation. So while our primary goals remain the demonstration of the existence of entangled legality and argument that entangled legality may be a good thing, our argument is of additional interest to the extent that it has implications for the project of general jurisprudence as an attempt to develop an explanation of law capable of scoping over all instances, without limitation to the post-Westphalian state which has dominated so much discussion at least since the initial 1961 publication of *The Concept of Law*.

[4] Ibid., p. 249 (emphasis added).

[5] J. Raz, *The Authority of Law*, 2nd ed. (Oxford University Press, 2009), p. 118.

[6] Ibid., p. 104.

[7] See, e.g., A. Marmor, *Positive Law and Objective Values* (Oxford University Press, 2001), p. 40; and B. Tamanaha, *A General Jurisprudence of Law and Society* (Oxford University Press, 2001), p. 140.

The utility and limitations of the supremacy claim are usefully explored in application of the claim to explain the Canadian context in both historic perspective, and as new evidence shows Canadian adoption of something other than a supremacy claim in the self-conception of the Canadian legal system and the Canadian polity. Claims of supremacy have certainly been prominent, but now seem to be withdrawn in certain instances with regards to some Indigenous peoples, creating an explanatory demand unmet by the supremacy claim. Let us set out an outline of the historical presence of the supremacy claim, in preparation for demonstration of its recent retreat.

The supremacy claim has (at least) three dimensions, divided as follows.

Supremacy of norms. Like other sovereign states, at the foundation of the Canadian legal system is a unitary constitution, first the Constitution Act, 1867, now the Constitution Act, 1982. And like other state constitutions, the Constitution Act, 1982 contains a common supremacy clause. Section 52(1) reads: 'The Constitution of Canada is the supreme law of Canada, and any law that is inconsistent with the provisions of the Constitution is, to the extent of the inconsistency, of no force or effect.'[8] There is of course more than just constitutional law in Canada: there is federal law and regulation, provincial law and regulation, and judicial precedents. Yet these all occupy a particular place in the hierarchy of norms in Canada, with constitutional law serving as the top-down source of validity or authorization for all other types of law. The supremacy claim of the Canadian constitution, and its associated hierarchy of sources of law, is readily observable. John Borrows, for example, recounts the first time he encountered the idea of hierarchy as a law student in Canada:

> I remember my property law professor telling me that all laws had to be consistent with the Constitution Acts to be valid. Then we were told that below the Constitution were parliamentary or legislative enactments, which were greater in authority than common law pronouncements made by judges. Underneath these sources came law's subsidiary origins, such as parliamentary privilege, the royal prerogative, particularly persuasive published commentaries, followed finally by customs and conventions. This pattern for organizing the sources of Canadian law is evident in many of today's legal textbooks. I could not help but notice that custom

[8] The Constitution Act, 1982, section 52, https://laws-lois.justice.gc.ca/eng/const/page-16.html#docCont.

> was at the bottom of Canada's legal structure, and that custom was the kind of law Indigenous peoples were presumed to have, if they were regarded as having any law at all.[9]

One might suppose that including Indigenous rights within the Constitution of Canada would raise the level of protection of Indigenous law and so place it higher up in the hierarchy of Canada's legal system. Such inclusion happened in 1982 with the creation of the Constitution Act, 1982. Section 35(1) reads: 'The existing aboriginal and treaty rights of the aboriginal peoples of Canada are hereby recognized and affirmed.'[10] Yet it must be remembered that such recognition and affirmation are granted by the Constitution of Canada, and subject to amendment according to the amendment formula laid out in the Constitution. While there is a constitutional obligation to consult with Indigenous peoples in Canada regarding any amendment to sections 25 or 35 of the Constitution Act, 1982 or other parts of the Constitution which refer to Indigenous rights, any subsequent amendment only requires approval by a combination of federal and provincial governments. The approval of Indigenous governments is not required.[11] This constitutional recognition of 'existing aboriginal and treaty rights' is evidently more substantial than mere recognition of the existence of residual customary Indigenous law, but that recognition remains an elaboration of the detail of the Canadian legal system's supremacy claim, subsuming Indigenous rights, interests and laws within the Canadian constitutional order.

Supremacy of institutions. Canadian supremacy claims relative to Indigenous peoples' law and legal order are also visible in the status and role of central institutions. Federal and provincial governments are granted exhaustive lawmaking authority under the Constitution, and federal and provincial courts are presumed to have exhaustive authority to resolve disputes. Indeed, as the highest court in Canada, the Supreme Court of Canada, through its judgements and opinions offers final, authoritative decisions on matters regarding Indigenous rights in Canada. As such, the Supreme Court of Canada naturally derives its authority and validity for its decisions through its place in the hierarchy of norms and institutions of the supreme, comprehensive, independent legal system in Canada. Viewing Indigenous rights through the lens of

[9] J. Borrows, *Canada's Indigenous Constitution* (University of Toronto Press, 2010), p. 13.
[10] See The Constitution Act, 1982.
[11] Ibid.

the Supreme Court of Canada is of course to view Indigenous rights through a lens which presumes the underlying supremacy of that court and the legal order it implements, and moreover, lacks the institutional means to interrogate or vary this presumption. The force of this presumption is usefully emphasized by Patricia Monture-Angus:

> There is an insurmountable problem in taking Aboriginal claims to territory before the courts. Courts owe their creation to the fact of Canadian sovereignty. They cannot question that sovereignty because, to find it wanting would in fact dis-establish their own legitimacy. Without legitimate claim and control over territory, the international definition of sovereignty collapses.[12]

Aaron Mills offers a similar observation in the context of discussion of the nature of treaty relationships in Canada:

> The structural relation of settler supremacy that characterizes Canada–Indigenous relationships means that even if somehow the Supreme Court of Canada could get the doctrine right, inequality between Indigenous and settler peoples would persist. Yet the overarching theme of this book is treaty *remedies*. It will be clear by now that I think that's the wrong frame for thinking about changing treaty relationships today because it assumes too much, namely that the courts have a leading role to play in reorganizing treaty relationships. The courts are an institution internal to Canada's constitutional order and, as creations by and under its authority, are by definition incapable of taking up the very issue at stake in treaty: the coordination of distinct constitutional orders.[13]

Similarly, Mark Walters identifies several instances where Indigenous peoples have denied – to little practical effect – the authority and sovereignty of the Canadian state and its institutions. That denial amounts to what Walters aptly calls an 'existential threat' to Canadian sovereignty, swiftly rejected by Canadian courts. Here is an example:

> When it was argued that an interlocutory injunction against protesters from the Lilwat people was invalid 'because the Lilwat People constitute a sovereign nation to which the laws of Canada do not apply and over which the Courts have no jurisdiction,' the response from provincial

[12] P. Monture-Angus, *Journeying Forward: Dreaming First Nations' Independence* (Fernwood Publishing, 1999), p. 65 (internal notes omitted).

[13] A. Mills, 'What Is a Treaty? On Contract and Mutual Aid', in J. Borrows and M. Coyle (eds), *The Right Relationship: Reimagining the Implementation of Historical Treaties* (University of Toronto Press, 2017), pp. 223–4 (internal notes omitted, original emphasis).

> lawyers, that this 'Indian sovereignty argument challenges the basic constitutional framework of Canada,' was probably fair, in the sense that the Aboriginal sovereignty claim was made against, not under or pursuant to, the Constitution of Canada ... Often Indigenous claimants ... invoke international law as well as the laws of their Indigenous nation against the validity of the Canadian state. In general, judges respond to existential threat cases by quickly denying the claims, often by citing the sovereignty-without-a-doubt passage from *Sparrow* and/or the act of state doctrine.[14]

While the Supreme Court of Canada and other Canadian courts have on occasion questioned their jurisdiction to hear certain disputes, and sometimes refuse to offer judgements or opinions on issues they find not (or not yet) justiciable, there is entirely unsurprisingly little historical indication that courts conceived of themselves as institutionally able to question their general legitimacy as institutions of the sovereign Canadian state.[15] Yet as sometimes happens in social affairs, a sea change in attitudes and eventually practice has occurred in recent years, for various reasons beyond easy traceability, but with significant effects.[16] For example, in a 2014 decision then Chief Justice McLachlin of the Supreme Court wrote this about the test for establishing Aboriginal title to land:

> what is required is a culturally sensitive approach to sufficiency of occupation based on the dual perspectives of the Aboriginal group in question – its laws, practices, size, technological ability and the character of the land claimed – and the common law notion of possession as a basis for title. It is not possible to list every indicia of occupation that might apply in a particular case. The common law test for possession – which requires an intention to occupy or hold land for the purposes of the occupant – must be considered alongside the perspective of the Aboriginal group which, depending on its size and manner of living, might conceive of possession of land in a somewhat different manner than did the common law.[17]

[14] M. D. Walters, '"Looking for a Knot in the Bulrush": Reflections on Law, Sovereignty, and Aboriginal Rights', in P. Macklem and D. Sanderson (eds), *From Recognition to Reconciliation: Essays on the Constitutional Entrenchment of Aboriginal and Treaty Rights* (University of Toronto Press, 2016), pp. 54–5 (author's notes omitted).

[15] Even more unlikely would be to find acknowledgment by the Supreme Court of Canada (or any other Canadian court) that its authority to decide disputes regarding the status and nature of Indigenous rights depends on delegation or recognition by First Nations.

[16] Among these causes it is worth identifying the work of the Truth and Reconciliation Commission emerging from an inquiry into residential schools in Canada. See generally: www.trc.ca/about-us/our-mandate.html.

[17] *Tsilhqot'in Nation* v. *British Columbia* [2014] 2 S.C.R. 256.

Consideration of the 'dual perspectives' of Aboriginal groups and the common law when establishing title is a marked change from the Indian Act and earlier Aboriginal title decisions, but it still presumes that authority to make binding decisions regarding Aboriginal title rests with state courts and institutions, not Aboriginal ones. It is nonetheless clear that the demand for judgement incorporating 'dual perspectives' is the foundation of not just recognition of de facto entanglement, but choice of entanglement in the growth of the body of constitutional norms.

Supremacy of force. A further characteristic claim of legal systems of sovereign states, found hand in hand with claims of supremacy of norms and supremacy of institutions, is the claim to a monopoly on the lawful use of force. The Supreme Court of Canada has expressed this dimension of the Canadian supremacy claim in the course of identifying limits to Aboriginal rights in its 2001 decision *Mitchell* v. *M.N.R.*:

> Canadian sovereign authority has, as one of its inherent characteristics, a monopoly on the *lawful* use of military force within its territory. I do not accept that the Mohawks *could* acquire under s. 35(1) a legal right to deploy a military force in what is now Canada, as and when they choose to do so, even if the warrior tradition was to be considered a defining feature of pre-contact Mohawk society. Section 35(1) should not be interpreted to throw on the Crown the burden of demonstrating subsequent extinguishment by 'clear and plain' measures [. . .] of a 'right' to organize a private army, or a requirement to justify such a limitation after 1982 under the *Sparrow* standard. This example, remote as it is from the particular claim advanced in this case, usefully illustrates the principled limitation flowing from sovereign incompatibility in the s. 35(1) analysis.[18]

At the risk of belabouring the point, claims of supremacy of norms, institutions and the use of force in Canada all support the central observation in this section, that Indigenous rights, norms and institutions, to the extent to which they have legal status and force in Canada, have depended on the authorization and permission of the Canadian legal system. The approach to characterization of law and legal system developed by Hart, Raz and following analytical legal theorists is readily capable of explaining the Canadian situation and the respects in which it resembles and varies from other legal systems. That approach is equally capable of reminding us that the patterns of recognition just surveyed may or may not be indicative of a durable legal system combining claims

[18] *Mitchell* v. *M.N.R.* [2001] 1. S.C.R. 911, para. 153 (original emphasis).

to authority in fact generally accepted and practised by the society with which the legal system exists in an intimate relationship. In a relatively durable system such as that found in Canada, supremacy claims are generally accepted, as when provincial and federal governments accept the supremacy of constitutional law over their legislative acts (e.g. where courts strike down some legislative provision citing violation of a Canadian Charter right or provision), or when the police cede authority to the military over the use of force in times of emergency or martial rule. In other instances, claims to supremacy can be rejected in ways that are not readily explained as mere rule-breaking, or as attempts at revolution resulting in the dissolution of the state. Rejection of claims of supremacy of the Canadian legal system by Indigenous peoples are easily found, in contexts of entanglement where durable models for social life are sought beyond the discourse available in a supremacy-presuming state and peoples subject to its supremacy claim. For example, in *This Is Not a Peace Pipe*, Dale Turner begins with the following observations about the legal status of Aboriginal rights in Canada:

> Aboriginal rights, as constitutional rights, are still developing in law; that said, one important principle is now embedded in Canadian law and politics: the meaning and content of Aboriginal rights is expressed in the legal and political discourses of the Canadian state, and therefore Aboriginal rights exist or have legitimacy only *within* the Canadian state [...] But many Aboriginal peoples do not understand their rights in terms that are amenable to the state's legal and political discourses. This is because many Aboriginal peoples do not perceive the political relationship as one of subservience; that is, they do not view their rights as somehow legitimated by the Canadian state. Rather, many Aboriginal peoples understand the political relationship as one of 'nation to nation'.[19]

In some instances, First Nations not only claim independence as sovereign nations alongside Canada, but assert a kind of reversal of the hierarchy and stream of supremacy claims. Some First Nations assert authority to validate the inclusion of settler peoples and institutions into the family of legal orders present in North America. For example, Turner notes this particular feature of an Iroquoian treaty known as 'the Guswentha' or 'Two Row Wampum', an agreement which symbolizes

[19] D. Turner, *This Is Not a Peace Pipe: Towards a Critical Indigenous Philosophy* (University of Toronto Press, 2006), pp. 3–4 (original emphasis).

'peace, friendship, and respect'[20] and serves to constitute the relationship and standing between Indigenous peoples and settlers:

> One reason why the Two Row Wampum is useful for a kind of 'pan-indigenous' political thinking is that it demonstrates that European nations became nations because of the forms of political recognition the Iroquois *bestowed* on them. The kind of nationhood that remains embedded in Iroquois has retained its normative force throughout the historical relationship. This supports McNeil and Borrows's thesis that the Canadian legal system has gained its legitimacy by virtue of indigenous law.[21]

This reversed supremacy claim is of interest as a matter of both the history of the relations between Indigenous peoples and the Canadian state, and for reasons internal to the Canadian state and its self-understanding. Borrows has done perhaps more than anyone else to show that the creation of the Canadian state and its legal system has in its roots a nation-to-nation treaty, recognized, for example, by the Royal Proclamation of 1763.[22] As Borrows argues, the Royal Proclamation of 1763 presumes, and was understood by Indigenous peoples at the time as recognizing, equal standing between Indigenous peoples and settler peoples, including the British Crown itself. On such a view there was no domination of one nation or government over another, but acknowledgement that the validity of agreements regarding the use and title of land, respective self-government and all other aspects of interaction required mutual recognition. Borrows sets this understanding of the relationship between Indigenous peoples and settler peoples in Canada in stark contrast to the view of a unilateral assertion of Crown sovereignty, which prevailed around the time of Confederation in 1867 and continues in many ways until the present day, marking a kind of deliberate Canadian forgetfulness made possible by the prevailing imbalance in political power between the thoroughly established settlers and the

[20] On the origins of the Guswentha or Two Row Wampum, see Turner, *This Is Not a Peace Pipe*, p. 48, quoting Grand Chief Michael Mitchell of Akwesane.

[21] Ibid., pp. 54–5 (original emphasis).

[22] See J. Borrows, 'Constitutional Law from a First Nation Perspective: Self-government and the Royal Proclamation' (1994) 28 *University of British Columbia Law Review* 1–47; J. Borrows, 'Canada's Colonial Constitution', in J. Borrows and M. Coyle (eds), *The Right Relationship: Reimagining the Implementation of Historical Treaties* (University of Toronto Press, 2017), pp. 17–38; J. Borrows, *Recovering Canada: The Resurgence of Indigenous Law* (University of Toronto Press, 2002); and J. Borrows, *Freedom and Indigenous Constitutionalism* (University of Toronto Press, 2016).

substantially displaced Indigenous peoples. There is nonetheless room in the content of the Canadian legal system's self-conception for a return to a collaborative, entangled stance with respect to Indigenous legal orders, warranting further attention to past and present conditions of engagement between Canadian and Indigenous legal orders.

Borrows' work is again instructive. In light of the Supreme Court's acknowledgement of the need for a 'dual perspective', we can ask the question of what, from a First Nations perspective, gives treaties between Indigenous peoples and settler peoples their validity, which sets terms for engagement and perhaps entanglement. Borrows notes that for many Indigenous peoples, there is an important idea of sacred law: 'Laws can be regarded as sacred if they stem from the Creator, creation stories or revered ancient teachings that have withstood the test of time. When laws exist within these categories they are often given the highest respect.'[23] Sacred laws, then, as supreme laws or laws deserving the highest respect, can serve as the source of validity for treaties. Borrows explains how this view can be found regarding treaties signed in parts of Western Canada:

> I encountered this view when working with Elders in Saskatchewan. They spoke of their treaties as being sacred because they brought Canada into existence within their territories [. . .] In listening to the Elders speak about the meanings of these legally binding promises, it was clear that they regarded the treaty as flowing from a sacred source. They did not rely on the written text of the treaty to arrive at this conclusion. Because First Nations followed their own legal traditions in creating treaties, their interpretation was that treaties were made with the Creator as well as the Crown.[24]

As Borrows explains, however, the Creator and Crown are not on equal footing in this respect. The Crown, much like Indigenous peoples, is subject to the laws of the Creator, who is supreme. Borrows quotes one particular Elder:

> It was the will of the Creator that the White man would come to live with us, among us, to share our lives together with him, and also both of us collectively to benefit from bounty of Mother Earth for all time to come [. . .] Just like the treaty, that's what it is, one law was given, Indian and white, we both gave something special, something to keep, something to reverence, just like the treaty, both Indian and white beneficiaries, we were

[23] Borrows, *Canada's Indigenous Constitution*, p. 24.
[24] Ibid., pp. 25–6.

> given a gift from the Creator. The Creator owns us, he is still the boss, nothing is hidden.[25]

As we saw earlier, there is a long history of assertions of the supremacy of the Canadian legal system over First Nations, largely matched by First Nations' acquiescence or practical inability to contest those claims even when the claims arguably amounted to Canadian self-misunderstanding omitting recognition of the force of prior treaty agreements. There is nonetheless an additional history of competing assertions of independence on the part of First Nations, although these assertions most often do not also claim to serve as authority over settler laws. In the passage just quoted, however, we do have an example where sacred Indigenous law is the source of validity for other Indigenous laws and treaties, and additionally claims to serve as the source of validity for the presence of settler peoples and their laws.

14.2 The Contingent Relation between Supremacy Claims and Law

We now arrive at a crucial question: are assertions of the existence of legal system, and in particular assertions of supremacy of the kind visible in the Canadian legal system, necessary or inevitable in understanding and constructing the relations between state governments and Indigenous governments in Canada? Historical evidence and recent agreements suggest the answer is 'no'. Historically, assertions of legal systems and claims of supremacy were not always the way that settler peoples and institutions related to Indigenous peoples in what is now Canada, and very recently there seem to be instances of a return – or at least steps towards a return – to older ways of conceiving such relations. Looking first at pre-Confederation times, we can find evidence of a preference, on the part of many Indigenous peoples, for the terms of the Royal Proclamation of 1763, issued by the British Crown, over the terms and understanding of the British North America Act of 1867 (also known as the Constitution Act, 1867) which created modern-day Canada. Borrows again offers a helpful account. He argues that while the Royal Proclamation has appeared to Canadian courts as an effective unilateral assertion of Crown sovereignty, it was understood by First Nations at the time to be an important nation-to-nation treaty of peace

[25] Ibid., p. 26.

and friendship, which would honour First Nations' ownership of land and self-government.[26] The Royal Proclamation, in this sense, was understood by First Nations to be a kind of sovereignty-protecting international treaty. This understanding and relationship was threatened, as many First Nations believed, by the Constitution Act, 1867, as well as the subsequent patriation of the constitution to include a domestic amending formula:

> For most Canadians, the lack of a domestic amending formula led them to seek constitutional reform in 1927, 1931, 1935–6, 1950, 1960–1, and 1964. Indigenous peoples were not part of these efforts, because they were not invited, and may not have even been interested had such an invitation been extended. As noted, many Indigenous people regarded the Queen as their ally and the Canadian state as their oppressor and thus saw domestication as a great political and legal evil. The substitution of the Canadian state for the British Crown would not have been regarded as a positive development. This fact has led many Indigenous peoples through the years to declare that they possessed or desired a stronger constitutional relationship with Britain, as opposed to a diminished one. When the British (rather than the Canadian) Crown was regarded as their partner, a nation-to-nation relationship with the British Crown made greater political sense.[27]

For many Indigenous peoples the idea of a nation-to-nation treaty or partnership is best exemplified by the Guswentha or Two Row Wampum mentioned in Section 14.1, a form of treaty which originated in agreements between Indigenous peoples (such as the Iroquois or Haudenosaunee) and European settlers. Turner quotes this well-known explanation of the Two Row Wampum:

> When the Haudenosaunee first came into contact with the European nations, treaties of peace and friendship were made. Each was symbolized

[26] Borrows, 'Constitutional Law from a First Nation Perspective'. Many First Nations continue to make reference to the Royal Proclamation of 1763 in their claims. For example, the Kingsclear First Nation cites the Royal Proclamation as law protecting their rights to land which was violated on several occasions throughout their history in what is now New Brunswick. See www.kingsclear.ca/about/history/.

[27] Borrows, *Freedom and Indigenous Constitutionalism*, p. 114. See also Borrows, *Canada's Indigenous Constitution*, pp. 26–7. For comparison, in New Zealand, renewed respect for the *Treaty of Waitangi* of 1840 began and has continued to grow since 1986, when the state introduced the first of several legislative acts recognizing the Treaty as a source of law in New Zealand. For an account of some of the similarities and differences in Indigenous–settler relations between Canada and New Zealand, see J. Ruru, 'Constitutional Indigenous Jurisprudence in Aotearoa, New Zealand', in P. Macklem and D. Sanderson (eds), *From Recognition to Reconciliation*, pp. 415–48.

> by the Gus-Wen-The or Two Row Wampum. There is a bed of white wampum which symbolizes the purity of the agreement. There are two rows of purple, and those rows have the spirit of your ancestors and mine. There are three beads of wampum separating the two rows and they symbolize peace, friendship, and respect.
>
> These two rows symbolize two paths or vessels, traveling down the same rivers together. One, a birch bark canoe, will be for the Indian people, their laws, their customs, their ways. The other, a ship, will be for the white people and their laws, their customs and their ways. We shall each travel the river together, side by side, but in our own boat. Neither of us will try to steer the other's vessel.
>
> The principles of the Two Row Wampum became the basis for all treaties and agreements that were made with the Europeans and later the Americans.[28]

Despite these First Nations perspectives, the idea of a nation-to-nation treaty or partnership did not survive in settler understanding and was simply given no recognition at the time of Confederation in 1867 and subsequent practice. As the above account showed, the Canadian state opted for the extinguishment and then subsumption of Indigenous legal orders. Recently, however, the idea of a nation-to-nation partnership has resurfaced. In various framework agreements, letters of understanding and reconciliation protocols signed by First Nations and provincial and federal governments, relations are being expressed and understood not in a hierarchical or delegated fashion, but rather as relations of 'government-to-government' or 'true partnership'.[29] Many of these agreements

[28] Turner, *This Is Not a Peace Pipe*, p. 48 (internal notes omitted). See also *Mitchell* v. *M.N.R.*, paras 127–30. Also valuable on the importance of such an understanding of state-settler relations is J. Tully, *Strange Multiplicity: Constitutionalism in an Age of Diversity* (Cambridge University Press, 1995). Tully does not examine the relations through the lens of the concept of legal system, but his account of the difference between ancient constitutionalism, modern constitutionalism and contemporary constitutionalism offers a nice parallel.

[29] See, for example, the Letter of Understanding between the Tsilhqot'in Nation and the Government of British Columbia (2014), www.tsilhqotin.ca/Portals/0/PDFs/LOU_Tsilhqotin_BC.pdf; the Letter of Understanding between the Tsilhqot'in Nation and the Government of Canada (2017), www.tsilhqotin.ca/Portals/0/PDFs/Press%20Releases/2017_01_27_Tsilhqotin_Canada_LOU.pdf; Kunst'aa guu – Kunst'aayah Reconciliation Protocol, signed between the government of British Columbia and the Haida Nation (2009), www.haidanation.ca/wp-content/uploads/2017/03/Kunstaa-guu_Kunstaayah_Agreement.pdf; and the Shíshálh Government-to-Government Agreement (2018), www2.gov.bc.ca/assets/gov/environment/natural-resource-stewardship/consulting-with-first-nations/agreements/shishalh_g2g_2016-06-21_final_-_public.pdf.

are quite recent, so have yet to be seen in full operation, but an early framework agreement and subsequent legislation and practice provide a good illustration of the way in which state and First Nations relations are evolving. The Framework Agreement on First Nation Land Management was created in 1996 and signed by the government of Canada and thirteen First Nations, and is expressly characterized as a 'government-to-government' agreement.[30] The central purpose of the Framework Agreement is to allow 'First Nations to opt out of the land management sections of the *Indian Act* and take over responsibility for the management and control of their reserve lands and resources'.[31] As its name suggests, the Framework Agreement has since served as a framework and source of law for both the government of Canada as well as First Nations:

> Canada enacted the *First Nations Land Management Act* (FNLMA), as part of its obligation to ratify the *Framework Agreement.* It was given royal assent on June 17, 1999. The FNLMA brought into effect the terms and conditions agreed to in the *Framework Agreement.* It is the *Framework Agreement* that is actively being implemented by First Nations and Canada.[32]

This statement from the Lands Advisory Board, an institution established under the Framework Agreement and comprising representatives of several First Nations, makes plain how First Nations understand the Framework Agreement and the First Nations Land Management Act. As First Nations see it, the Framework Agreement, which is not federal legislation or policy, or an amendment to the Canadian constitution, represents a foundational agreement and source of law outside the traditional hierarchy of legal norms in the Canadian legal system, giving rise to obligations on the part of the Canadian government. So while it might be observed that the First Nations Land Management Act is a federal statute, as it is, and so stands in a familiar place in the hierarchy of legal norms in the Canadian legal system, the First Nations Land Management Act must also be seen as deriving its ultimate validity and authority from recognition by *both* the Canadian government and First Nations.

[30] See a news release here: https://labrc.com/framework-agreement/, and the full text of the agreement here: https://labrc.com/wp-content/uploads/2016/08/FA-current-to-2013.pdf.

[31] See https://labrc.com/framework-agreement/. At the beginning of 2019, 153 First Nations already had their own land codes or were actively developing them. See: www.aadnc-aandc.gc.ca/eng/1327090675492/1327090738973.

[32] See https://labrc.com/framework-agreement/.

What makes the Framework Agreement, together with the First Nations Land Management Act and the many First Nations land codes now in operation, an example of entangled legalities, and why is it important to understand the social situation in this way? It might be tempting to suppose that First Nations gaining greater control over management of their lands, which also includes the authority to create a range of criminal offences,[33] authority which has historically been held in Canada by the federal government alone, represents a step towards independence of the sovereign state kind. If this were true, then we would not have an instance of entangled legalities but perhaps some form of secession then treaty under international law. However, under arrangements such as the Framework Agreement, fragmentation into several sovereign states within Canada is not contemplated. Rather, what is sought are forms of self-government which depend on mutual recognition and thick intermingling of norms and institutions from diverse sources of ultimate authority. A recent case provides a good illustration.

The K'omoks First Nation in British Columbia created their own land code in 2016 in accordance with the Framework Agreement and the First Nations Land Management Act. Section 31.1 of their land code reads: 'Any person who resides on, enters or remains on KFN [K'omoks First Nation] lands other than in accordance with a residence or access right under this *Land Code* or under a Law is guilty of an offence.'[34] Two non-K'omoks First Nation renters, Thordarson and Sorbie, had failed to pay their rent for several months on a property on K'omoks First Nation lands, and after having been given formal notice to vacate by the K'omoks First Nation, did not leave the premises. They were then considered trespassers by the K'omoks First Nation and guilty of an offence under the Land Code. As the Provincial Court of British Columbia recounts, the K'omoks First Nation requested assistance from the Provincial Prosecution Service and Federal Crown, a provincial institution and federal institution respectively, to help in prosecuting and enforcing the laws of the K'omoks First Nation Land Code, since the Land Code, in accordance with the Framework Agreement, makes reference to the Canadian Criminal Code, a federal statute, as establishing the process for prosecuting the range of criminal offences created in the

[33] Section 22 of the *First Nations Land Management Act*, https://laws-lois.justice.gc.ca/eng/acts/f-11.8/page-4.html#docCont.

[34] *K'omoks First Nation* v. *Thordarson and Sorbie* [2018] BCPC 114, www.canlii.org/en/bc/bcpc/doc/2018/2018bcpc114/2018bcpc114.html.

K'omoks First Nation Land Code. However, 'both the Provincial Prosecution Service and Crown Federal have declined to assist K'omoks'.[35] The court writes:

> This leaves the K'omoks First Nations in a situation where their case must be pursued under 22[3] [a] [of the *First Nations Land Management Act*]. The Band has a law on the books that may give relief from trespass, by way of a court order, but no ability to enforce the law without the cooperation of authorities outside the Band, unless it assumes the burden of prosecution.
>
> K'omoks First Nations, therefore, has applied to this Court pursuant to s.508 of the *Criminal Code* for what has been deemed as a private prosecution or prosecution by the Band. That section of the *Criminal Code* provides a justice who receives information laid under s.505 shall hear and consider *ex parte* the allegations of the informant and the evidence of witnesses where he considers it desirable to do so.[36]

The idea of a 'private prosecution' of a criminal offence is a novel development in Canada, where criminal offences have always been considered as offences against the state so prosecutable only by the state. Private prosecution, however, is made possible by the nature and provisions of the Framework Agreement, the First Nations Land Management Act and particular First Nations land codes.[37] The court concluded that the K'omoks First Nation was entitled to a remedy, and in this case to an order to remove Thordarson and Sorbie from the property on K'omoks First Nation land.

However, we need not take the characterization of 'private prosecution' at face value, as appearances might be deceiving, and there might be an alternative understanding available. What might look like private prosecution from one perspective could also be viewed as an assumption of public prosecution by a hitherto unrecognized institution. On this understanding the possibility of prosecution by the K'omoks First Nation was not a delegated power, expressly or implicitly provided by the federal government; the K'omoks First Nation did not, in this sense, pull on some chain of validity to initiate a criminal proceeding, but instead

35 *K'omoks First Nation* v. *Thordarson and Sorbie*, para. 15.

36 Ibid., paras 16–17.

37 For news coverage of the case, see B. Lindsay, 'They Did It "Their Own Damn Selves": First Nation Wins Unusual Bid to Evict Bad Tenants', *CBC News* (8 October 2018), www.cbc.ca/news/canada/british-columbia/they-did-it-their-own-damn-selves-first-nation-wins-unusual-bid-to-evict-bad-tenants-1.4852788.

assumed and so created the power itself. If we keep in mind as well that criminal offences are typically considered to be the most serious forms of voluntary wrongdoing, which therefore concern not just individual victims but political communities in their entirety, then assumption of the power to prosecute can easily be understood as assumption of a public power to address issues which are not merely of a private nature. Recognition by state courts of such a power might then be much more than simply toleration of a private exercise of power by federal and provincial courts; it might be part of the mutual recognition by state and Indigenous authorities to share in the creation, application and enforcement of criminal law, which was once within the sole purview of the federal government but no longer.

The details of the K'omoks case show, we suggest, that it is implausible to see First Nations law and state law (provincial and federal) as representing distinct legal systems, operating independently at the level of both norms and institutions. The entanglement is unmistakable. The ultimate source of law and authority of First Nations land codes such as the K'omoks First Nation Land Code is shared between First Nations and the federal government by virtue of the Framework Agreement. And at the level of application and enforcement of law, norms sourced in First Nations law as well as federal law coexist and complement each other, and institutions from both the K'omoks First Nation and state government (e.g. provincial courts) are envisioned in a relationship of coordination and assistance. *Thordarson and Sorbie* might become a precedent-setting case, and likely one which establishes some of the relations of entanglement required for First Nations law and state law, as well as their respective institutions, to coexist and operate within Canada.

Still, one might object, why could we not understand the relation between the state and First Nations, in instances such as those presented in *Thordarson and Sorbie*, as distinct but interacting legal systems, much like some claim we see in the European Union where there are longstanding rival supremacy claims made between member state courts and the Court of Justice of the European Union on behalf of their respective legal orders?[38] To see why, we must remember from earlier discussion that to be a legal system requires a distinctive claim to supremacy over all other legal and normative orders in the same social space, as the ultimate

[38] See, e.g., N. MacCormick, *Questioning Sovereignty: Law, State, and Nation in the European Commonwealth* (Oxford University Press, 1999), chapter 7.

foundation for all other applicable law, and this is precisely what is missing in the interaction between state and First Nation institutions regarding First Nation land codes. The foundation of such land codes is the Framework Agreement, a government-to-government framework of mutual understanding and recognition between the federal government and First Nation governments. In broader terms, as one of us elaborates elsewhere,[39] legal systems are social constructions, constructed out of the beliefs, intentions, self-understandings and practices of relevant actors. Supremacy claims are part of the beliefs, intentions, self-understandings and practices of relevant actors for the creation and existence of legal systems, so where these are absent, legal systems are absent as well. The framework agreements, letters of understanding and reconciliation protocols we find in Canada are evidence that, however incrementally, the relevant beliefs, intentions, self-understandings and shared practices of state institutions and First Nation institutions are moving away from supremacy-claiming systematicity towards something else. Simply put, we might be witnessing the social *re*construction of the character of legal relations between the state and First Nations.

To bring the argument of this section full circle, even while further coordination is required to manage the entanglement, for First Nations law and state law to coexist, all that is required is mutual recognition of each other's legal orders. Claims of one order to supremacy over the other are neither necessary nor inevitable as a matter of social fact regarding the existence of law in the durable alignment and intimate relationship between law and society most familiar from the life of the sovereign state. And as we have seen, claims of supremacy, and in particular claims of supremacy made by state institutions over First Nations institutions, would only act as political obstacles to shared goals of reconciliation and partnership.

14.3 A Conceptual Alternative to Legal System

We have sought in this chapter to demonstrate that entangled legality exists, and that in at least the case of Canada–First Nations relations, it is viewed as desirable. Along the way we have undermined the applicability of the concept of legal system and opened the way to asking whether there is an alternative to the concept of legal system (and primarily its

[39] See M. Giudice, *Social Construction of Law: Potential and Limits* (Edward Elgar, 2020).

state-based form) for thinking about law in general, and more particularly the relations between legal orders.[40] In previous work we have developed what we call an 'inter-institutional view of legality' amplifying themes found in Neil MacCormick's work on institutional normative order. The inter-institutional view is particularly useful for the explanation of relations between Canadian state institutions and First Nations legal institutions. The primary descriptive-explanatory benefit of our view lies in its showing how relations of mutual reference can arise between institutions within and across legal orders, operating in ways that need not be viewed as carrying implicit or explicit supremacy competitions as part of their purpose or function. Relations of mutual reference, whether codified in law or formal agreements, or simply found as a matter of social practice, may of course take the form and character of hierarchical relations of supremacy and comprehensiveness; but it is also possible for them to take the form and character of horizontal relations of partnership or shared governance, as we have seen in the case of Canada–First Nations relations. The actual form and character of relations of mutual reference, in other words, is variable, and contingent upon the particular ways in which social groups intend, practice and understand – that is, socially construct – their relations to each other.

The inter-institutional view is designed as a morally neutral descriptive-explanatory view of law, and as such, its possibility and success as a conceptual view of law stands or falls on its success in explaining in general terms (i.e. across as wide a range of contexts as possible) the social fact existence of law (including the existence of legal order between legal orders) wherever and whenever it exists. That said, if such a view is successful on descriptive-explanatory grounds, its adoption in practice may identify political options or possibilities of a morally desirable nature which might otherwise remain hidden from view under prevailing conceptual understandings, such as the understanding of law which ties it squarely to the idea of a state-based legal system. As we have seen in the context of Canada, where there is a politically desired goal of reconciliation between settler and Indigenous peoples, the inter-institutional view seems superior to the state system-centred view in making visible and characterizing a form of non-dominating, non-hierarchical relationship between legal orders. This reconceptualizing will not of course solve all legal, political, moral and economic problems, but it

[40] See again, Culver and Giudice, *Legality's Borders* and Culver and Giudice, *The Unsteady State*.

has the potential to address one particular challenge of reconciliation identified by Borrows, Turner and many others: the challenge of reconceiving the status of Indigenous peoples and their legal orders as something other than subordinate to the comprehensive and supreme Canadian legal system.[41] The inter-institutional view of law may be a particularly useful precursor or accompaniment to politically viable reconciliation between Canada and First Nations.

Relations of mutual reference between institutions are also a particularly helpful tool for detecting the emergence of new legal orders, especially in contexts where there is a plurality of entangled sources of law. In the Canadian context, we might be witnessing a shift away from recognition of a unitary constitution and towards a plurality of constitutional sources.[42] Since Confederation in 1867, the Constitution Act, 1867, then the Constitution Act, 1982, have served as the unitary Constitution of Canada. Yet if the socially accepted relations of mutual reference expand to include various foundational framework agreements, letters of understanding and the Royal Proclamation of 1763, these ultimate sources of rights and obligations might reasonably be viewed as constitutional moments, and so new (or revived) constitutional sources of law and authority. Unitary constitutions might be the ideal in some circumstances, but perhaps not so in others. Relations of mutual reference, which might follow existing, established law or might not, can be seen to have a kind of reconstitutional power if they occur at a basic, foundational level. Such reconstitutional power might not only be possible but highly desirable in some contexts.

Clearly, much remains to be done to specify how the inter-institutional view works as an alternative to system- or supremacy-centred views in particular contexts, including state–First Nations relations in Canada. This is not our aim here, as we aimed to demonstrate only the existence

[41] We also hope we are not read as supposing that such reconceptualization will be easy or straightforward. Like other social constructions, such as those of race, gender and disability, altering the social construction of law in Canada, beyond the handful of examples identified in this chapter, is likely to be slow and difficult, if it is accomplished at all. In general, the inter-institutional view is not a dominant, prevailing view. It is a mostly revisionary view.

[42] For sophisticated accounts of the nature and value of constitutional pluralism in a variety of contexts, see MacCormick, *Questioning Sovereignty*; N. Walker, 'The Idea of Constitutional Pluralism' (2002) 65 *Modern Law Review* 317–59; and N. Krisch, *Beyond Constitutionalism: The Pluralist Structure of Postnational Law* (Oxford University Press, 2010).

of entanglement and its desirability in some circumstances, and in that context articulate a broader lesson regarding the contingency of the system- or supremacy-centred view and the consequent importance of exploring alternative explanations such as that offered by our inter-institutional view. We plan to continue this line of argument in future work. What does remain to be done here is to return to the organizing theme of legal entanglement.

A system-centred concept of law is one way of characterizing relations between multiple legal orders, so setting the basic terms of entanglement as ones of hierarchy, supremacy and delegation. As we have demonstrated, however, the system-centred concept represents one choice of explanation among others. In particular contexts, such as that of Canada, the choice of a system-centred concept may pose an obstacle to both the explanation of changes occurring in an evolving constitution and its relation to adjacent legal orders, and a further obstacle to an imaginative exploration of ways to achieve particular political objectives such as recognition and reconciliation between state institutions and Indigenous peoples. Exploration and development of basic terms of entanglement of mutual reference, partnership and non-hierarchical shared authority is therefore important not only as a tool for successful descriptive-explanation of the range of possible social facts comprising law, but also for surfacing conceptual choices which might assist in achieving morally desirable political objectives. We followed in detail one instance of legal entanglement in the example of application and enforcement of a First Nation land code, finding in this example the elements of a new, positively entangled First Nations–state relation showing the possibility of durable coexistence in an era of 'nation-to-nation' or 'government-to-government' partnerships. Throughout our exploration of legal system, entangled legality and evolving state–First Nations relations, we have shown that there is choice in how to present, understand and reconceive foundational state–First Nations relations. This is a choice about the *basic terms* of legal entanglement, the basic terms about how relations among legal orders of different communities and cultures are to be characterized and practised, ahead of and during the task of working out the particular ways in which norms and institutions will interact and mutually refer to each other.

15

Entangled Hopes

Towards Relational Coherence

JULIA ECKERT

15.1 Entangling Law 'from Below'

In a world that is deeply entangled, the relations between different bodies of law, different legal systems and individual norms originating in different systems are necessarily called into question. 'Cases' increasingly traverse legal systems and implicate subjects of multiple jurisdictions; conflicts in places far apart are, moreover, deemed comparable and references to norms that were applied to similar cases in different places are made by all involved actors – judges, lawyers, plaintiffs and defendants – irrespective of the legal specificities that distinguish jurisdictions. '[B]odies of norms become "entangled" not only as a matter of fact, but also in discursive construction ... Actors – litigants, judges, dispute settlers, observers, addressees – make claims about the relation of norms from different backgrounds, and they thus define and redefine the relative weights and interconnection between the norms at play', writes Nico Krisch in Chapter 1.[1] Relations between different legal systems and different bodies of law today are increasingly relations of mutual information;[2] legal 'systems' are brought into conversation and challenged to influence and learn from each other by the various movements that are driving entanglement.[3]

I would like to express my gratitude to Laura Affolter, Keebet von Benda-Beckmann and Angela Lindt with whom discussing the questions raised in this article has been inspiring, illuminating and enriching.

[1] See Chapter 1, Section 1.2.

[2] J. Eckert, 'What Is the Context in "Law in Context"?', in S. P. Donlan and L. Heckendorn (eds), *Concepts of Law: Comparative, Jurisprudential, and Social Science Perspectives* (Ashgate, 2014), pp. 225–36.

[3] This is the case in some fields of law more than in others, and in some areas of the world and for some people more than for others: Since state sovereignty and autonomy take

Among the diverse processes that lead to an increasing entanglement of laws in the current global situation as sketched out in Chapter 1, I am here concerned with one specific movement of entanglement, namely the way in which law is entangled by its mobilizations in local social struggles. In a world in which ideas of justice, rights and entitlements circulate among people far apart and concerned with very different problems, people perceive themselves to be in situations comparable to those of others and shaped by similar forces. Such struggles have regularly invoked norms from international conventions and from hitherto unrelated bodies of law such as environmental law, trade law and human rights or constitutional law. They have referred to presumed precedents from other situations and claim that norms from different jurisdictions and various bodies of law are applicable to their concerns. They hold accountable actors far removed from the occurrences in question, but who are, in their reasoning, deeply implicated in the conflicts at issue. Last but not least, they mobilize norms not hitherto incorporated into state law or international law – moral norms or those stemming from other (non-state) normative orders – and 'translate' them into the available legal instruments.

With these mobilizations, new possibilities for negotiation and the pursuit of legal rights are being sought.[4] Evocations of other norms may be strategic, as they mostly are when activist lawyers campaign to have certain interpretations of harms be heard, such as when they claim that damage to the environment amounts to a violation of the human rights of those affected in their health or livelihoods by environmental degradation, and when they advocate specific avenues of redress.

contrasting forms in different regions of the world, people are subjected to varying bodies of law and different constellations of legal entanglement, some being more directly impacted by various international norms than those who happen to live in parts of the world that are governed by clear rules of subsidiarity. See T. Bierschenk, 'Sedimentation, Fragmentation and Normative Double-Binds in (West) African Public Services', in T. Bierschenk and J.-P. Olivier de Sardan (eds), *States at Work: Dynamics of African Bureaucracies* (Brill, 2014), pp. 221–45; L. Eslava, *Local Space, Global Life: The Everyday of International Law and Development* (Cambridge University Press, 2015), p. 258.

[4] K. von Benda-Beckmann, 'The Contexts of Law', XIIIth International Congress of the Commission on Folk Law and Legal Pluralism: 'Legal Pluralism and Unofficial Law in Social, Economic and Political Development', Chiang Mai, Thailand (9–13 April 2002), p. 3. PDF on file with the author.

Evocations of other norms might also result from lay views of rights that do not differentiate between different systems of law and are oblivious to the origin of a norm in a specific system, assuming a general validity of the legal norms that promise rights.[5] Their hopes in law make broad comparisons about what is to be treated as – structurally – the same in cases far apart and located in multiple jurisdictions, and by making claims about the comparability of such cases they seek access to norms that promise rights. They operate by ignoring – strategically or idealistically – any boundaries between systems or bodies of law, be they jurisdictional or material, and furthermore, they interpret such bodies and systems of law in the light of moral norms which give them a particular content. 'Often enough, these linkages may connect individual norms, rather than "bodies" of norms as such, thus taking us yet further away from the notion of closed systems' writes Nico Krisch in Chapter 1,[6] and we can see in these mobilizations of law 'from below' what he calls 'the trans-systemic, networked character of law' emerging.[7]

These entangling mobilizations of law 'from below' often occur in highly asymmetrical relations; they concern, in particular, struggles around human rights violations and the destruction of the environment along the long global chains of value production. I argue that because they mobilize law in such asymmetrical relations against more powerful adversaries, their entanglements of law most often strive – implicitly – for a trans-systemic coherence. Entanglement stops short of integration, as Nico Krisch explains. I would argue that the moves towards normative relationality that these mobilizations of law from below engage in are moves to overcome the boundaries around legal systems and bodies of law and towards a trans-systemic and unsystematic coherence. Their end is not integration in a systemic sense; in fact, they do not bother with systematicity, but operate with fluid relations between existing norms. Moreover, these moves are concurrent with moves towards the

[5] J. Eckert, B. Donahoe, C. Strümpell and Z.Ö. Biner, 'Introduction: Laws Travels and Transformations', in J. Eckert, B. Donahoe, C. Strümpell and Z.Ö. Biner (eds), *Law against the State: Ethnographic Forays into Law's Transformations* (Cambridge University Press, 2012), pp. 1–22, at p. 3.

[6] See Chapter 1, Section 1.6.2.

[7] B. de Sousa Santos and C. A. Rodríguez-Garavito, 'Law, Politics and the Subaltern in Counter-Hegemonic Globalisation', in B. de Sousa Santos and C. A. Rodríguez-Garavito (eds), *Law and Globalisation from Below: Towards a Cosmopolitan Legality* (Cambridge University Press, 2005), pp. 1–26.

'distancing' of legal orders and bodies of law, or their entanglement along different lines – what could be called 'counter-entanglements'.

However, at the same time that we see the plurality of legal orders moving into such fluid and dynamic relations of conversation, entanglement and distancing, we can also observe a tendency in law towards a particularization, or rather 'singularization', that not only distances normative orders from each other, but disentangles law. As in the case of entanglements, this is also a desystematization, but one that proceeds through the treatment of individual cases as singular. There appears to be a broader tendency in dispute resolution away from seeing the general norm in the particular case and towards treating incidents and constellations as solitary. This is evident most prominently in procedures such as arbitration, out-of-court settlements and alternative dispute resolution. These all focus on the specific circumstances of a single case, and the unique constellation of parties concerned, and aim at an agreement between those involved, rather than finding solutions according to a general norm. Even though the procedural norms governing these practices of singularization might become more alike, given that forms of arbitration and mediation are standardized and subject to increasing professionalization, cases are treated in their singularity. This might indicate an incremental but fundamental transformation in law that coincides with increasing entanglement, and counteracts it. In the following, I try to understand this coincidence and the dynamics of entanglement and disentanglement that ensue and which possibly prevent the legal change that is sought by movements towards relational coherence.

15.2 Cutting the Network

To understand movements of entanglement from below, we might consider in what way liberal law is at base an instrument of disentanglement, not only because it is so deeply shaped by its relation to the nation state and its borders, but also by way of its very categories, which – for better or worse – have at their horizon the protection of individual liberty and subjective private rights.[8] I find it useful to employ Marilyn Strathern's analysis of the specificities of modern liberal law to understand how our current legal instruments cut, into small segments, issues that are

[8] K. Pistor, *The Code of Capital* (Princeton University Press, 2019); C. Menke, *Kritik der Rechte* (Suhrkamp, 2018).

increasingly perceived by those concerned as crossing the boundaries of jurisdictions and entangling us in fundamental interdependencies. In her response to Bruno Latour's assumption about the prolongation of actor networks in modernity, she held that while the chains of interaction may become ever longer in modernity, modern institutions of law cut these chains at particularly short intervals. Strathern takes the example of intellectual property rights,[9] which privilege the 'invention' and the inventor, rather than accounting for the endless chains of actions that make a certain invention or innovation possible. She observes that many 'traditional' legal institutions take into account the sociality of property, and therefore reflect to some degree the actor networks that produce 'property', while modern legal institutions quintessentially abstract from, and thus disregard, these social relations.

From such an anthropological perspective, contemporary legal institutions could be said to 'cut' interdependent chains of action in several ways: first, as addressed by Strathern, they perform specific cuts around who is actually legally recognized to be a participant in the production of a situation or event. Such cuts can also take other forms. Stuart Kirsch, for example, when comparing the notions of liability that were raised by different Melanesian groups with those raised by multinational companies on the basis of scientifically established causal relationships, found that Melanesians hold accountable those who have created the context for a particular social interaction that has led to harm:

> The underlying principle of liability [relies on the idea that] social networks link specific losses to the person(s) or agent(s) responsible for the context (the road, the feast, the town) in which events occurred, regardless of their separation in time or the actions of other agents in the interim. In all of these claims, social networks are stretched to their logical limits.[10]

Such varying scopes of the social networks that are considered relevant for an issue concern not only the question of who is considered to have participated in bringing about a state of affairs, but also who can be considered affected by it in law. Here, too, liberal law relies on a narrow idea of who is personally affected and can thus appeal to law, and has instituted only a few exceptions in the form of public interest litigation.

[9] M. Strathern, 'Cutting the Network' (1996) 2(3) *Journal of the Royal Anthropological Institute* 517–35. See also K. Pistor, *The Code of Capital*, on the issue of intellectual property rights, particularly pp. 108–31, 211.

[10] S. Kirsch, 'Property Effects: Social Networks and Compensation Claims in Melanesia' (2001) 9 *Social Anthropology* 147–63, at 155.

Second, there are cuts around the time of an event. The most prominent temporal 'cuts' are forfeiture and limitation periods, which might fundamentally jar with the temporality of the effects of a contested action, the time of harm and suffering.[11] There are also more basic cuts in the temporal reach of law, which concern the narratives of when a situation actually begins and how long it lasts. This leads us back to Strathern's concern with the cuts within actor networks, which are, of course, also cuts in time.

The third set of cuts in liberal law are the ways that it separates different fields of practice. Particularly in international law, different bodies of law stand in relatively independent relations to each other,[12] separating trade from human rights, labour law from ecological issues, etc. More generally, the differentiation of various fields of law might not be entirely congruent with the factual interdependence of the fields of interaction that they regulate. Anthropologists have long questioned the adequacy of descriptions of social differentiation as conceived by understandings of modernity based on differentiation theory, observing the continuing interdependence of different fields of interaction even in what are considered highly differentiated societies.[13]

These cuts of liberal law culminate in distinctions concerning what can actually be addressed by legal measures, and between what is offered legal protection and what is not. These might constitute the most pressing cuts for the mobilizations of law from below, since such mobilizations address precisely the specific distribution of rights and privileges provided by current legal instruments. Human rights, for example, often the instrument of entangling legal struggles, protect only some concrete, specific individual rights. Although 'poverty, racism, sexism, imperialism, colonialism and exploitation' might be considered to violate the freedom and dignity of individuals,[14] these are forms of suffering that today cannot be addressed legally as injuries for which someone is liable. The loss of livelihood, or of employment, for example, is regulated via insurance and social welfare, or not at all, but is in most places not legally considered a violation of individual rights, because myriad forms of dispossession are

[11] D. Loher, 'Everyday Suffering and the Abstract Time-Reckoning of Law' (2020) 4 *Journal of Legal Anthropology* 17–38.

[12] Von Benda-Beckmann, 'The Contexts of Law', 4.

[13] See, for example, T. Thelen and E. Alber (eds), *Reconnecting (Modern) Statehood and Kinship: Temporalities, Scales, Classifications* (Pennsylvania University Press, 2018).

[14] R. Cotterrell, *Sociological Jurisprudence: Juristic Thought and Social Inquiry* (Routledge, 2018), p. 150.

legal. The fact that contemporary legal instruments rely at base on subjective private rights[15] makes for their inability to address what are still called structural issues or 'root causes'.[16]

These cuts are increasingly challenged by the mobilization of law 'from below' when people apply existing legal norms to their situations and entangle them with others, making claims that reinterpret and widen the scope of the norms' applicability to address the forms of suffering that they experience. They address the perceived inadequacies of current legal instruments to reflect the factual relations that shape our world and strive for (legal) change by advocating relations between different normative realms. Thus, the very legal norms that are in themselves inadequate to reflect the situations of suffering because of the diverse cuts through social relations in time and space that they entail are entangled in a way that produces novel meanings. They propose novel normative interpretations, thereby creating what Susanne Baer has called 'legal trouble',[17] claiming what does not – yet – exist in dominant legal discourse and hence opening up the possibility to think and speak it[18] – and possibly think and speak it into being.

15.3 Mending the Cuts: Entanglements from Below

Here I would like to consider the mobilization of law from below, which struggles against the cuts of liberal law by means of liberal law itself. There appear to occur two principal contestations in these mobilizations of law, each of which entangles law in specific ways to overcome specific 'cuts' of liberal law. One is the contestation over the attribution of

[15] Pistor, *The Code of Capital.*

[16] S. Marks, 'Human Rights and Root Causes' (2001) 74 *Modern Law Review* 57–78. See also D. Kennedy, 'The International Human Rights Movement: Part of the Problem?' (2002) 15 *Harvard Human Rights Journal* 101–26; S. Moyn, *Not Enough: Human Rights in an Unequal World* (Harvard University Press, 2018), particularly pp. 173–222.

[17] S. Baer, 'Inexcitable Speech: Zum Rechtsverständnis postmoderner feministischer Positionen am Beispiel Judith Butler', in A. Hornscheidt, G. Jähnert and A. Schlichter (eds), *Kritische Differenzen – geteilte Perspektiven* (Westdeutscher Verlag, 1998), pp. 229–43.

[18] See the arguments of Maksymilian del Mar on how legal imagination in legal fictions and other forms of legal reasoning provide new possibilities of interpretation 'hinting at the possibility, perhaps even desirability [. . .] of introducing, more explicitly, a new rule in the future'. See M. Mar, 'Legal Reasoning in Pluralist Jurisprudence', in N. Roughan and A. Halpin (eds), *In Pursuit of Pluralist Jurisprudence* (Cambridge University Press, 2017), pp. 40–63, at p. 51.

responsibility in the long chains of 'distributed agency' across the globe. The second type of contestation is over which norms actually apply to a case. This often also contests the limits of what can be addressed legally as a harm.

The field in which such struggles against the 'cuts' of liberal law are possibly most evident is struggles around human rights violations and environmental damages along the long global chains of value production. The transnational lawsuits brought by people affected by harm resulting from the activities of multinational corporations concern the question of who is to bear responsibility for this harm.[19] Such transnational lawsuits first attempt to expand the scope of responsibility from the person on the ground, whose actions directly lead to harm, to the headquarters of multinational companies. This move raises the question of where to sue, and thus, which jurisdiction and which legal system comes to bear on the case.[20] Transnational lawsuits thus entangle the laws of host states with those of the home states of multinational companies. Furthermore, they often try to distribute the burdens of liability anew by renegotiating mediate responsibility: actions and omissions that enable (rather than directly cause) situations of damage and injury are increasingly moving to the centre of litigation.[21] They address a wider range of actors than conventional legal treatments of global value chains, which typically cut short these chains into contractual relations between a limited number of actors. By addressing a larger set of actors, such struggles entangle the laws that regulate liability, tort and criminal responsibility in the various legal systems to which the actors partaking in these long chains of production and consumption are subject. In both tort and criminal law, claimants as well as lawyers are reaching ever farther, drawing causal and moral connections between events, actions, suffering and remedies.

[19] See e.g. M. Galanter, 'When Legal Worlds Collide: Reflections on Bhopal, the Good Lawyer, and the American Law School' (1986) 36 *Journal of Legal Education* 292–310; S. Sawyer, 'Disabling Corporate Sovereignty in a Transnational Lawsuit' (2006) 29 *Political and Legal Anthropology Review* 23–43.

[20] See N. Krisch, 'Entgrenzte Jurisdiktion: Die extraterritoriale Durchsetzung von Unternehmensverantwortung' (Jurisdiction Unbound: Extraterritoriality and Corporate Responsibility), in Deutsche Gesellschaft für internationales Recht (ed.), *Unternehmensverantwortung im internationalen Recht* (2020), pp. 11–38.

[21] In other fields, such as that of international criminal law, the role and responsibility of those who enable violent conflicts by legally exporting weapons, trading in 'conflict resources', etc. is also now receiving increasing attention, as is the role of states in human rights violations committed by third parties.

Current legal initiatives such as the French *loi de vigilance*, the *Lieferkettengesetz* debated in Germany or the *Konzernverantwortungsinitiative* in Switzerland all seek to transform both the delineations of jurisdictions[22] and, to a lesser degree, the relative weight of primary and secondary responsibility. However, to the extent that these laws and legal proposals concern very specific obligations, such as disclosure requirements or due diligence principles, and rely on rather nebulous identifications of a corporation's 'sphere of influence', they do not overcome the narrow spatial or temporal cuts of current conceptions of liability.[23]

At the same time, such struggles over the attribution of responsibility are now sometimes carried onto a different level. Litigation against states, the host states of multinational companies as well as – particularly in relation to climate change – the home state of companies that globally pollute or enable pollution, is increasingly chosen as an avenue of protest via law. For example, in a case brought against the Ministry of the Environment of Ecuador and the state-owned mining company ENAMI EP over a mining concession granted to the Canadian company Cornerstone, which Laura Affolter observed[24] – the 'Los Cedros case' as it is referred to – claims were made not against the corporation, and not for harms that had occurred. Rather, the plaintiffs targeted the government of Ecuador for issuing the licence for mining, thereby shifting responsibility to the state for making economic activities possible that would – in their perception – inevitably produce harms to the environment and the people living in the vicinity of the mine.

The shift from local causers to transnational enablers is now followed by a shift from those transnational enablers to the states that make their operation legally possible – the enablers of the enablers, so to speak. This puts at issue the legal structure in which corporations, or rather corporate activities, are embedded. Such legal structures are today not made by states alone, particularly as concerns international law, as multiple actors including corporations, international organizations and private law firms

[22] Krisch, 'Entgrenzte Jurisdiktion', 22f.

[23] They are often counteracted by bilateral or multilateral trade agreements, or the institution of special economic zones, which respond to movements of jurisdictional extension by limiting contractually what norms and regulations corporations are required to comply with.

[24] L. Affolter, 'The Responsibility to Prevent Future Harm: Anti-mining Struggles, the State, and Constitutional Lawsuits in Ecuador' (2020) 4 *Journal of Legal Anthropology* 78–99.

are increasingly involved in drafting law.[25] International organizations such as the World Trade Organization (WTO) and the International Monetary Fund (IMF) have developed their own norm-generating formats, and while they are formally constituted by their member states, only some states have an effective say in them. This should not deflect attention from legislatives as lawmakers, administrations as issuers of licences and governments as signatories to investment treaties and the governmental decisions that make corporate activities possible. Even if some states are severely restricted in their choices of whether or not to ratify international agreements, formally it is states that make the laws that regulate the global economy and give corporations their legal shape. More importantly, it is state governments that choose which laws to enact, and how and when to enact them.[26] This is what Shalini Randeria pointed to with her observation of the 'cunning' of states to avoid accountability towards their citizens.[27] Randeria also points to the differences among states in the degree of autonomy they have towards international organizations, corporations and international law. However, it could be claimed that even severely 'dependent' states have room to manoeuvre, and the way they do so is a matter of political choice. Ecuador is an interesting example in this regard, considering the different choices subsequent Ecuadorian governments have taken.

The ongoing claim against the state of Ecuador in the Los Cedros case mentioned above calls into question the mining policy adopted by the current government, and with it its entire economic policy. In this way, it inches closer to challenging the production of the structural possibilities of harm that have so often been overlooked in human rights struggles.

Such claims not only shift responsibility onto states – host states as well as the home states of multinational companies – but further, by focusing on the creation of the legal conditions for harmful activities by

[25] J. Mugler, 'Regulatory Capture? Fiscal Anthropological Insights into the Heart of Contemporary Statehood' (2019) *Journal of Legal Pluralism and Unofficial Law* 379–95; P. Dann and J. Eckert, 'Norm Creation beyond the State', in M. C. Foblets, M. Goodale, M. Sapignioli and O. Zenker (eds), *The Oxford Handbook of Law and Anthropology* (Oxford University Press, 2020).

[26] Dann and Eckert, 'Norm Creation beyond the State'; Krisch, 'Entgrenzte Jurisdiktionen', 34.

[27] S. Randeria, 'The (Un)making of Policy in the Shadow of the World Bank: Infrastructure Development, Urban Resettlement and the Cunning State in India', in C. Shore, S. Wright and D. Però (eds), *Policy Worlds: Anthropology and the Analysis of Contemporary Power* (Berghahn Books, 2011), pp. 187–204.

multinational corporations, they involve a move from retrospective responsibility to the prospective responsibility to prevent potentially harmful operations. It might be too early to speak of 'a (re)turn in the understanding of responsibility', as Klaus Bayertz[28] put it, with prospective, precautionary responsibility, and possibly even strict liability gaining in importance in law. However, such normative possibilities become part of the debate as a result of mobilizations of this kind, and it is to some degree independent of their legal outcomes whether they thereby provide a model for new legal 'imaginations'[29] that 'consider possible or alternative solutions to the problem',[30] and are taken up elsewhere, travelling to new sites and situations and yet further interpretative translations.[31]

15.4 The Import of Other Norms

The interpretations of the responsibilities of different actors thus challenge the jurisdictional cuts currently shaping liability. Beyond these jurisdictional entanglements engendered by the mobilization of law from below, it is the actual 'import' of other norms into the legal reasoning pertinent to a case that entangles law in these struggles over the harms that result from global capitalism. To come back to the case brought against the Ministry of the Environment of Ecuador and the state-owned mining company ENAMI EP over a mining concession granted to the Canadian company Cornerstone, potential harms addressed were those to a healthy environment, harms to livelihood and harms to nature. The lawyer for the plaintiffs argued on the basis of Articles 71, 73, 397 and 407 of the Constitution of Ecuador that enshrine the principle of '*buen vivir*' and the rights of nature as inherent in it. Other activist lawyers at first criticized the mixing up of claims to the rights of nature and the rights to a healthy environment, arguing that these were separate issues, and that the rights of nature were not well served by being mixed up

[28] K. Bayertz, 'Eine kurze Geschichte der Herkunft der Verantwortung', in K. Bayertz (ed.), *Verantwortung – Prinzip oder Problem?* (Wissenschaftliche Buchgesellschaft, 1995), pp. 3–71, at p. 29.

[29] Like the imagination in legal reasoning that Maksymilian del Mar call us to explore for providing models of possible interpretation for the future (see Mar, 'Legal Reasoning in Pluralist Jurisprudence'), such mobilisations suggest new normative possibilities. .

[30] See Mar, 'Legal Reasoning in Pluralist Jurisprudence', p. 45.

[31] For this notion of translation, see e.g. A. Behrends, S-J. Park and R. Rottenburg (eds), *Travelling Models in African Conflict Management: Translating Technologies of Social Ordering* (Brill, 2014).

with, or even identified with (and reduced to), rights to a healthy environment. They then changed course, and joined as *amici curiae* to invoke Article 11 of the Additional Protocol to the American Convention on Human Rights in the Area of Economic, Social and Cultural Rights (Protocol of San Salvador), which establishes the right to a healthy environment and states that everyone shall have the right to live in a healthy environment and to have access to basic public services, and that the signatory states shall promote the protection, preservation and improvement of the environment. They referred to the Stockholm Declaration of 1972 and to the judgement of the Inter-American Court of Human Rights (IACrtHR) in the case of *Indígena Yakye Axa* v. *The State of Paraguay*, which established property rights over ancestral land and the state's obligation to protect the traditional means of livelihood of Indigenous communities as part of the right to life. Furthermore, they referred to an Advisory Opinion of the IACrtHR (OC-23/17, 15 November 2017), the Rio Declaration on Environment and Development (1992), the Convention on Biological Diversity, the United Nations Framework on Climate Change and a judgement by the Columbian Constitutional Court. In the second instance, the 'Regional Agreement on Access to Information, Public Participation and Justice in Environmental Matters in Latin America and the Caribbean' was added to this list.

The claim thus brought into relation regulations on biodiversity with social and economic rights, judgements on Indigenous rights and resolutions on states' obligations to take measures preventing further climate change. Moreover, the concept of *buen vivir*, which was incorporated in the Ecuadorian constitution in 2008, could be said to directly challenge the cuts that liberal law makes to separate different fields of human action. Characteristic of the principle of *buen vivir* is that it overcomes the opposition between human and non-human nature that modern law creates by separating the bodies of law that regulate the economy, intimate relations, the use of resources and the treatment of non-human nature. Like the Indigenous approaches to law that Kirsten Anker describes in Chapter 3, *buen vivir* provides for norms that perceive all relations as inextricably entangled.[32]

[32] The lawyers bringing the case were initially criticised by colleagues who were otherwise in favour of their endeavour precisely for 'mixing up' the rights of nature and the right to a healthy environment, which it was claimed would weaken the claim. They were also critical of the employment of the instrument of a '*consulta previa, libre e informada*',

Everywhere, the constitutional claims made in the name of the rights of nature or in relation to the right to life and physical integrity aim at structural change that goes far beyond legislating binding due diligence norms for corporate legal responsibility. In this way, they transgress the conventional limitations of which harms can actually be addressed by law. The claim that issues regulated by different bodies of law are in fact intricately connected is a central proposition in such struggles. Keebet von Benda-Beckmann shows how, paradigmatically, in the dispute about the availability of low-priced AIDS medicine, the WTO accepted the argument that the prices of medicines were not only an issue of free trade regulation, but also one of human rights: 'In this dispute two bodies of law that had been regarded as separate, had been successfully linked. WTO could no longer reject the human rights as not belonging to its relevant context. From now on, arguments of human rights are in principle legitimate claims in WTO procedures.'[33] The World Health Assembly and the UN Human Rights Commission, following activist campaigns, urged an interpretative entanglement of the different areas of legal regulation. The discursive entanglement provided for the concepts and (legal) arguments to become part of negotiations where they had not been so before. The 'cuts' of liberal law around jurisdictions and the limited reach of liability, including temporally (and regarding the 'rights' of future generations), are thus contested; different fields of interaction and regulation are purported to be inseparable. In this contestation, claimants draw upon hitherto unrelated norms from various bodies of law and connect them in a 'situation'. In this situation, the distinctions between different bodies of law and between moral and legal norms are dissolved. What emerges is interlegality.[34] Interlegality, in the understanding of Santos, does not denote hybrids, but rather the mutual informing of different norms and normative orders, through which novel forms and meanings emerge.

which applies only to areas in which indigenous people and descendants of Africans live, which this was not. The opinion that ecological preservation and human rights were distinct legal fields and had little to do with each other was voiced, and different interpretations of *buen vivir* were articulated in the case in Ecuador by the amicus curiae of the defendants and that of the plaintiffs. See Affolter, 'The Responsibility to Prevent Future Harm'.

[33] Von Benda-Beckmann, 'The Contexts of Law', pp. 4–5.

[34] B. de Sousa Santos, *Toward a New Legal Common Sense: Law, Globalization, and Emancipation* (Cambridge University Press, 1995), p. 473.

15.5 Is This Entanglement?

We might debate at what point norms originating in different legal systems or different bodies of law are truly entangled. References to other norms and laws, which 'are not heard' and do not affect the way a case is interpreted in the last instance, or do not determine what harms are seen to be at issue, might arguably not actually entangle law. However, as Krisch argues in Chapter 1, entanglement proceeds here discursively, that is by way of the interpretative and argumentative realms that mobilizations of law(s) open up: 'If we understand law as ultimately socially constructed, a shift in the ways in which actors relate different parts of the legal order to one another reshapes the law itself'.[35] The actors that need to be taken into consideration are not only judges, Krisch insists:

> [W]e cannot limit ourselves to considering the formal rules that govern these relations or the occasional pronouncement of a court – too much of the postnational legal order only has loose connections with courts or other formal dispute settlers. Instead, we need to take into view the ways in which different kinds of actors – norm-makers, addressees, dispute settlers and other concerned societal actors – construe these relations and resolve (potential) conflicts between different norms.[36]

To return to the idea of legal trouble that Susanne Baer proposes:

> Legal trouble can be caused by judges who make a dissenting judgment in the lowest instance [. . .]. Legal trouble can be triggered by lawyers who simply claim what does not yet exist in the traditional, regularly dominant and discriminatory discourse. Or legal trouble can be created within the framework of a legal policy in which, last but not least, draft laws are presented that oppose the dominant discourses by dissident positions.[37]

One might thus argue that norms inform each other not only when incorporated into the effective normative legal realm through adjudication and the legal reasoning of judges,[38] but also when rejected in

[35] See Chapter 1, Section 1.2.

[36] Chapter 1, Section 1.5.

[37] Baer, 'Inexcitable Speech', p. 242 (my translation).

[38] Stuart Kirsch also points particularly to adjudication as a process of 'reverse translation' that is the import of norms from other normative orders into liberal law. See S. Kirsch, 'Juridification of Indigenous Politics', in J. Eckert, B. Donahoe, C. Strümpell and Z. O. Biner (eds), *Law against the State: Ethnographic Forays into Laws Transformations* (Cambridge University Press, 2012), pp. 23–43, at p. 39. See also F. von Benda-Beckmann, 'Pak Dusa's Law: Thoughts on Legal Knowledge and Power', in E. Berg, J. Lauth and A. Wimmer (eds), *Ethnologie im Widerstreit: Kontroversen über Macht,*

courts as invalid alternatives. Even when rejected, norms that remain in a dissident or minority position have an effect on the dominant norms that they are set in opposition to. The arguments made to deny their applicability themselves set norms in relation to each other. More importantly, the relational meaning established might be taken up by other struggles, and further imaginative interpretations.

Nonetheless, we can presume that not all actors' entanglements have the same effect on normative transformations. Judges import norms into legal reasoning in a different manner than the claims of lay people do. Therefore, different pathways of entanglement can be explored for their different normative effects and processes of homogenization,[39] standardization,[40] pluralization or coherence.

15.6 Counter-Entanglements

This is therefore not the end of the story. When local social struggles against multinational corporations succeed either in winning their cases, or in obliging their governments to regulate corporations' activities more strictly, the conflicts today often shift to arbitration between the corporations and host states on the terms of the investment regimes that host states have concluded with the home states of the corporations in question, or their national investment laws. In Ecuador, for example, after the civil lawsuit against Chevron, in the so-called 'oil dumping' case about the devastating pollution in relation to Texaco's[41] operations in the Lago Agrio oil field, was won in all instances, the international arbitral tribunal in the dispute between the government of Ecuador and Chevron obliged Ecuador to pay compensation for damages to the company's

Geschäft, Geschlecht in fremden Kulturen (Trickster Verlag, 1991), pp. 215–27. Here, Benda-Beckmann argues that it is ultimately judges who determine what is law.

39 J. Eckert, 'From Subjects to Citizens: Legalisation from Below and the Homogenisation of the Legal Sphere' (2006) 38 *Journal of Legal Pluralism and Unofficial Law* 45–75.

40 F. von Benda-Beckmann, K. von Benda-Beckmann and J. Eckert, 'Rules of Law and Laws of Ruling: Law and Governance between Past and Future', in F. von Benda-Beckmann, K. von Benda-Beckmann and J. Eckert (eds), *Rules of Law and Laws of Ruling: On the Governance of Law* (Ashgate, 2009), pp. 1–30.

41 Litigation against Texaco claiming for the clean-up of the polluted area and compensation to its inhabitants began in 1993. In 2001 Chevron acquired Texaco and in 2011 was ordered to pay compensation by an Ecuadorian court. However, a US court in 2014 overturned the verdict, arguing that the plaintiffs had used coercion and bribery, and opening a case against their lawyer under the RICO Act. The Permanent Court of Arbitration in The Hague in 2018 ruled in favour of Chevron, too.

reputation on grounds of the US–Ecuador Bilateral Investment Treaty. The arbitral tribunal also ordered Ecuador to quash the earlier Ecuadorian court ruling.[42] The tribunal held that the plaintiffs should be prohibited from filing any further class actions against the group.[43] Affected persons should only be able to file individual claims for damages. Furthermore, the arbitral tribunal suggested that Ecuador should see to it that the plaintiffs did not file lawsuits in other countries where Chevron has subsidiaries.[44] Pablo Fajardo, the chief lawyer in the Chevron case in Ecuador, presented a document at a lecture in Bern in October 2019 showing that the Ecuadorian Attorney General's Office had asked the courts in Argentina, Brazil and Canada to stop dealing with the cases there, and deny the plaintiffs the possibilities to collect the Ecuadorian judgement.[45] The General Prosecutor's Office thereby hoped to minimize the amount the Arbitration tribunal would allow Chevron to request from Ecuador.[46]

As well as being prohibited from filing suits against the company, Ecuador was also required to pay all outstanding debts it had accrued through such arbitration cases in order to be eligible for a loan from the IMF.[47] The government is apparently willing to comply with all of these requirements. Furthermore, when the bilateral investment treaty with the USA was terminated in 2018, Ecuador adopted its own investment law (*Ley de Fomento Productivo*), which provides that disputes arising out of investment agreements are to be resolved through arbitration, and arbitral awards arising therefrom are immediately enforceable in Ecuador, without the need for any further recognition by the courts.[48] The government repeatedly warned those organizing public consultation

[42] See *Chevron Corporation and Texaco Petroleum Company* v. *Ecuador*, PCA Case no. 2009-23, UNCITRAL, Partial Award, 30 August 2018, part X, para. 10.13 (i).

[43] Ibid., para. 10.13 (ii).

[44] Ibid., para. 10.13 (iii).

[45] *Informe Ejecutivo Sobre Estado Del Caso Chevron Corporation y Texaco Petroleum Company* v. *Republica del Ecuador* (Caso CPA No 2009–23), Procuraduría General del Estado, 2019), p. 2.

[46] Personal communication from Pablo Fajardo to Laura Affolter, received by the author 13 November 2019.

[47] Memorando No. MEF-SFP-2019-0036 (Subsecretario de Finanziamento Publico, 2019), p. 15.

[48] Article 37 of the law stipulates that the Ecuadorian state must agree to domestic or international arbitration to resolve disputes regarding investment agreements. In a further provision, the law states that for investment agreements whose value is over US$10 million, the investor may initiate proceedings before a number of arbitral institutions, namely the Permanent Court of Arbitration, the International Chamber of

meetings on international mining projects, such as those in the Los Cedros case described in Section 15.3, that if such consultations succeed in preventing mining, corporations would likely bring further disputes against the Ecuadorian government in international arbitration tribunals.[49] The costs would be borne by all citizens.

This could be said to be the counter-entanglement to the entanglements from below in transnational relations. It might be considered to fall under the third pathway of entanglement identified by Krisch: coercion. 'Today, for example, the adoption of World Bank rules on resettlement in the context of infrastructure programmes on the part of borrowing states is often a matter of conditionality and necessity rather than persuasion or attraction', he writes in Chapter 1.[50] In this particular case, and this holds for many others, coercion forced the entanglement of particular norms, counteracting other entanglements. Here, in several steps culminating in the conditionalities of the IMF, but significantly moving via the bilateral investment agreement between the USA and Ecuador that was, upon termination, immediately followed by the new investment law, Ecuador's environmental law, human rights law ratified by Ecuador, its trade law and even its administrative law are entangled.

Such coercive entanglements set the contexts for entanglements from below; they limit the possibilities of entanglements and drive them to strive for a trans-systemic coherence, so as to make binding norms for more powerful opponents, thereby limiting the latter's possibilities of forum shopping.

15.7 From the Particular to the Singular?

Beyond the different pathways of entanglement there is, it seems, yet another response to the protesting entanglements from below. This points neither towards plurality finding a form nor towards greater coherence, but in an entirely different direction: beyond its effects on normative developments 'within' systems of law, the entanglement of law created by appeals to other norms might actually lead to cases being treated increasingly as singular, that is, with regard to their unique

Commerce or the Interamerican Commercial Arbitration Commission. The arbitration will be governed by the UNCITRAL Rules or the relevant institutional rules.

49 Personal communication from Pablo Fajardo to Laura Affolter, received by the author 13 November 2019.

50 See Chapter 1, Section 1.4.2.

constellation rather than how they relate to general norms (regardless of which system they might stem from). Rather than entanglement leading to closer and more systematic relations between legal systems, entanglement might actually support – possibly inadvertently – another tendency in litigation, namely 'singularization'.

We observe that the legal struggles against multinational corporations that cross jurisdictional boundaries in seeking to attribute responsibility for harm that occurs in relation to these companies' economic activities are rarely adjudicated but tend rather to be settled out of court, if they are not simply dismissed beforehand.[51] As in many such litigations, in the Monterrico case analysed by Angela Lindt, an out-of-court settlement was reached three months before the trial date. Claimants had sued the British mining company Monterrico and its Peruvian subsidiary Rio Blanco Copper for human rights violations in relation to a protest against the mine, in which twenty-eight people were arrested. The claimants sought damages for the involvement of Monterrico and Rio Blanco personnel in the violence perpetrated against them during the three days of detention, as well as for the material support provided to the police, and the companies' failure to prevent police violence. In a way that was reminiscent of Union Carbide case in Bhopal and many others, Monterrico did not admit any liability, but agreed to pay compensation to the plaintiffs. In return, the plaintiffs withdrew their complaint by accepting the compensation and waived the need for a judgement on whether the parent corporation bore any responsibility.[52] The exact content of the settlement and the precise sum of compensation were not disclosed, and the plaintiffs were obliged not to make them public.

Settlements concentrate not on what is specific to a case and how that specificity might be related to a general norm. Rather, cases are treated as singular, as concerning a singular relationship between the parties

[51] See Chapter 8. See also A. Lindt, 'Transnational Human Rights Litigation: A Means of Obtaining Effective Remedy Abroad? (2020) 4 *Journal of Legal Anthropology* 57–77; J. A. Zerk, 'Corporate Liability for Gross Human Rights Abuses: Towards a Fairer and More Effective System of Domestic Law Remedies', report prepared for the UNHCHR (2014), www.ohchr.org/Documents/Issues/Business/DomesticLawRemedies/StudyDomesticeLawRemedies.pdf.

[52] Lindt, 'Transnational Human Rights Litigation'; C. Kamphuis, 'Foreign Investment and the Privatization of Coercion: A Case Study of the Forza Security Company in Peru' (2012) 37 *Brooklyn Journal of International Law* 529–78.

involved; they need not have any comparable aspects with others, and if they do, these need not become an issue in the negotiations leading to a settlement.

Since the settlement prevents a ruling on the question of whether a corporation actually is at fault and thus bears legal responsibility, it cannot be used as precedent in comparable cases.

> The practice of pursuing out of court settlements before disputes are finally determined, while benefiting the victims in the particular case, impacts upon the development of jurisprudence and precedent. As a litigation strategy, out of court settlement prevents the development of a settled body of law, which may pave the way for more victims to bring claims against corporations for human rights abuse.[53]

In fact, comparability is made irrelevant, as the settlement is a private agreement between the two parties involved in the particular case, a fundamentally unrepeatable situation.[54] Occurrences of harm turn from being 'cases' to being singular 'incidents', and the very legal entanglement created by the references to various norms that might possibly be relevant is dissolved in these cases, which are treated as private negotiations between the involved parties.

This prevention of precedent and, with it, a settled body of law that could be entangled with other such settled bodies of law is facilitated by the fact that settlements such as the one in the Monterrico case are conducted in private and as matters of private contract law. Even if we learn on what terms the settlement was reached, that is, what arguments about duties and responsibilities came to bear on it, it has no relevance for other cases because it is a private agreement that holds only for that specific constellation of actors and the claims which they make on each

[53] J. Robinson and L. Lazarus, *Report for the UN Special Rapporteur on Business and Human Rights – Obstacles for Victims of Corporate Human Rights Violations* (Oxford Pro Bono Publico, 2008).

[54] This unrepeatability is apparently not always strong enough for the defendants, and is therefore sometimes further enforced by the conditions they insist on for engaging in such negotiations: 'Several practitioners pointed to instances where the business defendant required that the law firms make commitment to not representing any other plaintiff in any similar case for a period of several years, or not providing even general information about the kinds of harms identified during the case to any other person. Such commitments may be enforced by a threat that a breach of the commitment by the law firm will result in the plaintiffs having to forfeit the settlement.' See M. B. Taylor, R. C. Thompson and A. Ramasastry, *Overcoming Obstacles to Justice: Improving Access to Judicial Remedies for Business Involvement in Grave Human Rights Abuses* (Amnesty International, 2010), p. 17.

other. The parties involved are free to agree over which norms come to bear on the settlement. The privacy of the agreement can 'convert [. . .] the accountability of the perpetrators into a private matter'.[55]

When the parties involved are furthermore obliged to keep the outcome secret, settlements and the norms that are activated within them are entirely removed from public view. Thus, singularization proceeds in several ways: the avoidance of a judgement about fault relating the case to a general norm, the private agreement between the parties involved and secrecy. Everything prevents the case from being a precedent, or simply an example or model, for others; by making comparability irrelevant, entanglement, too, is inhibited or at least left suspended.

The privatization inherent in such settlement negotiations thus introduces new 'cuts' in Strathern's sense, cuts around a single constellation of actors brought together by the specific legal limitations regarding legitimate claimants in the event of a harm. Even when settlements include compensation payments to collectives, or compensatory action in affected regions, the limitations of who can actually be a party to a settlement are decided by as yet unentangled law, as I mentioned earlier in this section. The question of who is to be considered 'involved', that is, who is a legitimate plaintiff, is most often determined according to the conventions of the jurisdiction where the corporation has its headquarters – its home country. As I briefly discussed in Sections 15.2 and 15.3, liberal law tends to rely on comparatively narrow conceptualizations of the reach of liability and likewise of identifying those who are affected, particularly in cases related to human rights, because of the concentration of human rights on specific violations of individual rights.

The avoidance of precedent, one could say, responds to entanglement by actively making the comparability of cases irrelevant. Singularization disentangles cases from the systematicity of law and redirects the hopes that had once aimed at 'justice'[56] towards individual remedy. The fact that these cases are settled out of court is not directly *caused* by the entanglement of law so much as triggered by the arguments and claims of the plaintiffs. They are settled out of court for various reasons,[57] foremost

[55] Kamphuis, 'Foreign Investment and the Privatization of Coercion', 562.

[56] See Lindt, 'Transnational Human Rights Litigation'; Loher, 'Everyday Suffering and the Abstract Time-Reckoning of Law'.

[57] See e.g. M. Galanter, 'A Settlement Judge, Not a Trial Judge' (1985) 12 *Journal of Law & Society* 1–18.

among them the many obstacles that stand in the way of plaintiffs successfully suing multinational corporations, such as the high costs and long durations, time limitations and jurisdictional limitations. It is commonly argued that such alternative forms of dispute resolution in fact particularly benefit those plaintiffs who cannot afford long and expensive court procedures. Settlements lessen the costs of procedures and make restitutive measures more accessible for the victims, and because they do not need to spend their efforts on attributing fault, can ameliorate suffering more effectively.[58] However, they often do not bring about a judgement about where fault lies, nor do they produce a precedent, the two issues which are often central to the plaintiffs' hopes, their ideas of justice and their desire for preventive signals.

We have here another form of the proximity-distancing dynamic Krisch describes in Chapter 1: the 'distancing' entailed in singularization not only preserves or increases the distance between different bodies of law or among different systems of law. Rather, it creates a distance between cases, so that cases cease to be 'cases' exemplary of a general type, but become unique, that is singular. Singularization is thus a specific form of distancing, possibly the most radical one, in as much as singularization does not preserve an earlier distance but introduces a new logic. This new logic concerns not merely the relation between different laws, but the idea of law in itself. Law ceases to operate by subsuming specific instances under a general principle, valid beyond the specific parties to a legal dispute, and turns into a tool of mediation.

Singularization thus not only prevents precedent but also makes the development of tertiary norms unnecessary, because it circumvents rather than regulates the interface.[59] A different logic emerges, one that develops neither systematicity, nor modes of dealing with normative

[58] See M. Galanter and M. Cahill, 'Most Cases Settle: Judicial Promotion and Regulation of Settlements' (1994) 46 *Stanford Law Review* 1339–91, for a critical discussion of the arguments for settlements as the preferred mode of conflict resolution.

[59] Could singularization be considered a kind of tertiary procedure in which plurality is accommodated by singularising cases? This conclusion could be drawn from the observation that judges, in response to the plurality of norms that could possibly be relevant for a case, tend to adopt relatively minimalist stances, avoiding broader principles and instead deciding cases on as narrow grounds as possible (just because the questions of general principle are so wide open). See e.g. Mar, 'Legal Reasoning in Pluralist Jurisprudence'; and N. Krisch, *Beyond Constitutionalism: The Pluralist Structure of Postnational Law* (Oxford University Press, 2010), in particular pp. 263–96. Theirs, however, is rather a reaction to pluralism than an accommodation of it, inasmuch as pluralism disappears from view in such minimalism.

pluralism, but rather entails a radical singularization where common ground can be found only in procedural norms at best. The paradox is that entanglements engendered by strategic comparisons across legal systems and bodies of law increase attention to the singular.

15.8 Plurality, Singularity or Coherence: Towards a Conclusion

Entanglements of law initiated by struggles for fairer relations, be they fairer trade relations, fairer labour relations, fairer distribution of the costs of climate change or a fairer attribution of responsibility in incidents of violence, not only bring into closer proximity norms originating in different legal systems or bodies of law, they also challenge the boundaries or cuts that current law establishes along the chains of distributed agency and around different fields of practice and interaction. These mobilizations aim to overcome the cuts established by current legal instruments, even the ones they are mobilizing, and to articulate new forms of (legal) relations that reflect the interdependence of different fields of social practice within the (global) chains of action. They are anti-pluralist in that they strive for trans-systemic coherence.

Krisch explains in Chapter 1 that entanglement is precisely not synthesis; it stops short of integration. I argue that, indeed, integration in a systemic sense is neither the goal nor the effect of entangling mobilizations of law from below. These mobilizations of law from below are not concerned with systematicity in the sense of an intra-systemic logic, and probably too fragmented and case-bound to produce it.

Nor are these movements much concerned with finding ways to accommodate the existing legal pluralism so as to avoid conflicts of law. There are indeed many struggles that strive for the possibility of pluralism, also struggles that mobilize law from below. Rachel Sieder, for example, has described the struggles for 'legal sovereignty' of the Maya in Mexico.[60] Such struggles for legal sovereignty, and for a realm of autonomy in legally plural situations, are, however, movements of 'distancing' rather than entanglement. They can mobilize liberal law because it provides for the recognition of some forms of plurality, such as those based in legal categories like indigeneity.

[60] R. Sieder, 'The Juridification of Politics', in M. C. Foblets, M. Goodale, M. Sapignioli and O. Zenker (eds), *Oxford Handbook of Law and Anthropology* (Oxford University Press, in press).

The entanglements produced by the mobilization of law from below I consider here do not strive for such accommodations of pluralism. In fact, they are often at base anti-pluralist, in that they produce novel relational meanings, thereby moving towards a trans-systemic and, at the same time, unsystematic coherence. In their position of relative weakness, they entangle law simply because they need to make use of any norm that might provide them with benefits. It is beneficial for them if all laws providing their claims with legal arguments, no matter where they stem from, are applicable to their situation. They need to strive for the normative amalgamation that comes to bear on their case to be binding for their opponents, and thus for its trans-systemic (trans-jurisdictional) validity. Hence, I argue that these entangling mobilizations of law from below strive for coherence. Such coherence is trans-systemic inasmuch as it refers to norms from various normative orders. It is unsystematic in the sense noted earlier in this section, not being concerned with systematicity, but rather with coherent relationality.

The vision of coherence that comes to the fore in these hopeful mobilizations of law leaves behind the systemic character of individual legal systems; it transcends global legal pluralism, and articulates a more universal notion of the coherence of law. These mobilizations claim that different norms, such as those of trade agreements or environmental conventions and those of civil or human rights, are intricately related to each other, inseparable even. This is a kind of 'legal holism', an approach to law that attempts to counteract the differentiation of various legal fields and the borders of different legal systems.

The fact that hopes are placed in the very law that underlies the unequal distribution of rights and privileges might be due to the 'appeal' of the norms invoked, their charisma.[61] Krisch distinguishes three pathways of entanglement, namely mutual benefit, appeal and coercion. The appeal of norms, as Krisch writes, might arise 'for their substantive content but also for the aura of progress they come with, the Zeitgeist they represent or the fit they produce with existing commitments. Likewise, the actors creating such norms may appear as appealing – as embodying the right values, as culturally superior, etc.'.[62] Such appeal might of course also indicate the hegemonic sway of liberal law and its power to shape people's understanding of the world, of themselves and of

[61] Philipp Dann and I have distinguished between structural privilege, similar to Krisch's coercion, expertise and charisma. Dann and Eckert, 'Norm Creation beyond the State'.

[62] See Chapter 1, Section 1.4.2.

their aims and conflicts. The question of whether an alternative imagination of the world is possible within the parameters of existing law has been much debated. I have argued elsewhere that when people turn towards legal norms to express their hopes and struggle for their future, they interpret norms in the light of these aspirations – rather than simply in terms of existing normative orders.[63] Of course, these aspirations are shaped by the normative orders that currently prevail in the historical situation in which they live. More than being simply evidence of the hegemonic power of the existing norms of liberal law, such mobilizations of law from below put forth specific interpretations of rights and entitlements and act upon them in order to shape institutions accordingly.[64] Concepts such as 'vernacularisation', as proposed by Sally Merry,[65] or 'reverse translation', as suggested by Stuart Kirsch,[66] provide us with instruments to turn this question into an empirical one.

Singularization that proceeds through the privatization of dispute settlement and the move from public courts to private agreements between specific parties runs counter to this. While circumventing rather than resisting the challenges to current legal instruments and norms posed by such entangling struggles, singularization prevents entanglements of law from producing novel legal meanings and thus obstructs legal change. By doing away with precedent, it inhibits the development of normative entanglements that could better reflect current relations of interdependence, position anew the various actors concerned in them and respond to the enabling mechanisms that produce the conditions that make harm possible.

Singularization does not revert the extensions of jurisdictions, nor does it refute the plurality of normative possibilities. It rather proceeds in a different way, namely by making comparability irrelevant, and relationality obsolete; the very idea of normative coherence that drives hopes in law is circumvented, and cases claimed to be equal to others are dissolved into the singular relationships among parties to the individual agreement. Singularization is a form of distancing that keeps not only different bodies or systems of law apart, but even individual cases.

[63] Eckert et al., 'Introduction: Laws Travels and Transformations', pp. 1–22.

[64] De Sousa Santos and Rodríguez-Garavito, 'Law, Politics and the Subaltern', 1–26. S. Kirsch, *Engaged Anthropology* (University of California Press, 2018).

[65] S. Merry, 'Transnational Human Rights and Local Activism: Mapping the Middle' (2006) 108 *American Anthropologist* 38–51.

[66] Kirsch, 'Juridification of Indigenous Politics', 36.

If hope in law is hope in the coherence of law in the sense of the promise of the applicability of norms to one's concerns irrespective of jurisdiction, the tendency to singularization does not bode well for it. Time and again the argument has been made that law operates for the 'haves' not merely because of its substantive content, but also because of the advantages the haves possess in negotiations.[67] We see here that the two are related, that is, that the substantive content, and above all the distinctive 'cuts' of current law, are protected by the turn to settlement, which prevents change. There is no hope in singularity.

[67] Galanter, 'A Settlement Judge, Not a Trial Judge'; Galanter and Cahill, 'Most Cases Settle'.

16

Tertiary Rules

RALF MICHAELS

16.1 Introduction

The entanglement between legal orders is a topic that legal theory has, until very recently, widely ignored or marginalized. For a long time, legal theory happened in the singular: it was mostly a theory of *law*, not a theory of *laws*. The object was one law, not many – whether that one law was confined and contingent (as in legal positivism) or all-encompassing and universal (as in natural law). In such a singular theory of *law*, relations between legal orders are ignored because, by definition, a multitude of laws is not conceptualized. Or, at best, multiple laws are subsumed, somewhere, under one ultimate law.

Such a multitude of legal orders is a theme of legal pluralism, a conceptualization of law as plural that has been discussed not only in legal anthropology and sociology but also in legal theory. Here, entanglement is recognized, but it is often not sufficiently theorized. In legal sociology, the interrelation between legal orders is often conceptualized as interlegality, a rather vague concept that obfuscates more than it actually explains.[1] In legal theory, attempts have been made to conceptualize entanglement, and some of these are discussed in this chapter. However, there is a wide disparity of views. Some discuss entanglement as a matter of social fact, others as a matter of legal ordering. Some discuss entanglement from a neutral perspective, others view it from the perspective of peculiar legal orders, some as both. Some authors discuss a plethora of mechanisms to reduce conflicts between legal orders, or to organize interactions, or the like. But it does not always become clear

Thanks for valuable suggestions to David Dyzenhaus, Nico Krisch, and Tomáš Morochovič.

[1] B. de Sousa Santos, 'Law: A Map of Misreading – Toward a Postmodern Conception of Law' (1987) 14 *Journal of Law and Society* 279–302; J. Klabbers and G. Palombella (eds), *The Challenge of Inter-Legality* (Cambridge University Press, 2019).

what holds these mechanisms together and what keeps them apart. What we lack is an overarching conceptualization of these mechanisms.

This chapter suggests that these mechanisms should be understood as a peculiar type of legal rules. These rules are different from primary rules because they do not provide commands, dos and don'ts. They are also different from secondary rules because they do not determine issues of validity and valid change of a legal system, at least not in the way in which we traditionally understand secondary rules. Instead, they are a different type of legal rules I propose to call tertiary rules. Tertiary rules are rules with which one legal order designates, relative to itself, the normative space of another legal order to which it is not hierarchically superior. In an earlier publication, I discussed a special case of these tertiary rules, namely the rule of external recognition.[2] In this chapter, I generalize the concept.

Tertiary rules are an element necessary for the development of a concept of laws instead of law. The argument for a concept of laws rests on the conviction that a proper understanding of global law is neither monist or pluralist but instead must transcend the difference between monism and pluralism. That global law is differentiated into distinct legal systems, which interrelate and organize their interrelations through tertiary rules. Such tertiary rules therefore presume that legal systems are at least partly autonomous from each other, but at the same time they also make such partial autonomy possible.

The argument rests on a number of assumptions. These assumptions are not self-evident and will require justification at some point, but here is not the right place to demonstrate why they are justifiable, and so I ask the reader to accept them, for the purpose of this argument, as given.

The first assumption is that global law is both one and many at the same time.[3] Global law is many in the sense that we have many separate legal orders, state and non-state, and we do not have a comprehensive meta-law that brings them all together. Global law is one in the sense that none of the many separate legal orders really exists in isolation from the other: they interrelate with each other, and none of them can be fully

[2] R. Michaels, 'Law and Recognition: Towards a Relational Concept of Law', in N. Roughan and A. Halpin (eds), *In Pursuit of Pluralist Jurisprudence* (Cambridge University Press, 2017), pp. 90–115. Some of the material in this chapter draws on that earlier chapter.

[3] Ibid; see also T. E. Riesthuis, 'The Intertwinement of Legal Orders - A Critical Reconstruction of Theories of Jurisprudence' PhD Thesis, Erasmus University Rotterdam (2019).

explained without regard to the other. In this sense, entanglement is a universal condition of law.[4] If this is so, then legal theory must change from a concept of *law* to a concept of *laws*, from a concept of law as essentially one to a concept of law as one and many at the same time. For this concept of *laws*, traditional legal theories, whether monist or dualist, are useful but insufficient.

The second assumption is that legal systems are separate from each other. This has become a minority position within pluralist theories of global law. Such theories often emphasize that borders between alleged systems are blurred, or that transnational law does not allow for such borders altogether.[5] In fact, there is a fascination with hybrid spaces that transcend borders. This is not the place to demonstrate comprehensively the assumption of this chapter in favour of separate legal systems, but two remarks may be helpful. First, the observation that borders are transcended is often a sociological and not a legal observation. As such it is important but not novel: it is a core insight of empirical legal pluralism that legal rules of different origins not only overlap but are also frequently mixed. But such sociological observations are of limited use for a legal theory that looks at the operation of legal rules. Second, the assumption is not that legal systems are natural entities to which the law only responds. In fact, the separatedness of legal systems is in no small part itself a creation of law, and most importantly by tertiary rules. Tertiary rules thus do not only respond to, and organize, a world of separated legal systems, they are themselves involved in the creation of such a system.

This last argument has already alluded to the third assumption, namely that entanglement between legal orders is organized by law.[6] Law organizes its own plurality through its own rationality: it is inadequate and incomplete to describe entanglement solely in extra-legal ways (just as it would be inadequate and incomplete to describe, for example, contractual relations solely in extra-legal ways). In this sense, the theory is a positivist theory: it assumes that not only the definition and the creation of law but also the way in which legal orders relate to

[4] I take it that this is what Nico Krisch has in mind with the concept of entanglements: see Chapter 1, Section 1.1.

[5] In this context, Nico Krisch, in Chapter 1, speaks of 'straddling norms' or 'straddling practices'.

[6] See also Section 16.4.2.

each other are themselves operations by the legal system.[7] To this extent, the concept of laws is autopoietic. However, in emphasizing that legal systems mutually constitute each other, the concept also includes an allopoietic aspect. While the law at large is autopoietic, individual legal systems are not; they constitute each other through mutual recognition. There may, of course, be other theories of law to describe legal entanglement, and it may even be the case that a positivist theory does not explain all aspects of entanglement – though it seems that positivist approaches to global law, which had fallen somewhat out of fashion, are becoming more defensible in recent times.[8] But, I would argue, any theory that is entirely non-positivist – that is, a theory that does not account for the fact that entanglement is organized in legal ways – is necessarily incomplete.

The fourth assumption is that this ordering takes place in a heterarchical way. This is the kind of ordering that presents the greatest challenge to legal theory. Where entanglement takes place between legal orders that are in a clear hierarchical relation, entanglement is relatively simple, because it is simply organized by the hierarchically superior order.[9] However, in many cases, entanglement takes place between legal orders none of which is clearly hierarchically superior to the other and therefore able to determine, with binding force for the other, how the entanglement is organized. It is in these heterarchical situations where we must understand and explain the way entanglement is organized.

[7] Legal positivism is here meant in the sense of normative positivism: the bindingness and legitimacy of legal rules depends on legal, not extra-legal criteria. (See, e.g., J.-R. Sieckmann, *Rechtsphilosophie* (Mohr Siebeck, 2018), pp. 14–15.) This definition is different from the one in F. Schauer, 'Normative Legal Positivism', in P. Mindus and T. Spaak (eds), *Cambridge Companion to Legal Positivism* (Cambridge University Press, 2021), pp. 61–78. It is not meant in the sense of sociological positivism: that legality is an observable social fact. In this sense, it follows Kelsen rather than Hart. For a forceful argument in favour of Kelsen's basic norm over Hart's rule of recognition for problems of cross-border normativity, see D. Dyzenhaus, 'The Janus-Faced Constitution', in J. Bomhoff, D. Dyzenhaus and T. Poole (eds), *The Double-Facing Constitution* (Cambridge University Press, 2020), pp. 17–53, p. 17.

[8] See, e.g., J. Kammerhofer and J. d'Aspremont (eds), *International Legal Positivism in a Post-modern World* (Cambridge University Press, 2014); L. Siliquini-Cinelli (ed.), *Legal Positivism in a Global and Transnational Age* (Springer 2019).

[9] See also Section 16.4.3.

16.2 Cross-Border Normativity

16.2.1 Primary and Secondary Rules within One Order

Because tertiary rules obviously present themselves as an addition to the idea of primary and secondary rules, it makes sense to describe first why the Hartian system of primary and secondary rules is incomplete.[10] Hart's own introduction of a distinction between primary and secondary rules, introduced in his *Concept of Law* in 1961, came in response to a perceived shortcoming of legal positivism at the time. As conceived by John Austin, legal positivism reduced the law to a system of commands. The problem with such a definition was its inability to differentiate between legal and other commands. Why was the order by a sheriff to hand out one's assets a legal command, but the similar order of a mugger was not? How, in short, should one distinguish legal rules from non-legal threats?

Hart's answer borrowed from the dual concept of internal and external sovereignty: 'The legal system of a modern state is characterized by a certain kind of *supremacy* within its territory and *independence* of other systems.'[11] He went on to find an ingenious explanation for the first of these aspects, that of supremacy, but not for the second.

For rules to count as law, Hart suggested, they have to emerge from a source recognized as competent to do so. The rule that determines who can competently set laws is the so-called rule of recognition – not a legal rule but a sociological fact for Hart, though others have suggested that the rule of recognition is better understood as a legal rule. The recognition of who is entitled to make laws does not yet, on its own, determine the conditions under which that person's orders actually are valid law. The determination of this is done by an additional set of rules that Hart calls secondary rules. Some of these rules determine who can make laws, some of these rules determine through what processes laws are made, some of these rules determine institutions and procedures of adjudication.

[10] My argument thus draws on Hart here in part for terminiological reasons, although it might actually fit better with a Kelsenian conception of validity. See Dyzenhaus, 'The Janus-Faced Constitution'.

[11] H. L. A. Hart, *The Concept of Law*, 3rd ed. (Oxford University Press, 2012), p. 24 (emphases in original). On internal and external sovereignty, see, e.g., S. Krasner, 'Sovereignty', in G. Ritzer (ed.), *The Blackwell Encyclopedia of Sociology* (Wiley-Blackwell, 2007).

The introduction of secondary rules created a significant advance for legal positivism. It was now possible to explain normativity without having to resort to natural law foundations for the law. The distinction between primary and secondary rules made it possible to distinguish between the effectiveness of a rule – that had essentially been Austin's only concern – and its validity and applicability. Legal rules as opposed to mere commands were now those rules that actually had legal validity – because they were made by recognized officials in the ways provided for by the law. Moreover, they were those rules that were not only followed by ordinary citizens (out of concern over the threat that backed them up) but also were those rules applied by officials asked to apply or enforce the law. In addition, the separation between effectiveness on the one hand, validity and applicability on the other, also enabled the construction of law as a system, or at least an order. Commands backed by threats can come in isolation. Primary rules created and validated through secondary rules, by contrast, become part of a bigger whole: they relate to each other. Where primary rules are in apparent conflict, secondary rules are able to resolve that conflict, though whether they succeed may depend on an additional account for law's systematicity, either a juridical one (like Kelsen's idea of law as a system) or an extra-legal one (like Dworkin's idea of law as integrity).[12]

16.2.2 The Challenge from Cross-Border Normativity

Helpful as it is for internal sovereignty,[13] the introduction of secondary rules does not help for external sovereignty. Here, Hart had little to offer. Granted, external sovereignty itself – the fact that foreign rules could not, *on their own*, bind subjects in England – is no problem for his theory. The challenge for jurisprudence emerges from the plurality of laws, but if plurality were all there is to it that challenge would not be very great. What is challenging, and insufficiently conceptualized in jurisprudence, is the relation and interaction between laws – the problem of cross-border normativity. In his *Concept of Law*, Hart dealt with the challenge through a (somewhat simplistic) idea of replication: in his view, the Russian law that an English court may apply is really not Russian law

[12] On potential parallels between Kelsen and Dworkin here, see Dyzenhaus, 'The Janus-Faced Constitution', 41–2.

[13] P. Eleftheriadis, 'Law and Sovereignty' (2010) 29 *Law & Philosophy* 535–69.

but English law modelled after Russian law.[14] Later, in a debate with Hans Kelsen, he rejected Kelsen's monist theory of a unity of all laws and even began conceptualizing types of relations between laws: completion, reception and delegation.[15] Nonetheless, his statement that 'there is a good deal of unfinished business for analytical jurisprudence still to tackle'[16] seemed true then and still seems true today, despite a growing and important body of scholarship tackling these questions.

Cross-border normativity describes the situation that legal rules from system A somehow have normative force within and for system B. Cross-border normativity plays a role in a number of contexts. The conflict of laws provides the best, though by far not only, example for this. Whether a marriage celebrated by two Syrians in Syria is considered valid in Germany is, with some exceptions, determined by Syrian, not German, substantive law. Article 13 of the German Introductory Act explicitly says as much: the substantive validity of a marriage is governed by the law of the parties' nationality. Syrian law, therefore, becomes in some ways part of German law – it will govern the relation of parties living in Germany, and it will be the applicable law for judges. But it remains Syrian law.

16.3 Three Strategies for Cross-Normativity

Such cross-normativity is difficult for legal theory to conceptualize. In this section, I look at three types of responses to the problem, hoping to cover a wide array of existing responses without having to address, or even name, each individual response. A first set of attempts denies that foreign law is *law*. A second set of attempts denies that foreign law is *foreign*. A third set of attempts, finally, denies the *interrelation* of laws.[17]

[14] This is similar to the so-called local law theory in private international law; see Section 16.3.2.

[15] H. L. A. Hart, 'Kelsen's Doctrine of the Unity of Law', in H. L. A. Hart, *Essays in Jurisprudence and Philosophy* (Oxford University Press, 1983), pp. 309–42. Cf. D. von Daniels, *The Concept of Law from a Transnational Perspective* (Ashgate, 2010), pp. 158–60.

[16] See Hart, 'Kelsen's Doctrine', 310.

[17] In an earlier publication I distinguished three modes of responding to foreign law outside of its recognition at law, namely incorporation, deference and delegation. See R. Michaels, 'The Re-*State*-Ment of Non-state Law: The State, Choice of Law, and the Challenge from Global Legal Pluralism' (2005) 51 *Wayne Law Review* 1209–59, at 1231ff. The three modes correlate with the three positions discussed in Sections 16.3.1–16.3.3 – deference denies normativity, incorporation denies (or overcomes) foreignness, delegation establishes hierarchy.

16.3.1 Denying Normativity

A first way to deal with foreign normativity is simply to deny its normative nature: to treat foreign normativity as fact. We used to find such approaches quite frequently in legal doctrine. They emerged from a concern about foreign normativity. But the responses proved to be neither convincing conceptually nor to lead to adequate normative results.

A first example is the fact doctrine in civil procedure. The doctrine emerges from English law, where the only law that could be applied was domestic law, and so foreign law had to enter the courts not as law but as fact.[18] This has implications in particular for the procedural treatment of foreign law – under the doctrine, its validity and content must be proven like that of any other law, and burdens of evidence can be allocated according to who relies on the foreign law. The fact doctrine is not entirely wrong: foreign law (like domestic law) is, of course, also a fact.[19] But the doctrine cannot explain the normative force that foreign law has in domestic courts – that it is applied as law, not merely referred to as fact. Insofar as claims and defences are based on foreign law, it seems impossible to deny that the foreign law has its own normativity within domestic courts, and thus differs from facts. Indeed, the procedural treatment of foreign law as fact demonstrates this (and is another reason for the doctrine's decline).[20]

A second example emerges from choice of law, in particular within an approach popular for some time in England and the United States and in a different way in France: the vested rights theory.[21] Under this theory, the applicable law in English courts is still only English law. But foreign law can enter English courts in the form of rights that parties have acquired abroad under foreign law and are now having enforced. This seemed a clever trick to justify normativity while denying that an English judge would actually apply foreign law, but it was an unsuccessful trick. The main problem of the theory had already been shown by Wächter in

[18] R. Fentiman, *Foreign Law in English Courts: Pleading, Proof and Choice of Law* (Oxford University Press, 1998).

[19] See N. Jansen and R. Michaels, 'Die Auslegung und Fortbildung ausländischen Rechts' (Interpreting and Developing Foreign Law) (2003) 116 *Zeitschrift für Zivilprozess* 3–55.

[20] Comparatively, see Y. Nishitani, 'General Report', in Y. Nishitani (ed.), *Treatment of Foreign Law: Dynamics towards Convergence?* (Springer, 2017), pp. 3–60, at pp. 18–19.

[21] See R. Michaels, 'EU Law as Private International Law? Reconceptualising the Country-of-Origin Principle as Vested Rights Theory' (2006) 2 *Journal of Private International Law* 195–242.

the nineteenth century: it is impossible to say that a right is 'vested' under foreign law unless we determine previously that the law under which it 'vested' is actually applicable.[22]

It is worth noting that the vested rights theory continues to have a (limited) existence in the enforcement of foreign judgements. Previously, foreign judgements were not actually enforced but merely treated as (irrebuttable) evidence for the existence of a claim that was then enforced under the forum's own law – they were, in other words, treated as facts. Even today, foreign judgements are, in principle, enforceable without a reference to the foreign law on which they may be based.

16.3.2 Internalization of Normativity

If these theories denied, unsuccessfully, the *lawness* of foreign law, other theories attempt to deny the *foreignness* of foreign law. One way to do so is through incorporation – turning the foreign rule into a domestic rule. Short of actual colonization of a foreign country, such incorporation will, however, rarely be complete.[23] The legal rule will remain foreign. It would be odd to say that rules of Soviet law become rules of English law merely because a judge applies them.[24]

Hart's replication theory provides an alternative explanation: in reality, he says, English law replicates a rule of Soviet law. It finds its equivalent in the so-called local law theory in private international law.[25] According to this theory, an Italian judge, when asked to apply English law, never really applies English law. What she does apply is a rule of Italian law that is modelled after English law. Here, the legal character of English law is accepted, but its normativity is derived from its character as a rule of Italian law. The doctrine has not been convincing either.

Cavers formulated the most compelling criticism:[26]

[22] The relevant passage is translated in K. H. Nadelmann, 'Some Historical Notes on the Doctrinal Sources of American Conflicts Law', in K. H. Nadelmann, *Conflict of Laws: International and Interstate. Selected Essays* (Nijhoff, 1972), pp. 1–20, at p. 16.

[23] See J. Raz, 'Incorporation by Law' (2004) 10 *Legal Theory* 1–17.

[24] Ibid., 10.

[25] W. W. Cook, 'The Logical and Legal Bases of the Conflict of Laws' (1924) 33 *Yale Law Journal* 457–88; R. De Novo, 'New Trends in Italian Private International Law' (1963) 28 *Law & Contemporary Problems* 808–21, at 812–13.

[26] D. F. Cavers, 'The Two "Local Law" Theories' (1950) 63 *Harvard Law Review* 822–32, at 823. See also Dyzenhaus, 'The Janus-Faced Constitution', 31–2.

> Theories that explain how it is that a foreign rule isn't foreign law when it is used in deciding a case in another country might seem more useful if I could forget the way in which my son resolved a like problem when, at the age of four, he encountered tuna fish salad. 'Isn't that chicken?' he inquired after the first bite. Told that no, indeed, it was fish, he restored his world to order and concluded the matter by remarking to himself, 'Fish made of chicken'.

Cavers' son seems right. When a judge has to apply foreign law, she must, to a great extent, attempt to apply that law in the way in which it is applied abroad. What is demanded from her, therefore, is the actual application of a foreign law. Replication is a cumbersome fiction, made necessary only if we assume that cross-boundary normativity is not possible. These shortcomings are consequences from Hart's thinking within one legal system, namely his own.[27]

16.3.3 *Sharing of Authority*

A third attempt to deal with cross-normativity exists in the literature on legal pluralism. Much of this literature does not conceptualize interactions between overlapping orders, beyond stating that they exist, but some does. A jurisprudentially ambitious attempt is what Nicole Roughan calls 'relative authority', by which she means 'shared or independently held normative power'.[28] Roughan recognizes, based on ideas from legal pluralism, that multiple legal orders may not only coexist but even claim normative force with regard to the same situation – a conflict-of-laws situation, if you will. In response, she suggests that multiple laws (or institutions) may share authority: they may, each, cover only part of the normative space. The prerequisite for this is a 'justified inter-authority relationship' between the different orders. Conflicts between such orders may be resolved by 'meeting in the middle' – effectively, the drawing of compromise.[29]

From an external perspective, such an idea of shared authority appears attractive. For a strictly positivist theory, by contrast, it runs into three problems. The first is that legal orders are not usually incomplete in the

[27] On Hart's 'parochialism' see D. Dyzenhaus, 'Kelsen's Contribution to Contemporary Philosophy of International Law' (2020), https://ssrn.com/abstract=3571343.

[28] N. Roughan, *Authorities: Conflicts, Cooperation, and Transnational Legal Theory* (Oxford University Press, 2013), pp. 136 et seq.

[29] N. Roughan, 'Meet Me in the Middle?' (2019) 29 *Duke Journal of Comparative & International Law* 423–36.

sense that they deliberately limit themselves without need. The English law on negligence is, potentially, universal. Granted, there are cases in which an English court will not apply that law, for example with regard to a tort committed in France, and in that sense there is a sharing of authority. But this is in consequence of (real or potential) conflicts, not intrinsic to English law itself.

This first problem may seem banal on its own, but it is exacerbated by a second one. Roughan calls her mechanism of cross-border authority a 'justified inter-authority relationship', but while she develops criteria for that justification, she does not say where the normative foundation of the justification derives from. The justification does not appear to come from one of the two authorities, but where does it rest instead? Morality? Natural law? Practical reasoning? None of these justifications is available to a positivist theory of law. And none of them seems to account for the way in which each legal order in fact mediates its relation to others.

A third problem concerns the border between the authorities: who determines it, and how? Roughan proposes that conflicting authorities should compromise, 'meet in the middle'. This sounds like an attractive solution, the likely result of a (real or hypothetical) agreement between the orders. But such difference-splitting is problematic.[30] Where exactly is that middle? Why should we think legal orders agree on the middle, rather than on any other point of the continuum between full authority for one or the other legal order? And how do we account for a situation in which the authorities actually do not agree where the middle is? Must we defer analysis until such agreement occurs or one authority 'wins'?

16.4 The Answer of Tertiary Rules

It is proposed that a better way to account for relations between legal orders is the concept of tertiary rules. Tertiary rules share characteristics with secondary rules insofar as they do not constitute commands; instead, they serve to identify the processes by which the applicable commands can be recognized. This is why several scholars, beginning with Hart himself, have viewed them as extensions of secondary rules.[31] They differ from secondary rules in one significant way however: they

[30] See D. Kennedy, 'Strategizing Strategic Behavior in Legal Interpretation' (1996) *Utah Law Review* 785–825, at 795–6, 808–9.

[31] J. P. Trachtman, *The Future of International Law: Global Government* (Cambridge University Press, 2013), p. 272; T. Schultz, 'Secondary Rules of Recognition and

determine the scope of foreign, not domestic, law. Ignoring this crucial difference leads to significant and consequential misunderstandings.

I am not the first to propose such a concept – my tertiary rules share certain characteristics with Nico Krisch's interface norms and with Detlef von Daniels' linkage rules.[32] Even the term tertiary rules has been used before: Joel Trachtman has used it to account for rules that 'allocate authority among constitutions: among state constitutions, between state constitutions and international organization constitutions, and among international organization constitutions'.[33] But the concept is not yet, I think, sufficiently precise. In the following I try to develop a precise concept of tertiary rules, and discuss in what ways it differs from the other projects mentioned.

A definition of tertiary rules is not easier than a definition of secondary rules, but here is an attempt: *Tertiary rules are rules with which one legal order designates, relative to itself, the normative space of another legal order to which it is not hierarchically superior*. This definition requires explanation, which takes place here. Perhaps more importantly, it requires application and examples, which will take place in Section 16.5, where three different types of tertiary rules are explicated at somewhat greater length.

16.4.1 *Designation of Normative Spaces*

A first element of this definition that requires explanation is the rather amorphous term normative spaces. Why not rather the validity or bindingness of foreign rules? After all, the question for a positivist theory of law (or laws) in the Hartian tradition is to determine what does and what does not count as normatively valid.

Relative Legality in Transnational Regimes' (2011) 56 *American Journal of Jurisprudence* 59–88.

32 N. Krisch, *Beyond Constitutionalism: The Pluralist Structure of Postnational Law* (Oxford University Press, 2010), pp. 285–96; von Daniels, *The Concept of Law from a Transnational Perspective*, pp. 158–66.

33 Trachtman, *The Future of International Law*, p. 272, see also pp. 286–87. For an earlier version of the argument, see J. P. Trachtman, 'The Constitutions of the WTO' (2006) 17 *European Journal of International Law* 623–46, at 627. Trachtman does not, however, provide a more extensive analysis of either the nature or the scope of tertiary rules, except to link the concept to an idea of global law as both one and plural. As a consequence, neither the legal character nor the origin of these tertiary rules becomes clear. A different concept of tertiary rules can be found in J. Hampton, 'Democracy and the Rule of Law' (1994) 36 *Nomos* 13–44, at 35–36: rules about changing secondary rules.

Tertiary rules do indeed give normative validity to (foreign) legal rules, but that alone does not distinguish them from secondary rules, and that similarity does not account for existing differences. The difference is this: secondary rules operate *within* one legal order – they give validity to rules that would otherwise have no validity at all. A legislative bill that does not obtain the required parliamentary majority does not become a valid legal rule at all. In the transnational realm, unlike in the domestic realm, we are confronted not only with the relations between legal rules within one system. We are additionally confronted with the limitations and cross-references existing between, not within legal orders. In response, tertiary rules operate *between* legal orders: they extend the validity that a rule in a foreign legal order already has into another legal order where it does not have that validity.

This focus on foreign normativity distinguishes tertiary rules from a whole number of techniques that respond to the existence of competing normativities through self-restraint. The presumption against extraterritoriality is one of many examples. According to this doctrine, courts should choose an interpretation of statutes that confines its scope of application to the home state's own territory. Such techniques are not tertiary rules, however. They determine the scope of application of a legal order's *own* rules and are, as such, secondary rules, insofar as they are directed at adjudicators or other norm interpreters. The restriction of a rule's scope of application is an ordinary process within domestic law; it does not change its nature when it happens in response to normative claims from another legal order any more than it does when it happens in response to other normative claims. Tertiary rules do something different: they provide normative space to *foreign* legal rules.

Unlike secondary norms, tertiary rules do not provide requirements for the change of rules and institutions of foreign orders, nor do they provide specific rules on adjudication. The courts and rules of legal order B never derive their validity exclusively from legal order A. Instead, tertiary norms deal with the recognition and application of foreign institutions and rules that are already valid under foreign law. Rules of Syrian marriage law are valid, within Syrian law, regardless of whether they are designated by a German conflicts rule or not. This is why it would be misleading to say that tertiary rules allocate authority. The German conflicts rule does not create the validity of the rule per se; all it does is extend that validity and bindingness into German law. The question for tertiary rules is not whether a law is binding or valid in the abstract – that is, in principle, determined by the legal order to which the law belongs – but to what extent it has normative force in the concrete case in the view of another legal order. This means, firstly, that the issue of normative space includes not only validity and normativity but also their respective space and limitations. The normative space granted to legal order B by legal order A may be narrower than that which legal order B grants to itself. It means, in addition, that what matters are not only questions of validity and general bindingness but also of *applicability*.

16.4.2 Legal Nature

Second, in accordance with the positivist aim of this approach, I understand tertiary rules as legal rules. The designation of normative spaces is an operation of law, and tertiary rules are part of the legal system of A. This means that choice-of-law rules are tertiary rules, as are rules on the recognition of foreign judgements. By contrast, diplomatic negotiations are not,[34] nor are ideas about inter-institutional dialogue, compromise and so on and so forth. Such processes have an existence of course, and they are also often legitimate, though not unsuspicious.[35] But they have no space within a positivistic theory of law that aims at determining normativity, not factual actions that are taken.

I can see two objections to this postulate. The first is that it would be unduly restrictive to exclude non-legal mechanisms. Functionally, legal and non-legal mechanisms both operate towards similar ends. Indeed, some mechanisms are not easily placed within one or the other category. Comity, for example, is often placed somewhere between law and politics – 'neither a matter of absolute obligation, on the one hand, nor of mere courtesy and good will, upon the other', to use the US Supreme Court's famous definition.[36] But what matters here is not function but mode. There are many ways in which legal claims can be negotiated between legal orders, just as there are many ways, legal and non-legal, to

[34] This does not deny that certain moves of diplomacy can be reconceptualized as conflict-of-laws moves: K. Knop and A. Riles, 'Space, Time and Historical Injustice: A Feminist Conflict-of-Laws Approach to the "Comfort Women" Settlement' (2016) 102 *Cornell Law Review* 853–928, at 885ff.

[35] See K. Knop, R. Michaels and A. Riles, 'From Multiculturalism to Technique: Feminism, Culture, and the Conflict of Laws Style' (2012) 64 *Stanford Law Review* 589–656, at 648–52.

[36] *Hilton* v. *Guyot*, 159 U.S. 113, 143 (1895).

resolve disputes. But we call only some of these ways legal, and they are distinct through their mode.

This leads to the second, more fundamental, possible objection. Maybe it is wrong to refer to any techniques of cross-boundary normativity as legal. It is now widely accepted that public international law is law. But maybe private international law is not.[37] Or, put more generally (and plausibly), the legal rules of private international law are not really different from secondary rules within a system, whereas the relation between legal orders, that is, cross-boundary normativity, is in reality regulated through extra-legal norms.

This would be a category error. It may of course be possible to describe tertiary rules as mere social practices. It is also possible to describe, in quasi-realist fashion, what factors courts actually use in order to resolve conflict-of-laws issues, perhaps regardless of the existing doctrine. Notably, however, that would not distinguish tertiary rules from other rules. For Hart, the rule of recognition was a social, not a legal rule. Andrei Marmor argues that all secondary rules are social and not legal rules: they describe the practice of legal officials in determining what should and what should not count as law.[38] Scandinavian legal realism explains even primary rules as social facts, not legal rules. But such attempts could not account for the particular mode in which such decisions are justified, namely through invocation of legal rules and techniques. A description of choice-of-law reasoning as the mere following of a certain social norm cannot account for the complexity in which this reasoning occurs, the complexity of legal technique. Non-legal modes of negotiating between legal orders – diplomacy, for example – may at times also be complex. But their complexity is of a very different kind.

16.4.3 Horizontal Nature

So far, tertiary rules are not significantly different from secondary rules. What sets them apart, what is in fact their most important characteristic, is their horizontal nature. Tertiary rules are part of one legal order that is not hierarchically superior to the legal order whose normative space is

[37] See R. Michaels, 'Post-critical Private International Law: From Politics to Technique', in H. Muir Watt and D. P. Fernández Arroyo (eds), *Private International Law and Global Governance* (Oxford University Press, 2014), pp. 54–69, at pp. 54, 57–8.

[38] A. Marmor, *Positive Law and Objective Values* (Oxford University Press, 2001).

designated. If English law designates the normative space of Moroccan law, it does so in a horizontal way. English law is not superior to Moroccan law, and yet designates the latter's normative space.

It is useful, first, to distinguish tertiary rules from two other types of rules that are not horizontal in nature. The first of these are vertical priority rules based on hierarchy within one legal system. The supremacy clause of the US Constitution, for example, creates, within the US legal system, a hierarchy between federal and state law. In this hierarchy, state law is valid only insofar as it does not exceed the normative space of the laws of the individual states (they are valid insofar they do not contradict federal law). Within the system of US law, the supremacy clause is a secondary rule, just like a rule that designates the later-in-time rule to trump the former-in-time, or the special rule to trump the general rule.

The other type are rules that exist in a legal system that is hierarchically superior to both legal orders between which it mediates. In this sense, public international law allocates jurisdictional authority among states. And in this sense, EU private international law rules allocate authority between the laws of France and Germany. These EU rules are choice-of-law rules, but although the relation between the laws of France and Germany may be horizontal, the relation between EU law and these two legal orders is not.

In several ways vertical priority rules look like tertiary rules: they designate normative spaces, and they act inter-systemically. However, they do not operate in a horizontal way, and this makes the difference. A tertiary hierarchy rule is uniform for all affected legal systems. By contrast, and this is crucial, tertiary rules are not uniform for all affected legal system. Instead, each legal system has its own tertiary rules, and because there is no hierarchy between the affected legal systems, all of them coexist. English law has rules designating the normative space of rules from Moroccan law, just as Moroccan law has rules designating the normative space of rules from English law.

As a consequence, tertiary rules are reciprocal. However, these rules are not necessarily symmetrical. The way in which English law designates the normative space of Moroccan law is independent from the way in which Moroccan law designates normative space for English law. A fortiori, the normative space given to Moroccan law by English law may be different from the normative space given to English law by Moroccan law.

It follows that there is not one but two borders between English law and Moroccan law.[39] Or, put differently, the resulting border may look different from the perspective of each system. As a consequence, a certain set of facts may be within the limits of English law from the perspective of English law, and within the limits of Moroccan law from the perspective of Moroccan law (a situation private international lawyers call a true conflict). Or, conversely, it may be within the limits of Moroccan law from the perspective of English law, and within the limits of English law from the perspective of Moroccan law (a situation that private international lawyers call renvoi).[40]

Often, there will be such symmetry, or at least mutuality, and agreement on the place of the border. Often, English law will only be willing to grant normative space to Moroccan law if and insofar as Moroccan law grants such normative space to English law in other cases. In this sense, reciprocity is often viewed as the foundation of international relations and, by extension, international law. But this is only a special case, and by far not uniformly true. Tertiary rules, as explained here, are rules of each domestic law, not of international law. Whereas reciprocity and mutual respect provide good reasons for having such rules, they are neither necessary for such rules to exist, nor are they sufficient in bringing such rules about.

16.4.4 Relationality

All of this brings about the possibility that conflicts – or, put more neutrally, disagreements about the place of the border between legal systems – may exist. Such conflicts are a problem of theories of law that are not plural in nature. One legal system cannot be a system, arguably, if it does not provide mechanisms with which conflicts are resolved. Indeed, most legal systems provide secondary rules to resolve such conflicts if they occur *within* one system. Tertiary rules make it possible to account for the fact that, as *between* legal systems, conflicts can continue to exist. Thus, it may be possible that a certain conduct is

[39] See R. Michaels, 'A Symmetry of Asymmetries? A Private-International-Law Reconstruction of Lindahl's Work on Boundaries' (2019) 29 *Duke Journal of Comparative and International Law* 405–22, at 419.

[40] Cf. H. Kelsen, 'Observations' (1957) 447 *Annuaire de l'Institut de droit international*, II, 115; republished in C. Leben (ed.), *Hans Kelsen - Écrits français de droit international* (PUF, 2001), p. 309.

governed by English law from the perspective of English law, and *at the same time* governed by Moroccan law from the perspective of Moroccan law. This means, however, that there no longer is an independent position from which to determine whether some rules do or do not count as valid and applicable law. Instead, there are separate legal systems, each of which determines what counts as law for itself (through a rule of internal recognition) and for other orders (through a rule of external recognition). The normative space of each legal system differs depending on the legal system from which it is designated.

The biggest challenge then from tertiary rules – the main reason why they are so hard to conceptualize from the perspective of traditional legal theory – is their relationality.[41] What is meant by relationality is this: the tertiary rules of English law designate normative spaces of foreign laws only relative to English law itself. English law cannot designate the normative space of Moroccan law with binding force for any order other than English law. It can certainly not bind Moroccan law: if a rule of Moroccan law is held to be inapplicable by a court in London, this does not mean that it is inapplicable from the perspective of Moroccan law. Nor can English law bind a third legal system, for example Japanese law with regard to Japan's own designation of the normative space of Moroccan law. If a rule of Moroccan law is held to be inapplicable by a court in London, Japan remains free to hold the rule applicable in relation to Japan.

On the flipside, a legal order cannot designate its own normative space with binding force for any other legal order. Certainly, it would be unusual for a court in Morocco to consider a rule of English law applicable even though an English court would not apply it. But it would be perfectly possible. For example, take a case in which Moroccan law designates the law of nationality to be the applicable law, whereas English law designates the law of the domicile to be applicable. In that case, arguably, Moroccan law would limit the normative space of its own legal order so that it would not include an Englishman domiciled in Morocco. Nonetheless, an English court would be free to apply Moroccan law to this person regardless.[42]

This relationality and relativity of a concept of law are necessary consequences of global legal pluralism. We no longer have an Archimedean point from which we can determine whether something

[41] See already Michaels, 'Law and Recognition'.

[42] The English court would indeed do so, provided it did not apply the doctrine of renvoi.

is or is not law. If we accept that the definition of law is itself the fruit of the operation of legal rules, then we have to find these rules in the law. And if laws are interrelated, then we can find these rules not merely within each legal system, but must instead look within other legal systems, too. Because such rules operate between legal systems only, they lead to a relational concept of law. The nature of law, the normative space of law, is no longer determined in an absolute fashion but only relative to other legal systems. Something can be a legal order vis-à-vis one other legal system, but not vis-à-vis another legal system. The nature of a legal system exists in relation to another legal system. The normative space of a legal system in the world is determined, in part, by other legal systems.

16.5 Examples of Tertiary Rules

All of this has been quite abstract. Some examples will hopefully both demonstrate that tertiary rules actually exist and will clarify the abstract concept. That most of these come from the discipline of private international law should not be surprising: private international law is the discipline specifically focused on cross-border normativity. But no claim is made that all tertiary rules belong to private international law.

16.5.1 External Recognition

The first and arguably most important tertiary rule is the rule of external recognition.[43] Under this rule, English law recognizes Moroccan law as a legal order. This means that legal order A is willing to designate a positive normative space to legal order B, without yet determining how far this space extends. The clearest example exists in public international law: if the United Kingdom recognizes Palestine as a state, it thereby also expresses a willingness to recognize, as to an as of yet undefined extent, Palestine's laws as having a normative space. But external recognition goes to laws and legal orders, not to sovereignty. It can therefore in theory also designate normative space for non-state law.

The rule of external recognition exists in partial analogy to Hart's rule of recognition, but there are important differences. First, Hart's rule of recognition determines binding force of law within one system; I therefore call it a rule of internal recognition. The rule of external

[43] This is discussed in more detail in Michaels, 'Law and Recognition'.

recognition, by contrast, determines the binding force of another legal system. It is therefore properly called a rule of external recognition. That external recognition cannot be universal, as was seen before. An Italian judge can recognize Islamic law as law with effect only for Italian law, not in general. On the other side, the rule of internal recognition is also relative in this way, as Hart himself recognized. The rule of recognition of English law designates English law as binding (as law) only with force for the English.

Second, although both rules of internal and of external recognition create the possibility of normative spaces, they do so in different ways. The rule of internal recognition creates lawmaking power – without it, the recognized institutions would have no lawmaking power at all. The rule of external recognition, by contrast, does not create lawmaking power. The lawmaking power of a Palestinian legislator does not depend on recognition by English law. What does depend on that recognition is the normative space of resulting law, with regard to English law.

Third, whereas there is debate over whether the rule of internal recognition is a legal rule or a social fact, the rule of external recognition, as understood here, is undoubtedly a legal rule. The recognition of Moroccan law for English law is an operation of English law. That operation may of course be brought about by factual acts, like a declaration of recognition by a head of state. But that does not distinguish it from other operations: most legal operations are brought about by a factual act. If a pronouncement by the head of state of legal order A can bring about the potential bindingness of laws and decisions of legal order B for legal order A, then this is not a social fact but a consequence of the rules of legal order B.

Fourth, whereas the rule of internal recognition is often discussed but rarely practically relevant, the rule of external recognition is actually important. The rule of internal recognition is largely irrelevant because the operation of legal orders depends largely on the self-reinforcing day-to-day operations of the law, based on the mutual and tacit, though rarely effectively expressed or doubted, assumption of a valid recognition. If, for example, some citizens in the southern states of the United States, or the so-called *Reichsbürger* in Germany, refuse to recognize the authority of their own governments, this is irrelevant not merely because they are unjustified in their refusal, but also (mainly) because their recognition is relatively unimportant. The rule of internal recognition is rarely questioned. By contrast, the recognition of foreign law as law is frequently relevant. This is not only the familiar question of illegitimate governments or of failed states, not even only that of non-recognized states, but also the question of the ability to make law more generally.

16.5.2 Recognition of Foreign Acts, Records and Judicial Proceedings

Just as Hart's rule of internal recognition alone is not sufficient for the functioning of a legal system, so the rule of external recognition alone is not sufficient to deal with cross-normativity as between normative orders. Another important set of tertiary rules concerns the recognition not of legal orders at large, but instead of individual products of other legal orders.

Such recognition is often required in federal systems. The US Constitution, in its Article IV Section 1 First Sentence, requires that 'Full Faith and Credit shall be given in each State to the public Acts, Records, and judicial Proceedings of every other State'. In a parallel way, EU law requires its member states to recognize a number of acts of other member states, so much so that one speaks of a principle of mutual recognition within EU law.[44] These rules are not, however, tertiary rules in the sense in which I speak of them here. Their root is not decentralized within each legal order itself (see characteristic 1 in Section 16.4.1). They emerge from a superior system of law, which can, due to its (presumed) hierarchical superiority, allocate normative spaces with effect on all affected states alike. They are vertical hierarchy rules.

For tertiary rules, the validity of products of Moroccan law for English law is in principle dependent on two factors. The first is internal to Moroccan law and depends on Morocco's secondary rules: was the act produced by the appropriate authorities and within the proper competence? The second factor, however, is external to Moroccan law and depends instead on the tertiary rules of English law: does English law recognize the products of Moroccan law as valid?

Take, for example, my German passport that I present at the border entering the United States. The USA will not admit me to its territory unless my passport is valid. That validity is determined not by US law but by German law. It is true that the acceptance of my passport as valid

[44] See C. Jannsens, *The Principle of Mutual Recognition in EU Law* (Oxford University Press, 2013); K. Lenaerts, 'The Principle of Mutual Recognition in the Area of Freedom, Security and Justice', The Fourth Annual Sir Jeremy Lever Lecture (All Souls College, University of Oxford 2015), www.law.ox.ac.uk/sites/files/oxlaw/the_principle_of_mutual_recognition_in_the_area_of_freedom_judge_lenaerts.pdf .

under these conditions is a function of US law (in addition to international law, which I will ignore for purposes of the argument here).[45] But it would be odd to claim that the United States, through its secondary rules, authorized the German authorities to create valid passports. The United States does have secondary rules for its own passports, which designate both the competent authorities to create passports and the processes through which this production takes place. It does not apply those rules to German passports, however.

The passport's validity under German law alone does not, however, make it binding on US authorities. Rather, whether the passport is recognized – and whether additional requirements must be met – is a function of a tertiary rule of US law. It is that rule that designates normative force to the passport vis-à-vis US authorities.

Documents may serve as the clearest example of recognition, but they are not the only one. Another example concerns the recognition of administrative acts. There is a question, for example, whether country A should, in regulating the conduct of corporation X, take into account that corporation X received a permit for its conduct from country B. Under the principle of mutual recognition, there is a wide-ranging duty to recognize such permits, but that duty, as emerging from a hierarchically superior order, does not count as a tertiary rule. Such recognition is the object of tertiary rules, however, insofar it emerges from rules of the recognizing legal order itself.

Another example can be found in the recognition of foreign arrest warrants. Take the European arrest warrant.[46] This warrant is issued not by a European authority but instead by one member state; it is, however, with few exceptions, recognized and enforced by other member states. Here, recognition does not go to a private privilege that an individual or a corporation wants to carry with them across boundaries, but instead expands the normative space of a foreign warrant beyond the territorial borders that would normally limit a sovereign's executive jurisdiction. Again, insofar as the duty emerges from EU law, it follows from a vertical

[45] International law obliges states to recognize foreign passports, but whether they do this remains a function of their own sovereign decision. For the interplay, see, R. A. C. Alton and J. R. Struble, 'The Nature of a Passport at the Intersection of Customary International Law and American Judicial Practice' (2010) 16 *Annual Survey of International and Comparative Law* 9–18.

[46] See V. Mitsilegas, 'Judicial Dialogue, Legal Pluralism and Mutual Trust in Europe's Area of Criminal Justice' (forthcoming) *European Law Review*.

hierarchy rule. By contrast, if one country recognizes a foreign arrest warrant on its own, such recognition is a matter of a tertiary rule.

Finally, the recognition and enforcement of foreign civil and commercial judgements can count as an example for this type of tertiary rule. The old common law rule, by which judgements provided rights which, by themselves, the winning party could enforce anywhere, was incompatible not only with the idea of sovereignty but also with the justified interest of legal orders to refuse recognition and enforcement to judgements they considered incompatible with certain important values. By themselves, judgements bind only within the borders of the sovereign whose courts issued them. This is why a French seventeenth-century statute declared all foreign judgements to be without force in France, and why some countries still, technically, refuse to recognize and enforce foreign judgements outside of a treaty. In such systems, a foreign judgement can be considered as a fact, perhaps even, as in some theories, as irrefutable evidence of the existence of the underlying right. It can also be internalized into the enforcing legal order, as is the case in the technique of naturalization of foreign judgements. Modern theories (and practices) of judgement recognition follow neither of these twisted techniques, however. Instead, foreign judgements are recognized and enforced and thereby given normative space beyond their traditional borders.

16.5.3 Application of Foreign Law

The most important tertiary rules are, arguably, choice-of-law rules that designate the application of foreign law, mainly within the context of private international law. Foreign law is applied as a matter of course today, despite the considerable theoretical difficulty to explain such application within traditional legal theory. Indeed, the absence of private international law from most theories of law, including those of (public) international law and of private law, may be a consequence of such difficulties.

The misnomer 'choice of law', frequent in the common law world, is already a sign for these difficulties. The applicable law is not determined by a discretionary choice of the judge. Instead, the application of foreign law is an operation of the law itself, in this case the private international law rules of the forum. Save for a few exceptions, most prominently the conflict-of-laws regime of the European Union, these rules are not hierarchically superior. Instead, they are horizontal rules in the sense given above.

Nonetheless, many explanations of private international law try to explain its rules by denying one of the criteria found here for tertiary rules. The vested rights theory as a theory denying normativity was already explained in Section 16.3.1. Another theory of private international law, the so-called datum theory, also denies foreign normativity and claims to consider foreign rules as mere facts (data). That approach has found a recent application in Article 17 of the Rome II Regulation, which mandates that 'account shall be taken, as a matter of fact and in so far as is appropriate, of the rules of safety and conduct which were in force at the place and time of the event giving rise to the liability'. The wording demonstrates the desire to avoid normativity, but it can hardly be denied that such 'taking into account' will often, effectively, amount to application. How else should such rules be taken into account if not in their normativity?

What choice-of-law rules do is to designate the normative space of law. An English rule that designates Moroccan law as applicable to a certain conduct thereby designates a normative space that Moroccan law would not otherwise have. Moroccan law might (or indeed might not) be applicable to the relevant facts relative to itself, that is, from the perspective of a Moroccan judge. But that normative space would not exist universally. An English private international law rule cannot make the space universal either. What it can do, however, is to designate a normative space relative to English law, that is, from the perspective of an English judge.

16.6 Conclusion

In this chapter I have argued that some rules that exist in legal systems cannot be understood as either primary or secondary rules but constitute a different type of rules, called tertiary rules. These are the rules with which a legal system organizes its own relation to other legal systems and also designates those other legal systems' normative space with regard to itself. Those rules have proven to be more complex than primary and secondary rules, and incompatible with certain postulates of traditional theories of legal systems that emphasize internal coherence and consistency. They are the consequence of a plural world in which law is not one but many.

Recognizing tertiary rules is thus necessary for a pluralistic theory of laws. However, the recognition of tertiary rules is not dependent on the recognition of such a theory. Tertiary rules are an actually observable category of rules within legal systems. This chapter does not invent them, it merely brings them together and describes their qualities. If anything, therefore, a pluralistic theory of laws is a necessary consequence of the recognition of tertiary rules which do not have a proper space in monist theories of law.

Regardless of such a theory, the concept of tertiary rules ought to be of both theoretical and practical interest. Theoretically, they represent an important category of rules and are instructive for the way in which such rules operate across borders. Practically, they help see commonalities between rules in different areas of law. And they help see differences from other rules, like rules of unilateral restraint, or from non-legal mechanisms to resolve normative conflicts. They thereby also provide ammunition against those who claim that conflicts of laws cannot be resolved except in extra-legal ways. The recognition of tertiary rules demonstrates that law is more varied and therefore more flexible that one may think on the basis of monist legal theories.

17

A Reconstruction of Transnational Legal Pluralism and Law's Foundations

BRIAN Z. TAMANAHA

An outpouring of writings on global or transnational legal pluralism has occurred in the past two decades. Despite its apparent popularity, however, it suffers from deep conceptual problems. After reviewing two decades of this proliferating literature, jurisprudent William Twining remarked, 'I have come away feeling that it is little better than a morass'.[1] This chapter is an attempt to clear up the morass. Three complicating factors bear mention at the outset. First, 'pluralism' is a capacious term that simply means two or more and can be applied to law in a multitude of ways. Second, 'law' is a contested notion that has been conceived of in numerous ways. Third, legal pluralism has been invoked in a variety of fields with very different orientations and objectives, including legal anthropology, legal sociology, postcolonial studies, law and development, human rights, comparative law, international law, transnational law and jurisprudence. The confluence of these factors has resulted in a tangled conceptual mess.

With these preliminary comments in mind, I address a series of central issues bearing on global/transnational legal pluralism (labels used interchangeably). The first several parts of this chapter critically examine certain prominent positions in global legal pluralism, showing why they are problematic, after which I construct an alternative account that avoids these problems. First, I demonstrate that, contrary to current accounts, global legal pluralism is not continuous with earlier versions of (postcolonial and sociological) legal pluralism; these are three completely distinct paradigms. Next, I expose the flaw of overinclusiveness that has plagued theoretical conceptions of legal pluralism from the

For their helpful critical comments on earlier drafts, I thank Nico Krisch, Hanna Birkenkotter, Sarah Nouwen and Ralf Michaels.

[1] W. Twining, 'Normative and Legal Pluralism: A Global Perspective' (2010) 20 *Duke Journal of Comparative and International Law* 473–518, at 487.

outset and reappears in global legal pluralism, particularly in the work of Paul Berman. Then I show why theoretical concepts of law cannot solve this flaw, which ultimately led John Griffiths – the foremost champion of legal pluralism – to repudiate the notion. I then address the profusion of private and hybrid regulatory forms on the domestic and transnational levels, and I mark the line between theory and practice. Thereafter, I expose problems with the relational concept of law formulated by Ralf Michaels, showing why it is unsuitable for many situations of legal pluralism. These critical examinations lay a basis for the constructive account that follows. The approach to legal pluralism I articulate involves social constructions conventionally identified as law that vary and change over time, which can be grouped in terms of three categories: community law, regime law and cross-polity law. Finally, I set forth a handful of specific lessons for a reconstructed transnational legal pluralism.

17.1 Three Distinct Paradigms of Legal Pluralism

It is common to characterize attention to legal pluralism as three successive waves building on earlier work: first came attention by anthropologists to postcolonial legal pluralism, then attention by sociologists to legal pluralism in every society, then attention by jurists to global/transnational legal pluralism. Global legal pluralist Ralf Michaels observed:

> Legal pluralism, long a special interest within the specialist discipline of legal anthropology, has recently moved into the mainstream of legal discourse. The most likely reason is globalization. Many of the challenges that globalization poses to traditional legal thought closely resemble those formulated earlier by legal pluralists. The irreducible plurality of legal orders in the world, the coexistence of domestic state law with other legal orders, the absence of a hierarchically superior position transcending the differences – all of these topics of legal pluralism reappear on the global sphere.[2]

This narrative of continuity is reinforced by frequent references in the third approach to major theorists and theories within the second approach, prominently including John Griffiths (anti-legal centralism, strong versus weak legal pluralism), Eugen Ehrlich (living law of social associations) and Sally Falk Moore (semi-autonomous social field).

[2] R. Michaels, 'Global Legal Pluralism' (2009) 5 *Annual Review of Law and Social Sciences* 243–62, at 244.

This narrative, however, is misleading. Other than being about 'law' (though in different senses) and shining the spotlight on 'pluralism' (albeit in different senses), these three approaches have little in common. John Griffiths, the leading proponent of the second approach, pointedly *rejected* the first approach. He labelled postcolonial legal pluralism 'weak' because it involved recognition by the state of customary law, which Griffiths construed as merely reinforcing legal centralism. '"Legal pluralism" in the weak [postcolonial] sense has little to do with the concept of legal pluralism which is the subject of this article',[3] he declared, sharply distancing his sociological conception from studies of postcolonial law.

Griffiths' essay centres on 'strong' legal pluralism – 'an empirical state of affairs, namely the coexistence within a social group of legal orders which do not belong to a single system'.[4] This legal pluralism is based on a sociological concept of law, which encompasses the normative ordering of social associations and institutionalized rule systems generally (more on this shortly). As Sally Engle Merry noted three decades ago in her astute overview of legal pluralism, which boosted its academic profile, these two contexts of legal pluralism 'make odd companions' in that they have different targets and 'they come out of different scholarly traditions'.[5] In Kuhnian terms, this is a revolutionary paradigm shift, not a cumulative building on previous insights.

Comparative, international and transnational legal scholars who came to legal pluralism changed the subject yet again, in multiple ways. Contemporary global/transnational legal pluralism is the product mainly of jurists who focus on public and private systems of law and regulation between and across states, giving rise to multiple coexisting regulatory forms with potential application in various contexts. Constitutional pluralism of the European Union involves the pluralism of coexisting, intertwined official systems of national and EU law; international legal pluralism (or fragmentation) involves a pluralism of different subject matter regimes and tribunals within international law. None of this resembles postcolonial legal pluralism or sociological legal pluralism.

The characteristic feature of postcolonial legal pluralism is the coexistence of bodies of law with profoundly different norms and processes – mainly state law, and customary and religious law – operating

[3] J. Griffiths, 'What Is Legal Pluralism?' (1986) 24 *Journal of Legal Pluralism* 1–56, at 8.
[4] Ibid., 8.
[5] S. E. Merry, 'Legal Pluralism' (1988) 22 *Law & Society Review* 869–96, at 874.

independently as well as intertwined in various ways. A report issued by the World Bank legal department observes:

> In many developing countries, customary systems operating outside of the state regime are often the dominant form of regulation and dispute resolution, covering up to 90% of the population in parts of Africa. In Sierra Leone, for example, approximately 85% of the population falls under the jurisdiction of customary law, defined under the Constitution as 'the rules which, by custom, are applicable to particular communities in Sierra Leone'. Customary tenure covers 75% of land in most African countries, affecting 90% of land transactions in countries like Mozambique and Ghana [. . .] In many of these countries, systems of justice seem to operate almost completely independently of the official state system.[6]

Many manifestations of customary law involve the application of informal (unwritten) legal norms by chiefs or village elders, with the participation of members of the community, oriented towards resolving the matter, taking into consideration not just the individuals and specific incident involved, but also broader social relations. In contrast, state law involves transplanted, formal legal norms applied by legal officials within legal institutions utilizing technical legal terminology and processes.

What stands out about postcolonial legal pluralism is not the multiplicity of law per se, but rather the stark *contrasts* and sheer *diversity* between the coexisting bodies of formal and informal law derived from different traditions involving fundamentally different world views (in certain respects incompatible), reflecting highly fragmented societies (ethnic, religious, urban/rural, educated/illiterate, commercial developers/subsistence farmers, etc.). Compare this with discussions in the global/transnational legal pluralism literature of the interaction between EU law and national law, the TRIPS (Trade-Related Aspects of Intellectual Property Rights) agreement, *lex mercatoria*, human rights, World Trade Organization (WTO) law and the Appellate Body, Codex Alimentarius, UNIDROIT, *lex sportiva* and so forth. What stands out about the latter group is the burgeoning *multiplicity* of transnational legal and regulatory regimes, many tied to the expansion of global capitalism. While these norms and bodies of law may conflict in various ways, they are virtually all Western derived and they involve formal written regulatory regimes and tribunals operating in standard ways familiar to jurists.

[6] L. Chirayath, C. Sage, and M. Woolcock, *Customary Law and Policy Reform: Engaging with the Plurality of Justice Systems* (World Bank Legal Department Paper, 2005), p. 3.

The point, again, is that these situations of legal pluralism have very little in common. The claim of continuity between the first (postcolonial) and third (global) approaches to legal pluralism trades on two distinct connotations of pluralism: *diversity* and *multiplicity*. The former is fundamentally about legal diversity while the latter is about legal multiplicity. The former is largely the product of legal anthropologists exploring the various social consequences of these contrasting coexisting bodies of law; and most of these works are not juristically oriented. The latter largely involves academic jurists – many of whom are Europeans grappling with the interaction between EU law and national law – focusing on harmonization, reconciliation, assimilation, discussing choice of law and conflicts of law, jurisdiction and the like.

The differences between the second (sociological) and third (global) approaches to legal pluralism are also substantial – again grounded in fundamentally different orientations and objectives. The second approach was pioneered by sociologists whose goal was to construct a science of society around a sociological concept of law. A scientific positivist, John Griffiths was explicit about this objective:

> Thus, if concepts such as law, legalness, and social control are to figure in sociological theory, they must be taken as referring to identifiable social facts, and variation in those social facts should ultimately be expressible in quantitative terms.
>
> The first problem for the sociology of law, given the preceding assumptions, is to identify the sort of social fact it takes as its subject matter.[7]

Griffiths believed that (strong) legal pluralism follows directly from a sociological conception of law, and thus (strong) legal pluralism provides a basis for the sociology of law.

Among global/transnational legal pluralists, Gunther Teubner early on constructed legal pluralism in terms of a science of society (taking off from Griffiths and Sally Falk Moore), applying his autopoietic theory of law as a communicative system to transnational law,[8] advocating that 'legal pluralism needs to shift emphasis and focus on the fragmentation of social reproduction in a multiplicity of closed discourses'.[9] A second

[7] J. Griffiths, 'The Division of Labor in Social Control', in D. Black (ed.), *Toward a General Theory of Social Control* (Academic Press, 1984), pp. 37–70, at p. 39 (italics added).

[8] G. Teubner, 'Two Faces of Janus: Rethinking Legal Pluralism' (1991) 13 *Cardozo Law Review* 1443–62.

[9] Ibid., 1457.

early theorist of transnational legal pluralism, Boaventura de Sousa Santos, also had a sociological orientation, though from a postmodern perspective that eschewed a systematic science of society.[10] However, most contemporary global/transnational legal pluralists are not sociologists engaged in scientific theorizing about law, but are academic jurists largely focusing on, mapping and grappling with the multiplicity of transnational regulatory forms and their various modes of interaction and entanglement.[11] Owing to these different backgrounds and objectives, what the second (sociological) approach to legal pluralism is about is radically different from what the third (global) approach is about. Understood on its own terms, this latest take on legal pluralism represents yet another revolutionary paradigm change. The only connective link is that global legal pluralists regularly refer to the work of Griffiths, Moore and Ehrlich, derived from the sociological approach. This link, however, gives rise to irresolvable conceptual difficulties and disputes and should be discarded for reasons I explain in Sections 17.2 and 17.3.

William Twining, who has written extensively about globalization as well as about legal pluralism,[12] found that 'the many extensions and applications of the idea of legal pluralism to new phenomena and situations are so many and so varied that it is difficult to construct a coherent answer to the question: what is the relevance of classical studies of legal pluralism to the emerging field of "global legal pluralism"?'[13] My point is that any relevance is minimal.[14]

17.2 The Overinclusiveness Flaw

In her 1988 overview of legal pluralism, Sally Merry flagged a conceptual flaw of sociological legal pluralism that has reappeared in global legal pluralism in the writings of Paul Berman. Merry remarked, 'Where do we

[10] B. de Sousa Santos, 'Law: A Map of Misreading – Toward a Postmodern Conception of Law' (1987) 14 *Journal of Law and Society* 279–302; B. de Sousa Santos, *Toward a New Common Sense: Law, Science and Politics in the Paradigmatic Transition* (Routledge, 1995).

[11] See Chapter 1.

[12] See W. Twining, *General Jurisprudence: Understanding Law from a Global Perspective* (Cambridge University Press, 2009).

[13] Twining, 'Normative and Legal Pluralism', 512–13.

[14] Twining denied 'any strong claims to continuity', though he observed that global legal pluralism exhibited a similar opposition to state centrism, recognition of non-state law, taking religion seriously and more of an empirical orientation. Ibid., 515.

stop speaking of law and find ourselves simply describing social life? Is it useful to call all these forms of ordering law? I find that once legal centralism has been vanquished, calling all forms of ordering that are not state law by the term law confounds the analysis.'[15] The sociological conception of legal pluralism construes the normative ordering of social associations (like the family) and institutionalized rule systems (like corporations and universities) as forms of law. In Section 17.3, I explain the source of this problem and why it cannot be resolved, but here I flag its appearance in global legal pluralism.

Paul Berman, a prolific contemporary theorist of global legal pluralism, asserts that there is no need to define law. Yet, in effect, he presupposes a conception of law tied to social associations, but without explicitly articulating it.[16] Berman identifies law with norm-generating communities: 'From religious institutions, to industry standard-setting bodies to not-for-profit accreditation entities to arbitral panels to university tenure committees to codes promulgated within ethnic enclaves to self-regulation regimes in semi-autonomous communities, the sites of non-state lawmaking are truly everywhere.'[17] (His reference to self-regulation of semi-autonomous communities incorporates Sally Falk Moore's analysis, which I take up in Section 17.3) Berman has also identified law within the family[18] and 'in day-to-day human encounters such as interacting with strangers on a public street, waiting in lines, and communicating with subordinates or superiors'.[19] These examples reveal that for Berman virtually all normative ordering is law. As a consequence, law is a fuzzy notion and legal pluralism is extraordinarily pervasive.

In a recently published 1,000-plus-page *Oxford Handbook on Global Legal Pluralism* (2020) that Berman edited, he makes a revealing statement. After acknowledging that global legal pluralism is not really global

15 Merry, 'Legal Pluralism', 878–9.

16 By not making his concept of law explicit, Berman shields it from critical scrutiny and denies the need to justify it. Berman has cited my position in support of his, but his position is not mine. He applies an implicit concept of law, while refusing to specify what it is. My position is that no abstract concept or definition of law comes into play in the analysis, implicitly or explicitly; instead, I utilize collective identification of law in the social arena at issue.

17 P. Berman, *Global Legal Pluralism: A Jurisprudence of Law beyond Borders* (Cambridge University Press, 2012), pp. 41–2.

18 P. Berman, 'The New Legal Pluralism' (2009) 5 *Annual Review of Law and Social Science* 225–42, at 236.

19 P. S. Berman, 'The Globalization of Jurisdiction' (2002) 151 *University of Pennsylvania Law Review* 311–545, at 505.

in reach and not fully pluralist (because he disallows illiberal values), Berman observes: 'Indeed, given the broad (and often undefined) vision of law embraced by legal pluralists, *it is perhaps not properly considered "legal" either!*'[20] Global legal pluralism, under his conception, extends far beyond law to encompass normative pluralism generally. This conceptually confused stance – the source of which lies in sociological legal pluralism – confounds the analysis, as Merry observed three decades ago.

Not only is this understanding of law *over*inclusive, but global legal pluralism is also *all inclusive* to an extent that borders on meaninglessness or totalizing ambition. *Global* legal pluralism apparently purports to encompass all legal orders in the world – local, state, transnational, customary, religious, non-state, etc. – considered together in a vast bottomless bucket. If the assertion is that all legal orders in the world in the aggregate constitutes legal pluralism, it is a true but empty claim; if the claim is that their framework applies to all legal orders in the world considered together or whenever legal multiplicities of any kind arise, it is an audacious claim. Legal pluralism is everywhere, in so many different manifestations and variations that no single framework can capture it all except in the most general descriptive terms.

17.3 The Problem with Sociological and Jurisprudential Concepts of Law

After two decades of forcefully promoting legal pluralism, John Griffiths acknowledged that sociological legal pluralism does not work:

> In the intervening years, further reflection on the concept of law has led me to the conclusion that the word 'law' could be better abandoned altogether for the purposes of theory formation in sociology of law [. . .] It also follows from the above considerations that the expression 'legal pluralism' can and should be reconceptualized as 'normative pluralism' or 'pluralism in social control'.[21]

[20] P. S. Berman, 'Understanding Global Legal Pluralism: From Local to Global, from Descriptive to Normative', in P. S. Berman (ed.), *The Oxford Handbook of Global Legal Pluralism* (Oxford University Press, 2020), p. 62, https://papers.ssrn.com/sol3/papers.cfm?abstract_id=3715553.

[21] J. Griffiths, 'The Idea of Sociology of Law and its Relation to Law and to Sociology' (2006) 8 *Current Legal Issues* 49–68, at 63–4. For helping him come to this realization, Griffiths cites a Dutch article by G. van den Bergh, and two of my articles, 'An Analytical Map of Social Scientific Approaches to the Concept of Law' (1995) 15 *Oxford Journal of Legal Studies* 501–36, and 'The Folly of the Social Scientific Concept of Legal Pluralism' (1993) 20 *Journal of Law and Society* 192–217.

This is a stunning reversal for Griffiths. To renounce a doctrine that brought him academic renown is a testament to his inestimable intellectual integrity. What doomed sociological legal pluralism is the problem of overinclusiveness.

This insurmountable problem is detailed in other work,[22] so here I present a drastically abbreviated account. Almost all sociological as well as jurisprudential concepts of law involve specifications of *function* and *form* (structure). (This is true of all efforts to define social artefacts; for example, a standard definition of a 'chair' is a seat (function) with legs and a back (form).) While numerous variations exist, conceptions of law fall into two basic streams. The first stream encompasses the normative ordering of social associations (focused on law's function) – put forth by Griffiths, who melded Eugen Ehrlich's living law with Sally Falk Moore's semi-autonomous social field. The second stream encompasses institutionalized rule systems (a combination of function and form) – put forth by Marc Galanter, who drew on H. L. A. Hart's union of primary and secondary rules.

The problem with identifying law as the normative ordering of social institutions (the first stream), as Eugen Ehrlich did, including clubs, community organizationsand business partnerships, is that a variety of social mechanisms – customs, morals, habits, reciprocity, etc. – are involved in the ordering of social associations. Defining law in terms of the ordering of associations inevitably encompasses all of this. Jurists at the time rejected his concept of law for this reason. Legal philosopher Morris Cohen objected: 'Ehrlich's book suffers from the fact that it draws no clear account of what he means by law and how he distinguishes it from customs and morals.'[23] John Griffiths concluded that Ehrlich's 'theory therefore lacks an independent criterion of "the legal". He seems to take it as obvious which sorts of rules of conduct are legal in character.'[24] Griffiths turned to Sally Moore's semi-autonomous social field (SASF), declaring: 'law is the self-regulation of a semi-autonomous social field'.[25] However, Moore herself refused to use the label 'law' (she proposed 'reglementation') owing to the same objection: an array of

[22] See B. Z. Tamanaha, *Legal Pluralism Explained: History, Theory, Consequences* (Oxford University Press, 2021).

[23] M. R. Cohen, 'Recent Philosophical Literature: Legal Literature in French, German, and Italian' (1916) 26 *International Journal of Ethics* 528–46, at 537.

[24] Griffiths, 'What Is Legal Pluralism?', 27.

[25] Ibid., 38.

mechanisms support the rule-bound ordering within social groups that her SASF centres on, including moral norms, reciprocity, potential loss of future benefits and social ostracism. Griffiths understood that his conception of law encompasses a broad continuum of normative ordering, from informal to institutionalized, which led him to conclude that 'all social control is more or less legal'.[26] This position results in the assertion (per Berman) that law encompasses people queuing at a bar or bank.

The conception of law as institutionalized rule systems (the second stream) is an abstract reduction of state legal systems, presenting law as an institutionalized rule system (form) that enacts and enforces norms for social ordering (function). An influential early work on legal pluralism, Marc Galanter's 'Justice in Many Rooms: Courts, Private Ordering, and Indigenous Law' (1981),[27] builds on H. L. A. Hart's account, defining law in terms of 'the organization and differentiation of norms and sanctions. The differentiation is the introduction of a second layer of control – or norms about the application of norms.'[28] Since society is filled with institutionalized norm-enforcement systems, it follows that law is 'found in a variety of institutional settings – in universities, sports leagues, housing developments, hospitals, etc.'.[29] A century ago, Italian jurist Santi Romano articulated a theory of legal pluralism that takes this line of thinking to its utmost extension, asserting that every institution is a legal order and every legal order is an institution.[30] Legal orders, in this view, include states, municipalities, corporations, factories, political parties, a prison, a church, a family, a criminal gang and much more.[31] In a recent essay acknowledging legal pluralism, legal philosopher Joseph Raz likewise identifies law in 'the rules and regulations governing the activities of voluntary associations, or those of legally recognized corporations, and more, including many very transient phenomena, like neighbourhood gangs'.[32] The legal institutions he has in mind, Raz elaborates, 'are themselves rule-governed, ultimately governed by practice-based

[26] Ibid., 39 n. 3.

[27] M. Galanter, 'Justice in Many Rooms: Courts, Private Ordering, and Indigenous Law' (1981) 19 *Journal of Legal Pluralism* 1–48, at 2.

[28] Ibid., 19.

[29] Ibid., 17–18.

[30] S. Romano, *The Legal Order* (Routledge 2017).

[31] For a concise description of Romano's account of law, see L. Vinx, 'Santi-Romano against the State?' (2018) 11 *Ethics and Global Politics* 25–36.

[32] J. Raz, 'Why the State?', in N. Roughan and A. Halpin (eds), *In Pursuit of Pluralist Jurisprudence* (Cambridge University Press 2017) pp. 136–62, at p. 138.

rules that determine if not all at least the most important aspects of their constitution, powers, and mode of operation'.[33] 'In this sense', he continues, 'both the rules of the Roman Republic and those of the University of Wales (disbanded 2011), just as the rules of the United States and of Columbia University, *are legal systems.*'[34]

At bottom, these two streams of conceptions of law involve exercises in *relabeling*. The first stream relabels the normative ordering of social associations as legal ordering; the second stream relabels institutionalized rule systems as law. Through this relabeling, both approaches immediately produce an immense profusion of law in society. However, their conflation of law with broader social phenomena is theoretically unjustified and results in confusion. Rather than assert that all forms of social control are more or less legal or that all institutionalized rule systems are law, it makes far more sense to assert that multiple forms of social control exist, some of which are law, and that innumerable institutionalized rule systems exist, some of which of are law.

The most straightforward way to identify law from among the multitude of normative orderings and institutionalized rule systems in society is via conventional recognition of what is 'law' (*droit*, *loi*, *lex*, *ius*, *recht*, *gesetz*, *diritto*, *prawo*, *horitsu*, *fa*, etc.) – which I elaborate further in Section 17.7. The legal systems of France and Massachusetts (etc.) are conventionally perceived as *law*, but not the internal rule systems of Saint Laurent or Harvard (etc.), which are seen as rule systems specific to the purposes of the organization. International law *is* law, not because it satisfies abstract criteria of legality based on form, function or some other basis (which no theorist has successfully formulated), but because it is conventionally recognized as law by jurists, political leaders and the public.[35]

17.4 The Ubiquity of Private Rule Systems and Regulatory Forms

Transnational legal pluralism scholars have emphasized the ubiquity of private and hybrid regulatory systems operating on the transnational level. Examples include the Court of Arbitration for Sport,[36] Codex

[33] Ibid., p. 142.
[34] Ibid., p. 143 (emphasis added).
[35] For a discussion showing the legal status of international law, see B. Z. Tamanaha, *A Realistic Theory of Law* (Cambridge University Press 2017), chapter 6.
[36] See Chapter 10.

Alimentarius Commission on food standards, voluntary 'soft law' provisions like corporate codes of conduct and UNIDROIT Principles of International Commercial Contracts, International Organization for Standardization and an increasing multitude more. The domestic level has also witnessed a proliferation of private and hybrid bodies carrying out legal functions, with the expansion of private arbitration, private policing (gated communities, universities, sports venues, shopping malls, etc.), private prisons (common in the USA) and private standard setting.

The underlying cause of the explosion of private and hybrid regulation is plain: governments and public bodies lack the capacity to produce and carry out the regulatory activities necessary to deal with countless transactions and intercourse within society and across societies. It has long been common for regulatory standards to be produced by private organizations tied to non-profit consumer associations or trade associations in specific industries, which have the requisite expertise as well as an interest in maintaining quality and safety standards (as well as creating barriers to entry against potential new competitors). Domestic and transnational private standard setting are frequently connected. The American National Standards Institute (ANSI), a private organization created in 1918, accredits standards produced by private standard-setting organizations (many of which have been adopted by state regulators) across a broad swath of matters (electrical standards, chemical standards, public health standards, and so forth); ANSI is a member of the International Organization for Standardization as well as the International Accreditation Forum, propagating American standards more broadly as well as introducing externally produced standards into the USA.

In addition, private organizations have long established and enforced their own rule systems on their employees and consumers and users of their goods and services. Twitter and Facebook famously demonstrated this power in the aftermath of the insurrection on the Capitol building when they banned President Donald Trump from using their platforms for repeated violations of their terms of service. Private companies can also directly enforce state law. Google enforces the EU's 'right to be forgotten law', thus far rendering judgements on over 845,000 requests, delisting 45 per cent of the links.[37] As Galanter made clear four decades ago, a far greater amount of rule enforcement affecting people's lives takes place within private institutionalized rule systems than through

[37] See L. Kelion, 'Google Wins Landmark Right to be Forgotten Case', *BBC News* (23 September 2019), www.bbc.com/news/technology-49808208.

state law, and private regulation has vastly increased since that time at domestic and transnational levels.

These private and hybrid regulatory phenomena are undoubtedly important. The issue for theorists and jurists is how they should be characterized. They carry out legal functions, many are structured like legal institutions and their rules and processes often supplement state law. Based on these similarities, leading transnational legal pluralist theorists have swept these phenomena within law – asserting that they *are* law or that *law is a matter of degree*, thereby encompassing these regulatory forms. This approach, however, inevitably results in the overinclusiveness problem identified above (including as law universities, hospitals or corporations). A simpler approach is to call them what they are – private and hybrid regulatory forms – noting the manifold respects in which they are *law-like* and identifying the various ways in which they interact with law. Rather than hold that all forms of regulation are law, it is more sensible to see regulation as a broad category, certain manifestations of which are law (conventionally recognized as such), while many others carry out legal functions but are not law per se. All the same observations can be made by jurists and theorists without stumbling over irresolvable theoretical hurdles involving the concept of law.

17.5 The Separation of Theory and Practice

The question 'What is law?' is almost entirely a theoretical exercise. Judges, lawyers and parties engaged in situations with multiple, coexisting forms of law rarely take up this abstract theoretical inquiry. The issues that typically arise in contexts of transnational legal pluralism mainly include questions like these: which of the various forms of law and regulation are relevant to the resolution of the dispute or problem at hand, how much weight should attach to each, and how should conflicts between them be resolved? These issues are resolved not by abstract theoretical inquiries into the concept of law, but by resort to applicable rules of legal relevance and validity, choice of law, conflicts of law and other standard legal mechanisms and analyses that jurists commonly utilize.

Transnational legal pluralist theorists engender confusion when they cross over the line between theory and practice. Roger Cotterrell asserts that lawyers dealing with transnational law need a theory of legal pluralism; after considering different concepts of law by a number of theorists, he proposes that law involves institutionalized doctrine.[38] Berman seeks to develop for jurists 'procedural mechanisms, institutions, and practices that aim to manage, without eliminating, the legal pluralism we see around us'.[39] But it is doubtful that lawyers need or will utilize theoretical concepts of law and legal pluralism, since they have been dealing with these phenomena for many decades without such theories – and how would they decide which is correct among the many theories of law proposed in the literature? Few, if any, judges or lawyers would find useful Berman's assertion that law includes people queuing to get into a bar. While it is common for academic jurists to construct frameworks for lawyers and judges, they typically do so working with the same legal materials, analysing applicable doctrines and legal mechanisms from the internal standpoint of a jurist. In contrast, sociological and theoretical concepts produced from an external standpoint – law as institutionalized normative orders, autopoiesis, networks, entanglement, interlegality, the semi-autonomous social field and other theoretical constructs referred to in the literature – have little application in juridical tasks. Theory and practice are different enterprises.

17.6 Flaws of a Relational Concept of Law

Ralf Michaels recently articulated a novel concept of law (or *laws*) grounded on pluralism as an intrinsic aspect of legal ordering, an account that transnational pluralist scholars have begun to cite.[40] To Hart's obligatory *primary rules* addressing social behaviour, and *secondary rules* used by legal officials to create and apply primary rules, Michaels adds *tertiary rules* for engaging with external legal orders. Michaels summarizes his definition of law:

> A concept of laws, appropriate for a situation of global legal pluralism, must take these challenges [postcolonial customary and religious law] seriously. It should accept the challenge that non-state law can be law. It should reject, however, the claim that non-state law must be viewed as law irrespective of recognition. Instead, it should generalize this

[38] R. Cotterrell, 'Do Lawyers Need a Theory of Legal Pluralism?', in Roughan and Halpin (eds), *In Pursuit of Pluralist Jurisprudence*, pp. 20–39.

[39] P. S. Berman, 'Jurisgenerative Constitutionalism: Procedural Principles for Managing Global Legal Pluralism' (2013) 20 *Indiana Journal of Global Legal Studies* 665–95, at 668–69.

[40] See Chapter 16; R. Michaels, 'Law and Recognition: Towards a Relational Concept of Law', in Roughan and Halpin (eds), *In Pursuit of Pluralist Jurisprudence*, pp. 90–115.

> recognition requirement and turn it into a general requirement of law – a requirement that exists not just for non-state law, but for state law as well. A legal order, in this definition, requires not two but three kinds of rules. It requires primary rules as its content. It requires secondary rules for its operation. And it requires tertiary rules to establish its relation with other legal orders, whether they are called interface norms, linkage rules or something else. The suggestion that such tertiary rules are a *necessary element of legal systems* should not be so provocative.[41]

He emphasizes that external recognition by *other* legal orders is *constitutive* of whether a given legal order *is* law: 'Under this theory, translated into legal theory, [external] recognition is constitutive for the identity of law as law.'[42] A given system is *not* a legal system absent external recognition.

To justify adding tertiary rules Michaels draws an analogy to recognition by other states as the basis for nationhood status under international law. He asserts that 'effectively a legal system cannot operate vis-à-vis other legal systems unless it is recognized by those other legal systems'.[43] Thus, legal systems are 'mutually constitutive', each becoming law through recognition by the other. This recognition is relative to the interaction between any two systems (hence it is relational). 'Something can be a legal order vis-à-vis one other legal system, but not vis-à-vis another legal system. The nature of a legal system exists in relation to another legal system.'[44] Since all existing state legal systems are externally recognized by other state legal systems via domestic conflicts of law rules (which are tertiary rules), all state legal systems qualify as law in his definition. For reasons I explain, however, his scheme heavily disadvantages non-state law.

Michaels' theory of law has three major problems relevant to legal pluralism, which I articulate up front then illustrate with examples. One problem is that a legal system can be highly effective within a community regardless of whether any external legal system recognizes it, and indeed even when its legal status is affirmatively denied by other

[41] Michaels, 'Law and Recognition', pp. 107–8 (emphasis added). The reference to interface norms is from N. Krisch, *Beyond Constitutionalism: The Pluralist Structure of Postnational Law* (Oxford University Press, 2012); and the reference to linkage rules is from D. von Daniels, *The Concept of Law from a Transnational Perspective* (Ashgate, 2010).

[42] Michaels, 'Law and Recognition', p. 105.

[43] Ibid., p. 106.

[44] Ibid., p. 110.

legal systems – which is a common occurrence in the history of legal pluralism. Since the vast bulk of what legal systems typically address relate to internal effectiveness, Michaels does not explain why a lack of external effectiveness – which it can function without – justifies the conclusion that an internally effective system is *not* law. A second problem is that a system can go from being *not law* until receiving external recognition, then becoming *law* upon recognition, then *not law* when recognition is withdrawn, then *law again* when recognition is restored (and so on) – with its legal status dictated entirely at the whims and interests of the external system (an example follows).

The third problem is a conceptual flaw within the relational theory itself. If a necessary element to qualify as law is *external* recognition by another legal system, as Michaels contends, then that in itself does not necessitate tertiary rules within the system to *establish relations* with others. As long as another legal system recognizes *it*, a given legal system exists even if *it* does not recognize any *other* legal system on its part. Since external recognition in his scheme is not conditioned upon reciprocal recognition, there is no logical basis in his theory for requiring tertiary rules within a given system as a necessary feature of law. His account requires only: (1) primary rules of content, (2) secondary rules of operation and (3) receiving external recognition. In Hart's account, to supplement his union of primary and secondary rules, he identified two minimum conditions for the existence of a legal system: the populace must generally obey the primary rules, and legal officials must accept the secondary rules.[45] Similarly, Michaels' requirement of *receiving* external recognition does not itself give rise to a third distinct body of rules, and indeed it is not about rules at all. Instead, what his justification calls for is another *existence condition*: an external legal system must recognize it as law to be effective.

This conclusion reveals that his tertiary rules are neither necessary nor sufficient to constitute law. Assume System A has primary, secondary and tertiary rules – thus possessing the three features he identifies as essential to law. However, if System B does not recognize A as a legal system, it is not a legal system with respect to B. As Michaels put it, 'System A can only determine whether and how it recognizes System B and insofar be constitutive for System B. It cannot determine whether

[45] Hart's justifications for these two conditions were functionality and efficacy. If legal officials do not accept the secondary rules the system cannot function, and if the populace does not obey the primary rules it would be ineffective.

and how System B recognizes System A.'[46] So having tertiary rules (on top of primary and secondary) is not *sufficient* to constitute A as law with respect to B. Now assume System A has primary and secondary rules, but not tertiary rules – thus lacking what he identifies as an essential feature of law. If System B nonetheless recognizes A as a legal system, it does count as law for B. So tertiary rules are not *necessary* to constitute law. It turns out that tertiary rules, Michaels' key addition to Hart's concept of law, are not actually essential to constituting law under his own conceptual scheme.

The conceptual soundness of his theory of *laws* (positing pluralism and interrelatedness as intrinsic) must be evaluated in terms of whether it makes sense when applied to account for legal phenomena. However, his theory construes law in counterintuitive ways. No system counts as law in isolation or as a general matter because its legal status is constituted only with respect to particular other legal systems that recognize it. It is law in relation to Systems B, C, D, etc., which recognize it, but not law with respect to Systems E, F, G, etc., which do not recognize it. Thus, System A can *be law* and *not law* at the same moment (depending on which relation one considers). Moreover, as we just saw, System A's legal status with respect to Systems B, C, and D, etc., can be turned on and off at the sole discretion of each external system. Michaels extrapolates from the correct proposition that System B alone has the power to determine what counts as law for *it* (a direct implication of legal rules of validity), but ratchets up the theoretical import of this proposition to be 'constitutive' of A's *nature* as law (an internal point about System B thereby determines the legal nature of System A). This conceptual move transforms a commonplace idea into a source of multiple puzzling implications.[47]

The distorting lens his relational theory provides is evident through application to actual situations of legal pluralism. Consider British treatment of Aboriginal customary law. Upon arrival, they declared Australia *terra nullius*, with no semblance of law or civil society, a blank legal slate, enabling the colonial government and settlers to seize Aboriginal land

[46] Michaels, 'Law and Recognition', p. 109.

[47] A strange implication of this theory, which he acknowledges, is that a legal system cannot exist unless another legal system exists that recognizes it, which itself is not a legal system unless it is recognized by another existing legal system, etc. – thus involving an infinite regress. Michaels dismisses this as a problem for all theories of law, but conventionalist theories based on social recognition do not face an infinite regress.

because no property rights existed.[48] This stance conceptually erased the reality that Aboriginal communities had lived for aeons, and continued to live, in accordance with customary law on property rights, personal injuries, marriage and so forth. In *Mabo* v. *Queensland* (1992), the Australian court finally recognized that Aboriginal customary law indeed conferred pre-existing property rights that must be respected.[49] Aborigines had all along viewed and lived in accordance with their customary law, but according to Michaels' relational theory, Aboriginal customary law was not law until external recognition by the Australian legal system *constituted* it as law, putting its status as law entirely at the leave of the state legal system.

Not only does this stance wholly discount the views and legal practices of Aborigines, it twists the court's inquiry into a logical pretzel. A court in this position is inquiring *whether* customary law was (or is) a genuine form of law. According to the court, the pre-existing legal status of customary law provides the *ground*s for its decision, but according to Michaels its legal status follows solely as a *consequence* of the decision itself. Under his theory, it is not conceptually possible for Aboriginal law to be law prior to recognition, so the court's inquiry into whether it was law (prior to the decision) is nonsensical.

In New Zealand, after a number of violent skirmishes, the British entered the Treaty of Waitangi (1840) with powerful Maori chiefdoms, acknowledging their right to rule in their home areas, and subsequent statutes were enacted recognizing customary law. But this initial recognition was withdrawn after the rapidly increasing settler population became dominant. In an 1877 case, *Wi Parata* v. *Bishop of Wellington*, Chief Justice Prendergast declared the Treaty of Waitangi a 'simple nullity', 'worthless', because it had been signed by 'barbarians without any form of law or civil government' incapable of entering a treaty with a civilized nation.[50] Furthermore, he concluded, the Native Rights Act of 1865 and Native Land Act of 1873, which recognized Maori customary law property rights, were nullities because '*no such body of law existed*', and '*a phrase in a statute cannot call what is non-existent in being*';

[48] See Australian Reform Commission, 'Recognition of Aboriginal Customary Laws (ALRC Report 31)' (1986) paras 39, 60, www.alrc.gov.au/publication/recognition-of-aboriginal-customary-laws-alrc-report-31/.

[49] *Mabo* v. *Queensland* [1992] HCA 23.

[50] *Wi Parata* v. *Bishop of Wellington* (1877) 3 NZ Jur. (N.S.) S.C., language cited in J. Tate, 'The Three Precedents of Wi Parata' (2004) 10 *Canterbury Law Review* 273–308, at 293, 294 n. 92.

subsequent statutes withdrew recognition of customary law. Only in recent decades has Maori customary law again received recognition by the New Zealand state legal system. Ironically, contrary to Justice Prendergast's assertion, according to Michaels' theory, recognition of customary law in a state statute or case does indeed *bring previously non-existent Maori law into being* – but by the same reasoning the withdrawal of said recognition *also extinguishes it*. External recognition has a kind of magical ontological power to snap law into and out of existence by declaration, a power wielded by the state legal system, while Maori legal understandings and practices do not matter.

Now I shift from colonial settings to show how the relational theory fails to adequately account for Jewish law and Sharia law in Western legal systems, both mentioned by Michaels. Jewish law recognizes the law of the state, but most state legal systems do not recognize Jewish law as *law*. In the United States, the decisions of Jewish tribunals (Beth Din) are enforced not as Jewish law, but rather as contractually binding arbitration decisions, no different from contract-based private arbitration generally. From the standpoint of believers, in contrast, these decisions are based on Jewish *law*. The rules of Beth Din America declare: 'The Beth Din of America accepts that *Jewish law* as understood by the Beth Din will provide the rules of decision and rules of procedure that govern the Beth Din or any of its panels.'[51] Thus Jewish adherents see two legal systems operating. But according to Michaels' theory, Jewish law is *not law* unless state law recognizes it as such, which it refuses to do, so state law is the exclusive form of law as far as it is concerned (enforcing private arbitration grounded in state contract law is not recognition of the status of Jewish law as a legal system, nor does it involve conflicts of law rules). A number of states in the USA prohibit courts from recognizing religious law of any kind. Since state legal systems typically assert a monopoly over law, the consequence of his theory is to disqualify non-state law at the outset, eliminating legal pluralism by automatically granting the monopolistic claim of state law.

The situation of Sharia law is even more problematic for Michaels' theory. The UK government recently enacted provisions that would give limited recognition (again as arbitration, not law) to decisions by Sharia tribunals that meet specified criteria, but a number of Sharia councils have expressed reluctance to obtain formal recognition under state law,

[51] Rules and Procedures: Beth Din America, p. 5 (emphasis added), https://bethdin.org/wp-content/uploads/2018/04/BDA118-RulesProcedures_Bro_BW_02.pdf.

which they consider to be 'un-Islamic'.[52] In this instance, one form of law *rejects* an offer of recognition from an external legal system, viewing such recognition as unnecessary and perhaps an insult to its own independent legal status – whereas for Michaels this very rejection disqualifies it from constituting law. Both state law and religious law assert that their law is *binding* and *superior*. The direct clash is evident in a *fatwa* on divorce issued by the Islamic Council of Europe:

> In conclusion, I would like to affirm that the divorce issued by the civil court in response to the wife's request *is neither a valid divorce nor legitimate marriage dissolution*. This means that such a wife remains a wife and is not free to marry another man. Marrying another man while the original marriage is still in place is *a violation of Islamic law and a crime*. What is more dangerous than this is the fact that all children she gives birth to before obtaining a proper marriage dissolution may be considered to be of the first husband from whom she assumed she had been divorced. Wives who face intolerable situations may seek marriage dissolution by a recognized body that is known and accepted in acting as a judiciary body for Muslims.[53]

State law asserts a parallel position on the opposite side. In February 2020, a British Court of Appeal ruled that a *nikah* (Islamic) marriage is a 'non-marriage' under state law, so no legally cognizable marital rights attach to Islamic marriages.[54] This mutual standoff of non-recognition has significant actual consequences: over half of Muslim marriages in the UK, many of which take place in mosques or private homes, are not registered as civil marriages.[55] Oddly, under Michaels' relational theory, in the relations between the two, *neither* is a legal system. This is yet another way in which the relational theory conceptually erases manifest legal pluralism.

[52] See S. Bano, 'In Pursuit of Religious and Legal Diversity: A Response to the Archbishop of Canterbury and the "Sharia Debate" in Britain' (2008) 10 *Ecclesiastical Law Journal* 283–309, at 299.

[53] S. H. Al-Haddad, 'Fatwa: A Civil Divorce Is Not a Valid Islamic Divorce', Islamic Council of Europe (17 February 2017), https://iceurope.org/fatwa-a-civil-divorce-is-not-a-valid-islamic-divorce/ (emphasis added).

[54] H. Sherwood, 'Islamic Faith Marriages Not Valid in English Law, Appeal Court Rules', *The Guardian* (14 February 2020), www.theguardian.com/world/2020/feb/14/islamic-faith-marriages-not-valid-in-english-law-appeal-court-rules.

[55] See G. Douglas, N. Doe, S. Gilliat-Ray, R. Sandberg and A. Khan, 'The Role of Religious Tribunals in Regulating Marriage and Divorce' (2012) 24 *Child & Family Law Quarterly* 139–57.

The relational theory of law is antithetical to the thrust of legal pluralism for reasons revealed by these examples. Law throughout history and today is the product of recognition within communities that live by and recognize their own forms of law. This holds for the Indigenous law of the Maori, Australian Aborigines and Native American tribes of North America, as well as Jewish law, Sharia law, Hindu law and other forms of religious law, as well as customary law across Africa, Asia and the Pacific Islands, and many other forms of law. To condition their status as law on recognition by an external legal system, the state legal system in particular, denies communities their own agency in determining what counts as law. Michaels asserts, 'In all but the rarest cases, we will be faced with external recognition from both sides.'[56] This is true among state legal systems, which uniformly recognize one another, but there are many examples past and present of state legal systems not extending reciprocal recognition to customary and religious law.

The examples in this section also illustrate that whether external recognition is extended is not always a matter of comity and respect, but rather is a function of relative power and self-interest. Under the ideal of the monist law state, the state characteristically *claims* a monopoly over law backed by force of arms. Many forms of community-based law have vigorously disputed this monopolistic assertion for centuries. What Michaels clinically presents as 'external recognition' has often involved *existential* contests in which a state legal system asserts its dominance over community-recognized forms of law struggling to survive.[57] His theory gives the state legal system determinative say over legal status (a common assumption of jurists), while many communities around the globe observing non-state law resolutely insist otherwise. Although he is correct that state law determines what counts as law for its own purposes, this does not, and should not, dictate the status of other legal systems on their own terms.

These objections to the relational theory reinforce a point made earlier. Michaels' theory of law might fit state law recognition of other state laws through conflicts of law rules (his scholarly expertise), and it might work for transnational forms of law and regulation, but it is not suitable for many contexts of legal pluralism.

[56] Michaels, 'Law and Recognition', p. 114.

[57] Chapters 3 and 14 discuss Indigenous legal orders in Canada struggling to maintain their existence against state declarations of its legal dominance.

17.7 Foundations of Legal Pluralism in Conventional Recognition of Law

It is a commonplace that the social world we inhabit is socially constructed. The social world is the product of our meaningful beliefs, actions and projects, and their intended and unintended consequences. People are born into, assume a place in, partake of and modify existing language, knowledge, social practices and institutions, conventions and technology, generated on an ongoing basis by the community of actors – collectively giving rise to a common social world made up of hospitals, schools, petrol stations, factories, government offices, courts, movie theatres, grocery stores, universities and everything else in society. These are the ubiquitous social phenomena in which we are daily immersed and take for granted. Socially constructed institutions, furthermore, are interconnected within surrounding cultural, social, economic, political, legal, ecological and technological factors, and their existence endures over time (until they expire), developing and changing in relation to exogenous and endogenous factors.

The socially constructed Catholic Church, for example, has changed immensely over its two millennia history. Put in grossly broad strokes: from the claim that Christ designated the bishop of Rome as the head; to the edict establishing Christianity as the official religion of the Roman Empire; to a gradual split between the Western and Eastern churches; to the investiture conflict; to the development of canon law influenced by Roman law; to independent legal authority exercised by the Church across Western Europe on marriage, inheritance, defamation, moral crimes and other matters, alongside regal law, law of the manor, local customary law, etc.; to the Reformation and Counter-Reformation and decades of devastating religious wars; to changing relations with consolidating state systems in Europe and the stripping of ecclesiastical law from authority over the public; to the immensely wealthy Catholic Church today, governing its own affairs, operating its own legal system and ensconced in a sovereign state, Vatican City.

Notice that *law* and *legal pluralism* in various respects, evolving over time, have a prominent role in the history of the Catholic Church, interacting with politics, religion, economics and everything else. Accounts of this sort can be provided for all socially constructed, historically enduring, socially interconnected, varying and changing manifestations of law throughout history and today.[58] Whatever people collectively recognize as 'law' (and its translations) *is* law – recognition of legal status that has attached to innumerable instantiations and variations of law over time: European Union law, United Kingdom law, Scottish law, New York municipal and state law, international law, Halakha (Jewish law), Sharia law, Yapese customary law, Adat law in Indonesia and countless more. These manifestations of law cannot be captured in a single concept of law because their functions and features vary and have changed over time. Informal customary law, and international and transnational law, do not have the same structures as state law, which is why Hart, who explicitly based his concept on state law, concluded that they are not fully fledged law, but pre-legal.

To know what law is for the purposes of legal pluralism does not require an abstract concept or definition of law stating essential or defining features – instead one must inquire into what people in a given social arena collectively (conventionally) identify as law.[59] As with any social artefact, this inquiry presupposes a rudimentary sense of what is law (likewise, one must begin with a sense of what a chair is to identify what people collectively identify as chairs). Collective senses of what counts as law – including customary and religious law, state law and others – extend back millennia to a shared Western and Near-Eastern tradition (Hammurabi's Code, Greek law, Torah, Sharia, etc.). These notions of law have spread around the world through contact, trade, migration and interaction among peoples generally. Colonization spread state legal systems globally through imposition or imitation, as well as entrenched the notion of customary law in many societies, and international law was a companion of colonization, so these forms of law are familiar in every society around the globe today. Translations for law exist in all classical and contemporary languages – often in multiple terms, like *ius* and *lex*, and *recht* and *gesetz*, all of which count as conventionally identified law – instantly available on Google Translate.

[58] See Tamanaha, *A Realistic Theory of Law*.

[59] Collective recognition involves the shared conventional identification within a group of something as possessing legal status. Since law has substantial connotations of authority within a group, the conventional attachment of this label is relatively restricted, applying to a limited number of phenomena within societies. Under this approach, an interesting question for examination is why in given arenas certain institutional forms are conventionally identified as 'law', while others are not, which may relate to power, rhetorical import, normative authority and other factors.

In many social contexts today and in the past, multiple collectively recognized forms of law coexist – *this* is legal pluralism.

The key constitutive factor in particular social constructions of law is conventional recognition within social groups (including groups of legal officials). Conventional recognition determines *who* counts as legal officials, *which* specified legal powers they exercise and *what* they must do for their actions to count as legal.[60] In highly institutionalized formal legal systems this recognition is tied to official positions occupied by legislators, prosecutors, judges, police, etc., exercising roles with attendant legal powers. But a multitude of socially constructed arrangements of conventionally recognized law exist. In many informal customary law systems, village chiefs or elders preside in collective gatherings and render decisions on the resolution of disputes over matters of property, personal injuries, inheritance, property claims, etc. A single version of law can come in many variations across different contexts. For Islamic law, for example, respected Islamic jurists issue authoritative rulings (*fatwa*) based on the Quran, Hadith (sayings of the prophet Muhammad) and juristic teachings, although they do not operate within official legal systems; in Iran, an Islamic theocracy, judges occupy positions within the state system applying Islamic law; and in Indonesia, informal Adat tribunals apply mixtures of locally infused Islamic law and customary law. In many contexts, collectively recognized official state legal systems *and* non-state legal systems both operate, and can be potentially invoked by parties, and sometimes international and transnational forms of law can be invoked as well. *That* is legal pluralism.

17.8 Community Law, Regime Law and Cross-polity Law Juxtaposed

When thinking about situations of legal pluralism, it is useful to keep in mind three roughly distinguishable general categories of bodies of law that have been collectively recognized across many societies, which I descriptively label community law, regime law and cross-polity law.[61] (These categories are inductively derived generalizations, not analytically derived.) *Community law* encompasses basic laws and institutions of

[60] See N. MacCormick, *Institutions of Law: An Essay in Legal Theory* (Oxford University Press, 2007), pp. 289–93; J. R. Searle, *The Construction of Social Reality* (Free Press, 1995), pp. 27–51.

[61] The basis for these categories is in Tamanaha, *Legal Pluralism Explained.*

social intercourse within communities addressing property, personal injuries, marriage, divorce, sexual restrictions, inheritance, debts and obligations and others; the body of rules through which people arrange their daily affairs. Every society has rules addressing these matters, which vary greatly across societies and change over time. Many existing systems of customary and religious law involve the lengthy continuation of fundamental rules of social intercourse going back many centuries, predating the establishment of state legal systems and evolving to adjust to the presence of the state (and the state to them). *Regime laws* are laws tied to ruling polities. They constitute, support and enforce the power of the governing regime, including taxation and customs fees, forced labour and military service, laws against sedition, border controls and much more, with governing regimes frequently nested within or encompassing in whole or part other subregimes. *Cross-polity laws* deal with matters between and across organized polities, consisting of national law (including conflicts of law), international law, transnational law and non-state forms of law that extend across states (like *fatwa*).

Community law has remained roughly the same in its ambit across place and time. Regime law has expanded enormously in the past two centuries with the consolidation and proliferation of bureaucratic state law and the rise of instrumental lawmaking to address a full range of social, economic and political matters. Cross-polity law has multiplied greatly in conjunction with modern globalization, accelerating in the past half-century to deal with transnational capitalism, transportation, communications, financial transactions, legal and illegal migration, ecological harms and more.

All three categories of law are contained within many unified state legal systems today, though significant exceptions remain. This unification is a recent arrangement. Throughout history, from the Roman Empire to the Ottoman Empire to the British Empire, empires have imposed regime law to maintain imperial interests, while allowing local community-based customary and religious laws and tribunals to address matters of everyday social intercourse. Postcolonial legal pluralism across the Global South today is the continuing legacy of Western imperialism. Large polities that span multiple communities often comprise some arrangement (officially or unofficially) in which pockets of community law continue to function.

Many situations of legal pluralism involve juxtapositions of inconsistent versions of community law, state law and cross-polity law (forms of law from different categories and/or within the same category). In many regions across the Global South, people in rural communities manage their affairs through customary law and tribunals, apart from and often inconsistent with official state laws and tribunals. Disputes over the inheritance of land from a male who dies can involve, on the one side, male brothers of the deceased invoking customary law on patrilineal inheritance (community law), backed by the UN Declaration of Rights of Indigenous Peoples (cross-polity law), to support their claim to the land; while on the other side, widows (with help from non-governmental organizations) may invoke state inheritance law on widow's shares (state law), backed by the Convention on the Elimination of All Forms of Discrimination Against Women (cross-polity law).[62] Across Asia, subsistence farmers invoke customary land tenure rights (community law), clashing with governments and developers seizing land to establish plantations or commercial projects, who invoke transplanted official property rights and titling systems enacted by states (state law) at the behest of the World Bank and Western development agencies (cross-polity organizations transplanting law). European constitutional pluralism involves the juxtaposition of national law of the states (regime law) with EU treaties and law (cross-polity law); the pluralism of coexisting subject matter regimes in international law (WTO, TRIPS, World Health Organization, environmental treaties, etc.) involves multiple examples of cross-polity law with different orientations and objectives, interacting with the laws of nations (regime law).[63] Legal pluralism is thus manifested around the globe in myriad variations. In pluralistic contexts it is useful to pay attention to three different directions: (1) at the coexisting complex of legal and regulatory institutions and their interaction; (2) at individuals, entities and groups operating within contexts of coexisting legal and regulatory institutions; and (3) at the broader social, cultural, economic, political and legal consequences of the coexisting legal systems (at the consequences of 1 and 2). In the first direction, one should look at the relative power of each set of legal institutions, and the power and resources of the social, economic and political interests that support or align with each; at the normative commitments and personal interests of the officials who operate within each form of law; and at whether, and how, coexisting forms of law operate cooperatively, competitively or combatively (or all three). In the second direction, one should observe how people navigate legal pluralism for normative and strategic reasons:

[62] For other combinations, see Chapters 2, 7 and 15.

[63] For examples, see Chapters 8, 10 and 12.

they may resort to a particular form of law for moral, cultural or economic reasons; they may engage in forum shopping to achieve their objectives; they may pit one legal system against another or enlist multiple systems for support.[64] In the third direction, one should examine the broader cultural, social, economic, political and legal consequences of how the coexisting legal systems interact and how people, entities and groups operate within these contexts. These three directions will expose entanglements between the coexisting forms of law, entanglements between people and coexisting forms of law and entanglements of both with the surrounding interconnected society (culture, economics, politics, etc.). This trifold lens helps expose many of the dynamics at play in contexts of legal pluralism.

17.9 Transnational Legal and Regulatory Pluralism

To conclude, let me briefly state five main implications of the foregoing analysis for a reconstructed transnational legal pluralism.

The first lesson, repeated throughout, is that transnational legal pluralism has little in common with postcolonial legal pluralism (first approach) and sociological legal pluralism (second approach). Rather than look to the earlier literature on legal pluralism and emphasize continuity, which tends to mislead more than illuminate, transnational legal pluralists should embrace the understanding that they are jurists constructing a wholly new paradigm to address juristic concerns relating to proliferating forms of transnational law and regulation (public, private, hybrid).

The second lesson is that transnational legal pluralists should not attempt to build on an abstract concept or definition of law (implicitly or explicitly). Not only is a concept of law unnecessary and superfluous (stated next), but engaging in this theoretical project is a roadblock to progress. Theorists who attempt to base transnational legal pluralism on a definition of law will go in circles with other similarly engaged theorists and no prospect of resolution. Be forewarned by the example of John Griffiths – the most often cited theorist of legal pluralism – who finally abandoned this project because it could not be solved.

The third lesson is that what counts as law for transnational legal pluralism is what communities take for granted as law: European Union

[64] See Chapter 1.

law, UK law, individual treaties, national constitutions, international law, human rights, German municipal, state and administrative law, etc. These conventionally recognized manifestations of law are what transnational legal pluralists already discuss. That is why an abstract definition of law is unnecessary. We know what is law because we – jurists, government officials, citizens, native peoples, members of religious communities, etc. – collectively identify them as law. Coexisting clashing conventional identifications of law may exist in given contexts (for example state law and Sharia), but they still count as law when they are seen as such by communities of actors.

The fourth lesson, following directly from the second and third, is that 'transnational legal and regulatory pluralism' is a more suitable label for the concerns of global/transnational legal pluralists. The label '*global* legal pluralism' is misleading and should be dropped, for it is neither global nor exclusively legal. The label 'transnational *legal* pluralism' is problematic because it prompts theorists to explain why what they study counts as law (thereby generating the definitional problem). There is no juristic or conceptual reason to assert that they *are* law – a superfluous claim that inevitably runs into trouble. Adding 'regulatory' to the label immediately dissolves this issue and recognizes that their work encompasses public, private and hybrid regulatory regimes, a significant amount of which is not collectively considered law – which does not diminish the fact that they are important and accomplish a great deal. They are what they are: private and hybrid regulatory forms that carry out and complement legal functions, and frequently interact with manifestations of law. They bear directly on the concerns of transnational legal pluralists and merit inclusion in the label.

The final lesson, already mentioned but worthy of separate emphasis, is that, beyond state, international and transnational law, many communities also collectively identify and constitute forms of non-state law, mainly manifestations of customary law, religious law and Indigenous law (though other forms exist, like Romani law). These *are* law as well, which a huge number of people around the globe recognize and live by, especially in rural areas or within insular communities. State legal officials frequently assert state law's claim to supremacy and exclusivity, but this ambition (never fully achieved) does not trump what people collectively recognize, construct and live by as law. State legal systems are themselves collectively recognized forms of law – so state law, international law, transnational law and non-state law are *all* built on the same foundation of collective recognition.

The unifying thrust of these five lessons is that we should simplify how we view the complicated contexts of transnational legal and regulatory multiplicities – and the best way to accomplish this is to engage in modest, tailored theorizing that fits the matters at hand. Much of the morass of transnational legal pluralism lamented by Twining is the self-inflicted product of unnecessarily grand theories. The effort to construct a theory that encompasses everything and addresses every context of legal pluralism – as *global legal pluralism* suggests – is bound to lead us astray.

INDEX

www.ingramcontent.com/pod-product-compliance
Lightning Source LLC
LaVergne TN
LVHW052016200926
848481LV00005B/1509

* 9 7 8 1 1 0 8 8 2 3 7 9 1 *